P9-ARJ-459

AMERICAN HISTORY

VOLUME II

Early Modern Through the 20th Century

Eleventh Edition

A Library of Information from the Public Press

Editor

Robert James Maddox
Pennsylvania State University
University Park

Robert James Maddox, distinguished historian and professor of American history at Pennsylvania State University, received a B.S. from Fairleigh Dickinson University in 1957, an M.S. from the University of Wisconsin in 1958, and a Ph.D. from Rutgers in 1964. He has written, reviewed, and lectured extensively, and is widely respected for his interpretations of presidential character and policy.

Cover illustration by Mike Eagle

The Dushkin Publishing Group, Inc.
Sluice Dock, Guilford, Connecticut 06437

The Annual Editions Series

Annual Editions is a series of over fifty volumes designed to provide the reader with convenient, low-cost access to a wide range of current, carefully selected articles from some of the most important magazines, newspapers, and journals published today. Annual Editions are updated on an annual basis through a continuous monitoring of over 200 periodical sources. All Annual Editions have a number of features designed to make them particularly useful, including topic guides, annotated tables of contents, unit overviews, and indexes. For the teacher using Annual Editions in the classroom, an Instructor's Resource Guide with test questions is available for each volume.

VOLUMES AVAILABLE

Africa
Aging
American Government
American History, Pre-Civil War
American History, Post-Civil War
Anthropology
Biology
Business and Management
Business Ethics
Canadian Politics
China
Comparative Politics
Computers in Education
Computers in Business
Computers in Society
Criminal Justice
Drugs, Society, and Behavior
Early Childhood Education
Economics
Educating Exceptional Children
Education
Educational Psychology
Environment
Geography
Global Issues
Health
Human Development
Human Resources
Human Sexuality

Latin America
Macroeconomics
Management
Marketing
Marriage and Family
Microeconomics
Middle East and the Islamic World
Money and Banking
Nutrition
Personal Growth and Behavior
Psychology
Public Administration
Race and Ethnic Relations
Social Problems
Sociology
Soviet Union and Eastern Europe
State and Local Government
Third World
Urban Society
Violence and Terrorism
Western Civilization,
    Pre-Reformation
Western Civilization,
    Post-Reformation
Western Europe
World History, Pre-Modern
World History, Modern
World Politics

Library of Congress Cataloging in Publication Data
Main entry under title: Annual editions: American history, volume two.
    1. United States—History—Periodicals. 2. United States—Historiography—Periodicals.
3. United States—Civilization—Periodicals. I. Title: American history, volume two.
ISBN 1-56134-011-1   973'.05   75-20755

Eleventh Edition

Manufactured by The Banta Company, Harrisonburg, Virginia 22801

To the Reader

In publishing ANNUAL EDITIONS we recognize the enormous role played by the magazines, newspapers, and journals of the *public press* in providing current, first-rate educational information in a broad spectrum of interest areas. Within the articles, the best scientists, practitioners, researchers, and commentators draw issues into new perspective as accepted theories and viewpoints are called into account by new events, recent discoveries change old facts, and fresh debate breaks out over important controversies.

Many of the articles resulting from this enormous editorial effort are appropriate for students, researchers, and professionals seeking accurate, current material to help bridge the gap between principles and theories and the real world. These articles, however, become more useful for study when those of lasting value are carefully *collected, organized, indexed,* and *reproduced* in a *low-cost format,* which provides easy and permanent access when the material is needed. That is the role played by *Annual Editions.* Under the direction of each volume's *Editor,* who is an expert in the subject area, and with the guidance of an *Advisory Board,* we seek each year to provide in each *ANNUAL EDITION* a current, well-balanced, carefully selected collection of the best of the public press for your study and enjoyment. We think you'll find this volume useful, and we hope you'll take a moment to let us know what you think.

Many Americans appear fascinated with their history, provided it is presented to them in palatable form. In the fall of 1990, a television documentary on the Civil War and its aftermath attracted a huge audience and engendered considerable controversy over various aspects of the conflict. Other documentaries, such as "The Twentieth Century" and "The World at War," although originally produced years ago, still are being shown. Popular historical journals attract even greater readership, and new ones seem to appear every year.

The essays included in *American History* also are intended to present history in palatable form. That is, they are selected from publications oriented toward general readers rather than specialists. They are for the most part free of jargon and do not include academic paraphernalia such as footnotes that are appropriate in professional journals. Some focus on prominent men and women, some on racial or ethnic groups, while still others discuss events or trends that affect all of us. The volume can stand alone or be used as a supplement to textbooks which, because of space limitations, necessarily are limited in the variety of subjects that can be included and the number of pages allotted to those subjects. More than half the articles in the previous edition have been replaced by new ones.

American History contains a number of features designed to be useful to students, researchers, and professionals. These include a *topic guide* to locate articles on specific subjects; the *table of contents abstracts* that summarize each essay, with key concepts in bold italics; and a comprehensive *index.* Articles are organized into six units. Each unit is preceded by an overview that provides background for informed reading of the articles, emphasizes critical issues, and presents *challenge questions.*

A new edition of *American History* is published every two years. Selections made to replace existing articles are culled from a variety of journals, magazines, and newspapers. Publications devoted to history are the most common source, but some of the best essays may appear in unexpected places. We seek two kinds of help from readers of this edition: We welcome your opinions of the selections included so as to help us judge which should be retained, and we urge you to recommend others (or better yet, send along a copy) of those you think should be included in the next edition. Please complete and mail the post-paid article rating form included in the back of the book. Your suggestions will be carefully considered and appreciated.

Robert James Maddox
Editor

Contents

Unit 1

Reconstruction and the Gilded Age

Five articles examine the development of the United States after the Civil War. Society was changed by expansion, technology, merchandising, and agricultural development.

The concepts in bold italics are developed in the article. For further expansion please refer to the Topic Guide and the Index.

Unit 2

The Emergence of Modern America

Six articles review the beginnings of modern America. Key issues of this period are examined, including the rise of capitalism, racial consciousness, and the larger role of women in America.

The concepts in bold italics are developed in the article. For further expansion please refer to the Topic Guide and the Index.

Unit 3

From Progressivism to the 1920s

Seven articles examine American culture in the early twentieth century. The economy began to reap the benefits of technology, women gained the right to vote, Henry Ford ushered in mass production, and the Jazz Age arrived.

The concepts in bold italics are developed in the article. For further expansion please refer to the Topic Guide and the Index.

Unit 4

From the Great Depression to World War II

Five selections discuss the severe economic and social trials of the Great Depression of the thirties, the slow recovery process, and the enormous impact of World War II on America's domestic and foreign social consciousness.

The concepts in bold italics are developed in the article. For further expansion please refer to the Topic Guide and the Index.

Unit 5

From the Cold War to the Reagan Revolution

Eight articles cover the post-World War II period in the United States. The Truman Doctrine influenced America's foreign policy, equality of education became the law of the land, the Vietnam War changed the way America looked at conflict, Nixon's Watergate tested the United States' system of balanced political power, and the poor of America increasingly affected society's conscience.

The concepts in bold italics are developed in the article. For further expansion please refer to the Topic Guide and the Index.

The concepts in bold italics are developed in the article. For further expansion please refer to the Topic Guide and the Index.

Unit 6

New Directions for American History

Four articles discuss the current state of American society, considering the effects of the "Reagan Revolution," the state of women's rights, and the arguable decline of America.

The concepts in bold italics are developed in the article. For further expansion please refer to the Topic Guide and the Index.

Topic Guide

This topic guide suggests how the selections in this book relate to topics of traditional concern to American history students and professionals. It is useful for locating articles that relate to each other for reading and research. The guide is arranged alphabetically according to topic. Articles may, of course, treat topics that do not appear in the topic guide. In turn, entries in the topic guide do not necessarily constitute a comprehensive listing of all the contents of each selection.

TOPIC AREA	TREATED IN:	TOPIC AREA	TREATED IN:
African Americans	11. George Washington Carver 18. Jazz 27. Trumpet of Conscience	Farming	3. Winning of the West Reconsidered 5. Upward Bound 11. George Washington Carver 32. Changing Face of a Restless Nation
Asians	13. Angel Island 22. An American Tragedy 32. Changing Face of a Restless Nation	Ford, Henry	17. Citizen Ford
Barton, Clara	2. Clara Barton	Government	12. Theodore Roosevelt 20. 'Give Us Roosevelt' 28. Lyndon B. Johnson 31. Change in the Weather
Business	9. Gospel of Andrew Carnegie 17. Citizen Ford		
Carnegie, Andrew	9. Gospel of Andrew Carnegie	Hispanics	32. Changing Face of a Restless Nation 34. Push for Power
Carver, George Washington	11. George Washington Carver	Immigrants	7. Hope, Tears, and Remembrance 13. Angel Island 18. Jazz 32. Changing Face of a Restless Nation
Children	1. First Chapter of Children's Rights 26. Rebels Without a Cause?		
Culture	10. Cleaning Up the Dance Halls 15. Unknown Hollywood 18. Jazz 26. Rebels Without a Cause?	Johnson, Lyndon B.	28. Lyndon B. Johnson
		King, Martin Luther, Jr.	27. Trumpet of Conscience
Depression, the Great	19. How Hollywood Fixed an Election 20. 'Give Us Roosevelt' 21. 1940: America on the Eve of Conflict	Korean War	24. The Forgotten War
		Labor	4. Haymarket Bomb 5. Upward Bound 14. Rose Schneiderman and the Triangle Fire 20. 'Give Us Roosevelt'
Diplomacy	8. Our First Southeast Asian War 29. Lessons From a Lost War 35. (Relative) Decline of America		
		Movies, the	15. Unknown Hollywood
		Music	18. Jazz
		Native Americans	30. New Indian Politics

TOPIC AREA	TREATED IN:	TOPIC AREA	TREATED IN:
Politics	6. Cycle of Reform 12. Theodore Roosevelt 19. How Hollywood Fixed an Election 20. 'Give Us Roosevelt' 28. Lyndon B. Johnson 30. New Indian Politics 31. Change in the Weather 33. "Remember the Ladies"	**Society**	1. First Chapter of Children's Rights 3. Winning of the West Reconsidered 5. Upward Bound 6. Cycle of Reform 21. 1940: America on the Eve of Conflict 26. Rebels Without a Cause? 32. Changing Face of a Restless Nation
Progressivism	12. Theodore Roosevelt 14. Rose Schneiderman and the Triangle Fire	**Urban Problems**	14. Rose Schneiderman and the Triangle Fire 32. Changing Face of a Restless Nation
Racism	8. Our First Southeast Asian War 11. George Washington Carver 22. An American Tragedy 27. Trumpet of Conscience 30. New Indian Politics 32. Changing Face of a Restless Nation 34. Push for Power	**Vietnam War**	29. Lessons From a Lost War
		West, the	3. Winning of the West Reconsidered
Reform	1. First Chapter of Children's Rights 6. Cycle of Reform 10. Cleaning Up the Dance Halls 14. Rose Schneiderman and the Triangle Fire 15. Unknown Hollywood 20. 'Give Us Roosevelt' 27. Trumpet of Conscience 30. New Indian Politics	**Women**	2. Clara Barton 3. Winning of the West Reconsidered 10. Cleaning Up the Dance Halls 14. Rose Schneiderman and the Triangle Fire 23. Rosie the Riveter Remembers 33. "Remember the Ladies"
		World War I	16. Saint-Mihiel Salient
Roosevelt, Franklin D.	20. 'Give Us Roosevelt' 21. 1940: America on the Eve of Conflict	**World War II**	21. 1940: America on the Eve of Conflict 22. An American Tragedy 23. Rosie the Riveter Remembers
Roosevelt, Theodore	12. Theodore Roosevelt		

Reconstruction and the Gilded Age

During the first years of the Civil War, Abraham Lincoln claimed it was being fought to preserve the Union. It became a war against slavery after he issued the preliminary Emancipation Proclamation in September 1862. Ending slavery was a first step, but what status would former slaves occupy in the postwar society? What became known as "Radical Reconstruction" constituted an effort to assure full political and economic equality. Enthusiasm waned as the years passed, however, and whites gradually regained control over the Southern states. Blacks were pushed back to the bottom of the order through denial of civil rights and liberties.

Westward expansion continued during the years after Reconstruction. Improved equipment and farming techniques permitted cultivation of land previously deemed unsuitable. But farming remained a risky business. Too little or too much rain could ruin crops, locusts and other pests periodically caused great damage, and farm prices fluctuated wildly. Cattle and sheep ranching proved equally hazardous. And the growth of farms and ranches impinged upon the remaining areas occupied by Native Americans. Some tribes sought accommodation, some resisted, but in the end whites relegated them to the most undesirable regions.

The rapid growth of industry brought its own troubles. Workers, many of them immigrants, toiled long hours under harsh, frequently unhealthy conditions. Their efforts to better their way of life at times resulted in violence as many businessmen bitterly resisted unionization. Cities became more crowded and slum areas grew rapidly.

A great deal in what became known as the "Gilded Age" was shoddy, garish, and superficial. Corruption flourished at all levels, and the newly rich flaunted their wealth in the most vulgar and ostentatious ways. At the same time, scholars have pointed out, it was an era of great vitality, innovation, and of considerable accomplishment in art and literature.

The first article provides an early example of a problem that is with us still. What role should society play in trying to prevent child abuse within families? "Clara Barton: Founder of the American Red Cross," also deals with reform or attempted reform. Barton, a driven and controversial humanitarian, created an organization to mitigate the effects of catastrophe both in war and peace.

The process of settling the West has exercised a great impact on the American imagination. Brave pioneers in covered wagons trekking across the plains, the U.S. Cavalry arriving in the nick of time to prevent massacres by savage Indians, and heroes in white hats shooting down bad guys in ritualistic gunfights have been staples in popular literature, films, and television. Recent scholars have challenged this view, and tend to paint an almost unrelieved picture of hard times, brutal treatment of individuals and groups, and thoughtless despoilment of the environment. "The Winning of the West Reconsidered" attempts a balanced assessment.

"The Haymarket Bomb" provides a graphic account of an incident in 1886 that strongly influenced attitudes toward organized labor.

This unit ends with "Upward Bound," that deals with both farmers and working people, and challenges popular beliefs about the "rags to riches" theme in American history.

Looking Ahead: Challenge Questions

How can society protect children against child abuse without exercising authoritarian interference in family life?

Have the "new" western historians significantly added to our understanding of the westward movement? Or have they demolished convenient straw men and sacrificed evenhandedness in order to stress the darker side of the westward migration?

A popular notion in the United States has been that people are free to go as far and as fast as his/her abilities and ambitions can take them. How true was this in the nineteenth century? How true is it today?

THE FIRST CHAPTER OF CHILDREN'S RIGHTS

Peter Stevens and Marian Eide

I n the quiet New York courtroom, the little girl began to speak. "My name is Mary Ellen McCormack. I don't know how old I am. . . . I have never had but one pair of shoes, but can't recollect when that was. I have had no shoes or stockings on this winter. . . . I have never had on a particle of flannel. My bed at night is only a piece of carpet, stretched on the floor underneath a window, and I sleep in my little undergarment, with a quilt over me. I am never allowed to play with any children or have any company whatever. Mamma has been in the habit of whipping and beating me almost every day. She used to whip me with a twisted whip, a raw hide. The whip always left black and blue marks on my body. I have now on my head two black and blue marks which were made by mamma with the whip, and a cut on the left side of my forehead which was made by a pair of scissors in mamma's hand. She struck me with the scissors and cut me. I have no recollection of ever having been kissed, and have never been kissed by mamma. I have never been taken on my mamma's lap, or caressed or petted. I never dared to speak to anybody, because if I did I would get whipped. . . . Whenever mamma went

More than a century ago an abused child began a battle that is still being fought today

out I was locked up in the bedroom. . . . I have no recollection of ever being in the street in my life."

At the beginning of 1874 there were no legal means in the United States to save a child from abuse. Mary Ellen's eloquent testimony changed that, changed our legal system's view of the rights of the child.

Yet more than a century later the concerns that arose from Mary Ellen's case are still being battled over in the courts. The classic dilemmas of just how deeply into the domestic realm the governmental arm can reach and what the obligations of public government are to the private individual take on particular urgency in considering child abuse.

Early in 1989, in the case of *DeShaney* v. *Winnebago County*, the Supreme Court declared that the government is not obligated to protect its citizens against harm inflicted by private individuals. DeShaney brought the case be-

fore the court in a suit against county social service agencies that had failed to intervene when her estranged husband abused their son, Joshua, who, as a result of his father's brutality, suffered permanent brain damage. The father was convicted, but his former wife believes that fault also lies with the agencies, whose failure to intercede violated her son's Fourteenth Amendment right not to be deprived of life or liberty without due process of the law. Chief Justice William H. Rehnquist wrote that intervening officials are often charged with "improperly intruding into the parent-child relationship." Justice William J. Brennan, Jr., dissenting, wrote: "Inaction can be every bit as abusive of power as action, [and] oppression can result when a State undertakes a vital duty and then ignores it."

The difficulty in bringing Mary Ellen McCormack into the New York Supreme Court in 1874 grew from similar controversy over the role of government in family matters, and Mary Ellen's sad history is not so different from Joshua DeShaney's.

When Mary Ellen's mother, Frances Connor, immigrated to the United States from England in 1858, she took a job at the St. Nicholas Hotel in New

York City as a laundress. There she met an Irishman named Thomas Wilson who worked in the hotel kitchen shucking oysters. They were married in April 1862, shortly after Wilson had been drafted into the 69th New York, a regiment in the famous Irish Brigade. Early in 1864 she gave birth to their daughter, whom she named Mary after her mother and Ellen after her sister.

The birth of her daughter seems to have heralded the beginning of Frances Wilson's own decline. Her husband was killed that same year in the brutal fighting at Cold Harbor, Virginia, and with a diminished income she found it necessary to look for a job. In May 1864, unable to pay someone to watch the baby while she was at work, she gave Mary Ellen over to the care of a woman named Mary Score for two dollars a week, the whole of her widow's pension. Child farming was a common practice at that time, and many women made a living taking in unwanted children just as others took in laundry. Score lived in a tenement in the infamous warrens of Mulberry Bend, where thousands of immigrants crowded into small, airless rooms, and it is likely that providing foster care was her only means of income.

Finally Frances Wilson became unable to pay for the upkeep of her child; three weeks after the payments ceased, Score turned Mary Ellen over to the Department of Charities. The little girl—whose mother was never to see her again—was sent to Blackwells Island in July 1865. Her third home was certainly no more pleasant than Mulberry Bend. Mary Ellen was among a group of sick and hungry foundlings; fully two-thirds of them would die before reaching maturity.

The same slum-bred diseases that ravaged the children on Blackwells Island had also claimed all three children of a couple named Thomas and Mary McCormack. So when Thomas frequently bragged of the three children he had fathered by another woman, his wife was more receptive to the

idea of adopting them than she might otherwise have been. Those children, he told her, were still alive, though their mother had turned them over to the care of the city.

On January 2, 1866, the McCormacks went to the Department of Charities to reclaim one of the children Thomas's mistress had abandoned. The child they chose as their own was Mary Ellen Wilson. Because the McCormacks were not asked to provide any proof of relation to the child and gave only the reference of their family doctor, there is no evidence that Thomas was in any way related to the child he brought home that day. More than a month later an indenture was filed for Mary Ellen in which the McCormacks promised to report on her condition each year. There were no other requirements.

Shortly after bringing the child home, Thomas McCormack died, and his widow married a man named Francis Connolly. Little more than that is known of the early childhood of Mary Ellen. She came to her new home in a flannel petticoat, and when her clothing was removed from Connolly's home as evidence six years later, there was barely enough to fill a tiny suitcase. She was beaten, set to work, deprived of daylight, and locked in closets for days at a time; she was rarely bathed, never kissed, and never addressed with a gentle word. During the six years she lived with Connolly, only two reports on her progress were filed with the Commissioners of Charities and Correction.

Late in 1873 Etta Angell Wheeler, a Methodist caseworker serving in the tenements of New York City, received a disturbing report. It came from Mar-

garet Bingham, a landlord in Hell's Kitchen, and told of a terrible case of child abuse. The child's parents had been tenants of Bingham for about four years, and almost immediately after they moved in, Bingham began to observe how cruelly they treated their child, Mary Ellen. They confined her in close quarters during hot weather, kept her severely underdressed in cold, beat her daily, and left her unattended for hours at a time. On several occasions Bingham tried to intervene; each time the child's mother said she would call upon the fullest resources of the law before she would allow any interference in her home. Finally Bingham resorted to threat: The beatings and ill treatment would have to stop, or the family would be evicted. When her plan backfired and the family left, Bingham, in a last-ditch effort, sent for Etta Wheeler. In order to observe Mary Ellen's predicament, Wheeler went to the Connollys' neighbor, an ailing tubercular woman named Mary Smitt. Enlisting Smitt's aid, she proposed that Mary Ellen be sent over each day to check on the patient. Smitt reluctantly agreed, and on the pretext of inquiring about this sick neighbor, Wheeler knocked on Mary Connolly's door.

Inside she saw a "pale, thin child, bare-foot, in a thin, scanty dress so tattered that I could see she wore but one garment besides.

"It was December and the weather bitterly cold. She was a tiny mite, the size of five years, though, as afterward appeared, she was then nine. From a pan set upon a low stool she stood washing dishes, struggling with a frying pan about as heavy as herself. Across the table lay a brutal whip of twisted leather strands and the child's meager arms and legs bore many marks of its use. But the saddest part of her story was written on her face in its look of suppression and misery, the face of a child unloved, of a child that had seen only the fearsome side of life. . . . I never saw her again until the day of her rescue, three months later. . . ."

Though social workers often witnessed scenes of cruelty, poverty, and grief, Wheeler found Mary Ellen's plight especially horrifying. She went first to the police; they told her she must be able to furnish proof of assault in order for them to act. Charitable institutions she approached offered to care for the child, but first she must be brought to them through legal means. There were none. Every effort Wheeler made proved fruitless. Though there were laws to protect children—laws, in fact, to prevent assault and battery to any person—there were no means available for intervention in a child's home.

Finally Wheeler's niece had an idea. The child, she said, was a member of the animal kingdom; surely Henry Bergh, the founder of the American Society for the Prevention of Cruelty to Animals, who was famous for his dramatic rescue of mistreated horses in the streets of New York, might be willing to intervene. Within the hour Wheeler had arranged a meeting with Bergh. Despite its apparent strangeness, this sort of appeal was not new to Bergh. Once before he had tried to intervene in a case of child abuse and had failed. This time he was more cautious.

"Very definite testimony is needed to warrant interference between a child and those claiming guardianship," Bergh told Wheeler. "Will you not send me a written statement that, at my leisure, I may judge the weight of the evidence and may also have time to consider if this society should interfere? I promise to consider the case carefully."

Wheeler provided a statement immediately, including in it the observations of neighbors to whom she had spoken. Bergh was convinced. "No time is to be lost," he wrote his lawyer, Elbridge T. Gerry. "Instruct me how to proceed."

The next day Wheeler again visited the sick woman in Hell's Kitchen and found in her room a young man who, on hearing Wheeler's name, said, "I was sent to take the census in this house. I have been in every room." Wheeler then knew him to be a detective for Bergh.

On the basis of the detective's observations and the testimony provided by Etta Wheeler, Bergh's lawyers, Gerry and Ambrose Monell, appeared before Judge Abraham R. Lawrence of the New York Supreme Court to present a petition on behalf of Mary Ellen. They showed that Mary Ellen was held illegally by the Connollys, who were neither her natural parents nor her lawful custodians, and went on to describe the physical abuse Mary Ellen endured, the marks and bruises on her body, and the general state of deprivation that characterized her existence. They offered a list of witnesses willing to testify on behalf of the child and concluded by stating that there was ample evidence to indicate that she was in clear danger of being maimed or even killed. The lawyers requested that a warrant be issued, the child removed from her home and placed in protective custody, and her parents brought to trial.

Bergh testified that his efforts on behalf of the child were in no way connected to his work with abused animals and that they did not make use of the special legal provisions set up for that purpose. Because of Bergh's association with animal rescue, to this day the case is often described as having originated in his conviction that the child was a member of the animal kingdom. Bergh, however, insisted that his actions were merely those of any humane citizen and that he intended to prevent cruelties inflicted on children through any legal means available.

Judge Lawrence issued a warrant under Section 65 of the Habeas Corpus Act as requested. This provision read in part: "Whenever it shall appear by satisfactory proof that any one is held in illegal confinement or custody, and that there is good reason to believe that he will . . . suffer some irreparable injury, before he can be relieved by the issuing of a *habeas corpus* or *certiorari*, any court or officer authorized to issue such writs, may issue a warrant . . . [and] bring him before such court or officer, to be dealt with according to law."

The press of the day hailed Gerry's use of Section 65 of the Habeas Corpus Act as brilliant. The act was rarely invoked, and the legal means for removing a child from its home were nonexistent. In using the little-known law, Gerry created a new method for intervention.

That same day, April 9, 1874, Mary Ellen was taken from her home and brought into Judge Lawrence's court. Having no adequate clothing of her own, the child had been wrapped in a carriage blanket by the policemen who held her in custody. A reporter on the scene described her as "a bright little girl, with features indicating unusual mental capacity, but with a care-worn, stunted, and prematurely old look. . . . no change of custody or condition could be much for the worse."

The reporter Jacob Riis was present in the court. "I saw a child brought in . . . at the sight of which men wept aloud, and I heard the story of little Mary Ellen told . . . that stirred the soul of a city and roused the conscience of a world that had forgotten, and as I looked, I knew I was where the first chapter of children's rights was being written." Her body and face were terribly bruised; her hands and feet "showed the plain marks of great exposure." And in what almost instantly seemed to condemn Mrs. Connolly before the court, the child's face bore a fresh gash through her eyebrow and across her left cheek that barely missed the eye itself. Mary Ellen was to carry this scar throughout her life.

Interestingly, there is no further mention in the ample reports surrounding Mary Ellen's case of her foster father, Francis Connolly. He was never brought into court, never spoke publicly concerning the child. All her life Mary Ellen exhibited a frightened timid-

> Jacob Riis "saw a child brought in at the sight of which men wept aloud, and heard the story that roused the conscience of a world."

ity around men, yet it was against her foster mother that she testified.

On the evening of her detention, Mary Ellen was turned over to the temporary custody of the matron of police headquarters. The next day, April 10, the grand jury read five indictments against Mary Connolly for assault and battery, felonious assault, assault with intent to do bodily harm, assault with intent to kill, and assault with intent to maim. Once the stepmother had been brought into the legal system, there were ample means to punish her.

Mary Ellen herself was brought in to testify against the woman she had called her mother. On her second appearance in court she seemed almost wholly altered. She was clothed in a new suit, and her pale face reflected the kindness that surrounded her. She carried with her a new picture book, probably the first she had ever owned. She acted open and uninhibited with strangers, and interestingly, seemed to show no great fear of her mother or any apparent enmity toward her.

The lawyers Gerry and Monell gathered several witnesses against Mary Connolly, among them neighbors, Wheeler, and Mary Ellen herself. Margaret Bingham said she had seen the child locked up in a room and had told other neighbors, but they said there was no point in interfering since the police would do nothing. Bingham had tried to open the window of the child's room to let in some air, but it would not lift more than an inch. As a constant presence and reminder, a cowhide whip was locked in the room with the child. Wheeler recounted her first visit to Mary Ellen, during which the child washed dishes that seemed twice her size and was apparently oblivious of the visitor's presence. The whip lay on the table next to her. The next day, when Wheeler came by again, the child was sewing, and the whip lay on a chair near her.

Then it was the mother's turn to testify. On the witness stand Mary Connolly showed herself to be a woman of some spirit. Despite her treatment of the child, there is something compelling in Connolly's strength and humor. At one point the prosecutor asked if she had an occupation beyond housekeeping. "Well," she said, "I sleep with the boss." As the trial wore on, she became enraged at Gerry's prodding questions; finally she accused him of being "ignorant of the difficulties of bringing up and governing children." Yet she admitted that contrary to regulations, in the six years she had Mary Ellen in her custody, she had reported on her condition to the Commissioners of Charities and Correction only twice.

Two indictments were brought against Connolly, the first for her assault on the child with scissors on April 7, the second for the continual assaults inflicted on the child throughout the years 1873 and 1874. After twenty minutes of deliberation the jury returned a verdict of guilty of assault and battery. Connolly was sentenced to one year of hard labor in the city penitentiary, then known as the Tombs. In handing down this sentence, the judge defined it not only as a punishment to Connolly but also as a statement of precedence in child-abuse cases.

Mary Ellen never returned to the Connollys' home. In the ensuing months the publicity that her case received brought in many claims of relation. But on investigating, her guardian, Judge Lawrence, discovered the stories were fictions, and he finally placed the child in the Sheltering Arms, a home for grown girls; soon after, she was moved to the Woman's Aid Society and Home for Friendless Girls. This mirrors another critical problem in the system's treatment of minors. All juveniles were handled by the Department of Charities and Correction, and whether they were orphaned or delinquent, their treatment was the same. And so it was that the ten-year-old Mary Ellen was placed in a home with mostly delinquent adolescents.

Etta Wheeler knew this was wrong for Mary Ellen, and she expressed her hesitations to Judge Lawrence. He, in turn, consulted with Henry Bergh, and eventually they agreed to turn the girl over to Etta Wheeler herself. Unable to imagine giving up her work in the slums of New York City but believing that Mary Ellen deserved a better envi-

ronment, Wheeler brought the child to her mother in North Chili, New York. Wheeler's mother became ill shortly afterward, and Mary Ellen was raised mostly by Wheeler's sister.

Here began a new life," Wheeler wrote. "The child was an interesting study, so long shut within four walls and now in a new world. Woods, fields, 'green things growing,' were all strange to her, she had not known them. She had to learn, as a baby does, to walk upon the ground,—she had walked only upon floors, and her eye told her nothing of uneven surfaces. . . . But in this home there were other children and they taught her as children alone can teach each other. They taught her to play, to be unafraid, to know her rights and to claim them. She shared their happy, busy life from the making of mud pies up to charming birthday parties and was fast becoming a normal child."

The happiness of her years in the upstate New York countryside lies in stark contrast to her early childhood. And indeed, as Wheeler wrote, she learned by example the ways of normal childhood. She grew up strong and well, learning how to read and playing with friends and pet kittens. In 1875 Wheeler reported to Gerry that Mary Ellen was growing up as a normal child. "She has some faults that are of the graver sort. She tells fibs and sticks to them bravely, steals lumps of sugar & cookies and only confesses when the crumbs are found in her pocket—in short she is very much like other children, loving—responding to kindness & praise, hating a task unless there be a play, or a reward thereof, and inevitably 'forgetting' what she does not wish to remember—what children do not do some or all of these forbidden things! She is a favorite with nearly all the people who have come to know her."

When she was twenty-four, Mary Ellen married a widower named Louis Schutt and with him had two children, Etta—named after the woman who had rescued her—and Florence. She adopted a third, orphaned child,

9

Eunice. She also raised Louis Schutt's three children from his first wife.

In 1911 Wheeler visited her protégé in her home, "finding her well and happy. . . . The family income is small, but Mary Ellen is a prudent housewife & they are comfortable. The two daughters are promising girls." The eldest daughter, Etta, worked industriously through that summer, finished high school, and became a teacher. Florence followed her sister's path, teaching first grade for thirty-eight years. When she retired, the elementary school in North Chili was renamed in her honor. Eunice earned a business degree, married, and raised two sons.

Florence remembers her mother as a solemn woman who came alive whenever she listened to Irish jigs and especially to "The Irish Washerwoman." She was unfailingly generous with her time and her affection. Her years in North Chili had saved her from the vicious cycle abused children often suffer of becoming abusers themselves. According to Florence her mother was capable of sternness and certainly willing to punish her daughters, but the terrible experiences of her early childhood never spilled into her own child rearing. As Etta Wheeler wrote, "To her children, two bright, dutiful daughters, it has been her joy to give a happy childhood in sharp contrast to her own."

Etta and Florence often asked their mother about the Connollys, but Mary Ellen was reluctant to speak of her early years. She did show her daughters the scars on her arms where she had been burned with a hot iron, and of course they could see the scissors scar across her face. Florence distinctly recalls that in the few times they spoke of her mother's years in New York City, she never mentioned a woman inflicting her injuries; it was always a man.

In October of 1913 Mary Ellen Schutt attended a meeting of the American Humane Society in Rochester. She was accompanied by Etta Wheeler, who was there to present a paper entitled "The Finding of Mary Ellen." The paper con-

Mary Ellen was survived by three daughters—and by a movement that would help avert tragedies like hers.

cluded: "If the memory of her earliest years is sad, there is this comfort that the cry of her wrongs awoke the world to the need of organized relief for neglected and abused children."

Mary Ellen died on October 30, 1956, at the age of ninety-two. She was survived by her two daughters, her adopted daughter, three stepchildren, three grandchildren, and five great-grandchildren. More important, she was survived by the beginning of a movement to prevent the repetition of tragedies like her own. On December 15, 1874, Henry Bergh, Elbridge Gerry, and James Wright founded the New York Society for the Prevention of Cruelty to Children (SPCC) with the ample assistance of Cornelius Vanderbilt. It was the first organization of its kind in America. At the outset of their work the founders signed a statement of purpose: "The undersigned, desirous of rescuing the unprotected children of this city and State from the cruelty and demoralization which neglect and abandonment engender, hereby engage to aid, with their sympathy and support, the organization and working of a Children's Protective Society, having in view the realization of so important a purpose."

The SPCC saw its role essentially as a legal one. As an agent or a friend of the court, the society endeavored to intervene on the behalf of children, enforcing the laws that were in existence to prevent cruelty toward them and at the same time introducing new legislation on their behalf.

At the first meeting of the SPCC on December 16, 1874, Gerry stressed the fact that the most crucial role of the society lay in the rescue of children from abusive situations. From there, he

pointed out, there were many excellent groups available to care for and shelter children and many state laws to punish abusive parents. He went on to predict that as soon as abusers learned that the law could reach them, there would be few cases like that of Mary Ellen.

Bergh was less optimistic. At the same meeting, he pointed out that neglected and abused children were to become the mothers and fathers of the country and that unless their interests were defended, the interests of society in general would suffer.

In its first year the SPCC investigated more than three hundred cases of child abuse. Many people felt threatened by the intrusion of the government into their private lives; discipline, they believed, was a family issue, and outside influence was not only unwelcome but perhaps even unconstitutional. When, with the aid of a state senator, James W. Booth, Gerry introduced in the New York legislature a law entitled "An Act to Prevent and Punish Wrongs to Children," the proposal was immediately and vigorously attacked. The New York *World* wrote that Bergh was to be authorized to "break into the garrets of the poor and carry off their children upon the suspicion of spanking." According to the *World*, the law would give Bergh "power to discipline all the naughty children of New York. . . . We sincerely hope that it may not be finally kicked out of the legislature, as it richly deserves to be, until the public mind shall have had time to get itself thoroughly enlightened as to the state of things in which it has become possible for such a person as Mr. Bergh to bring the Legislature to the point of seriously entertaining such an impudently senseless measure. This bill is a bill to supersede the common law in favor of Mr. Bergh, and the established tribunals of justice in favor of an irresponsible private corporation." The bill was passed in 1876, however, and became the foundation upon which the SPCC performed its work.

From its initial concentration on preventing abuse in the home, the society broadened its franchise to battle neglect, abandonment, and the exploitation of children for economic gain. In 1885, after considerable effort by the SPCC and in the face of yet more opposition, Gerry secured passage of a bill that made labor by children under the age of fourteen illegal.

As the explosive story of the death of Lisa Steinberg in the home of her adoptive parents revealed to the nation in 1987, abuse still haunts American society. There are still legal difficulties in removing a child from an abusive situation. In 1987 the House Select Committee on Children, Youth, and Families reported that the incidence of child abuse, particularly sexual abuse and neglect, is rising; in 1985 alone almost two million children were referred to protective agencies. In part, the committee said, this increase was due to a greater awareness of the issue, and there has also been an increased effort to educate children themselves about situations that constitute abuse or molestation and about ways to get help.

Despite a plethora of programs designed to address abuse, the committee concluded that not enough is being done. The most effective programs were found to be those that worked to prevent the occurrence of abuse at the outset through education in parenting techniques, through intervention in high-risk situations, such as unwanted pregnancies, and through screening for mental and emotional difficulties. However, funding for public welfare programs has fallen far below the demands, and what funding there is must frequently be diverted to intervene in more and more sensational and hopeless cases.

If there is still much hard, sad work ahead, there is also much that has been accomplished. And all of it began when Mary Ellen McCormack spoke and, in speaking, freed herself and thousands of other children from torment.

Peter Stevens, who lives in Quincy, Massachusetts, writes frequently on historical themes. Marian Eide is a graduate student in the Comparative Literature and Critical Theory Program at the University of Pennsylvania. We would like to thank Dr. Stephen Lazoritz for his contributions to the research of this article. Lazoritz, a pediatrician specializing in child-abuse cases, first became interested in Mary Ellen's history when, preparing for a lecture on child abuse, he read "The Great Meddler," Gerald Carson's profile of Henry Bergh in the December 1967 issue of American Heritage. Lazoritz was fascinated by the child and traced her history through a trail of documents and newspaper articles. In the story of Mary Ellen's childhood he found the roots of a movement to prevent child abuse in which he is very much involved today. Lazoritz's youngest daughter was born during his pursuit of the case. Her name is Mary Ellen. Thanks, too, to the New York Society for the Prevention of Cruelty to Children, whose archives contain full documentation of the Mary Ellen case.

CLARA BARTON

FOUNDER OF THE AMERICAN RED CROSS®

Cathleen Schurr

Cathleen Schurr is the author of several books and has contributed articles to national magazines and newspapers. Schurr's account of her ordeal as a survivor of the first U-boat attack of World War II appeared in the February 1988 issue of this publication. She lives in Maryland.

Opposition and inner turmoil haunted this tireless, driven humanitarian who drew inspiration for her life work from Civil War battlefields.

Red Cross director Clara Barton and her aides arrived in flooded Johnstown, Pennsylvania five days after the May 1889 catastrophe, on board the first train to get through to the site where more than two thousand people had died. General Daniel H. Hastings, the Pennsylvania militia officer in charge of the stricken city, had never heard of Barton or the Red Cross. He was skeptical as to how a small, cheerful sixty-seven-year-old woman in long skirts and muddy boots could help in the chaos that followed the disaster. But within a week, Hastings, like others, sought her help. And within five months, Johnstown residents had learned what Barton and the Red Cross meant to those in trouble.

At that Pennsylvania city, Barton, through the seven-year-old Red Cross, executed one of the greatest relief missions of her long career. Later she harbored vivid memories of her first day in Johnstown: "wading in the mud, climbing over broken engines, cars, heaps of iron rollers, broken timbers, wrecks of houses, bent railway tracks tangled with piles of iron wires, bands of workmen, squads of militia and getting around the bodies of dead animals, and often people being borne away, the smouldering [sic] fires and drizzling rain. . . ." Nor could she forget the thirty-foot heaps of rubbish, the thousands dead in the river beds, and the twenty thousand with no food but bread.

Improvising as always, Barton began working out of an abandoned railroad car, then from a tent, using a dry goods packing crate as a desk. Here she marshalled supplies and workers: the Philadelphia Red Cross responded with doctors and nurses to establish the area's only official field hospital; Iowa and Illinois sent lumber for shelters; and others contributed desperately needed clothing. In the beginning everything was distributed by hand; three weeks passed before a cart could get through the mud. From her makeshift desk, Barton directed a half-million-dollar relief program with about fifty workers. She answered requests, mounted a vast publicity campaign, and ultimately helped about twenty-five thousand flood victims.

For the first time at a disaster site, the Red Cross built shelters—three "Red Cross hotels" consisting of long central communal halls flanked by suites of private rooms furnished with pieces salvaged from the heaps of debris. (Eventually, wood from the housing units was shipped to Washington, D.C., and in 1891 portions of it were used in building a new Red Cross headquarters in Glen Echo, Maryland.)

When Barton left Johnstown, the local newspapers eulogized her— "We bow to the idea which brought her here. God and humanity!"— and the governor added his public praise. Grateful Johnstown women gave Barton a pendant encrusted with diamonds and sapphires, which she added to her growing collection of medals and decorations.

Contrary to popular belief, Barton was not a nurse, though her name is forever associated with the care of the ill and suffering. Although she is world-renowned for founding the American Red Cross, lesser known is Barton's active participation in many of the other major issues of nineteenth-century America: equal rights for women and blacks, free public education, foreign aid, and international diplomacy. Barton knew and worked with nine U.S. presidents, the Russian czar, the Austrian emperor, the

From *American History Illustrated*, November/December 1989, pp. 50-64. Reprinted through the courtesy of Cowles Magazines, publishers of *American History Illustrated*.

Useful works marked Clara Barton's life of service from an early age, assuring her a lasting legacy of humanitarianism. This daguerreotype, the earliest known photograph of Barton, was likely taken during her studies at progressive Clinton Liberal Institute following a successful teaching career.

COURTESY OF THE AMERICAN ANTIQUARIAN SOCIETY, WORCESTER, MASSACHUSETTS

Duke and Duchess of Baden, and countless cabinet ministers, generals, army surgeons, and government officials all over the world. She was the most decorated woman in American history and the first woman ever to receive Germany's Iron Cross and Russia's Imperial Cross.

Barton was known in her day, and in the legend that survives, as a bright and cheerful angel. But behind this facade was a troubled soul, a woman of massive contradictions subject throughout her life to crippling depression and illness.

Beginnings

Clarissa Harlowe Barton was born in the small rural village of North Oxford, Massachusetts on Christmas Day 1821. The fifth and last child of Sarah and Captain Stephen Barton, she was ten years younger than her closest sibling, Sally.

Her mother was a strong, iron-faced woman with a violent temper, whose eccentricities, among them unforgiving parsimony and profanity, were well-known. A story goes that after a grandchild viewed Sarah in her coffin, the child reported: "I saw grandma and she never swored once."

Despite her erratic ways, Sarah Barton was an "involved" woman, an early abolitionist and supporter of women's rights. Sarah taught young Clara the domestic arts: cooking, sewing, weaving, soap-making, and gardening. These skills were of inestimable value to her in later life.

Clara's father, born in 1774, had served in "Mad" Anthony Wayne's army during the Indian Wars of the Northwest Territory. He was committed to the liberal views of the Universalist church and to public charity and philanthropy. His twin occupations were farming and milling, but his greatest joy was the military, an interest he early transferred to daughter Clara, who preferred war stories to Mother Goose.

Clara was a shy child among her grown-up siblings, anxious to please and morbidly afraid of "being a burden, or giving trouble." Despite her timidity, however, Barton early learned to identify with male accomplishments. She became a tomboy, proud that her father said she was "more boy than girl." Instead of dolls, she played at soldiers, rode bareback before she was five,

played ball, and joined her male cousins in excursions and adventures around the countryside, exhilarated by daring and danger.

But it was through useful work that the young Clara began a pattern of conduct she would repeat throughout her long life. As a child she performed endless farm and domestic chores. When she was eleven, she nursed her brother David when he suffered severe headaches and fever following an accident. For two years Clara rarely left his side, giving him medicines, applying "great loathsome crawling leeches," and dressing his blisters.

Once David recovered, Clara found other ways to be of service, briefly working in the family mill, caring for Sally's children, and helping to nurse poor families in the community. Her future was decided when a visiting phrenologist told Sarah Barton that Clara's sensitive nature would always remain, but that she had all the qualities of a teacher.

Teacher and Office Worker

Barton was still in her teens when she began teaching in the Oxford school. She soon earned a reputation for discipline and scholarship. Barton treated her students as individuals, dealing with each according to his needs. They were her "boys" Barton said, and scores of affectionate letters to her years after when she had become famous attest to how much she had affected them. As her work continued, she grew more self-assured, less introverted—confident enough to demand pay equal to a man's. She might work for nothing, she said, but if paid, "I shall never do a man's work for less than a man's pay."

In 1850, when she was twenty-nine and after more than ten years of successful teaching, Barton enrolled at Clinton, New York's Liberal Institute, almost two hundred miles away from Oxford, to further her own education. Although Clinton with its progressive ideas on women's education was a good choice for Barton, she ran out of funds before she completed her studies.

Barton returned to teaching, first at Hightstown, New Jersey and later at nearby Bordentown. Accustomed to the Massachusetts tradition of free education, Barton persuaded the school board to establish a free school, improve the curriculum, and install her as teacher. School enrollment jumped from six to six hundred in the first year, and a second school had to be added.

But instead of Barton, town officials appointed a dictatorial male to head the new school, classifying her only as a "female assistant" with a salary of $250 annually to her chief's $650. Barton and other instructors chafed under their supervisor's strict rule, and the teachers' squabbles soon became public. Under the pressure of rivalry and the collapse of her hopes, Barton be-

Barton was not a nurse, though her name is forever associated with the care of the ill and suffering.

came ill, a pattern that was oft-repeated during other stressful periods of her life. She resigned.

Next she moved to Washington, D.C. There Barton became a recording clerk in the U.S. Patent Office—and one of the first women to be so employed by the federal government. Commissioner of Patents Charles Mason, impressed by her exquisite penmanship and trustworthy character (confidentiality was important at patents), hired her at a $1,400 annual salary—equivalent to that of male clerks. In 1854 this was good pay even for men.

There were few women in government offices at the time, and male workers were generally uncomfortable in their presence. Secretary of the Interior Robert McClelland, under whom the patent office operated, said there was an "obvious impropriety in the mixing of the sexes within the walls of a public office." Mason was careful not to advertise Barton's presence; her name did not appear on the congressional list during the six years she worked for the government.

When Mason resigned, Barton lost her status and was relegated to being a "copyist" at home. Although McClelland disapproved of women in offices, he had no objection to their working at home for much less pay.

Later, however, Mason came out of retirement to rescue the patent office, where fraud and alcoholism had become rampant. He reinstated Barton to help him sort out the difficulties.

Barton's reappearance further annoyed already disgruntled male employees. Daily she faced a gauntlet of jeering men who spit tobacco juice at her and blew smoke in her

face. And like all women employed in Washington in the mid-nineteenth century, her morals became an issue. Popular opinion held that "nice" women did not work for money; therefore office women must be of low character, given to promiscuity, drink, and debauchery. Rumors of lax sexual conduct by Barton surfaced. Such talk was to be repeated throughout her life (even when she was in her eighties) as she appeared in places and situations thought to be unsuitable for women.

Barton's life in Washington was socially pleasant, however, and she advanced her political education by friendships with important political figures and visits to the Senate gallery. Senator Henry Wilson, chairman of the Senate Committee on Military Affairs, became her lifelong friend and ally, visiting Barton almost daily.

The "Homely" Angel

The Confederate attack on Fort Sumter in April 1861 changed forever the course of Barton's life. Soon after, the Massachusetts Sixth Regiment was attacked by secessionist mobs while traveling through Baltimore. The regiment, temporarily housed in the U.S. Senate, included Barton's former pupils—her "boys" and friends—and she rushed to help them. The soldiers' luggage had been seized in the Baltimore riots, and they needed such things as towels, blankets, handkerchiefs, kitchen utensils, candles, and preserved food. Barton quickly collected and delivered these items.

On her own initiative, Barton then began a year-long campaign to solicit and collect supplies for future needs. Her home became a warehouse for ordinary necessities as well as medical and nursing supplies. Eventually she had to rent additional storage space. She soon became a familiar sight on Washington's streets, her small frame bouncing uneasily atop a lumbering wagon loaded with goods. But as the wounded began to pour into the city, and as she read reports of the suffering at the front, she wanted to do more. "I'm well and strong and young enough to go to the front," she said. "If I can't be a soldier, I'll help soldiers."

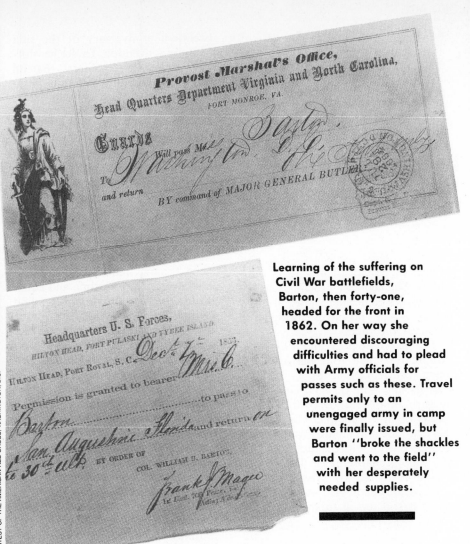

Learning of the suffering on Civil War battlefields, Barton, then forty-one, headed for the front in 1862. On her way she encountered discouraging difficulties and had to plead with Army officials for passes such as these. Travel permits only to an unengaged army in camp were finally issued, but Barton ''broke the shackles and went to the field'' with her desperately needed supplies.

doctor described her ''. . . with her sleeves rolled up . . . her dress skirt pinned around her waist . . . a lady of pleasing countenance . . . besides a huge iron kettle . . . over a roaring fire, using a ladle to stir . . . a barrelful of soup.''

Her field work was marked by her inventiveness and timeliness as trains and wagons brought her bandages, drugs, coffee, wine, brandy, cans of soup, beef, jars of jellies, juices, and crackers.

Barton was in the field for subsequent battles: Fairfax Court House, Chantilly, and Antietam. And at Fredericksburg the carnage of more than twelve thousand men lost by Union forces would remain forever in her mind. Barton recalled piles of amputated arms, legs, and feet at the door of Lacy Mansion, which, used as a hospital, had floors so slippery with blood that Barton had to wring it from her skirts before she could walk.

In spring 1864, she was again at the front in the campaigns of the Wilderness and Spotsylvania where more than fifty thousand were killed or wounded. Next she worked out of invalid camps receiving wounded from Petersburg and other battles near Richmond. The controversial General Benjamin F. Butler, who became a lifelong friend, appointed her supervisor of nurses for the Army of the James. ''Honor any request Miss Barton makes without question,'' he ordered. ''She outranks me.''

Barton organized nurses and directed daily activities. She wrote letters for the soldiers and tended to their needs, working at her own frenzied pace. She refused to delegate work; she could not supervise without dictating, and she would not accept criticism or suggestions.

The difficulties were exacerbated by the need to be constantly on the move before the enemy: ''I cannot tell you how many times I have moved with my whole family of 1,000 or 1,500,'' she wrote her cousin. Barton made an important contact at this time, nursing a wounded young Swiss soldier named Jules Golay, who would later figure in Barton's Red Cross work.

As the war drew to a close, she was drained and exhausted. Her

Clara was forty-one when she went to the battlefields, after first returning to Oxford to receive her dying father's blessing and his gold masonic badge, which she carried throughout the war. But Barton did not reach the war theater without discouraging difficulties. After she pleaded without success for a pass to the front from one army official after another, a permit was finally issued only for travel to an unengaged army in camp. Undeterred, Clara ''broke the shackles and went to the field'' anyway with her sorely needed supplies.

In August 1862, dressed in a jacket, kerchief, and a dark skirt with no crinolines to hinder movement, Barton rode to the front near Culpeper, Virginia with her four-mule team and supplies a few days after the Battle of Cedar Mountain. The North had been badly beaten and had suffered several thousand casualties. Surgeon James L. Dunn

watched in astonishment as Barton, arriving at midnight at the hospital tent, delivered her wagonload of precious surgical dressings and supplies. She stayed to hand out shirts and soup to the wounded.

Dunn, in a letter to his wife, which was later unofficially publicized in newspapers throughout the country, wrote, ''I thought that night if heaven ever sent out a homely angel, she must be one, her assistance was so timely.'' His original letter clearly shows he used the word ''homely.'' (Apparently Barton or one of her followers did not like the connotation, for the letters ''m'' and ''e'' are carefully blocked out in the clippings she kept.) So it was that Barton came to be known as the ''holy'' angel, ''the true heroine of the age,'' as Dunn described her.

In the fields Barton cooked gruel, baked hardtack, aided doctors, and distributed medical supplies. One

Civil War record was marked by unflinching courage under dangerous and difficult conditions. Although a Union sympathizer, she had treated soldiers on both sides with the same touching compassion.

When the war ended, Barton sought a new cause. Postwar conditions presented another need: locating thousands of missing soldiers. Through her patron, Senator Wilson, Barton received President Abraham Lincoln's authorization to conduct the search that led to the establishment of a National Cemetery at the notorious Confederate prison in Andersonville, Georgia. Throughout the war, Barton had listed the names of missing, wounded, and dying soldiers. Now, using regional newspaper advertising, she published long lists of men whose families had inquired about them. The response was overwhelming.

Barton realized the value of public support for her work, and she undertook a series of lecture tours, covering the missing soldiers search and such topics as "How the Republic Was Saved," "Work and Incidents of Army Life," and "War Without the Tinsel." Despite chronic stage fright, she captivated

> ## "I'm well and strong and young enough to go to the front," said Barton. "If I can't be a soldier, I'll help soldiers."

audiences, moving them to tears and cheers. She kept to a grueling schedule despite rain and snow, at the mercy of the primitive transportation of the time.

The psychological and physical strains took their toll. Barton suffered recurrent earaches, bronchial distress, and sore throats. During a lecture in Portland, Maine one snowy night in 1868, her voice gave out and she was unable to utter a sound. Barton was on the verge of the major collapse of her life.

She returned to Washington, D.C., deeply depressed. A year later she was still too ill to speak at the twentieth anniversary of the first feminist convention. Under her doctor's order for total rest, Barton sailed for Europe with her sister Sally.

The Geneva Treaty and the Red Cross

Barton's "rest" cure involved traveling all over the continent. At Golay's family home in Switzerland, she met Dr. Louis Appia, a representative of the International Committee of the Red Cross. This organization had grown out of the 1864 Geneva Convention, which advocated humane treatment of sick and wounded during wartime and equal treatment for both sides. The United States was the only major nation that had not signed the Geneva Convention, though the American government had been approached at least three times.

The Red Cross had first been envisioned by Jean Henri Dunant, a Swiss who had been shocked at the horrors he saw at the 1859 battle of Solferino in northern Italy. There he aided the suffering and was touched by Italian peasant women murmuring "tutti fratelli" ("all are brothers") while caring for the hated Austrians.

Like many others, Barton was immensely moved by Dunant's book *A Memory of Solferino*, and she determined to support its aims. But before she could act she again became ill and despondent, moaning over her "useless" days and unproductivity. When Appia invited her to join the International Red Cross relief in the Franco-Prussian war, her spirits rose, hearing "the bugle call to arms . . . and it nerved me to action for which the physical strength had long ceased to exist."

Barton cared for Civil War soldiers both in the field and in invalid camps such as those that received wounded from Petersburg and other battles near Richmond, Virginia. Although sympathetic to the Union cause, Barton treated members of both armies with equal compassion.

She worked first for the Red Cross in Basel, France, where well-stocked warehouses and ready-for-action volunteers suggested a model organization. Next, she set out for the front with a young Swiss companion, Antoinette Margot, who acted as interpreter.

According to Barton's diary, the two women failed to reach the front in the Franco-Prussian war, but publicly she asserted she had been with the fighting men—an example of a lifelong predilection for amending facts. Barton *did* serve in another equally important area: helping the destitute and starving civilian population, under the patronage of Grand Duchess Louise of Baden, daughter of Germany's Kaiser Wilhelm I. The Duchess, a noted philanthropist and promoter of women in charitable ventures, became a lifelong friend, showering Barton with gifts, precious jewels, and medals.

After establishing a women's sewing center in Strasbourg, France, Barton and Margot traveled to Paris to aid the poor there. They then went to the Franco-German border to help civilians desperate for work and money. Once again, Barton's health began to erode; depression, backaches, and failing eyesight resulted. She went to England to recover, but there only added chronic bronchitis to her ailments. In 1873, physically broken, she returned to America with her niece Mamie.

Barton had once again driven herself to exhaustion, working long hours under difficult conditions without enough sleep or food. She was in a Washington, D.C. hospital when her closest sister, Sally, died of cancer. Unable to reach her in time, Barton suffered another breakdown. She collapsed again when her dear friend and political patron, the former senator, now Vice President Wilson, died a year later in 1875. For months Barton clung to her bed, sobbing and whimpering, an emotional and physical wreck.

Dansville

Barton's rehabilitation began in a flourishing sanatorium in Dansville, New York, a small town near the Finger Lakes. The facility was run by new-age thinker Dr. James Jack-

A surgeon at the Battle of Cedar Mountain wrote of Barton: "I thought that night if heaven ever sent out a homely angel, she must be one, her assistance was so timely."

son and his adopted daughter, Dr. Harriet Austin, who became Barton's close friend. The sanatorium followed the so-called "water-cure," emphasizing wearing of uncorseted clothing, exercising, intellectual stimulation, and a diet of whole grains, fresh fruits, and vegetables.

Barton's improved health led her to buy a house in Dansville, where she lived intermittently for the next ten years. From her new home she began an intensive campaign for ratification of the Geneva Convention and the establishment of an American Red Cross.

For fourteen years American officials had resisted signing the Geneva Convention, interpreting such action as contrary to the Monroe Doctrine that prohibited foreign "entanglements." By discrediting earlier Red Cross promoters, Barton received official sanction from the International Red Cross as the *sole* U.S. representative. She began lecturing and writing, churning out press releases and informational pamphlets, including a booklet titled *What the Red Cross Is*, which emphasized the neutral nature of the organization's potential relief work in peacetime disasters. She installed her nephew, Stephen E. Barton, as her aide. Together they petitioned Presidents Rutherford B. Hayes and James A. Garfield. The Bartons were well received by Garfield's new secretary of state, James G. Blaine,

and plans were made to submit the Geneva Convention to the Senate for ratification. Barton lobbied the senators.

In June 1881, Barton and a few friends announced the formation of the first American Association of the Red Cross, with twenty-two charter members. Barton was president, and the organization's goal was ratification of the Geneva Treaty. In August, Dansville residents established the first local chapter. Soon, with Susan B. Anthony's help, other chapters were established in upstate New York.

In Dansville Barton met a shy young chemistry teacher named Julian Hubbell, who was to become one of the most important people in her life and that of the Red Cross. Hubbell had idolized Barton from his boyhood in Iowa and now offered her his help. When she told him to get a medical degree, Hubbell quit teaching and enrolled in the University of Michigan medical school. Dr. Hubbell became Barton's lifelong foot soldier and aide. He referred to himself as Barton's "boy," and he called her "Mamie." Later, as the chief Red Cross field agent, Hubbell was involved in more direct relief work than Barton herself.

President Garfield's assassination in July 1881 was a tragedy for the country and a potential catastrophe for Barton's new organization. But Garfield's successor, former Vice President Chester A. Arthur, announced his unconditional support for "that humane and commendable engagement" in his first annual message to Congress. With presidential support, the Senate's March 1882 vote in favor of ratification was unanimous. It was a major achievement in Clara Barton's long career. She wept because she had waited so long "and got so weak and broke that she could not even feel glad."

New Challenges and Problems

Not only had Barton established the internationally recognized Red Cross in America, she had vanquished competing organizations. With her new success, Barton began building an entourage from which

Clara Barton called to order a May 21, 1881 meeting (notes from which appear here) of those interested in forming an American Red Cross. The following month she and some friends announced the creation of such an organization, with twenty-two charter members over whom Barton was president.

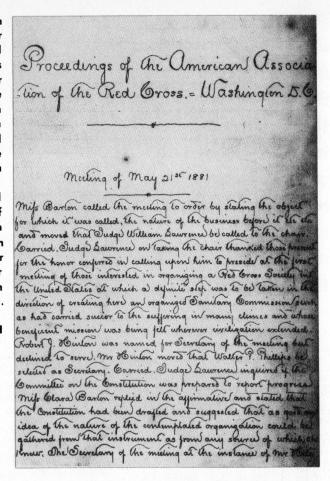

Proceedings of the American Association of the Red Cross. — Washington D.C.

Meeting of May 21st 1881

Miss Barton called the meeting to order by stating the object for which it was called, the nature of the business before it &c &c and moved that Judge William Lawrence be called to the chair. Carried. Judge Lawrence on taking the chair thanked those present for the honor conferred in calling upon him to preside at the first meeting of those interested in organizing a Red Cross Society in the United States at which a definite step was to be taken in the direction of creating such an organized Sanitary Commission such as had carried succor to the suffering in many climes and whose beneficent mission was being felt wherever civilization extended. Robert J. Hinton was named for Secretary of the meeting but declined to serve. Mr Hinton moved that Walter P. Phillips be selected as Secretary. Carried. Judge Lawrence inquired if the Committee on the Constitution was prepared to report progress Miss Clara Barton replied in the affirmative and stated that the Constitution had been drafted and suggested that as good an idea of the nature of the contemplated organization could be gathered from that instrument as from any source of which she knew. The Secretary of the meeting at the instance of Mr ...

she demanded loyalty, obedience, and total acceptance of her rule. Some aides adored her. There was always the infinitely patient Hubbell, who slavishly and unquestioningly did Barton's bidding. But other aides called her "The Great I Am" or "The Queen."

Barton did not work easily with others; she could not give or take orders, and she would not tolerate criticism. Building up the organization required administrative skills for which she was temperamentally unsuited. Her plan was for loosely organized local Red Cross chapters with a small national group at the head. But local societies were slow to form, and either could not make a move without Barton or wanted to act autonomously in emergencies. Part of the slow growth was due to the peacetime absence of urgency. But Barton's inability to delegate caused endless problems.

Then several natural calamities helped spur the growth of the American Red Cross. The Mississippi and Ohio rivers flooded disastrously in 1882. Hundreds were homeless and destitute; property damage was extensive, and repeated floodings washed out replanted crops. The Red Cross delivered aid immediately, even before the government could arrive.

In 1883, at a crucial juncture in the Red Cross's development, Barton accepted a position as superintendent of the Women's Reformatory Prison in Sherborn, Massachusetts. She went reluctantly, chiefly as a political favor to her old friend and supporter from Civil War days, General Butler, now Massachusetts governor. She found the job lonely and depressing, "the most foolhardy thing" she ever did, and was glad to resign when Butler was not re-elected.

As always during Barton's absences, the American Red Cross had suffered. Correspondence had piled up, requests about forming chapters had gone unanswered; one Philadelphia group thought the organization was defunct and wrote the international office in Geneva to revive it.

But no sooner was Barton back at headquarters, when, in February 1884, the Ohio River flooded again. Barton took to the field for another three months. The river area had been devastated, whole towns swept away. Property damage was acute. Setting up warehouses in Ohio and Indiana, Barton hired a crew and a steamer, the *Josh V. Throop*, to travel up and down the river distributing food, fuel, clothing, blankets, and small but vital essentials such as scissors, needles, and thread. One victim said the *Throop* came out of the mist and sleet like a phantom ship, an answer to a prayer.

In the spring, Barton hired another relief ship, the *Mattie Belle*, to travel the Mississippi, distributing fodder for starving animals, lumber, and tools with which to rebuild. Barton, aware of the dramatic appeal of the mission, mounted a widespread publicity campaign, writing some of the most poignant human interest stories herself. More than $175,000 in donations poured in as a result; in the two previous years, the total had been only $26,000.

But trouble brewed aboard the *Mattie Belle*. The St. Louis Red Cross chapter president reported that long stretches of the river were passed without supplies being distributed. He was also concerned about the project's muddled financial state. Most distressing was Barton's obvious physical exhaustion; at one point she directed the expedition from her bed. Aides worried about her health, but Barton would not acknowledge her weak condition.

Back in Washington, D.C., she tried to regain her strength, but when the secretary of state urged her to attend the Third International Conference of the Red Cross in Geneva as the country's official representative, she could not refuse. It was the first time a woman had ever been appointed to such a diplomatic mission. In Barton's honor, an amendment at the conference committing the international organization to provide relief in peacetime disasters was called the "American amendment." Her mission to Geneva was a personal triumph.

In 1888, a yellow fever epidemic

Although renowned as American Red Cross founder, Barton was also a dedicated advocate of human rights and equality who lectured on many vital topics of the day. She believed that her individual actions and attitudes demonstrated that women equaled men in intellect, abilities, and courage. Notable nineteenth-century reformers such as Frederick Douglass, Lucy Stone, Susan B. Anthony, and William Lloyd Garrison often appeared in company with her.

EMINENT WOMEN
WHO WILL BE PRESENT AND SPEAK AT THE
NEW ENGLAND
Woman Suffrage Festival,
AT
MUSIC HALL,
Wednesday Evening, May 30th.

Mrs. Laura Ormiston Chant, of London.
Miss Alli Trygg, of Finland.
Baroness Gripenberg, of Finland.
Mrs. Zerelda G. Wallace, of Indiana.
Mrs. Lucy Stone,
Mrs. Mary A. Livermore,
Mrs. Elizabeth Cady Stanton,
Miss Susan B. Anthony,
Miss Clara Barton,
Mrs. Ednah D. Cheney,
Miss Mary F. Eastman,
and others.

THE FOLLOWING GENTLEMEN HAVE ALSO PROMISED TO SPEAK AT THE FESTIVAL:
Frederick Douglass,
William Lloyd Garrison, Jr.
Henry B. Blackwell,
Rev. Charles G. Ames,
AND OTHERS.

☞ Every one of the 900 supper tickets has been sold, and no more can be issued, but admission tickets (with reserved seats) can be obtained to the lower balcony for 50 cents, or to the upper balcony for 25 cents each, at the Ticket Office, Music Hall, or at the office of the WOMAN'S JOURNAL, 3 Park Street.

No such gathering of distinguished women has occurred in Boston for years, and as there is a great demand for tickets application should be made promptly in order to secure seats.

MUSIC BY THE MARIAN OSGOOD ORCHESTRA.

the Sea Islands off the South Carolina coast, killing five thousand and leveling crops, buildings, and boats. Barton agreed to deliver relief, though reluctantly, because resources were limited. With the region desolate and the largely black population demoralized, the task was gargantuan. The islands stretched out for a hundred miles, with small boats the only transport. Lack of food was a major problem; the island people grew little of their own.

Islanders were given seeds and taught how to plant and grow their own vegetables. Eager workers, they dug drainage ditches to prepare the soil for planting, returning borrowed tools each night to the Red Cross. Volunteers taught them financial responsibility concepts and provided medical attention for more than two thousand malaria cases.

Barton was a celebrity; parents named babies after her, children tagged behind her. Many, who recalled her nursing care thirty years before, walked miles to see her again. One old man, asked on what he depended for the winter, replied "God and Miss Barton."

Opposition Grows

But criticism of Barton was mounting, both within and outside the Red Cross. The powerful Philadelphia chapter, which had refused to cooperate with her on two occasions including the Johnstown flood, began communicating directly with the international society in Geneva, urging an investigation of Barton's activities.

Primary criticism alleged Barton's unaccountability, and inaccuracy in the official reports she did make. The *Review of Reviews* in 1894 reported that it could not get clear, itemized financial statements or specific details about Red Cross work.

Much of the criticism about accountability was justified; Barton kept Red Cross financial records on scraps of paper and in scattered notebooks, omitting important details and explanations. Records for Johnstown, for example, had receipts without amounts, and official reports of expenditures there varied from $40,000 to $250,000. In Geneva, the International Red Cross

in Jacksonville, Florida marked the first use of trained Red Cross nurses, both black and white. Barton, not immune to the fever, called on a Louisiana chapter member, Col. F.R. Southmayd, to replace her as leader of the relief project.

The Louisiana nurses from the Red Cross's New Orleans chapter had had wide exposure to the deadly disease, and, for the most part, did heroic work. Some nurses, unfortunately, were less admirable, refusing to work for three dollars a day when the hospitals paid four. One got drunk; another was arrested for theft; one vanished with Red Cross

funds; and several were branded as prostitutes and ordered to leave.

Southmayd's inability to cope with the local problems and his refusal to dismiss the offenders resulted in widespread unfavorable publicity about Red Cross nurses, haunting them for years to come. New York City papers ran stories about "Drunken Red Cross Nurses" who had come to New Orleans to "prey on the sick." The Florida experience strengthened Barton's determination to take field command herself, as she did the following year at Johnstown.

In 1893, a hurricane devastated

expressed dismay at the situation, warning that relations with the parent body were reaching a breaking point.

The confusion caused dwindling contributions; businessmen increasingly withdrew support. Personal attacks on Barton multiplied: she was a tyrant, she lacked administrative skills, she was too old. Barton, demoralized as always by criticism, considered the critics enemies, and marshalled her forces against them. In 1895, her supporters unanimously elected her "permanent" president of the American Red Cross. Barton replied to the international society's objections by saying that she was "too burdened to fuss with accurate reports" and that her "extreme modesty and humility" prevented her from making a full statement about her accomplishments.

Beginning in 1894, the American press had publicized barbarous warfare atrocities committed by Turkish Moslems against the largely Christian Armenians who were resisting incorporation into the Ottoman Empire. When U.S. missionaries were harassed while aiding victims, American indignation exploded into action.

Barton was reluctant to undertake the relief work because of lack of funds and the uncertainty of the Turkish reception, given the American criticism. A special relief committee raised the necessary funds, but Turkey agreed to the mission only on condition that Barton work as an individual, not as a representative of any official body, including the Red Cross.

From Constantinople in 1896, the seventy-four-year-old Barton sent relief teams into the field, where they found appalling conditions. Victims had been robbed of basic necessities: pots, water bags, hand tools, and looms. Typhoid and typhus were spreading, dysentery and diarrhea were rampant. The place was full of "walking skeletons," one doctor reported. Barton's medical teams in five short weeks prevented a potentially catastrophic epidemic. Field workers set about rehabilitation—distributing seeds and teaching hygiene, sewing, and tool-making.

With her new success, Barton began building an entourage from which she demanded loyalty, obedience, and acceptance of her rule.

Barton and her workers faced innumerable problems: language barriers, suspicion of foreigners, long delays in communication with the field, and threats to their safety. Difficulties with the Turkish government, questions from American fund raisers, and the fact that Barton aided Turks as well as Armenians, led to further criticism from home. But in five months, Barton and her followers helped thousands. Missionaries as well as the Turkish government praised and honored her work.

In 1898 Barton was in Cuba, aiding victims of a rebellion against Spanish rule. The insurgents, *reconcentrados* as they were called, had been driven into concentration camps where filthy conditions, lack of food, water, and medical attention prevailed. "The massacres of Armenia seemed merciful in comparison," Barton reported.

While Barton was in Cuba, the battleship USS *Maine* was blown up in Havana Harbor. Barton's famous wire to President William McKinley, "I am with the wounded," was factually inaccurate, but she was in a strategic position to offer aid in field and boat hospitals. War was declared in April 1898, and once again, Barton found alarming inadequacies in medical and relief supplies.

Meanwhile, the powerful New York chapter of the Red Cross jockeyed for position as the *sole* government relief agency. The New York Relief Committee was run by professionals critical of Barton's small force and her casual, independent style that had changed little since the Civil War. The New Yorkers had warehoused supplies, and had two hundred relief auxiliaries, a hospital, and a nursing school. Barton's relief ship, the SS *State of Texas*, on the other hand, was held in Florida for nearly two months before being cleared to enter the Cuban war zone.

Once in Cuba, Barton as usual aided both sides. Supplies had to be ferried in on flat, skimpy scows during the few hours that the tide allowed; men waded waist-deep to land basic foods. Doctors performed more than four hundred operations in two days. And at seventy-seven, Barton again worked sixteen hours a day. Malaria, typhoid, dysentery, and yellow fever broke out both in recruit camps and American bases. Some of Barton's own staff contracted the fever and were hospitalized.

The national Red Cross ultimately distributed about six thousand tons of provisions, but the New York Relief Committee contributed much more, and sent a greater number of trained medical personnel. The army, siding with neither faction, offered little cooperation, and the surgeon general adamantly refused to allow women nurses in the field. Thus the Cuba relief effort fell short of its potential and ended with a divided American Red Cross.

As always, Barton responded to all criticism with anger, accusing even her devoted nephew-aide, Stephé, of trying to bypass her authority. She issued a directive that all Red Cross doctors and nurses be approved by her personally, and forbade all employees from even discussing Red Cross affairs with outsiders. She refused to consider reorganization.

Retreating to her home in suburban Glen Echo, Maryland, then also the official Red Cross headquarters, Barton turned to writing a long-overdue account of the Red Cross and its activities. A cabal of trusted writing associates helped her produce a long, haphazard, poorly organized work titled *The Red Cross in Peace and War* that in no way substituted for missing field reports or financial accounts.

Soon she returned to Cuba, where people still suffered. Her trip became a personal public relations mission as she toured hospitals and orphanages—a little old lady in fussy black silk and a quaint flower-trimmed bonnet. She was cheered by everyone but her own staff, who saw her presence as mistrust, and her manner dictatorial and old-fashioned. She believed they were plotting against her, and returned to America depressed and exhausted.

The American National Red Cross was finally incorporated in 1900 by Congressional action, securing its national position with a federal charter. Despite criticism, Barton, nearing seventy-nine, was again elected Red Cross president.

In September 1900, a brutal hurricane swept across the Gulf of Mexico, savaging Galveston, Texas, among other coastal areas. About six thousand were killed. Hospitals, homes, and communication lines were destroyed. Barton arrived to assist the devastated city, buried in thick smog from huge piles of burning bodies and trash. Corpses dumped into the gulf floated back; they had to be burned. The peculiar sickening smell of burning flesh "became horribly familiar . . ." Barton wrote: ". . . for two months we lived in it and breathed it, day after day." Ill and exhausted, Barton directed relief work from her hotel bed. But she arranged for an orphanage, shelter, and daily hot soup for the disaster victims. As always, Red Cross articles were practical, geared to rehabilitation and recovery: seeds, clothing, lumber, and bandages.

Crisis and Defeat

In Washington, the simmering Red Cross conflict rapidly reached a boil. Chief among the critics was powerful society leader and humanitarian Mabel T. Boardman, a woman of haughty, regal presence who spearheaded the attack on Barton.

Boardman and Barton were diametric opposites in taste, training, and temperament. Barton was a self-made woman who worked for a living. Boardman derived her prom-

The bitter brew of half-truths, petty gossip, lies, rumors, and inventions about the Red Cross founder served only to sensationalize and distort the real problems.

inence from her father's position and wealth. Boardman was elegant; Barton was frumpy. Boardman, who walked easily among the powerful, was a formidable foe and, more important, a skillful organizer. She had joined the Red Cross in 1900, serving on the financial committee, where she soon began collecting information about mismanagement and inaccountability. With easy access to prominent individuals in New York and Washington, Boardman set about reform. When Barton was unanimously reelected Red Cross president in 1901, Boardman was on the executive committee and ten other Barton opponents were made national directors. This faction was known as the "remonstrants."

In 1902 Barton was again summoned by the secretary of state to attend the International Red Cross conference, this time in St. Petersburg, Russia. A representative from the "remonstrants" was also present, creating tense social moments.

Back home, Barton marshalled her forces to meet the opposition at the 1902 annual meeting, drafting new by-laws abolishing the directorial board, and giving the president total control over appointments. She collected enough proxy votes to support her position, and she was elected president once again, this time for life.

Boardman's faction now took up the anti-Barton battle with a vengeance, with a letter to President Theodore Roosevelt (signed by his sister Anna Roosevelt, among others) complaining about Barton's high-handed tactics at the annual meeting and her absolute rule. Roosevelt's reply censured Barton on both counts, and in a stunning blow he resigned as honorary chairman of the Red Cross advisory board, taking his cabinet with him. Crushed by the president's rebuff, Barton defended her use of proxies and begged him to reconsider. When twenty-three dissatisfied Red Cross members petitioned Congress demanding reorganization, Barton suspended them all, including Roosevelt's sister.

Boardman, who until the suspensions had worked primarily for reorganization within the Red Cross while urging Barton to accept an honorary presidency with an annuity, now loosed a virulent, full-scale personal attack on Barton. She enlisted many who had been estranged from Barton to tell their stories; Boardman recorded every rumor about Barton's sex life, including the scurrilous gossip that Barton and the late Senator Wilson had had several mulatto children together, and that Barton and Hubbell's adjoining rooms at Glen Echo were further proof of Barton's immorality. Boardman alleged misappropriation of funds, declared Barton's Civil War work largely fanciful, and branded her an "adventuress from the beginning and a clever one."

The bitter brew of half-truths, petty gossip, lies, rumors, and inventions about the Red Cross founder served only to sensationalize and distort the real problems. Barton refused to surrender and never publicly acknowledged the validity of any of Boardman's charges. Reinstating the suspended "remonstrants," she invited them to the 1903 annual meeting (they did not attend) where her presidency was reaffirmed. She also agreed, reluctantly, to allow an investigating committee headed by Senator Redfield Proctor to examine the records.

The major charges against Barton involved financial accounting; her

She could not accept the fact that the Red Cross had grown beyond her management ability. She believed she had been repudiated, expatriated by the country she had served for so long.

field records were notoriously lax, and she consistently failed to differentiate between her private funds and those of the Red Cross. Through the years she had repeatedly used her own money in relief work, but she also had used organization funds for private purposes. Allegations regarding various properties Barton acquired for the Red Cross were also brought into the testimony. But when none of the "remonstrants" appeared in the Senate Caucus Room to produce hard, demonstrable evidence against Barton, Senator Proctor declared the charges against her false and completely exonerated her.

Crushed and humiliated by the investigation, Barton realized that her exculpation would not end the dispute within the Red Cross. On May 14, 1904, at eighty-two, she resigned as Red Cross president, refusing to accept either an honorary position or an annuity.

She retired to Glen Echo brokenhearted and grieving. She could not accept the fact that the Red Cross had grown beyond her ability to manage it. She believed she had been repudiated, expatriated by the country she had served for so long. She toyed with exiling herself.

Boardman's obsessive campaign against her did not stop with Bar-

ton's resignation; it persisted long after Barton's death. The new Washington, D.C. Red Cross headquarters was dedicated in 1916, and although the then-secretary of state honored Barton during the ground breaking, the building contains no plaque or memorial recognizing the organization's founder. Barton has been relegated to the second floor, where, ironically, her portrait hangs not far from Boardman's.

Barton, a workaholic even in old age, took on new projects during her "retirement." In 1905 she founded the National First Aid Association of America (NFAA), established to teach first aid to private citizens, and to educate private manufacturing firms and auxiliary services such as fire and ambulance companies in emergency first aid. The association developed the original "first aid kit" that contained not only bandages, iodine, and splints, but ingredients for making a mustard plaster. Barton worked for the NFAA for five years in an unofficial capacity, lecturing and writing and allowing use of her name to promote the work.

In 1908 the American Red Cross decided that the NFAA belonged under its jurisdiction because Barton had first developed the program prior to resigning from the Red Cross. The following year, with War Department backing, first aid became an integral part of the Red Cross, and the NFAA disbanded.

Eventually Barton began to slow down, tiring quickly, refusing assistance—impatient, as always, of "coddling." On her ninetieth birthday, newspapers reported her fierce independence, quoting her recipe for longevity: "low fare, hard work."

Two bouts of pneumonia, one in 1911 and another the following year, hastened the end. Two days before her death, Barton told Hubbell of a dream of being back on a battlefield, wading through blood, seeing soldiers having their limbs sawed off without opiates, never complaining or murmuring, "and I woke to hear myself groan because I have a stupid pain in my back . . . I am ashamed that I murmur."

Her last words were from the

On Barton's ninetieth birthday, newspapers reported her fierce independence, quoting her recipe for longevity: "low fare, hard work."

poem "The Old Soldier" by the Rev. John Purves: "Let me go," she said, "let me go." She died on April 12, 1912.

While newspapers all over the world carried tributes, neither the White House nor the Red Cross gave any official recognition. There were funeral services at Glen Echo, and she was buried alongside her parents in Oxford, Massachusetts.

On April 15, 1912, the *Worcester [Massachusetts] Evening Post* carried two headlines on its front page: "Clara Barton at rest in town of her birth" and "All passengers taken off; *Titanic* still afloat." Even in death notices, there was a disaster at her side.

Recommended additional reading: Clara Barton: Professional Angel by Elizabeth Brown Pryor (Philadelphia: University of Pennsylvania Press, 1987) is the definitive in-print biography of the founder of the American Red Cross. This book is available as a quality paperback from the university press for $19.95. In 1981 the National Park Service published an excellent handbook, Clara Barton, illustrated in color and featuring a profile of Barton by Pryor. A limited number of copies are still available for $3.95 each plus postage through the bookshop at the Clara Barton National Historic Site. For ordering information for this title contact the historic site at 301-492-6245.

THE WINNING OF THE WEST RECONSIDERED

Brian W. Dippie

Brian W. Dippie is professor of history at the University of Victoria in Canada. Born in Edmonton, Alberta, he received a B.A. (1965) from the University of Alberta, an M.A. (1966) from the University of Wyoming, and a Ph.D. (1970) from the University of Texas, Austin. He is the author of several books, including most recently Looking at Russell *(1987) and* Catlin and his Contemporaries: The Politics of Patronage *(1990).*

We are now within easy striking distance of 100 years since Frederick Jackson Turner, following the lead of the Superintendent of the Census, proclaimed the end of the frontier and, with it, "the closing of a great historic moment": "The peculiarity of American institutions is, the fact that they have been compelled to adapt themselves to the changes of an expanding people—to the changes involved in crossing a continent, in winning a wilderness, and in developing at each area of this progress out of the primitive economic and political conditions of the frontier into the complexity of city life."

Then, in 1890, it was all over.

Turner, a young historian at the University of Wisconsin, delivered his paper on "The Significance of the Frontier in American History" at the 1893 meeting of the American Historical Association in Chi-

cago. The setting gave point to his observations. Chicago was then playing host to a gargantuan fair, the World's Columbian Exposition, commemorating the 400th anniversary of the discovery of the New World. The session at which Turner spoke met on the Exposition grounds, where buildings coated in plaster of Paris formed a White City, symbolizing civilization's dominion over what not long before had been a wilderness on the shore of Lake Michigan. Chicago's magical growth was, in microcosm, the story of America. Four centuries after Columbus's landfall, a century since white settlers began occupying the interior of the continent, there was no frontier left, no vast reserve of "free land" to the west.

Turner's timing was acute, the psychological moment perfect to find symbolic meaning in recent events. The rise of the Ghost Dance movement, with its vision of a rejuvenated Indian America, the arrest and killing of Sioux leader Sitting Bull on December 15, 1890, the culminating tragedy at Wounded Knee two weeks later—all attested that the "winning of the West" was no longer a process but a *fait accompli*. Indian wars, a fact of American life since the first English colony was planted at Jamestown, were finished. There was no longer an Indian domain to contest; it had disappeared, along with the Jeffersonian vision of an agrarian democracy resting on an abundance of cheap land.

Whatever else farmer discontent represented in the 1890s, it manifested an awareness of the new urban-industrial order.

From *The Wilson Quarterly*, Summer 1990, pp. 71-85. Adapted from a longer version that appeared in *American Studies International*, October 1989, pp. 3-25.

America's 20th-century future was reaffirmed in Chicago the year after the Exposition, when labor unrest erupted into violence and troops that had served on distant frontiers "taming" Indians were shipped in to tame Chicago's unemployed instead.

When Turner read his paper, then, portents were everywhere. Near the Exposition grounds, Buffalo Bill's Wild West show was offering the public its immensely popular version of the frontier experience. Sitting Bull's horse and the cabin from which the chief was led to his death were both on display. Frederic Remington, the artist most responsible for the public's perceptions of life in the West, was on hand to tour the Exposition's midway and to take in Buffalo Bill's show; a year later he was back in Chicago to cheer George Armstrong Custer's old unit, the "gallant Seventh," against, as he put it, "the malodorous crowd of anarchistic foreign trash."

It did not take a prophet to discern a pattern in all this, but Turner reached beyond the obvious. Frontiering, he argued, was not merely a colorful phase of American history. It had actually shaped the American character. On the frontier, environment prevailed over inherited culture. The frontier promoted individualism, self-reliance, practicality, optimism, and a democratic spirit that rejected hereditary constraints. In Turner's reading of U.S. history, the significance of the frontier was simply enormous. To understand American history, one had to understand western history. Whatever distinguished Americans as a people, Turner believed, could be attributed to the cumulative experience of westering: "What the Mediterranean Sea was to the Greeks, breaking the bond of custom, offering new experiences, calling out new institutions and activities, that, and more, the ever retreating frontier has been to the United States."

Turner's audience in Chicago received these ideas with polite indifference. In time, however, the frontier thesis gained influential adherents. For almost half a century, it served as the master explanation of American development. Problems of fact and interpretation were acknowledged. But Turner's essay offered a coherent, self-flattering vision of the American past, and it seemed prophetic in anticipating American involvement abroad. It would be "rash," Turner wrote, to "assert that the expansive character of American life has now entirely ceased . . . . [T]he American energy will continually demand a wider field for its exercise." Cuba and the Philippines soon proved him right. Like any good historical explanation, the frontier thesis seemed to account for past *and* future. Finally, its sweeping imagery and elegiac tone nicely matched the nostalgic mood, which, during the 20th century, would make the mythic Wild West a global phenomenon.

The inadequacy of the frontier thesis did not become plain until the 1940s, after the complex industrial civilization it sought to explain had suffered through the Great Depression and risen to become a world power. But if American history was only temporarily under Turner's shadow, western history has never quite emerged.

Begin with the basics: time and place. Turner's West was a fluid concept, an advancing frontier line and a retreating area of free land. If one instead defined the West as a geographical entity— that old standby "the trans-Mississippi West," for example—then over half of western American history proper has transpired since Turner's 1890 cutoff date. What the Louisiana Purchase inaugurated in 1803 is an ongoing story of growth and change. The boundaries of this geographic West are usually set at the 49th parallel to the north, the Mexican border to the south, the Mississippi to the east, and the Pacific Ocean to the west, though historians have found each of these too arbitrary. Some see these boundaries as too inclusive to be meaningful, others as too restrictive. Historians of the fur trade might want to embrace all of North America, historians of the borderlands all of Mexico, students of outlawry the Old Southwest, and students of the Indian wars the Old Northwest.

Then there is the matter of time. Turner's frontier West ended with the 19th century. To effect a revolution in western history one need simply move forward into the 20th. Immediately, most of the familiar signposts are missing: fur trade and exploration, Indian wars and Manifest Destiny (overland migration, war with Mexico, Mormonism, the slavery expansion contro-

Frederic Remington, one of the creators of the frontier myth, painted The Fall of the Cowboy *(above) in 1895 as a lament for a way of life that seemed to be vanishing as cattle ranchers enclosed the open range with barbed wire. It was not only the cowboy's supposed freedom that Remington and others admired; it was his status as a kind of Anglo-Saxon ideal at a time when "foreign swarms" were taking over the eastern cities. Nearly a century later, in the* San Jose Mercury-News *(April 15, 1990), reporter Michael Zielenziger added a new twist to the cowboy's saga:*

Wyoming, the Cowboy State, is facing a shortage of cowboys.

One would not think so. On every state license plate, cowboys ride broncos. The university football team is the Cowboys. Likenesses of cowboys gallop through restaurants and saunter across billboards throughout this large, lonesome state.

But to ranch owners like Georgie LeBarr, those symbols represent the romance of the Old West, not the reality of the new. Truth is, no one wants the job these days.

"Nobody wants to work that hard," said LeBarr, who grew up on a ranch and never intends to leave her rolling spread.

As a result, LeBarr is among the first U.S. ranchers to legally import Mexican cowboys to work on her 400,000-acre ranch properties straddling two states. She can do that because the federal government has for the first time certified that no qualified American citizens are interested in the work.

"Nobody wants to be a cowboy," said Oralia Mercado, executive director of the Mountain Plains Agricultural Service, which helps ranchers like LeBarr find suitable workers. "It's hard work, it's dirty work, it's round-the-clock work. It's not something a U.S. worker wants to do."

This month, for the first time, Mercado's organization imported Mexican *vaqueros*, or cowboys, to work with cattle on the open range of Wyoming and the Dakotas. It is a formal acknowledgment that efforts to hire qualified cow hands have met with failure.

It is also a reminder to the families still working the range in this sparsely populated state that their traditional, even romantic, way of life is quickly disappearing.

"We advertised in the newspapers and on radio, but we got zero results," Mercado said, displaying a classified ad that appeared in a Denver newspaper. "I can't see that there's anyone in the U.S. that wants this job. The status of being a cowboy just doesn't exist anymore."

versy), gold rushes and railroad building, vigilantism and six-gun violence, trail drives and the open-range cattle industry, the farmers' frontier and the Populist revolt. Beyond 1900, a different West emerges, a hard-scrabble land rich in scen-

ery and resources, perhaps, but thinly populated for the most part, chronically short of capital and reliant on government aid (such as cheap water and access to federal lands), a cultural backwater whose primary appeal nationally is as the setting for a romantic historical myth. Writing in a bitter-sweet key about the creation of these myths in *The Mythic West in Twentieth-Century America* (1986), historian Robert G. Athearn began by recalling his own boyhood sojourn at his grandfather's Montana ranch: "To me, the wilderness just couldn't hold a candle to indoor plumbing. Of course, I was just a kid, an unformed man whose regard for the freedom of the untouched country was yet nascent. I had not yet developed a sense of romance or the appreciation of idealized landscapes. I never before had felt suppressed or imprisoned. Not until I was locked into the Missouri River breaks and banished from the world, so to speak."

A romantic myth that is untrue for the present is probably untrue for the past as well. By redefining western history's subject-matter, a 20th-century perspective encourages a reassessment of the 19th century. That process began in 1955, when Earl Pomeroy of the University of Oregon published a breakthrough essay, "Toward a Reorientation of Western History: Continuity and Environment."* Not only did it pull together many scholars' dissatisfactions with the frontier thesis; it offered a persuasive alternative.

The crux of Pomeroy's revision was in the word "continuity." "America was Europe's 'West' before it was America," a pair of literary critics once observed. Frontiering was a global phenomenon, as old as the idea of the West, which was freighted with significance even for the ancient Greeks. More than a direction or a place, the West was a cultural ideal signifying quest and the prospect of fulfillment in some elusive Elysium. To the west, then, myths ran their course, and America was simply a new stage for an old dream.

Charging the Turnerians with a "radical environmental bias," Pomeroy argued that inherited culture had strongly persisted in the West. Indeed, cultural continuity, imitation in everything from state constitutions to architectural styles, a deep conservatism only intensified by the process of moving away from established centers, and a constant search for respectability and accep-

tance—these, not individualism, inventiveness, and an untrammeled democratic spirit, were the real characteristics of the West. "Conservatism, inheritance, and continuity bulked at least as large in the history of the West as radicalism and environment," Pomeroy wrote. "The westerner has been fundamentally [an] imitator rather than [an] innovator.... He was often the most ardent of conformists."

For the popular image of the West as pathbreaker for the nation, Pomeroy substituted the West as a kind of colonial dependency, an area dominated by eastern values, eastern capital, eastern technology, eastern politics. To understand American development, one need no longer look west; but to understand western development, one *had* to look east. That was the essence of Earl Pomeroy's reorientation.

To historians born during the 20th century, Pomeroy's version of the western past seems much nearer the mark than Turner's. Moreover, Pomeroy reinvigorated western history by suggesting subjects outside the frontier thesis that merited investigation—frontier justice, constitution-making, and politics and parties. His call was answered, most notably, by Yale's Howard Lamar, who sought to rectify the historical neglect of the later territorial period with *Dakota Territory, 1861–1889* (1956) and *The Far Southwest, 1846–1912: A Territorial History* (1966). In the latter, Lamar showed that the various cultures imported into the Southwest remained remarkably impervious to what Turner had regarded as the homogenizing influence of the frontier environment. "Throughout the territorial period New Mexico remained stubbornly and overwhelmingly Spanish-American in culture, tradition-directed in habits, and Roman Catholic in religion. Indeed, Anglo-American citizens remained the minority ethnic group in New Mexico until 1928. Colorado, on the other hand, was essentially an American frontier mining society, which retained close business and social connections with the American East. The settlers of Utah, though partly native American in origin, felt so persecuted because of their firm belief in the Mormon religion—and the accompanying doctrine of polygamous marriage—that they deliberately developed their own unique social and political systems. . . . The di-

---

*Pomeroy's essay appeared in *The Mississippi Valley Historical Review* (March 1955).

One would not know it from watching John Wayne movies, but after the Civil War up to 25 percent of all cowhands were black. Here, black cowboys gather at a fair in Bonham, Texas, in 1910.

verse pioneer settlers of Arizona Territory, hailing from Mexican Sonora, the Confederate South, the American Northeast, and Mormon Utah, formed a conglomerate American frontier society not quite like any of the other three."

Another staple of revisionist western history is economic studies emphasizing the West's dependence on eastern investment capital. In his 1955 essay, Pomeroy wrote that the economic history even of "the pre-agricultural frontiers" would come to rest "on the cold facts of investment capital." However, he said, "we still know the homesteader better than the landlord, the railroad builder better than the railroad operator. The trapper, the prospector, and the cowboy, moving picturesquely over a background of clean air and great distances, hold us more than the tycoons and corporations that dominated them."

The revisionists had their work cut out. They showed, in William H. Goetzmann's memorable phrase, that even the trappers, those legendary embodiments of wanderlust, were Jacksonian men, expectant capitalists out to make their fortune. In *Bill Sublette, Mountain Man* (1959), John E. Sunder detailed the career of one of the most famous beaver trappers of the early 19th century. Sublette frequently relied on eastern capital or credit to keep his dreams alive, and was almost as familiar with the business hotels of New York, Philadelphia, and Washington as he was with the backwoods.

According to legend, cowboys were second-generation mountain men, fiddle-footed wanderers with guns on their hips. Their status as what we now refer to as seasonal agrarian workers might be obscured by romance, but, Lewis Atherton noted in *The Cattle Kings* (1961), cowboys were simply hired hands who lived with the environment while their employers, the ranchers, were businessmen out to dominate it. "The cowboy's life involved so much drudgery and loneliness and so little in the way of satisfaction that he drank and caroused to excess on his infrequent visits to the shoddy little cowtowns that dotted the West.... Most of his physical dangers scarcely bordered on the heroic, necessary as they were in caring for other men's cattle, and they served primarily to retire him from cowpunching." Atherton shared the disparaging view of Bruce Sibert, a rancher in the Dakotas during the 1890s: "Only the few good ones got into the cow business and made good." For those who did become ranchers in "the cow business," Gene M. Gressley observed in *Bankers and Cattlemen* (1966), profit was the motive, capitalization a major problem. Again, eastern money figured prominently.

Nowhere was eastern domination more evident than on the mining frontier. Gold rushes thoroughly disrupted the stately progression of Turner's frontier line, making a shambles of his East-West advance and the stages of social evolution preceding urban civilization. As Richard Wade asserted in *The Urban Frontier* (1959), his history of early Pittsburgh, Cincinnati, Lexington, Louisville, and St. Louis, "The towns were the spearheads of the frontier."

Mining was a case in point. "On the mining frontier the camp—the germ of the city—appeared almost simultaneously with the opening of the region," Duane A. Smith wrote in *Rocky Mountain Mining Camps: The Urban Frontier* (1967). In California, the flood of gold-hungry Forty-Niners created an overnight urban civilization with eastern values. In his history of the Far West, *The Pacific Slope* (1965), Pomeroy noted that in 1860 California had a population three times that of Oregon, Washington, Idaho, Utah, and Nevada combined, and an economy thoroughly integrated into that of the Atlantic Seaboard. A network of eastern

SHOWDOWN IN DODGE CITY

Was it really a wild, wild West before settlers tamed the frontier? More like a mild, mild West, concluded historian Robert Dykstra. The Cattle Towns (1968), his relentlessly factual study of Dodge City and four other fabled Kansas towns during the supposedly wild years between 1870 and 1885, suggests that neither outlaws nor lawmen spent much on ammunition.

Many legendary desperadoes and gunfighters sojourned in the cattle towns at one time or another, but few participated in slayings. Among those with clean records were such famed killers as Clay Allison, Doc Holliday, and Ben Thompson. The teen-aged gunman John Wesley Hardin was responsible for only one verifiable cattle-town homicide, apparently having fired through the wall of his hotel room one drunken night to silence a man snoring too loudly in the adjoining cubicle. Nor did famous gunfighters serving as officers add much to the fatality statistics. As city marshal of Abilene in 1871, his only term as a cattle-town lawman, the formidable Wild Bill Hickok killed just two men—one, a "special" policeman, by mistake. Wyatt Earp, who served as an officer (but never actually as marshal) at both Wichita and Dodge City, may have mortally wounded one law violator, though he shared credit with another policeman for this single cattle-town homicide. The now equally renowned lawman William B. ("Bat") Masterson, at least according to contemporary sources, killed no one in or around Dodge, where he lived for several years.

With these celebrated personalities contributing far less than their supposed share, it is hardly surprising that the overall homicide statistics are not particularly high . . . .

The number of homicides never topped five in any one cattle-season year between 1870 and 1885, and reached this figure only at Ellsworth in 1873 and at Dodge City five years later. In both instances, homicides may have been said to have manifested "wave" dimensions, and were in fact thus considered by local residents. In at least six years no fatalities occurred at all . . . . The zeros recorded for two busy [cattle trade] years at Dodge City seem particularly meaningful. The average number of homicides per cattle-town trading season amounted to only 1.5 per year.

In the case of at least six of these killings—or well over 10 percent—it is hard to identify any connection whatever with the existence of the cattle trade. Besides a Wichita insurance murder, and the murder of an Abilene tailor and the lynching of *his* murderer, already noted, these included the shootings of a Wichita hotel keeper resisting arrest on a federal warrant, that of one Wichita Negro by another, and that of a Caldwell housewife by her drunken husband.

The majority of those involved in homicides, however, were indeed law officers, cowboys and drovers, or gamblers—the last a somewhat elastic category to accommodate four ex-lawmen without obvious means of support. Of homicide victims, nine were

merchants and investors supplied the California miners through West Coast middlemen. As miners dug deeper into the ground, overhead soared, and the need for capital with it. Thus, the network even stretched across the Atlantic. British investors contributed so heavily that they made the Far West part of Britain's "invisible empire," and provided the leadership to draw out more cautious American investors as well, Clark C. Spence explained in *British Investments and the American Mining Frontier, 1860–1901* (1958). It was not long before the fabled individual prospector and his trusty mule were eclipsed.

In advocating a reorientation of western history, Pomeroy had suggested various paths historians might follow to discover East-West continuities. The study of frontier justice would open into an examination of western legal history. Inquiry into frontier religion, literacy, education, and architecture would establish the westerners' cultural conservatism. Likewise, scrutiny of the U.S. Army in the West would show it to be only intermittently a fighting force but continuously a visible manifestation of the federal government and its role in promoting western development. Forest G. Hill's *Roads, Rails, and Waterways: The Army Engineers and Early Transportation* (1957) and Goetzmann's *Army Explorations in the American West, 1803–1863* (1959) responded to the challenge. Goetzmann went on to redirect the history of western exploration from the exploits of hardy individuals to a collective, nationalistic enterprise in which the federal government played a decisive part, the theme of his Pulitzer Prize-winning *Exploration and Empire: The* cowboys or drovers and nine were gamblers. Six were officers of the law. Aside from the non-cattle-trade killings mentioned above, victims included five townsmen with conventional occupations, three local rural settlers, two dance house proprietors, two miscellaneous visitors (one lawyer and a Pawnee Indian), and one female theatrical entertainer. The status of the remaining two victims is obscure. Analyzed in terms of perpetrators, 16 cattle-town homicides can be attributed to law officers, or citizens legitimately acting as such, 12 to cowboys or drovers, and eight to gamblers. The other nine homicides are distributed evenly among some of the categories already mentioned. These included two lynchings evidently carried out by cattle-town residents rather than transients. Besides the episode at Abilene, a Caldwell gambler and bootlegger was hanged in somewhat mysterious circumstances.

With the exception of killings by law officers and lynchings, the homicidal situations varied considerably. Seventeen apparently resulted from private quarrels, four were accidental or without discernible motive, two were committed by resisters of arrest, two avenged prior homicides, and two consisted of murders for profit. Homicidal disputes involving women, incidentally, exceed by eight to one those mainly resulting from gambling disagreements. Of the six lawmen killed, interestingly enough, half met death in circumstances that must be termed accidental, although two of them—Ellsworth's Sheriff Whitney and the Abilene policeman killed by Marshal Hickok—were attempting to help quell trouble when shot. Only two

Formula for Justice

ONE JOB—To head off trouble in a town where trouble was just around the corner.

ONE BADGE—To show the lawless element that the rights of Dodge citizens would be protected.

TWO GUNS—To back the play for law and order in the face of the toughest opposition on the Western frontier.

PUT THEM TOGETHER AND YOU HAVE **WYATT EARP,** FRONTIER MARSHAL

officers died attempting to make arrests; the other fell in a private quarrel.

Lest tradition be completely overthrown, let it be noted that gunshots were far and away the principal medium of death. But tradition would also have it that the cattle-town homicide typically involved an exchange of shots—the so-called gunfight. Actually, though 39 of the 45 victims suffered fatal bullet or buckshot wounds, less than a third of them returned the fire. A good share of them were apparently not even armed.

Explorer and the Scientist in the Winning of the American West (1966). Other histories showed that western communities routinely exaggerated the Indian threat in order to enjoy the benefits—payrolls, improved transportation and communication facilities, even a livelier social life—that an army presence brought. The link between East and West, metropolis and hinterland, federal government and frontier citizen, was everywhere a fact of western life. Even today, the federal government owns vast areas of the West.

By submerging regional in national concerns, "colonial" histories make western history, as such, of limited significance. Regional history is based on the assumption that there are meaningful differences between local and national developments. The South's claim to distinctiveness, histo-

rian C. Vann Woodward has argued, arose from its unique past, marked by the un-American experience of guilt arising from slavery, military defeat, and occupation. History, more than any other factor, accounted for southern uniqueness. But Pomeroy's argument robbed the West of its distinctiveness, making it simply an appendage of the East that was neither exceptional nor especially consequential in the history of the nation.

Opposition to that point of view was not long in coming, and it has usually worked some variation on the exceptionalist premise. Gerald D. Nash, the first historian to attempt a synthesis of 20th-century Western history, rejects Turner's 1890 cutoff date and agrees with Pomeroy that colonialism remained a fact of western life well into the 20th century. But Nash argues that

WOMEN ON THE ROAD WEST

The five-month ordeal of traveling to California or Oregon offered pioneer women many opportunities to shed traditional feminine roles. Most, wrote Julie Roy Jeffrey in Frontier Women: The Trans-Mississippi West, 1840–1880 *(1979), declined to take them.*

Women's work? Collecting buffalo chips for the campfire on the Great Plains, about 1880.

As they catalogued each sign of the passing of civilization, women coped with their sense of desolation by reproducing aspects of the world they had left behind. Thus, women arranged their wagons, writing in their journals of the little conveniences they had fixed, the pockets in the wagon's green cloth lining which held "looking-glasses, combs, brushes, and so on," the rag carpet to keep the floor of the tent snug at night, the bedding, sleeping, and dressing arrangements. As one woman explained, she was busy making "our home" comfortable so that there would be little time "for that dreaded disease, 'home-sickness.'" Another hoped to maintain some continuity by dressing as neatly on the trip as she might at home, in a blue traveling dress with white collar and cuffs rather than homespun, linsey-woolsey, or calico.

These attempts to reproduce the rudiments of a home setting and to perpetuate a sense of the familiar, though they might appear trivial, were not. Publicists of domesticity had encouraged women to believe that the physical arrangements of their homes exerted a powerful influence over their families. The makeshifts of the journey were an unconscious way of asserting female power and reassuring women of their sexual identity. And, of course, the objects symbolized an entire way of life temporarily in abeyance. When her husband grumbled about the quantity of her baggage, Lucy Cooke revealed how vital her knickknacks were. Fearing she would have to discard some . . . , she confessed, "I had a cry about it . . . as I seemed to have parted with near everything I valued."

Although Cooke's husband promised to stop complaining about belongings which provided so much comfort for her, other women would find it difficult to maintain symbolic ties with home life and the female world. The woman who started out in a traveling dress with clean collar and cuffs soon found she had to abandon it for clothes she originally had refused to wear. Indeed, changes in clothing hinted at the social disruption the frontier could cause women. By 1852, some women on the trail were wearing the bloomer costume, finding the "short skirt and pantletts" a "very appropriate dress for a trip like this." Although bloomers were practical, the costume, espoused by feminists as dress for liberated women, carried a radical sexual and political message and was, in the words of one magazine, "ridiculous and indecent." So one woman who had brought bloomers with her found she lacked the "courage" to wear them and vowed, "I would never wear them as long as my other two dresses last." Women bickered over the pros and cons of the costume. Supporters accused women in dresses of being vain and preoccupied with appearance, while they, in turn, replied that bloomers led to male gossip. Said one opponent, "She had never found her dress to be the least inconvenient. . . . [S]he could walk as much in her long dress as she *wanted to, or was proper for a woman* among so many men."

World War II liberated the West from its political, economic, and cultural dependency on the East. The year 1945 becomes a new dividing line in western history, signifying the moment not when the frontier passed into oblivion but when the West passed out of colonialism to become "a pace-setter for the nation."

Yet only by focusing on the Sun Belt, and especially on Southern California, is Nash able to make much of a case for the West as a 20th-century pace-setter. One must be cautious in making parts of the West synonymous with the whole and, out of regional pride, discarding too readily the unflattering fact of western dependency.

Such caution characterizes Patricia Nelson Limerick's provocative new synthesis, *The Legacy of Conquest: The Unbroken Past of the American West* (1987). Limerick is skeptical about talk of the New West, arguing instead for a continuity in western history uninterrupted by any turning points. In her mind, it is this continuity—not links to the East, but the defining western experience "of a place undergoing conquest and never fully escaping its consequences"— that validates a regional approach.

A legacy of conquest, of course, is consonant with Pomeroy's colonial thesis. But Limerick in effect views the East-West relationship from a western perspective rather than a national one. "With its continuity restored," she writes, "western American history carries considerable significance for American history as a whole. Conquest forms the historical bedrock of the whole nation, and the American West is a preeminent case study in conquest and its consequences."

"Celebrating one's past, one's tradition, one's heritage," she concludes, "is a bit like hosting a party: one wants to control the guest list tightly . . . . To celebrate the western past with an open invitation is a considerable risk: The brutal massacres come back along with the cheerful barn raisings, the shysters come back with the saints, contracts broken come back with contracts fulfilled."

Limerick calls her introduction "Closing the Frontier and Opening Western History," as if summoning her fellow historians to put away the toys of childhood and get on with the sterner duties of adulthood. Western historians today regularly berate themselves for failing to keep up with trends in the discipline, for glorying in narrative at the expense of analysis, for favoring the colorful and peripheral to the neglect of the ordinary and substantial. Hard riding makes for easy reading. The very qualities that explained the public's love affair with the West also explained western history's decline in academic circles.

Over the years, suggestions for revitalizing western history have been pretty conventional: Find out where everyone else is going and follow. Learn to quantify. Adopt social-science methodologies. Alter the very nature of historical inquiry and expression or fade into academic oblivion, western historians were warned. But the most extravagant claims for the new social history, for example, have been recanted, and dire predictions about the early demise of "old-fashioned" history have failed to come true. It is apparent now that the advocates of new history too often adopted the strategy of Melville's lightning-rod salesman and sold fear rather than necessity. To date, the net effect of the new history revolution has been new topics rather than a consistent new direction for western history, fragmentation rather than synthesis.

Turner's thesis is now notorious for excluding women and everyone whose skin was dark or whose language was not English. Indians were obstacles handy for demarking the frontier line and eliciting pioneer traits in the white men who would overcome them; women apparently stayed in the East until the land was tidied up and made presentable; Mexicans and other ethnics never existed.

Women have been a favorite topic of the new history. Studies of army wives and daughters, women teachers, women on the overland trails, farm women, prostitutes, divorcees, widows, and urban women have forever altered the sentimental stereotypes of sunbonneted pioneer mothers and soiled doves with hearts of gold.

Pomeroy's argument for cultural continuity has been echoed in discussions of one key issue: Did the move West liberate women from conventional sex roles or not? John Mack Faragher concludes *Women and Men on the Overland Trail* (1979) with a flat negative: "The move West called upon people not to change but to transfer old sexual roles to a new but altogether familiar environment." While confessing that she had hoped to find otherwise, Julie Roy Jeffrey, in *Frontier Women: The Trans-Mississippi West, 1840–1880* (1979), is forced to agree with Faragher: "The frontier experience served to reinforce many conven-

31

Among the many westerners who found it profitable to promote the Western mystique was Jesse James's brother Frank, shown here about 1914 at the family farm in Excelsior Springs, Missouri.

tional familial and cultural ideas.... The concept of woman as lady, the heart of domestic ideology, survived."

Jeffrey did detect some changes in women's roles. Prostitutes, for instance, were treated as individuals in the West rather than simply as a pariah class. Polly Welts Kaufman in *Women Teachers on the Frontier* (1984) also strains against the limitations implied by the colonial interpretation, noting that the 250 women who went west to teach for the National Board of Popular Education before the Civil War decided to do so largely out of a desire for independence and control over their lives. Kaufman concedes, however, that teaching was among the few occupations that met "society's expectations for women." Liberation plays an even larger part in Paula Petrik's *No Step Backward: Woman and Family on the Rocky Mountain Mining Frontier, Helena, Montana, 1865–1900* (1987). The move west, Petrik maintained, did change things for some women, at least during the frontier period.

Another prominent strain of western historical scholarship takes the western myth itself as its subject. Americans have loved the Wild West myth with an abiding, though some say waning, passion. It has circled the globe in its appeal. To its critics, however, the myth is an invitation to the wrong set of values. It embodies an essentially conservative ethos—rugged individualism, stern justice, indifference or hostility to women and ethnics, exploitation of

the environment, development at any cost. But it also embodies the American dream, and has served as the polestar for generations of immigrants who sought a greater measure of human happiness in a land of unrivaled wealth and opportunity.

It should come as no surprise, then, that the popular image of the Wild West is largely the work of outsiders meeting outside needs. There seems no escaping eastern domination. Pomeroy himself traced an aspect of this cultural imperialism in his imaginative *In Search of the Golden West: The Tourist in Western America* (1957). The West, he found, became whatever the eastern tourist wanted it to be: "[F]or 60 or 70 years...tourists had to be reassured, and westerners felt that they had to assure them, that the West was no longer wild and woolly—until fashions changed and it was time to convince them that it was as wild as it ever had been."

How wild was it to begin with? There is an established tradition in western history of separating fiction from fact to get at the truth behind the frontier's most storied individuals and episodes. Don Russell's *The Lives and Legends of Buffalo Bill* (1960), Joseph G. Rosa's *They Called Him Wild Bill: The Life and Adventures of James Butler Hickok* (1964, rev. 1974), William A. Settle, Jr.'s *Jesse James Was His Name; or, Fact and Fiction Concerning the Careers of the Notorious James Brothers of Missouri* (1966), Robert K. De Arment's *Bat Masterson: The Man and the Legend* (1979), and Jack Burrows's *John Ringo: The Gunfighter Who Never Was* (1987) are good examples of this approach to biography.

Cultural historians find the legends more arresting—and revealing—than the facts. Strip Billy the Kid of his myth and little of historical consequence remains. Even the number of his victims does not hold up under scrutiny. But the mythic Billy the Kid is full of interest, as Stephen Tatum explains in *Inventing Billy the Kid: Visions of the Outlaw in America* (1982). During the first 40 years after his death at the hands of Pat Garrett in 1881, writers (including Garrett himself in his *The Authentic Life of Billy, the Kid*) portrayed the Kid as the villain in "a romance story dramatizing civilization's triumph over a stubborn, resistant, and savage wilderness."

For roughly the next 30 years, however, Billy was portrayed in a more positive light. Disillusioned by the power of gangsters and the weakness and corruption of government, the Kid's "creators"—including the composer Aaron Copland, who wrote the score for the 1938 ballet, *Billy the Kid*—conjured up a new image. Because society is "unable to defend itself or recognize the evil within its own ranks," Tatum writes, "the outsider like the Kid enters the scene to save the day and restore a society of common people being threatened by evil bankers and their henchmen. Yet no matter how noble his actions, in this era the Kid is not integrated into society at story's end."

But after 1955, Tatum continues, inventions of the Kid "typically omit the romance framework of civilization's progress or foundation, and instead present a dehumanizing society at odds with an authentic individual's personal code." No longer is there much hope that the hero can transform the world; the Kid "appears in works that dramatize the individual at odds with society, a civil law unrelated to moral law, and violence hardly legitimated or regenerative." This culminated in the purely meaningless cinematic violence of Sam Peckinpah's famous *Pat Garrett and Billy the Kid* (1973). Today, the Kid awaits new mythmakers.

Since cultural values shift over time, myths, in order to remain relevant, shift their meanings as well. If the major challenge facing western history is to relate past to present in a meaningful way, the mythic approach has much to offer. It accounts for continuity *and* change. George Armstrong Custer is dead, his Last Stand long over. Why then do so many people continue to refight it? Why can they still see it in their minds? Why are passions still aroused by the man? We may dismiss Custer as a minor figure historically, but he was once a national hero, a martyr to cause and country, held up as a model for America's youth. His defenders still think him a paragon, if not a saint, and he has been compared to Jesus. His detractors regard him as a racist villain, fit symbol for America's mistreatment of its native peoples. In 1988, a Sioux activist likened him to Adolf Hitler and argued that the Custer Battlefield National Monument was as welcome in Indian country as a Hitler monument would be in Israel.

Myths have consequences, and Richard Slotkin's *Regeneration Through Violence: The Mythology of the American Frontier, 1600–1860* (1973) and *The Fatal Environment: The Myth of the Frontier in the Age of Industrialization, 1800–1890* (1985) are the most ambitious attempts yet to trace patterns of frontier mythology, from Cotton Mather through Walt Whitman and Theodore Roosevelt. So deeply has the language of the frontier myth been woven into our popular culture, he writes, "that it still colors the way we count our wealth and estimate our prospects, the way we deal with nature and with the nations so that the Myth can still tell us what to look for when we look at the stars."

Works like Slotkin's assume something Turner labored to prove: American exceptionalism. On the other hand, they encourage a reexamination of the qualities supposedly fostered by frontiering and which, according to Turner, combined to form the American character.

The character-forming western myth is marked by some notable omissions. "Where are the women in this tradition?" asked Helen Winter Stauffer and Susan J. Rosowski in *Women and Western American Literature* (1982). It is a question that cuts to the heart of a male myth steeped in escapist fantasies. The myth does include Indians, but simply as part of the savage Nature that the white pioneer was expected to subdue, a test of the sort that meets any quester after Elysium. The native *fact* offers its own rebuttal: The white man's occupation of America was an armed invasion, nothing more, nothing less.

When one moves from individuals and events and omissions to the qualities or traits revered in western myth, it is apparent that the myth generates its own critiques, its own counter-images.

Rugged individualists taming a raw wilderness? Roderick Nash's *Wilderness and the American Mind* (1967, rev. 1982) and Lee Clark Mitchell's *Witnesses to a Vanishing America: The Nineteenth-Century Response* (1981) show that frontiering and its apotheosis of axe and plow created a contrary reaction, a conservationist outlook that deplored the wastefulness inherent in pioneering and opened the way to resource management and federal controls.

Buoyant optimism and the mastery of material things? The lunacy of such hopeful frontier slogans as "Rain follows the plow" was revealed during the 1930s, when the interior of the continent turned into a dust bowl, spurring a massive internal migration that exposed the hollow promise of western opportunity. The California Dream? Ask the Okies.

Cowboy freedom in a spacious land where all were equal? Ask the multitude of western wage-earners who found the pay low, conditions hard, strife endemic, upward mobility limited, and independence illusory. Or ask any racial minority struggling to get ahead in the West.

Six-gun justice and self-reliance? The horrifying rate of contemporary violence would seem rebuttal enough to such a cherished tradition, but in *The Cattle Towns* (1968), Robert Dykstra shoots down the Hollywood version of Dodge City and its ilk. [See box, p. 28.]

Abundant natural resources ensuring all a chance to prosper? The antimyth points to the depletion and spoliation of a rich heritage, a destructive "Myth of Superabundance," and the rise of resource monopolization and agribusiness, the creation of a boom-and-bust economy, and a continuing reliance on the federal government. More colonialism, and precious little individual opportunity. Myth, after all, is myth.

For the historian, the western myth offers a skewed but revealing national portrait, a study not in what was but in what once seemed desirable. To the extent that it was always false, we have a measure of the distance between expectation and reality in western and American history. To the extent that it now seems unbecoming, we have a measure of the distance between the values of yesterday and today. The myth and the antimyth are keys to the western past and the western present that can also unlock the American past and the American present.

The Haymarket Bomb

Burton Schindler

Burton Schindler is a newspaper reporter and feature writer who also does extensive free-lance writing for business and general interest publications.

A trail of sparks followed the small dark object as it soared over the throng. A few in the shoving, scrambling, shouting crowd looked up. But most were trying to avoid rank after rank of policemen who were marching steadily toward them. In the dimness of the few gas lights, only twinkles from the police badges could be seen.

Then the bomb exploded.

The repercussions from that blinding flash in Haymarket Square in Chicago one hundred years ago, May 4, 1886, were far-reaching. Eventually the bomb blast and its aftereffects would leave seven policemen dead and sixty others wounded, an unknown number of civilians killed and injured, four men hanged, another a suicide, a judge and a lawyer disgraced, a governor's career wrecked, and a mighty labor union destroyed. Its echoes can still be faintly heard today.

Haymarket—like Watergate eighty-six years later—was a place that lent its name to a particular event in time and to the violent emotions accompanying that event. Haymarket Square was, as it is today, a wide place on Randolph Street just west of Desplaines Avenue, near Chicago's open-air produce market. It gained its place in history because it happened to be a convenient location for a mass-meeting of workers who were protesting the long hours, low pay, and oppression they claimed were the results of unfair government action.

The circumstances that would set the stage for the events of May 1886 had been taking form for more than a decade. America's working class had been hard-hit by economic severity and depression during the 1870s. Especially apparent was the wide gulf between the world of a few industrial millionaires and that of three million unemployed and fifteen million others who lived in poverty. Such conditions led to riots, the starting of labor union organizations, and the questioning by some of the viability of the capitalist system.

By 1886 one national labor union, the Knights of Labor, had grown to over seven hundred thousand members, and workers all around the country were demand-

From *American History Illustrated*, June 1986, pp. 20-27. Reprinted through the courtesy of Cowles Magazines, publishers of *American History Illustrated*.

ing improved conditions. In particular, they were marching and striking for an eight-hour workday. A deadline for making the eight-hour day a reality was set for May 1, 1886.

Chicago, especially, was a hotbed of labor unrest. In 1871 much of Chicago had been destroyed by fire, and within three years thousands of workers who had come to rebuild the city were unemployed. Making the situation even worse over the next several years was an influx of thousands of Irish and German immigrants. The result was that there were simply not enough jobs to go around, and many of those who did have work labored under poor conditions. In addition, a group of radicals had taken over much of the labor and union leadership, especially among the German immigrant workers, who had seen employers use other immigrant groups as strikebreakers against them whenever they attempted to enforce demands.

But the Germans who headed the most vocal groups were not just seeking changes in the number of working hours—they wanted an end to the entire capitalist system that seemed to create millionaires at the expense of the poverty-stricken. And they saw violence as the means to that end. They called themselves Socialists sometimes, but they often preferred the name the newspapers used: Anarchists.

Two men were the leaders of this group: August Spies, who was editor of the German-language Socialist newspaper *Arbeiter-Zeitung* ("Workers' Newspaper"), and Albert Parsons, editor of another activist newspaper, *The Alarm.*

Spies, born in Germany in 1855, had emigrated to the United States in 1872. He moved to Chicago the following year and in 1876 opened a furniture store. Spies soon made enough money to bring his widowed mother, sister, and three brothers to America. His interest in socialism began in the mid-1870s, when he felt the irony of his own success in the face of the poverty around him.

Parsons was born in Montgomery, Alabama, in 1848 and was orphaned at an early age. He served in the Confederate Army during the Civil War but became a strong believer in black civil rights, a cause he addressed in *The Spectator,* a newspaper he started in Texas in 1867. Parson's marriage to a woman of mixed racial background made him unwelcome in Texas, and in 1873 the couple moved to Chicago to become involved with the labor struggle that was centered there.

By 1886 both men had been politically active for years, making speeches throughout the country to any group that would listen, expounding their ideas of a new society without property rights, in which every man would be equal. Only a year earlier Parsons had spoken at a workingman's picnic attended by more than ten thousand, calling for a society in which there would be "neither masters nor slaves, neither governors nor governed, no law but the natural law."

As the drive for an eight-hour workday gained momentum, the anarchists saw it as an opportunity for promoting their own militant causes, and Spies and Parsons became the leading spokesmen for the campaign in the Chicago area. The two men frequently issued calls for violence in the columns of the *Arbeiter-Zeitung* and *The Alarm;* later these words would help to place nooses around their necks.

With the arrival of the May deadline for an eight-hour day, more than forty thousand Chicago workers went on strike. No violence occurred on May 1, as had been feared by officials, but it erupted just two days later at the McCormick Reaper Works on Blue Island Avenue. During a bitter labor struggle that had begun at McCormick several months earlier, the plant management had locked out striking union workers and hired nonunion men.

On the afternoon of May 3, August Spies was asked to speak to a group of striking lumber shovers a few blocks from the McCormick works. While he was addressing a crowd of some six thousand men, nonunion workers began leaving the nearby plant at the end of their shift, and strikers there attacked them with rocks. Police quickly moved in; shots were fired; and within minutes two men were dead. Early newspaper reports erroneously claimed that six had been killed.

Spies rushed to the scene following his speech and witnessed some of the violence. Infuriated by what he saw as police brutality, he returned to his office and printed up leaflets, in English and German, with the headlines "Revenge!" and "Workingmen, to Arms!!!" The following morning other anarchists associated with Spies printed up additional handbills calling for a mass meeting of workers that night in Haymarket Square. Because of the emotions that were building up over the McCormick deaths, they expected a crowd of twenty thousand, and Haymarket was the only spot that could accommodate such numbers. The organizers knew that the Desplaines Avenue police station was only a half-block from the site, but though there would be angry speeches they neither planned nor expected violence.

The night of May 4 was mild, but the skies were heavy with clouds and an intermittent mist blew through the square where a few groups were beginning to gather. At about 8:15 P.M., Spies arrived on the scene and found only about two thousand people waiting. There was no organization and no speeches were yet in progress, just small clumps of people talking together around the intersection. Spies headed a few yards up Desplaines Avenue, away from the square, to a wagon that he selected as a speakers' platform. Calling the crowd over, he began his talk while hoping that other speakers would soon arrive. He continued for an hour. Eventually, a few others of his group began to arrive.

While Spies was speaking, Chicago Mayor Carter Harrison wandered through the crowd. Earlier he had personally given permission for the rally and now he made himself conspicuous by lighting and relighting his cigar. "I want the people to know their mayor is here," he

August Spies

said to a bystander, who warned him that his action might bring him harm. Harrison knew that Police Captain William Ward and Inspector John Bonfield were waiting with 176 officers at the nearby station in case of trouble. After listening for a while, Harrison strolled down to the alley where the police were assembled and told Bonfield that although the speech was angry, there seemed to be nothing dangerous in the situation. With that, he left and rode to his home on Ashland Avenue.

As Spies finished, another speaker arrived. Albert Parsons had been hurriedly located and brought to the wagon before the crowd could leave. Parsons spoke for an hour more, and while most of his speech supported the eight-hour day and the usual calls for an end to oppression, a *Chicago Tribune* reporter recalled later that he also told the listeners, although in a calm voice, to "arm, arm yourselves." He also referred to a "Gatling gun ready to mow you down." A *New York Times* story over the weekend had mentioned that members of Chicago's Commercial Club, an association of business leaders, had raised over two thousand dollars among themselves to purchase a Gatling machine gun for the local militia regiment to be used in the event of disorder.

Parsons then introduced Samuel Fielden as the last speaker. Parsons and his wife Lucy soon headed up Desplaines Avenue to a beer hall, Zepf's, to await the end of the rally.

Fielden, who was born in 1847 in Lancashire, England, had begun working in a cloth mill at age eight — an experience that would have a formative influence on his later involvement in labor and union causes. Emigrating to the United States in 1868, he found employment as a stonehauler in Chicago. One of the more radical activists, Fielden was nevertheless popular and respected

among workers for his eloquent and impassioned speeches on labor issues.

As Fielden started to speak, the skies rumbled and drops of rain began to pelt the crowd in Haymarket Square. Most of the listeners drifted away, until fewer than three hundred remained around the speakers' wagon. As Spies listened from the back of the wagon, Fielden said that the law was nothing of value. He told his listeners "to lay hands on it and throttle it until it makes its last kick."

Two detectives who had been mingling with the crowd hurried away from the wagon as Fielden spoke these words. They rushed down the street to Inspector Bonfield at the Desplaines Street station and told him that the atmosphere was growing violent. Bonfield and Ward mustered their squads and ordered them forward. The men moved out of the darkened alley next to the police station, filling the street and heading across the half-block of Randolph to a spot just north of the corner where Fielden was speaking.

At first the crowd was unaware of the approaching policemen. As the ranks of officers began to shove into their midst, Captain Ward shouted, "I command you, in the name of the people of the State of Illinois, immediately and peaceably to disperse!" Fielden saw the police and responded, "But we are peaceable," and began to climb down from the wagon. At just that moment the trail of sparks flew overhead. The bomb landed just in front of the first police rank. It burst with a roar that was heard by Mayor Harrison, who was preparing for bed in his home blocks away.

For an instant afterward there was silence. Then shouts, screams, and soon the roar of shots as the police fired into the crowd. Most of the crowd started to run up the street, away from the police. The shots followed them, dropping some blocks or more away. The scene around the explosion was one of horror. Maimed and dying policemen lay scattered along the pavement. Injured and shot workers lay moaning against the darkened buildings. The firing continued for almost five minutes.

Many of those who were injured by the bullets or the trampling crowd burst into saloons and stores along Desplaines and other streets, ignoring the threats of the owners, and piled up tables and boxes for protection. The police, meanwhile, began to drag their injured comrades back toward the station. Soon the floor there was covered with mangled and bleeding men, some calling for help, others pale and silent in shock and approaching death. Eventually, seven policemen would die and more than sixty would recover from wounds. According to the *Chicago Tribune*, "a very large number of the police were wounded by each other's revolvers."

Of the civilian casualties, no exact count was ever made. Many of the injured were hauled away by their friends, some riding streetcars to get away from the scene. Others treated themselves as best they could, fearing to report their wounds lest they be arrested.

1. RECONSTRUCTION AND THE GILDED AGE

As the night descended on the city, police raced from rumor to rumor of impending riot and rebellion. Alarmed, Mayor Harrison issued orders approaching martial law. Suspects were routed out of bed, often without the legality of a warrant. Men were jailed without evidence, and questioning was often harsh. Over the next days, all meetings would be banned. The city trembled in fear. Even display of the color red was prohibited because of its association with the anarchists.

Newspapers and civic leaders across the country demanded action and revenge. The *New York Times* headlined its lead story the next morning, "Anarchy's Red Hand." And, from the respected *Albany Law Review* came demands for punishment "for the few long-haired, wild-eyed, bad-smelling, atheistic, reckless foreign wretches."

By midmorning on May 5, the Chicago police had arrested dozens. Among them were seven who would eventually stand trial. August Spies and Adolph Fischer, a typesetter at Spies's newspaper, were arrested just after nine o'clock in their office. Samuel Fielden was taken from his home early in the morning. He was wearing a bandage and told the police he had been wounded in the knee and needed treatment. According to his testimony, a detective responded that "they ought to put strychnine in it." While Fielden was being rushed to a cell, the police turned his house inside-out, but found nothing incriminating. Other activists arrested included George Engel, Oscar Neebe, Michael Schwab, and Louis Lingg.

Albert Parsons was not found. While he and his wife were waiting at Zepf's Hall they heard the explosion and shots. Knowing that her husband would be a prime suspect, Lucy urged him to leave the city. Borrowing five dollars from a friend, Parsons made his way to the Chicago & Northwestern Railroad station and took the next train to Wisconsin.

After staying one night with a friend in Lake Geneva, Parsons went to Waukesha, where he remained in hiding while the search continued in Chicago. His escape caused even further outrage.

While Chicago seethed in fear and rumor, other cities, too, reacted with alarm. According to many historians, this was America's first actual terrorist bombing. For many, the threat of true anarchy now was made real. The Knights of Labor sought to distance themselves from the unknown bomb-thrower and issued statements denouncing the act and urging the conviction of Parsons, Fielding, and Spies. The demands for swift justice were heard everywhere.

Indictments were handled quickly and the trial began on June 21, only a few weeks after the Haymarket explosion. It lasted until August 19 and, despite the heat of a Chicago summer, the courtroom was continually packed. Judge Joseph E. Gary was chosen to preside. His actions—such as refusing to allow the case to be postponed until public hysteria had died down and refusing to disqualify clearly prejudiced jurors—would

eventually become cause for the claims of bias.

The Cook County state's attorney was Julius S. Grinnell. For a time, the defendants were without a lawyer. No one in Chicago was willing to risk his career in their behalf. Finally, after being asked to find an attorney for the seven, William P. Black, a respected corporation lawyer and Civil War veteran, decided to handle the case himself even though he, too, feared that it might cause him damage.

Meanwhile, hiding out in Wisconsin, Albert Parsons considered his situation. There he was safe. But his conscience demanded that he join his comrades on the dock, even though he guessed the outcome of the trial. Before the trial began, after talking with his friends and on the advice of William Black, Parsons decided to return to be tried. Black had hoped that Parsons's voluntary surrender would improve the court's attitude. Unfortunately for Parsons, his return only sealed his fate.

Both the prosecution and defense had difficult jobs ahead of them. Grinnell's first problem was to connect the defendants with the bomb itself. One witness, Harry L. Gilmer, told the police that he had seen August Spies actually lighting the fuse at the rear of the wagon. But others discounted that testimony, saying they had seen the bomb coming from a spot near the northeast corner of Desplaines Avenue and Randolph.

Each of the defendants turned out to have a clear alibi for his whereabouts, which meant that none of those on trial could have actually thrown the bomb. Samuel Fielden was actually talking with Captain Ward as the bomb flew overhead. August Spies was seen by the crowd and policemen at the back of the wagon. Louis Lingg was on the north side of town, George Engel and Oscar Neebe were at home, and Michael Schwab was five miles away. Adolph Fischer and Albert Parsons were known to have been in Zepf's Hall when the explosion occurred.

Determined to obtain a conviction nevertheless, Grinnell now changed his tactics, going for a charge of conspiracy. "Although perhaps none of these men personally threw the bomb," he argued, "they each and all abetted, encouraged and advised the throwing of it and are therefore as guilty as the individual who in fact threw it."

Judge Gary aided the prosecutor's cause mightily with his charge to the jury that if any of the men had "by print or speech advised, or encouraged the commission of murder, without designating time, place or occasion at which it should be done . . . then all of such conspirators are guilty of such murder." August Spies's handbill and the speeches of the others were coming back to convict them of a crime they did not commit.

After dozens of witnesses (many of whom gave conflicting testimony that was later discredited) and extensive exhibited evidence that told of the defendants' years of inciting anarchy, the trial came to a close. The jury received its instructions and retired to deliberate on the afternoon of August 19. It needed only three hours to reach its verdict.

On the following morning Judge Gary convened the court, and the verdict was read. Oscar Neebe was considered to have played a minor role in the alleged conspiracy and was sentenced to fifteen years in prison; all of the other defendants were found guilty of murder and sentenced to death. The verdict exceeded even the expectations of state's attorney Grinnell, who had anticipated at most four death sentences.

According to defense attorney William Black, "not a [defendant's] face blanched" as the verdict was read. Albert Parsons, who was standing near an open window, coolly waved a red handkerchief to the hostile crowd waiting in the street below. Then, to advise them of the penalty, he tied the cords of the window shade to form a noose. His action was greeted by wild cheers.

Black immediately filed for a retrial, but Judge Gary denied all motions on October 7, the day set for formal sentencing. Prior to his statements, Gary allowed each prisoner the right to speak. They all took full advantage of the opportunity: their speeches lasted for three days.

The defendants remained unrepentant regarding both their beliefs and actions. "I am an Anarchist," Albert Parsons loudly stated. "I declare again, openly and frankly," said Louis Lingg, "that I am in favor of using force." "I am sorry that I am not to be hung with the rest of the men," said Oscar Neebe. Nevertheless the men maintained that they had been tried for their radical political beliefs, not their actions; that they had been found guilty by public opinion from the beginning; and that they were innocent of the crime for which they had been convicted.

Gary told the condemned men that their trial had been "unexampled for these days, in the patience with which an outraged people have extended you every protection and privilege of the law which you have derided and defied." He then set December 3, 1886, for their execution.

Black promptly filed an appeal with the Supreme Court of Illinois. On November 25, Chief Justice John M. Scott ordered a stay of execution until the appeal was decided. That body took months to deliberate, but in the end, its decision on September 14, 1887, confirmed the verdict. On November 2, 1887, the United States Supreme Court refused to consider the case as it lacked jurisdiction. A new date, November 11, 1887, was set for the executions.

In the interim, however, emotions had subsided a bit. Some of those who had earlier been crying for instant vengeance now were wondering if the trial had been completely fair. Petitions began to pour into the office of Governor Richard J. Oglesby in Springfield. After an Amnesty Association was formed, the mass of petitions and personal appeals for clemency for the seven condemned men grew even more. Among the powerful petitioners was Samuel Gompers, the first president of the new American Federation of Labor (AFL) that had been founded in 1886. The fledgling organization would eventually supplant Terence Powderly's faltering Knights of Labor as the strongest organization behind labor reform. "I abhor anarchy," stated Gompers, "but I also abhor injustice when meted out even to the most despicable being on earth."

Illinois law required that a condemned man had to ask personally for clemency before the governor could legally act on the matter. Only Samuel Fielden, August Spies, and Michael Schwab did so. After many hours and a full day devoted to listening to petitions, Oglesby prepared to make his decision. But two events intervened before he could make a statement.

On November 6, guards at the Cook County Jail conducted a surprise search of the cells. They discovered four dynamite bombs hidden under the bunk in Louis Lingg's cell. Reports that the prisoners had planned a mass suicide attempt ran through the city. Lingg was moved to another cell and the other prisoners were separated from each other. Visitors, however, were permitted.

Then, at about 9:00 A.M. on November 10, a loud explosion resounded through the cell block. Guards rushed into Lingg's cell to find him slumped on his cot in a mass of blood and torn flesh. He had exploded a dynamite cap in his mouth and blown the lower half of his face away. Despite attempts by doctors to sew up the shattered face, Lingg continued to bleed and he died at 2:50 P.M. His body was dumped into a tub to await the execution of his comrades the following day.

Governor Oglesby was told of Lingg's suicide. It is not known how the event weighed on his decision. His final announcement on November 10 was that Michael Schwab and Samuel Fielden would have their sentences commuted to life in prison. The others would hang.

At 11:30 A.M. on the following day, November 11, 1887, Sheriff Canute R. Matson entered the prison with a squad of armed guards. Outside, Chicago was an armed camp: the Cook County Jail was ringed with armed officers, and police and soldiers were on alert at key points throughout the city. They feared not only a possible attempt to rescue the prisoners, but citywide rebellion.

Robed in white shrouds, the four condemned men were led to a scaffold that had been erected in a corridor of the jail building. Rows of benches, occupied by 170 witnesses, faced the scaffold. As each man was brought forward to stand under a hangman's rope, his ankles were bound with a leather strap. The noose was then placed around his neck and a hood put over his head.

From behind one hood, the muffled voice of Adolph Fischer cried out in German, "Hurrah for Anarchy!" George Engel echoed his cry in English. The witnesses strained to hear August Spies who shouted through his hood, "The day will come when our silence will be more powerful than the voices you strangle today!" Albert Parsons, too, attempted to speak, but as he started, the trap was sprung and the four dropped. Eight minutes later they were declared dead; all four had died from strangulation.

Afterward, the bodies were taken to their respective homes for mourning by their friends. (The remains of Louis Lingg, because he had no relatives in America, were taken to Engel's house.) On Sunday, November 13, a funeral procession wound through downtown Chicago to the central railroad station. By this time public opinion had reversed itself; many now viewed the five men as martyrs who had died unjustly. More than twenty thousand people followed the caskets to the depot, while over two hundred thousand others lined the streets. Then a special train carried the bodies and ten thousand mourners toward the German village of Forest Park on Chicago's west side and its Waldheim Cemetery. It was the largest funeral in the city's history.

Six years later, on June 25, 1893, another eight thousand people assembled at Waldheim Cemetery for the dedication of a monument to the condemned men. The memorial featured a bronze sculpture by Albert Weinert, depicting a hooded woman placing a wreath on the head of a fallen worker. August Spies's last words from the scaffold were carved into the base of the memorial.

On the following day the new governor of Illinois, John Peter Altgeld, announced that he was pardoning the three remaining members of the "Haymarket Eight." At the same time he issued a strongly worded, detailed statement condemning the Haymarket trial as blatantly unfair and the actions there by the police, prosecuting attorneys, and judge as prejudiced. Michael Schwab, Samuel Fielden, and Oscar Neebe were free men.

Governor Altgeld's actions, however, drew hostile reactions from many newspapers around the country and ignited a storm of controversy. Later the governor would be defeated in his bid for a second term—a result at least in part attributable to his stand on the Haymarket trial.

Altgeld was not the only one to suffer from association with the Haymarket controversy. Corporation lawyer William P. Black, who had defended the anarchists at the risk of his reputation, saw his worst fears realized. Following the trial Black was ostracized by the city's business community, lost most of his clients, and his once-thriving law partnership dissolved.

Even more far-reaching in consequence was Haymarket's effect on the labor movement. Although labor unions had had no direct connection with the bombing—and sought to distance themselves from it—such association in the public mind was nevertheless inevitable. The campaign for an eight-hour workday suffered a severe setback, and the powerful Knights of Labor, which had boasted seven hundred thousand members in 1886, soon shriveled to a shadow of its former strength.

And what of the man who should have been convicted, the actual bomb-thrower? He was never caught or identified. Some suspected that he was an *agent provocateur* against the eight-hour movement. The police, and many others, suspected that the killer was Michael Schwab's brother-in-law, Rudolph Schnaubelt. Although no proof was ever presented, many have claimed that it was indeed Schnaubelt who stood in a darkened doorway near the corner of Randolph and Desplaines and hurled the bomb ninety-two feet to its point of impact. It would have taken a very strong man to toss it that far. Schnaubelt was a big man, standing over six feet tall and weighing two hundred pounds. He was arrested and questioned during the furor following the bombing, but claimed innocence. Shortly after Schnaubelt was released he fled to England and then to Argentina. Eventually he married, became a prosperous manufacturer, and faded into anonymity.

The true identity of the person responsible will probably never be known. However, research by historian Paul Avrich indicates that Dyer Lum, an anarchist who committed suicide in 1893, knew who the bomb-thrower was. Lum's letters give tantalizing hints—but no specific name—about the man: he was a militant activist and anarchist, he was probably German, and he was not one of the men tried and convicted of the crime.

Thirteen years after the tragic day, on Memorial Day in 1899, a monument was dedicated to the fallen policemen of Haymarket Square. The bronze figure of a policeman with his arm raised, demanding peace, was placed on a granite base about a block from the site of the actual events. Twice, in 1969 and 1970, the policeman's figure was blown from its pedestal by bombs put there by modern anarchists. After the second explosion, Chicago's Mayor Richard Daley denounced the acts and pledged a full-time police guard over the monument. But a year later, this measure having proved too costly, the figure was removed from its base and placed in the lobby of the main Chicago police station.

Today the site of the bombing is a desolate corner of rubble and decrepit buildings. Traffic roars down the nearby Kennedy Expressway, and fruit and vegetable vendors fill the marketplace with activity. The empty pedestal for the police memorial stands in Haymarket Square, visited only by pigeons and an occasional vacant-eyed drunk from nearby Skid Row.

But twice each year at Waldheim Cemetery, on May 4 and November 11 (the anniversaries of the bombing and executions), someone places a single, long-stemmed red rose at the base of the memorial for the condemned men. After one hundred years, the controversy still lingers on over the anarchists . . . or the martyrs . . . depending on the point of view.

Suggested additional reading: The Haymarket Tragedy *by Paul Avrich (Princeton University Press, 1984).*

UPWARD BOUND

Clyde C. Griffen

Clyde C. Griffen, 58, is professor of history at Vassar College. Born in Sioux City, Iowa, he received a B.A. from the University of Iowa (1952) and a Ph.D. from Columbia University (1960). He is author, with Sally Griffen, of Natives and Newcomers: The Ordering of Opportunity in Mid-Nineteenth-Century Poughkeepsie *(1978).*

Land of opportunity, of self-made men, where newcomers from every nation can slough off old habits and restrictions and strive for advancement. That is one of the ways Americans like to think of their country. And it seems as if they always have. In 1782, the French-born New York farmer-author, J. Hector St. John Crèvecoeur, wrote of the immigrant in the New World: "He forms schemes of future prosperity, he proposes to educate his children better than he has been educated himself; he thinks of future modes of conduct, feels an ardor to labor he never felt before."

In one sense, the contemporary ring of Crèvecoeur's observation is misleading, for the popular meanings of "self-improvement" and "opportunity" have varied over the years. Chattel slaves aside, Crèvecoeur's America was mostly a nation of farmers, savoring the freedom of thought and action that comes with tilling one's own land. The early goals that he described were those of sturdy independence or a modest rise in earnings and status. Later came visions of "rags-to-riches," and, especially during the 20th century, notions of success as "self-fulfillment" and psychic well-being.

But, in another sense, the freshness of Crèvecoeur's words is a reminder of the tension that has always existed between American ideas of material success and other notions of self-improvement—moral, religious, and intellectual. Today, in academe, in the popular press, and in opinion polls, Americans still seem to vacillate among these diverse ideas, even as "social mobility" is generally equated with individual movement up or down the socioeconomic ladder.

Moreover, only during the past few decades have historians looked closely at the changing visions and realities of social mobility in American history. Easiest to see were the heroes and maxims held aloft by authors of popular fiction (e.g., Horatio Alger, Jr.) and advice books. Even with the help of computers, the more difficult task has been the analysis of masses of data (censuses, tax lists, probate records, and other quantifiable sources) in an attempt to reconstruct changing patterns of Americans' fortunes during individual careers and between generations. Archives vary in quality and coverage. Scholars' confidence in generalizing from these sources also varies. But historians have enough of an outline to see that the story of social mobility—up and down—in America is much more complex and significant than was previously thought.

Anglo-Americans began life in America with Old World visions of a static social order. In 1630, when John Winthrop addressed his Puritan shipmates aboard the *Arbella* before leading them ashore in Massachusetts, he reminded them that a fixed social hierarchy was God's ordering of "differences for the preservation and good of the whole . . . in all times some must be rich some poor, some high and eminent in power and dignity; others mean and in subjection."

In Winthrop's austere Massachusetts Bay Colony, personal ambition received no encouragement. The well-being of the community required that all individuals fulfill the responsibilities of their respective ranks in life. The vast majority would follow in the footsteps of their fathers and become farmers. (In a more unusual example of continuity, Winthrop, his son, and his grandson all served as colonial governors.) The few colonists who rose from lowly origins to grander positions would simply adopt the customs, dress, and manners of their new peers.

A century and a half later, Benjamin Franklin signaled the beginning of a shift in American conceptions of both individual mobility and community. Once a poor boy, now rich and famous, the plump, bespectacled Franklin sailed to Europe at age 70 in 1776 to enlist the aid of France in the war against Britain. Presenting himself to the elegant court of King Louis XVI "plainly dressed," he served notice on the world that upward mobility in the United States need not entail putting on the trappings of aristocracy. The French adored the author of *Poor Richard's Almanack* (1733–58); the Comte de Ségur marveled that such a "rustic" sage could appear in "our effeminate and slavish age."

Much earlier, Franklin had begun

shedding the habits of deference and dependence bred by the hierarchical Anglo-Saxon social order. He had started his career as a printer in colonial Boston during the 1720s with the traditional hope of finding helpful patrons in high places. Sadly disabused of that notion by Sir William Keith, the colonial governor, who had deceived him with empty promises, Franklin moved to Philadelphia and turned to self-reliance. With 11 other artisans and tradesmen, he founded the Junto, a voluntary association devoted to civic uplift—it created a subscription library and a volunteer fire company—and to the advancement of its members' business interests.

In effect, Franklin pointed the way from an Anglo-American tradition of order and hierarchy to new ideals of voluntary association designed to meet collective needs and to provide opportunities for individual social and economic progress for everyone.

AN ARISTOCRACY IS BORN

Ironically, this change began even as upward mobility was, in fact, declining in some areas of the country, notably parts of the South.

Many of the first Southern settlers had made extraordinary gains. During the early 1600s, Maryland and Virginia were the extreme cases, where economics (i.e. a tobacco boom) and demographics conspired to create striking opportunities. The profits from producing and exporting tobacco leaf spurred growers to import hundreds of young male indentured servants from England. They contracted to labor for roughly five years in the tobacco fields and curing sheds, in return for passage to the New World and room and board once there. Typhoid fever and other diseases took a heavy toll of the new arrivals in the humid Chesapeake lowlands. But, perversely, the high mortality rate opened possibilities for those who survived.

They prospered amid adversity, often quite visibly. In 1618, John Pory of Virginia noted that "a wife of one that in England had professed the black arte not of a scholler but of a collier of Croydon, weares her rough bever hatt with a faire perle hattband, and a silken suite therto correspondent." (The next year, the colonial authorities felt impelled to enact an ordinance

banning such flamboyant dress.) Of the indentured Englishmen who entered Maryland before 1642, and who survived for a decade or more, only about one-tenth failed to become landowners. Their holdings—usually 50 to 400 acres—might be enough only to allow a "rude sufficiency" of living, but the owners were independent.

By the 1660s, however, falling tobacco prices sharply reduced opportunities for ex-servants. Only half of the young indentured English who stepped ashore in Maryland during that decade eventually obtained their own land. Ordinary farmers struggled just to stay out of debt. It generally took money—enough capital or credit to support large-scale enterprises, or to branch out into trade—to make money. Throughout the Chesapeake region, this disparity between rich and poor promoted a new social structure, a nascent Southern "aristocracy." The self-made men acquired titles—mister, gentleman, esquire—and demanded deference from the less fortunate souls who were now their social inferiors. The *nouveaux riches* presumed, as people back in England did, that hierarchy was the Divinely intended order of things, even though their own ranking within it had changed. Upward mobility had not yet emerged as a popular ideal.

In New England, the 17th-century settlers were soon established in well-regulated towns and villages. Religious faith, poorer soils, the least dynamic economy in the colonies, and a healthier climate combined to create a more stable society. Often surviving into old age, Yankee parents did not designate their heirs early, thus giving older people subtle influences over the careers of the young. Individual progress largely followed the life cycle. The men at the bottom of society at a given moment, mostly young and single, would generally gain entry to the middling ranks of established farmers if they lived long enough to inherit their parents' farms. Those who lost the favor of their parents might light out for the frontier to acquire land, or seek jobs in the coastal towns and cities as dockworkers, stable boys, or sailors.

LOOKING WEST

Few struck it rich. Colonial seaport

cities, even in New England, were not showcases of rapid individual advancement. During the decades before the Revolution, thanks in part to windfall profits reaped by merchants who secured contracts to provision British troops and warships in the colonies, the size of the largest fortunes in Boston and Philadelphia increased dramatically—and so did conspicuous consumption. The wealthy built fine new homes and purchased country estates. In the City of Brotherly Love, John Cadwalader, a hugely successful merchant, rode through the cobblestone streets during the early 1770s in an elegant new English-made coach behind a coachman and six horses, with two of his 12 slaves riding postilion.

At the other extreme, the harsh Northern winters often brought joblessness and uncommon hardships to dockworkers, bricklayers, and ordinary laborers. The rising cost of living reduced even journeymen in some crafts (e.g., tailors, cobblers) nearly to the subsistence level. The indigent filled almshouses. But historians know relatively little about mobility in the middling ranks, among men in the professional, commercial, and artisan classes, who in theory had fair prospects for self-employment and at least modest prosperity.

What is clear is that by the 1770s, a small but influential patriotic gentry had emerged in Boston, New York, and other cities, and in the plantation colonies of the South. These were the men who would lead the Revolution. When Thomas Jefferson proposed in 1778, during the Revolution, that 20 bright but poor Virginia boys "be raked from the rubbish" and educated at state expense, he consciously did so to enlarge, as historian Robert Wiebe says, "the small pool of leaders at the top of the pyramid where gentlemen of breeding, wealth, and talent made their contribution 'to the general happiness' by forming and directing the revolutionary republics."

But the gentry's heyday was brief. Only a few decades after Jefferson made his proposal, the nation's rapid expansion toward the midwestern prairies mixed and dispersed the population, creating new societies where even those settlers who had been leaders in the East had to prove themselves anew. "The feeblest and most obscure do not now despair of exerting influence," declared temperance leader Justin Edwards.

"No longer looking upward within a contained system," writes Wiebe, Americans "looked outward, saw the land stretching endlessly ahead, and followed it."

By the 1820s, universal white manhood suffrage had been achieved in nearly every state, as property qualifications and other restrictions were dropped by well-to-do Federalists in some states, and by their equally well-heeled Jeffersonian opponents in others. Each party hoped that the new voters would remain loyal out of gratitude to their upperclass benefactors. Instead, the spokesmen for the unwashed engaged in egalitarian reforms. "We find ourselves oppressed on every hand," complained Philadelphia's "Unlettered mechanic," a pamphleteer, in 1827. "We labor hard in producing all the comforts of life for the enjoyment of others, while we ourselves obtain but a scanty portion."

BEING FIRST IS BEST

After Andrew Jackson, widely perceived as the candidate of "King 'Mob,'" defeated the Old Guard's John Quincy Adams in the election of 1828, American politicians learned to portray themselves and their allies as men with a common touch. In 1832, Senator Henry Clay of Kentucky found it prudent to describe the home state manufacturers whom he wished to aid with the protective tariff as "self-made men, who have acquired whatever wealth they possess by patient and diligent labor."

Generally, as historian David Brion Davis notes, "mobile men began boasting of their humble origins and their ability to have made it on their own, without influence and patronage, even without education, or at least a gentleman's education."

It is now easy to forget, says Davis, how "novel, indeed, radical" this was. The new American obeisance to the self-made and the self-taught baffled English visitors like Mrs. Trollope, mother of the famous novelist, to whom these labels meant badly made and badly taught. In Europe, kings, generals, and poets might be considered worthy of respect; the entrepreneur as hero was a preposterous notion. The London *Daily News*

was still flying in the face of received opinion at mid-century when its editors wrote, "It is time that the *millionaire* should cease to be ashamed of having made his fortune."

During the 1830s, Alexis de Tocqueville emphasized how restless and mobile Americans were, endlessly abandoning homes, occupations, and half-completed projects to pursue new opportunities. In fact, recent research shows, population turnover was dizzying: Because of out-migration and deaths, for example, 56 percent of the men living in Boston in 1830 had disappeared by the end of the decade, replaced by new arrivals. (Similarly, today in Boston and other cities, 40 to 60 percent of the inhabitants depart every decade.) Tocqueville and some American conservatives worried about the social costs of this continual upheaval. But most Americans seemed to find change exhilarating. Ralph Waldo Emerson cheered the "sturdy lad from New Hampshire or Vermont, who in turn tries all the professions, who teams it, farms it, peddles, keeps a school, preaches, edits a newspaper, goes to Congress, buys a township, and so forth . . . and always like a cat falls on his feet."

The path of advancing settlement from Ohio to Iowa comes closest to Tocqueville's portrait of a bubbling, restless society, uncongenial to the aristocrat. In the towns that sprang up on the frontier, deference to "gentlemen" vanished, and so did many an Eastern fortune, lost in land speculation. The first settlers honed their political skills building local governments and campaigning for roads, bridges, and canals. Possession of at least some capital gave many a head start, but, generally, first arrivals made greater gains than either their descendants or latecomers. Being first was best. Here and there, "first families"—such as the Coulters, Fogles, Shorbs, Lathrops, and Stidgers of Canton, Ohio—managed to preserve their local pre-eminence for generations.

Back East, as factories began to develop, opportunities for artisans to work for themselves dwindled. As early as 1802, a New York City journeyman in Benjamin Franklin's trade complained that "the business of Printing being very expensive to establish, from the high price of materials, very few of those, who are obliged to resort

to journey-work . . . ever have it in their power to realize a capital sufficient to commence business on their own account."

THE RICH GET RICHER

Yet opportunity contracted so unevenly in different places and in different industries that urban Americans could easily fail to see that, for the majority, industrialization was destroying the old dream of becoming one's own boss.

In Paterson, New Jersey, for example, only a small number of workingmen actually became iron, machinery, and locomotive manufacturers after 1830. But most of Paterson's successful industrialists had been apprentices and journeymen before opening small shops or factories of their own, so it was tempting for artisan wage-earners to imagine becoming entrepreneurs themselves. In the bigger cities, most workers probably saw that aspiration as fantasy by 1860. Indeed, the first stirrings of class-conscious labor activity had already appeared in the metropolises; in 1828, Philadelphia's Mechanics' Union of Trade Associations created the first of many local workingmen's political parties.

But, even before the Civil War, industrialization created a host of new white-collar jobs in the towns and cities—downtown retailer, mill supervisor, bookkeeper. From Baltimore to Chicago, the new middle class enjoyed important advances in consumption—wool carpets, indoor toilets, pianos, and other "luxuries" that few had known earlier.

Ironically, the new age also brought the first marked overall rise in economic stratification since the late 17th century, chiefly because the profits from emerging industries, such as textiles and iron, lined the pockets of the well-to-do. The rich got richer. Among the 52 men in Boston worth more than $200,000 in 1848, notes Edward Pessen of the City University of New York, 75 percent had been rich already in 1833, and most of the rest had been at least well-off. By 1860, five percent of the nation's families owned more than half of its wealth.

Amid the economic ferment of the era, Americans struggled to reconcile different models of success—fulfilling the obligations of one's calling, improving one's character, becoming a

THE GOLDEN DOOR

"With me bundle on me shoulder,/Faith! there's no man could be bolder;/I'm lavin' dear old Ireland without warnin'/For I lately took the notion/For to cross the briny ocean,/ And I'm off for Philadelphia in the mornin'."

So went a 19th-century ditty, hummed, presumably, by many of the 650,000 Irish who fled the Great Potato Famine of the 1840s. Between 1820 and 1880, they were joined by some nine million other immigrants—Germans, Britons, Scandinavians. A "second wave" of some 23 million immigrants, mainly from Italy, Greece, Poland, Russia (mostly Jews), and other Slavic countries, arrived between 1880 and 1920.

Many of the immigrants sailed into New York Harbor, hoping, as the famous inscription at the base of the Statue of Liberty promised, that they were passing through a "golden door." But a good number were driven across the Atlantic less by dreams of wealth than by the lash of necessity. Some, such as the Irish, were escaping economic misfortune, or, in the case of Russian Jews, religious persecution. Others hoped chiefly to win better pay for their toil. At the turn of the century, for example, a Hungarian mechanic could multiply his wages fivefold simply by emigrating to the United States.

Disillusionment awaited more than a few. "I looked out into the alley below and saw palefaced children scrambling in the gutter," recalled Russian-born novelist Anzia Yezeirska (1885–1970) of her early years in New York City. " 'Where is America?' cried my heart." But Yezeirska, like many others, did finally make her way out of the slums.

How the various ethnic groups fared in the New World depended not only on what attitudes and skills they brought with them, but also on where they settled. Many mid-19th century Irishmen, for example, clustered in relatively stagnant, pre-industrial Yankee Boston. Having worked mostly as unskilled farm laborers at home, Irishmen took jobs as bartenders, teamsters,

and dockworkers; women often served as maids or mill hands. Only a handful managed to escape to Dorchester or other "lace curtain" neighborhoods. The Irish knack for politics—Hugh O'Brien's Democratic machine captured City Hall in 1885—yielded Thanksgiving turkeys and street-cleaning jobs for the party faithful, but upward career mobility for only a few.

Several generations later, many Irish of South Boston work at the same jobs as their forefathers did. But, in cities where economic opportunities were greater, such as San Francisco and Detroit, the Irish moved somewhat more easily into the economic mainstream.

By contrast, the German immigrants tended to arrive with useful skills, as shoemakers, tailors, and butchers. In St. Louis, Milwaukee, and other cities, they often advanced relatively quickly; many opened their own shops. Likewise, many Jews of the "second wave" were experienced in the needle trades, and arrived in the United States just as New York City's garment industry was beginning its rapid expansion.

The Jews quickly embraced the American "success ethic." Like the Germans, they opened their own small shops as soon as they were able, or became subcontractors to garment manufacturers. One such "sweater" family was described by Danish-born New York Journalist Jacob Riis in his 1890 classic, *How the Other Half Lives:* The family "hoards up $30 a month, and in a few years will own a tenement somewhere and profit by . . . rent collecting. It is the way the savings of [the Jews] are universally invested."

With their traditional respect of learning, the Jews emphasized the education of their young at all costs, while Irish, Polish, and Italian Catholic families, if forced to choose, tended to send their children to work instead of to school. In 1907, the editors of New York's Italian-language *Bolletino della Sera* complained that "Italian families falsify even the ages of their children in order to send them to the factories."

The Italians, as well as the Jews, Poles, and Scandinavians, benefited from active religious traditions, and the various charitable and mutual-aid organizations that revolved around their churches or synagogues. Strong families and a commitment to community seem to have helped all of these groups adjust to life in America. But, as in Irish South Boston, too much ethnic solidarity could hinder assimilation.

In certain enclaves, such as the working-class Italian North End in Boston, cloistered immigrant groups simply rejected the success ethic as destructive to church, family, and community life. Studying these "urban villagers" as late as the 1950s, sociologist Herbert Gans found that "the idea that work can be a central purpose of life . . . organized into a series of related jobs that make up a career is virtually nonexistent." In the close-knit Scandinavian farming communities of Minnesota and Wisconsin, "overachievers" were discouraged. Garrison Keillor recalls in his fictional memoir of his Minnesota boyhood, *Lake Wobegon Days* (1985), that the firing of Bernie Carlson, host of the local radio station's "Farm Hour," was held up by local folk as an example of "what happens to people who get too big."

By the second generation, differences in the mobility of the various groups became more pronounced. Jews progressed the fastest, followed by Italians, Catholic Slavs, and Scandinavians. The Irish lagged behind. But, as historians Alice Kessler-Harris and Virginia Yans-McLaughlin observe, the link between ethnic background and individual progress weakens dramatically by the third generation, except among Jews. By 1969, for example, Italian-Americans and Irish-Americans had achieved nearly identical levels of schooling, income, and occupational status. After three generations, the "golden door" had finally swung wide for them, and new immigrants—Mexicans, Koreans, Chinese—were arriving to test Miss Liberty's promise again.

—C.G.

---

capitalist. They devoured popular almanacs, advice books for the young, and sentimental fiction, penned mostly by men from "proper" middle-class families, who tended to uphold the old notion of achievement only within limited bounds. "Instruct them that the farmer's frock and the mechanic's apron are as honorable as the merchant's and clerk's paletot or the student's cap," wrote Sylvester Judd, a

Massachusetts minister and popular novelist. "Show them how to rise *in* their calling, not out of it."

THE WHEEL OF FORTUNE

Franklin remained the great symbol and teacher for all Americans, but it was possible to draw different lessons from his writings. At mid-century, Connecticut's famous "learned black-

smith," Elihu Burritt, who had schooled himself in ancient languages, mathematics, and geography while working at the forge, gained national fame as a living incarnation of Franklin's credo that the dignity of manual labor could be reinforced through self-education.

Businessmen emphasized Franklin's view that success depended upon practice of the simple economic virtues—

thrift, zeal, honesty, hard work. But strains appeared as the marketplace changed and the size of fortunes increased. When John Jacob Astor, fur trader and real-estate speculator *extraordinaire,* died in 1848, leaving almost all of his $20 million to his relatives and a pittance to charity, newspaper obituary writers hinted darkly that Astor had made part of his fortune by illicit means. The New York *Herald* accused the "self-invented money-making machine" of trying to create an "Astor dynasty"; another newspaper noted that Astor's estate was "much less than was expected, but still too much for any man."

As attacks on the rich grew sharper, many conservatives feared that the rights of property—and the future of the Republic—might be in jeopardy. They insisted even more vehemently that the wealthy in America generally succeeded by their virtues, that every American could be a capitalist. "The wheel of fortune is in constant operation," declared Governor Edward Everett of Massachusetts, "and the poor in one generation furnish the rich of the next."

Even after the Civil War, many Americans probably accepted one of these idealized visions of self-improvement. But also popular were dozens of satires that undercut all the solemn talk about sticking with the daily grind as the way to succeed. "It is good to be shifty in a new country," was the motto of J. J. Hooper's fictional Simon Suggs.

By the end of the 19th century, the wealth of the very rich both awed and alarmed the American public. Carnegie, Vanderbilt, Rockefeller, and Duke became household names; the New York *Tribune* astonished its readers in 1892 when it published a list of reputed millionaires containing more than 4,000 names. That year, the Populist Party platform of presidential candidate General James Baird Weaver warned that the nation was splitting into two classes: tramps and millionaires. "The fruits of the toil of millions are boldly stolen to build up colossal fortunes for a few, unprecedented in the history of mankind."

"The problem of our age," declared steel magnate Andrew Carnegie, one of the few truly self-made men among the millionaires, "is the proper administration of wealth, so that the ties of brotherhood may still bind together the

rich and poor." As Carnegie noted, the transformation of the economy by big corporations meant that, in many cases, fact to face contact between employer and employees "is at an end. Rigid Castes are formed, and, as usual, mutual ignorance breeds mutual distrust." But Carnegie argued that the change was both inevitable and beneficial, that cheaper and better goods provided by the modern economy meant that the "poor enjoy what the rich could not before afford."

He had a point. Real wages had increased after the Civil War, so that skilled workers, and even ordinary factory hands with children who brought home wages, could acquire decent housing, sewing machines, and other comforts that helped take the edge off the huge disparities in wealth during the Gilded Age. A workingman might resent those who dined at Delmonico's or owned mansions in Newport, but a rising standard of living could be enough to resign him to his lot.

DOING BETTER THAN DAD

Redefining the meaning of opportunity in an age of Big Business proved to be a long and often confusing process. Dozens of new books about success appeared, increasingly with that word in their title. Many were soothing but largely irrelevant sermons, harking back to the bygone world of small shops and counting rooms, defining success in terms of "living an earnest, honest, pure life." Contrary to today's popular impression, even the prolific Horatio Alger, Jr. (1832–99) did not emphasize money-getting. As historian John G. Cawelti writes, Alger's young heroes did not go from "rags to riches," but (often with more luck than hard work) from "rags to respectability."

White Americans who extolled the "land of opportunity" before 1990 did not have blacks or women in mind. Unless economic hardship forced women to work after marriage, they belonged at home. Their social status depended on that of their menfolk. The feminization of teaching did provide careers, and, in the larger city school systems, some upward mobility for single women. But female achievement was discouraged and remained exceptional, and so, like that of blacks, invisible in the literature on success.

Not until 1891 did an American dictionary, *The Century Dictionary,* define success as the "art of gaining money." By then, the careers of the notorious "robber barons"—Daniel Drew, Jay Gould, and Cornelius Vanderbilt—rendered largely implausible the traditional notion that wealth was a reward for personal virtue. The defenders of the very rich increasingly emphasized not their personal virtues or how they made or disposed of their money, but simply the number of jobs which their capital created—a far more utilitarian justification.

Neither the robber barons nor the growth of corporate business, nor sermons on success seemed to have any effect on American opportunities during the late 19th century. Surveying studies of U.S. cities, Stephan Thernstrom found that little changed; indeed, mobility remained the same at least through the early 20th century. Overall, he discovered much more upward mobility in individual careers (12 to 22 percent of his sample population per decade) than downward (seven to 12 percent). Progress *between generations* was even greater: In Boston, more than two-fifths of the sons in every generation climbed at least one rung above their fathers on the ladder.

The men who managed to get ahead within their own lifetimes generally took small steps: A casual laborer might land a regular factory job; a wage-earning shoemaker might open his own shop; or a clerk in a hardware store might become a partner in the enterprise. During the mid-19th century in Boston, the nation's fourth largest metropolis, and Poughkeepsie, a small Hudson River city, 60 percent of skilled manual workers remained at that level. But an impressive one-fourth or more rose (mostly to run their own small workshops and stores), and just one-seventh or less sank into lower status jobs.

In the two cities, according to Thernstrom, one-third or more of the men who started work in menial jobs (e.g., porter, stable man) managed to better themselves. In Boston, the largest percentage found low-paying white-collar jobs, probably reflecting the greater opportunities for sales and clerical workers in a commercial entrepôt; in Poughkeepsie, more found their way into the higher-paid skilled trades as masons, coopers, or machinists.

1. RECONSTRUCTION AND THE GILDED AGE

MENTAL SUNSHINE

Beyond showing how differences among cities and their occupational structures affected one's chances of getting ahead—best in a commercial center like Boston, worst in a one-industry mill town—historians have been unable to pin down other factors affecting individual mobility during the nation's 19th-century industrial surge. We can say, however, that the school of "hard knocks" had more graduates than did formal institutions of learning. In 1870, only two percent of the nation's teenagers received high school diplomas; by 1910, only nine percent did. But many professionals, shopkeepers, and some craftsmen saw that the future lay in the expanding world of white-collar work. Increasingly, they sent their children to the new public high schools.

As if to reconcile urban Americans to their dwindling chances of becoming their own bosses, a number of popular writers around the turn of the century offered a new definition of success that seemed more compatible with the emerging economy of affluence and large firms. With the right outlook these writers suggest, one could make just about any confining corporate job satisfying. Ralph Waldo Trine, Orison Swett Marden, and other advocates of "New Thought" saw success chiefly in terms of "fulfillment" and "self-realization." They spoke of the "creative life" and of the pleasures of achievement rather than of competition in the world of work. Philosopher William James lent crucial support: *Believe what is in the line of your needs,* for only by such belief is the need fulfilled. . . . Have faith that you can successfully make it, and your feet are nerved to its accomplishment."

The New Thoughters also advised middle-class readers to cultivate "mental sunshine" and to take time to savor nature, family, and hobbies; they warned against total obsession with business.

Even writers who clung to more materialistic notions of success began to emphasize new virtues, such as "personality" and "psychic energy," which seemed useful in getting ahead within the new corporate bureaucracies. Americans would have to learn to sell themselves. In *The Man Nobody Knows* (1925), adman Bruce

Barton portrayed Jesus as both the exemplar of these qualities and the founder of modern business. Jesus, wrote Barton, had "picked up 12 men from the bottom ranks of business and forged them into an organization that conquered the world."

Jesus was no "kill-joy," he said, but "the most popular dinner guest in Jerusalem" who could teach modern Americans "a happier more satisfying way of living."*

At various times later in the 20th century, popular writers, politicians, and academics would reconsider the challenge that the rise of Big Business (and, later, Big Government) posed to traditional American notions of success and independence. Few would take so complaisant a view of the challenge as did these early writers.

The rise of Big Business may have made self-employment a receding prospect for most urban Americans, but studies of the early 20th century show an increase in upward *occupational* mobility, most of it due to the massive American exodus from the farms to the cities (which began around the time of the Civil War). Already by 1900, 20 farmers were leaving the land for every city dweller who became a farmer. A man fresh from the hinterland might land a job in a Dayton, Ohio, cash register factory or as a shipping clerk in a Chicago warehouse; his sons could expect to do better.

MOVING UP IN EUROPE, TOO

Helping them along was the influx of cheap labor, chiefly from Italy and Eastern Europe (1.2 million people in 1907), which pushed many earlier immigrants and American-born white unskilled factory workers up into foremen's jobs and other supervisory occupations [see box]. The immigrants, or their sons, could hope eventually to follow the same route, although members of different ethnic groups would progress at widely different rates. "If America was the land of promise,"

---

* Later writers, such as the Reverend Norman Vincent Peale and Dale Carnegie, expanded on the notion of reshaping one's personality in order to get ahead. Peal's 1952 best-seller, *The Power of Positive Thinking,* is still in strong demand.

writes Hartmut Kaelble of West Berlin's Free University, "this was more true for the unskilled workers . . . than for any other social group."

But many scholars now believe that for everybody else, from carpenters to schoolteachers to business executives, opportunities were no greater in the United States after 1850 than they were in Europe. In essence, industrialization seems to have had the same effect on both sides of the Atlantic. In cities as diverse as Graz, Austria, and Waltham, Massachusetts, Kaelble found that 17 to 25 percent of the male workers moved up or down at least one rung on the class ladder during every decade through 1930.

Why, then, this notion of America as a *unique* "land of opportunity?" It simply may have been the legacy of the years before 1850, when opportunities probably were greater in the United States than anywhere else. Or perhaps the existence of hereditary aristocracies at the top of society in Europe discouraged the expression of yearnings that Europeans felt as keenly as Americans did. In the United States, where all it took to join the "aristocracy" was enough money, anybody could hope, in theory, to scale the very summit. Today, the persistence of the "rags to riches" myth and its variants testifies to the depth of American's belief in the ideal of opportunity. But historians still do not know how strong or pervasive the hunger actually was to "make it," and especially to make it big, among Americans in the past.

Tocqueville gave us lasting images of the restless American, forever hoping to better his lot: "Death at length overtakes him, but it is before he is weary of his bootless chase of that complete felicity which forever escapes him." But labor historians during the last decade have suggested that the visions of personal advancement among many farmers and workers before 1900 were relatively modest. To Americans with strong community or ethnic loyalties, happiness meant staying put. If they were farmers, they aimed chiefly to secure the family patrimony, while many urban workers aspired simply to a decent standard of living, to job security, and to dignity in the workplace.

Thus, then as now, individual Americans' ambitions for themselves or their children varied; not everyone aspired

46

to reach the top, despite the impression often given by best-selling writers of the day. But broadly popular goals did seem to change. If during the early 1800s one ideal appears to have been independence through self-employment, something new had begun to emerge by the turn of the century.

That something new was simple consumerism.

Higher average incomes, the rapid proliferation of widely advertised goods, and the availability of consumer credit whetted the appetites of Americans for everything from washing machines to automobiles. As time went on, people of all classes seemed increasingly to measure personal accomplishment by the ability to satisfy growing material expectations. Indeed, by the late 1920s, more Americans than ever before seemed to embrace Tocqueville's "bootless chase," which continues to this day.

The Emergence of Modern America

By the 1890s issues such as urbanization, industrialization, and unionization preoccupied many people. The unprecedented growth of corporations had enabled them to exercise inordinate influence on the economy and the political process. Both farm and labor groups sought to use government to prevent what they called "the interests" from dominating the entire society. Although often condemned as radicals, these reformers claimed they were merely trying to "restore" a more equitable system as had existed in the past. Their efforts produced modest results that did not halt the trends they deplored.

America's continental expansion had long since ended by the latter part of the nineteenth century. Beginning in the 1880s, more obvious by the 1890s, a number of ideas and theories influenced attitudes toward expansion abroad. These included, but were not limited to, the need for foreign markets, taking up the "white man's burden" to civilize and Christianize peoples of different colors, and the search for "new frontiers" to prevent American society from stagnating. Such notions culminated in the Spanish-American War, and the decision to acquire overseas possessions such as Hawaii, the Philippines, Puerto Rico, and Guam. Already dominant in the Western Hemisphere, the United States became a world power.

The 1890s was a decade of labor strife and rural unrest. There also was a great deal of intellectual ferment, as individuals challenged existing wisdom in economics, history, and the law. "The Cycle of Reform" examines this period and speculates on its relevance for the 1990s. Beginning in 1892, Ellis Island became the primarily U.S. immigration center on the East Coast. The text of "Hope, Tears, and Remembrance" tells of those who sought a new life in America. When the United States acquired the Philippines following the Spanish-American War, Filipino insurgents began a bloody war for independence. "Our First Southeast Asian War" analyzes the struggle and shows how closely it resembled the more recent involvement in Vietnam.

"The Gospel of Andrew Carnegie" shows how this titan of industry promoted the idea that the existing system of capitalism was the best of all possible worlds.

Early twentieth century social workers believed modern urban society threatened the traditional family and community controls that used to protect the young, especially females. "Cleaning Up the Dance Halls" provides insights on prevailing attitudes about morality.

This section concludes with an article about George Washington Carver, a man who overcame enormous obstacles to become a leading agricultural scientist. His greatest contribution, however, was that he "made the results of both his and others' research available and understandable to thousands whose lives were thereby enriched.

Looking Ahead: Challenge Questions

How did farmers and laborers try to curb the enormous power exercised by large corporations? How could the deplorable conditions of workers, especially children, be justified? Why did businessmen so bitterly resist unions?

Many Americans genuinely believed it was the duty of the United States to dominate other peoples in order to "civilize" and uplift them. Why was this "help" so fiercely resisted?

Unit 2

The Cycle of Reform

William L. O'Neill

William L. O'Neill is professor of history at Rutgers University. He is the author of, among other books, A Better World *and* Feminism in America, *both published by Transaction.*

1890 has a special meaning to historians of the United States, for the census taken that year revealed a momentous fact. The Census Bureau put it as follows: "Up to and including 1890 the country had a frontier of settlement, but at present the unsettled area has been so broken into by isolated bodies of settlement that there can hardly be said to be a frontier line." A young historian, Frederick Jackson Turner, would soon use this sentence to begin one of the most influential articles ever written about our past. "The Significance of the Frontier in American History," a paper first given by Turner in July 10, 1893 during the World's Columbian Exposition in Chicago, has probably inspired the writing of more books and articles than any other piece of scholarship by an American historian. The central idea, advanced by Turner in this and later works, was that "the existence of an area of free land, its continuous recession, and the advance of American settlement westward explain American development."

What became known as "the frontier thesis" stimulated generations of historians, first to spread Turner's gospel, then to demolish it. Almost every key point that Turner made has since been refuted, and few if any accept today that the existence of free land determined the American character. Yet, like the Columbian Exposition itself – perhaps the greatest world's fair and arguably the most exuberant – Turner's thesis remains a monument to the boldness and optimism of his time. His daring is self-evident. Turner was 31, his Ph.D only three years old, and yet at a meeting of the American Historical Association he informed his seniors that they had contrived to miss the point of the entire national experience. His optimism is less manifest since, if American development was produced by a wilderness that had just disappeared, the future might seem gloomy. But Turner's thesis suggested that the frontier had done its work so well that it was no longer needed. Having triumphed over nature, American democracy was now self-renewing. Americans would go on to greater things, using their pioneer virtues to build a great industrial nation.

The Turnerians were right for the wrong reasons. Turner argued that, in addition to democracy, the "composite nationality" of Americans, our blend of ethnic groups, resulted from the frontier experience. But most historians believe that both the integration of people from many different nations and the extension of democratic rights are products of urbanization. No matter, he had identified many of the most important national traits, and by provoking historians to look at America in a fresh way stimulated lines of inquiry that would later prove more fruitful. Historians still admire Turner, for attacking the hard questions, for his originality, for his eloquence, for the breadth of his learning – he drew upon all the contemporary social sciences – for his love of research, and for his democratic values.

We also envy Turner his optimism, which now seems remarkable given the misery around him. Today many consider the fact that at least 15 percent of all Americans live in poverty to be a national disgrace. Yet in 1890 when Jacob Riis wrote his powerful exposé of destitution in New York City he called it *How the Other Half Lives,* and understated the case at that since actually three fifths of the nation fell below the poverty line. Others besides Riis were troubled by the great distance between the few who monopolized America's industrial wealth, and the many who toiled to produce it. Edward Bellamy spoke to the worriers in his utopian novel *Looking Backward* (1888). Set in the year 2000, it described a cooperative social order which had replaced the cutthroat capitalism of America's Gilded Age. Although *Looking Backward* sold a million copies to a population one quarter the size of ours, and prompted the formation of many "Nationalist" clubs devoted to Bellamy's gospel, the tangible results were slight. Most educated Americans were unmoved by the suffering of the poor and did nothing about it.

Yet poverty declined all the same. By 1920 the earlier figure had been reversed, three-fifths of the

From *Society,* Vol. 27, No. 5, July/August 1990, pp. 63-68. Copyright © 1990 by Transaction Publishers. Reprinted by permission.

population now being above, rather than below, the poverty line. And, irregularly to be sure, poverty would go on declining until the 1970s. In a sense, the optimism of Turner's generation has been justified by events. To us that generation often seems complacent beyond belief, quarreling about tariffs and currency questions while ignoring the distress of millions. But they did not view their era as we do, from the vantage point of a century of further development. In 1890 there were men and women still alive who could remember when nine out of ten Americans scratched a bare living from the soil, when the line of settlement was drawn east of the Mississippi, when travel proceeded no faster than a horse could walk or a ship under canvas sail. To Americans the nineteenth century was an age, not just of steam, but of miracles.

Class Conflict

Even so the basic confidence of the Gilded Age is all the more extraordinary considering that it was a time of savage industrial warfare, labor-management disputes often being settled by those with the greatest firepower. In the summer of 1877 a wave of railroad strikes, together with sympathetic walkouts by factory workers and miners, brought the nation literally to a halt. In Baltimore after nine strikers were killed by state militiamen, riots broke out that took the lives of another 50 persons. In Chicago 19 perished when police and cavalry attacked an unauthorized demonstration. Twenty-six were killed in Pittsburgh during a night of rioting and looting that saw 2,000 railroad cars destroyed and a wall of fire three miles long engulf the center city. Though the death rate was never so high again, shooting strikers remained a management tool as late as 1937, when guards at a Republic Steel plant killed or wounded almost a hundred unarmed people.

Few issues troubled thoughtful men and women in the 1890s so much as class conflict, which involved not only workers but farmers – who were more numerous than workingmen and more political. In 1892 many of them organized as the People's, or Populist Party, and subsequently gained control of a handful of western states. With a platform calling for nationalization of the railroad and telegraph companies, extensive government aid to agriculture, and soft money, they threw a fright into the middle classes. Predictions of a bloody apocalypse more often involved workers than farmers, but some alarmists managed to include both. During the presidential campaign of 1896, when William Jennings Bryan inherited the Populists' following – though, except for

soft money, not their program – young Theodore Roosevelt compared prominent Democrats and union heads to the leaders of the Paris Commune. They would try to make a revolution, he was sure, and he expected to meet them on the field of battle. Alternatively, or perhaps afterward, he favored "taking ten or a dozen of their leaders out, standing them against a wall, and shooting them dead."

To Americans, the nineteenth century was an age, not just of steam, but of miracles

Of course Roosevelt was excitable, others beside Mark Hanna regarding him as a "madman." But fantasies of revolution aside, the 1890s were a remarkably turbulent decade, marred by a series of brutal strikes, notably against Carnegie Steel and the Pullman Sleeping Car Company, the Populist uprising, and a market panic in 1893 followed by the worst depression Americans had yet experienced. The last massacre of the Indian wars took place at a creek known as Wounded Knee in South Dakota, where, on December 28, 1890, almost 200 Sioux, men, women, and children alike, were shot by troopers of the 7th U.S. Cavalry. There were more lynchings by far during the 1890s than in any subsequent decade, 230 during one year alone. The level of collective domestic violence was higher than it ever would be again, including even the riot-plagued 1960s.

Great Events Have Antecedents

What does this mean as we look to the end of our own century? One thing it fails to suggest is that rioting will become popular again. The bloody strikes of the 1890s resembled previous ones, while lynchings and urban mob actions had an even longer tradition. The Populists too were foreshadowed by earlier agrarian movements. Conversely, little has happened in recent years to indicate that the 1990s will be a stormy decade. Anything is possible, and we remember that much of the violence of the 1960s seemed to come out of nowhere. But it remains a rule of thumb that great events have antecedents, which, though easier to recognize after the fact, are usually visible before it. If such exist today they have escaped attention.

On the other hand, the fallow years we have been passing through must end sooner or later. Long ago Arthur M. Schlesinger, Sr. observed that there was a cycle in American political life which produced waves of reform every few decades. Today the pattern seems less regular than he supposed, but that it exists is hard to dispute. In the 1860s Republicans abolished slavery, passed the Homestead Act, and introduced other important measures, before taking the position Andrew Carnegie expressed in 1886: "If asked what important law I should change I must perforce say none; the laws are perfect." The ideology behind his remark was that of laissez-faire, which had created a great body of literature to the effect that government meddling in social and economic affairs always made things worse. In practice advocates of laissez-faire found exceptions to the rule, as when manufacturers secured tariffs to preserve "infant" industries long after they had become giants. Its imperfections notwithstanding, middle class people seemed thoroughly committed to laissez-faire in 1890, and yet, before very long, they would turn their backs upon it.

Knowing this does not help us determine what the prospects are for reforms in the 1990s, but history suggests the kind of indicators we ought to be looking for. Forceful social and political criticism often prepares the way for change, and did so toward the end of the nineteenth century. Edward Bellamy was one such critic, and so also was Henry George, whose great tract *Progress and Poverty* (1879), identified the "unearned increment" owners derived from rising land values as the curse of the laboring classes. Though his proposal for a "single tax" on real estate failed, George, like Bellamy, made people think about the sources of inequality. So too did Henry Demarest Lloyd, whose *Wealth Against Commonwealth* (1894) brilliantly attacked monopolies as a whole and Standard Oil in particular. It, and Lloyd's personal efforts, led the Populist convention that year to call for public ownership of all monopolies.

The Social Gospel movement was another precursor to the age of reform. Under laissez-faire Protestant clergymen saw inequality as part of the divine order. Henry Ward Beecher, the most famous minister of his day, announced that "God has intended the great to be great and the little to be little." Poverty was thus predestined, and yet at the same time deserved, for Beecher also said "no man suffers from poverty unless it be more than his fault – unless it also be his sin." This had to change if the leading denominations were not to remain obstacles to reform, and change it did, thanks to Walter Rauschenbusch and other progressive church leaders. Rauschenbusch – then a Baptist preacher in New York, later a theologian – was inspired by Henry George and

the English Fabians to believe that it was not the church's role simply to interpret poverty and injustice, but actively to combat them. In 1892 he helped found the Brotherhood of the Kingdom as a means of doing so. Though fundamentalists were beyond reach, Rauschenbusch and his allies would in time win over the mainstream denominations, making them engines of reform instead of barriers to it.

The social settlement movement would also contribute much to the coming struggle, though few could have guessed this in 1890, when there were only a handful of settlements and Hull House was just a year old. Social settlements enabled middle class men and women, usually recent college graduates, to live in slums and mingle with the local population. In time settlements would provide many social services, but the original intent was for residents to be helpful neighbors rather than case workers, to teach by example and establish rapport between the social classes. For many, including Jane Addams, living with the urban poor was a radicalizing experience. The need was so great, their resources so meager, that residents usually came to believe government alone could provide solutions. Settlements were training camps for young men and women who would become officers in the reform army when it finally mustered.

Most educated Americans were unmoved by the suffering of the poor and did nothing about it

---

George, Bellamy, and Lloyd were journalists and best selling authors, but the seeds of reform were being sown by professors, too. The end of the last century was a time of enormous intellectual vitality in a broad range of disciplines. The Ph.D, today often regarded as stultifying, had just been introduced and the first generation of scholars to possess it was notable both for ability and intellectual courage. William James and John Dewey in philosophy, Richard T. Ely, John Commons, Thorstein Veblen, and Simon Patten in economics, Lester Ward, E.A. Ross, and Albion Small in sociology, Turner, Charles Beard and James Harvey Robinson in history, among many others, destroyed the assumptions upon which laissez-faire depended.

Oliver Wendell Holmes, Jr. argued that legal principles were based on history and experience, not logic. The law is made by judges, he insisted, and can be unmade by them as well when circumstances warrant. Veblen struck out against orthodox economics for being static, abstract, and preoccupied with discovering non-existent natural laws. His economics was an evolutionary science that saw man as much more than simply a producer and consumer of wealth. Morality also, Dewey held, was evolutionary and progressive. He denounced contemporary ethics for being archaic survivals that stood in the way of needed social and political improvements.

Under laissez-faire, Protestant clergymen saw inequality as part of the divine order

---

Together they staged what Morton White called "the revolt against formalism." By formalism White meant traditional logic, classical economics and jurisprudence, deductive reasoning, and all ways of thinking that were not pragmatic, experimental, and inductive. The rebellious scholars were, or tried to be, scientific, not in the sense of establishing new laws in their disciplines to replace old ones, but rather by employing sophisticated methods in their research, and by challenging the received wisdom. Formalists upheld a status quo based, as they saw it, upon immutable truths, unlike the rebels, who believed that truth was whatever worked for the good of society. Many of their students went on to become a new kind of reformer, a social technician equipped with the latest tools for practical problem solving. Some of these were what we would now call technocrats, but the best were imbued with the humane, rational, tolerant, flexible, and democratic spirit of their teachers.

Though the rebels against formalism did not create progressivism all by themselves, they performed several essential functions in addition to destroying the ideology of laissez-faire. Their work supplied a generation of reformers with arguments and ideas. And they fashioned the academic culture as we know it. We too believe that scholarly as well as scientific research ought to be pragmatic, instrumental and deductive and, many of us still think that ideas should be used to better the human condition. Dewey and Veblen and their colleagues set the standard liberal academicians have measured themselves against ever since.

Urban Reform

Besides intellectual excitement, there was another

way in which the 1890s were less barren than they seemed at the time. Though frustrated at the national level, reform blossomed in the cities. Eastern urban reformers tended to be businessmen and professionals mobilized against what they saw as corrupt and incompetent political machines. Their ambitions were often confined to making local government honest and business-like. William L. Strong, mayor of New York from 1895 to 1897, was this kind of reformer. Another type, more common in the Midwest, was epitomized by Hazen S. Pingree, mayor of Detroit from 1890 to 1897. Pingree and his colleagues not only wanted good government, but welfare services for the poor, the regulation of utilities and transport companies, and many other changes.

Urban reform was made necessary by the phenomenal growth of cities, especially in the Midwest. In 1880 one out of every five Midwesterners lived in towns over 4,000, a decade later one in three. In only ten years the urban population had doubled, Chicago, for example, growing from 500,000 to a population of about one million. It would have been difficult even for well run urban governments to cope with this breakneck expansion, which put intolerable strains upon even the most basic services. But the cities, far from being efficiently led, were under the control of bosses who, in connivance with dishonest businessmen, ran them for personal profit. The function of urban government, as they saw it, was to generate bribes and graft.

Middle class people resented this system, but, while times were good, not enough to challenge it. Then came the four year business collapse which followed the panic of 1893. Hard times greatly increased demands upon city governments, while their revenue base declined. Public utilities such as trolley systems, telephone companies, and water works, faced with shrinking earnings tended to raise their rates – despite the fact that most of their customers had less money to spend than before. This outrageous behavior, made possible by monopolization and the corrupt public officials who sustained it, aroused widespread anger. Since it affected virtually everyone in their roles as consumers, the arrogance of power had a unifying effect, bringing together small businessmen, professionals, women's organizations, trade union leaders and others who had never joined forces before.

David Thelen has shown in detail how this process worked in Wisconsin. The high levels of unemployment, as much as 50 per cent in some cities, and sharp declines in income experienced by the business and professional classes, undermined faith in the status quo. Investigative journalists, discussion clubs, extension lectures by economists and sociologists from the state university, stirred citizens, got them to talking with one another, and helped them define their problems and seek collective solutions. Political organizations were formed to eliminate graft and corruption, place more employees under civil service, and reduce taxes. The discovery that lower taxes meant fewer services at a time when more were needed led to calls for action against wealthy individual and corporate tax evaders. In order to reduce the power of venal or unresponsive officials, reformers fought for instruments of "direct democracy," such as the recall and referendum.

In the nineteenth century, like today, Congress could not lead and the presidents refused to

---

Then came efforts to effectively regulate utilities, and even replace privately owned utilities with cooperative or municipally owned institutions. As many problems could only be solved with the aid or approval of state government, reformers in different communities reached out to one another. Robert M. La Follette was won over to reform in 1897 and elected governor three years later. Under La Follette Wisconsin became the most politically advanced state in the nation, initiating many reforms that were copied elsewhere. In a few more years "progressivism," as the movement came to be called, was a national phenomenon.

Every state had a somewhat different experience, reform did not always prevail, and even when it did the results often fell short of what was expected. Even so, American political life was dramatically altered in the first decade of this century because of what had gone on earlier. The 1890s, and especially the years from 1893 to 1897, which had been a dark period shadowed by economic collapse and abortive farmer and worker uprisings, came in retrospect to assume a larger significance. It turned out to have been the seed time for an age of reform, an overture to greatness. And when the Progressive Era was born its midwife would be none other than Theodore Roosevelt, the onetime conservative having become a liberal in response to changing circumstances.

Uncertain Parallels

What this means for us today is uncertain despite some obvious parallels. In 1890, as in 1990, the United States was suffering from decades of feeble government. Then, as now, the major parties were evenly balanced, Republicans winning most presidential elections while Democrats usually controlled the House and sometimes also the Senate. While partisanship was much more intense than today, the parties did not offer strikingly different programs and neither possessed a mandate for change. Unable to cope with poverty or the consequences of growth, politicians fought over the currency question, which, though hardly the nation's most urgent problem, seemed within their power to answer. Like today, Congress could not lead and the presidents refused to.

Our federal system of government requires presidential leadership to solve problems, but in the late nineteenth century chief executives were so retiring that Woodrow Wilson called his study of how the nation conducted its affairs *Congressional Government* (1885). Being locally oriented Congress cannot define the national interest and is always under pressure to service powerful constituents. Congressional government consisted largely of log rolling, pork barreling, and the delivery of favors. In 1890 there had been no strong presidents since Lincoln. We have not had a strong president since Nixon, who was no Lincoln to be sure, yet who made some historic changes.

Ronald Reagan might seem an exception, but though he was politically formidable, he was also the first activist president since Andrew Jackson to weaken the federal government. Reagan destroyed government's ability to solve problems by raising the national debt to paralyzing levels, while at the same time fixing in stone the twin rules that defense spending must not be cut nor new taxes levied. Until the budget is brought under control there can be no new or expanded government programs, but that cannot be accomplished without reducing defense spending or increasing taxes. This fiscal Catch-22 is Reagan's legacy to America and, so long as it lasts, there can only be presidents like Bush – who, weight apart, reminds one of Grover Cleveland.

Yet there remains the hope that a dynamic new leader has arisen who may lead us out of stagnation. That man is, of course, Mikhail Gorbachev. If he brings the cold war to an end, as seems entirely possible, the defense budget will no longer be sacred.

And reductions in defense spending can hardly fail to benefit the nation, by reducing the deficit, or funding new programs, or by some combination of both. Most of the traditional harbingers of reform do not now exist. There is no great literature of protest, except against Reaganomics: there are no promising political movements on the state and local level; neither war nor a great depression quickens the pace of change. But if post-cold war America enjoys the kind of affluence this country once knew, that itself might encourage progress. After all, two of the three twentieth-century reform eras came during periods of record abundance. Even now, just off stage, another Roosevelt may be waiting.

READINGS SUGGESTED BY THE AUTHOR:

Billington, R. *Frederick Jackson Turner*. New York: Oxford University Press, 1973.

Davis, A. *Spearheads for Reform: The Social Settlements and the Progressive Movement, 1890-1914.* New York: Oxford University Press, 1967.

Link, A. & R. McCormick. *Progressivism.* Arlington Heights, Ill.: Harlan Davidson, Inc., 1983.

Thelen, D. *The New Citizenship: Origins of Progressivism in Wisconsin, 1885-1900.* Columbia, Mo.: University of Missouri Press, 1972.

White, M. *Social Thought in America: The Revolt Against Formalism.* New York: Viking Press, 1949.

Hope, Tears, and Remembrance

For more than twelve million immigrants, Ellis Island was a place of new beginnings.

Edward Oxford

New York writer Edward Oxford is a frequent contributor to American History Illustrated.

Ellis Island. The end of passage. The door of dreams. "Island of Hope" for those who found refuge here, "Island of Tears" for those who were turned away here.

For more than sixty years, from 1892 until 1954, Ellis Island in New York harbor served as the U.S. government's primary immigration center. Today, the three dozen buildings that crowd this twenty-seven-acre patch of land still loom sentinel-like above the cobalt-blue waters, just as they have for close to a century. A half-mile to the southwest, the Statue of Liberty beckons; a mile and a quarter in the opposite direction the towers of lower Manhattan reach skyward like a mirage.

This September, after seven years of painstaking restoration, Ellis Island reopens—not as a reception depot but as the site of a magnificent new Immigration Museum, part of the Statue of Liberty National Monument.

The tiny island has a strong claim on the hearts of Americans. One of the greatest migrations in human history—more than twelve million people—passed through here. Today four out of every ten of us claim a forebear who stepped ashore at this place. Just as the Statue of Liberty has become the universal symbol of our nation's ideals, so Ellis Island has become the symbol of the peopling of our land.

Although the long lines of immigrants that once filled the cavernous Registry Room in Ellis Island's Main Building have long since gone, visitors to the restored structure can still, with a bit of imagination, sense their presence. In the stray echoes and the play of lights and shadows, phantom traces of these seekers of a better life linger on.

A Slavic woman in a babushka, carrying a bundle of clothing on her back . . . Hungarians in high boots and rough jackets . . . an Italian couple bearing battered suitcases . . . Irish women in shaggy woolen shawls . . . gypsies from the kingdom of Serbia . . . dark-hatted Armenian Jews . . . Greeks in white, kilt-like foustanellas . . . Mohammedan dervishes . . . Germans wearing sturdy farm clothes . . . women from the French West Indies wearing long dresses . . . Cossack soldiers carrying sheathed swords.

Their reasons for undertaking this uncertain journey mirrored the entire range of human hopes, fears, and aspirations. Ambition. Famine. Persecution. Revolution. Poverty. Restlessness. Debt. Oppression. War. Drought. Adventure. Unemployment. Plague. Despair.

"The happy and powerful do not go into exile," Alexis de Tocqueville, the brilliant French observer of the American scene, wrote in 1835, "and there are no surer guarantees of equality among men than poverty and misfortune."

America was ever the place of seekers. In the historical scheme of humankind, it was a nation of strangers. In the chronicles of civilization, it represented the last, best hope of earth.

Immigration to America began before recorded time, and it has never ceased. Even native Americans are said to have migrated from other continents. The Founding Fathers were of varied strains.

From *American History Illustrated*, September/October 1990, pp. 28-42, 68-70. Reprinted through the courtesy of Cowles Magazines, publishers of *American History Illustrated*.

All of us, it seems, came from someplace else.

During the country's formative years, immigrants were thought of as a "given good" who would bring to bear their skills and strengths, settle the vast open spaces of the land, and help move America into the industrial age. George Washington looked upon America as a receiving place for "the oppressed of all nations and religions." His vision became self-fulfilling.

For nearly a century after the nation's founding, the federal government took little official note of the growing numbers of newcomers, leaving their reception in the hands of the coastal states through which the immigrants arrived. About all an "alien passenger" needed to do to enter the United States was to walk off the ship that brought him here. The door stood open and had no keeper.

During the nineteenth century, more than twenty million people throughout Europe packed their belongings and left their homelands for America.

They had heard tales—some true, some tall—about the land westward across the sea. Of farmlands waiting to be worked. Of cities to be built. Of railroads to be driven across the continent. Of money to be made. Americans, stories went, had so much gold they didn't know what to do with it—so they used it to fill their teeth.

But an even greater allure grasped spirit and soul: the simple, splendid chance—as set forth in the Declaration of Independence—for "Life, Liberty, and the Pursuit of Happiness."

The immigrant tide surged during the closing decades of the century, as millions of additional newcomers—southern Italians, Greeks, Austro-Hungarians, Poles, and Jews fleeing the pograms of Eastern Europe and Russia—joined the waves of Northern and Western Europeans already moving across the Atlantic.

Many Americans began to look askance at these newcomers sweeping in from "the other side," whose look, language, and ways differed from their own. They viewed such arrivals as "beaten men from beaten lands," "the alien menace," or simply, "those damn foreigners."

As the tide of immigrants grew, legislators and federal officials joined the ranks of Americans growing more aware—and apprehensive—of the new arrivals. Increasing numbers of immigrants carried diseases, or wound up on charity rolls, or in prison.

At the same time, government agents viewed with increasing alarm the slipshod processing of immigrants at New York's notoriously corrupt Castle Garden and other state-administered processing centers, where record-keeping was tenuous at best and where immigrants were often robbed and abused.

Congress and the U.S. government finally responded to these pressures during 1890-91, with passage of an immigration act that included restrictive legislation to curtail the influx of "undesirable" aliens, and with the transfer of immigration affairs from individual states to federal control. Ellis Island in New York harbor was designated as the site of a huge receiving station to be administered by the Treasury Department's new Bureau of Immigration.

The three-acre mud flat had an undistinguished history. Located just three hundred yards from the New Jersey shore, it had at various times been a hanging ground for pirates, a fort, a munitions depot, and site of a fishermen's tavern owned by one Samuel Ellis, a merchant whose name eventually became the islet's own.

The first Ellis Island Immigration Station, a sprawling four-hundred-foot-long structure made of Georgia pine, opened amid much fanfare on New Year's Day 1892. Officials bestowed a $10 goldpiece on a bewildered young woman from Ireland—the first immigrant to pass through the new reception center. Unfortunately, the building was a tinderbox. One midnight five years later, fire collapsed it into a heap of ashes.

In its place slowly rose the Ellis Island that stands today. Its centerpiece: the imperious, 220,000-square-foot Main Building, a $1.5

Gradually expanded from a three-acre mud flat to more than twenty-seven acres of landfill with three dozen buildings, the federal immigration center on New York harbor's Ellis Island eventually included dormitories, dining halls, hospitals, laundries, and other support facilities. During Ellis Island's peak years (1905-1914), as many as five thousand immigrants per day disembarked from transatlantic steamers onto the piers of lower Manhattan, then boarded ferries for the mile-and-a-quarter trip to the processing center.

Most newcomers spent only a few hours on Ellis Island before proceeding to their American destinations, but thousands of others were detained overnight or for several days or even weeks. These included immigrants with cases awaiting official review, others waiting for funds from relatives already in America, and those who would be met by family members.

ton, Baltimore, Philadelphia, New Orleans, and Galveston.)

More than a half-million immigrants a year passed through Ellis Island during its peak decade, 1905-1914. In 1907, its busiest year, the reception depot processed more than one million people. On April 17 of that year, the center handled its record volume: 11,747 in a single day.

The influx nearly overwhelmed even the grand new facilities and the well-intentioned immigration officials. "To receive, examine, and dispose of [more than a half-million] aliens in one fiscal year is a work so stupendous," Immigration Service officer Robert Watchorn pointed out when he took over Ellis Island in 1905, "that none but painstaking students of the immigration service could possibly have any intelligent conception of what arduous duties and unusual considerations it involves."

And while Ellis Island saw apprehension, suffering, and despair, a remarkable 98 percent of all those seeking entrance to the United States through this portal were ultimately admitted, most in a few hours' time. Few would ever forget the experience.

million fireproof red-brick and limestone structure large enough to house four Independence Halls. Four seventy-five-foot-high copper-domed towers rose above the vast roof, giving the wide-winged building the appearance of an Old-World palace.

On the morning of December 17, 1900—with the mighty Main Building still taking form, the enlarged depot received its first immigrants—654 Italians debarking from the *Kaiser Wilhelm II*. Steerage passengers from three other ships followed. By nightfall, 2,251 newcomers had made their way through the processing center.

They were the vanguard of millions to come. During the decades that followed, seven out of every ten immigrant ships leaving Europe for the United States headed for New York. (Others docked at a score of American ports that included Bos-

The long list of those who made their way through Ellis Island includes many illustrious Americans-to-be, including songwriter Irving Berlin (Russia), football great Knute Rockne (Norway), Supreme Court Justice Felix Frankfurter (Austria), entertainer Al Jolson (Lithuania), film mogul Samuel Goldwyn (Poland), labor leader Philip Murray (Scotland), director Frank Capra (Italy), Boys Town founder Father Edward Flanagan (Ireland), impresario Sol Hurok (the Ukraine), comedian Bob Hope (England), producer Spyros Skouras (Greece), and author Isaac Asimov (Russia). "[On] Ellis Island," actor Edward G. Robinson (Rumania) later stated, "I was born again."

The wider meaning of Ellis Island, however, is not to be found in the famous who passed through there. The island has instead become indelibly associated with the millions of immigrants who subsequently lived out their lives known but to their own families, friends, and neighbors. It was the concourse of the common man—"common people," as one writer described them, "who made an uncommon decision."

"People got twenty cents a day in the old country," recalled an immigrant who left Sicily in 1911. "Then you hear that you get a dollar a day in America. From twenty cents a day, you know, you're gonna try your very best to come to America. Those days that's all everybody talked about—America."*

Representatives of the leading transatlantic steamship companies aggressively canvassed the Continent from Scandinavia to Sicily, spreading the word that even the poorest of the poor could book passage to America. In the early 1900s a steerage-class ticket sold for about $20 (though prices ranged from $10 to $35 any given year). A person could travel in higher style—second- or cabin-class—for $40, or in truly grand style—first class—for about $80.

Despite its seemingly insignificant cost today, a steerage-class ticket represented the equivalent of months—even years—of a poor family's savings. Sometimes, a friend in America sent the ticket to a would-be immigrant. Often, family members pooled all their money to pay for the voyage of a loved one. Such was the case in 1913 of sixteen-year-old Hannah Murphy, a servant girl from Ireland, mother of the author of this article.

Under Immigration Service regulations, the steamship companies agreed to examine, disinfect, and vaccinate prospective immigrants before their departure from Europe, and to screen out persons forbidden by American law to enter: those who had "loathsome or dangerous contagious diseases" or who could not earn a living. The lines would—at their own expense—return to the Old World any applicants found unable to meet immigration requirements upon reaching Ellis Island.

Traveling by train, or riding horse-drawn wagons, or pushing handcarts, the dreamward-bound

*Quotations of immigrants in this article are drawn, in the main, from oral histories on file at the Ellis Island Immigration Museum.

seekers converged on ports such as Bremen, Antwerp, Cork, Rotterdam, Le Havre, Palermo, Liverpool, Glasgow, Southampton, Naples, Constantinople, Pireaus, Hamburg, Trieste, and Fiume. Thousands of them—Europe's lost, America's found—walked up the gangways of the ships that waited to take them away from the places and the people and the lives they had known.

They carried what refugees had always carried—the last of their possessions: straw hampers, battered suitcases, iron pans, candlesticks, sewing machines, prayer books. . . .

"What did we bring with us?" Fanny Shook reminisced of her 1921 departure from Poland. "Our clothes, our pillows, our big, thick comforters made from pure goose feathers—not chicken feathers—and a barrel of pickles."

Johanne Gentsch Kusche, aged eighteen upon her arrival from Germany, remembered: "In the trunk, odds and ends. I had no gold, no jewelry, no anything. . . . I didn't have anything!"

Fourteen-year-old Florio Vincenzo announced to an inspector at the pier: "I am a nobleman, seeking my fortune." The official opened Florio's paper valise. It was empty, save for a pair of old shoes. One shoe was packed with bologna wrapped in paper, the other with a small bag of cheese. These articles, the sum of $1.80 in coins, and the ragged clothes in which he stood, represented the beginnings of Florio's fortune.

T he voyage to America, immigrants learned too late, was not the picturesque passage depicted on steamship company posters. "Steerage," they found out during their ten to thirty spirit-rending days on the high seas, was not only the cheapest but also the lowest and meanest way to cross the Atlantic Ocean. It meant being quartered near the bottom of a ship—usually below the waterline, in near-darkness, with no portholes and almost no ventilation.

Hundreds of steerage passengers were jammed into barracks-like spaces six to eight feet high. They

slept on straw or thin mattresses laid upon two- or three-tiered bunk racks, five or six across. "It was horrible, horrible!" recalled Josephine Reale with bitterness. "Very sad. My poor mother had me, I was five-and-a-half. And she had an eleven-month-old boy. And she was three months pregnant. Sleeping was, like, one over the other. Very terrible."

Foul air, rampant lice, and vomit-covered decks drove the immigrants to spend as much time on the meager third-class deck as weather permitted. Toilet facilities barely worked; on some ships these consisted of plain openings over the under-rushing seas. Many steerage passengers were unable to wash for the duration of the voyage. The few who tried to bathe—in open stalls—had to use cold ocean water that trickled in from rusted faucets. In rough weather, the hatches were locked shut. "I couldn't lift my head for four days," remembered a Czech immigrant of his ordeal. "I thought I would never see the United States."

On many ships the food was scarcely palatable—thin soup, boiled potatoes, and stringy beef; or perhaps herring and soggy rye bread for the Scandinavians, Slavs, Germans, and Jews traveling the northern routes; sardines and soggy wheat bread for the Italians, Greeks, and Armenians sailing out of the Mediterranean.

Ships' crewmen, known to berate immigrants, gave the voyagers a foretaste of what life might hold for them on the promised shore. Sailors made unbidden advances on women in steerage or tried to sell families "genuine" U.S. citizenship certificates for $5 apiece.

Few immigrants survived the voyage without encountering dreaded, unlisted passengers—sickness and disease. The pitching and rolling of the ship almost guaranteed seasickness, while the rank miasma of the wretched steerage environment engendered epidemics.

Fannie Kligerman and her family, after fleeing the Russian pogroms, sailed on the *Batavia*, a leaky hulk that barely made it across the Atlantic. "We got water in the ship," she remembered, "and all the children got measles."

Moshe Lodsky crossed on the *Klist*: "It took four weeks. A lot of the people took sick, terrible."

Dominick Piccolo, a nine-year-old from Italy, never forgot his voyage: "We have a storm at sea. Lightning, thunder, the waves like mountains. The ship is rocking. I fall on my nose. I start bleeding. [One] woman—her husband is sick. During the night, he dies. They give him the prayers. Then they throw him overboard. His wife is screaming, 'My husband! My husband!'"

During the peak immigration years, as many as one out of ten steerage passengers succumbed to disease while en route to America.

But despite such odds, the immigrants would not be deterred. "I would rather cross the Atlantic ten times over," said one mother, "than to hear my child cry once."

As ships reached the approaches to New York harbor, they hoisted a yellow quarantine flag. The vessels hove to while U.S. Public Health Service doctors boarded and quickly scanned the passengers for signs of cholera, yellow fever, or typhoid. Once "cleared," the ships continued through the Narrows.

For those who had at last come within sight of the New World's shores, the first view of America would often remain foremost in their memory. Nineteen-year-old Totunno Pappatore of Italy kept a record of his 1906 crossing: "On the morning of May 15th we could make out a thin thread of land on the horizon. By midday we could clearly see a string of communities and farms spread along the coast in a continuous line of habitation. It was five o'clock when the ship entered the harbor."

As the landing hour approached, steerage passengers dressed in their best clothes. Women dug out their finest shawls. Men put on derbies. Girls appeared on deck in bright hats. Here and there stood boys in white suits.

Before Ellis Island: Castle Garden

From America's beginning, most immigrants came to the Promised Land by way of the port of New York. During the early 1800s, ships discharged hundreds of newcomers each day, unchecked and unregulated, at docks along Manhattan's notorious waterfront. Thugs and thieves, in what was to become a traditional welcome, pounced on the new arrivals as soon as the gangplanks went down.

By 1855 matters had gotten so out of hand that New York State leased Castle Garden, at the southern tip of Manhattan, for use as an immigration depot. The half-century-old circular structure, two hundred yards in circumference, had in its time served as a fort (Castle Clinton), a setting for band concerts, and a theater. Jenny Lind, "the Swedish Nightingale," had sung there in 1850, selling out the six-thousand-seat house for six performances. Castle Garden was the crowning jewel of Battery Park, a gracious promenade overlooking New York harbor.

Well-to-do residents of lower Manhattan were horrified by the notion of an immigrant landing-place in so elegant a setting. Battery Park, they predicted, would become a place of "riff-raff," and the glory would depart from Castle Garden. Their concerns proved prophetic.

In the early years of Castle Garden, immigrants arrived on small sailing ships, some aboard the same vessels that had carried black slaves from Africa. Their voyage took five or six weeks in cramped, filthy, disease-ridden quarters. For weeks after landing, the passengers and their possessions reeked of "the smell of the ship"—described by one young Russian man as "a distillation of bilge and putrescence, impervious to the cleaning agents available to the poor."

Many would-be immigrants never reached their destination. The immigrant ship *Liebnitz*, from Hamburg, was forced by head winds to detour through the tropics. By the time it finally arrived in New York harbor in January 1868

after a fourteen-week voyage, 108 of the 544 passengers had died of typhoid fever. A young German girl, asked at dockside where her parents were, pointed to the ocean and said, "Down there."

After arriving ships anchored near Castle Garden, customs inspectors boarded the vessels and examined the baggage; then two 150-ton barges ferried the immigrants to the Castle Garden wharf. As many as three thousand newcomers a day streamed into the rotunda. Clerks registered the new arrivals in ledger books by name, nationality, former residence, and intended destination. Physicians gave them cursory inspections for disease. A labor bureau provided assistance in finding work. Each immigrant was given a jug of fresh water with which to bathe in twenty-foot-long troughs. Because there were no sleeping quarters, newcomers had to cart away their baggage before nightfall.

Under the protection of Castle Garden, so its commissioners claimed, immigrants were "en-

They waited, massed on deck, voices stilled, eyes straight ahead—seeking, through the spray of sea, the figuration of a statue.

And there, finally appearing out of the mist, she loomed—the sea-green figure of Liberty, torch high, seemingly striding toward the newcomers as though she had sighted them in greeting at the same instant they had sighted her in gratitude.

"The first thing some people did," recalled Polish immigrant Stephanie Okunewitch, "was they got down on their knees. And they prayed to God, in their language, to thank God."

Arnold Weiss arrived in 1921: "Seeing the Statue of Liberty was the greatest thing I've ever seen. What a wonderful sight! To know you're in this country . . . just think of it!"

"I was looking," related Tessie Argianas, who came from Greece at the age of nine. "There was the statue. This is the liberty. The freedom of the world. This lady opened her arms for people. The prettiest thing I had ever seen in my life."

Some of the crowd on deck sang, or danced, or threw their hats into the air. One woman remembered that "the people were screaming, some were crying. It was the feeling of coming to a land of freedom, a land of love."

"When we arrived, it was like a dream," a man said. "I tell you the God's truth, it felt like a dream."

At times as many as thirty ships, jammed with more than ten thousand immigrants, rode at anchor in New York harbor while awaiting their turn to dock and discharge their passengers. Recalled Hungarian Endre Bohem of his winter night's arrival: "They wouldn't land us in the dark. I was a frightened boy. There had been typhoid on the ship. In the night, someone stole my one blanket. Snow blew in, right down the hatch. I woke up covered with snow."

Immigrants quickly discovered that in America—perhaps scarcely

---

abled to depart for their future homes without having their means impaired, their morals corrupted, their persons diseased." Nevertheless, contingents of hardened con men, swindlers, and ladies of pleasure energetically plied their trades just outside the twelve-foot-high wooden fence that encircled the facility. Boarding-house "runners" steered the new arrivals to outrageously overpriced, run-down lodgings. Baggage handlers demanded drinking money—"trinkgelt"—if the newcomers wanted to see their belongings again.

Harper's Weekly, in 1858, painted this picture of the immigrant's plight: "Authorities regarded him as a bale of goods. Scoundrels seized him. If he had any money, they robbed him of it. If he had a pretty wife or daughters, they stole them too, if they could. If he had neither money nor wife nor daughters, they took his luggage. It was well for him if, after having been robbed of all he had, he was not beaten to death."

Immigrants who settled in the city found themselves trapped in tenement enclaves such as Hell's Kitchen, Bandits' Roost, and Thieves Alley—catch-basins of crime, filth, and disease. Many others, perhaps fortuitously, boarded trains for the open spaces westward.

New York officials connivingly looked the other way as the depredations of Castle Garden continued year after year.

Joseph Pulitzer's newspaper, the *World*, ran a series of scathing articles on Castle Garden in 1887, terming it "a place of unlawful detention, a place for tyranny and whimsical rule, a place for the abuse and insult of helpless women, for the inhuman treatment of mothers and children, for the privation of the poor, for the lecherous pursuit of shielded employees, for the disgrace of the nation in the eyes of those who desire to become citizens."

Conditions finally grew so deplorable that Congress held investigations of the depot. They found that the local inspectors couldn't keep up with the growing volumes of immigrants. Money-changers shortchanged the newcomers. Railroad agents gouged them on ticket prices. Runners fleeced them. Some immigrants were made to pay twice for their baggage. One agent matter-of-factly told investigators, "We call Castle Garden 'Hell,' and don't expect to change Hell."

The federal government, dismayed by the nasty doings at Castle Garden, decided in 1890 to order its closure and take over from the states the inglorious business of admitting immigrants to America.

Some eight million people passed through Castle Garden during its thirty-five years as a reception depot—about seven in ten of all entering the United States during that period. Most were German (3,425,000), Irish (2,541,000), and English (1,178,000). Among the newcomers were future greats such as social reformer Jacob Riis (Denmark), physicist Michael Pupin (Serbia), labor organizer Samuel Gompers (England), and scientist Charles Steinmetz (Germany).

Castle Garden registered its last immigrants on April 18, 1890. The big rotunda thereupon closed its doors.*

Just days before, President Benjamin Harrison had officially designated the site of the first—and destined to become the most famous—federal immigration station. Strollers near old Castle Garden could see the mud flat about a mile away, not far from the Statue of Liberty. It was small, it was low, and it was in water so shallow that no ship could land there.

Ellis Island. ★

From 1896 to 1941, Castle Garden served as the New York City Aquarium. Then, after the structure sat vacant for more than thirty years, the U.S. National Park Service restored it to its original appearance as a War of 1812 fort. It is now operated by the Park Service in conjunction with Ellis Island and the Statue of Liberty.

RAILROAD TICKETS TO ALL POINTS
EISENBAHN BUREAU. BIGLIETTI FERROVIARII.
JÆRNBANE BILLET KONTOR.
VASUTI JEGYEK. ZELESNICKI KARTI.

Before leaving Ellis Island, many immigrants stopped at a money exchange window to obtain U.S. currency, and those continuing to points beyond New York City visited the processing center's railroad ticket office

less than in Europe—an economic class system separated the "haves" from the "have nots." Ships bearing immigrants usually docked at one of the piers jutting out from lower Manhattan. First- and second-class (or cabin) passengers— the upper and middle crust—moved through customs and immigration stages with no worry and little delay. Immigration authorities boarded the vessels as they reached New York harbor, passing through a quick, cursory examination those well-to-do aliens who traveled in the relative comfort of cabin or first class. These privileged newcomers walked right down the gangways and onto the streets of New York, avoiding Ellis Island entirely.

Finally, the hundreds of steerage-class immigrants trudged ashore with their few shabby possessions. Large paper tags tied to their coats identified the arrivals not by name but by their place on the ship's manifest. Exhausted and subdued, the steerage passengers waited on the pier for the small wooden ferries that would carry them the final mile to Ellis Island. Wrote a journalist: "Their stolid faces hide frightened, throbbing hearts. They obey the signs, gestures, and directions of the attendants as dumbly as cattle, and as patiently."

Film-footage shot in 1903 by a cameraman from the Thomas Edison studios captured the dramatic arrival of one contingent of immigrants at Ellis Island. Like a beleaguered army on the move, they marched off the ferry, fathers hefting suitcases tied with ropes; mothers carrying infants; boys and girls bearing tattered bags of belongings. Uniformed guards hurried them along toward the Main Building— for their appointment with destiny.

A New York newspaper reporter,

writing in the summer of 1896, told of "rugged, sun-browned faces . . . lit up with hope and fear, joy and sorrow . . . Hope for success in the new land to which they are voluntary exiles; fear of the unknown future; joy that the long-dreaded voyage is over; and sorrow at the memories tugging at their heartstrings . . ."

Inside the stately Beaux-Arts-style Main Building, as many as five thousand immigrants were processed on a typical, busy day. On the first floor, they could deposit their baggage in a cavernous Baggage Room. Some who did later wished they hadn't; their luggage was misplaced. Many who didn't later wished they had, after carrying their belongings up twenty or so steps to the second floor.

Unknown to the immigrants, U.S. Public Health Service doctors in military-style uniforms carefully observed the arrivals as they made their way, single file, up the staircase—watching for lameness of gait, shortness of breath that might mean heart weakness, and physical deformities. At the top of the staircase, an interpreter shouted, "This way! Hurry up!" in several languages.

Ushered into the Registry Room, many a new arrival felt diminished by its vastness. This Great Hall was by far the largest room many of the immigrants had ever seen—a two-hundred-foot-long, vaulted-ceilinged chamber that seemed big enough to contain an entire Old-World village. The grand scale of the Hall's design was intentional—in practical terms, the space was needed to cope with large volumes of immigrants; in poetic terms, it impressed them with the majesty of their new homeland.

The Hall was as bewildering as it was impressive. A babel of voices sounded from the lines of immigrants awaiting processing. Many of the Irish had never seen an Italian or a Jew; some Italians had never seen a Slav or a Russian. The German could not understand the Swede's language, nor could the Pole gather the meaning of the Turk's words. All the world, it seemed, had come to this vast room.

"The noise was deafening," recalled Stephen Peters, an immigrant from Albania who reached Ellis Island when he was fourteen years old. "There were children crying and women crying." The scene resembled a human stockyard. Separated into lots of thirty—the number of names contained on a single page of a ship's manifest—the immigrants were herded through a maze of aisles and pens formed by seven-foot-high iron railings. (By 1906, benches took the place of the railings.)

Making two right-angle turns through the aisles, arrivals passed medical officers who, seer-like, could supposedly "read" expressions that bespoke mental abnormalities. In the last, lonely, twenty-five paces to the examining doctor, an immigrant underwent even closer scrutiny. The sure-eyed physician took particular note of the man who wheezed, the woman trying to hide her limp behind the big bundle she carried, the girl with a glaring rash, the boy with a bewildered gaze, the child who couldn't walk well.

A knowing glance at head, face, and throat was enough for a doctor to reach his decision. In the early 1900s, the examination took from six to sixty seconds. Each of ten doctors examined as many as five hundred immigrants a day.

The doctors were on particular watch for so-called "immigrant diseases"—cholera, yellow fever, typhoid, leprosy, ringworm, scarlet fever, and tuberculosis. Unfortunates found to be afflicted with one of these "loathsome" diseases would in most cases be sent back to their ports of embarkation.

Even before they left the Old Country, immigrants were warned to "beware of the eye man" on Ellis Island. A medical officer would place an ordinary glove-buttonhook over each of the newcomer's eyelids in turn, swiftly folding the lid back to expose and examine the lining for signs of trachoma, a disease leading to blindness. Fairly common in Southern Europe, the then-incurable ailment spread rapidly among shiploads of immigrants. Although the examination took but a few seconds, its consequences could be devastating. A diagnosis of trachoma meant certain deportation—accounting for more than half of the medical turn-backs at Ellis Island.

"They were all lined up—a motley crowd in colorful costumes," recalled an interpreter, "Doctors put them through their examinations. If one stirred their suspicion, the alien was set aside from the rest, and his coat lapel or shirt marked with colored chalk, the color indicating why he had been isolated."

One in six arrivals was so branded during the review: an "H" indicated possible heart trouble; "K" for hernia; "F" signifying a facial rash; "S" for senility; "X" for a suspected mental disorder. Immigrants bearing the telltale mark were shunted into "cages" to await more thorough re-examinations that for some spelled deportation.

America, immigrants learned in the Great Hall, welcomed newcomers—provided they posed no future menace as health risks, public charges, or lawbreakers. At various times the nation refused to admit anarchists, paupers, criminals, prostitutes, imbeciles, polygamists, illiterates, and Orientals. By 1917, an immigrant faced thirty-three separate reasons for exclusion from America.

After the newcomers had cleared the medical inspectors at one end of the Registry Room, they were directed through the aisleways to the legal inspectors at the other end. Seated on uncomfortable benches, the immigrants nervously awaited their turn to face men in dark uniforms who would perform something akin to a judging of souls.

Perched behind high desks like so many clerks from a Charles Dickens novel, twenty or more inspectors pored over ship manifests. One by one, leaning across the desktops to look the newcomers in the eye, they beckoned immigrants to come forward. Interpreters stood by to assist the inspectors with more than twenty languages and numerous dialects. (One interpreter—a New Yorker by the name of Fiorello H. La Guardia—spoke French, German, Italian, Yiddish, and Serbo-Croatian. La Guardia served on Ellis Island from 1910 to 1912, and eventually went on to become New York City mayor.)

In interviews that lasted about two minutes, the examiners asked

each immigrant more than two dozen questions in rapid succession, seeking to verify whether the applicant was "clearly and beyond a doubt entitled to land." "What is your name?" "Where were you born?" "Where did you last live?" "Are you married?" "Where is your wife?" "Do you have children?" "Where are they?" "Have you ever been in jail?" "How did you make your living?" "How will you make a living in America?" "Do you have a job waiting for you?" "What kind of job is it?" "Is someone meeting you?" "Who?" "How much money do you have with you?" "Would you please show it to me now?" "Where did you get it?" "Where are you going?" "Who paid for your passage?" "Is that person in the United States?"

At times the dialogue between inspector and immigrant took Kafka-esque turns. One Polish girl, asked how she would wash stairs—from top to bottom or bottom to top—calmly replied: "I didn't come to America to wash stairs."

A puzzled Slav, when asked if he was an "anarchist," thought the word meant a religious believer. "Yes," he responded, "a very devout one."

An Armenian woman who could not read—even in her own language—was fortunate enough to encounter a kind-hearted inspector. The woman whispered something to the interpreter, who passed it on to the inspector, who then asked the woman to read a passage at random from an Armenian book. She put her finger on the page and, without looking at it, recited the Lord's Prayer in Armenian. The inspector waved her and her children on their way.

Able-bodied men trod a thin line when asked whether they had a job waiting for them. Many miners, for example, had been lured to America by unscrupulous mineowners who wanted to use immigrants as strikebreakers. If a newcomer sounded too sure of employment, he might be turned back for taking a job away from an American. But if he was too indefinite, he could be rejected as a potential charity case.

"From morning to night, we were examining immigrants," recalled

Frank Martocci, an inspector during Ellis Island's peak years. "Every twenty-four hours from three to five thousand people came before us. I myself examined from four to five hundred a day. We were swamped by that human tide."

Even a simple question—"What is your name?"—could become a complicated task for an inspector, who had to match the spoken name against that recorded on the steamship companies' handwritten manifests. Among the more daunting names were "Andrjuljawierjus," "Grzyszczyszn," "Koutsoghianopoulos," and "Zemiszkicivicz."

Scores of people who passed through Ellis Island later contended that during processing their names were changed or simplified. Although such acts have never been officially documented, stories of people receiving new names as they stood before the inspectors' desks are a revered part of America's oral history tradition.

An immigrant bearing the name Honnes Gardashian upon his arrival at Ellis Island left with the name Joe Arness. An Irish woman surnamed McGeoghegan somehow became McGaffighan. A man named Mastroianni emerged as Mister Yanni.

One Russian Jew had been told that some people changed their own names at Ellis Island. When he arrived, he asked a clerk to suggest a good name for use in America. "Rockefeller," the clerk advised. During his four-hour wait for an interview, the newcomer tried to remember how to say this odd name. When an inspector finally asked the Russian his name, the man sputtered "Shoyn feggessen!"—Yiddish for "I have already forgotten!" The inspector wrote "Sean Fergusson" on the fellow's landing card, and a dazed new American-to-be wondered long and hard about his new name.

Despite the astounding numbers of arrivals and the grueling paces through which they were taken, eighty percent of the immigrants passing through Ellis Island were on their way to their American destination within three to four hours.

As the flood of immigrants pushed Ellis Island beyond its limits, its land area was increased ninefold. Ballast from ships, mixed with dirt dug from New York City's subway tunnels, comprised much of the landfill used to enlarge the island from less than four to more than twenty-seven acres. With thirty-six buildings, the facility eventually became a city unto itself, generating its own electricity and heat, and boasting kitchens, laundries, a dining room that could feed one thousand people at a sitting, dormitories for overnight detainees, and hospitals with beds for more than seven hundred patients. Pianos, a baseball field, and play space for children were ultimately added, along with a post office, library, chapel, greenhouse, and morgue.

Many steerage passengers had become infested with lice during their voyage; on Ellis Island they were scrubbed down, their hair cut off or soaked with kerosene, and their clothing fumigated. "They put my mother and me in the shower room," recounted a woman who had been detained with her parents for a week. "They hosed us down. I cried. I yelled that they were burning me with the hot water. It was bitter tears I shed!"

Many immigrants got their first taste of American food at long tables in the dining hall. The foods baffled, delighted, or repelled them—depending upon who was eating what. Many had never previously tasted oatmeal, doughnuts, tomatoes, Fig Newtons, or oranges. Given bananas, a few devoured the fruit skin and all. Frenzied by their first taste of granulated sugar, thirteen men were injured as they fought over a bowl of the flavorsome substance.

One Ellis Island commissioner lamented his difficulty in pleasing the wide range of immigrant tastes: "If I added spaghetti, the Italians sent me an engrossed testimonial—and everybody else objected. If I put pirogi and Mazovian noodles on the table, the Poles were happy and the rest discontented. Irish stew was no good for the English, and the English marmalade was gunpowder to the Irish. The Scotch distrusted both. The Welsh took what they could get."

Life-and-death struggles filled the island's fifteen hospital buildings.

Contagious disease wards housed victims of scarlet fever, smallpox, chicken pox, measles, ringworm, or tuberculosis. In the children's wards, nurses were taught: "Never kiss them."

Martha Strahm, a Swiss immigrant, reached Ellis Island in 1920 with her husband and her son. "My boy Walter was sick," she reflected, "They put him in the ward six weeks. Only one of us could go see him at a time—five minutes, once a week. We had to put on a gown. We were not allowed to touch him. He died late at night. They took him down the hall wrapped in a sheet."

Between 1900 and 1925, an estimated 3,500 immigrants died on Ellis Island—many from typhoid fever, dysentery, or measles. Nearly half were children. But as life ended in the grim wards, so new life began. More than three hundred babies were born there. Robert Rodojcsin—whose name was later shortened and Americanized to Robert Rath, came into the world in 1921 as the seven-and-one-half-pound son of Yugoslavian parents. To this day he carries "Ellis" as his middle name, in memory of his birthplace.

Sadly, for some new arrivals, Ellis Island was all they would ever experience of America. As many as two thousand disconsolate detainees at a time whiled away hours, days, even weeks on the island, awaiting rulings on their cases.

Boards of Special Inquiry, composed of three or four inspectors and an interpreter, heard up to seventy thousand pleadings a year. Struggling to be fair-minded, the inquiry boards generally gave detained aliens the benefit of the doubt. They ultimately admitted about five of every six immigrants who appeared before them.

Hearing stenographer Jack Rund said of the sessions: "A lot of times immigrants would break down and cry. For some, to go back meant death. Their foot, their toe is in the door. They have clawed their way to this point and now someone's going to tear their fingers away from it. So they're going to fight and they're going to give it everything they've got."

But board members drew a harsh

line when the law of the land so decreed. They might be compelled to rule against the laborer who had agreed to take a job in America in exchange for his free steamship ticket; the woman with a history of "moral terpitude"; the sixteen-year-old with a contagious disease; the shipboard stowaway; the teen-aged girl deemed "insane"; the enfeebled man judged "likely to become a public charge"; the unmarried, pregnant woman; the criminal sought by police in his own country.

About one thousand persons each month—two percent of those processed—were proclaimed "undesirable aliens." These unfortunate travelers would have bittersweet remembrances of Ellis Island, of gazing across the harbor at the Statue of Liberty and the towers of Manhattan and realizing that they would never see any more of America than that vision. The long, bitter voyage home for some 250,000 immigrants meant sailing back to the very fates they had hoped to flee. It was the end of a dream.

Most heart-rending of all were deportation rulings that broke up households, with most family members admitted to the Promised Land but with a husband, wife, or child disqualified for health or other reasons. Families then faced the immediate, agonizing decision of either leaving one of their number behind or of sorrowfully returning to Europe together.

Henry Curran, a commissioner of Ellis Island, wrote of the deportees in 1923: "Day by day the barges took them from Ellis Island back to the ships again, back to the ocean, back to—what? As they trooped aboard the big barges under my window, carrying their heavy bundles, some in their colorful native costumes worn to celebrate their first glad day in free America, some carrying little American flags, most of them quietly weeping, they twisted something in my heart."

If there were tears, there was also hope. Some of those detained were awaiting funds from relatives already in America; inspectors would not clear immigrants carrying less than $25 in cash. Immigrants suffering from minor illnesses were cared for until well. Unaccompanied women were detained until inspectors could be assured of their safety once they left the island. Many women arrived to join husbands or fiancés who had gone ahead to America to find jobs. A telegram, letter, or railway ticket from a relative in the United States usually assured these women's release.

A wooden pillar stood near the point where released immigrants and their anxious loved ones rushed into one another's arms. It became known as the "Kissing Post." Unmarried couples thus united sometimes chose to be wed immediately, in a hall used as a chapel.

Ellis Island brightened with romance when, from time to time, shiploads of "picture brides" arrived. These young immigrant women had exchanged photographs with American men who had courted the women by mail. Introduced to their waiting swains, the brides-to-be went on their presumably blissful way with their future husbands. Sometimes, however, Cupid misaimed his arrow. On occasion, a "picture bride" fell in love with a fellow immigrant during the long voyage, leaving her hopeful American suiter waiting on Ellis Island with just a photograph by which to remember his intended. Upon first laying eyes on her intended husband, more than one prospective bride chose deportation rather than joining him; and a few suitors never came to Ellis Island to claim their waiting brides

Immigrants shall be treated with kindness and civility," announced a framed notice on a wall at Ellis Island. To a remarkable degree, despite overcrowding and an overworked staff, they were.

Ellis Island's employees, assisted by volunteers from forty immigrant aid societies, labored to ease the passage—and the waiting—that immigrants experienced. A rooftop playground entertained youngsters. Some detainees saw their first Charlie Chaplin movie on the island. One Christmas Eve, famed performer Enrico Caruso raised immigrants' spirits. "Caruso! The real Caruso!" Helen Cohen, of Poland, related years later. "He sang for us. His voice is still ringing in my ears! But then the loudspeaker called out our family's name. My cousin had come to take us out. We ran out quick—even on Caruso—to get out of Ellis Island."

Ellis Island was never meant to be a Czar's palace. "A saint from heaven actuated by all his saintliness would fail to give satisfaction at this place," declared commissioner Robert Watchorn in 1907, the facility's peak year. His predecessor, William Williams, lamented that while he believed it was possible to keep evil practices well within bounds and give immigrants proper treatment during their stay, he doubted "that the millennium can ever exist here." The sheer size and complexity of the task defied perfection.

At last waved onward, immigrants hefted their boxes and bundles. A pause at the money exchange booth brought them U.S. dollars for their lire, marks, pounds, rubles, and drachmas. Hundreds then hurried down a corridor to doors marked "Push, To New York," and onto the ferry that would carry them that last mile and a quarter to Manhattan.

Others bought railroad tickets to the far reaches of the country. Railroad agents did their best to figure out the destinations scrawled on baggage tags: "Detrayamis" (Detroit), "Linkinbra" (Lincoln, Nebraska), "Deas Moyness Youa" (Des Moines, Iowa), "Szekenevno Pillsburs" (Second Avenue, Pittsburgh)—or simply "Main Street."

Right town or wrong, the newcomers could at least be sure that they had reached the right country. America. ★

Recommended additional reading: Ellis Island: Echoes from a Nation's Past *(Aperture Books and National Park Service, 1990) contains essays and numerous photographs documenting the history of the immigration depot and its subsequent restoration. Other excellent accounts include* Island of Hope, Island of Tears *by David M. Brownstone, Irene M. Franck, and Douglass L. Brownstone (Rawson, Wade, 1948),* Strangers at the Door: Ellis Island, Castle Garden, and the Great Migration to America *by Ann Novotny (Chatham Press, 1971),* Keepers of the Gate: A History of Ellis Island *by Thomas M. Pitkin (New York University Press, 1975), and* Gateway to Liberty: The Story of the Statue of Liberty and Ellis Island *by Mary J. Shapiro (Vantage Books, 1986).*

BATTLES WON AND LOST

OUR FIRST SOUTHEAST ASIAN WAR

DAVID R. KOHLER
AND JAMES WENSYEL

David R. Kohler, Commander, U.S. Navy, is a Naval Special Warfare officer who has served multiple tours in UDT (underwater demolition) and SEAL (sea, air, land) teams. He has a master's degree in national security affairs from the Naval Postgraduate School in Monterey, California.

James W. Wensyel, a retired Army officer, is the author of three published books and numerous articles. His article on the crash of the dirigible Shenandoah *appeared in the February 1989 issue of this magazine. He resides with his wife Jean in Newville, Pennsylvania.*

Guerrilla warfare . . . jungle terrain . . . search and destroy missions . . . benevolent pacification . . . strategic hamlets . . . terrorism . . . ambushes . . . free-fire zones . . . booby traps . . . waning support from civilians at home. These words call forth from the national consciousness uncomfortable images of a war Americans fought and

America's turn-of-the-century military campaign against Philippine insurgents consumed three years, involved 126,000 troops, and cost 4,000 lives. The lessons we learned could have been used in Vietnam sixty years later.

died in not long ago in Southeast Asia. But while the phrases may first bring to mind America's painful experience in Vietnam during the 1960s and '70s, they also aptly describe a much earlier conflict—the Philippine Insurrection—that foreshadowed this and other insurgent wars in Asia.

The Philippine-American War of 1898-1902 is one of our nation's most obscure and least-understood campaigns. Sometimes called the "Bolo War" because of the Filipino insurgents' lethally effective use of razor-sharp bolo knives or machetes against the American expeditionary force occupying the islands, it is often viewed as a mere appendage of the one-hundred-day Spanish-American War. But suppressing the guerrilla warfare waged by Philippine nationalists seeking self-rule proved far more difficult, protracted, and costly for American forces than the conventional war with Spain that had preceded it.

America's campaign to smash the

From *American History Illustrated,* January/February 1990, pp. 19-30. Reprinted through the courtesy of Cowles Magazines, publishers of *American History Illustrated.*

Philippine Insurrection was, ironically, a direct consequence of U.S. efforts to secure independence for other *insurrectos* halfway around the world in Cuba. On May 1, 1898, less than a week after Congress declared war against Spain, a naval squadron commanded by Commodore George Dewey steamed into Manila Bay to engage the Spanish warships defending that nation's Pacific possession. In a brief action Dewey achieved a stunning victory, sinking all of the enemy vessels with no significant American losses. Destroying the Spanish fleet, however, did not ensure U.S. possession of the Philippines. An estimated 15,000 Spanish soldiers still occupied Manila and the surrounding region. Those forces would have to be rooted out by infantry.

President William McKinley had already ordered a Philippine Expeditionary Force of volunteer and regular army infantry, artillery, and cavalry units (nearly seven thousand men), under the command of Major General Wesley Merritt, to "reduce Spanish power in that quarter [Philippine Islands] and give order and security to the islands while in the possession of the United States."

Sent to the Philippines in the summer of 1898, this limited force was committed without fully considering the operation's potential length and cost. American military and government leaders also failed to anticipate the consequences of ignoring the Filipino rebels who, under Generalissimo Don Emilio Aguinaldo y Famy, had been waging a war for independence against Spain for the past two years. And when American insensitivity toward Aguinaldo eventually led to open warfare with the rebels, the American leaders grossly underestimated the determination of the seemingly ill-trained and poorly armed insurgents. They additionally failed to perceive the difficulties involved in conducting military operations in a tropical environment and among a hostile native population, and they did not recognize the burden of fighting at the end of a seven-thousand-mile-long logistics trail.

Asian engagements, the Americans learned for the first time, are costly. The enterprise, so modestly begun, eventually saw more than 126,000 American officers and men deployed to the Philippines. Four times as many soldiers served in this undeclared war in the Pacific as had been sent to the Caribbean during the Spanish-American War. During the three-year conflict, American troops and Filipino insurgents fought in more than 2,800 engagements. American casualties ultimately totaled 4,234 killed and 2,818 wounded, and the insurgents lost about 16,000 men. The civilian population suffered even more; as many as 200,000 Filipinos died from famine, pestilence, or the unfortunate happenstance of being too close to the fighting. The Philippine war cost the United States $600 million before the insurgents were subdued.

The costly experience offered valuable and timeless lessons about guerrilla warfare in Asia; unfortunately, those lessons had to be relearned sixty years later in another war that, despite the modern technology involved, bore surprising parallels to America's first Southeast Asian campaign.

Origins

America's war with Spain, formally declared by the United States on April 25, 1898, had been several

Manila-bound soldiers on a troopship pulling away from a San Francisco pier watch as the last man climbs aboard (above). At the height of the Spanish-American War, President William McKinley sent a seven-thousand-man expeditionary force to occupy the Philippines; during the next three years nearly twenty times that number of Americans would become involved in operations against Filipino insurgents.

years in the making. During that time the American "yellow press," led by Joseph Pulitzer's *New York World* and William Randolph Hearst's *New York Journal*, trumpeted reports of heroic Cuban *insurrectos* revolting against their cruel Spanish rulers. Journalists vividly described harsh measures taken by Spanish officials to quell the Cuban revolution. The sensational accounts, often exaggerated, reminded Americans of their own uphill fight for independence and nourished the feeling that America was destined to intervene so that the Cuban people might also taste freedom.

Furthermore, expansionists suggested that the revolt against a European power, taking place less than one hundred miles from American shores, offered a splendid opportunity to turn the Caribbean into an American sea. Businessmen pointed out that $50 million in American capital was invested in the Cuban sugar and mining industries. Revolutions resulting in burned cane fields jeopardized that investment. As 1898 opened, American relations with Spain quickly declined.

In January 1898 the U.S. battleship *Maine* was sent to Cuba, ostensibly on a courtesy visit. On February 15 the warship was destroyed by a mysterious explosion while at anchor in Havana harbor, killing 262 of her 350-man crew. The navy's formal inquiry, completed on March 28, suggested that the explosion was due to an external force—a mine.

On March 29, the Spanish government received an ultimatum from Washington, D.C.: Spain's army in Cuba was to lay down its arms while the United States negotiated between the rebels and the Spaniards. The Spanish forces were also told to abolish all *reconcentrado* camps (tightly controlled areas, similar to the strategic hamlets later tried in Vietnam, where peasants were regrouped to deny food and intelligence to insurgents and to promote tighter security). Spain initially rejected the humiliation of surrendering its arms in the field but then capitulated on all points. The Americans were not satisfied.

On April 11, declaring that Spanish responses were inadequate, Pres-

ident McKinley told a joint session of Congress that "I have exhausted every effort to relieve the intolerable condition . . . at our doors. I now ask the Congress to empower the president to take measures to secure a full and final termination of hostilities in Cuba, to secure . . . the establishment of a stable government, and to use the military and naval forces of the United States . . . for these purposes. . . ."

Congress adopted the proposed resolution on April 19. Learning this, Spain declared war on the 24th. The following day, the United States responded with its own declaration of war.

The bulk of the American navy quickly gathered on the Atlantic coast. McKinley called for 125,000 volunteers to bolster the less than eighty-thousand-man regular army. His call was quickly oversubscribed; volunteers fought to be the first to land on Cuba's beaches.

The first major battle of the war, however, was fought not in Cuba but seven thousand miles to the west —in Manila Bay. Dewey's victory over Spanish Admiral Patricio Montojo y Pasarón (a rather hollow victory as Montojo's fleet consisted of seven unarmored ships, three of which had wooden hulls and one that had to be towed to the battle area) was wildly acclaimed in America.

American leaders, believing that the Philippines would now fall into America's grasp like a ripe plum, had to decide what to do with their prize. They could not return the islands to Spain, nor could they allow them to pass to France or Germany, America's commercial rivals in the Orient. The American press rejected the idea of a British protectorate. And, after four hundred years of despotic Spanish rule in which Filipinos had little or no chance to practice self-government, native leaders seemed unlikely candidates for managing their own affairs. McKinley faced a grand opportunity for imperialistic expansion that could not be ignored.

The debate sharply divided his cabinet—and the country. American public opinion over acquisition of the Philippines divided into two ba-

sic factions: imperialists versus anti-imperialists.

The imperialists, mostly Republicans, included such figures as Theodore Roosevelt (then assistant secretary of the navy), Henry Cabot Lodge (Massachusetts senator), and Albert Beveridge (Indiana senator). These individuals were, for the most part, disciples of Alfred Thayer Mahan, a naval strategist who touted theories of national power and prestige through sea power and acquisition of overseas colonies for trade purposes and naval coaling stations.

The anti-imperialists, staunchly against American annexation of the Philippines, were mainly Democrats. Such men as former presidents Grover Cleveland and Rutherford B. Hayes, steel magnate Andrew Carnegie, William Jennings Bryan, union leader Samuel Gompers, and Mark Twain warned that by taking the Philippines the United States would march the road to ruin earlier traveled by the Roman Empire. Furthermore, they argued, America would be denying Filipinos the right of self-determination guaranteed by our own Constitution. The more practical-minded also pointed out that imperialistic policy would require maintaining an expensive army and navy there.

Racism, though demonstrated in different ways, pervaded the arguments of both sides. Imperialists spoke of the "white man's burden" and moral responsibility to "uplift the child races everywhere" and to provide "orderly development for the unfortunate and less able races." They spoke of America's "civilizing mission" of pacifying Filipinos by "benevolent assimilation" and saw the opening of the overseas frontier much as their forefathers had viewed the western frontier. The "subjugation of the Injun" (wherever he might be found) was a concept grasped by American youth —the war's most enthusiastic supporters (in contrast to young America's opposition to the war in Vietnam many years later).

The anti-imperialists extolled the sacredness of independence and self-determination for the Filipinos. Racism, however, also crept into their argument, for they believed that "protection against race min-

Stymied by the Filipinos' use of guerrilla warfare, the Americans were forced to change their strategy.

gling'' was a historic American policy that would be reversed by imperialism. To them, annexation of the Philippines would admit ''alien, inferior, and mongrel races to our nationality.''

As the debate raged, Dewey continued to hold Manila Bay, and the Philippines seemed to await America's pleasure. President McKinley would ultimately cast the deciding vote in determining America's role in that country. McKinley, a genial, rather laid-back, former congressman from Ohio and one-time major in the Union army, remains a rather ambiguous figure during this period. In his Inaugural Address he had affirmed that ''We want no wars of conquest; we must avoid the temptation of territorial aggression.'' Thereafter, however, he made few comments on pacifism, and, fourteen weeks after becoming president, signed the bill annexing Hawaii.

Speaking of Cuba in December 1897, McKinley said, ''I speak not of forcible annexation, for that cannot be thought of. That, by our code of morality, would be criminal aggression.'' Nevertheless, he constantly pressured Madrid to end Spanish rule in Cuba, leading four months later to America's war with Spain.

McKinley described experiencing extreme turmoil, soul-searching, and prayer over the Philippine annexation issue until, he declared, one night in a dream the Lord revealed to him that ''there was nothing left for us to do but to take them all [the Philippine Islands] and to educate the Filipinos, and uplift, and civilize, and Christianize them.'' He apparently didn't realize that the Philippines had been staunchly Roman Catholic for more than 350 years under Spanish colonialism. Nor could he anticipate the difficulties that, having cast its fortune with the expansionists, America would now face in the Philippines.

Prosecuting the War

Meanwhile, in the Philippine Islands, Major General Wesley Merritt's Philippine Expeditionary Force went about its job. In late June, General Thomas Anderson led an advance party ashore at Cavite. He then established Camp Merritt, visited General Aguinaldo's rebel forces entrenched around Manila, and made plans for seizing that city once Merritt arrived with the main body of armed forces.

Anderson quickly learned that military operations in the Philippines could be difficult. His soldiers, hastily assembled and dispatched with limited prior training, were poorly disciplined and inadequately equipped. Many still wore woolen uniforms despite the tropical climate. A staff officer described the army's baptism at Manila: ''. . . the heat was oppressive and the rain kept falling. At times the trenches were filled with two feet of water, and soon the men's shoes were ruined. Their heavy khaki uniforms were a nuisance; they perspired constantly, the loss of body salts inducing chronic fatigue. Prickly heat broke out, inflamed by scratching and rubbing. Within a week the first cases of dysentery, malaria, cholera, and dengue fever showed up at sick call.''

During his first meeting with Dewey, Anderson remarked that some American leaders were considering annexation of the Philippines. ''If the United States intends to hold the Philippine Islands,'' Dewey responded, ''it will make things awkward, because just a week ago Aguinaldo proclaimed the independence of the Philippine Islands from Spain and seems intent on establishing his own government.''

A Filipino independence movement led by Aguinaldo had been active in the islands since 1896 and, within weeks of Dewey's victory, Aguinaldo's revolutionaries controlled most of the archipelago.

Aguinaldo, twenty-nine years old in 1898, had taken over his father's position as mayor of his hometown of Kawit before becoming a revolutionary. In a minor skirmish with Spanish soldiers, he had rallied the Filipinos to victory. Thereafter, his popularity grew as did his ragtag but determined army. Aguinaldo was slight of build, shy, and soft-spoken, but a strict disciplinarian.

As his rebel force besieged Manila, Aguinaldo declared a formal government for the Philippines with himself as president and generalissimo. He proclaimed his ''nation's'' independence and called for Filipinos to rally to his army and to the Americans, declaring that ''the Americans . . . extend their protecting mantle to our beloved country. . . . When you see the American flag flying, assemble in numbers: they are our redeemers!'' But his enthusiasm for the United States later waned.

Merritt put off Aguinaldo's increasingly strident demands that America recognize his government and guarantee the Filipinos' independence. Aguinaldo perceived the American general's attitude as condescending and demeaning.

On August 13, Merritt's forces occupied Manila almost without firing a shot; in a face-saving maneuver the Spanish defenders had agreed to surrender to the Americans to avoid being captured—and perhaps massacred—by the Filipino insurgents. Merritt's troops physically blocked Aguinaldo's rebels, who had spent weeks in the trenches around the city, from participating in the assault. The Filipino general and his followers felt betrayed at being denied a share in the victory.

Further disenchanted, Aguinaldo would later find his revolutionary government unrepresented at the Paris peace talks determining his country's fate. He would learn that Spain had ceded the Philippines to the United States for $20 million.

Officers at Merritt's headquarters had little faith in the Filipinos' ability to govern themselves. ''Should our power . . . be withdrawn,'' an early report declared, ''the Philippines would speedily lapse into anarchy, which would excuse . . . the intervention of other powers and the division of the islands among them.''

Meanwhile, friction between American soldiers and the Filipinos increased. Much of the Americans' conduct betrayed their racial bias. Soldiers referred to the natives as ''niggers'' and ''gu-gus,'' epithets whose meanings were clear to the Filipinos. In retaliation, the island inhabitants refused to give way on sidewalks and muscled American officers into the streets. Men of the expeditionary force in turn escalated tensions by stopping Filipinos at gun point, searching them without cause, ''confiscating'' shopkeepers' goods, and beating those who resisted.

On the night of February 4, 1899 the simmering pot finally boiled over. Private William ''Willie'' Walter Grayson and several other soldiers of Company D, 1st Nebraska Volunteer Infantry, apprehended a group of armed insurgents within their regimental picket line. Shots were exchanged, and three Filipino *insurrectos* fell dead. Heavy firing erupted between the two camps.

In the bloody battle that followed, the Filipinos suffered tremendous casualties (an estimated two thousand to five thousand dead, contrasted with fifty-nine Americans killed) and were forced to withdraw. The Philippine Insurrection had begun.

Guerrilla Warfare

The Americans, hampered by a shortage of troops and the oncoming rainy season, could initially do little more than extend their defensive perimeter beyond Manila and establish a toehold on several islands to the south. By the end of March, however, American forces seized Malolos, the seat of Aguinaldo's revolutionary government. But Aguinaldo escaped, simply melting into the jungle. In the fall, using conventional methods of warfare, the Americans first struck south, then north of Manila across the central Luzon plain. After hard marching and tough fighting, the expeditionary force occupied northern Luzon, dispersed the rebel army, and barely missed capturing Aguinaldo.

Believing that occupying the remainder of the Philippines would be easy, the Americans wrongly concluded that the war was virtually ended. But when the troops attempted to control the territory they had seized, they found that the Filipino revolutionaries were not defeated but had merely changed strategies. Abandoning western-style conventional warfare, Aguinaldo had decided to adopt guerrilla tactics.

Aguinaldo moved to a secret mountain headquarters at Palanan in northern Luzon, ordering his troops to disperse and avoid pitched battles in favor of hit-and-run operations by small bands. Ambushing parties of Americans and applying terror to coerce support from other Filipinos, the insurrectionists now blended into the countryside, where they enjoyed superior intelligence information, ample supplies, and tight security. The guerrillas moved freely between the scattered Ameri-

U.S. troops found the tropical climate and Southeast Asian terrain almost as deadly as combat. Thousands of soldiers were incapacitated by dysentery, malaria, and other tropical maladies. The first troops sent to the archipelago wore unsuitable woolen uniforms; these men, photographed in 1900, had at least been issued ponchos for use during the rainy season.

can units, cutting telegraph lines, attacking supply trains, and assaulting straggling infantrymen. When the Americans pursued their tormentors, they fell into well planned ambushes. The insurgents' barbarity and ruthlessness during these attacks were notorious.

The guerrilla tactics helped to offset the inequities that existed between the two armies. The American troops were far better armed, for example, carrying .45-caliber Springfield single-shot rifles, Mausers, and then-modern .30-caliber repeating Krag-Jorgensen rifles. They also had field artillery and machine guns. The revolutionaries, on the other hand, were limited to a miscellaneous assortment of handguns, a few Mauser repeating rifles taken from the Spanish, and antique muzzle-loaders. The sharp-edged bolo knife was the revolutionary's primary weapon, and he used it well. Probably more American soldiers were hacked to death by bolos than were killed by Mauser bullets.

As would later be the case in Vietnam, the guerrillas had some clear advantages. They knew the terrain, were inured to the climate, and could generally count on a friendly population. As in Vietnam, villages controlled by the insurgents provided havens from which the guerrillas could attack, then fade back into hiding.

Americans soon began to feel that they were under siege in a land of enemies, and their fears were heightened because they never could be sure who among the population was hostile. A seemingly friendly peasant might actually be a murderer. Lieutenant Colonel J.T. Wickham, commanding the 26th Infantry Regiment, recorded that "a large flag of truce enticed officers into ambushes . . . Privates Dugan, Hayes, and Tracy were murdered by town authorities . . . Private Nolan [was] tied up by ladies while in a stupor; the insurgents cut his throat . . . The body of Corporal Doneley was dug up, burned, and mutilated . . . Private O'Hearn, captured by apparently friendly people was tied to a tree, burned over a slow fire, and slashed up . . . Lieutenant Max Wagner was assassinated by insurgents disguised in American uniforms."

As in later guerrilla movements, such terrorism became a standard tactic for the insurgents. Both Filipinos and Americans were their victims. In preying on their countrymen, the guerrillas had a dual purpose: to discourage any Filipinos disposed to cooperate with the

Americans, and to demonstrate to people in a particular region that they ruled that area and could destroy inhabitants and villages not supporting the revolution. The most favored terroristic weapon was assassination of local leaders, who were usually executed in a manner (such as beheading or burying alive) calculated to horrify everyone.

By the spring of 1900 the war was going badly for the Americans. Their task forces, sent out to search and destroy, found little and destroyed less.

The monsoon rains, jungle terrain, hostile native population, and a determined guerrilla force made the American soldiers' marches long and miserable. One described a five-week-long infantry operation: ". . . our troops had been on half rations for two weeks. Wallowing through hip-deep muck, lugging a ten-pound rifle and a belt . . . with 200 rounds of ammunition, drenched to the skin and with their feet becoming heavier with mud at every step, the infantry became discouraged. Some men simply cried, others slipped down in the mud and refused to rise. Threats and appeals by the officers were of no avail. Only a promise of food in the next town and the threat that if they remained behind they would be butchered by marauding bands of insurgents forced some to their feet to struggle on."

News reports of the army's difficulties began to erode the American public's support for the war. "To chase barefooted insurgents with water buffalo carts as a wagon train may be simply ridiculous," charged one correspondent, "but to load volunteers down with 200 rounds of ammunition and one day's rations, and to put on their heads felt hats used by no other army in the tropics . . . to trot these same soldiers in the boiling sun over a country without roads, is positively criminal. . . . There are over five thousand men in the general hospital."

Another reported that the American outlook "is blacker now than it has been since the beginning of the war . . . the whole population . . . sympathizes with the insurgents. The insurgents came to Pasig [a local area whose government cooperated with the Americans] and their

first act was to hang the 'Presidente' for treason in surrendering to Americans. 'Presidentes' do not surrender to us anymore.''

New Strategies

Early in the war U.S. military commanders had realized that, unlike the American Indians who had been herded onto reservations, eight million Filipinos (many of them hostile) would have to be governed in place. The Americans chose to emphasize pacification through good works rather than by harsh measures, hoping to convince Filipinos that the American colonial government had a sincere interest in their welfare and could be trusted.

As the army expanded its control across the islands, it reorganized local municipal governments and trained Filipinos to take over civil functions in the democratic political structure the Americans planned to establish. American soldiers performed police duties, distributed food, established and taught at schools, and built roads and telegraph lines.

As the war progressed, however, the U.S. commanders saw that the terrorism practiced by Aguinaldo's guerrillas was far more effective in controlling the populace than was their own benevolent approach. Although the Americans did not abandon pacification through good works, it was thereafter subordinated to the "civilize 'em with a Krag" (Krag-Jorgensen rifle) philosophy. From December 1900 onward, captured revolutionaries faced deportation, imprisonment, or execution.

The American army also changed its combat strategy to counter that of its enemy. As in the insurgents' army, the new tactics emphasized mobility and surprise. Breaking into small units—the battalion became the largest maneuver force—the Americans gradually spread over the islands until each of the larger towns was occupied by one or two rifle companies. From these bases American troops began platoon- and company-size operations to pressure local guerrilla bands.

Because of the difficult terrain, limited visibility, and requirement for mobility, artillery now saw limited use except as a defensive weapon. The infantry became the main offensive arm, with mounted riflemen used to pursue the fleeing enemy. Cavalry patrols were so valued for their mobility that American military leaders hired trusted Filipinos as mounted scouts and cavalrymen.

The Americans made other efforts to "Filipinize" the war—letting Asians fight Asians. (A similar tactic had been used in the American Indian campaigns twenty years before; it would resurface in Vietnam sixty years later as "Vietnamization.") In the Philippines the Americans recruited five thousand Macabebes, mercenaries from the central Luzon province of Pampanga, to form the American-officered Philippine Scouts. The Macabebes had for centuries fought in native battalions under the Spanish flag—even against their own countrymen when the revolution began in 1896.

Just as a later generation of American soldiers would react to the guerrilla war in Vietnam, American soldiers in the Philippines responded to insurgent terrorism in kind, matching cruelty with cruelty. Such actions vented their frustration at being unable to find and destroy the enemy. An increasing number of Americans viewed all Filipinos as enemies.

"We make everyone get into his house by 7 P.M. and we only tell a man once," Corporal Sam Gillis of the 1st California Volunteer Regiment wrote to his family. "If he refuses, we shoot him. We killed over 300 natives the first night. . . . If they fire a shot from a house, we burn the house and every house near it."

Another infantryman frankly admitted that "with an enemy like this to fight, it is not surprising that the boys should soon adopt 'no quarter' as a motto and fill the blacks full of lead before finding out whether they are friends or enemies."

That attitude should not have been too surprising. The army's campaigns against the Plains Indians were reference points for the generation of Americans that took the Philippines. Many of the senior officers and noncommissioned offi-cers—often veterans of the Indian wars—considered Filipinos to be "as full of treachery as our Arizona Apache." "The country won't be pacified," one soldier told a reporter, "until the niggers are killed off like the Indians." A popular soldiers' refrain, sung to the tune of "Tramp, tramp, tramp, the boys are marching," began, "Damn, damn, damn the Filipinos," and again spoke of "civilizing 'em with a Krag."

Reprisals against civilians by Americans as well as insurgents became common. General Lloyd Wheaton, leading a U.S. offensive southeast of Manila, found his men impaled on the bamboo prongs of booby traps and with throats slit while they slept. After two of his companies were ambushed, Wheaton ordered that every town and village within twelve miles be burned.

The Americans developed their own terrorist methods, many of which would be used in later Southeast Asian wars. One was torturing suspected guerrillas or insurgent sympathizers to force them to reveal locations of other guerrillas and their supplies. An often-utilized form of persuasion was the "water cure," placing a bamboo reed in the victim's mouth and pouring water (some used salt water or dirty water) down his throat, thus painfully distending the victim's stomach. The subject, allowed to void this, would, under threat of repetition, usually talk freely. Another method of torture, the "rope cure," consisted of wrapping a rope around the victim's neck and torso until it formed a sort of girdle. A stick (or Krag rifle), placed between the ropes and twisted, then effectively created a combination of smothering and garroting.

The anti-imperialist press reported such American brutality in lurid detail. As a result, a number of officers and soldiers were court-martialed for torturing and other cruelties. Their punishments, however, seemed remarkably lenient. Of ten officers tried for "looting, torture, and murder," three were acquitted; of the seven convicted, five were reprimanded, one was reprimanded and fined $300, and one lost thirty-five places in the army's seniority list and forfeited half his pay for nine months.

Officers and soldiers, fighting a cruel, determined, and dangerous enemy, could not understand public condemnation of the brutality they felt was necessary to win. They had not experienced such criticism during the Indian wars, where total extermination of the enemy was condoned by the press and the American public, and they failed to grasp the difference now. Press reports, loss of public support, and the soldiers' feeling of betrayal—features of an insurgent war—would resurface decades later during the Vietnam conflict.

Success

Although U.S. military leaders were frustrated by the guerrillas' determination on one hand and by eroding American support for the war on the other, most believed that the insurgents could be subdued. Especially optimistic was General Arthur MacArthur, who in 1900 assumed command of the seventy thousand American troops in the Philippines. MacArthur adopted a strategy like that successfully used by General Zachary Taylor in the Second Seminole War in 1835; he believed that success depended upon the Americans' ability to isolate the guerrillas from their support in the villages. Thus were born "strategic hamlets," "free-fire zones," and "search and destroy" missions, concepts the American army would revive decades later in Vietnam.

MacArthur strengthened the more than five hundred small strong points held by Americans throughout the Philippine Islands. Each post was garrisoned by at least one company of American infantrymen. The natives around each base were driven from their homes, which were then destroyed. Soldiers herded the displaced natives into *reconcentrado* camps, where they could be "protected" by the nearby garrisons. Crops, food stores, and houses outside the camps were destroyed to deny them to the guerrillas. Surrounding each camp was a "dead line," within which anyone appearing would be shot on sight.

Operating from these small garrisons, the Americans pressured the guerrillas, allowing them no rest. Kept off balance, short of supplies, and constantly pursued by the American army, the Filipino guerrillas, suffering from sickness, hunger, and dwindling popular support, began to lose their will to fight. Many insurgent leaders surrendered, signaling that the tide at last had turned in the Americans' favor.

In March 1901, a group of Macabebe Scouts, commanded by American Colonel Frederick "Fighting Fred" Funston, captured Aguinaldo. Aguinaldo's subsequent proclamation that he would fight no more, and his pledge of loyalty to the United States, sped the collapse of the insurrection.

As in the past, and as would happen again during the Vietnam conflict of the 1960s and '70s, American optimism was premature. Although a civilian commission headed by William H. Taft took control of the colonial government from the American army in July 1901, the army faced more bitter fighting in its "pacification" of the islands.

As the war sputtered, the insurgents' massacre of fifty-nine American soldiers at Balangiga on the island of Samar caused Brigadier General Jacob W. "Hell-Roaring Jake" Smith, veteran of the Wounded Knee massacre of the Sioux in 1890, to order his officers to turn Samar into a "howling wilderness." His orders to a battalion of three hundred Marines headed for Samar were precise: "I want no prisoners. I wish you to kill and burn, the more you kill and burn the better it will please me. I want all persons killed who are capable of bearing arms against the United States." Fortunately, the Marines did not take Smith's orders literally and, later, Smith would be court-martialed.

On July 4, 1902 the Philippine Insurrection officially ended. Although it took the American army another eleven years to crush the fierce Moros of the southern Philippines, the civil government's security force (the Philippine Constabulary), aided by the army's Philippine Scouts, maintained a fitful peace throughout the islands. The army's campaign to secure the Philippines as an American colony had succeeded.

American commanders would have experienced vastly greater difficulties except for two distinct advantages: 1) the enemy had to operate in a restricted area, in isolated islands, and was prevented by the U.S. Navy from importing weapons and other needed supplies; and 2) though the insurgents attempted to enlist help from Japan, no outside power intervened. These conditions would not prevail in some subsequent guerrilla conflicts in Asia.

In addition to the many tactical lessons the army learned from fighting a guerrilla war in a tropical climate, other problems experienced during this campaign validated the need for several military reforms that were subsequently carried out, including improved logistics, tropical medicine, and communications.

The combination of harsh and unrelenting military force against the guerrillas, complemented by the exercise of fair and equitable civil government and civic action toward those who cooperated, proved to be the Americans' most effective tactic for dealing with the insurgency. This probably was the most significant lesson to be learned from the Philippine Insurrection.

Lessons for the Future

Vietnam veterans reading this account might nod in recollection of a personal, perhaps painful experience from their own war.

Many similarities exist between America's three-year struggle with the Filipino *insurrectos* and the decade-long campaign against the Communists in Vietnam. Both wars, modestly begun, went far beyond what anyone had foreseen in time, money, equipment, manpower, casualties, and suffering.

Both wars featured small-unit infantry actions. Young infantrymen, if they had any initial enthusiasm, usually lost it once they saw the war's true nature; they nevertheless learned to endure their allotted time while adopting personal self-survival measures as months "in-country" lengthened and casualty lists grew.

Both wars were harsh, brutal, cruel. Both had their Samar Islands and their My Lais. Human nature being what it is, both conflicts also included acts of great heroism, kindness, compassion, and self-sacrifice.

Both wars saw an increasingly disenchanted American public withdrawing its support (and even disavowing its servicemen) as the campaigns dragged on, casualties mounted, and news accounts vividly described the horror of the battlefields.

Some useful lessons might be gleaned from a comparison of the two conflicts. Human nature really does not change—war will bring out the best and the worst in the tired, wet, hungry, and fearful men who are doing the fighting. Guerrilla campaigns—particularly where local military and civic reforms cannot be effected to separate the guerrilla from his base of popular support—will be long and difficult, and will demand tremendous commitments in resources and national will. Finally, before America commits its armed forces to similar ventures in the future, it would do well to recall the lessons learned from previous campaigns. For, as the Spanish-born American educator, poet, and philosopher George Santayana reminded us, those who do not learn from the past are doomed to repeat it.

Recommended additional reading: Benevolent Assimilation: The American Conquest of the Philippines, 1899-1902 *by Stuart C. Miller (Yale University Press, 1982);* In Our Image: America's Empire in the Philippines *by Stanley Karnow (Random House, 1989);* Little Brown Brother *by Leon Wolff (Doubleday & Co., Inc., 1961);* Muddy Glory *by Russell Roth (Christopher Publishing House, 1981); and* Soldiers in the Sun *by William T. Sexton (Books for Libraries Press, 1971).*

THE GOSPEL OF ANDREW CARNEGIE

Milton Goldin

The explosion of capitalism in late nineteenth-century America also spawned, via one of its key figures, a philanthropic ideal 'in which the surplus wealth of the few will become... the property of the many'.

FOR THIRTY-FIVE YEARS AFTER THE CIVIL War, the United States of America sustained the greatest period of economic growth of any country in history. Its wealth quadrupled. Fifth among the world's major powers in 1865, it was first by 1901. Its citizenry came to believe that nothing was impossible and that anything wrong could be made right, provided enough energy was applied to a problem.

One of the great symbols of American wealth and dynamism was a slight, Scottish immigrant with pale, penetrating eyes and a broad nose. Andrew Carnegie rose to fame and fortune in a way that made Horatio Alger look phlegmatic. After retiring from business activity, he donated some $350 million to philanthropic causes and shipped free Scotch whisky to the White House.

What largely accounted for both the surge in American wealth and Carnegie was a development still imperfectly understood today – the extent to which the North's victory affected the capitalist spirit. Nearly all writers on American history now agree that the conflict actually impeded economic growth, instead of stimulating industry as was thought by earlier scholars. But, after 1865, expansionist outlooks characteristic of the country's early history re-emerged, and wartime profiteers invested in railroads, built factories, and, with notable energy, manipulated stocks and bonds. So monumental was their sheer greed that they were called 'robber barons' with justification. By 1890, the United States census bureau estimated that 9 per cent of the nation's families owned 71 per cent of its wealth.

Not unnaturally, the rest of the population noticed significant changes in the distribution of wealth and also grasped that businessmen who wanted to control raw materials, markets, workers, and the legal system might also have greater power than ordinary citizens in local, state, and federal governments. Its assumptions were correct. By 1888, the Pennsylvania Railroad had gross receipts of $115 million and employed 100,000 men. In the same year, the entire State of Massachusetts had gross receipts of $7 million and employed 6,000 persons.

On the face of it, robber barons were so far ahead in the race for power as early as 1870 that the rest of the population feared it would never catch up. Revolution became a distinct possibility. The personal fortunes of the rich beggared anything seen before in America. When George Washington died in 1799, he left an estate of only $500,000 and was accounted one of the richest men of the time. Not until 1847 was the word 'millionaire' used in a New York newspaper to denote a person of unusual wealth, and before the Civil War there were only a handful of multi-millionaires.

Forum magazine estimated 120 men worth over $10 million in 1891, and the following year, the *New York Times* listed 4,047 millionaires. Robert Lincoln, the son of a president whose later life was dedicated to the preservation of the Union, became a corporation lawyer and a multi-millionaire. Apparently because his mother annoyed him, Robert had her committed to an insane asylum.

By the early 1870s, when the unbridled speculation of post-war America reached its first major crisis in a depression, the result was a near-breakdown of society. Hundreds of thousands of people were thrown

First published in *History Today*, June 1988, pp. 11-17. Reproduced by kind permission of History Today, Ltd., 83-84 Berwick Street, London W1V 3PJ, England.

out of work and off farms. State militias and federal troops mobilised to crush strikes and to put down expected insurrections. In New York, some 70,000 men left their jobs to strike for an eight-hour day at no decrease in pay, as provided for in an 1870 state law. Around them, writes one social historian, 'multitudes of the lowest grades of the city poor' begged for food on the streets, and shelters were overwhelmed by the homeless, who had to be lodged in police stations. Yet, among city fathers, the major question was, 'How can we get rid of the transients at the least cost and trouble to the community?'

This harsh attitude toward the poor reflected a Calvinist philosophy that had informed Americans since Colonial days. During that period, Americans did not interpret poverty as a personal or as a communal failing, mainly because the needy were neighbours. Churches took poor relief as their responsibility, stressed that the existing social order was right and reasonable, and bestowed special praise on generous givers for rising above the common herd with donations for families in need. Typically, colonists cared for dependents in their own homes, disrupting lives as little as possible. This was in sharp contrast to practices in the motherland, where the British had a bewildering array of almshouses, workhouses, and other institutions to house and to feed swarms of beggars.

The Colonial period was an age of emerging humanitarianism, and throughout the western world prosperous citizens led the middle classes in providing succour for the less fortunate. On the other hand, destitute strangers were not welcomed anywhere in North America because of the high costs of maintaining them. The purpose of poor-relief legislation was as much to keep non-residents out as it was to help neighbours. When the first Jews in North America arrived in New Amsterdam from Recife in 1654, Governor Peter Stuyvesant, whose intolerance of Quakers was already notorious, wanted the newcomers ousted at once. The refugees wrote to brethren in Amsterdam, who were directors of the Dutch West India Company, and pleaded to be allowed to stay. The

Company finally ordered Stuyvesant to permit them to remain – not because of humanitarian considerations, but because the Jews pledged that they would care for their own in cases of need.

Until the Civil War, philanthropic practices remained largely the same as during the Colonial period, with clerics taking major roles in raising and disbursing funds. What changed was the manner in which funds were raised. In addition to taxes and collections in churches, an Assistance Society in New York, organised in December 1808, raised relief funds via printed appeals and house-to-house solicitations. During the war, a great Metropolitan Fair was held in the city for the benefit of sick and wounded Union soldiers, which helped set an example for future fund-raising events.

No previous experience prepared anyone for the 1870s, however, thanks to the staggering dimensions of the economic disaster. The State of Massachusetts dumped 7,000 unwanted homeless on the State of New York. In both states, public welfare agencies were permeated not only by gross inefficiency but by the wholesale corruption that marked government at all levels in the post-Civil War years. The gentry, or more specifically the descendants of men and women who had invented America, abandoned hope for government's ability to deal with any problem, let alone charity.

Yet, impressed by post-war strides in industry made possible through technology, a group of militant reformers thought that philanthropy could become 'scientific'. They believed that charity could be rationalised and the poor saved from alcoholism, commonly thought to be the basic cause of impoverishment. Scientific philanthropy would eliminate crafty paupers who took advantage of soup kitchens and cast-off clothing provided by givers. Scientific philanthropy would make better men and women of givers and receivers alike and end poverty altogether. Finally, scientific philanthropy would cut mounting public expenditures for the poor.

But who would pay for philanthropy, scientific or otherwise? The people who had the most money were the robber barons, and so far as

reformers could see, robber barons were not so much threatening American standards of living as they were threatening American ways of life.

Inevitably, reformers had two questions to answer. Did robber barons care about the poor? And, if they did care, on what basis would they give?

With amusing regularity, interpretations of the robber barons' business tactics and generosity have changed from generation to generation, since the early years of the twentieth century. The muckrakers, notably Ida Tarbell and Lincoln Steffens, accounted them despoilers, thieves, and threats to the public welfare, whose donations were devices to assuage guilty consciences. A quarter of a century later, President Herbert Hoover acclaimed them industrial statesmen and magnificent benefactors. Then came the Depression of the 1930s and Hoover, himself, fell into disgrace for his economic policies, despite his reputation as a businessman, engineer, and humanitarian organising relief in Europe during and after the First World War. Writers such as Gustavus Myers (whose earlier *History of the Great American Fortunes* was updated) and Matthew Josephson again accounted robber barons despoilers and thieves, partly on the basis of Balzac's dictum that behind every great fortune there must lie a great crime.

Early in the 1950s, after the Rockefeller family had given away $2.5 billion since John D. Senior's earliest contributions, former despoilers and thieves received acclaim in the press as business pioneers and model givers. Then came the 1960s, when the doctrines of Social Darwinism and WASP superiority that the rich of the early 1900s espoused were in especially bad repute. The robber barons were hauled out to be demolished yet again in Ferdinand Lundberg's, *The Rich and the Super Rich.*

Today, in the midst of untrammeled economic growth, Andrew Carnegie, Jay Gould, John D. Rockefeller, Charles Schwab, J.P. Morgan, Leland Stanford, and Henry Frick – the *crême-de-la-crême* of robber barons – are again described as managerial geniuses and outstanding philanthropists, instrumental in moving mankind forward to its present and exalted status.

In many ways, the most puzzling of these men is Carnegie. The first robber baron to accumulate a fortune of nearly $450 million, he is also accounted the model philanthropist for being the first robber baron to give unprecedented amounts to universities, institutes, libraries, to churches for organs, to a foundation that provides pensions for professors, to a fund that honours 'heroes', and to innumerable individuals and smaller causes. Admiring contemporaries put his name on hundreds of buildings, avenues, and streets. John D. Rockefeller wrote, 'I would that more men of wealth were doing as you are doing with your money but be assured your example will bear fruit'.

Like so much else in his extraordinary career, the picture of a warm and generous tycoon, which Carnegie assiduously cultivated, is deceptive. All his life, he was a mass of contradictions.

During an eighty-four-year lifetime, he had time to play not only the role of self-made man and multimillionaire but of intellectual and spokesman for the new entrepreneurial classes. His energy, like his duplicity, was limitless. The same man who courageously assailed American imperialism in the Phillipines and sincerely worked for world peace, deceitfully sold overpriced and underdone armour plate to the American Navy. Carnegie boasted about his close personal relations with workers and said, 'The best workmen do not think about money'. To reinforce this claim, he constantly demanded that his subordinates reduce wages so that he could earn higher profits.

In 1892, Carnegie ordered Frick, his junior, to cut overheads at the huge Homestead steel plant, near Pittsburgh. He then left for a vacation in the Scottish Highlands. There followed a bloody strike at Homestead during which an anarchist shot Frick, and Irish immigrants fought gun battles with Pinkerton agents. Carnegie later said publicly that he knew nothing about the disorders until they were over but would have handled matters differently had he known. In private, he praised Frick for breaking the strike.

Ironically, Andrew Carnegie's father, William, by trade a linen weaver in Dunfermline, Scotland, was a local leader of the Chartists.

His mother, Margaret, was the daughter of a shoemaker and political and social reformer. After William Carnegie's business failed in 1848, the family, including thirteen-year-old Andrew, emigrated to Allegheny, Pennsylvania (later a suburb of Pittsburgh), where two of Mrs Carnegie's sisters were living.

William failed for a second time in a handloom business and, with his son, sought work in local cotton mills. Andrew began his labours as a bobbin boy working from 6 a.m. to 6 p.m., earning $1.20 a week. A short time later, his father quit – factory work turned out to be impossible for this small enterpriser – and Andrew got another job dipping newly-made spools in an oil vat. He was paid $3 a week for work in a foul-smelling basement. Thereafter, just a whiff of oil could make him deathly sick.

A game of chequers between his uncle and the manager of the local telegraph office set Carnegie on the road to wealth. The manager mentioned that he was looking for a messenger boy. Andrew got the job and diligently memorised the name of every street in Pittsburgh. He also arrived earlier each day at the telegraph office than any other worker, stayed later, learned the Morse code, and astounded fellow workers by the speed with which he took down words. Among those he impressed was Thomas A. Scott, superintendent of the Pennsylvania Railroad at Pittsburgh. Scott hired him as secretary, telegrapher, and general factotum for $35 a week, a hefty increase over the $800 a year he had been earning.

Carnegie continued to arrive earlier at the office and to leave later than other employees. It is to his hard work and telegraphic skills that biographers ascribe his early successes. But thousands of other young men in hundreds of other places also arrived earlier, stayed later, and learned Morse code but did not become multi-millionaires. The differences between them and Carnegie were that he had business acumen, a willingness to gamble, made salesmanship into an art form, and was a born courtier, adept at outrageous but irresistible flattery. Applying this talent to Scott, he became the superintendent's favourite. Scott passed on tips on investments, including one

to buy $500-worth of Adams Express stock. Carnegie, who probably did not have even $50, told his mother about the offer, and she mortgaged the family home to raise the money.

When the first dividend payment arrived, writes Carnegie in his autobiography, 'I shall remember that check as long as I live. It gave me the first penny of revenue from capital – something that I had not worked for with the sweat of my brow. "Eureka!" I cried, "Here's the goose that lays the golden eggs."' Thus was Andrew Carnegie introduced to capitalist enterprise.

Some time later, Carnegie was riding on a company train when approached by a rustic named T.T. Woodruff who asked whether he was an employee of the Pennsylvania Railroad. Receiving an answer in the affirmative, Woodruff opened a green bag and produced a model of the first sleeping car. An impressed Carnegie arranged for Woodruff to meet Scott. In appreciation, Woodruff offered the go-getter a one-eighth interest in his sleeping-car company, which Carnegie financed with a bank loan of $217.50. The investment was soon to be worth more than $5,000 a year to the young investor.

In 1859, Carnegie replaced Scott as superintendent, Scott having advanced to a vice-presidency. During the Civil War, much too busy with his career to bother with the armed forces, Carnegie bought himself out of the draft. He helped the North use railroads and the telegraph, however, to win a victory.

By 1873, Carnegie already had extensive interests in bridge building, telegraphy, and in sleeping cars, but it was to be during the depression that he would make the move into the steel industry which was to lift him out of the ranks of the rich into those of the super-rich. On a trip to England, he visited a mill in which the new Bessemer converter was being used to manufacture steel. Overnight, he grasped the implications of the process and became a booster of steel products.

Back in the United States, he displayed that sycophantic skill that was his hallmark. His first steel plant was named for J. Edgar Thomson, president of the Pennsylvania Railroad. The name was chosen not only to indicate that there existed no bad blood between the two men (Carnegie left the Railroad in 1865) but because Thomson was a buyer of steel rails and could also transport steel products to customers.

By 1899, a Carnegie Steel Company was making 695,000 tons more of steel every year than the total output of Great Britain. Carnegie had always refinanced internally, through surpluses of earnings, and consequently, he owed nothing to banks. The practice insulated him from the stock market but left no way to publicly evaluate the worth of his steel company. He rectified the problem by setting his own value on the factories – $157,950,000 – which was later artificially inflated to $250 million when John D. Rockefeller indicated interest in buying him out. The price led the oil magnate to drop out of the running.

Charles Schwab, a subordinate, broached the subject of a purchase with J.P. Morgan, who wanted to include Carnegie Steel in a super-trust of steel corporations he was organising. Morgan agreed to a price of $447 million, which was two-thirds more than Carnegie had thought it was worth only months before, and, on January 4th, 1901, the deal was consummated.

Carnegie received $303,450,000 in 5 per cent bonds and stock with a market value of about $144 million. Shrewd to the very end, he also held a mortgage on Morgan's new United States Steel Corporation – a detail that nearly put him back in possession of the whole overpriced monstrosity when it almost went bankrupt a few years later.

In 1868 at the age of thirty-three Carnegie was already earning $50,000 a year, but had given no major gifts to charity. In papers discovered by executors after his death, there was a memorandum that had been written in December of the year. 'By this time two years I can so arrange all my business as to secure at least $50,000 per annum', he wrote. 'Beyond this never earn – make no effort to increase fortune, but spend the surplus each year for benevolent purposes. Cast aside business forever, except for others'.

Carnegie did not cast aside business in two years, and his philanthropies began with modest gifts for

public baths in Dunfermline, during the late 1860s. What he concentrated on, before he had $447 million to give, was writing about the glories of American business and philanthropy in a series of books and articles. The most influential of these on the philanthropic practices of the American rich was 'Wealth', an article published in the June 1889 issue of the North American Review and republished shortly afterwards in Great Britain, in the Pall Mall Gazette, under the title, 'The Gospel of Wealth'. The American publication of the article was followed six months later in the North American Review by 'The Best Uses of Philanthropy' and in 1900 by a collection of his essays in book form, The Gospel of Wealth.

Carnegie's masterful salesmanship is immediately evident in these writings. A true Dr Pangloss, he does not even suggest the possibility that his may not be the best of all possible worlds. His basic assumptions in 'Wealth' are that the rich deserve their money and know what is best for society. What, then, is there left to discuss? In Carnegie's view, how the rich should spend their fortunes.

Considering the orgies, banquets on horseback, sixty-room mansions, and works of art with which his fellow robber barons happily indulged themselves, this would seem to have been a pressing issue only to Carnegie. But he shifts the argument from the present to the future and from idle frivolities to matters of moral substance. Because no one can take his fortune with him when he dies, Carnegie argues, the man of great wealth (and virtue) actually has only three ways to dispense his fortune: he can leave it to his family; he can bequeath it for public purposes; or he can spend it during his lifetime for public purposes and take an active pleasure in the good that he does.

In Carnegie's view, the first mode is undesirable because its consequences are to make a god of money ('The thoughtful man must shortly say, "I would as soon leave to my son a curse as the almighty dollar..."'), and the second mode will inevitably result in disappointed heirs contesting wills in courts. 'There remains, then, only one mode of using great fortunes', he concludes, 'and in this we have the true antidote for the temporary unequal distribution of

wealth, the reconciliation of the rich and the poor and a reign of harmony...'

The rich man, he believes, should spend his fortune during his lifetime in ways that will benefit mankind and influence society for the better, and:

under its sway we shall have an ideal State, in which the surplus wealth of the few will become, in the best sense, the property of the many, because administered for the common good, and this wealth passing through the hands of the few, can be made a much more potent force for the elevation of our race than if distributed in small sums to the people themselves.

His views did not go unchallenged. In London, the Reverend Hugh Price Hughes agreed that if tensions between haves and have-nots grew in intensity, social disaster threatened. In an article, 'Irresponsible Wealth', in the magazine Nineteenth Century, Hughes also wrote:

In a really Christian country – that is to say, in a community reconstructed upon a Christian basis – a millionaire would be an economic impossibility. Jesus Christ distinctly prohibited the accumulation of wealth.

In Massachusetts, the Reverend William Jewett Tucker, professor of religion at Andover Seminary and later president of Dartmouth College, acknowledged in the June 1891 issue of the Andover Review:

... the great benefit to society from the gifts of the rich, from those which have been received and from those which are likely to be received. But I believe that the charity which this gospel enjoins is too costly, if taken at the price which the author puts upon it; namely the acceptance of his doctrine of the relation of private wealth to society.

Tucker concluded:

The assumption...that wealth is the inevitable possession of the few, and is best administered by them for the many, begs the whole question of economic justice now before society... But charity, as I have claimed, cannot solve the problems of the modern world.

When Morgan bought him out, Carnegie was sixty-five years old, and generosity was still not his strong suit. Donations had hardly made a dent in his fortune – except for gifts to libraries in the United States and in Great Britain. He insisted that receiving libraries match his building donations by providing annual operating expenses and purchasing books. He also donated organs to churches, for which the applying church had to prove that it was not in debt.

Carnegie rejected contributions to medical causes, a field in which John D. Rockefeller was specialising, and social reform, for which he thought government should be the prime giver, to concentrate on education. His first great benefaction was for a Carnegie Institute in Pittsburgh. His second was to the Carnegie Trust for the Universities of Scotland, but many Scots were suspicious. *Blackwood's Edinburgh Magazine* flatly thought him nothing but an American money-making machine, adding, 'In old days, a rich man enjoyed his wealth – and if he did the community "no good", at least he did not insult it with patronage'.

As usual ignoring criticism, Carnegie gave the trust a $10 million endowment, half of which was to be used to finance the education of 'students of Scottish birth or extraction'. But this, too, inspired protest. British upper classes feared that lower orders would forget 'their proper station in life', if given free access to education.

When he returned to the United States from his annual trip to Scotland in 1901 – from this point on, the British would be just as happy to see him travel west each year as to welcome him back – Carnegie found a host of volunteers, including every college president in the country, ready to help him spend his money. At his new mansion in New York, he thought about creating a national university in Washington DC, an idea that went back to the country's founding fathers. The university took form, however, as the Carnegie Institution of Washington, an establishment without students but with departments of research in evolution, marine biology, history, economics, and sociology.

The Carnegie Institution, which established an outstanding reputation, required large contributions to

sustain operations but did not use up the bulk of Carnegie's fortune. One of his philanthropic tenets was to avoid 'indiscriminate charity' and Carnegie still faced the problem of where to make a really large gift. In 1905, he endowed a Carnegie Teachers Pension Fund Foundation with $10 million. From this seed grew the Carnegie Foundation for the Advancement of Teaching, which eventually received a national charter by Act of Congress and $125 million from Carnegie himself.

Carnegie demanded that educational institutions that applied to the Foundation, which was originally conceived to provide pensions for underpaid professors, meet certain standards. Among them, no school could have an endowment of less than $200,000, no school could receive a substantial portion of its operating funds from public sources, and no school could accept applicants with less than minimum preparation for college studies. Above all, he prohibited colleges under sectarian control from receiving grants.

By insisting on these criteria, and certainly with no plan beforehand to reform education in America, Carnegie did more to advance standards of higher education in the United States than any contemporary educator or government official. As usual, he was roundly attacked for his efforts, this time by heads of institutions who wished to be included but wanted denominational controls maintained. One such was Abram W. Harris, president of Northwestern University, who wrote that his institution was 'really non-sectarian in spirit', although a majority of its trustees were Methodists. Carnegie responded:

I [have seen] in my travels around the world what denominationalism really [means] – several sects each claiming to proclaim the truth and by inference condemning the others as imperfect.

Northwestern did not get a grant.

The $125 million he gave to the Foundation was by far the largest single amount that he would give to any of the organisations he founded, or to which he contributed. Thereafter, large-scale philanthropy ceased to be of prime interest to him. Carnegie had discovered that giving away

money gave him no special place in the hearts of recipients. For the public, there were two classes of men – those who were rich and had money to give and those who were poor and needed contributions from the rich. Those who wanted money were interested in immediate and direct benefits, not in the philosophy of the giver.

By 1910, Carnegie was increasingly involved in problems of world peace. Benefactions went to the Peace Palace at the Hague (1903) and to the Carnegie Endowment for International Peace (1910). It would come as a shock to him in 1914 that the world's great powers had as little interest in his exertions for peace as the public had had earlier in his philosophy of philanthropy.

On those who had money to give, however, Carnegie's philanthropy had a profound influence. His benefactions offered proof that no single private sector giver or group of givers, no matter how rich, could decide for a whole community the terms of its welfare programmes.

On the other hand, the philanthropic foundation, which Carnegie pioneered, became the standard gift-giving vehicle for the rich. After Carnegie, every self-respecting robber baron had to have at least one foundation. There were only five such entities at the end of the nineteenth century. Six more were created in the first decade of the century, twenty-two during the second decade, and forty-one in the third. Today, there are over 25,000 foundations in the United States.

The most dedicated students of Carnegie's philanthropy were John D. Rockefeller, his son, John, Jr., and his five grandsons. It would not only be the enormous wealth of this family that made it the core of the American Establishment, but a network of think-tanks, institutes and experts financed through Rockefeller grants. Andrew Carnegie could indirectly be thanked for these results.

FOR FURTHER READING:
E. Digby Baltzell, *The Protestant Establishment* (Vintage, 1966); Robert H. Bremner, *American Philanthropy* (University of Chicago, 1970); Carl Bridenbaugh, *Cities in Revolt* (Capricorn, 1964); Andrew Carnegie, *Autobiography of Andrew Carnegie* (Houghton Mifflin, 1948); John M. Dobson, *Politics in the Gilded Age* (Praeger, 1972); John A. Garraty, *Interpreting American History* (Macmillan, 1970).

CLEANING UP THE DANCE HALLS

Life in the fast lane – but was it the girl who paid the price? **Elisabeth Perry** looks at the campaign to clean up the dance palaces of America's cities at the turn of the century.

Elisabeth Perry *is Associate Professor of history at Vanderbilt University, Tennessee, and author of* Belle Moskowitz: Feminine Politics and the Exercise of Power in the Age of Alfred E. Smith *(Oxford University Press, 1987).*

In 1903, a sixteen-year-old girl named Frieda left a small Eastern European village to emigrate to America. An uncle, who lived in New York City with his three daughters, took her in. Frieda knew little of the language, nothing of American customs. Her cousins, who grew up in America but who had a busy life of their own, did not take the time to teach her. They were happy that she spent her days in the kitchen, looking after their needs. After a while Frieda discovered life outside the kitchen. Brightly lit halls and images of forms moving to the strains of upbeat music drew her in. There she discovered laughter, joy, and other young people much like herself. As girls were always in demand at such places, and she was pretty, she soon became a popular patron at this and other dance halls. But she also learned that to keep her popularity she had to drink 'stylish drinks', for dancing without drinking was 'slow'.

According to the social welfare workers of Frieda's day, the dance halls, then proliferating in American cities, were initiating many girls into a 'fast' life. Here's how one social worker, writing about the problem for a national magazine, described Frieda's dénouement:

> One night, when her head was whirling from excitement and dazed with drink, the man who had been playing with her for weeks... took her not home, but to a place where she offered on the altar of her 'good time' the sacred gift of her girlhood – all she had to lose. She never turned again from the path... She followed it through the mazes of wretched slavery to men and walked to its end five years later in a reformatory to which she had been committed and where her nameless baby was born. It was the price paid.

Several assumptions about sexual relations in the early 1900s lie behind the way this story was told. First, that men 'play' with girls, almost for sport. Second, when left to their own devices, lonely girls cannot resist the offer of a man's 'love', even though accepting it means losing their 'girlhood'. Third, that sex for young unmarried girls leads inevitably to some form of criminal activity or worse.

Whether these assumptions were based on reality need not concern us. The important thing is that early twentieth-century social workers believed they were. They also believed that modern urban society had weakened if not destroyed the traditional family and community controls that used to protect innocent girls. In their view, men should control their urges toward sexual conquest. But since most men did not, society had to control the venue – namely, the dance hall – which clearly increased a girl's vulnerability. Thus began the campaign to clean up America's dance halls, a campaign that aroused wide public support and lasted for over two decades.

Dance halls were run for profit. Their owners or managers gave patrons, most of whom were

First published in *History Today*, October 1989, pp. 22-26. Reproduced by kind permission of History Today, Ltd., 83-84 Berwick Street, London W1V 3PJ, England.

young and unattached, what they wanted – the fast, rhythmic music of Tin Pan Alley, no restrictions on dancing styles, and plenty of drinks, usually alcoholic, to quench the thirst and arouse the spirits. Dance halls also offered girls unprecedented freedom in finding amusement and making new acquaintances. Unescorted girls often got in for half-price or free. Worse, from the point of view of social workers, dance halls made no provision for social chaperonage. Complete strangers accosted girls and invited them to dance. Such easy affability was in part what excited youth most about the dance-hall environment, but it appalled social workers.

Dance-hall reform officially began in 1908. In that year, Belle Israels (later, Moskowitz), a social worker associated with the New York Council of Jewish Women, became concerned about rising numbers of Jewish girls in homes for unwed mothers and in reformatories. Interviews with the girls produced evidence that the dance halls were where the girls had first fallen into 'bad' company. Mrs Israels formed a Committee on Amusements and Vacation Resources of Working Girls to find out why. Its report disclosed that nine out of every ten girls considered dance halls their favourite resort, forty-nine out of seventy-three New York City dance halls sold alcohol, and twenty-two of these were attached to hotels known to be brothels.

Having established the popularity of dance halls among city youth, and associated them in the public mind with alcohol and sex, the report then went on to distinguish several types of halls. Most were 'inside' or saloon halls that merely cleared away space for dancing to piano music. 'Spielers' worked for the management, bringing customers in and dancing with wall-flowers. Frequenting such places night after night, the report surmised, girls assuaged their loneliness, felt popular, and dreamt of romance. Soon they found themselves accepting 'treats' (usually alcoholic drinks) from men, in return for which they sat with them in the dark alcoves and balconies that ringed the dance floors. There, of course, they 'paid the price'.

Another type of dance hall was the 'outside' hall or casino that offered unlimited beer and dancing during the day. At night, prices dropped and 'immoral persons' arrived to use adjacent parks for assignations. Yet a third type was the 'dancing academy'. Some had good reputations; others were fly-by-nights that kept little order, allowed close body contact in dancing styles, improper dress, and smoking, and encouraged gambling and prostitution in back rooms. The report lamented that girls, some only fourteen, paid high fees for lessons at these places, often learning more than they bargained for.

Belle Israels and her committee recognised that commercial dance halls provided essential recreation to urban youth. They knew that the halls could not be abolished. But they did believe the halls could and ought to be controlled. Their strategy was two-pronged: first, to regulate existing halls through a licensing act; then, using both private and public funds, to substitute 'decent' halls for the sleazy ones, and 'proper' dancing for the 'tough' or 'sensual' styles then popular. These complementary themes of regulation and substitution, which seemed so sensible and moderate, drew prominent adherents to the cause.

Over the next months, committee members lobbied city and state legislators for action. Success came in 1910, when the committee proposed a bill that prohibited the sale of alcohol on dance floors and in adjoining rooms, and made conformity to strict safety and sanitation codes compulsory in both dance halls and dance academies. Few critics objected to the codes, but many fought the alcohol ban. Brewers and saloon dance-hall owners pressured legislators to reject the bill. Immigrant groups, for whom a dance without wine or beer was unthinkable, joined in. For her part, Belle Israels insisted that she was not making a temperance argument, but that her experience with hundreds of girls who had learned the taste of alcohol from the dance hall or amusement park had made her realise its 'stupefying effect on the moral sensibilities'.

A compromise bill passed. It stipulated that saloons could not allow dancing unless they were licenced also as dance halls. Further, no alcohol could be sold in places that taught dancing and advertised as such. The bill passed, but left reformers dissatisfied. It delayed enforcement until 1911 and exempted all hotels

'The Danger Line'—this 1911 cartoon appeared in a Cleveland paper after a report on the dance halls by Mildred Chadsey of the Committee on Amusements.

A 1912 engraving of Belle Israels, the driving force behind dance hall reform.

with more than fifty bedrooms. There were other problems, such as an inadequate budget for dance-hall inspection. Members of the Committee on Amusements became volunteer inspectors themselves, a development neither they nor the city wanted.

While awaiting the result of the licensing legislation, Mrs Israels and her committee worked on the companion side of their strategy-substitution. They opened model dance halls designed to show businessmen that decent places could be run at a profit. Such halls planned to serve only non-alcoholic drinks and be free of other objectionable features of commercial resorts.

The committee opened its first model hall the following year. Hundreds of youngsters flocked to the place, advertised by a plain sign, 'General Dancing, Fifteen Cents'. Because of recent dance-hall shootings, a bouncer checked for weapons at the door. Soft drinks sold briskly for five cents. The dance floor was large, the ceiling high, the room well lit and ventilated. In a space reserved for beginners, a stout dancing master — a 'mixture of artist and pugilist', a reporter observed — called out the 'Lancers'. A young man resting his head on his partner's shoulder found himself expelled. College students dancing too wildly were told to stop. In the place of spielers, male relatives of the Committee on Amusements took care of wallflowers.

Over the next two years, the Committee on Amusements sponsored model dance halls in Manhattan, Brooklyn, and Newark. Newark's Palace Ballroom was its showplace. Located in a large rectangular building with an enclosure for a fourteen-piece orchestra and a balcony for spectators, the hall featured close supervision, especially in the balconies where an 'introducer' helped young people meet 'properly'. There was 'barn dancing' once a week, complete with two or three farmers forking hay; German dancing or waltz tournaments took place on other nights. But the hall's most dazzling feature was its streamers of rainbow-coloured lights hung from a central chandelier. Operated by a switchboard, the lights blinked on and off in time to the music, changing hues to suit moods. The hall was a splendid mixture of old-fashioned dancing decorum with the novelties of the electrical age.

In addition to regulating existing dance halls and creating model ones, the Committee on Amusements also addressed dancing styles. In the late 1890s, the waltz, polka, two-step, and 'set and figure' dances were standard. But by the turn of the century, ragtime and cakewalks had moved into northern cities. There they evolved into a variety of 'animal' dances named after turkeys, bunnies, monkeys, and bears. The Turkey Trot required couples to move in fast one-step circles occasionally flapping their arms. The Grizzly Bear, Bunny Hug, and Kangaroo Dip encouraged close body contact. Soon, enterprising songwriters such as Irving Berlin were putting suggestive words to the new tunes, telling dancers to 'hug up close to your baby', and 'everybody's doin' it'. Then South American dances such as the Argentine Tango appeared, its medley of dips, glides, and sways suggesting sexual conquest and submission.

Clergymen, dancing masters, and upper-class citizens denounced the new dances as ugly and indecent. But their attempts to keep them out of ballrooms were in vain. Even at society balls, couples slipped out into the corridors to learn the forbidden steps. By 1912, letters to editors dwelled incessantly on whether to 'trot' or not, and the 'nots' were losing.

The Committee on Amusements took a remedial approach. Belle Israels argued that repression without substitution would fail. Her substitution plan began with a conference on the 'real nature' of the new dances. Meeting in a fancy ballroom early in 1912, the conference attracted 600 observers. Israels introduced a dancing master who demonstrated how the new dances start out innocently, but then become passionate, gliding embraces. The audience gasped in horror. Next, entertainers Al Jolson and Florence Cable performed. Jolson told how he had learned to dance on San Francisco's infamous Barbary Coast. Drunken tars who could barely stand up would come alive when the orchestra 'ragged it up', hitting seductive minor keys. Jolson then grabbed his partner, snapped his fingers, and drew her daringly close. The audience gasped again, but when the dancers finished they broke out with thunderous applause.

Perhaps unhappy with such a positive response to 'offensive' dancing, the Committee on Amusements focused subsequent demonstrations only on the 'graceful' dances that illustrated the 'best standards'. These promised to be 'just as much of a romp' as the offensive dances, Mrs Israels declared. The committee also won the co-operation of a 'better class' of dance halls and ballrooms. In return for being on an approved list, their owners and managers posted signs forbidding 'immoral dancing' and inserted clauses in musicians' contracts against the playing of 'rags' and 'shivers'.

In time, the controversy over dancing styles died down. Professional dancers 'sanitised' the new dances, turning them into the elegant Castle Walk, Hesitation, or Maxixe. Popular magazines and newspapers published 'how-to' dance articles, complete with photographs and diagrams. The dances forced clothing styles to change to accommodate them, skirts becoming looser, or slit at the side to allow for dips. Even the infamous Turkey Trot won admirers as physicians assured young and old that its effects benefited the circulation. 'Honi soit qui mal y danse', quipped one writer in *Collier's* in 1913. Even Belle Israels admitted in 1914 that the tango was beautiful, if danced well.

Between 1910 and 1913, dance-hall reform spread across the country. By 1914, many cities, including Cleveland, Detroit, Chicago, Cincinnati, Kansas City, Minneapolis, Los Angeles, and Portland, had passed dance hall ordinances or planned to. The new ordinances shared certain features: licence fees, compliance with city codes, and controls or bans on alcohol. But on other issues of social chaperonage, such as ages of admission for minors, free admission for females, 'moonlight' dancing, and correct dancing positions, there was almost no agreement.

By the end of this first stage of American dance-hall reform, reformers had won the passage of a number of laws, but felt disappointed on other grounds. On the substitution side of reform, several cities set up supervised summer dance pavilions in parks or on docks, but in some cities clergy campaigned against such uses of public funds, and in Denver and Milwaukee, after the defeat of progressive governments, experiments at public dancing foundered. Worse, enforcement of the laws was never properly funded. As a result, many regulatory provisions remained dead letters.

Despite such setbacks, agitation for dance-hall reform continued throughout the 1910s, reviving vigorously after the First World War. In the 1920s, with the rise of the cheap automobile and the spread of the paved road system, urban dance halls began to crop up in mid-sized provincial cities as well as in the countryside (in this instance called roadhouses). When rural communities found themselves thus 'contaminated' with city ways, they pressed for county- and state-wide regulation.

In addition, new types of dancing resorts

Decorous but not dull? The reformers believed that offering properly-lit, ordered and policed dance pavilions would produce wholesome but enjoyable scenes.

began to appear in major northern cities. One type that reformers found particularly appalling was the 'closed dance hall', so called because it was closed to women customers but not women employees. This kind of dance hall arose out of a combination of circumstances. In the 1920s, many cities were experiencing an unprecedented influx of working-class immigrants, many of whom were single, male, and of new racial and ethnic types. When these men sought amusement in dance halls, either they were denied admission or native-born girls refused to dance with them. Capitalising on this situation, and on the lack of well-paid jobs for young, unskilled urban women, entrepreneurs hired such women to provide 'dance instruction' to the men in return for a commission — usually five cents on a ten-cent ticket. Halls that offered this kind of amusement became known as 'taxi-dance halls', since they allowed men who 'paid the fare', as in a taxi, to dance with a partner. Reformers opposed the existence of these halls because they seemed exploitative of women and to promote, if not prostitution, then at least some forms of sexual 'disorder'. Indeed, in the so-called 'tougher' halls, women

Irene and Vernon Castle, popularisers of sanitised versions of the new dances, who made ballroom dancing into an art form.

Maintaining standards; Joseph Guyon's vociferous campaign for his clean dance hall in Chicago almost bankrupted him but made him a hero for the moralists as these posters and press reports show.

engaged in what observers euphemistically called 'sensual' dancing. This was, in fact, the masturbation of their partners on the dance floor.

To deal with these developments, dance-hall reform revived, reaching a peak in mid-decade. The result was legislation that, by the end of the decade, covered 70 per cent of all American cities over 15,000 in population. Reformers were interested in more than just the extension of dance hall regulation, however. They wanted to use regulation to control the conditions in dance halls that permitted young people to flout standards of social decorum. Reformers argued that unrestrained and unsupervised dancing to jazz music was dangerous, especially to girls. Sexually aroused by the dancing, sometimes lubricated with 'hooch', innocent young women left the dance halls (often in men's automobiles) to go straight to seduction. Again, as in the case of the immigrant 'Friedas' of an earlier decade, there may have been some basis to such fears. But it is also clear that, in the 1920s, when the pace of change in sexual morality was accelerating, dance-hall reform became a way of resisting the prevailing trends of the day.

The story of Joseph Louis Guyon, former soap salesman turned Chicago dance-hall entrepreneur, illustrates how this resistance could be effective. Guyon had first invested in a dance hall in 1909. Then the modern dance craze hit Chicago. Tangos, Bunny-Hugs, and Turkey

Trots became the rage. Worried about the falling-off of their trade, the city's dancing masters got together and voted to 'go with the crowd'. But not Guyon. 'I am going to stick to the waltz and two-step', he declared. 'In my hall, I'll make everybody keep six inches from his partner'. His colleagues called him a fool. His partner left him and his hall began to fail. Even when jazz came to the Chicago dance floor in the form of 'walking the dog', 'ballin' the Jack', and finally the 'shimmy', Guyon held out.

In 1914 Guyon invested in poster and newspaper advertisements for a new Dreamland Ballroom where 'No Modern Dances Would be Allowed', and partners had to keep at least six inches between them. Young people who came to the ballroom to test him found themselves warned three times and then out on the street — Guyon, six feet tall and fifteen stone, acted as his own bouncer. The ballroom did not do well, and Guyon almost went bankrupt. Desperate, he mortgaged his household furniture, sinking the money into one final clean-dancing advertisement. At last (as he told the story at least) *women* responded. Juvenile protection associations, women's clubs, and other similar groups endorsed him, and gradually people in ever-increasing numbers started coming to his hall. A year later he had recouped his losses and was well on his way to making a small fortune. The continued support of reformers enabled him to carry on his campaign against jazz and improper dance-floor etiquette long into the next decade.

Much of Guyon's efforts in this campaign focused on the behaviour of girls. Every night, Guyon, his wife, and twenty staff members enforced the rules, including those against hugging, a man walking his partner backward, or any of the 'clutching, writhing postures of the new dances'. Most significantly, however, Guyon took direct action against any display of female sexuality:

> If a girl's skirts are too high, or her dress too low, we bundle her up and send her home to her mother in the automobile that always stands outside. If she is too highly rouged, we make her take it off – if she is too young – we allow no one in the ballroom under seventeen – we send a private letter to her mother, telling just why we cannot admit her daughter. I send hundreds of letters to mothers whose daughters I see keeping undesirable company, or developing dangerous mannerisms. I accept responsibility for much of the moral standard of those who dance on my floor. Parents and preachers are my strongest supporters.

The twenties were a time when young women were freeing themselves from many restraints. Yet many Americans resisted this trend, even in a large cosmopolitan community such as Chicago, but especially in mid-sized American communities where rules like Guyon's were standard fare. Perhaps only some parts of urban America were prepared to accept, or at best tolerate, the 'flapper'. The successful and widespread passage of dance hall regulation indicates broad popular support for the six-inch rule.

The story of dance-hall reform offers insights into the American response to changing sexual mores in the early part of the modern era. There were some repressive variations of the reform, but most reformers argued that repression would only drive youth to experiment with worse forms of amusement. They therefore pressed communities to adopt substitution programmes, and to provide young women, especially, with a wider range of recreational choices than they had before.

Many of reformers' concerns about maintaining 'standards' and protecting young women from seduction seem silly and naive to us now. But as a result of their efforts they established the principle that public amusements should be regulated in the interests of youth. They also convinced many municipalities and even some church-related groups that they ought to provide safe recreational facilities for youth where none exists, that is, facilities that do not cater to a lowest common denominator in standards of human behaviour. As we struggle today to provide our youth with drug- and alcohol-free environments, we realise that some of the concerns of the dance hall reformers of the 1910s and 1920s are still with us.

FOR FURTHER READING:
Elisabeth Israels Perry, *Belle Moskowitz: Feminine Politics and the Exercise of Power in the Age of Alfred E. Smith* (New York: Oxford University Press, 1987). Don S. Kirschner, 'The Perils of Pleasure: Commercial Recreation, Social Disorder and Moral Reform in the Progressive Era', *American Quarterly* 21/2 (1980); Lewis Erenberg, *Steppin' Out: New York Nightlife and the Transformation of American Culture, 1890-1930* (Greenwood Press, 1981); Kathy Peiss, *Cheap Amusements: Working Women and Leisure in Turn-of-the-Century New York* (Temple University Press, 1986). Russell B. Nye, 'Saturday Night at the Paradise Ballroom: or, Dance Halls in the Twenties', *Journal of Popular Culture* 7/1 (Summer 1973); Paul G. Cressey, *The Taxi-Dance Halls: A Sociological Study in Commercialized Recreation and City Life* (University of Chicago Press, 1932).

GEORGE WASHINGTON CARVER: CREATIVE SCIENTIST

In the early twentieth century, this prolific and charismatic scientist played a key role in spreading the benefits of scientific agriculture throughout the southern United States.

VIVIAN E. HILBURN

Vivian E. Hilburn is a guidance counselor and instructor of Spanish at Paul Quinn College in Waco, Texas. She has been the director of the Black Studies Club on campus for many years.

Few scientists—and particularly few specialists in botany or chemistry—have a monument erected in their memory, and still fewer can boast of having a foundation or museum carrying their name. All of these and numerous other honors have come to George Washington Carver, a man of humble birth who, until his death in the middle of this century, etched indelible marks on the history and lives of his people and his nation.

Carver, the son of a female slave in the home of Moses and Susan Carver, was born near Diamond Grove, Missouri, circa 1864. His childhood was tumultuous because of the unstable conditions of the times. Southwest Missouri, a frontier area, was bordered by the slaveholding, secession-oriented Arkansas, "Free Kansas," and the Oklahoma Indian Territory. Moses Carver, a slaveholding Unionist, was caught in the middle of the issues dividing the nation. Linda McMurry writes in *George Washington Carver: Scientist and Symbol,* "Throughout the war, area residents were prey to looting and killing by Confederate bushwackers, Union raiders, and ordinary outlaws taking advantage of the unsettled conditions." Moses Carver's homestead was raided by Confederate bushwackers several times, and on one of those raids, George and his mother were kidnapped and taken to Arkansas.

The Carvers were fond of Mary and her two sons —their only slaves—and wanted to find them. A neighbor, who was familiar with the guerrilla bands in the area, said he knew their whereabouts and agreed to hunt for them. His search uncovered George, who was returned to the Carvers, but Mary was never found. George and his brother Jim had always lived with their mother in a smaller cabin on the Carver property, but with the disappearance of Mary, the Carvers moved the boys into the main cabin with them and they lived as a family.

George was a frail and sickly child due to an earlier bout with whooping cough. He stuttered because of a speech impediment and had a falsetto voice about which he was often teased. The heavier chores on the farm were allotted to Jim, who was older, healthier, and stronger. George helped Susan around the house, and learned cooking, sewing, laundering, and needle work.

The young George was untiringly inquisitive and could often be seen in the woods, scraping earth, gathering bark from trees, and coddling weeds and flowers. He gathered cans and gourds in which he

From *The World & I*, July 1987, pp. 189-197. *The World & I*, a publication of The Washington Times Corporation, copyright © 1990.

grew sprouts. He became so adept at cultivating plants that neighbors called him the Plant Doctor. His desire "to know" and "to do" became a lifelong obsession. Until his death Carver enjoyed making things, and his rapport with nature was nurtured by early morning walks in the woods.

From a very early age Carver was recognized as having exceptional intelligence. His desire to learn, however, was thwarted for a while. Although the Missouri Constitution of 1865 made free schooling mandatory for black youngsters from age five, George could not attend school at that time because there were not enough blacks of a qualifying age in his township to warrant a school. There was, however, a school for blacks in the county seat of Neosho, and around age twelve, George left the Carvers to attend school there. In Neosho, only eight miles from Diamond Grove, George lived with his first set of black parents, Mariah and Andrew Watkins. Mariah was a midwife and she, like Susan, cultivated his homemaking skills. He also attended worship serv-

---

Carver turned down an offer of a permanent position at Iowa State to "be of the greatest good" to his fellow blacks.

---

ices with her at the African Methodist Episcopal Church, where religion became a central focus of his life.

Neosho had a large black population and there George felt a sense of belonging. By now, he had learned that he was black, and being so, he could not dream of fame, affluence, or lofty achievements. But his drive "to know" and "to do" spurred him on. What was rain?—the question constantly nagged him. What was creation, order and design? What gives soil different colors? These questions echoed through his mind and strengthened his determination to discover truth.

But his excitement about the schooling in Neosho was short-lived. Carver soon learned that the teacher knew little more than he did. Carver's disillusionment with the Neosho school and his desire for knowledge started him on a long trek through several towns in Kansas in search of an education. Eventually, he became an art major at Simpson College in Indianola, Iowa. His cooking and laundering skills provided a livelihood wherever he went.

At Simpson, despite his talent and interest in painting, his art teacher advised him to enroll in the state agricultural college at Ames, where her father was a horticulture professor. She was convinced that his botanical skills offered him more financial security than would a career as a black artist. Despite his desire to cease his wandering, he took her advice and enrolled at Ames.

He quickly overcame the initial reservation of the other students to him as the only black on campus, and he became an active and popular member of the student body. Carver graduated in 1894 with a bachelor of science degree from Iowa State College, and took a position at the Ames Experiment Station as an assistant to Louis Pammell, a noted botanist and mycologist. He also taught freshman biology while pursuing graduate work. By the time he earned a masters degree in 1896, his abilities in mycology and plant hybridization were already remarkable.

EMPLOYMENT AT TUSKEGEE

That same year he was asked by Booker T. Washington, then widely known as an educator, author, lecturer, and reformer, to head the newly established Department of Agriculture at Tuskegee Institute in Alabama. Washington advocated industrial and agricultural education as the key to black advancement. He understood the plight of the farmers, white and black. The one-crop system that had consisted principally of cotton production had drained them of energy and incentive. Most of these farmers were tenants and sharecroppers who eked out a bare existence by borrowing money for planting in the spring and paying it back after harvest in the fall.

Washington sought to free farmers from the burden of debt, and he found an ally in George Washington Carver. Carver turned down an offer of a permanent position at Iowa State to "be of the greatest good" to his fellow blacks. He arrived in Alabama wearing a too-tight gray suit, the top button of his jacket fastened, and a pert pink rose in his lapel. He presented a striking figure with a handlebar moustache, pointed nose, and deep, burning eyes. Thin stooped, he resembled a question mark. While waiting at the Chehaw railroad station for someone to take him to the campus, he immediately began plucking plants and surveying the red clay hills in the distance. "Red! Yellow! Oh! the handiwork of God!" he thought. He saw the undeveloped natural resources that could improve the lives of all Southerners.

As a trained researcher, the first item on Carver's agenda was setting up a proper laboratory. Although Tuskegee was the second best-endowed black school in the nation, it was still poor in comparison to similar white schools. With exceedingly limited funds, Washington sought to elevate an entire people. Thus Carver made his own equipment with retrievals from junk piles. His lamp served as a heater for his hands when they became stiff from the cold, as a Bunsen burner for his scientific experiments, and as a reflector for his microscope. For graders, he punched holes in pieces of tin. He used reeds as pipettes, cut broken bottles clean-edged with string, and pulverized his material using a cracked china bowl as a mortar. And since zinc sulphate was costly, he picked up discarded zinc tops from fruit jars.

It was a far cry from the equipment he had used

at Iowa State. One consolation was that soon after he arrived in Tuskegee, the Institute was granted $1,500 annually by the state legislature to establish and run an agricultural experiment station. It became the only all-black-manned station, and not coincidentally the lowest-funded one. Carver's station never received more than $1,500 a year, while a nearby white station got between $60,000 and $100,000 for its annual budget.

Over the years his desire for a better and more adequate laboratory and more time to do research, free from teaching responsibilities, became the main source of a growing rift between him and Booker T. Washington. He clashed with Washington largely because Carver was a gifted teacher and researcher, but not much of an administrator. His assistant, George Bridgeforth, eventually became the head of the Department of Agriculture and Carver was named the director of agricultural research. Although this move freed Carver from the administrative details he hated, it did not sit well with him to have anyone over him. These basic conflicts were never resolved and only ameliorated with Washington's death in 1915.

ROLE AS AN EDUCATOR

In Carver's laboratory, which he called "God's Little Workshop," the students learned the techniques of analyzing soils to determine which elements were lacking. They tested fertilizers and feeds to find out what ingredients increased tissue, fat, or milk. He taught the "trinity of relationship" between the soil, the plants growing on it, and the human beings or animals consuming the plants. He insisted that only by knowing the components of the soil could one determine the proper quantities of minerals needed to nourish each particular crop. He argued that a mastery of the economics of plant life can improve human existence. And above all, Carver preached the unity of the universe and the interrelatedness of all its parts.

Farming was unpopular at the Alabama school because blacks had been the major victims of farming's failures. Carver had to make the vocation attractive. He possessed two essential qualities of a good teacher—a thorough knowledge of his subject and an intuitive sense of how to transmit and instill it while he was able to convey his own motivating compulsion—"I don't know, but I'll find out"—he also knew "you can't teach people anything, you can only draw out what is in them." He was extraordinarily effective. Even when Washington was deeply exasperated with Carver, he admitted that the professor was "a great teacher, a great lecturer, a great inspirer of young men and old men."

Most of his students had only average intelligence, but he brought out the best points in each. He made each of them feel proud of his own ability and fostered a desire to extend it. He moved them to action with scoldings. "Get the drones off you! Remember, the more ignorant we are the less use God has for us." Carver was able to instill the "Tuskegee

Carver graduated in 1896 with a master's degree in botany from Iowa State College. Recruited by Booker T. Washington, he then accepted a position at the fledgling Tuskegee Institute. He arrived in Alabama wearing a flower in his lapel, which became an enduring symbol.

Ideal"—that the benefits of a student's education were to be shared with his community. Most of his students returned to their homes and spread the gospel of scientific agriculture.

He also promoted a philosophy of thrift and conservation. He thought that saving was not enough; there must be order also. To demonstrate this he showed his students a box of string, saved but snarled and entangled. "This is ignorance," he said. "And this"—he held up another box in which each piece was neatly tied or rolled into balls—"is intelligence."

In 1903 a boy's dormitory, Rockefeller Hall, was erected on the Tuskegee campus and Carver moved into two ground-floor rooms which he was to occupy for 35 years. Initially controversy arose over this special treatment. Many of the other teachers felt it unfair that he be given more space than they and that he was arrogant to expect such treatment. Carver prevailed though, and weathered quite a bit of resentment over a bachelor's occupying so much space on a crowded campus. At the same time, the students loved having him near, and for many of them he played the role of teacher, father, and spiritual adviser.

DEMONSTRATION AS TEACHING

Carver had come South to help farmers, and the Experiment Station at Tuskegee was the nucleus of this effort. Tuskegee had long engaged in extension activities such as an annual Farmers' Conference. Carver improved and expanded such efforts. He added farmers' institutes, an annual colored fair, and easy-to-read agricultural bulletins.

Throughout the years, he did not limit his scientific demonstrations to the classroom. Believing that demonstration is the purest form of teaching, Carver went into the community to give hands-on illustrations of his theories. He would not rely on publications to relay the results of experiments because many farmers could not read. Since there were no home and farm demonstration agents, he developed the "Jesup Wagon"—a wagon equipped with demonstration materials—to communicate his ideas. Money for the project was donated by Morris K. Jesup. The Jesup Wagon, "a farmers' college on wheels," started its career in May 1906. It was operated by Thomas M. Campbell, a former student of Carver's. In November of that year, the U.S. Department of Agriculture (USDA) employed Campbell as the first "Negro Demonstration Agent." He took the wagon to surrounding communities for regularly scheduled demonstrations of plowing and planting, usually at a house where neighbors had gathered. He returned later at the appropriate time to give instructions on cultivation and harvesting.

Tuskegee was a leader in the development of movable schools. In the United States, Iowa State College was the first to experiment with a "Seed Corn Gospel Train." But the success of Tuskegee's later version was the prime reason for the idea's success. It has since helped to shape educational policies with respect to disadvantaged groups and underdeveloped countries throughout the world. Similar projects were adopted in China, India, Macedonia, and Southern Rhodesia. In regions where road systems could not accommodate motor vehicles, donkeys were used to transport educational materials as "a gift of knowledge" to farmers.

Encouraged by Washington, Carver also published numerous agricultural bulletins. By 1908 he had published fourteen bulletins and devoted many hours to his column, "Professor Carver's Advice." Here he warned farmers of impending dangers such as hog cholera, and he cautioned stockmen against poisonous weeds that their livestock might eat. One bulletin, *Some Cercosporae of Macon County, Alabama,* reflected Carver's favorite field of research, which was largely denied to him by his circumstances. He did not have the equipment or time needed for the proper identification of the many species of fungus. Nevertheless, he continued to collect fungi, and he was the first to identify several species, one of which was named *Taphrina carveri.* In 1935 the USDA made him a "collaborator," and his specimens are still preserved in the USDA herbarium in Beltsville, Maryland.

RESEARCH IN CROPS AND NATURAL RESOURCES

In 1904 the boll weevil invaded American cotton fields. By 1910 it was a full-grown menace. Spraying each plant with calcium arsenate would be financial-

ly prohibitive. Only by planting, cultivating, and harvesting early might the damage be minimized. Carver advised farmers to obtain cotton of the greatest vitality—the fastest-growing and the earliest ripening. He developed his own hybrid and distributed its seeds at the Farmers' Conference. At the same time, he urged farmers to plant less cotton and to replace this cash crop with sweet potatoes, cowpeas, and peanuts.

Cowpeas, or black-eyed peas as they were commonly called, had proved to be "the poor man's bank" as a soil health builder and excellent livestock food. At that time few people in the United States had heard of the soybean, another leguminous nitrogen fixer. Only much later did the USDA experiment with imported soybeans and adapt them to American soils and climatic conditions. Carver had successfully experimented with them, and they eventually became a major crop in the region.

But Carver's most important studies revolved

He made the results of his and others' research available and understandable to thousands whose lives were thereby enriched.

---

around the peanut. Farmers already knew about the peanut. Indigenous to South America, it had been relished by conquistadors who carried it to Spain. It found its way to Africa in the seventeenth century, and came back again to the New World with slave traders as their chief bill-of-fare for their human cargo. The African word *goober* for peanut is today an active part of the Southern vocabulary. The peanut is leguminous, and easy to plant, grow, and harvest.

The peanut is equal to sirloin beef in protein content and to potatoes in carbohydrates. Before 1913, Carver published recipes for cooking peanuts in one of his bulletins. By 1916, this bulletin was in its sixth edition, carrying directions for growing peanuts and 105 ways to prepare and eat them. Carver taught a class of senior girls who were studying dietetics the varied usages of the peanut. They served a tasty five-course lunch to Booker T. Washington and nine guests—soup, mock-chicken, vegetable, salad, bread, candy, cookies, ice cream, and coffee—all made from peanuts!

The peanut, soybean and sweet potato had not only helped enrich the soil, but they had provided bumper crops. Yet the market place was still not profitable for farmers due to the lack of viable products from these commodities. Carver's research turned to developing new uses for them in three distinct stages: finding, adapting, and creating. First he used the raw materials nature had provided. Second he rearranged these materials—wood, stones, ores, fibers, skins, metals—targeting their potential industrial

A MAN OF FAITH

I came to know George Washington Carver during the time we were together at Tuskegee Institute, where I was a student and he an instructor. At least three times a day, over a period of eight years, I observed the posture and mood of his daily life. Since both of us were housed on the east end of campus, he at Rockefeller Hall and I at Thrasher Hall, this gave me a splendid opportunity to see him as he went to and from his quarters. We also ate in the same main dining hall—he with the members of the faculty and I with the other students.

Often on long evenings, he would leave the dining room and walk toward the agriculture building. Sometimes, he took a similiar route in the early morning, but frequently in the morning hours he could be found examining the roots, plants, shrubbery, and soil around campus. The area of campus where the science building, the Hollis Burke Frissell Library and Logan Hall now stand was then an open field and Dr. Carver spent a lot of time there also. During these excursions, he communed with God and nature.

I believe his intellectual resources profited from his spiritual life. He was able to accomplish so much because he prayed so much. The more difficult the task he confronted, the more time he spent preparing through prayer and meditation. Even though he kept a busy schedule, he took time for reflection and always took stock of his spiritual condition. He labored to be right with God and he often expressed that he did not want to come to the edge of the grave before manifesting a concern about eternity. He advised that every young person should find a little time to be alone with God each day.

Many mornings I would hear a low-sounding voice under my window, only to look out and observe Dr. Carver examining a lump of dirt or a root or a growth of some kind, asking God to reveal its secrets. He knew the truth of William Cullen Bryant's words: "To him who in the love of Nature holds Communion with her visible forms, she speaks a various language."

TUSKEGEE UNIVERSITY ARCHIVES

Carver knew the truth of William Cullen Bryant's words: "To him who in the love of Nature holds Communion with her visible forms, she speaks a various language."

He was not only a great scientist, but a great man of faith. Every Sunday, many students and faculty at Tuskegee Institute attended chapel services at 11:00 A.M. Later Dr. Carver would lead a Bible class of about 200 students. He told the same stories I had heard so many times before, but he made the characters in the Bible come alive. Once, while he was discussing a Bible figure, he characterized him in relation to the people with whom he associated. He pointed out his virtues and vices as he walked from one side of the room to the other. Suddenly, he astounded the entire assembly by saying that the character under consideration suffered from hemorrhoids. This is only one example of his uncanny insights into the human character.

The themes of his Bible classes, as well as chance conversations with him on campus, were pure and uplifting. He was guileless and gentle. For a while, because of his modest and peaceful nature, I had a feeling that he didn't know how to be stern, but that opinion was changed upon several occasions when I heard him strongly scold a student for misbehaving.

His life has had a quiet influence on my own. He was so dedicated to his area of expertise that he had a great deal to do with the deepening and confirming of my own dedication to lifelong goals.

—*Rev. Andrew Fowler*
Capitol View Baptist
Washington, D.C.

use. Third he transformed these materials into new ones for the benefit of people and society.

He knew that a large portion of any farm crop was inedible and was therefore wasted. Carver abhorred waste. His solution was simple and direct: Find uses for a product's waste and thus enlarge its usefulness. He had a vision of farms as not merely food factories but as sources of raw materials for industry. In the meantime, he sought to produce cheap substitutes for the expensive goods whose purchase helped to keep sharecroppers in debt.

From soybeans he had made flour, starch, meal, stains, dyes, ink, breakfast food, oil, milk, and wood fillers. But he knew that soybeans could not be promoted for industrial purposes because of Southern unfamiliarity with them. Instead, Carver concentrated on the peanut. From his research on peanuts emerged such products as beverages, pickles, sauces, meal, coffee, salve, bleach, wood filler, washing powder, metal polish, paper, ink, plastics, shaving cream, rubbing oil, linoleum, shampoo, axle grease, and synthetic rubber.

Carver's interest in the dormant mineral wealth of Alabama became more pressing. In the clay hills near Tuskegee, he discovered marble, limestone, malleable copper, azurite, iron, manganese, sugar quartz, bentonite (a de-inker for newspapers), and heat-resisting and nonconducting micas for the electrical industry. He also discovered and developed various fertilizers and dyes. He was most enthusiastic about the use of native dyes for paints. In one bulletin he told farmers how to make and use such paints for their homes, fences, and barns. Later, he got two patents on processes for paint production and an unsuccessful company was formed to market them.

With World War I the danger of a food shortage came to the United States. Because Carver had always believed that a weed was merely a plant out of place, he began teaching the virtues of eating wild vegetables, both fresh and dehydrated. In January 1918, Carver was summoned to Washington to demonstrate products made from the sweet potato and to exhibit how it could be used to make bread. He demonstrated before Army bakers, chemists, dieticians, technicians, and transportation authorities. This last group was invited because of Carver's work on a method of food dehydration that not only preserved foods indefinitely, but greatly decreased their weight and bulk.

In a press conference at this meeting he said, "I do not like the word *substitute* applied to my products. I prefer to let each stand on its own merits." He defined *synthetic* as a "fourth kingdom of nature," in man's control and in which incompatible elements could unite. He predicted "a new world coming—The Synthetic World."

AWARDS AND LEGACY

George Washington Carver died on January 5, 1943, and was buried on the Tuskegee campus next to Booker T. Washington. His outstanding service to humanity had been recognized in the many awards given to him during his lifetime and has been preserved in his legacy.

International recognition was given Carver as a botanist and chemurgist. He was elected a fellow of the Royal Society of Arts of Great Britain in 1918 and awarded the Spingarn Medal in 1923. Carver received an honorary Doctor of Science degree from Simpson College in 1928 and was appointed collaborator for the USDA Mycology and Plant Disease Survey Bureau of Plant Industry. The George Washington Carver Museum was established on the Tuskegee campus in 1935.

Carver was awarded the Franklin Delano Roosevelt Medal in 1939, and received an honorary doctorate from the University of Rochester in 1941. Carver also received many medals, scrolls, citations, and honorary degrees for his achievements in creative and scientific research and for his contributions to the improvement of health and living conditions of the Southern farmer. The United States honored him with a three-cent postage stamp in 1948, and Congress authorized the establishment of the George Washington Carver National Monument near the site of his birth in 1953.

Carver's fame was also enhanced by his adoption as a symbol by a myriad of causes.

CARVER AS SYMBOL

Few scientists have become as well known and widely acclaimed as Carver, which raises intriguing questions. He made no great theoretical breakthroughs and did not develop a single new commercially successful product. Many scientists, both white and black, have accomplished more through their research. Why then did Carver become so famous? The answers are found in the nature of his personality and the symbolic value of his work and life story.

Carver was both a complex and compelling person with many interests and activities. His prize-winning art, his mastery of the piano and several other musical instruments, and his creativity in such crafts as knitting and weaving bespeak his versatility. Some of his paintings were exhibited at the World's Fair in Chicago in 1893. One of them, *Three Peaches*, done with his fingers and with pigments he developed from the clays of Alabama, was requested by the Luxembourg Gallery.

Considered by many to be an introvert and mystic, Carver was little understood during his lifetime. He was often described by those who knew him as modest, unassuming, yet profound. At the same time, he courted and relished publicity. Deeply religious, he attributed his success in developing new products to divine guidance. He found little pleasure in material goods and frequently refused to accept payment for his services to peanut processors and others. He never asked for an increase in his starting salary of $1,200 during his four decades at Tuskegee Institute. Some of his monthly salary checks were still in his desk drawer when the banks crashed during the Depression. He had just not bothered to deposit them. However, since he rarely spent anything on himself—he continued to wear a suit given to him by his Iowa teachers and fellow students until his death—he did accumulate a sizeable savings.

In 1940, when Carver realized that he would not be able to continue his work much longer, he contributed these savings, more than $60,000 in all, to the establishment of the George Washington Carver Research

Foundation, "dedicated to the progress of humanity through the application of science to the problems of agriculture and industry." During his remaining three years, Carver continued to work in the foundation with the aid of his young assistant, Austin W. Curtis.

During the next thirty years the foundation grew from a one-man operation on a meager budget to its current status as a multifaceted research organization with over 100 faculty and staff investigators and an annual operational budget in excess of $5 million. These projects include pure research, training and demonstration, and outreach projects, all proper extensions of such a creative life.

His appeal was and is based on more than his idiosyncrasies or physical legacies, however. After hearing Carver speak, one person wrote, "You are the most seductive person I have ever met." His was not a surface charisma—he had a talent for making people feel special. Most acquaintances became intimate friends, and dozens of people, black and white, believed themselves to be Carver's "closest friend." The force of his personality captivated many, including journalists who wrote scores of articles about him.

Carver's fame was also enhanced by his adoption as a symbol by a myriad of causes. The romance of his rise from slavery to success was used to motivate youth to work hard and to prove the fairness of the economic system. Race relations improvement groups, such as the Commission on Interracial Cooperation, publicized his achievements and sponsored talks by him at white colleges to demonstrate the capabilities of blacks. Ironically, at the same time supporters of segregation used his story and unassuming manner to deny the crippling effects of legalized separation. Because of his publicly proclaimed reliance on divine inspiration, a number of religious groups made him a patron saint in the battle against secularism and materialism. Also, the United Peanut Association and "New South" advocates of crop diversification and industrialism saw obvious value in publicizing his work.

In the end, Carver became famous for inventing hundreds of products and saving the South from cotton dependency. This assessment both exaggerates and distorts the nature of his work. His original goal was not to produce commercially feasible commodities, but to provide impoverished sharecroppers with a way out by the use of available resources to improve their circumstances. What he advocated would later be called "appropriate technology." A lot of what he taught was not original, but he was without equal as a popularizer of scientific agriculture. He made the results of both his and others' research available and understandable to thousands whose lives were thereby enriched.

From Progressivism to the 1920s

Most reform movements in American history have occurred during periods of economic depression. What came to be known as "progressivism" arose in a time of relative prosperity, and many of its leaders were themselves well-off. Yet there was discontent over the directions in which American society seemed to be moving. Inspired by "muckrakers," who exposed corruption in high and low places, corporate misdeeds, and the blight of urban poverty, men and women joined in a crusade to correct the system's ills. Although a few wished to establish some type of socialism, most did not. They merely wanted to reform the system so that it would function more equitably and efficiently.

America's entry into World War I for all practical purposes ended the Progressive Era. The nation's energies were devoted to winning the war, and dissent was often equated with disloyalty. Intolerance flourished during the conflict, directed especially toward anyone suspected of harboring sympathy for Germany. This atmosphere of suspicion and hatred for all things "foreign" continued after the armistice, except that now "bolshevism" (communism) became the target. American failure to join the League of Nations led to a retreat into political isolationism, although mushrooming trade and investment abroad inevitably influenced the affairs of other nations.

The 1920s witnessed a curious blend of political conformity and sociocultural change. Neither Warren G. Harding nor Calvin Coolidge were activist presidents, and Congress was not disposed to take the lead. Herbert Hoover might have provided more energetic leadership, but his presidency was undermined by the onset of economic depression soon after he took office. At the same time, there were great innovations in the arts and in literature, and young men and women everywhere were challenging existing social and sexual customs. The darker side was an increase in crime and in repression of minority racial and ethnic groups.

Theodore Roosevelt personified progressivism to some, to others he was a latecomer who merely adapted to political currents. "Theodore Roosevelt, President" is an affectionate portrait of this dynamic individual who seemed to attract attention to whatever he did. The Progressive Era witnessed no great change in attitudes toward Orientals, whose immigration to the United States had been slowed to a trickle by restrictive legislation. "Angel Island" describes the indignities endured by Chinese who tried to gain entry into the "Promised Land." "Rose Schneiderman and the Triangle Fire" is the story of a determined woman's fight to change the dreadful—and often dangerous—conditions under which many people worked. Most films of the period were made to entertain audiences, according to "The Unknown Hollywood," but "many of the issues that dominated Progressive-era politics were also portrayed on the screen."

For the first time in its history, the United States sent an army to fight in Europe during World War I. The British and French wanted to absorb American units into the existing command structure, but General John J. "Black Jack" Pershing insisted that they occupy their own sector of the front. "The Saint-Mihiel Salient" tells of this dispute and how the first American offensive operation affected the outcome of the war.

In 1913 the Ford Motor Company made almost as many cars as all the other auto builders combined. Ford's Model T was tough, reliable, and above all, inexpensive. Henry Ford's unwillingness to improve or abandon this workhorse helped cause the company's decline during the 1920s. David Halberstam's "Citizen Ford" traces the career of this brilliant but willfull and eccentric man. F. Scott Fitzgerald dubbed the 1920s "The Jazz Age." Jazz was the creation of black musicians, but whites such as Paul Whiteman "sanitized" it and made it popular with larger audiences. "Jazz: Red Hot & Cool" describes the emergence of this distinctive art form and its pioneers.

Looking Ahead: Challenge Questions

Discuss the major issues of the Progressive Era. What type of legislation did Theodore Roosevelt sponsor, and what did he hope to achieve? What does the article on the Triangle Shirtwaist fire tell us about labor conditions during that period?

"Henry Ford's strengths," writes David Halberstam, "eventually became his weaknesses." How and why did this early innovator later lose touch with public tastes?

Theodore Roosevelt, President

Edmund Morris

If Theodore Roosevelt seems to push his way into our pages with extraordinary frequency, it is because the force and variety of this "giant," "over-engined" man appear to be endless. The following study of TR's personality— which so well illustrates this point—was written by Edmund Morris, who won the Pulitzer Prize for The Rise of Theodore Roosevelt *in 1980. This essay was delivered as a speech, in somewhat longer form, at a symposium on presidential personality at the National Portrait Gallery in Washington.*

Let us dispose, in short order, with Theodore Roosevelt's faults. He was an incorrigible preacher of platitudes; or to use Elting E. Morison's delicious phrase, he had "a recognition, too frequently and precisely stated, of the less recondite facts of life." He significantly reduced the wildlife population of some three continents. He piled his dessert plate with so many peaches that the cream spilled over the sides. And he used to make rude faces out of the presidential carriage at small boys in the streets of Washington.

Now those last two faults are forgivable if we accept British diplomat Cecil Spring-Rice's advice, "You must always remember the President is about six." The first fault—his preachiness—is excused by the fact that the American electorate dearly loves a moralist. As to the second and most significant fault—Theodore Roosevelt's genuine blood-lust and desire to destroy his adversaries, whether they be rhinoceroses or members of the United States Senate—it is paradoxically so much a part of his virtues, both as a man and a politician, that I will come back to it in more detail later.

One of the minor irritations I have to contend with as a biographer is that whenever I go to the library to look for books about Roosevelt, Theodore, they infallibly are mixed up with books about Roosevelt, Franklin—and I guess FDR scholars have the same problem in reverse. Time was when the single word "Roosevelt" meant only Theodore; FDR himself frequently had to insist, in the early thirties, that he was not TR's son. He was merely a fifth cousin, and what was even more distant, a Democrat to boot. In time, of course, Franklin succeeded in preempting the early meaning of the word "Roosevelt," to the point that TR's public image, which once loomed as large as Washington's and Lincoln's, began to fade like a Cheshire cat from popular memory. By the time of FDR's own death in 1945, little was left but the ghost of a toothy grin.

Only a few veterans of the earlier Roosevelt era survived to testify that if Franklin was the greater politician, it was only by a hairsbreadth, and as far as sheer personality was concerned, Theodore's superiority could be measured in spades. They pointed out that FDR himself declared, late in life, that his "cousin Ted" was the greatest man he ever knew.

Presently the veterans too died. But that ghostly grin continued to float in the national consciousness, as if to indicate that is owner was meditating a reappearance. I first became aware of the power behind the grin in Washington, in February of 1976. The National Theater was trying out an ill-fated musical by Alan Lerner and Leonard Bernstein, *1600 Pennsylvania Avenue.* For two and a half hours Ken Howard worked his way through a chronological series of impersonations of historic Presidents. The audience sat on its hands, stiff with boredom, until the very end, when Mr. Howard clamped on a pair of pince-nez and a false mustache, and bared all his teeth in a grin. The entire theater burst into delighted applause.

What intrigued me was the fact that few people there could have known much about TR beyond the obvious cliches of San Juan Hill and the Big Stick. Yet somehow, subconsciously, they realized that here for once was a positive President, warm and tough and authoritative and funny, who believed in America and who, to quote Owen Wister, "grasped his optimism tight lest it escape him."

In the last year or so Theodore Roosevelt has made his long-promised comeback. He has been the subject of a *Newsweek* cover story on American heroes; Russell Baker has called him a cinch to carry all fifty states if he were running for the White House today; he's starring on Broadway in *Tintypes,* on television in *Bully,* and you'll soon see him on the big screen in *Ragtime.* Every season brings a new crop of reassessments in the university presses, and as for the pulp mills, he figures largely in the latest installment of John Jakes's Kent Chronicles. No time like the present, therefore, to study that giant personality in color and fine detail.

When referring to Theodore Roosevelt I do not use the word "giant" loosely. "Every inch of him," said William Allen White, "was over-engined." Lyman Gage likened him, mentally and physically, to two strong men combined; Gifford Pinchot said that his normal appetite was enough for four people, Charles J. Bonaparte estimated that his mind moved ten times faster than average, and TR himself, not wanting to get into double figures, modestly remarked, "I have enjoyed as much of life as any nine men I know." John Morley made a famous comparison in 1904 between Theodore Roosevelt and the Niagara Falls, "both great wonders of nature." John Burroughs wrote that TR's mere proximity made him nervous. "There was always something imminent about him, like an avalanche that the sound of your voice might loosen." Ida Tarbell, sitting next to him at a musicale, had a sudden hallucination that the President was about to burst. "I felt his clothes might not contain him, he was so steamed up, so ready to go, to attack anything, anywhere."

Reading all these remarks it comes as a surprise to discover that TR's chest measured a normal forty-two inches, and that he stood only five feet nine in his size seven shoes. Yet unquestionably his initial impact was physical, and it was overwhelming. I have amused myself over the years with collecting the metaphors that contemporaries used to describe this Rooseveltian "presence." Here's a random selection. Edith Wharton thought him radioactive; Archie Butt and others used phrases to do with electricity, high-voltage wires, generators, and dynamos; Lawrence Abbott compared him to an electromagnetic nimbus; John Burroughs to "a kind of electric bombshell, if there can be such a thing"; James E. Watson was reminded of TNT; and Senator Joseph Foraker, in an excess of imagination, called TR "a steam-engine in trousers." There are countless other steam-engine metaphors, from Henry Adams' "swift and awful Chicago express" to Henry James's "verily, a wonderful little machine: destined to be overstrained, perhaps, but not as yet, truly, be-

traying the least creak." Lastly we have Owen Wister comparing TR to a solar conflagration that cast no shadow, only radiance.

These metaphors sound fulsome, but they refer only to TR's physical effect, which was felt with equal power by friends and enemies. People actually tingled in his company; there was something sensually stimulating about it. They came out of the presidential office flushed, short-breathed, energized, as if they had been treated to a sniff of white powder. He had, as Oscar Straus once said, "the quality of vitalizing things." His youthfulness (he was not yet forty-three at the beginning of his first term, and barely fifty at the end of his second), his air of glossy good health, his powerful handshake—all these things combined to give an impression of irresistible force and personal impetus.

But TR was not just a physical phenomenon. In many ways the quality of his personality was more remarkable than its quantity. Here again, I have discovered recurrences of the same words in contemporary descriptions. One of the more frequent images is that of sweetness. "He was as sweet a man," wrote Henry Watterson, "as ever scuttled a ship or cut a throat." But most comments are kinder than that. "There is a sweetness about him that is very compelling," sighed Woodrow Wilson. "You can't resist the man." Robert Livingstone, a journalist, wrote after TR's death: "He had the double gifts of a sweet nature that came out in every hand-touch and tone . . . and a sincerely powerful personality that left the uneffaceable impression that whatever he said was right. Such a combination was simply irresistable." Livingstone's final verdict was that Theodore Roosevelt had "unquestionably the greatest gift of personal magnetism ever possessed by an American."

That may or may not be true, but certainly there are very few recorded examples of anybody, even TR's bitterest political critics, being able to resist him in person. Brand Whitlock, Mark Twain, John Jay Chapman, William Jennings Bryan, and Henry James were all seduced by his charm, if only temporarily. Peevish little Henry Adams spent much of the period from 1901 to 1909 penning a series of magnificent insults to the President's reputation. But this did not prevent him from accepting frequent invitations to dine at the White House and basking gloomily in TR's effulgence. By the time the Roosevelt era came to an end, Adams was inconsolable. "My last vision of fun and gaiety will vanish when my Theodore goes . . . never can we replace him."

It's a pity that the two men never had a public slanging match over the table, because when it came to personal invective, TR could give as good as he got. There was the rather slow British ambassador whom he accused of having "a mind that functions at six guinea-pig power." There was the State Supreme Court Justice he called "an amiable old fuzzy-wuzzy with sweetbread brains." There was that "unspeakable villainous little monkey," President Castro of Venezuela, and President Marroquin of Colombia, whom he described in one word as a "Pithecanthropoid." Woodrow Wilson was "a Byzantine logothete" (even Wilson had to go to the dictionary for that one); John Wanamaker was "an ill-constituted creature, oily, with bristles sticking up through the oil," and poor Senator Warren Pfeffer never quite recovered from being called "a pin-headed anarchistic crank, of hirsute and slabsided aspect." TR did not use bad language—the nearest to it I've found is his description of Charles Evans Hughes as "a psalm-singing son of a bitch," but then Charles Evans Hughes tended to invite such descriptions. Moreover, TR usually took the sting out of his insults by collapsing into laughter as he uttered them. Booth Tarkington detected "an undertone of Homeric chuckling" even when Roosevelt seemed to be seriously castigating someone—"as if, after all, he loved the fun of hating, rather than the hating itself."

Humor, indeed, was always TR's saving grace. A reporter who spent a week with him in the White House calculated that he laughed, on average, a hundred times a day—and what was more, laughed heartily. "He laughs like an irresponsible schoolboy on a lark, his face flushing ruddy, his eyes nearly closed, his utterance choked with merriment, his speech abandoned for a weird falsetto. . . . The President is a joker, and (what many jokers are not) a humorist as well."

If there were nothing more to Theodore Roosevelt's personality than physical exuberance, humor, and charm, he would indeed have been what he sometimes is misperceived to be: a simple-minded, amiable bully. Actually he was an exceedingly complex man, a polygon (to use Brander Matthews' word) of so many political, intellectual, and social facets that the closer one gets to him, the less one is able to see him in the round. Consider merely this random list of attributes and achievements:

He graduated *magna cum laude* from Harvard University. He was the author of a four-volume history of the winning of the West which was considered definitive in his lifetime, and a history of the naval war of 1812 which remains definitive to this day. He also wrote biographies of Thomas Hart Benton, Gouverneur Morris, and Oliver Cromwell, and some fourteen other volumes of history, natural history, literary criticism, autobiography, political philosophy, and military memoirs, not to mention countless articles and approximately seventy-five thousand letters. He spent nearly three years of his life in Europe and the Levant, and had a wide circle of intellectual correspondents on both sides of the Atlantic. He habitually read one to three books a day, on subjects ranging from architecture to zoology, averaging two or three pages a minute and effortlessly memorizing the paragraphs that interested him. He could recite poetry by the hour in English, German, and French. He married two women and fathered six children. He was a boxing champion-

ship finalist, a Fifth Avenue socialite, a New York State Assemblyman, a Dakota cowboy, a deputy sheriff, a president of the Little Missouri Stockmen's Association, United States Civil Service Commissioner, Police Commissioner of New York City, Assistant Secretary of the Navy, Colonel of the Rough Riders, Governor of New York, Vice-President, and finally President of the United States. He was a founding member of the National Institute of Arts and Letters and a fellow of the American Historical Society. He was accepted by Washington's scientific community as a skilled ornithologist, paleontologist, and taxidermist (during the White House years, specimens that confused experts at the Smithsonian were occasionally sent to TR for identification), and he was recognized as the world authority on the big-game mammals of North America.

Now all these achievements *predate* his assumption of the Presidency—in other words, he packed them into his first forty-three years. I will spare you another list of the things he packed into his last ten, after leaving the White House in 1909, except to say that the total of books rose to thirty-eight, the total of letters to 150,000, and the catalogue of careers expanded to include world statesman, big-game collector for the Smithsonian, magazine columnist, and South American explorer.

If it were possible to take a cross section of TR's personality, as geologists, say, ponder a chunk of continent, you would be presented with a picture of seismic richness and confusion. The most order I have been able to make of it is to isolate four major character seams. They might be traced back to childhood. Each seam stood out bright and clear in youth and early middle age, but they began to merge about the time he was forty. Indeed the white heat of the Presidency soon fused them all into solid metal. But so long as they were distinct they may be identified as aggression, righteousness, pride, and militarism. Before suggesting how they affected his performance as President, I'd like to explain how they originated.

The most fundamental characteristic of Theodore Roosevelt was his aggression—conquest being, to him, synonymous with growth. From the moment he first dragged breath into his asthmatic lungs, the sickly little boy fought for a larger share of the world. He could never get enough air; disease had to be destroyed; he had to fight his way through big, heavy books to gain a man's knowledge. Just as the struggle for wind made him stretch his chest, so did the difficulty of relating to abnormally contrasting parents extend his imagination. Theodore Senior was the epitome of hard, thrusting Northern manhood; Mittie Roosevelt was the quintessence of soft, yielding Southern femininity. The Civil War—the first political phenomenon little Teedie was ever aware of—symbolically opposed one to the other. There was no question as to which side, and which parent, the child preferred. He naughtily prayed God, in Mittie's presence, to "grind the Southern troops to powder," and the victory of Union arms reinforced his belief in the superiority of Strength over Weakness, Right over Wrong, Realism over Romance.

Teedie's youthful "ofserv-a-tions" in natural history gave him further proof of the laws of natural selection, long before he fully understood Darwin and Herbert Spencer. For weeks he watched in fascination while a tiny shrew successively devoured a mass of beetles, then a mouse twice her size, then a snake so large it whipped her from side to side of the cage as she was gnawing through its neck. From then on the rule of tooth and claw, aided by superior intelligence, was a persistent theme in Theodore Roosevelt's writings.

Blood sports, which he took up as a result of his shooting for specimens, enabled him to feel the "strong eager pleasure" of the shrew in vanquishing ever larger foes; his exuberant dancing and whooping after killing a particularly dangerous animal struck more than one observer as macabre. From among his own kind, at college, he selected the fairest and most unobtainable mate—"See that girl? I'm going to marry her. She won't have me, but I am going to have *her!*"—and he ferociously hunted her down. That was Alice Lee Roosevelt, mother of the late Alice Longworth.

During his first years in politics, in the New York State Assembly, he won power through constant attack. The death of Alice Lee, coming as it did just after the birth of his first child—at the moment of fruition of his manhood—only intensified his will to fight. He hurried West, to where the battle for life was fiercest. The West did not welcome him; it had to be won, like everything else he lusted for. Win it he did, by dint of the greatest physical and mental stretchings-out he had yet made. In doing so he built up the magnificent body that became such an inspiration to the American people (one frail little boy who vowed to follow the President's example was the future world heavyweight champion, Gene Tunney). And by living on equal terms with the likes of Hashknife Simpson, Bat Masterson, Modesty Carter, Bronco Charlie Miller, and Hell-Roaring Bill Jones, he added another mental frontier to those he already had inherited at birth. Theodore Roosevelt, Eastern son of a Northern father and a Southern mother, could now call himself a Westerner also.

TR's second governing impulse was his personal righteousness. As one reviewer of his books remarked, "He seems to have been born with his mind made up." No violent shocks disturbed his tranquil, prosperous childhood in New York City. Privately educated, he suffered none of the traumas of school. Thanks to the security of his home, the strong leadership of his father, and the adoration of his brother and sisters, Teedie entered adolescence with no sexual or psychological doubts whatsoever. Or if he had any, he simply reasoned them out, according to the Judeo-Christian principles Theodore Senior had taught him, reached the proper moral decision, and that was that. "Thank heaven!" he wrote in his diary after falling in love with Alice Lee, "I am perfectly pure."

His three great bereavements (the death of his father in 1878, and the deaths of his mother and wife in the same house and on the same day in 1884) came too late in his development to do him any permanent emotional damage. They only served to convince him more that he must be strong, honest, clean-living, and industrious. "At least I can live," he wrote, "so as not to dishonor the memory of the dead whom I so loved," and never was a cliche more heartfelt. Experiment after experiment proved the correctness of his instincts—in graduating *magna cum laude* from Harvard, in marrying successfully, in defying the doctors who ordered him to live a sedentary life, in winning international acclaim as writer and politician long before he was thirty. (He received his first nomination for the Presidency, by the Baltimore *American,* when he was only twenty-eight; it had to be pointed out to the newspaper's editors that he was constitutionally debarred from that honor for the next seven years.)

In wild Dakota Territory, he proceeded to knock down insolent cowboys, establish the foundations of federal government, pursue boat thieves in the name of the law, and preach the gospel of responsible citizenship. One of the first things he did after Benjamin Harrison appointed him Civil Service Commissioner was call for the prosecution of Postmaster General William Wallace of Indianapolis—who just happened to be the President's best friend. "That young man," Harrison growled, "wants to put the whole world right between sunrise and sunset."

TR's egotistic moralizing as a reform Police Commissioner of New York City was so insufferable that the *Herald* published a transcript of one of his speeches with the personal pronoun emphasized in heavy type. The effect, in a column of gray newsprint, was of buckshot at close range. This did not stop TR from using the personal pronoun thirteen times in the first four sentences of his account of the Spanish-American War. In fact, a story went around that halfway through the typesetting, Scribner's had to send for an extra supply of capital I's.

The third characteristic of Theodore Roosevelt's personality was his sense of pride, both as an aristocrat and as an American. From birth, servants and tradespeople deferred to him. Men and women of high quality came to visit his parents and treated him as one of their number. He accepted his status without question, as he did the charitable responsibilities it entailed. At a very early age he was required to accompany his father on Sunday excursions to a lodging house for Irish newsboys and a night school for little Italians. It cannot have escaped his attention that certain immigrant groups lacked the intellectual and social graces of others. Extended tours of Europe and the Levant as a child, teen-ager, and young man soon taught him that this was not due to ethnic inferiority so much as to centuries of economic and political deprivation. Prosperous, independent countries like England and Germany were relatively free of slums and disease; but in Italy women and children scrabbled like chickens for scraps of his cake, and in Ireland people lay down in the road from sheer hunger. From what he read, things were no better in the Slavic countries.

Only in America, with its limitless economic opportunities and freedom from political bondage, might these peasants begin to improve their stock. And only in America could they revitalize their racial characteristics. His own extremely mixed ancestry proved that a generation or two of life in the New World was enough to blend all kinds of European blood into a new, dynamic American breed. (As President, he had a habit when shaking hands with ethnic groups of saying, "Congratulations, I'm German too!" and "Dee-lighted! I'm also Scotch-Irish, you know!" Newspapermen privately referred to him as "Old Fifty-seven Varieties.")

TR knew the value of an ethnic vote as well as the next man. There is a famous—alas, probably apocryphal—story of his appointment of Oscar Straus as the first Jewish Cabinet officer in American history. At a banquet to celebrate the appointment, TR made a passionate speech full of phrases like "regardless of race, color, or creed" and then turned to Jacob Schiff, the New York Jewish leader, and said, "Isn't that so, Mr. Schiff?" But Schiff, who was very deaf and had heard little of the speech, replied, "Dot's right, Mr. President, you came to me and said, 'Chake, who is der best Choo I can put in de Cabinet?'"

TR realized, of course, that the gap between himself and Joe Murray—the Irish ward-heeler who got him into the New York Assembly—was unbridgeable outside of politics. But in America a low-born man had the opportunity—the *duty*—to fight his way up from the gutter, as Joe had done. He might then merit an invitation to lunch at Sagamore Hill, or at least tea, assuming he wore a clean shirt and observed decent proprieties.

Here I must emphasize that TR was not a snob in the trivial sense. He had nothing but contempt for the Newport set and the more languid members of the Four Hundred. When he said, at twenty-one, that he wanted to be a member of "the governing class," he was aware that it was socially beneath his own. At Albany, and in the Bad Lands, and as Colonel of the Rough Riders, he preferred to work with men who were coarse but efficient, rather than those who were polished and weak. He believed, he said, in "the aristocracy of worth," and cherished the revolution that had allowed such an elite to rise to the top in government. On the other hand (to use his favorite phrase) the historian John Blum has noted that he rarely appointed impoverished or unlettered men to responsible positions. He made great political capital, as President, of the fact that his sons attended the village school at Oyster Bay, along with the sons of his servants, of whom at least one was black; but as soon as the boys reached puberty he whisked them off to Groton.

Only the very young or very old dared call him "Teddy" to his face. Roosevelt was a patrician to the tips of his tapering fingers, yet he maintained till death what one correspondent called an "almost unnatural" identity with the masses. "I don't see how you understand the common people so well, Theodore," complained Henry Cabot Lodge. "No, Cabot, you never will," said TR, grinning triumphantly, "because I am one of them, and you are not." TR deluded himself. His plebian strength was due to understanding, not empathy.

The fourth and final major trait of Theodore Roosevelt's character was his militarism. I will not deal with it in much detail because it is a familiar aspect of him, and in any case did not manifest itself much during his Presidency. There is no doubt that in youth, and again in old age, he was in love with war; but oddly enough, of all our great Presidents, he remains the only one not primarily associated with war (indeed, he won the Nobel Peace Prize in 1906).

He did not lack for military influences as a child; four of his Georgian ancestors had been military men, and stories of their exploits were told him by his mother. Two of his uncles served with distinction in the Confederate navy—a fact of which he proudly boasts in his *Autobiography,* while making no reference to his father's civilian status. (The *Autobiography,* by the way, is one of history's great examples of literary amnesia. You would not guess, from its pages, that Theodore Senior ever hired a substitute soldier, that Alice Lee ever lived or died, that TR was blind in one eye as President, that anything called the Brownsville Affair ever occurred, or that Elihu Root ever sat at his Cabinet table. As James Bryce once said, "Roosevelt wouldn't always *look* at a thing, you know.")

When TR learned to read, he reveled in stories "about the soldiers of Valley Forge, and Morgan's riflemen," and confessed, "I had a great desire to be like them." In his senior year at Harvard, he suddenly developed an interest in strategy and tactics and began to write *The Naval War of 1812;* within eighteen months he was the world expert on that subject. As soon as he left college he joined the National Guard and quickly became a captain, which stood him in good stead when he was called upon to lead a cavalry regiment in 1898. Throughout his literary years he made a study of classical and modern campaigns, and he would wage the great battles of history with knives and forks and spoons on his tablecloth. No doubt much of this fascination with things military related to his natural aggression, but there was an intellectual attraction too: he read abstract tomes on armaments, navigation, ballistics, strategy, and service administration as greedily as swashbuckling memoirs. Nothing is more remarkable about *The Naval War of 1812* than its cold impartiality, its use of figures and diagrams to destroy patriotic myths. Roosevelt understood that great battles are fought by thinking men, that mental courage is superior to physical bravado. Nobody thrilled more to the tramp of marching boots than he, but he believed that men must march for honorable reasons, in obedience to the written orders of a democratically elected Commander in Chief. In that respect, at least, the pen was mightier than the sword.

Now how much did these four character traits—aggression, righteousness, pride, and militarism—affect TR's performance as President of the United States? The answer is, strongly, as befits a strong character and a strong Chief Executive. The way he arrived at this "personal equation" is interesting, because he was actually in a weak position at the beginning of his first administration.

When TR took the oath of office on September 14, 1901, he was the youngest man ever to do so—a Vice President, elevated by assassination, confronted by a nervous Cabinet and a hostile Senate. Yet from the moment he raised his hand in that little parlor in Buffalo, it was apparent that he intended to translate his personal power into presidential power. The hand did not stop at the shoulder; he raised it high above his head, and held it there, "steady as if carved out of marble." His right foot pawed the floor. *Aggression.* He repeated the words of the oath confidently, adding an extra phrase, not called for in the Constitution, at the end: "And so I swear." *Righteousness.* His two senior Cabinet officers, John Hay and Lyman Gage, were not present at the ceremony, but TR announced that they had telegraphed promises of loyalty to him. Actually they had not; they were both considering resignation, but TR knew any such resignations would be construed as votes of no confidence in him, and he was determined to forestall them. By announcing that Hay and Gage would stay, out of loyalty to the memory of the dead President, he made it morally impossible for them to quit. *Pride.*

As for *militarism,* TR was seen much in the company of the New York State Adjutant General the next few days, and an armed escort of cavalrymen accompanied him wherever he went. This was perhaps understandable, in view of the fact that a President had just been assassinated, but it is a matter of record that more and more uniforms were seen glittering around TR as the months and years went on. Toward the end of his second administration, *Harper's Weekly* complained that "there has been witnessed under President Roosevelt an exclusiveness, a rigor of etiquette, and a display of swords and gold braid such as none of his predecessors ever dreamed of."

As the theatrical gestures at TR's Inauguration make plain, he was one of the most flagrant showmen ever to tread the Washington boards. He had a genius for dramatic entrances—and always was sure the spotlight was trained his way before he made one. The first thing he asked at Buffalo was, "Where are all the newspapermen?" Only three reporters were present. His secretary explained that there was no room for more. Ignoring him, TR sent out for the rest of the press corps.

Two dozen scribes came joyfully crowding in, and the subsequent proceedings were reported to the nation with a wealth of detail.

Here again we see a pattern of presidential performance developing. The exaggerated concern for the rights of reporters, the carefully staged gestures (so easy to write up, such fun to read about!)—it was as if he sensed right away that a tame press, and an infatuated public, were his surest guarantees of political security. To win election in his own right in 1904—his overriding ambition for the next three years—he would have to awake these two sleeping giants and enlist their aid in moral warfare against his political opponents, notably Senator Mark Hanna. (Hanna was chairman of the Republican National Committee and the obvious choice to take over McKinley's government after "that damned cowboy," as he called TR, had filled in as interim caretaker.)

The new President accordingly took his case straight to the press and the public. Both instantly fell in love with him. Neither seemed to notice that administratively and legislatively he accomplished virtually nothing in his first year in office. As David S. Barry of the *Sun* wrote, "Roosevelt's personality was so fascinating, so appealing to the popular fancy, so overpowering, so alive, and altogether so unique that . . . it overshadowed his public acts; that is, the public was more interested in him, and the way he did things . . . than they were about what he did."

This does not mean that TR managed, or even tried, to please all the people all the time. He was quite ready to antagonize a large minority in order to win the approval of a small majority. The sods had hardly stopped rattling on the top of McKinley's coffin when the following press release was issued: "Mr. Booker T. Washington of Tuskegee, Alabama, dined with the President last evening." Now this release, arguably the shortest and most explosive ever put out by the White House, has always been assumed to be a reluctant confirmation of the discovery of a reporter combing TR's guest book. Actually the President himself issued it, at two o'clock in the morning—that is, just in time for maximum exposure in the first edition of the newspapers. By breakfast time white supremacists all over the South were gagging over their grits at such headlines as ROOSEVELT DINES A NIGGER, and PRESIDENT PROPOSES TO CODDLE THE SONS OF HAM. This was the first time that a President had ever entertained a black man in the first house of the land. The public outcry was deafening—horror in the South, acclamation in the North—but overnight 9,000,000 Negroes, hitherto loyal to Senator Hanna, trooped into the Rooseveltian camp. TR never felt the need to dine a black man again.

Although we may have no doubt he had the redistribution of Southern patronage in mind when he sent his invitation to Washington, another motive was simply to stamp a bright, clear, first impression of himself upon the public imagination. "I," he seemed to be saying,

This famous photograph of Roosevelt—his eyes crinkled shut with laughter and grinning his toothy grin—was taken at Oyster Bay during the 1912 campaign.

BROWN BROTHERS

"am a man *aggressive* enough to challenge a hundred-year prejudice, *righteous* enough to do so for moral reasons, and *proud* enough to advertise the fact."

Again and again during the next seven years, he reinforced these perceptions of his personality. He aggressively prosecuted J.P. Morgan, Edward H. Harriman, and John D. Rockefeller (the holy trinity of American capitalism) in the Northern Securities anti-trust case, threw the Monroe Doctrine at Kaiser Wilhelm's feet like a token of war in the Caribbean, rooted out corruption in his own administration, and crushed Hanna's 1904 presidential challenge by publicly humiliating the Senator when he was running for re-election in 1903. He righteously took the side of the American worker and the American consumer against big business in the great anthracite strike, proclaimed the vanity of muckrake journalists, forced higher ethical standards upon the food and drug industry, ordered the

dishonorable discharge of 160 Negro soldiers after the Brownsville Affair (on his own willful reading of the evidence, or lack thereof), and to quote Mark Twain, "dug so many tunnels under the Constitution that the transportation facilities enjoyed by that document are rivalled only by the City of New York."

For example, when the anthracite strike began to drag into the freezing fall of 1902, TR's obvious sympathy for the miners, and for millions of Americans who could not afford the rise in fuel prices, began to worry conservative members of Congress. One day Representative James E. Watson was horrified to hear that the President had decided to send federal troops in to reopen the anthracite mines on grounds of general hardship. Watson rushed round to the White House. "What about the Constitution of the United States?" he pleaded. "What about seizing private property for public purposes without the due processes of law?"

TR wheeled around, shook Watson by the shoulder, and roared, *"To hell with the Constitution when the people want coal!"* Remarks like that caused old Joe Cannon to sigh, "Roosevelt's got no more respect for the Constitution than a tomcat has for a marriage license."

Pride, both in himself and his office, was particularly noticeable in TR's second term, the so-called imperial years, when Henry James complained, "Theodore Rex is distinctly tending—or trying to make a court." But this accusation was not true. Although the Roosevelts entertained much more elaborately than any of their predecessors, they confined their pomp and protocol to occasions of state. At times, indeed, they were remarkable for the all-American variety of their guests. On any given day one might find a Rough Rider, a poet, a British viscount, a wolf hunter, and a Roman Catholic cardinal at the White House table, each being treated with the gentlemanly naturalness which was one of TR's most endearing traits. His pride manifested itself in things like his refusal to address foreign monarchs as "Your Majesty," in his offer to mediate the Russo-Japanese War (no American President had yet had such global presumptions), and, when he won the Nobel Peace Prize for successfully bringing the war to a conclusion, in refusing to keep a penny of the forty-thousand-dollar prize money. This was by no means an easy decision, because TR could have used the funds: he spent all his presidential salary on official functions and was not himself a wealthy man. He confessed he was tempted to put the Nobel money into a trust for his children, but decided it belonged to the United States.

Pride and patriotism were inseparable in Theodore Roosevelt's character; indeed, if we accept Lord Morely's axiom that he "was" America, they may be considered as complementary characteristics. And neither of them was false. Just as he was always willing to lose a political battle in order to win a political war, so in diplomatic negotiations was he sedulous to allow his opponents the chance to save face—take all the glory of settlement if need be—as long as the essential victory was his.

As I have noted earlier, TR's militarism did not loom large during his Presidency. The organizational structure of the U.S. Army was revamped in such a way as to strengthen the powers of the Commander in Chief, but Secretary of War Elihu Root takes credit for that. TR can certainly take the credit for expanding the American Navy from fifth to second place in the world during his seven and a half years of power—an amazing achievement, but quite in keeping with his policy, inherited from Washington, that "to be prepared for war is the most effectual means to promote peace." The gunboat TR sent to Panama in 1903 was the only example of him shaking a naked mailed fist in the face of a weaker power; for the rest of the time he kept that fist sheathed in a velvet glove. The metaphor of velvet on iron, incidentally, was TR's own; it makes a refreshing change from the Big Stick.

If I may be permitted a final metaphor of my own, I would like to quote one from *The Rise of Theodore Roosevelt* in an attempt to explain why, on the whole, TR's character shows to better advantage as President than in his years out of power. "The man's personality was cyclonic, in that he tended to become unstable in times of low pressure." The slightest rise in the barometer outside, and his turbulence smoothed into a whir of coordinated activity, while a core of stillness developed within. Under maximum pressure Roosevelt was sunny, calm, and unnaturally clear." This explains why the first Roosevelt era was a period of fair weather. Power became Theodore Roosevelt, and absolute power became him best of all. He loved being President and was so good at his job that the American people loved him for loving it. TR genuinely dreaded having to leave the White House, and let us remember that a third term was his for the asking in 1908. But his knowledge that power corrupts even the man who most deserves it, his reverence for the Washingtonian principle that power must punctually revert to those whose gift it is, persuaded him to make this supreme sacrifice in his prime. The time would come, not many years hence, when fatal insolence tempted him to renege on his decision. That is another story. But the self-denial that he exercised in 1908 gives us one more reason to admire Old Fifty-seven Varieties.

Angel Island: The Half-Closed Door

Brian McGinty

Brian McGinty is a frequent contributor to American History Illustrated. *His history of earthquakes in California appeared in the March/April 1990 issue.*

From 1910 to 1940, the principal immigration station on the West Coast of the United States occupied a remote site on the northern shore of Angel Island in San Francisco Bay. Facing the blue waters of one of the world's most renowned natural harbors, the Angel Island Immigration Station was the point of entry—or of deportation—for tens of thousands of Chinese and other Asian immigrants. Located only six miles from downtown San Francisco, the processing center was isolated from the mainland by deep water, imposing gray walls, and barbed-wire fences. Immigrants detained there were within easy sight of the "Promised Land," yet still a world away from it— separated from their goal by treacherous straits, discriminatory immigration laws, and bureaucratic obstacles that at times seemed insurmountable.

The history of Asian immigration to the United States is long and painful, fraught with the prejudice of the Western world. During the early years of California settlement, Oriental immigrants (mostly Chinese) were welcomed with civility if not enthusiasm. The Chinese were hard workers, and their labor was badly needed to build the burgeoning frontier's cities, bridges, and railroads. They were good businessmen, too, with rigorously frugal habits and a seemingly natural sense for the give-and-take of commerce.

So successful were the Chinese in the economic life of the West that within a few years demagogic politicians began to blame the newcomers for the economic slowdowns that periodically beset the region. Adopting "The Chinese must go!" as their slogan, these politicians proposed a series of stern laws that would make it difficult for Chinese to live in the United States—and harder yet for new Chinese immigrants to enter the country.

American hostility toward alien cultures ultimately resulted in the Chinese Exclusion Act, passed by Congress in 1882. A series of increasingly restrictive laws that followed were designed to cut the flow of Chinese immigrants to a trickle. The laws worked as planned; in California alone, the number of Chinese declined from almost 9 percent of the total population in 1880 to less than 1 percent in 1940.

But the new legislation did not totally bar Chinese immigration. A small class of "exempts" (officials, merchants, teachers, students, and tourists) were still permitted to enter the country, as were individuals who could prove a claim to U.S. citizenship by birth or by descent from an American citizen.

Beginning in the 1880s, a stream of Chinese claiming the right to enter the country as children of native-born Chinese-Americans arrived in San Francisco. Many of these would-be immigrants were known as "paper sons and daughters," for their claims were frankly based on fraudulent documents. The destruction in the great 1906 earthquake and fire of records that verified citizenship made it easier for many new arrivals in California to fabricate claims to citizenship by right of inheritance. Driven by the poverty and privation that gripped their native land, and desperate to penetrate the legal wall Americans had erected against them, the Chinese were willing to risk their fortunes, their freedom, and even their lives to make new homes in the country they called "The Land of the Flowery Flag."

Before 1910, Chinese arrivals in San Francisco were detained in a dismal wooden shed on the waterfront while their papers were reviewed or, if they had no papers, while witnesses were questioned to prove or disprove their claims. But conditions in the detention shed were so appalling that in 1903, under pressure from Chinatown's community leaders, the Bureau of Immigration announced its intention to build a new immigration station—on the shore of Angel Island.

The largest island in San Francisco Bay, Angel Island

From *American History Illustrated*, September/October 1990, pp. 50-51, 71. Reprinted through the courtesy of Cowles Magazines, publishers of *American History Illustrated*.

covers 740 acres and measures about a mile and a quarter from shore to shore at its widest point. Rising to 781 feet above sea level, the steep and hilly chunk of land lies due north of San Francisco's downtown financial district. Separated from Marin County's Tiburon Peninsula by Raccoon Strait—one of the deepest and most treacherous channels in the bay—the island, first sighted in 1769 by Gaspar de Portolá's overland expedition to Monterey, was named *Isla de Nuestra Señora de Los Angeles* by Spanish explorers under the command of Juan Manuel de Ayala, who anchored there in 1775 while charting San Francisco Bay. When Americans took control of California in the 1840s, they anglicized the name to Angel Island.

During the nineteenth century, the island served many purposes. For nearly twenty-five years, Russian settlers from Fort Ross on the nearby coast used it as a camp from which to hunt sea otters. The island was a Mexican cattle ranch during the 1840s, and a decade later a quarry on its rugged eastern shore supplied stone for San Francisco buildings. During the Civil War, the U.S. Army fortified the island against possible Confederate attacks on San Francisco Bay. Over the years, the Army expanded its presence there until the island contained three main camps with officers' quarters, hospitals, parade grounds, and barracks for several thousand troops.

Taking advantage of Angel Island's isolation, the government in 1892 opened the San Francisco Quarantine Station on the northwest shore of the island. There it built housing for surgeons, pharmacists, and attendants, and dormitories and bathhouses for detainees. Passengers arriving in San Francisco were checked for signs of communicable diseases and, if infected, held at the station until they were either certified healthy or returned to their ports of origin. Although the quarantine station's activities slowed after 1915, it continued to operate well into the 1930s.

But it was as Ellis Island's Pacific counterpart that Angel Island became best-known. The new immigration station was designed to alleviate the unsafe and unsanitary conditions that had long prevailed in San Francisco's waterfront detention shed; to prevent newly arriving immigrants from communicating with friends or relatives in the city while they awaited processing; and to establish an escape-proof facility. Although construction was completed in 1908, the processing center did not officially open until January 21, 1910. The following morning, more than four hundred would-be Americans were moved into the two-story barracks serving as the station's main detention center.

Upon arrival at Angel Island, immigrants were ordered to leave their luggage in a warehouse on the wharf while they climbed the hill to the barracks. Separated by race and sex, they were led into drafty dormitories furnished with long rows of steel bunks in tiers of three. As soon as the doctors were ready to receive them, groups of newcomers were led to the hospital and examined for signs of disease. The detainees ate their meager and often scarcely palatable meals in a dining hall in the administration building. Lights went out in the station at about 9:00 P.M., at which time the massive doors to the dormitories were closed and securely locked.

Between two hundred and five hundred immigrants were housed at the Angel Island facility at any one time. Nearly all of the detainees were Asians, and the bulk of these were Chinese.

Immigrants with convincing "papers" were normally detained for only a few days. others, who had either suspicious documents or no documents at all, had to wait until immigration officers scheduled hearings to examine the newcomers' claims. Witnesses were ferried from San Francisco. To prevent collusion between witnesses and interpreters, the interpreters were rotated on a random basis.

If a young Chinese immigrant claimed to be the son of an American citizen, immigration examiners questioned him closely. What was his mother's name? In what village was his father born? How many houses were there in the village? Did he have any brothers or sisters? What were their names? Did they have a dog in the family house? Where was the rice bin kept? The witnesses, always questioned separately, were asked the same questions. Discrepancies in the testimony often resulted in rejection and swift repatriation to China. Reflecting the overwhelmingly hostile American policy toward admitting Chinese, immigration regulations specified that "in every doubtful case the benefit of the doubt shall be given . . . to the United States government." As many as 30 percent of those examined were ultimately rejected and deported.

Depending on the circumstances of the case and the attitudes of the examiner, hearings could end in an hour or drag on as long as a week. Decisions in the applicant's favor were announced immediately; unfavorable decisions were withheld until all testimony had been transcribed and the examiner's report was completed. If an applicant decided to appeal to immigration authorities in Washington, D.C., the case could continue for months—or sometimes even years. All the while, the detainees languished in their barracks, reading the newspapers they managed to obtain from San Francisco, playing Mah-Jongg, and listening to Chinese opera on a scratchy, hand-wound Victrola.

During the long, dreadful wait, some of the detainees inscribed poetry on the walls of the barracks with knives or brushes. Composed in the classical Tan dynasty style, the poems provided a moving record of the immigrants' fears and hopes and served as a link between succeeding boatloads of detainees. One poet wrote:

This place is called an island of immortals,
When, in fact, this mountain wilderness is a prison.
Once you see the open net, why throw yourself in?
It is only because of empty pockets I can do nothing else.

And another:

Lin, upon arriving in America,
Was arrested, put in a wooden building,
And made a prisoner.

I was here for one autumn.
The Americans did not allow me to land.
I was ordered to be deported.
When the news was told,
I was frightened and troubled about returning to my
country.
We Chinese of a weak nation
Can only sigh at the lack of freedom.

Even before the Angel Island Immigration Station was completed, proposals were made to move it back to the mainland where the detainees would be less isolated and witnesses more accessible. The government resisted all of these suggestions until a fire broke out in the administration building on August 12, 1940, reducing the structure to rubble. Less than three months later, the island's last immigrants—about two hundred in all—were transferred to a new station in San Francisco.

During World War II, the former immigrant center housed federal convicts and even some prisoners of war. In 1954—by which time immigrants were screened overseas by American consular officials prior to emigrating— the State of California took over the old quarantine station on the northwest side of the island, creating Angel Island State Park. The park was expanded in 1962 to include the immigration station and other parts of the island, excepting a seven-acre Coast Guard facility.

After a park ranger drew attention to the poems on the walls of the old barracks in 1970, a systematic effort was made to photograph, transcribe, translate, and catalog the inscriptions. In 1976 the State of California appropriated funds for preservation of the barracks building, which was converted into the Angel Island Museum. A thirty-minute walk from the island's visitor center at Ayala Cove, the museum is now one of the best-known sites on the island. There, docents offer tours of the old building. Although the last detainees left fifty years ago, the poem-covered walls still bear silent testimony to their suffering and despair.

Today Angel Island is easily accessible via ferries that regularly ply the waters between Fisherman's Wharf in San Francisco, the town of Tiburon in Marin County, and Ayala Cove. The island boasts picnic grounds, campsites, and miles of well-maintained hiking trails. But the remains of the old immigration station speak most eloquently of the history made there—and of the indelible memories that refuse to be forgotten.

Recommended additional reading: Island: Poetry and History of Chinese Immigrants on Angel Island, 1910–1940 *by Him Mark Lai, Genny Lim, and Judy Yung (Hoc Doi, 1980) contains a representative collection of the poems inscribed by immigration station detainees on their barracks walls, together with interviews and a well-researched history of the station.*

Rose Schneiderman and the Triangle Fire

Bonnie Mitelman

Bonnie Mitelman, a freelance writer, is currently an adjunct lecturer in the Department of History at Mercy College in Dobbs Ferry, New York. For further reading on Rose Schneiderman and the March 1911 Triangle Fire, Ms. Mitelman suggests Leon Stein's THE TRIANGLE FIRE *(1962).*

On Saturday afternoon, March 25, 1911, in New York City's Greenwich Village, a small fire broke out in the Triangle Waist Company, just as the 500 shirtwaist employees were quitting for the day. People rushed about, trying to get out, but they found exits blocked and windows to the fire escape rusted shut. They panicked.

As the fire spread and more and more were trapped, some began to jump, their hair and clothing afire, from the eighth and ninth floor windows. Nets that firemen held for them tore apart at the impact of the falling bodies. By the time it was over, 146 workers had died, most of them young Jewish women.

A United Press reporter, William Shepherd, witnessed the tragedy and reported, "I looked upon the heap of dead bodies and I remembered these girls were the shirtwaist makers. I remembered their great strike of last year in which these same girls had demanded more sanitary conditions and more safety precautions in the shops. These dead bodies were the answer."

The horror of that fire touched the entire Lower East Side ghetto community, and there was a profuse outpouring of sympathy. But it was Rose Schneiderman, an immigrant worker with a spirit of social justice and a powerful way with words, who is largely credited with translating the ghetto's emotional reaction into meaningful, widespread action. Six weeks following the tragedy, and after years of solid groundwork, with one brilliant, well-timed speech, she was able to inspire the support of wealthy uptown New Yorkers and to swing public opinion to the side of the labor movement, enabling concerned civic, religious, and labor leaders to mobilize their efforts for desperately needed safety and industrial reforms.

The Triangle fire, and the deaths of so many helpless workers, seemed to trigger in Rose Schneiderman an intense realization that there was absolutely nothing or no one to help working women except a strong union movement. With fierce determination, and the dedication, influence, and funding of many other people as well, she battled to regulate hours, wages, and safety standards and to abolish the sweatshop system. In so doing, she brought dignity and human rights to all workers.

The dramatic "uprising of the 20,000" of 1909-10, in which thousands of immigrant girls and women in the shirtwaist industry had endured three long winter months of a general strike to protest deplorable working conditions, had produced some immediate gains for working women. There had been agreements for shorter working hours, increased wages, and even safety reforms, but there had not been formal recognition of their union. At Triangle, for example, the girls had gained a 52 hour week, a 12-15 percent wage increase, and promises to end the grueling subcontracting system. But they had not gained the only instrument on which they could depend for lasting change: a viable trade union. This was to have disastrous results, for in spite of the few gains that they seemed to have made, the workers won no rights or bargaining power at all. In fact, "The company dealt only with its contractors. It felt no responsibility for the girls."

There were groups as well as individuals who realized the workers impotence, but their attempts to change the situation accomplished little despite long years of hard work. The Women's Trade Union League and the International Ladies' Garment Workers' Union, through the efforts of Mary Dreier, Helen Marot, Leonora O'Reilly, Pauline Newman, and Rose Schneiderman had struggled unsuccessfully for improved conditions: the futility that the union organizers were feeling in late 1910 is reflected in the WTUL minutes of December 5 of that year.

A scant eight months after their historic waistmakers' strike, and three months before the

From *American History Illustrated*, July 1981. Reprinted through the courtesy of Cowles Magazines, publishers of *American History Illustrated*.

105

The Triangle Shirtwaist Company fire, Washington Square and Green Streets, New York City, 1911. The Bettmann Archive, Inc.

deadly Triangle fire, a Mrs. Malkiel (no doubt Theresa Serber Malkiel, who wrote the legendary account of the strike, *The Diary of a Shirtwaist Striker: A Story of the Shirtwaist Makers' Strike in New York*) is reported to have come before the League to urge action after a devastating fire in Newark, New Jersey killed twenty-five working women. Mrs. Malkiel attributed their loss to the greed and negligence of the owners and the proper authorities. The WTUL subsequently demanded an investigation of all factory buildings and it elected an investigation committee from the League to cooperate with similar committees from other organizations.

The files of the WTUL contain complaint after complaint about unsafe factory conditions; many were filled out by workers afraid to sign their names for fear of being fired had their employers seen the forms. They describe factories with locked doors, no fire escapes, and barred windows. The New York *Times* carried an article which reported that fourteen factories were found to have no fire escapes, twenty-three that had locked doors, and seventy-eight that had obstructed fire escapes. In all, according to the article, 99 percent of the factories investigated in New York were found to have serious fire hazards.

Yet no action was taken.

It was the Triangle fire that emphasized, spectacularly and tragically, the deplorable safety and sanitary conditions of the garment workers. The tragedy focused attention upon the ghastly factories in which most immigrants worked; there was no longer any question about what the strikers had meant when they talked about safety and sanitary reform, and about social and economic justice.

The grief and frustration of the shirtwaist strikers were expressed by one of them, Rose Safran, after the fire: "If the union had won we would have been safe. Two of our demands were for adequate fire escapes and for open doors from the factories to the street. But the bosses defeated us and we didn't get the open doors or the better fire escapes. So our friends are dead."

The families of the fire victims were heartbroken and hysterical, the ghetto's *Jewish Daily Forward* was understandably melodramatic, and the immigrant community was completely enraged. Their Jewish heritage had taught them an emphasis on individual human life and worth; their shared background in the *shtetl* and common experiences in the ghetto had given them a sense of fellowship. They were, in a sense, a family—and some of the most helpless among them had died needlessly.

The senseless deaths of so many young Jewish women sparked within these Eastern Europeans a new determination and dedication. The fire had made reform absolutely essential. Workers' rights were no longer just socialist jargon: They were a matter of life and death.

The Triangle Waist Company was located on the three floors of the Asch Building, a 10-story, 135-foot-high structure at the corner of Greene Street and Washington Place in Greenwich Village. One of the largest shirtwaist manufacturers, Triangle employed up to 900 people at times, but on the day of the fire, only about 500 were working.

Leon Stein's brilliant and fascinating account of the fire, entitled simply *The Triangle Fire*, develops and documents the way in which the physical facilities, company procedures, and human behavior interacted to cause this great tragedy. Much of what occurred was ironic, some was cruel, some stupid, some pathetic. It is a dramatic portrayal of the eternal confrontation of the "haves" and the "have-nots," told in large part by those who survived.

Fire broke out at the Triangle Company at approximately 4:45 P.M. (because time clocks were reportedly set back to stretch the day, and because other records give differing times of the first fire alarm, it is uncertain exactly what time the fire started), just after pay envelopes had been distributed and employees were leaving their work posts. It was a small fire at first, and there was a calm, controlled effort to extinguish it. But the fire began to spread, jumping from one pile of debris to another, engulfing the combustible shirtwaist fabric. It became obvious that the fire could not be snuffed out, and workers tried to reach the elevators or stairway. Those who reached the one open stairway raced down eight flights of stairs to safety; those who managed to climb onto the available passenger elevators also got out. But not everyone could reach the available exits. Some tried to open the door to a stairway and found it locked. Others were trapped between long working tables or behind the hordes of people trying to get into the elevators or out through the one open door.

Under the work tables, rags were burning; the wooden floors, trim, and window frames were also afire. Frantically, workers fought their way to the elevators, to the fire escape, and to the windows— to any place that might lead to safety.

Fire whistles and bells sounded as the fire department raced to the building. But equipment proved inadequate, as the fire ladders reached only to the seventh floor. And by the time the firemen connected their hoses to douse the flames, the crowded eighth floor was completely ablaze.

For those who reached the windows, there seemed to be a chance for safety. The New York *World* describes people balancing on window sills, nine stories up, with flames scorching them from behind, until firemen arrived: "The nets were spread below with all promptness. Citizens were commandeered into service, as the firemen necessarily gave their attention to the one engine and hose of the force that first arrived. The catapult force that the bodies gathered in the long plunges made the nets utterly without avail. Screaming girls and men, as they fell, tore the nets from the grasp of the holders, and the bodies struck the sidewalks and lay just as they fell. Some of the bodies ripped big holes through the life nets."

One reporter who witnessed the fire remembered how,

> A young man helped a girl to the window sill on the ninth floor. Then he held her out deliberately, away from the building, and let her drop. He held out a second girl the same way and let her drop. He held out a third girl who did not resist. They were all as unresisting as if he were helping them into a street car instead of into eternity. He saw that a terrible death awaited them in the flames and his was only a terrible chivalry. He brought around another girl to the window. I saw her put her arms around him and kiss him. Then he held her into space—and dropped her. Quick as a flash, he was on the window sill himself. His coat fluttered upwards—the air filled

his trouser legs as he came down. I could see he wore tan shoes.

Those who had rushed to the fire escape found the window openings rusted shut. Several precious minutes were lost in releasing them. The fire escape itself ended at the second floor, in an airshaft between the Asch Building and the building next door. But too frantic to notice where it ended, workers climbed onto the fire escape, one after another until, in one terrifying moment, it collapsed from the weight, pitching the workers to their death.

Those who had made their way to the elevators found crowds pushing to get into the cars. When it became obvious that the elevators could no longer run, workers jumped down the elevator shaft, landing on the top of the cars, or grabbing for cables to ease their descent. Several died, but incredibly, some did manage to save themselves in this way. One man was found, hours after the fire, beneath an elevator car in the basement of the building, nearly drowned by the rapidly rising water from the fire-men's hoses.

Several people, among them Triangle's two owners, raced to the roof, and from there were led to safety. Others never had that chance. "When Fire Chief Croker could make his way into the [top] three floors," states one account of the fire, "he found sights that utterly staggered him . . . he saw as the smoke drifted away bodies burned to bare bones. There were skeletons bending over sewing machines."

The day after the fire, the New York *Times* announced that "the building was fireproof. It shows hardly any signs of the disaster that overtook it. The walls are as good as ever, as are the floors: nothing is worse for the fire except the furniture and 141 [*sic*] of the 600 men and girls that were employed in its upper three stories."

The building *was* fireproof. But there had never been a fire drill in the factory, even though the management had been warned about the possible hazard of fire on the top three floors. Owners Max Blanck and Isaac Harris had chosen to ignore these warnings in spite of the fact that many of their employees were immigrants who could barely speak English, which would surely mean panic in the event of a crisis.

The New York *Times* also noted that Leonora O'Reilly of the League had reported Max Blanck's visit to the WTUL during the shirtwaist strike, and his plea that the girls return to work. He claimed a business reputation to maintain and told the Union leaders he would make the necessary improvements right away. Because he was the largest manufacturer in the business, the League reported, they trusted him and let the girls return.

But the improvements were never made. And there was nothing that anybody could or would do about

Above: Interior of the Asch Building after the Triangle fire. Brown Brothers.

An inadequate fire escape collapsed under the weight of victims struggling to safety. Even had it held, the flimsy stairway reached only to the second floor. Brown Brothers.

it. Factory doors continued to open in instead of out, in violation of fire regulations. The doors remained bolted during working hours, apparently to prevent workers from getting past the inspectors with stolen merchandise. Triangle had only two staircases where there should have been three, and those two were very narrow. Despite the fact that the building was deemed fireproof, it had wooden window frames, floors, and trim. There was no sprinkler system. It was not legally required.

These were the same kinds of conditions which existed in factories throughout the garment industry; they had been cited repeatedly in the complaints filed with the WTUL. They were not unusual nor restricted to Triangle; in fact, Triangle was not as bad as many other factories.

But it was at Triangle that the fire took place.

The *Jewish Daily Forward* mourned the dead with sorrowful stories, and its headlines talked of "funerals instead of weddings" for the dead young girls. The entire Jewish immigrant community was affected, for it seemed there was scarcely a person who was not in some way touched by the fire. Nearly everyone had either been employed at Triangle themselves, or had a friend or relative who had worked there at some time or another. Most worked in factories with similar conditions, and so everyone identified with the victims and their families.

Many of the dead, burned beyond recognition, remained unidentified for days, as searching family members returned again and again to wait in long lines to look for their loved ones. Many survivors were unable to identify their mothers, sisters, or wives; the confusion of handling so many victims and so many survivors who did not understand what was happening to them and to their dead led to even more anguish for the community. Some of the victims were identified by the names on the pay envelopes handed to them at quitting time and stuffed deeply into pockets or stockings just before the fire. But many bodies remained unclaimed for days, with bewildered and bereaved survivors wandering among them, trying to find some identifying mark.

Charges of first- and second-degree manslaughter were brought against the two men who owned Triangle, and Leon Stein's book artfully depicts the subtle psychological and sociological implications of the powerful against the oppressed, and of the Westernized, German-Jewish immigrants against those still living their old-world, Eastern European heritage. Ultimately, Triangle owners Blanck and Harris were acquitted of the charges against them, and in due time they collected their rather sizable insurance.

The shirtwaist, popularized by Gibson girls, had come to represent the new-found freedom of females in America. After the fire, it symbolized death. The reaction of the grief-stricken Lower East Side

was articulated by socialist lawyer Morris Hillquit:

> The girls who went on strike last year were trying to readjust the conditions under which they were obliged to work. I wonder if there is not some connection between the fire and that strike. I wonder if the magistrates who sent to jail the girls who did picket duty in front of the Triangle shop realized last Sunday that some of the responsibility may be theirs. Had the strike been successful, these girls might have been alive today and the citizenry of New York would have less of a burden upon its conscience.

For the first time in the history of New York's garment industry there were indications that the public was beginning to accept responsibility for the exploitation of the immigrants. For the first time, the establishment seemed to understand that these were human beings asking for their rights, not merely trouble-making anarchists.

The day after the Triangle fire a protest meeting was held at the Women's Trade Union League, with representatives from twenty leading labor and civic organizations. They formed "a relief committee to cooperate with the Red Cross in its work among the families of the victims, and another committee . . . to broaden the investigation and research on fire hazards in New York factories which was already being carried on by the League."

The minutes of the League recount the deep indignation that members felt at the indifference of a public which had ignored their pleas for safety after the Newark fire. In an attempt to translate their anger into constructive action, the League drew up a list of forceful resolutions that included a plan to gather delegates from all of the city's unions to make a concerted effort to force safety changes in factories. In addition, the League called upon all workers to inspect factories and then report any violations to the proper city authorities and to the WTUL. They called upon the city to immediately appoint organized workers as unofficial inspectors. They resolved to submit the following fire regulations suggestions: compulsory fire drills, fireproof exits, unlocked doors, fire alarms, automatic sprinklers, and regular inspections. The League called upon the legislature to create the Bureau of Fire Protection and finally, the League underscored the absolute need for all workers to organize themselves at once into trade unions so that they would never again be powerless.

The League also voted to participate in the funeral procession for the unidentified dead of the Triangle fire.

The city held a funeral for the dead who were unclaimed. "More than 120,000 of us were in the funeral procession that miserable rainy April day," remembered Rose Schneiderman. "From ten in the morning until four in the afternoon we of the Women's Trade Union League marched in the procession with other trade-union men and women, all of us filled with anguish and regret that we had never been able to organize the Triangle workers."

Schneiderman, along with many others, was absolutely determined that this kind of tragedy would never happen again. With single-minded dedication, they devoted themselves to unionizing the workers. The searing example of the Triangle fire provided them with the impetus they needed to gain public support for their efforts.

They dramatized and emphasized and capitalized on the scandalous working conditions of the immigrants. From all segments of the community came cries for labor reform. Stephen S. Wise, the prestigious reform rabbi, called for the formation of a citizens' committee. Jacob H. Schiff, Bishop David H. Greer, Governor John A. Dix, Anne Morgan (of *the* Morgans) and other leading civic and religious leaders collaborated in a mass meeting at the Metropolitan Opera House on May 2 to protest factory conditions and to show support for the workers.

Several people spoke at that meeting on May 2, and many in the audience began to grow restless and antagonistic. Finally, 29-year-old Rose Schneiderman stepped up to the podium.

In a whisper barely audible, she began to address the crowd.

I would be a traitor to these poor burned bodies, if I came here to talk good fellowship. We have tried you good people of the public and we have found you wanting. The old Inquisition had its rack and its thumbscrews and its instruments of torture with iron teeth. We know what these things are today: the iron teeth are our necessities, the thumbscrews the high-powered and swift machinery close to which we must work, and the rack is here in the fire-proof structures that will destroy us the minute they catch on fire.

This is not the first time girls have burned alive in the city. Every week I must learn of the untimely death of one of my sister workers. Every year thousands of us are maimed. The life of men and women is so cheap and property is so sacred. There are so many of us for one job it matters little if 140-odd are burned to death.

We have tried you, citizens; we are trying you now, and you have a couple of dollars for the sorrowing mothers and daughters and sisters by way of a charity gift. But every time the workers come out in the only way they know to protest against conditions which are unbearable, the strong hand of the law is allowed to press down heavily upon us.

Public officials have only words of warning to us—warning that we must be intensely orderly and must be intensely peaceable, and they have the workhouse just back of all their warnings. The strong hand

of the law beats us back when we rise into the conditions that make life bearable.

I can't talk fellowship to you who are gathered here. Too much blood has been spilled. I know from my experience it is up to the working people to save themselves. The only way they can save themselves is by a strong working-class movement.

Her speech has become a classic. It is more than just an emotional picture of persecution; it reflects the pervasive sadness and profound understanding that comes from knowing, finally, the cruel realities of life, the perspective of history, and the nature of human beings.

The devastation of that fire and the futility of the seemingly successful strike that had preceded it seemed to impart an undeniable truth to Rose Schneiderman: They could not fail again. The events of 1911 seemed to have made her, and many others, more keenly aware than they had ever been that the workers' fight for reform was absolutely essential. If they did not do it, it would not be done.

In a sense, the fire touched off in Schneiderman an awareness of her own responsibility in the battle for industrial reform. This fiery socialist worker had been transformed into a highly effective labor leader.

The influential speech she gave did help swing public opinion to the side of the trade unions, and the fire itself had made the workers more aware of the crucial need to unionize. Widespread support for labor reform and unionization emerged. Pressure from individuals, such as Rose Schneiderman, as well as from groups like the Women's Trade Union League and the International Ladies' Garment Workers' Union, helped form the New York State Factory Investigating Commission, the New York Citizens' Committee on Safety, and other regulatory and investigatory bodies. The League and Local 25 (the Shirtwaist Makers' Union of the ILGWU) were especially instrumental in attaining a new Industrial Code for New York State, which became "the most outstanding instrument for safeguarding the lives, health, and welfare of the millions of wage earners in New York State and . . . in the nation at large."

It took years for these changes to occur, and labor reform did not rise majestically, Phoenix-like, from the ashes of the Triangle fire. But that fire, and Rose Schneiderman's whispered plea for a strong working-class movement, had indeed become the loud, clear call for action.

THE UNKNOWN HOLLYWOOD

In the first two decades of the twentieth century escapist fantasy was not the sole diet offered to American audiences by the emerging film industry. **Steven Ross** relates the mixture of social realism and biting political commentary that inspired both film-makers and reformers to the silver screen in the Progressive era.

Steven J. Ross is Associate Professor of History at the University of Southern California, and the author of Working-Class Hollywood: Labor, Radicals, and the Movies *'forthcoming'.*

Hollywood remains endlessly fascinating to academics and audiences throughout the world. Histories of film, film-makers, and movie stars cram the shelves of bookstores, while video stores constantly expand their stock to meet the seemingly insatiable need for entertainment. In the last two years alone, American readers have been flooded with popular books about Samuel Goldwyn, Darryl Zanuck, Cary Grant, Francis Coppola, the rise of the studio system, and the first generation of Jewish entrepreneurs who 'invented' Hollywood. Frequent studio shake-ups, mergers, and takeovers by foreign corporations provide seemingly endless copy for movie-hungry newspapers. More recently, the fascination with Hollywood's past led the British film-makers, David Gill and Kevin Brownlow — who gave us several wonderful series on Hollywood's silent era – to offer transatlantic audiences a two-part documentary on the silent film comedian, Harold Lloyd.

Yet, for all the printed and visual materials about films and the film industry, there is another history of Hollywood that remains relatively unknown to scholars and audiences. When we think of Hollywood — a term I use loosely to describe American movie production in general, not simply films made in Los Angeles

— we think of films aimed at amusing audiences and making money for producers. Social realism and biting political commentary have not been the hallmarks of the modern film industry. Yet, there was a time when a wide array of liberal, conservative, and radical organisations made theatrical films — films produced for regular cinemas — aimed at politicising millions of viewers. During the early decades of the twentieth century, when the Progressive movement was in its heyday and the fledging film industry in its infancy, suffragettes, labour unions, socialists, religious groups, business associations, government agencies, and a wide array of reformers used film as a means of challenging or defending ideas about society, authority, and political life. While many contemporary groups and organisations, Left and Right, complain about the biased depictions of film and television, it is interesting to see how, during an earlier time, similar organisations altered visual perceptions of the world not by putting pressure on the studios but by making their own films.

During the early years of the new century, as workers won their demands for higher wages and a shorter working week, leisure assumed an increasingly important role in everyday life. Amusement parks, professional baseball games, nickelodeons, and dance halls attracted a wide array of men and women anxious to spend their hard earned dollars in the pursuit of fun and relaxation. Yet of all these new cultural endeavours, films were the most important and

First published in *History Today,* April 1990, pp. 40-46. Reproduced by kind permission of History Today, Ltd., 83-84 Berwick Street, London W1V 3PJ, England.

widely attended source of amusement. For a mere five or ten cents, even the poorest worker could afford to take himself and his family to the local nickelodeon or storefront theatre. Taking root in urban working-class and immigrant neighbourhoods, cinemas soon spread to middle-class districts of cities and into small communities throughout the nation. 'Every little town that has never been able to afford and maintain an opera house,' observed one journalist in 1908, 'now boasts one or two "Bijou Dreams".' By 1910 the appeal of films was so great that nearly one-third of the nation flocked to the cinema each week; ten years later, weekly attendance equalled 50 per cent of the nation's population.

Early films were primarily aimed at entertaining audiences, but entertainment did not always come in the form of escapist fantasies. Many of the issues that dominated Progressive-era politics were also portrayed on the screen. 'Between 1900 and 1917,' observes Kevin Brownlow, 'literally thousands of films dealt with the most pressing problems of the day – white slavery, political corruption, gangsterism, loan-sharking, slum landlords, capital vs labour, racial prejudice, etc.' While most of these films were produced by studios and independent companies, a significant number were made by what we might call today 'special interest groups'. As films quickly emerged as the nation's most popular form of mass entertainment, they attracted the attention of a wide range of organisations that recognised the medium's enormous potential for disseminating propaganda to millions of viewers. Before 1918, when the rise of the studio and expensive feature-length films squeezed out most small companies, the movies were still an artisanal industry with large numbers of small producers, distributors, and exhibitors. The modest cost of making simple one- or two-reel films – $500 to $1,000 in most instances – allowed a wide range of organisations to make movies advancing their cause. Moreover, exhibitors' need for several films to fill their daily bill, meant that these independently produced films would be shown in hundreds or thousands of cinemas.

For many Americans, especially the millions of immigrants who could neither read nor speak English, films were the newspapers of the screen. Films and newsreels not only entertained audiences but they served as important political documents that allowed them to see what was happening in the nation – or at least what producers wanted them to use. 'Far more people are today reached by the moving picture than by the daily press,' a Moving Picture World reporter observed in 1908, and 'while we read the newspaper only in parts, the moving picture we see complete.' Socialists, labour organisations, business associations, civic groups, religious bodies, and reform groups understood this and used films as political vehicles to portray their particular vision of the problems vexing the nation and the possible solutions to those ills. And, while speeches and newspapers might reach thousands and tens of thousands, films could reach millions of potential allies.

The largest number of early political films – that is, films consciously intended to influence and exert power over others – were produced by organisations espousing the varied causes of reform. By 1912, social workers, educators, ministers, and civic leaders who once denounced earlier films as morally corrupt and 'ministering to the lowest passions', came to embrace their elevating potentials. When 'rightly conducted', insisted settlement-house leader Jane Addams, motion pictures 'are a benefit and not a menace, especially to the poorer classes'. Capitalising upon the popularity of movies, ministers around the country began showing films at Sunday sermons to boost church attendance, while schools, prisons, and settlement houses screened films to educate their charges in proper values and habits.

A number of more venturesome reformers went a step further and actually made their own films. While specific messages varied with the perspective and agenda of the particular reform organisation, as a collective body their films – which they either made in co-operation with studios, or hired producers to make – reflected the liberal strand of Progressive-era ideology. In dramatising the social, economic, and political ills of the day, reformers advocated solutions that would create more just conditions without radically altering the basic structures of business or government. They defined proper class boundaries by prescribing acceptable forms of behaviour and action from above and below. Their films denounced monopolists, trusts, money-lenders, greedy landlords, and well-meaning but unthinking factory owners. Yet, while sympathetic to the plight of the urban poor and working class, reformer-made movies rarely endorsed collective action by the exploited. Instead, these people were told to wait patiently while reformers, clergy, and government officials tended to their cause.

Children Who Labor, which appeared in 1912, offers us a good example of the visual and ideological perspectives of one widely distributed reform film. Produced by the National Child Labor Committee in co-operation with the Thomas Edison Company, this well-made melodrama reflected the organisation's attempt to expose and end the evils of child labour. The film opens upon a depressing scene of down-trodden children shuffling into a factory to begin their day's work. Just before entering this hell-hole, they lift their arms and implore Uncle Sam – dressed in his usual top hat, stars-and-stripes suit, and white beard – to help them. But

Sam ignores their pleas, and over the skies of the factory appears in white smoke the word 'GREED'. Subsequent scenes show us how childhood and family life are shattered as the callous factory owner, Mr Hanscomb, ignores the pleas of reformers and continues to hire cheap child labour instead of more expensive able-bodied men. Conditions at the factory are only changed through a series of bizarre circumstances: Hanscomb's beloved daughter accidentally falls out of a train, is taken in by an impoverished immigrant family, and is unknowingly sent to work in her father's factory, where she collapses from exhaustion. Only after the inevitable reunion of father and daughter does the former come to realise and remedy his wrongful ways. The penultimate scene shows happy children passing the factory gate with school books in hand, while fathers and elder sons proudly enter the factory. The film ends on a more sombre note. An inter-title flashes the message, 'Lest We Forget', and the camera cuts to a scene of children vainly imploring Uncle Sam for help as dollar signs flash across the skies.

This very dramatic and engaging film was well received by contemporary audiences and reviewers. And yet, despite its clearly reformist aims, the film offers little insight into why this situation had arisen. Like most other reformist films, there is no attempt to analyse the roots of economic or political crises. The evils of child labour and factory exploitation are simply reduced to the greed of individuals. Similarly, the only solution offered comes through the personal conversion of the factory owner and not through any kind of collective action. *The Awakening of John Bond* (1911), a collaborate effort between the government and the Edison Company that warned of the dangers of tuberculosis in crowded slums, offered a similar conclusion. A rapacious 'slumlord' is transformed into a caring landlord only after his wife contracts the disease after coming into contact with his tenants. In neither film do we ever see workers or slum residents rising up in their own defence.

Outside intervention was more forthcoming in a number of other films made by reformers. Shifting its focus from the workplace to urban slums, *The Usurer's Grip*, produced in 1912 by the Russell Sage Foundation in co-operation with Edison, alerted audiences to the dangers of unscrupulous money-lenders who preyed upon hard-up working men and women. The film's hero and heroine are eventually rescued by a kindly businessman who sends them to the loan division of the Russell Sage Foundation. A sympathetic portrayal of the problems of urban life, the film nevertheless assumes an underlying tone of condescension toward the urban poor, who are rescued only through the paternal actions of the foundation. *The Other Half*, a

dramatisation of Jacob Riis' popular book produced in 1912 by the New York Association for Improving the Condition of the Poor in co-operation with Thanhouser, exposed audiences to the dire poverty of tenement life and the need for greater charity work. Yet neither it nor *The Usurer's Grip* ever asked *why* these conditions arose, or challenged the capitalist system that created them. Instead, they accepted the evils of modern urban industrial life as a given and simply went about trying to reform them.

A somewhat more radical perspective was offered by suffragists who made films eschewing outside intervention in favour of direct action by women's rights advocates. The National American Women's Suffrage Association (NAWSA) and the Women's Political Union (WPU), which collectively produced four films between 1912 and 1914, understood that this newest form of mass culture could serve the aims of mass movements by presenting their cause before large and diverse populations and trying to inspire them to action. Although the plot lines varied somewhat, all four films reversed conservative stereotypes of suffragettes as unattractive hysterical women and portrayed them, as the film historian Kay Sloan observes, 'as deeply moral, attractive women who were devoted to their families or to their sweethearts' and their cause. *Votes for Women*, a two-reel film produced by the NAWSA in 1912, shows suffragettes overcoming male apathy and political corruption and instituting important reforms in slums and sweatshops. Similarly, *Your Girl and Mine*, produced by NAWSA two years later, dramatises scenes of modern troubles – wives abused by drunken husbands, exploited working women, mistreated children – and suggests, through the repeated appearance of a young girl representing Votes For Women and accompanying inter-title, that 'It would not be so if you could get the state to accept me'. Depictions of suffragettes as attractive women and astute political activists are also the dominant themes of *Suffrage and the Man* (1912) and *Eighty Million Women Want – ?* (1913), both produced by the Women's Political Union. Reflecting on the power of these films, one *Moving Picture World* reviewer predicted in 1914 that they 'will accomplish more for the cause than all that eloquent tongues have done since the movement was started'.

The success of these films, which played at cinemas, auditoriums, and political meetings throughout the nation, led other reformers to embrace the screen. Between 1913 and 1917, theatrical films were made by or with the co-operation of organisations espousing the cause of temperance, prison reform, workmen's compensation, aid for widowed mothers, abolition of capital punishment, and birth control. Not all 'reform' films aspired to massive social change. A group of Chicago women, tired of the excessive drinking habits of their husbands, had the Rothacker Film Company secretly shoot several reels of film showing their inebriated mates staggering home 'after the cocktail hour.' When subsequently shown the film, the husbands were either cured or they went out on a drinking binge 'to forget how [they] looked'.

The most numerous and contentious of Hollywood's 'unknown' films revolved around the bitter struggles between labour and capital. The rise of monopolies, oligopolies, trusts, and massive corporations during the late nineteenth and early twentieth centuries, hailed as symbols of progress and efficiency by the nation's business élite, was greeted by massive strikes and sharp upsurges in labour and radical organising among workers. Despite national claims of being a classless society, few countries of the time experienced more labour related violence and deaths than the United States. As the war between labour and capital grew more intense, film emerged as a new weapon which both sides employed to present their cause before a mass public. Attacks and defences of corporate paternalism, factory safety records, unionisation, socialism, and government benevolence were waged not only in workplace and political campaigns, but in cinemas throughout the country.

As big business came under scathing attack by muckraking journalists and Progressive politicians, various corporations and business associations moved to counter negative public images by using film to sway popular opinion in their favour. As with other groups, the particular message of business-made films varied with the needs of the maker. Yet, taken collectively, they stressed a paternalistic ideology similar to that given by the railway president George Baer in 1902:

> The rights and interests of the laboring man [he declared] will be protected and cared for not by the labor agitators, but by the Christian gentlemen to whom God has given control of the property rights of the country.

Organisations like the National Association of Manufacturers (NAM), the most powerful employers' association and most rabidly anti-union organisation in the United States, set out to make films that would bring these words to life.

Concerned about the public outcry that followed the Triangle Fire (in which 146 garment workers perished) and the mushrooming deaths and dismemberments caused by accidents at work, NAM produced two films in 1912, *The Crime of Carelessness* and *The Workman's Lesson*, which portrayed employers' tremendous concern for ensuring the safety and well-being of their employees. The *Crime of Carelessness* attempted to reshape

public memory by implying that the Triangle Fire was caused by worker carelessness, and not, as was really the case, by callous employers who ignored factory safety laws and ensured the deaths of their employees by locking all fire exits. *The Workman's Lesson*, drove home similar messages by attributing the blame for the massive number of industrial deaths and accidents to the stubbornness of workers and not the cupidity of employers. The message was effectively conveyed through a repeated series of self-consciously political images. Employers and foreman in a machine shop are consistently shown teaching and reminding workers to use safety equipment. Opposition to safety, the inter-title tells us, comes from 'older workmen [who] do not like to bother with new-fangled safety devices'. When a new employee starts work in the shop, he is told by 'Old Wentzel' not to bother with the safety devices. As a result of following the advice of a fellow worker rather than the company, the young man's hand is mangled in the machinery. However, his arm is saved when the company doctor rushes to his side in world-record time and swiftly transports him to the company's luxurious infirmary. The final message is clear: blame for accidents rests entirely upon the stubbornness, carelessness, or ignorance of workers. Corporate benevolence – shown here in the form of safety equipment, efficient medical care, and scenes of prosperous workers' houses bought with the high wages paid by the company – is preferable to union selfishness and antagonism.

The success of these films, which, as one historian notes, 'circulated through the nation's movie houses as if they were no different from slapstick comedies, westerns, and historical dramas', led other big businesses to turn to the screen. Railway corporations parried union attacks on the industry's deplorable safety records – 180,000 injuries and 10,000 fatalities in 1912 alone – by producing films, such as *Steve Hill's Awakening* (1914), *The House That Jack Built* (1917), and *The Rule of Reason* (1917), which ascribed workplace accidents to the carelessness and drunkenness of company employees. The American Bankers' Association rebutted organised labour's complaints about low wages by making *The Rewards of Thrift* (1914), a film that showed how conscientious workmen who saved their money – rather than spend it on drink – were able to purchase houses. The Ford Motor Company took these cinematic endeavours a step further by producing *The Ford Educational Weekly*, a regular series of newsreels that, amongst other things, depicted the enormous safety advances made by assembly-line production and the paternalistic policies of enlightened companies like Ford. Business-made films and studio features with similar ideologies grew so popular that employers, observes the film historian Diane Waldman, 'used them as part of an overall strategy to diffuse worker discontent, to discourage union activity, and to exert corporate influence over areas of employees' lives outside the workplace itself'. Large manufacturers like the ketchup-magnate H. J. Heinz built cinemas in their factory grounds, while others incorporated film into company-sponsored recreational programmes.

Labour and radical organisations responded to these cinematic assaults by producing their own films. 'In the motion picture,' proclaimed one labour newspaper in 1914, 'there is a mighty agency for the working class.' Corporate claims of paternal benevolence, workplace safety, employee prosperity, and steadfast adherence to law and order were soon countered by worker-made films and newsreels that told of capitalist exploitation, greed, deceit, and lawlessness. These seemingly sombre messages, however, were told in the form of highly entertaining melodramas that appealed to mass audiences and not simply the already converted. Labour film-makers like Frank Wolfe, a socialist activist and former union organiser, understood that film would be a successful political weapon only if it 'amuses while it instructs'. Unsympathetic audiences, he insisted, 'will watch the message eagerly when they would not listen to it for a moment'. Consequently, labour films followed the dominant melodramatic conventions of the period, but gave them radical twists. The heroes and heroines of these dramas were union or socialist men and women who, unlike their counterparts in business or reform films, solved their problems through direct action and not by trusting in corporate benevolence or awaiting the intercession of some kindly outside figure. Collective activity, whether in the form of workplace militance, unionisation, or socialist politics, was the constant message of these films.

From Dusk to Dawn, a five-reel film produced by Frank Wolfe, was a popular drama filled with love, violence, politics, class conflict, and a spectacular cast of 10,000. It begins with a rebuke of the smug safety messages of business films: we see how an employer's flagrant disregard of employee warnings about unsafe working conditions leads to the explosion of his iron foundry and the death of several men. Rather than simply chastise businessmen, Wolfe provides audiences with a blueprint for change. During the course of a love story between an iron-moulder, Dan Grayson, and Carla Wayne, a laundress whose brother was killed in the foundry explosion, we see men and women picketing their shops, winning union recognition and safer working conditions, putting up socialist candidates for state elections, and eventually capturing the governor's office. The film comes to a politically and romantically satisfying end as Governor Dan signs a 'right to

work bill' that plunges the state into socialism, and then marries the lovely Carla.

While films like the *Crime of Carelessness* tried to distance corporations from complicity in contemporary tragedies like the Triangle Fire, labour-made films like *What Is to Be Done?* placed them right back in the middle of controversy. A five-reel film made by socialists in New York, *What Is to Be Done?* told the 'true' story of the Ludlow (Colorado) massacre. As in *From Dusk to Dawn*, the film's politics are delivered in the palatable form of a love story between a capitalist's liberal son and the radical stenographer who organises workers at his father's factory. During the course of an arbitration hearing, the film dissolves to a scene of the tent colony at Ludlow and the audience is shown how hired thugs in the employ of John D. Rockefeller's Colorado Fuel and Iron Company machine-gunned and then set fire to the tents of striking workers, killing sixteen men, women, and children. The film then cuts back to the present where the factory owner, fearing similar public disapproval of his tainted activities, agrees to the workers' demands. *What Is To Be Done?* proved successful enough to command several commercial runs in New York, while the even more popular *From Dusk to Dawn* was booked into cinema chains throughout the country. In addition to producing feature films, labour film-makers also made a number of shorter films and newsreels that played in union halls, municipal auditoriums, and cinemas.

The decline of the Progressive movement in the wake of American entry into the First World War was paralleled by the decline of social realist films made by reformers and Hollywood studios. 'In the pre-war atmosphere of confidence, order and limited pluralism,' explains the historian Robert Sklar, film-makers were able 'to explore political, religious, economic, and ethnic themes. After the war it became much more difficult.' Audiences, or so producers believed, now preferred films devoted to escapist amusement rather than serious social criticism. The rise of an oligarchic studio system that squeezed out independent producers and the accompanying trend toward expensive multi-reel feature films made participation in the cinematic world much more difficult. Organisations that were able to pay a few thousand for films could no longer afford the tens of thousands needed to produce well-made features after the war.

Radical and reformist film-makers found the problems of rising costs and changing audience tastes compounded by the frequent opposition of film censorship boards. The ability of organisations to recover expenses by exhibiting their films was greatly hampered as conservative state and local film censors banned labour-made films that portrayed class conflict (*From*

3. PROGRESSIVISM TO THE 1920s

Dusk to Dawn), or reformer-made films that explored controversial issues like birth control (*Birth Control*, also known as *The New World* – made by Margaret Sanger in 1917). The tendency towards class-biased censorship increased during the war as the Committee on Public Information, the government's propaganda arm, banned the export of liberal Hollywood-made films showing strikes and labour riots (*Intolerance, The Fourth Estate*), hunger and poverty (*A Corner in Wheat, The Eternal Grind*), or ghetto slums (*Little Italy*).

Despite these many problems, radicals, reformers and conservatives did not abandon the screen. Films continued to serve as battlegrounds for competing ideas in the post-war era. Instead of making commercial features for cinemas, many organisations produced less expensive non-theatrical films – what we would today call 'educational' films – that were shown in the 22,000 schools, churches, voluntary organisations, YMCAs, chambers of commerce, businesses, civic organisations, and union halls that regularly screened films. Yet, while most reformers and conservatives left the theatrical field, trade unionists, socialists, and Communists continued turning out feature films that would inspire working men and women to action and present the 'aims and hopes of the workers before the masses'. By the mid-1920s, the cinematic struggle between labour and capital was once again in full force as union and radical organisations produced features blasting capitalists and promoting the causes of industrial unionism, worker-control of production, socialism, and trade unionism. These efforts were quickly parried by state authorities who censored labour-made films, film industry personnel who blocked their distribution and exhibition, and capitalists who created production companies devoted to making anti-union, anti-Bolshevik feature films. This renewed era of screen wars persisted until the end of the decade when the rise of exorbitantly expensive 'talkies' finally forced labour and the Left out of the theatrical field.

As Hollywood's 'unknown' producers disappeared from the scene, the political issues which fuelled the passions of reformers, radicals, and conservatives were left largely in the hands of more established studios. Audiences continue to see films with liberal (*Norma Rae*) or conservative (*F.I.S.T.*) messages. But production companies, which are big businesses after all, rarely make films offering positive depictions of mass movements and their struggles. Those interested in seeing American workers, radicals, or women winning battles through their collective efforts must turn to the 'unknown' films of an earlier, and in many ways, more political era.

FOR FURTHER READING:
Kay Sloan, *The Loud Silents: Origins of the Social Problem Film* (University of Illinois Press, 1988); Lary May, *Screening Out the Past: The Birth of Mass Culture and the Motion Picture Industry* (New York: Oxford University Press, 1980); Robert Sklar, *Movie-Made America: A Cultural History of American Movies* (Random House, 1975); Charles Musser and Robert Sklar, eds., *Resisting Images: Radical Perspectives On Film and History* (Temple University Press, 1990); Kevin Brownlow, *Behind the Mask of Innocence* (forthcoming).

The Saint-Mihiel Salient

Pershing's "magnificent" victory

Robert Maddox

With approximately three books, twenty professional, and thirty popular articles to his credit, Robert J. Maddox has become a popular writer of recent United States history. He is currently a Professor of American History at the Pennsylvania State University. For further reading he recommends Frank Freidel's OVER THERE (1964) and THE DOUGHBOYS by Laurence Stallings (1963).

On September 12, 1918, the American First Army launched an attack against the Saint-Mihiel Salient. The salient, which began just southeast of Verdun, was a wedge-shaped area of about 200 square miles, its point projecting twenty miles into allied lines. It had been held by the Germans since early in the war when several bloody French assaults against it had failed. The American operation went according to schedule and by the 16th all objectives had been reached; the salient no longer existed. During those four days United States forces captured almost 16,000 enemy prisoners and 450 field guns, while suffering approximately 7,000 casualties. Not a large battle by World War I standards, it nonetheless had a profound psychological impact on both sides.

That the First Army existed at all was because of the stubbornness and tenacity of General John J. "Black Jack" Pershing, commander of the American Expeditionary Forces in France. Having for all practical purposes no standing army when we entered the war, the United States for many months could do no more than send "show-the-flag" detachments to Europe. American divisions in significant numbers did not begin arriving until the spring of 1918. They got there barely in time to play a key role in blunting the last great German drive of the war. They had fought, however, as elements of French and British armies, having been injected into the lines where needed. Pershing, supported by Secretary of War Newton D. Baker and President Woodrow Wilson, was determined to create an American army which would occupy its own sector of the lines.

A bitter struggle followed. The British and French had been fighting for four years. They suffered enormous casualties and most of their available troops were battle-weary. The French were in particularly bad shape; some of their divisions could no longer be relied on in combat. They looked upon the Americans as fresh reinforcements whose presence would invigorate and strengthen their own forces. Besides, they argued, their commanders had gained the experience American officers lacked.

Pershing saw it differently. He believed American troops would fight far more effectively under their own leadership and flag. And the argument about experience left him unmoved. Indeed, Pershing thought that four years of trench warfare had rendered both allied officers and men unsuited for the open warfare he predicted would mark the last stages of the struggle. His own ego and patriotism undoubtedly colored Pershing's views, but to what extent cannot be determined precisely.

It seemed that the Americans had won their case when, in early August, the Allied Commander in Chief Field Marshal Ferdinand Foch assented to the creation of the First Army and Pershing's plan for the reduction of the Saint-Mihiel Salient. But it only seemed that way. To Pershing's great astonishment and dismay, Foch visited the First Army's headquarters at Ligny-en-Barrois (about twenty-five miles from Saint-Mihiel) late in the month and announced new plans which would have dispersed American forces again, and which provided for only a limited attack against the salient. Foch defended his position by pointing to recent British successes in other sectors which, he said, must be exploited. The marshal expressed regrets over the necessity of separating American units again, but he could not see any other way.

Pershing refused to budge, and the meeting grew heated. The American government and the American people, Pershing argued, insisted that U.S. troops fight as an independent entity. With both men on their feet, Foch rather insultingly asked the American: "Do you

From *American History Illustrated*, April 1981, pp. 42-50. Reprinted through the courtesy of Cowles Magazines, publishers of *American History Illustrated*.

wish to go to battle?" "Most assuredly," Pershing replied, "but as an American Army." When Foch protested that this would take too long, he was told, "Give me a sector anywhere you decide and I will take it over at once." Further exchanges accomplished nothing. At last, referring to his new plan, the marshal stated that he "must insist upon the arrangement." "You may insist all you please," Black Jack retorted, "but I decline absolutely to agree to your plan." Foch left the room. So there would be no misunderstanding as to his position, on the next day Pershing sent a written message to the marshal. Acknowledging Foch's role as overall commander, Pershing nonetheless stood firm that "there is one thing that must not be done and that is to disperse the American forces among the Allied Armies."

Apparently convinced at last that Pershing meant what he said, Foch now gave the Americans what they wanted—and a great deal more. The task of eliminating the Saint-Mihiel Salient was again assigned to the U.S. First Army, but this was merely the first stage of a larger operation. As soon as the salient was taken, according to Foch's new plans, American forces were to move in a northwesterly direction beyond Verdun to take up positions in the Meuse-Argonne sector where another offensive was scheduled to begin on September 26. Poor roads and the fact that columns could move only at night presented the Doughboys with an awesome challenge. As Pershing himself later put it, "We had undertaken to launch, with the same army . . . two great attacks on battlefields sixty miles apart," and all in a period of two weeks!

The salient was less formidable than it appeared. It had the weakness of all salients because it could be attacked from both sides. Although enemy troops occupied commanding positions along parts of the salient's faces, they were vulnerable in others. The troops themselves were not first-rate; they were a mixed bag of Austrians, Hungarians, Bavarians, and Saxons who had long since settled into the dull routines of an inactive sector. Finally, the deeply dug emplacements and barbed wire belts in many places had fallen into disrepair and were easily breached when the fighting began.

About 450,000 Doughboys and 110,000 French colonial troops surrounded the salient. On the south face, where the major blow would fall, stood Major General Hunter Liggett's First Corps and to its left the Fourth Corps commanded by Major General Joseph T. Dickman. The French Colonial Corps was placed at the nose of the salient, and along its western face was the Fifth Corps under Major General George H. Cameron. The French and British were generous in providing air and artillery support. Almost 1,500 planes were made available for the operation, the largest fleet assembled up until that time. French field pieces, some operated by Americans, helped bring the total number of guns to over 3,000. Pershing and chief of operations Colonel George C. Marshall failed, however, to get the number

of tanks they wanted. The British were heavily engaged in their own sector and could spare no heavies, and the 267 light Renaults provided by the French failed to accomplish much once the fighting began. Almost completely equipped by their European allies, the Doughboys could boast of only two innovations: enormous sets of wire cutters left over from the Spanish-American War, and roles of chicken wire which they threw over barbed wire emplacements and walked across. French observers noted this latter practice with interest, but concluded it was useful only for American soldiers because they had such big feet.

Marshall originally asked for fourteen hours of artillery bombardment before the attack began, but Pershing decided on four in order to achieve a tactical surprise. The Germans knew something was brewing, of course, but they did not know how many divisions they faced nor when the assault would come. For some days Pershing's staff was engaged in a ruse designed to make the Germans think the real danger lay to the south, around a city called Belfort. An inordinate number of reconnaissance missions were ordered out in the area, new radio installations were set up to broadcast fictitious coded messages, and tanks were driven back and forth leaving poorly concealed tracks for German planes to spot. In case the Germans failed to notice these "preparations," an officer was dispatched to Belfort where, in a hotel room, he made out a report to Pershing on how the fictitious operation was proceeding. He sent both copies of the report out by courier, but carefully deposited the carbon paper in a wastepaper basket. When he returned from a few drinks at the hotel bar he was pleased to find the carbon had been taken.

German commanders responded to the American trick by sending three divisions and a number of field guns to the Belfort region, but still they anticipated an assault against the salient. Unfortunately for them, they woefully underestimated what they faced. As late as September 9, they believed the Americans would launch a limited attack against the south face only. This they hoped to crush by counterattack. When they finally realized they were going to be hit on both sides, the Germans again guessed wrong. They decided they would have to abandon the salient, but were mistaken as to the time they had left. The gradual evacuation they planned would begin on the 10th and be completed by the 18th. The Doughboys did not know it at the time, but they would be attacking an army already in retreat. This prompted some British wits to refer to the battle of Saint-Mihiel as "the show in which the Americans relieved the Germans."

At 1:00 A.M. on the 12th, more than 3,000 allied guns began pouring shells into the salient. Since part of the bombardment was interdiction fire directed against roads, the Americans unwittingly caught many enemy troops heading toward the rear. At dawn, after a rolling barrage lifted, forward elements of the First and Fourth Corps moved out against the south face of the salient in a cold, drizzling rain. Divisions such as the 1st, 2d, and 42d, which had seen action elsewhere, spearheaded the drive while "green" units were given less ambitious tasks. The resistance they met varied widely. In some instances the Germans fought bravely and inflicted heavy casualties before being grenaded out of their strongholds. More often, however, they surrendered without much struggle. Many Doughboys encountered no enemy troops at all, and trudged through undefended woods and fields with their rifles at the sling. By noon the Americans had taken most of the objectives set for the entire first day; by nightfall they occupied positions the planners had thought would take them another day.

On the western face of the salient the Fifth Corps found the going tougher, as the Germans were well dug in and evacuation had not really gotten under way. General Cameron had three divisions: on the left the 4th, in the center a French division, and on the right the 26th. The 4th and the French had relatively short distances to cover as they pivoted in a northeasterly direction against the Germans. The 26th had a more difficult assignment. It was to push more than six miles almost due east to the town of Vigneulles where, provided things went according to schedule, it was to meet units advancing from the south face, thereby pinching off the salient at its midsection. By nightfall, however, the 26th had advanced only half the distance set for it on the first day and still faced heavy German concentrations.

A most remarkable thing happened next. When he learned that there was heavy traffic on the roads leading out of the salient, Pershing ordered his divisions to continue their attack through the night. Officers of the 26th's 102d Regiment thereupon gathered their men into columns on the main road leading to Vigneulles and began heading through the enemy lines. Although the Germans occupied positions on both sides of the highway, they had neglected to set up any roadblocks. The Doughboys made it to Vigneulles a little after 3:00 A.M. without having a shot fired at them. A little after dawn advance units of the 1st Division coming up from the south were astonished to find the town already in the hands of American troops. Through a stroke of great luck the First Army had cut the salient in half in only twenty-four hours.

The battle for the Saint-Mihiel Salient for all practical purposes was over. Although some mopping up had to be done, the Germans still inside surrendered in droves. Then, after other units reached the line established by the advance regiments, the Americans pushed on. The Germans mounted counterattacks in some sectors, but by the 16th the entire salient had been taken. Pershing would have liked nothing better than to continue his drive. "Without doubt continuation of the advance," he wrote in his final report, "would have carried us well beyond the Hindenburg line and possibly into Metz [a strategically located city just inside the German border]." He had committed himself to the Meuse-Argonne offensive, however, and elements of the First Army began moving in that direction even before the salient had been consolidated.

How well had the Americans performed? Pershing's staff, particularly George C. Marshall, had constructed an almost flawless plan of operations. Mistakes were made in the field, particularly with regard to communications and transport. Units too frequently lost contact with one another, and there were colossal traffic jams on some of the roads. These were mistakes caused by inexperience and could be corrected. What was most noticeable to observers, and to the Germans as well, was the excellent spirit the Doughboys showed. Unlike their allied counterparts who had spent exhausting years in the trenches, the Americans were fresh and bold. One German soldier noted in his diary that they advanced under fire with "praiseworthy indifference." Another wrote that even though "one could see Americans, tall as trees, crash to the ground," they kept coming on. Granted that they engaged only second-line troops who already had been ordered to abandon withdrawal, the Doughboys seemed to warrant Pershing's confidence in them.

One incident in particular typifies both the lack of experience and the spirit. On the morning of the first day a road to the rear of the 26th Division was being used to transport supplies. Despite the fact that a portion of the road was in clear view of German observers and within easy range of their artillery, the American vehicles traveled bumper to bumper as though they were on their way to a Sunday outing. Unaccountably the Germans let this go on for a long time before they began firing. When they did, of course, the procession came to a screeching halt behind the section being shelled. The Americans then began playing a dangerous game. First it was a motorcyclist. Making his way to the head of the stalled vehicles, he turned, waved his hat to his comrades, and gunned his machine across the open area. Several other cyclists followed suit. Not to be outdone, a number of men on horseback galloped across the clearing under sporadic shellfire. Even a couple of automobiles ran the gauntlet as audiences at both ends of the zone cheered them on. "There is something fascinatingly American about this performance," one author has written, "but it cannot be classified as scientific war." Indeed not.

There were Americans in the air over the Saint-Mihiel salient as well. None performed more heroically than Lieutenant Frank Luke of Phoenix, Arizona. Luke was one of a kind, a man who followed orders only when he chose, and who fought the Germans without regard for his own personal safety. Having been told that attacking observation balloons was the riskiest task a fighter pilot could undertake, Luke naturally made balloons his specialty. The gas bags themselves were easy to hit but usually they were strongly protected by anti-aircraft fire, and often had pursuit planes hovering about ready to swoop down on attacking fighters. Luke sent his first balloon down in flames on the opening day of the attack. He bagged two more on September 14, and still another three the next day. Production held steady on the 16th as he and a friend destroyed three more, but his finest hour was yet to come.

On the morning of September 18 Luke took out after two balloons located near a body of water the pilots referred to as "Three Finger Lake." He got the first one on his initial pass, but as he headed for the second he saw three enemy fighters waiting for him. Luke attacked them and shot down two Fokkers, after which the third plane tried to escape. As he took off in pursuit Luke realized that the remaining balloon was between him and his prey. Making a slight detour, he proceeded to destroy the balloon quickly enough to permit him to catch up with, and shoot down, the third plane. In less than ten minutes Lieutenant Luke had scored five victories!

His career as the top "balloon buster" was short-lived. After a brief leave in Paris, Luke returned to the Saint-Mihiel area late in September. He quickly shot down another fighter and a balloon, but continued to disobey orders given him. By the end of the month he had managed to be recommended for the Distinguished Flying Cross and placed under arrest at the same time. Unwilling to stay on the ground, he made one last flight. This time he attacked and destroyed three German balloons, but shrapnel crippled his plane. Unable to gain altitude, he fired his remaining rounds strafing German ground troops and landed in a clearing. The Germans called on him to surrender but, defiant to the end, he shot at them with his pistol until they killed him. Captain Eddie Rickenbacker, who certainly ought to have known, declared that "Luke was the greatest fighter who ever went into the air."

The victory at Saint-Mihiel cannot be weighed properly by merely adding up the number of square miles taken, prisoners captured, or observation balloons shot down. Its symbolic value was important to all the combatants. For the first time an American army, under its own command, had fought and defeated the Germans. Some say the Americans were made over-confident by the ease of their success, and paid for it later during the Meuse-Argonne Offensive. It provided a

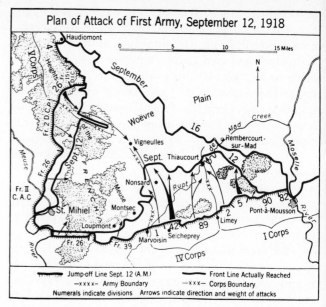

Map taken from American Armies and Battlefields in Europe.

great boost as well to the British and French. The salient, which had jutted imperviously into their lines for over four years, had been reduced in a twinkling by an ally who was pouring fresh troops into the conflict daily. Marshal Foch termed it a "magnificent" victory, and both French Prime Minister Georges Clemenceau and President Raymond Poincaré visited the scene. The latter had lived near Saint-Mihiel, and French newspapers made much of the fact that at last he was able to return to his home. It had, unfortunately, been blown into rubble.

To the Germans Saint-Mihiel was ominous. Their armies had been badly mauled during the summer, and the German high command realized that time was running out. What the generals hoped to do was to give ground grudgingly, inflict as many casualties as possible, and gain from the allies the best peace terms they could get. That had been their intention at the salient before they realized what the Americans were preparing to throw at them. The injection of hundreds of thousands of Doughboys into the struggle meant that stalling tactics would not work. "That St. Mihiel drive was the deciding blow," wrote an American soldier, with pardonable exaggeration. "Since then," he added, "the Huns have had no spirit."

Citizen Ford

He invented modern mass production. He gave the world the first people's car, and his countrymen loved him for it. But at the moment of his greatest triumph, he turned on the empire he had built—and on the son who would inherit it.

David Halberstam

Part One

The Creator

Late in the life of the first Henry Ford, a boy named John Dahlinger, who more than likely was Ford's illegitimate son,* had a discussion with the old man about education and found himself frustrated by Ford's very narrow view of what schooling should be. "But, sir," Dahlinger told Ford, "these are different times, this is the modern age and—" Ford cut him off. "Young man," he said, "I invented the modern age."

The American century had indeed begun in Detroit, created by a man of simple agrarian principles. He had started with scarcely a dollar in his pocket. When he died, in 1947, his worth

---

*Dahlinger, who died in 1984, was baptized in the Ford christening gown and slept as an infant in the crib Henry had used as a baby. His mother was a secretary at the Ford company. —*Ed.*

was placed at $600 million. Of his most famous car, the Model T, he sold 15,456,868. Mass production, he once said, was the "new messiah," and indeed it was almost God to him. When he began producing the Model T, it took twelve and a half hours to make one car. His dream was to make one car every minute. It took him only twelve years to achieve that goal, and five years after that, in 1925, he was making one every ten seconds. His name was attached not just to cars but to a way of life, and it became a verb—to *fordize* meant to standardize a product and manufacture it by mass means at a price so low that the common man could afford to buy it.

When Ford entered the scene, automobiles were for the rich. But he wanted none of that; he was interested in transportation for men like himself, especially for farmers. The secret lay in mass production. "Every time I reduce the charge for our car by one dollar," he said early in the production of the T, "I get a thousand new buyers," and he ruthlessly brought the price down, seeking—as the Japanese would some sixty years later—size of market rather than maximum profit per piece. He also knew in a shrewd, intuitive way what few others did in that era, that as a manufacturer and employer he was part of a critical

cycle that expanded the buying power of the common man. One year his advertising people brought him a new slogan that said, "Buy a Ford—save the difference," and he quickly changed it to "Buy a Ford—SPEND the difference," for though he was innately thrifty himself, he believed that the key to prosperity lay not in saving but in spending and turning money over. When one of the children of his friend Harvey Firestone boasted that he had some savings, Ford lectured the child. Money in banks was idle money. What he should do, Ford said, was spend it on tools. "Make something," he admonished, "create something."

For better or worse Ford's values were absolutely the values of the common man of his day. Yet, though he shared the principles, yearnings, and prejudices of his countrymen, he vastly altered their world. What he wrought reconstituted the nature of work and began a profound change in the relationship of man to his job. Near the end of this century it was clear that he had played a major part in creating a new kind of society in which man thought as much about leisure time as about his work. Ironically, the idea of leisure itself, or even worse, a leisure culture, was anathema to him. He was never entirely comfortable with the fruits of his success, even though he lived in

From *American Heritage,* October/November 1986, pp. 49-64. Adapted from THE RECKONING by David Halberstam. Copyright © 1986 by David Halberstam. Reprinted by permission of William Morrow & Company, Inc.

a magnificent fifty-six-room house. "I still like boiled potatoes with the skins on," he said, "and I do not want a man standing back of my chair at table laughing up his sleeve at me while I am taking the potatoes' jackets off." Of pleasure and material things he was wary: "I have never known what to do with money after my expenses were paid," he said, "I can't squander it on myself without hurting myself, and nobody wants to do that."

Only work gave purpose: "Thinking men know that work is the salvation of the race, morally, physically, socially. Work does more than get us our living; it gets us our life."

As a good farm boy should, he hated alcohol and tobacco, and he once said that alcohol was the real cause of World War I—the beer-drinking German taking after the wine-drinking Frenchman. His strength, in his early years—which were also his good years—was in the purity of his technical instincts. "We go forward without facts, and we learn the facts as we go along," he once said. Having helped create an urbanized world where millions of God-fearing young men left the farm and went to the cities, he was profoundly uneasy with his own handiwork, preferring the simpler, slower America he had aided in diminishing. For all his romanticizing of farm life, however, the truth was that he had always been bored by farm work and could not wait to leave the farm and play with machines. They were his real love.

When Ford was born, in 1863, on a farm in Dearborn, Michigan, the Civil War was still on. His mother died at the age of thirty-seven delivering her eighth child. Henry was almost thirteen at the time. He had idolized her, and her death was a bitter blow. "I thought a great wrong had been done to me," he said. Later in his life he not only moved the house in which he grew up to Greenfield Village, and tracked down the Ford family's very own stove, whose serial number he had memorized, he also had a cousin who resembled his mother dress up in an exact imitation of the way she had and wear her hair in just the same style.

His father's people were new Americans. When the great potato blight had struck Ireland in 1846, ruining the na-

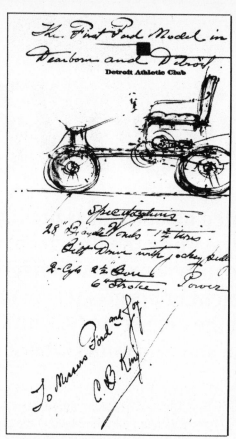

On the fiftieth anniversary of Ford's first car, in 1946, his adviser Charles Brady King made this sketch of it.

tion's most important crop, that country had been devastated. Of a population of eight million, one million had died, and one million had emigrated to America. Among the migrants was William Ford, who had set off to the magic land with two borrowed pounds and his set of tools. He was a skilled carpenter, and when he arrived, he moved quickly to Michigan, where some of his uncles had already settled, and found work laying railroad track. With his savings he bought some land and built a house, in awe of an America that had so readily allowed him to do so. To William Ford, Ireland was a place where a man was a tenant on the land, and America was a place where he owned it.

Henry Ford started school when he was seven. The basic books were the McGuffey Reader; they stressed moral values but included sections from Dickens, Washington Irving, and other major writers, which enticed many children into a genuine appreciation of literature. Although Ford loved McGuffey, he did not like books or the alien ideas they

sometimes transmitted. "We read to escape thinking. Reading can become a dope habit. . . . Book-sickness is a modern ailment." By that he meant reading that was neither technical nor functional, reading as an end in itself, as a pleasure without a practical purpose. But he was wary even of practical volumes. "If it is in a book, it is at least four years old, and I don't have any use for it," he told one of his designers.

What he truly loved was machinery. From the start, he had a gift for looking at a machine and quickly understanding it, not only to repair it but to make it work better. "My toys were all tools," he wrote years later. "They still are!" In his early teens he designed a machine that allowed his father to close the farm gate without leaving his wagon. Watches fascinated him. When he was given a watch at thirteen, he immediately took it apart and put it back together. He soon started repairing watches for his friends. His father complained that he should get paid for this, but he never listened, for it was a labor of love.

His father wanted him to become a farmer, but it was a vain hope. Henry Ford hated the drudgery of the farm. In 1879 he entered his seventeenth year, which in those days was considered maturity. On the first day of December of that year, he left for Detroit, a most consequential departure. He walked to the city, half a day's journey.

Detroit was a town of 116,000, a place of foundries and machine shops and carriage makers. There were some nine hundred manufacturing and mechanical businesses, many of them one-room operations but some of them large. It was an industrial city in the making. Ten railroads ran through it. As New York City, in the next century, would be a mecca for young Americans interested in the arts, Detroit was just becoming a city with a pull for young men who wanted to work with machines. The surge in small industries was beginning, and a young man who was good with his hands could always find a job.

Ford went to work at James Flower & Brothers, a machine shop with an exceptional reputation for quality and di-

Ford at Detroit Edison in 1893.

By 1896, at the age of thirty-three, Ford finally had his first car on the street. He couldn't sleep for forty-eight hours before driving it.

versity of product. As an apprentice there, Ford was immersed in the world of machinery, working among men who, like himself, thought only of the future applications of machines. He made $2.50 a week, boarded at a house that charged him $3.50 a week, and walked to work. His salary left him a dollar a week short, and as a good, enterprising young man, he set out to make up the difference. Hearing that the McGill Jewelry Store had just gotten a large supply of clocks from another store, Ford offered to clean and check them. That job added another two dollars to his weekly salary, so he was now a dollar a week ahead.

His fascination with watches led him to what he was sure was a brilliant idea. He would invent a watch so elementary in design that it could be mass-produced. Two thousand of them a day would cost only thirty cents apiece to make. He was

absolutely certain he could design and produce the watch; the only problem, he decided, was in marketing 600,000 watches a year. It was not a challenge that appealed to him, so he dropped the project. The basic idea, however, of simplifying the product in order to mass-produce it, stayed with him.

He went from Flower & Brothers to a company called Detroit Dry Dock, which specialized in building steamboats, barges, tugs, and ferries. His job was to work on the engines, and he gloried in it, staying there two years. There was, he later said, nothing to do every day but learn. In 1882, however, at the age of nineteen, he returned to the farm, and his father offered him eighty acres of land to stay there. William Ford did that to rescue his wayward son from the city and his damnable machines; Henry Ford took it because he momentarily needed security—he was about to marry Clara Bryant. Nothing convinced him more of his love of machines than the drudgery of the farm. Again he spent every spare minute tinkering and trying to invent and reading every technical magazine he could. He experimented with the sawmill on the farm; he tried to invent a steam engine for a plow. Crude stationary gasoline engines had been developed, and Ford was sure a new world of efficient gasoline-powered machines was about to arrive. He wanted to be part of it. In 1891, with all the timber on the farm cut, he asked Clara to go back to Detroit with him. "He just doesn't seem to settle down," his father said to friends. "I don't know what will become of him."

The last thing Henry Ford was interested in was settling down. He intended, he told his wife, to invent a horseless carriage. But first he needed to know a good deal more about electricity. So he took a job with Detroit Edison at forty-five dollars a month. The city had grown dramatically in the few years since he had first arrived; its population was now more than 205,000. The railroads had begun to open up the country, and, except for Chicago, no town in America had grown as quickly. Detroit now had streetlights. There were more machine shops than ever before. In this city the age of coal and steam was about to end.

By 1896, at the age of thirty-two, Ford

finally had his first car on the street. He was so excited by the prospect of his inaugural ride that he barely slept for the forty-eight hours before it. He had been so obsessed and preoccupied during the creation of the car that not until it was time for the test drive did he find that the door of the garage was too small for it to exit. So he simply took an ax and knocked down some of the brick wall to let the automobile out. A friend rode ahead on a bike to warn off traffic. A spring in the car broke during the ride, but they fixed it quickly. Then Henry Ford went home so he could sleep for a few hours before going to work. Later he drove the car out to his father's farm, but William Ford refused to ride in it. Why, he asked, should he risk his life for a brief thrill?

Henry Ford sold that first car for $200 and used the money to start work immediately on his next. It was consid-

Ford at the turn of the century.

The way to make cars, Ford said in 1903, is to make one like another, "just as one pin is like another pin, or one match like another match."

erably heavier than the first, and he persuaded a lumber merchant named William Murphy to invest in the project by giving him a ride. "Well," said Murphy when he reached home safely, "now we will organize a company." In August 1899 Murphy brought together a consortium of men who put up $15,000 to finance Ford's Detroit Automobile Company. Ford thereupon left Detroit Edison to work full time on his car.

In February 1900, at the threshold of the twentieth century, Ford was ready to take a reporter from the Detroit *News-Tribune* for a ride. The car, he said, would go twenty-five miles an hour. The reporter sensed that he was witness to the dawn of a new era. Steam, he later wrote, had been the "compelling power of civilization," but now the shriek of the steam whistle was about to yield to a new noise, the noise of the auto. "What kind of a noise is it?" the reporter asked. "That is difficult to set down on paper. It is not like any other sound ever heard in this world. It was not like the puff! puff! of the exhaust of gasoline in a river launch; neither is it like the cry! cry! of a working steam engine; but a long, quick, mellow gurgling sound, not harsh, not unmusical, not distressing; a note that falls with pleasure on the ear. It must be heard to be appreciated. And the sooner you hear its newest chuck! chuck! the sooner you will be in touch with civilization's latest lisp, its newest voice." On the trip, Ford and the reporter passed a harness shop. "His trade is doomed," Ford said.

Ford, however, was not satisfied. The cars he was making at the Detroit Automobile Company were not far behind the quality of the cars being made by Duryea or Olds, but they remained too expensive for his vision. Ford desperately wanted to make a cheaper car. His stockholders were unenthusiastic. By November 1900 the company had died. But Ford was as determined as ever to make his basic car, and he decided that the way to call attention to himself and pull ahead of the more than fifty competing auto makers was to go into racing. In 1901 he entered a race to be held in Grosse Pointe. He won and became, in that small, new mechanical world, something of a celebrity. That propelled him ahead

of his competitors.

Two years later, in 1903, he set out to start the Ford Motor Company. He was forty years old and had, he felt, been apprenticing long enough. There were 800 cars in the city at that time, and some owners even had what were called motor houses to keep them in. Ford soon worked up his plan for his ideal, inexpensive new car, but he needed money —$3,000, he thought, for the supplies for the prototype (the actual cost was $4,000). He got the financing from a coal dealer named Alexander Malcomson. Ford and Malcomson capitalized their original company for $150,000, with 15,000 shares. Some of the early investors were not very confident. John Gray, Malcomson's uncle, made a 500 percent return on his early investment but went around saying that he could not really ask his friends to buy into the company. "This business cannot last," he said. James Couzens, Malcomson's assistant, debated at great length with his sister, a schoolteacher, on how much of her savings of $250 she should risk in this fledging operation. They decided on $100. From that she made roughly $355,000. Couzens himself managed to put together $2,400 to invest, and from that, when he finally sold out to Ford in 1919, he made $29 million.

This time Ford was ready. He was experienced, he hired good men, and he knew the car he would build. "The way to make automobiles," he told one of his backers in 1903, "is to make one automobile like another automobile . . . just as one pin is like another pin when it comes from a pin factory, or one match is like another match when it comes from a match factory." He wanted to make many cars at a low price. "Better and cheaper," he would say. "We'll build more of them, and cheaper." That was his complete vision of manufacturing. "Shoemakers," he once said, "ought to settle on one shoe, stove makers on one stove. Me, I like specialists."

But he and Malcomson soon split over the direction of the company: Malcomson, like Ford's prior backers, argued that fancy cars costing $2,275 to $4,775 were what would sell. At the time, nearly half the cars being sold in America fell into this category; a decade later, largely

because of Ford, those cars would represent only 2 percent of the market. Malcomson wanted a car for the rich, Ford, one for the multitude. Though the early models were successful—the company sold an amazing total of 1,700 cars in its first 15 months—it was the coming of the Model T in 1908 that sent Ford's career rocketing.

It was the car that Henry Ford had always wanted to build because it was the car that he had always wanted to drive —simple, durable, absolutely without frills, one that the farmer could use and, more important, afford. He was an agrarian populist, and his own people were farmers, simple people; if he could make their lives easier, it would give him pleasure. He planned to have a car whose engine was detachable so the farmer could also use it to saw wood, pump water, and run farm machinery.

The Model T was tough, compact, and light, and in its creation Ford was helped by breakthroughs in steel technology. The first vanadium steel, a lighter, stronger form developed in Britain, had been poured in the United States a year before the planning of the Model T. It had a tensile strength nearly three times that of the steel then available in America, yet it weighed less and could be machined more readily. Ford instantly understood what the new steel signified. He told one of his top men, Charles Sorensen, that it permitted them to have a lighter, cheaper car.

The T was a brilliantly simple machine: when something went wrong, the average owner could get out and fix it. Unimproved dirt tracks built for horses which made up most of the nation's roads and which defeated fancier cars, posed no problem for it. Its chassis was high, and it could ride right over serious bumps. It was, wrote Keith Sward, a biographer of Ford, all bone and muscle with no fat. Soon the Ford company's biggest difficulty was in keeping up with orders.

Because the Model T was so successful, Ford's attention now turned to manufacturing. The factory and, even more, the process of manufacturing, became his real passions. Even before the T, he

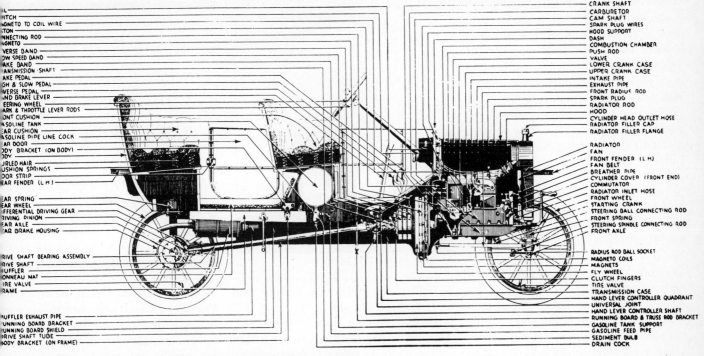

The Ford company issued this diagram showing every component of the Model T in 1913, five years after the car's birth. It was accompanied by the explanation, "The better you know your car the better will you enjoy it."

had been concerned about the production process. In 1906 he had hired an industrial efficiency expert named Walter Flanders and offered him a whopping bonus of $20,000 if he could make the plant produce 10,000 cars in 12 months. Flanders completely reorganized the factory and beat the deadline by two days. He also helped convince Ford that they needed a larger space. Flanders understood that the increasing mechanization meant that the days of the garage-shop car maker were over. There was a process now, a *line,* and the process was going to demand more and more money and employees. Flanders understood that every small success on the line, each increment that permitted greater speed of production (and cut the cost of the car), mandated as well an inevitable increase in the size of the company. "Henceforth the history of the industry will be the history of the conflict of giants," he told a Detroit reporter.

Ford thereupon bought his Highland Park grounds. Here he intended to employ the most modern ideas about production, particularly those of Frederick Winslow Taylor, the first authority on scientific industrial management. Tay-

lor had promised to bring an absolute rationality to the industrial process. The idea was to break each function down into much smaller units so that each could be mechanized and speeded up and eventually flow into a straight-line production of little pieces becoming steadily larger. Continuity above all. What Ford wanted, and what he soon got, was a mechanized process that, in the words of Keith Sward, was "like a river and its tributaries," with the subassembly tributaries merging to produce an ever-more-assembled car.

The process began to change in the spring of 1913. The first piece created on the modern assembly line was the magneto coil. In the past a worker—and he had to be skilled—had made a flywheel magneto from start to finish. An employee could make 35 or 40 a day. Now, however, there was an assembly line for magnetos. It was divided into 29 different operations performed by 29 different men. In the old system it took twenty minutes to make a magneto; now it took thirteen.

Ford and his men quickly imposed a comparable system on the assembly of engines and transmissions. Then, in the summer of 1913, they took on the final assembly, which, as the rest of the proc-

ess had speeded up, had become the great bottleneck. Until then the workers had moved quickly around a stationary metal object, the car they were putting together. Now the men were to remain stationary as the semifinished car moved up the line through them.

One day in the summer of 1913, Charles Sorensen, who had become one of Ford's top production people, had a Model T chassis pulled slowly by a windlass across 250 feet of factory floor, timing the process all the while. Behind him walked six workers, picking up parts from carefully spaced piles on the floor and fitting them to the chassis. It was an experiment, but the possibilities for the future were self-evident. This was the birth of the assembly line, the very essence of what would become America's industrial revolution. Before, it had taken some thirteen hours to make a car chassis; now they had cut the time of assembly in half, to five hours and fifty minutes. Not satisfied, they pushed even harder, lengthening the line and bringing in more specialized workers for the final assembly. Within weeks they could complete a chassis in only two hours and thirty-eight minutes.

Now the breakthroughs came even more rapidly. In January of 1914 Ford installed his first automatic conveyor belt. It was, he said, the first moving line ever used in an industrial plant, and it was inspired by the overhead trolley that the Chicago meat-packers employed to move beef. Within two months of that innovation, Ford could assemble a chassis in an hour and a half. It was a stunning accomplishment, but it merely whetted his zeal. Everything now had to be timed, rationalized, broken down into smaller pieces, and speeded up. Just a few years before, in the days of stationary chassis assembly, the best record for putting a car together had been 728 minutes of one man's work; with the new moving line it required only 93 minutes. Ford's top executives celebrated their victory with a dinner at Detroit's Pontchartrain Hotel. Fittingly, they rigged a simple conveyor belt to a five-horsepower engine with a bicycle chain and used the conveyor to serve the food around the table.

An oddly wistful 1912 portrait.

When Ford began making the Model T, the company's cash balance was $2 million; when production ceased, it was $673 million.

It typified the spirit, camaraderie, and confidence of the early days.

Henry Ford could now mass-produce his cars, and as he did so, he cut prices dramatically. In 1909 the average profit on a car had been $220.11; by 1913, with the coming of the new, speeded-up line it was only $99.34. But the total profits to the company were ascending rapidly because he was selling so many more cars. When the company began making the Model T, its cash balance was slightly greater than $2 million. Nineteen years

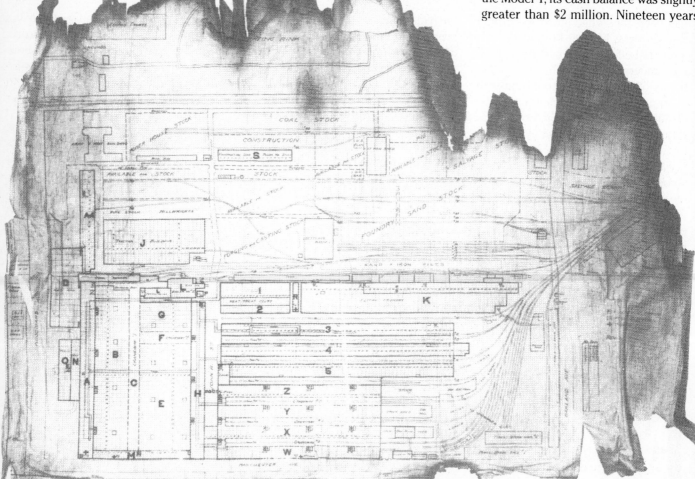

The only surviving plan of the production line that changed the world and made Ford a billionaire is this badly charred 1918 blueprint of the Highland Park plant.

and more than 15 million cars later, when Ford reluctantly came to the conclusion that he had to stop making the T, the company balance was $673 million. But this was not the kind of success that merely made a company richer; it was the beginning of a social revolution. Ford himself knew exactly what he had achieved—a breakthrough for the common man. "Mass production," he wrote later, "precedes mass consumption, and makes it possible by reducing costs and thus permitting both greater use-convenience and price-convenience." The price of the Model T touring car continued to come down, from $780 in the fiscal year 1910–11 to $690 the following year, to $600, to $550, to, on the eve of World War I, $360. At that price he sold 730,041 cars. He was outproducing everyone in the world.

In 1913 the Ford Motor Company, with 13,000 employees, produced 260,720 cars; the other 299 American auto companies, with 66,350 employees, produced only 286,770. Cutting his price as his production soared, he saw his share of the market surge— 9.4 percent in 1908, 20.3 in 1911, 39.6 in 1913, and with the full benefits of his mechanization, 48 percent in 1914. By 1915 the company was making $100 million in annual sales; by 1920 the average monthly earning after taxes was $6 million. The world had never seen anything remotely like it. The cars simply poured off the line. An early illuminated sign in Cadillac Square said, "Watch the Fords Go By." Ford's dreams, in a startlingly brief time, had all come true. He had lived his own prophecy.

There was a moment, however, in 1909 when Ford almost sold the entire company. William C. Durant, the entrepreneur who put General Motors together from several fledgling companies, felt him out about selling the company. An earlier offer of $3 million had fallen through because Ford wanted cash. This time, his company more successful, Ford demanded $8 million. But again he wanted what he called "gold on the table."

Durant couldn't get the financing.

Ford's timing in holding on to his company, it turned out, had been exquisite.

There was no point in designing an Everyman's Car unless the average man could buy fuel cheaply as well. The coming of Ford was almost perfectly synchronized with the discovery in the American Southwest of vast new reserves of oil.

If, as has been said, the American century and the oil century were one and the same thing, then that century began on January 10, 1901, in a field just outside of Beaumont, Texas. The name of the field was Spindletop, so called because of the spindly pines that grew there. For years local children had tossed lighted matches into the field; as the flames hit the strong petroleum vapors seeping up through the soil, there would be a satisfying bang. But anyone who believed that there was real oil beneath the ground was thought an eccentric. Oil was not found in Texas; it was found in places like Pennsylvania, West Virginia, and Ohio. Those states were all Standard Oil territory, and the Rockefeller people had no interest in the Southwest. "I will drink any drop of oil west of the Mississippi," boasted John D. Archbold of Standard.

It was Patillo Higgins, a Beaumont man, who had insisted that there was oil underneath Spindletop, and he had been trying to tap it for several years. It had cost him $30,000 of his own money, and he owed friends an additional $17,000. As each attempt had failed and he had been forced to go to others for financial help in order to continue drilling, his own share of the operation shrank. Higgins's faith had never flagged, but he had become more and more a figure of ridicule in his hometown. "Millionaire," his neighbors nicknamed him. The drilling had gotten harder and harder; just before New Year's Day they had gone through 140 feet of solid rock. That had taken them to a level of 1,020 feet. On January 10 it happened. A geyser of oil roared out of the ground and shot a hundred feet above the derrick. No one had ever seen anything like it before; with it, the word *gusher* came into use.

At first no one could figure out how much oil the field was producing. Some said 30,000 barrels a day, some said 40,000. Capt. Anthony Lucas, who had become a partner of Higgins, said 6,000,

because he had never heard of a larger hole in America. In fact, that one gusher was producing 100,000 barrels a day, roughly 60 percent of the total American production. One new well at Spindletop produced as much as the total from all the 37,000 wells back East in the Rockefeller territory. Within a short time there were five more hits. Eventually analysts found that the oil from the first six holes, some 136 million barrels annually, more than twice surpassed what Russia, then the world's leading petroleum producer, could generate.

Spindletop changed the nature of the American economy and, indeed, the American future. Before the strike, oil was used for illumination, not for energy. (Until 1911 the sales of kerosene were greater than the sales of gasoline.) Spindletop inaugurated the liquid-fuel age in America. The energy of the new age was to be oil, and America suddenly was rich in it.

Texas was providing the gas; Henry Ford was providing the cars. The only limits on him were those imposed by production, and he continued to be obsessed by it. He wanted to put as much of his money as he could back into the factory. He hated bankers and financial people anyway, and he did not want to waste the company's money on stockholders. They were, to his mind, parasites, men who lived off other men's labor. In 1917 the Dodge brothers, who had manufactured many of the early components for Ford and who had been rewarded with sizable amounts of stock, sued him for withholding stock dividends. Some $75 million was at stake. During the trial, Ford testified that putting money back into the plant was the real fun he got from being in business. Fun, the opposing attorney retorted, "at Ford Motor Company expense." Retorted Ford, "There wouldn't be any fun if we didn't try things people said we can't do."

That was the trial in which he referred to the profits he was making as "awful," and when questioned about that by attorneys for the other side, he replied, with absolute sincerity, "We don't seem to be able to keep the profits down." Ford lost the suit, and the court ordered him to pay $19 million in dividends, $11 million of which went to him. The decision probably persuaded him to take as complete control of the company's stock as he could, so that as little money would be wasted as possible. Money to stockholders was a waste, money gone idle; money for the factory was not.

Out of that suit came both the means and the determination to build the River Rouge plant, his great industrial masterpiece, a totally independent industrial city-state. Nothing in the period that followed was too good for the Rouge: it had the best blast furnaces, the best machine tools, the best metal labs, the best electrical systems, the most efficient efficiency experts. Dissatisfied with the supply and quality of the steel he was getting, Ford decided to find out how much it would cost to build a steel plant within the Rouge. About $35 million, Sorensen told him. "What are you waiting for?" asked Ford. Equally dissatis-

The Model T and its creator, 1921.

As he became one of the most popular men in America, the forces he had set in motion began to summon the darkness in his character.

The major production problems had been solved, but labor problems lay ahead when this picture of workers in the Highland Park plant was taken in the 1920s.

fied with both the availability and the quality of glass, he built a glass factory at the Rouge as well. The price of glass had been roughly thirty cents a square foot early in the life of the T; soon it had soared to $1.50 a foot. With the glass plant at the Rouge, the price came down to twenty cents a foot.

At the Rouge, barges carrying iron ore would steam into the inland docks, and even as they were tying up, huge cranes would be swinging out to start the unloading. Some sixty years later Toyota would be credited for its just-in-time theory of manufacturing, in which parts arrived from suppliers just in time to be part of the final assembly. But in any real sense that process had begun at the Rouge. As Eiji Toyoda, of the Toyota family said in toasting Philip Caldwell, the head of Ford, who in 1982 was visiting Japan: "There is no secret to how we learned to do what we do, Mr. Caldwell. We learned it at the Rouge."

All of this, the creation of the Rouge as the ultimate modern plant, speeded up production even more. Before the opening of the Rouge as an auto plant in 1920 (it had produced submarine chasers for World War I in 1918), it had taken 21 days from the receipt of raw material to the production of the finished car. The Rouge cut that time to 14 days. With the opening of the Rouge steel plant in 1925, it took only 4 days.

The Rouge was Henry Ford's greatest triumph, and with its completion he stood alone as the dominant figure in America and the entire developed world. He had brought the process of manufacture to its ultimate moment; he had given the world the first people's car and by dint of his inventive genius had become America's first billionaire. He was an immensely popular man as well, the man who had lived the American dream. But even then, forces he had helped set in motion would begin to summon forth the darkness in his character.

Part Two

The Destroyer

Henry Ford's strengths eventually became his weaknesses. One notorious example was staying with his basic car far too long, ignoring technological change in the cars themselves while obsessively pursuing technological change in their manufacture. From the very start he fought off every attempt to perfect the Model T. In 1912, while he was off on a trip to Europe, his top engineers made some changes intended to improve the car. Their version of the T was lower and some twelve inches longer. It was a better, smoother-riding vehicle, and his associates hoped to surprise and please him. When he returned, they showed it to him. He walked around it several times, finally approaching the left-hand door and ripping it off. Then he ripped off the other door. Then he smashed the windshield and bashed in the roof of the car with his shoe. During all this he said nothing. There was no doubt whose car the T was and no doubt who was the only man permitted to change it. For years anyone wanting to improve a Ford car ran into a stone wall.

What had been another Ford strength, his use of manpower, also turned sour. The early workers at Ford had been skilled artisans, tinkering with designs as they worked. A job at Ford's, as it was known, had been desirable because Henry Ford was at the cutting edge of technology, always trying to do things better, and men who cared about quality wanted to be a part of his operation. In the early days he had his pick of the best men in Detroit. But the mechanized line changed the workplace. These new jobs demanded much less skill and offered much less satisfaction. The pressure to maximize production was relentless. Men who had prided themselves on their skills and had loved working with machines found themselves slaves to those machines, their skills unsummoned. The machines, they discovered to their rage, were more important than they were. The more the plant was mechanized, the more the work force began to unravel. Men began walking out of the Ford plant.

The turnover in the labor force in 1913, the year of the great mechanization, was 380 percent. It soon became even worse. In order to keep one hundred men working, Ford had to hire nearly a thousand. Ford and his principal business partner, James Couzens, realized they had to stabilize the work force. So they came up with the idea of the five-dollar day—that is, of doubling the existing pay. There were some who thought it was Couzens's idea, though Ford later took credit for it. Perceived by many observers as an act of generosity, it was also an act of desperation. Ford calculated that a five-dollar day would attract the best workers, diminish labor unrest, and thus bring him even greater profits. Besides, he believed, it was a mistake to spend money on the finest machinery and then put those precious machines into the hands of disgruntled, unreliable, perhaps incompetent men.

Ford's instincts were right. Not only did the decision solidify the work force; it was so successful a public relations gesture that it allowed Ford to cut back sharply on his advertising. He liked to refer to it as one of the finest cost-cutting moves he had ever made and insisted that he had no philanthropic intent. This denial of altruism, a young Detroit theologian named Reinhold Niebuhr said later, was "like the assurance of an old spinster that her reputation as a flirt has been grossly exaggerated." Indeed in 1914, 1915, and 1916, the first three years of the five-dollar wage, the Ford Motor Company's profits after taxes were $30 million, $20 million, and $60 million.

To workingmen, the five-dollar day was electrifying. Ford had also instituted an eight-hour workday and with it a third shift, and the day after his announcement of the new wage, 10,000 men turned up at the gates of the plant looking for work. Ford had wanted the pick of workers; the pick he now had. For days the crowds grew, and policemen were needed to keep them under control. It was probably the first time that the fruits of the oil-fueled industrial age had reached down to the average worker. A worker had a grim and thankless job that rarely let him get ahead. He would end his life as he began it, and his children were doomed to the same existence. Now, however, with cheap oil and mass production, the industrial cycle was different. It was more dynamic; it generated much more profit and many more goods, which required customers with money to buy them. The worker became the consumer in an ever-widening circle of affluence.

Ford became perhaps the greatest celebrity of his time. Reporters hung out at his office, and his every word was quoted. That both helped and hurt him, because although he was a certifiable genius in manufacturing and perhaps a semi-genius for a long time in business, much of what he said was nonsense, albeit highly quotable nonsense. On cigarettes: "Study the history of almost any criminal, and you will find an inveterate cigarette smoker." On Jews: "When there is something wrong in this country, you'll find Jews." The Jews, he thought, were particularly unproductive people, and he once vowed to pay a thousand dollars to anyone who would bring him a Jewish farmer, dead or alive. He hated the diet of Americans of his generation —"Most people dig their graves with their teeth," he once said. He was prophetic about the nutritional uses of the soybean and intuitive about the value of whole wheat bread, and he wanted his friends to eat no bread but whole wheat. He felt that people who wore glasses were making a serious mistake; they should throw away their glasses and exercise their eyes. For almost all his adult life, he used unadulterated kerosene as a hair cream. He did this because he had observed, he said, that men who worked in the oil fields always had good heads of hair. "They get their hands filled with the oil, and they are always rubbing their hands through their hair," he said, "and that is the reason they have good hair." One of the jobs of E. G. Liebold, his private secretary, was to

At the peak of his power, about 1914.

Every year on his birthday, Ford said, he put on one old shoe to remind himself that he had once been poor and might be poor again.

keep a gallon of No. 10 light kerosene on hand for Ford's hair and constantly to watch that it did not turn rancid.

On one occasion someone noticed that his shoes did not match; he replied that every year on his birthday he put on one old shoe to remind himself that he had once been poor and might be poor again.

He was in some ways a shy man. In the old Ford factory his office had a window through which he used to crawl in order to escape visitors. Nonetheless he was acutely aware that his name was the company name and that his personal publicity generally helped the company. All news from the Ford Motor Company was about him. He was also a hard man, and he became harder as he became older. He distrusted friendship and thought it made him vulnerable: friends might want something from him. He used

a company group called the Sociological Department—allegedly started to help workers with personal problems in finances or health—to check up on employees and find out whether they drank at home or had union sympathies. If they were guilty of either, they were fired. For all his populism, he always took a dim view of the average employee. Men worked for two reasons, he said. "One is for wages, and one is for fear of losing their jobs." He thought of labor in the simplest terms—discipline. He once told a journalist named William Richards, "I have a thousand men who, if I say, 'Be at the northeast corner of the building at 4:00 A.M.,' will be there at 4:00 A.M. That's what we want—obedience."

Even in the days before he became isolated and eccentric, he liked playing cruel tricks on his top people. He loved pitting them against one another. A favorite ploy was to give the identical title to two men without telling either about the other. He enjoyed watching the ensuing struggle. The weaker man, he said, would always back down. He liked the idea of keeping even his highest aides anxious about their jobs. It was good for them, he said. His idea of harmony, his colleague Charles Sorensen wrote, "was constant turmoil." The same sort of thing was going on in the factories. The foremen, the men who ruled the factory floor, were once chosen for their ability; now, increasingly, they were chosen for physical strength. If a worker seemed to be loitering, a foreman simply knocked him down. The rules against workers talking to each other on the job were strict. Making a worker insecure was of the essence. "A great business is really too big to be human," Ford himself once told the historian Allan Nevins.

Slowly, steadily, in the twenties, Henry Ford began to lose touch. He had played a critical role in breeding new attitudes in both workers and customers. But as they changed, he did not, and he became more and more a caricature of himself. "The isolation of Henry Ford's mind is about as near perfect as it is possible to make it," said Samuel Marquis, a Detroit minister who had headed the Sociological Department when its purpose had been to help the employees and who later became its harshest critic.

The Ford Motor Company was no longer a creative operation focused on an exciting new idea and headed by an ingenious leader. For its engineers and designers, the company, only a decade earlier the most exciting place to work in America, was professionally a backwater. Sycophants rose, and men of integrity were harassed. Rival companies were pushing ahead with technological developments, and Ford was standing pat with the Tin Lizzie. His own best people became restless under his narrow, frequently arbitrary, even ignorant, policies. He cut off anyone who disagreed with him. Anyone who might be a threat within the company because of superior leadership ability was scorned as often and as publicly as possible.

Edsel and Henry Ford stand with the ten millionth Model T—and the original quadricycle, Ford's first car—shortly after the T made a transcontinental trip in 1924.

Eventually he drove out Big Bill Knudsen, the Danish immigrant who was largely responsible for gearing up the Ford plants during World War I and was widely considered the ablest man in the company. Knudsen was a formidable production man who had been in charge of organizing and outfitting the Model T assembly plants; he had set up fourteen of them in two years. But his prodigious work during World War I made him a target of perverse attacks by Henry Ford. Knudsen was a big, burly man, six foot three and 230 pounds, and he drank, smoked, and cursed, all of which annoyed the puritanical Ford. Worse, Knudsen was clearly becoming something of an independent figure within the company. He was also drawing closer to Ford's son, Edsel, believing him a young man of talent, vision, and, most remarkable of all, sanity. Together they talked of trying to improve the Model T. All of this merely infuriated the senior Ford and convinced him that Knudsen was an intriguer and becoming too big for his place. Ford took his revenge by making a great show of constantly countermanding Knudsen's production decisions. Knudsen became frustrated with these public humiliations and with the company's failure to move ahead technologically. He finally told his wife that he did not think he could work there any longer. He was sure he was going to have a major confrontation with Henry Ford.

"I can't avoid it if I stay," he said, "and I can't stay and keep my self-respect. I just can't stand the jealousy of the place any more."

"Then get out," she said.

"But I'm making $50,000 a year. That's more money than we can make anywhere else."

"We'll get along," she said. "We did before you went to work there."

In 1921 he quit, virtually forced out. "I let him go not because he wasn't good, but because he was too good—for me," Ford later said.

Knudsen went to General Motors for a starting salary of $30,000, but GM soon put him in charge of its sluggish Chevrolet division. It was the perfect time to join GM. Alfred P. Sloan, Jr., was putting together a modern automotive giant, building on Ford's advances in simplifying the means of production and bringing to that manufacturing success the best of modern business practices. Within three years of Knudsen's arrival, GM became a serious challenger to Ford.

By the early twenties the rumblings from Ford's dealers were mounting. They begged him to make changes in the Model T, but he had become so egocentric that criticism of his car struck him as criticism of himself. Ford defiantly stayed with the Model T. Perhaps 1922 can be considered the high-water mark of Ford's domination of the market. The company's sales were never higher, and

with an average profit of $50 a car, it netted more than $100 million. From then on it was downhill. As Chevy made its challenge, the traditional Ford response —simply cutting back on the price—no longer worked. The success of that maneuver had been based on volume sales, and the volume was peaking. From 1920 to 1924 Ford cut its price eight times, but the thinner margins were beginning to undermine Ford's success. The signs got worse and worse. For the calendar year ending February 1924, the Ford company's net profit was $82 million; of that only $41 million came from new cars, and $29 million came from the sales of spare parts. If anything reflected the stagnation of the company, it was that figure.

In 1926 Ford's sales dropped from 1.87 million to 1.67. At the same time, Chevy nearly doubled its sales, from 280,000 to 400,000. America's roads were getting better, and people wanted speed and comfort. In the face of GM's continuing challenge, Henry Ford's only response was once again to cut prices—twice in that year. The Model T was beginning to die. Finally, in May of 1927, on the eve of the manufacture of the fifteenth million Model T, Henry Ford announced that his company would build a new car. The T was dead. His domination over a market that he himself had created was over. With that he closed his factories for retooling, laying off his workers (many of them permanently).

3. PROGRESSIVISM TO THE 1920s

The new car was the Model A. It had shock absorbers, a standard gearshift, a gas gauge, and a speedometer, all things that Chevy had been moving ahead on and that Ford himself had resisted installing. In all ways it seemed better than its predecessor, more comfortable, twice as powerful, and faster. When it was finally ready to be revealed, huge crowds thronged every showplace. In Detroit one hundred thousand people turned up at the dealerships to see the unveiling. In order to accommodate the mob in New York City, the manager moved the car to Madison Square Garden. Editorials ranked the arrival of the Model A along with Lindbergh's solo transatlantic flight as the top news story of the decade. The car was an immense success. Even before it was available, there were 727,000 orders on hand. Yet its success was relatively short-lived, for once again Henry Ford froze his technology. Even the brief triumph of the Model A did not halt the downward spiral of the company. Henry Ford remained locked into the past. The twenties and thirties and early forties at Ford were years of ignorance and ruffianism. Henry Ford grew more erratic and finally senile. At the end of his life he believed that World War II did not exist, that it was simply a ploy made up by the newspapers to help the munitions industry. No one could reach the old man any more. His became a performance of spectacular self-destructiveness, one that would never again be matched in a giant American corporation. It was as if the old man, having made the company, felt he had a right to destroy it.

With Knudsen's departure, the burden of trying to deal with Ford fell on his son, Edsel. Gentle and intelligent, Edsel Ford reflected the contradictions in his father's life. He had been born while the Fords were still poor. (As a little boy, Edsel had written Santa Claus a letter complaining: "I haven't had a Christmas tree in four years and I have broken all my trimmings and I want some more.") By the time he entered manhood, his father was the richest man in the country, unsettled by the material part of his success and ambivalent about the more privileged life to which his son was being introduced. Henry Ford wanted to be-

In 1927, last year of the Model T.

After he built his fifteen millionth Model T, Ford's domination over a market that he himself had created came to an end.

stow on his son all possible advantages and to spare him all hardship, but, having done that, he became convinced that Edsel was too soft to deal with the harsh, brutal world of industry, symbolized by nothing better than the Ford Motor Company.

Edsel was not a mechanical tinkerer himself, but he had spent his life in the auto business, and he knew who in the company was good and who was not; he was comfortable with the engineers and the designers. Edsel knew times were changing and that the Ford Motor Company was dying. During his father's worst years, Edsel became a magnet for the most talented men in the company, who came to regard his defeats as their defeats. He was a capable executive, and an exceptionally well-trained one: his apprenticeship was full and thorough—and

it lasted thirty years. Absolutely confident in his own judgment about both people and cars, Edsel Ford was beloved by his friends and yet respected in the automobile business for his obvious good judgment. "Henry," John Dodge, Henry Ford's early partner and later his rival, once said, "I don't envy you a damn thing except that boy of yours."

Edsel was the first scion of the automotive world. He married Eleanor Clay, a member of the Hudson family that ran Detroit's most famous department store. They were society, and the marriage was a great event, the two worlds of Detroit merging, the old and the new, a Ford and a Clay. Henry Ford hated the fact that Edsel had married into the Detroit elite and had moved to Grosse Pointe. He knew that Edsel went to parties and on occasion took a drink with his friends, not all of whom were manufacturing people and some of whom were upper class —worse, upper-class citified people— and was sure all this had corrupted him. It was as if Edsel, by marrying Eleanor, had confuted one of Henry Ford's favorite sayings: "A Ford will take you anywhere except into society."

On top of all his other burdens, it was Edsel's unfortunate duty to represent the future to a father now absolutely locked in a dying past. Genuinely loyal to his father, Edsel patiently and lovingly tried to talk Henry Ford into modernizing the company, but the old man regarded his son's loyalty as weakness and spurned him and his advice.

When everyone else in the company agreed that a particular issue had to be brought before the old man, Edsel became the designated spokesman. With Knudsen now gone, he usually stood alone. He was probably the only person who told the truth to his father. Others, such as Sorensen, were supposed to come to Edsel's defense during meetings with Henry, but they never did. Sorensen, brutal with everyone else in the company but the complete toady with the founder, always turned tail in the face of Henry Ford's opposition.

All the while the competition was getting better faster. Chevy had hydraulic brakes in 1924; Ford added them four-

The young man—he was just twenty-eight—had not served the long apprenticeship his father had, and he had only the scantest knowledge of the vast and complicated world he inherited. But it soon became clear that he was shrewd and tough. Through the most unsparing work he mastered the business; and he got rid of Harry Bennett. "You're taking over a billion-dollar organization here that you haven't contributed a thing to!" Bennett yelled. But, having no other recourse, he left.

In the end Henry Ford II broke all of Bennett's cronies and put an end to the bad old era. But there was no way to escape the complex legacy of the founder.

Once a popular figure with the average man, Henry Ford had become known as one of the nation's leading labor baiters. He had helped usher in a new age of economic dignity for the common man, but he could not deal with the consequences. His public statements during the Depression were perhaps the most pitiless ever uttered by any capitalist. He repeatedly said that the Depression was good for the country and the only problem was that it might not last long enough, in which case people might not learn enough from it. "If there is unemployment in America," he said, "it is because the unemployed do not want to work." His workers, embittered by his labor policies, marched against him and were put down by Bennett's truncheons and guns. His security people were so vicious that when Ford's workers marched against the company, the workers wore masks over their faces to hide their identities—something rare in America. Nothing could have spoken more eloquently of tyrannical employment practices.

In business Henry Ford was overtaken by General Motors, which relentlessly modernized its design, its production, and its marketing. GM fed the appetites Ford had helped create. In addition, GM inaugurated a dynamic that haunted the Ford company for the next fifty years; buyers started out driving Fords when they were young and had little money, but slowly, as their earnings rose, they graduated to more expensive GM cars. As a workingman's hero, Ford was replaced by FDR. What had once been charming about his eccentricity now became contemptible.

Nothing reflected his failures more tellingly than the fate of the River Rouge manufacturing complex. It was an industrial masterpiece, and it should have stood long after his death as a beacon to the genius of its founder. But the treatment of human beings there had been so mean and violent, the reputation of the Rouge so scurrilous, that in the postwar era it stood as an embarrassment to the new men running Ford, a reputation that had to be undone.

The bequeathment had other unfortunate aspects. By fighting the unions so unalterably for so long, Ford and the other Detroit industrialists had ensured that, when the unions finally won power, they would be as strong as the companies themselves, and that there would be a carry-over of distrust and hatred. There were other, more concrete, burdens as well. Because he had been locked in the past and had frozen his technology, the company was on the verge of bankruptcy.

Probably no major industrial company in America's history was ever run so poorly for so long. By the beginning of 1946, it was estimated, Ford was losing $10 million a month. The chaos was remarkable, but some of it, at least, was deliberate. The old Henry Ford hated the government and in particular the federal income tax, and by creating utter clerical confusion he hoped to baffle the IRS. He also hated bookkeepers and accountants; as far as he was concerned, they were parasitical. When Arjay Miller, who later became president of the company, joined Ford in 1946, he was told to get the profit forecast for the next month. Miller went down to the Rotunda, where the financial operations were centralized, or at least supposed to be. There he found a long table with a lot of older men, who looked to him like stereotypes of the old-fashioned bookkeeper. These men were confronted by bills, thousands of bills, and they were dividing them into categories—A, B, C, D. The piles were immense, some several feet high. To Miller's amazement the bookkeepers were actually estimating how many million dollars there were per foot of paper. That was the system.

Miller asked what the estimates for the following month's profits were. One of the men working there looked at him and asked, "What do you want them to be?"

"What?" asked Miller.

"I can make them anything you want."

He meant it, Miller decided. It was truly a never-never land.

It was not surprising, then, that the young Henry Ford, seeking to bring sense to the madness he found all around him, turned to an entirely new breed of executive—the professional managers, the bright, young financial experts who knew, if not automobiles and manufacturing plants, then systems and bottom lines. To them Henry Ford II gave nearly unlimited power. And they, in turn, would in the years to come visit their own kind of devastation on the company. The legacy of what the old man had done in his last thirty years left a strain of tragic unreason in the inner workings of the company. So, once again did the past influence the future. For the past was always present.

■■■■■■■■■■■■■■■ **TO FIND OUT MORE**

There has been a great deal written about Henry Ford—in fact two large new biographies have come out this year —but one older book that David Halberstam found particularly readable was Keith Sward's "irreverent" *The Legend of Henry Ford,* originally published in 1948 and reissued as a paperback by Atheneum in 1968. There is also, he said, a "very good small book" by Anne Jardim, *The First Henry Ford,* published by the MIT Press in 1970. Allan Nevins's trilogy, *Ford,* much praised by scholars, is no longer in print but is still available in libraries. For a vivid sense of the man's life, readers can visit Henry Ford's Greenfield Village in Dearborn, Michigan, which is open year-round. Writing about this "stupendous" museum in the December 1980 issue of American Heritage, Walter Karp said that the collection reflects Ford's mind so intimately that it becomes almost a three-dimensional autobiography.

JAZZ:
Red Hot & Cool

Musical America boogie-woogies from Tin Pan Alley and the Big Band Era to the doorstep of Rhythm and Blues.

Brian McGinty

It was F. Scott Fitzgerald, an Irish-American, who gave the era a name—"The Jazz Age." It was Paul Whiteman, a white Anglo-American, who made jazz "respectable" by playing it in prestigious concert halls and commissioning serious composers to produce works in the new style. It was Jewish-Americans like Irving Berlin and George Gershwin who welded jazz to Tin Pan Alley, firmly anchoring the syncopated idiom in the mainstream of American popular music. And it was black Americans like Louis Armstrong, Fletcher Henderson, Bessie Smith, Huddie Ledbetter, Ma Rainey, Duke Ellington, and Count Basie who provided the seemingly endless source of invention that kept jazz perpetually young and fresh. What began in the South as an ethnic phenomenon became in the 'twenties and 'thirties a multicultural endeavor to which Americans of all races and national origins eagerly and productively contributed.

When Fitzgerald labeled the 1920's "The Jazz Age" (the name appeared in his short story collection, *Tales of the Jazz Age*, in 1922), he was less interested in the music than in the mood that it represented. But the name made musical as well as literary sense, for jazz dominated the music of the 'twenties as completely as ragtime had dominated that of the 'nineties. The Original Dixieland Jazz Band made jazz a household word in 1917, but many still frowned on the music. It was vulgar, they said, uncouth, unpolished. It violated every established rule of musical performance. "Modern jazz may be here to stay," one critic gibed, "but it can never replace the old-fashioned earache."

Black musicians took such barbs in stride. They did not expect to be accepted by "polite" white society, and when their music raised cultural hackles they were far from surprised. Whites who admired the new style were not as resigned. They sought to demonstrate jazz's artistic integrity, to show that it was a worthy idiom compatible even, with the classics.

Paul Whiteman did more than any other white musician in the early 'twenties to plead the cause of jazz. Whiteman's music was only remotely related to the "hot" jazz of New Orleans and the "down-and-out" blues of such authentic creators as W. C. Handy and Huddie "Leadbelly" Ledbetter, but it was a palatable concoction of popular melodies, light-classical techniques, and genuine jazz. The roly-poly Whiteman, born in Colorado in 1890, had begun his career as a violinist and dance bandleader. In 1920 he made some recordings that were enormously popular, and soon thereafter he took up the cause of jazz. Whiteman's orchestra was fuller and smoother than any previous jazz band, and his performances were carefully rehearsed. By 1922 he controlled twenty-eight bands that played in various locations on the East Coast and grossed more than a million dollars a year.

In February 1924 Whiteman staged a concert at New York's Aeolian Hall, prestigious home of serious classical music. His program included compositions by Sir Edward Elgar, Edward MacDowell, and Victor Herbert, as well as a lively rendition of *Livery Stable Blues*. But the concert was most notable for the premier performance of a "symphonic jazz" work by a young graduate of Tin Pan Alley named George Gershwin. Especially commissioned by Whiteman for the concert, Gershwin's *Rhapsody in Blue* was an impressive welding of jazz and symphonic techniques that celebrated jazz's auspicious graduation from the bordellos and honky-tonks of America's tenderloin to the serious world of concert music.

Whiteman's claim to be known as the "King of Jazz" seemed ridiculous to many jazz purists, but he worked hard to deserve the title. By combining jazz with light classics and popular dance music, he introduced it to a whole new world of music lovers. Though his own band played a watered-down version of jazz, he permitted his musicians to play "hot" music on their own

From *American History Illustrated*, January 1980, pp. 12, 15-20. Reprinted through the courtesy of Cowles Magazines, publishers of *American History Illustrated*.

time and to cut records in the latest styles. A dozen or more of Whiteman's musicians were ranked among the most brilliant jazz artists of the era—including trombonists Jack Teagarden and Tommy Dorsey, saxophonist Frankie Trumbauer, xylophonist Red Norvo, trumpeter Bunny Berigan, clarinetist and alto saxophonist Jimmy Dorsey.

But the best of them all was Leon (Bix) Beiderbecke. Beiderbecke was born in Iowa in 1903, cut his teeth as a jazz performer with King Oliver in the early 'twenties, and joined Whiteman's band in 1927. His short, unhappy life (an alcoholic, he died in 1931) contributed much to his posthumous legend, as did Dorothy Baker's novel, *Young Man With a Horn*, which was inspired by his life. Beiderbecke was a sensitive pianist and composer (his piano compositions were influenced by the French composer Debussy), but his greatest claim to fame was as a cornetist. His tone was strong and sweet, his improvisations smooth and sure. Before his untimely death, Beiderbecke had become one of the few white musicians in jazz who enjoyed the unreserved admiration of black performers.

Whiteman's was the largest jazz orchestra of its era, but it was not the first of what jazz fans throughout the country were soon to call the "big bands." That honor properly belonged to a group of black musicians led by a young university graduate from Atlanta named Fletcher Henderson.

Henderson had come to New York in 1920 to study at Columbia University but he soon took a job playing the piano in a music publishing house. A short time later the black singer, Ethel Waters, asked him to become her accompanist. In 1923 the newly organized Fletcher Henderson Orchestra opened at the Club Alabam in New York.

Henderson's band included some of the leading black instrumentalists of the day—trumpeters Tommy Ladnier, Joe Smith, and Rex Stewart, trombonist Jimmy Harrison, clarinetist Buster Bailey, and saxophonists Coleman Hawkins and Benny Carter—but his most brilliant star was undoubtedly Louis Armstrong. In 1924 Armstrong left King Oliver in Chicago to join Henderson in New York. His return to the Windy City after only a year robbed Henderson of his greatest musician, but not of his influence, for Armstrong's bold instrumental ideas continued to shape the mood and style of Henderson's band for years to come.

As important, perhaps, as Armstrong's instrumental inspiration in the molding of Henderson's band was the arranging done for it by saxphonist Don Redman. Well-planned, carefully synchronized arrangements were essential to the smooth operation of large orchestras, and Redman's instrumental combinations—notably his brilliant juxtaposition of alternating blocks of brasses and reeds—created a rich, full sound. Poor business management forced Henderson to abandon

his band for a few years in the early 'thirties. During this time he worked as an arranger for a bespectacled young clarinetist-turned-bandleader named Benny Goodman. Goodman was soon to become one of America's most popular musical performers, though few of his fans would realize that his distinctive instrumental combinations—blaring brasses alternating with sweet, rocking reeds—owed more to Henderson than to any other man.

Goodman did not reach his musical peak until the late 'thirties and early 'forties, but he was well along the road to jazz immortality when Henderson arranged for him in 1933 and 1934. Born in Chicago in 1909, he was 10 years old when he took up the clarinet and 12 when he made his debut on the stage of a local vaudeville house. During the middle and late 'twenties he played for Charles (Murph) Podalsky, Ben Pollack, and Ernest (Red) Nichols. He formed special bands for recording sessions and ballroom engagements, played with orchestras in Broadway theaters, and appeared on numerous radio shows. In June 1934 he formed his first regular band, a group that was warmly received when it appeared on the nationwide radio program "Let's Dance" in 1934 and 1935. In late 1935 Goodman's band opened an engagement at the Palomar Ballroom in Los Angeles. Playing special arrangements of *Sugarfoot Stomp, When Buddha Smiles,* and *Stomping at the Savoy,* the Goodman band drew huge and enthusiastic audiences. Goodman's appearance at the Palomar is generally considered the beginning of the "Swing Era."

From California, the band moved east to the Congress Hotel in Chicago. They made a film appearance in *The Big Broadcast of 1937,* and in January 1938 delighted an overflow crowd in New York's Carnegie Hall with swinging renditions of *Don't Be That Way, Bie mir bist do schoen,* and *Sing, Sing, Sing.*

At least as early as the 'twenties, the word "swing" had been used as a general mark of jazz quality (i.e. "good jazz should swing"), but it had not yet become a generic name for a whole school of music. The story has often been told that the British Broadcasting Company thought the expression "hot jazz" was somehow immoral and, when jazz musicians appeared on their programs, announcers referred to their work as "swing music." The phrase was adopted by promoters and, in time, by millions of music fans. "Swing" was played on juke boxes and over the radio, performed in ballrooms, on stages, and in the movies. "Jitterbugs" invented new dance steps to express the free spirit of the music. "Bobby-soxers" thronged dance halls and college gymnasiums to listen, enthralled, to the latest bands and cheer the popular singers who fronted them. The years 1935–1945 were generally known as the "Swing Era," and Benny Goodman was everywhere acclaimed as the "King of Swing."

Blacks joined in the new music as enthusiastically as whites. Goodman himself has often been credited with breaking down the racial barriers that had previously segregated jazz performers, hiring such blacks as pianist Teddy Wilson and drummer and vibraphonist Lionel Hampton to play with his white musicians. But even before then, all-black ensembles were playing in Kansas City, helping to mold the distinctive shapes and rhythms of what Americans everywhere would soon recognize as the "big band sound."

Situated at the confluence of the Kansas and Missouri rivers, Kansas City had always been a lively musical center. After World War I an influx of blacks made it an important rendezvous for jazz musicians. In the late 'twenties and early 'thirties, a new musical style evolved in Kansas City. Based on the blues, on the special demands of dance audiences, and on "jam sessions" (musical competitions, like the "carving contests" of New Orleans), the music was stronger and simpler than the old New Orleans style. Short, propulsive phrases called "riffs" were repeated throughout the twelve-bar duration of traditional blues songs. Riffs rocked back and forth between sections, chorus after chorus, from simple declamations to powerful climaxes.

The most important jazz figure in Kansas City in the 'twenties was Bennie Moten, who began playing New Orleans-style music in 1922 and, by 1930, was leading a large and powerful "big band." William (Count) Basie, a black pianist who was born in New Jersey in 1905, had played with Moten since about 1930. After Moten died in 1935, Basie formed his own orchestra. It was still playing in Kansas City in 1936 when critic John Hammond heard Basie on a local radio station and invited him to come to New York. The Count met with great success in the East, where his reputation soon rivaled that of Goodman. As Basie was influenced by Goodman's smoothness and precision, so Goodman was influenced by Basie's relaxed and powerful beat. When the "King of Swing" recorded *One O'Clock Jump*, one of Basie's best numbers, it became a runaway best-seller—the first record by Goodman to sell over a million copies.

With the exceptions of Henderson and Basie, the most influential black bandleader of the 'twenties and 'thirties was Edward Kennedy (Duke) Ellington. Ellington had been born in Washington, D.C. in 1899, cut his teeth as a jazz pianist in Washington and New York in the late 'teens and early 'twenties, and made his first recording in New York in 1924. Although his earliest efforts were unimpressive, Ellington was a flexible musician and an indefatigable innovator. Endlessly searching for new and arresting harmonies, seeking out fresh and expressive instrumental combinations, he built a solid reputation as an instrumentalist, a composer, and a bandleader. He traveled widely in the 1930's, taking his band from New York to California, then across the Atlantic to Europe. Composing, recording, appearing on radio and in motion pictures, Ellington was an endless source of inspiration to jazz lovers.

Big bands proliferated during the 'thirties and early 'forties. Goodman's popularity with the musical public was rivaled by that of Ellington, Basie, the Dorsey brothers, Artie Shaw, Glenn Miller, Harry James, and Woody Herman. Big bands were regular attractions in fashionable hotels in large American cities, and in smaller towns lesser-known ensembles played for Saturday night dances and high school proms. But while the big bands captured most of the spotlight, less celebrated jazz performers were continuing to develop other aspects of the music.

The blues were still a vital force in jazz. One of the oldest forms of Afro-American music, the blues proved to be one of the most durable. The Alabama-born W. C. Handy, who began his career as a minstrel-show performer and bandleader in the 1890's, had published several blues compositions before 1917—the immortal *St. Louis Blues* among them. The Georgia-born Gertrude (Ma) Rainey had also been a minstrel-show performer, but she was a more inspired performer than Handy and, when minstrelsy lost popularity, she continued her career in vaudeville. During the 1920's she was eagerly sought after by recording companies, for whom she cut such classics as *Boll Weevil Blues*, *Moonshine Blues*, and *Barrelhouse Blues*.

Bessie Smith was eight years younger than Ma Rainey, but she had a more powerful voice and ultimately attracted a larger following. She toured with Ma for a few years in vaudeville and, in 1923, made her recording debut with *Gulf Coast Blues*, *Down Hearted Blues*, and *Tain't Nobody's Business If I Do*. An attractive woman with a unique ability to touch the innermost feelings of her listeners, Bessie became the musical idol of millions of black Americans.

Huddie "Leadbelly" Ledbetter was a different kind of blues singer whose music was born in the folk tradition of the Gulf Coast and changed little before his death in the late 1940's. Born near Mooringsport, Louisiana, about 1888, Leadbelly sang hundreds, perhaps thousands, of worksongs, hollers, and blues as he worked his way across the South. A violent man who served several terms in prison (one for murder, another for attempted homicide), Leadbelly was an unpolished but genuine performer whose rough, natural artistry was powerfully revealed when he made a series of recordings for the Library of Congress in the late 'thirties.

The black piano tradition, too, was alive and well in the 'twenties and 'thirties. Black keyboard music was no longer called ragtime, but it was performed by many of the same men who had played popular rags before and after World War I. In New York such onetime "ragmen" as Willie "The Lion" Smith and Luckey Roberts roamed the streets and cafes of Harlem as Jelly Roll Morton and Tony Jackson had once roamed the streets and cafes of Storyville. The New Jersey-born James P. Johnson was one of the most skillful of the black pianists, famed as a master of the Harlem school of "stride piano" (so named because its characteristic left-hand figures were single notes or tenths that alternated with chords in a vigorous, "striding" pattern).

The most notable of all the black pianists of the period was Thomas "Fats" Waller, who was born in New York the son of a Baptist minister and who began his musical career as a ragtime pianist in the stride tradition. Waller was 10 when he began to play the organ in church, 15 when he wrote his first rag (his disapproving father condemned ragtime as "music from the Devil's workshop"), and 21 when he made his first phonograph recording. He was a skillful pianist, a talented composer, an occasional bandleader, and an inspired comedian. Waller's untimely death in 1943, when he was only 39, robbed the jazz world of one of its most versatile performers.

Another style of black piano music had been developing in the Midwest. Drawing from the blues, and employing the characteristic instrumental patterns of the guitar (an instrument that was often used to accompany blues vocalists), the style was transferred to the piano by largely unskilled musicians. In place of the tenths and chords of the stride pianists, the blues pianists used simple patterns of fifths and sixths. In their most rudimentary form, the figures were monotonous. When complicated with triplets or broken up with octaves in a "walking bass" pattern, they were hypnotic. Elaborate melodies in the right hand—liberally ornamented with trills, glissandos, and a plethora of sharps and flats—contrasted strikingly with the repetitious figures of the left hand. The music had a variety of names in the early days, such as "fast western" and "western rolling blues." It was played through much of the South and Midwest before World War I, but it did not achieve national popularity until the late 'thirties. By then it was known everywhere as "boogie-woogie." Jimmy Yancey and Meade Lux Lewis were the best known exponents of the style, though they had scores of imitators. From about 1938 to 1944, juke boxes and radios across the country blared forth a profusion of boogie recordings, and the names of such tunes as *Beat Me Daddy, Eight to the Bar,* and *Scrub Me Mama with a Boogie Beat* became household words.

By the end of World War II it was clear that the musical tastes of Americans were changing. The "Swing Era" was drawing to a close. Boogie-woogie was seldom heard on juke boxes or radios. The big bands were losing their audiences to smaller combos as ballroom dancing became less popular and television viewing occupied more and more of the nation's leisure time. Jazz musicians like trumpeter John (Dizzy) Gillespie, saxophonist Charlie (Bird) Parker, and pianist Theolonious Monk were leading the "bop" revolution, a bold and, to many, disturbing reshaping of harmonies, rhythms, and melodies. A little while later, white bandleaders like Boyd Raeburn, Earle Spencer, and Stan Kenton began to play what they called "progressive jazz." The word "hot," which had long been a measure of jazz virtuosity, gave way to its opposite, "cool," the new epithet of highest praise. As jazz modernists urged their audiences to "Be cool, man," jazz traditionalists were reviving the styles and techniques of early New Orleans—organizing small bands that recreated the "hot" styles of King Oliver and the Original Dixieland Jazz Band.

Jazz had come a long way since the ragtime era, a long way since the days when Buddy Bolden blew his horn in New Orleans and the sound was heard miles away. It had become a diverse art form with different schools, different values, different goals—a form that was taught in universities, performed in concert halls, discussed in scholarly journals and books, celebrated in festivals. It had grown older and more diffuse, but it had lost little of its vitality. There was scarcely a popular song or hit parade record of the 1940's that was not touched in some way by jazz—by its free-swinging rhythms, its pervasive syncopation, its "blue" harmonies, its improvisation. In the early 1950's jazz continued to dominate the musical consciousness of America (and, indeed, of the whole world) as "rhythm and blues" became the newest musical fad. But rhythm and blues was nothing more than a revival of traditional Negro blues songs, and few jazz observers were surprised when, in the late 'fifties, rhythm and blues (with an emphasis on the "rhythm") evolved into rock and roll.

The influence of jazz, it seemed, was endless—but hardly surprising. From its earliest days, jazz had been more than a fad, more than a style, more than a musical passion of the moment. It was, in truth, a whole world of music—a way of creating and a way of understanding, a vehicle for expression and a key to appreciation. It was a monument to the creative genius of a race and a nation. But, unlike monuments of bronze and stone, jazz was too vital, too immediate, to be politely ignored or forgotten. It was, in its own way, a living monument, destined to survive as long as signers sing and trumpeters blow their horns.

Brian McGinty is a frequent contributor to national and regional magazines and journals. Suggestions for further reading on the history of jazz are Barry Ulanov's History of Jazz in America *(1952), Dave Dexter, Jr.'s* The Jazz Story *(1964), Dan Morgenstern's* Jazz People *(1967), and Marshall W. Stearns'* The Story of Jazz *(1956).*

From the Great Depression to World War II

"The Roaring Twenties" crashed along with the stock market in October 1929. President Herbert Hoover's periodic reassurances that the situation was temporary rang more hollow as the economy began a long slide into the worst depression in the nation's history. Having taken credit for the prosperity of the 1920s, Hoover and the Republicans understandably were blamed for the catastrophe. Hoover, by temperament and because of this faith in the capitalist system, was unwilling to do more than what amounted to placing bandages on a fracture. He and his party went down in humiliating defeat in the presidential election of 1932.

Franklin Delano Roosevelt had compiled an enviable record as governor of New York, but the truth was that virtually any Democrat would have won. FDR met the crisis with an avalanche of measures during the "first 100 days" of what became known as the "New Deal." Most of the early legislation was designed to prime the economic pump, but as time wore on more permanent reforms were enacted. Most scholars agree that the New Deal palliated the effects of the Depression but did not "cure" it. Growing opposition toward the end of the decade blocked further change, and it was the onset of war in Europe that began to restore prosperity.

President Woodrow Wilson had hoped to create a lasting peace at the end of the Great War. In reality the peace settlement planted the seeds of future conflict. Germany, Japan, and Italy were dissatisfied with the existing structure and by the 1930s began to openly challenge it. The League of Nations, which the United States had failed to join, proved a frail obstacle to the rising tide of aggression. Americans were dismayed by events abroad, but the majority were determined to avoid involvement. A series of neutrality laws were passed in hopes that the United States could remain aloof in the event of war.

President Roosevelt moved hesitantly at first but then gradually developed a growing conviction that the nation must take an active role in deterring aggressors. The United States remained deeply divided between those who advocated cooperation with the "peace loving" nations and those who sought impartial neutrality. FDR's increasingly bold steps to help Great Britain and China aroused great opposition, as critics charged he was leading the country into war. His policies remain controversial. When the Japanese bombed Pearl Harbor, however, the public united behind the war effort.

Well before the United States entered the war, American planners had concluded that Nazi Germany provided the greater threat and must be dealt with first. Even at that, the tide of Japanese expansion was halted by the naval battles of the Coral Sea and Midway in the late spring of 1942. In Europe, after delays bitterly resented by our Soviet allies, an invasion of the continent was launched on June 6, 1942. The war ended less than a year later as the Germans were crushed between the western allies and the Soviet juggernaut advancing from the east. By this time allied forces had fought their way across the Pacific and were nearing the home islands of Japan. Whether an invasion of Japan would have been necessary to compel surrender is debatable, but the dropping of atomic bombs on Hiroshima and Nagasaki proved sufficient. The bloodiest war in history was over.

Unemployment figures and other statistics are useful in gauging the impact of the Depression, but they cannot convey a feeling of what it was like for ordinary people. Even in the midst of this disaster, hard-line conservatives resisted what they considered "radical" movements. "How Hollywood Fixed an Election" tells how extraordinary campaign tactics were used to assure the defeat of writer Upton Sinclair's bid for the governorship of California. " 'Give Us Roosevelt': Workers and the New Deal Coalition" analyzes how FDR attracted the support of labor.

With the Great Depression entering its 11th year and many workers still out of work, the public was ready for a new beginning. "1940: America on the Eve of Conflict" examines what American society was like on the eve of World War II.

The United States was the only major nation in the war to escape physical destruction. During the early months of the war, however, many Americans feared that the Japanese might attack the West Coast. Longstanding racial dislike of Japanese-Americans erupted into hysteria after Pearl Harbor. In February 1942, FDR signed an executive order that resulted in the internment of 110,000 people of Japanese ancestry—60 percent of whom were American citizens. "An American Tragedy" tells this story, and of recent efforts of make amends.

Roosevelt's description of America as the "arsenal of democracy" became a reality as the war went on and the economy produced staggering amounts of matériel for itself and its allies. The combination of booming production and the induction of millions of white males into the armed forces resulted in unprecedented opportunities for those who previously had not been part of the industrial workforce. "Rosie the Riveter Remembers" consists of reminiscences by women of the experiences they had in holding jobs previously reserved for men.

Looking Ahead: Challenge Questions

Although the Great Depression threw millions of people out of work or cost them their farms through no fault of their own, individuals suffered psychological damage as well as physical deprivation. Discuss what it must have been like for husbands to lose their positions as breadwinners and for parents to be unable to provide for their children. Try also to evaluate how Franklin D. Roosevelt appeared as a champion to workers and their families.

Americans of German and Italian ancestry were not relocated during World War II. Why were those of Japanese ancestry?

Many women had not held jobs outside the home before World War II. What did some of them learn about themselves when called upon to do "men's work"?

How Hollywood Fixed An Election

It took fake newsreels, extortion and intimidation, but industry moguls derailed Upton Sinclair's "Bolshevist" campaign for governor—and forever altered the conduct of American politics.

Greg Mitchell

VOTE SOCIALIST
"FOR PEACE, FREEDOM and PROSPERITY FOR ALL"

UPTON SINCLAIR   CHAIM SHAPIRO

NOT POLITICIANS, BUT SOCIAL ENGINEERS, UNDERSTANDING THE NEEDS OF HUMANITY. DEVOTING THEIR LIVES TO THE CAUSE OF SOCIALISM HAS MADE THEM BETTER MEN. WHEN VOTING FOR THEM YOU ARE NOT ONLY VOTING FOR REAL MEN BUT ALSO FOR THE PRINCIPLES FOR WHICH THEY STAND

FOR GOVERNOR
UPTON SINCLAIR
FOR LIEUTENANT GOVERNOR
CHAIM SHAPIRO

We Demand | Freedom of Mooney and Billings
Unemployment Insurance   Five-Day Week
Abolition of Capitol Punishment
Abolition of Child Labor   Six-Hour Day
Public Ownership of Power and Natural Resources | We Demand

VOTE SOCIALIST

Up-to-Date Print Shop — 221 S. Spring St., Room 306

Greg Mitchell researched the EPIC campaign for about six years.

SHORTLY AFTER election day, 1934, a number of celebrities gathered at a party given by noted Hollywood liberals Fredric March and his wife, Florence Eldridge. Many of the guests were still angry about what had transpired during the fall campaign for governor of California. One after another they denounced the movie industry for its role in defeating Democratic candidate Upton Sinclair, muckraking author and prominent socialist.

The guests charged that studio executives had coerced their employees into contributing to a secret slush fund and threatened writers (such as Dorothy Parker) and stars (including Katharine Hepburn) with dismissal if they supported Sinclair. The Hollywood moguls bankrolled an unprecedented smear campaign, utilizing press agents and advertising consultants imported all the way from New York. They had even made spectacular threats to move the entire film industry to Florida if Sinclair was elected.

Most disturbingly, the studio bosses had, for the first time, used the power of the silver screen against a candidate for political office. *The Hollywood Reporter* had labelled this "the most effective piece of political humdingery that has ever been effected." No one knew who was behind the outrageous newsreels that helped scuttle Sinclair's "End

From *American Film*, November 1988, pp. 26-31. Copyright © 1988 by Billboard Publications, Inc.

Poverty in California" (EPIC) crusade, but speculation centered on MGM's Louis B. Mayer, vice-chairman of the state's Republican Party.

Then, as the denunciations from the guests died down, Irving Thalberg—"Boy Wonder" producer at MGM and model for F. Scott Fitzgerald's *The Last Tycoon*—quietly admitted that, "I made those shorts."

The guests reeled in disbelief. Thalberg, a former socialist, was now believed to be apolitical.

"But it was a dirty trick!" Fredric March protested, referring to the newsreels. "It was the damnedest unfair thing I've ever heard of."

"Nothing," Thalberg replied, "is unfair in politics . . ."

Fair or not, the success of the movie industry's attack on Upton Sinclair had a profound effect on subsequent political campaigns. It marked the first use of motion pictures to influence an election, the "first all-out public relations Blitzkrieg in American politics," as historian Arthur Schlesinger Jr. put it. "In another twenty years," he observed, "the techniques of manipulation employed so crudely in 1934 would spread East, achieve a new refinement and begin to dominate the politics of the nation." Not to mention Europe.

When Upton Sinclair, popular author of *The Jungle*, announced his candidacy for governor in September 1933, no one in Tinseltown was alarmed. Sinclair had just gone broke financing the filming of Sergei Eisenstein's ill-fated *Que Viva Mexico*. In two previous campaigns for governor, Sinclair had gathered barely 50,000 votes running as a Socialist.

However, this time, in a bid to broaden his appeal, the amiable, 55-year-old Sinclair was running as a Democrat at a time when the Depression was deepening; 300,000 people were out of work in the Los Angeles area alone. And Sinclair had come up with a catchy program to "End Poverty in California."

The EPIC plan called for, among other things, higher property taxes, a steeply graduated income tax, and a special tax on movie studios. But Sinclair also proposed putting the unemployed to work in idle factories, or in the case of Hollywood, empty studios. This would have catapulted the state of California into the picture-making business. Sinclair said he would ask Charlie Chaplin to take charge of production. "We don't intend to interfere with capitalistic industry," Sinclair

said, while vowing to make pictures "superior to those now being produced by private enterprise."

Naturally, this kind of talk did not go over well with the studio heads, most of whom were known to be politically reactionary (Jack Warner being the notable exception). The industry was just pulling out of a recession and the studio bosses had no intention of yielding power or profits to a Socialist in Democratic clothing. Billy Wilder, who had only recently come to Hollywood from Austria, observed that Sinclair seemed to scare the hell out of the community. "They all thought him to be a most dangerous Bolshevik beast."

Still, they were not very concerned until August 1934, when Sinclair unexpectedly swept the Democratic primary in a landslide, and appeared headed for the governorship. Then the moguls swung into action.

Louis B. Mayer was in Europe the summer of 1934 but when urgent cables and telephone messages alerted him to what was happening, he denounced Sinclair and threatened to move at least part of MGM's production to New York if the Socialist was elected.

Most of the other bosses followed Mayer's cue. "The studios only acted in concert when it would benefit them all," recalled Joseph L. Mankiewicz, a budding screenwriter at the time. A September 17 article in *The Hollywood Reporter* declared that at least four, and possibly six, major studios were threatening to "close their doors" and move East. Paramount, for example, would purportedly move back to Astoria, Queens, while Columbia and Universal would return to studios they had once used in Ft. Lee, New Jersey.

A short time later the trades reported that New York was out of the question due to high taxes and real estate prices. Florida then became the potential new haven. The Sunshine State was so intent on welcoming the orphans from Hollywood that its legislature placed on the November ballot an amendment calling for a fifteen-year tax exemption for movie studios. Real estate speculators began buying land. Another sunny city, Phoenix, offered free land to the studios. A kind of Gold Rush in reverse was on. *Time* magazine labelled it "California Here I Run."

On October 1, 1934, the United Press reported that "Louis B. Mayer, head of the Metro-Goldwyn-Mayer Corporation, is rushing home on the liner *Paris* to organize the fight of the film industry

against Upton Sinclair's candidacy for Governor." Five days later, Mayer reached Los Angeles and offered his "services," as he put it, to Sinclair's opponent, Frank Merriam, the incumbent. "From the day of Mayer's arrival in California," the *New Yorker* would later comment, "Sinclair was a doomed politician."

By the time Mayer reached Hollywood, the studios' threat to move to Florida had run out of steam. The danger of a pull-out lost credibility when several of the studios began building new sound stages in Hollywood. Frank Scully in *Variety* called on the movie industry "to mind its own business, put its own house in order and stick to making pictures." Sinclair had mocked the idea from the beginning. "Think of what those big Florida mosquitoes would do to some of our screen sirens," Sinclair remarked. "Why, one bite on the nose could bring a $50,000 production loss."

Mayer realized that the moguls would have to go beyond mere threats and rhetoric if they were to defeat Sinclair. Mayer concocted a scheme to finance an effective smear campaign whereby every MGM employee, from writers and actors to stenographers, would be asked to donate one day's pay to the campaign of Sinclair's Republican opponent. Although Sam Marx, story editor at MGM, says the contribution was voluntary, "a suggestion from the executive suite," most lower-ranking employees believed that they had to contribute or risk losing their jobs. Blank checks, made out to Mayer, were distributed among employees at some of the studios.

At Columbia, the set department built a huge thermometer and as studio employees contributed to the stop-Sinclair fund, the red line approached the 100 percent mark. According to screenwriter John Wexley, Columbia's Harry Cohn "threatened everyone. Robert Riskin and Frank Capra didn't want to contribute but they finally gave in." Cohn told Wexley that if he did not contribute to Merriam he would be "marked lousy"—blacklisted. The last holdouts, in Wexley's recollection, were himself and screenwriter John Henry Lawson, "and finally he [Cohn] fired Jack."

The rank-and-file at Warner Brothers were simply assessed a modest $3 each by studio head Jack Warner, a Democrat. Overall the levy generated half a million dollars, an enormous sum for a state political campaign in the 1930s.

Several stars rebelled against enforced contributions, including James Cagney, Jean Harlow and Katharine Hepburn.

For her impertinence, Hepburn was reportedly threatened with dismissal. The star's father, perhaps attempting to take the heat off her, announced that Hepburn actually favored Merriam.

Yet the only big star to actually campaign for the EPIC candidate was Charlie Chaplin. Chaplin, who considered Sinclair his "mentor" in the study of socialism, took time out from filming *Modern Times* to speak for Sinclair at meetings and rallies, and reportedly contributed money to his campaign.

But Chaplin was up against the full power of the movie industry. The studios' slush fund became a key factor in the campaign. Hundreds of billboards, dozens of phony anti-Sinclair front groups, thousands of leaflets and countless newspaper ads and radio programs were paid for by the fund, all with the purpose of smearing Sinclair in the most vicious way.

Sinclair was accused of being out to "Sovietize" California. His followers were referred to as a "maggot-like horde." Sinclair was said to be a "Bolshevik beast," a "dynamiter of churches" who was in favor of "nationalizing children." He was compared, sometimes unfavorably, to Hitler, Stalin and Mussolini. Screenwriter John Bright recalls advising Sinclair to buy time on radio to rebut the smears. But Sinclair, he says, "thought it was all nonsense."

Orchestrating this campaign of villification and innuendo was the prominent Los Angeles advertising firm, Lord and Thomas. Press agents were imported to design campaign strategy, perhaps the first time this had ever been done. Heading the GOP effort were Louis B. Mayer and state Republican chairman Earl Warren (a future governor of California and chief justice of the U.S. Supreme Court).

Having successfully tapped their employees for funds, the studio execs wanted to make sure they would also vote the right way on election day. Signs exhorting a huge turnout for Merriam were posted around the studio lots. Anyone backing Sinclair risked retaliation. When screenwriter Dorothy Parker spoke up for Sinclair, she was reportedly told, "you're cutting your own throat."

At one studio an official called in a group of screenwriters and instructed them to shun Sinclair. "After all," he told them, "what does Sinclair know about anything? He's just a writer."

As election day grew near, a sign was posted above the time clock at one studio, reading: "If you expect to punch this a week from now, don't vote for Sinclair."

These tactics outraged many of Hollywood's top young screenwriters, such as John Bright, Allen Rivkin and Philip Dunne. Rivkin, who wrote *The Farmer's Daughter,* among other films, formed an authors' committee which raised funds for Sinclair. "We rebelled," Rivkin recalls, "simply because we felt the man [Sinclair] had the right to a fair campaign and that we had the right to speak for ourselves. It was democracy in action and a rebellion against the control of the studios over our non-studio life." Rivkin and Dunne credit this protest with spurring the formation of the Screen Writers' Guild, which had held its first exploratory meetings only the year before.

Some writers, however, went along with efforts to enlist them in the Merriam campaign. Joseph Mankiewicz, who was then writing scripts for Joan Crawford at MGM, contributed at least one anti-Sinclair skit to the "Young Crusaders" radio show, according to *The Hollywood Reporter.* Mankiewicz has no specific recollection of this but remembers he found Sinclair's ideas "nutsy," and recalls writing "simple-minded" radio scripts warning people that they might "have their swimming pools uprooted and taken away."

Meanwhile, studio personnel were hard at work creating the notorious fake newsreels that would destroy Sinclair's chances once and for all. On September 18, 1934, *Variety* had issued a call—"with theatres available to provide Sinclair opposition, so far as propaganda is concerned, let the picture business assert itself"—and the studios responded. At least two studios (MGM and Fox), and possibly others, produced anti-Sinclair trailers. Newsreels had previously played little role in electoral politics, and only rarely had propaganda raised its ugly head.

It is impossible to identify with certainty the architect of the "bogus newsreel" scheme. By the time Mayer returned from Europe, Thalberg had already ordered writer Carey Wilson and director Felix Feist Jr. to start shooting. Mayer may have given the orders from abroad. "All Mayer would have had to do was call his secretary, Ida Koverman, from Europe," Sam Marx observes, "and things would have gotten rolling."

Whether as creator or executioner, Thalberg's involvement in the anti-Sinclair production was ironic. Just three years earlier he had paid Sinclair $20,000 for rights to his novel, *The Wet Parade.* "Buy it," Thalberg had told Sam Marx, "but keep that Bolshevik out of the studio." After the picture was made, Thalberg paid Sinclair another $10,000 to develop a second film for MGM, to be entitled *The Star-Spangled Banner.* Sinclair had rechristened the project *The Gold-Spangled Banner,* and it never got off the ground.

A third suspect in the case of the bogus newsreels was William Randolph Hearst. His California newspapers led the attack on Sinclair, whom Hearst considered "an unbalanced and unscrupulous political speculator," and it was Hearst's Metrotone Newsreels, distributed by MGM, which carried the anti-Sinclair material. MGM had also been producing films featuring Marion Davies. Hearst could have dreamed up the newsreel scheme and passed the idea along to Mayer or Thalberg.

What is known for certain is that Felix Feist Jr. took camera and sound crews up and down the state, filming a series of shorts featuring "The Inquiring Reporter." The raw film was processed through MGM's lab, edited down to six minutes, and added to the Metrotone Newsreels, which were then supplied free of charge to theaters throughout California twice a week. According to John Bright, who wrote Jimmy Cagney's *The Public Enemy,* Mayer "blackmailed" the theatres into showing the trailers by threatening to withhold MGM features from them if they did not.

The newsreels were "expertly done," Sam Marx says, just subtle enough to have an enormous impact. Asked by the Inquiring Reporter who they favored in the campaign, respectable and well-dressed citizens invariably selected Merriam. A nice old lady, sitting in a rocking chair on her front porch, said she would vote for Merriam because she wanted to "save my little home."

Those who backed Sinclair scratched themselves, stammered or rubbed their bleary eyes. A shaggy man with whiskers and fanaticism in his eyes favored Sinclair because "his system vorked vell in Russia, vy can't it vork here?" And so it went.

According to the *New York Times,* low-paid "bit" players reading prepared scripts took the part of Merriam or Sinclair supporters. But some observers, such as MGM's Sam Marx, believe that the newsreels' vivid bias was achieved through selective editing, with "respectable people who favored Sinclair left on the cutting room floor."

Staged or merely one-sided, the effect of the newsreels was to make many of those in the audience leaning to Sin-

> "THE THREATS
> AGAINST US WERE REAL,
> NOT EMPTY.
> THE STUDIOS TOLERATED
> NO NONSENSE.
> YOU DID IT THEIR WAY
> OR GOT OUT."

clair feel that they no longer wanted to be associated with him.

Sinclair called for a congressional investigation of the motion picture industry's activities. Undeterred, the studios tried for a knockout blow, producing newsreels showing a legion of hoboes—or actors in whiskers and rags—trudging across California or arriving by rail, seeking admission to the EPIC utopia. At the same time, photos depicting the same mass immigration started appearing on the front pages of the "news photos" as a still from a Frankie Darro movie, *Wild Boys of the Road*—thoughtfully provided to the newspapers by Warner Brothers. Another pho-

to had been staged using actors straight from central casting.

◄§ §►

By election day it was clear that Upton Sinclair was a beaten man. In a front-page column, *Hollywood Reporter* editor/publisher W.R. Wilkerson gushed: "Never before in the history of the picture business has the screen been used in direct support of a candidate. . . . It will undoubtedly give the bigwigs in Washington and politicians all over the country an idea of the real POWER that is in the hands of the picture industry." Wilkerson, according to Allen Rivkin, "took instructions from the studios throughout the campaign, and got lots of advertising from the studios in appreciation."

Final election returns gave Merriam the edge over Sinclair by more than 250,000 votes. The wonder of it all, considering the studios' scare-campaign, was that Sinclair got as many votes as he did—900,000—and that 30 EPIC candidates were elected to the state legislature. As much as $10 million, for over 40 years the most ever spent in a state campaign, had been expended to defeat Sinclair. Much of it was raised or contributed by the film industry.

On election night, Frank Merriam thanked Louis B. Mayer for his "splendid" hard work. Two days later, a *Hol-*

lywood Reporter headline boomed: "With Sinclair Danger Gone/Studios Announce New Pix/And Add To Their Personnel." A few days after that, the big news was that David O. Selznick was leaving MGM and Harpo Marx, of all people, had agreed to do a "voice test." All was right again in Tinseltown.

In 1938, when Merriam ran for re-election, an army of Hollywood actors, writers and directors, led by people like Melvyn Douglas and Philip Dunne, mobilized to defeat him. "After 1934," Dunne recalls, "we said, 'Never again.' EPIC created a liberal climate in California for the first time." The liberals raised money, printed leaflets, put on radio shows and held rallies for Culbert Olson, the Democratic nominee, who had been elected to the state senate as an EPIC candidate four years earlier. In a classic gesture, the Hollywood Democrats asked Governor Merriam to contribute one day of *his* salary to *their* campaign fund.

Olson won the election, becoming the state's first Democratic governor in forty years. One pro-Merriam movie producer remarked sadly: "I guess we started something in 1934."

Indeed, the EPIC campaign, concluded Arthur Schlesinger, "marked a new advance in the art of public relations in which advertising men now believed they could sell or destroy political candidates as they sold one brand of soap or defamed its competitors."

'GIVE US ROOSEVELT' WORKERS AND THE NEW DEAL COALITION

Bruce Nelson traces how the magic of FDR and his practical social programmes welded American labour to the Democratic Party, and discusses the tensions that eventually weakened that union.

Happy days are here again – clothing workers at a 'Re-elect FDR' rally in Baltimore, 1936.

Bruce Nelson is Assistant Professor of History at Dartmouth College, New Hampshire, and the author of Workers on the Waterfront *(University of Illinois Press, 1988).*

Nearly forty-five years after his death, Franklin D. Roosevelt's reputation as one of the greatest vote-getters in the history of American politics remains intact. His smashing victory over Alf Landon in 1936 marked not only the zenith of his own popularity and power but a decisive step in the major political realignment that made the Democrats the nation's majority party after nearly forty years of Republican dominance. Although FDR attracted support from many sectors of the population, workers constituted the heart of the Roosevelt coalition.

Before the 1930s American workers had seldom if ever voted as a bloc at the national level. Cultural, ethnic, and racial divisions had driven them into different electoral camps. However, an erratic but increasingly persistent trend toward a more unified labour vote had begun developing early in the twentieth century. By 1928, the votes of urban, foreign-stock, and largely working-class voters for the Democrat Al Smith had provided a clear harbinger of the realignment that would become evident with Roosevelt's defeat of Herbert Hoover in 1932 and would solidify during his presidency.

In 1936 FDR won a then unprecedented 60.8 per cent of the popular vote and outpolled Landon by 523 to 8 in the electoral college. His landslide victory reflected the apparent willingness of the New Deal to 'deliver the goods' to the working class and to millions of other Americans who had suffered unprecedented losses during the depths of the Great Depression. The administration's commitment to relief payments and public works projects for the unemployed and hungry, along with the passage of the Social Security and National Labor Relation Acts, convinced working people that the president was on their side. Critics on the left could point out that even at its peak the principal federal relief agency provided jobs for

First published in *History Today*, January 1990, pp. 40-48. Reproduced by kind permission of History Today, Ltd., 83-84 Berwick Street, London W1V 3PJ, England.

only about a quarter of those counted as unemployed. But working people revered the president not only for what he had done, but for the things he wanted to do that remained undone, for the contrast between a compassionate FDR and an apparently uncaring and immobile predecessor, for the hatred he generated among the wealthy and others who were identified as oppressors of the 'forgotten man'. As major sectors of corporate capital went all out to defeat Roosevelt in 1936, he deftly sharpened the lines of division to his advantage with a series of verbal assaults on 'organised money' and the 'economic royalists'. Desperately, Republican nominee Alf Landon protested that the president was violating sacred American norms by injecting class conflict into the realm of politics. But Roosevelt's strategy worked brilliantly. In the aftermath of the election, the anonymous interviewee who stated that 'Mr. Roosevelt is the only man we ever had in the White House who would understand that my boss is a son-of-a-bitch' apparently spoke for millions of his fellow workers.

However, the euphoria of 1936 quickly gave way to unanticipated stumbling blocks that would bedevil the president's second administration and cast a long shadow on the 1940 election. Bitter class conflict – generated by virulent employer resistance to the aggressive organising campaigns of the Committee for Industrial Organization, or CIO – threatened to shatter the new and fragile Roosevelt coalition; another sharp economic downturn, dubbed the 'Roosevelt recession', rapidly eroded the president's aura of invincibility. By the end of 1938, attempts to implement the New Deal's increasingly social-democratic intellectual premises had run up against the impenetrable political reality of an effective congressional bloc of Republicans and conservative Democrats who were determined to thwart any new social welfare initiatives. In addition, the coming of war in Europe turned Roosevelt's priorities away from domestic reform and towards a new politics of national unity, which meant the embrace of prominent individuals in the business community who were ambivalent at best about the New Deal but shared the president's determination to mobilise the nation to resist the expansion of German power.

Moreover, by 1940, in sharp contrast to 1936, a number of organised labour's most influential spokesmen bitterly condemned Roosevelt's course and outspokenly opposed his re-election. The outstanding example is John L. Lewis, the charismatic leader of the United Mine Workers and the CIO, who believed that the president had betrayed his working-class supporters by remaining aloof from the bloody class warfare in the steel industry during the spring and summer of 1937. Lewis' disenchantment only increased as the second Roosevelt administration unfolded, and in October 1940 he went on nationwide radio and called upon the CIO faithful to join him in voting for the Republican candidate, Wendell Willkie. The Communists and their sympathisers, who held leadership positions in a number of important CIO unions could not bring themselves to swallow Willkie and the Republicans, but by 1940 they had turned against the president and were calling upon their followers to sit out the election.

Roosevelt broke the third term taboo and won a comfortable 55 per cent of the popular vote, in an election where the 'index of class polarisation' reached its highest point in American history. Compared to 1936, there was a decline in the level of support for FDR among virtually every segment of the population. The president lost from a quarter to a third of the votes of white-collar workers and the middle classes generally. But the erosion of working-class support was much smaller. Overall, in 1940 as in 1936, blue-collar workers voted overwhelmingly for FDR and were a critical factor in his continued success. Moreover, in spite of the stance of Lewis and a number of popular left-wing unionists, the CIO rank and file, which included the most militant and radicalised sectors of the American working class, were among Roosevelt's strongest supporters. According to a Gallup poll taken shortly after the election, 79 per cent of CIO members voted for the president, along with 71 per cent of the membership of the more conservative American Federation of Labor and 64 per cent of non-union workers. After taking the pulse of the electorate, journalist Samuel Lubell declared that 1940 signified 'a class-conscious vote for the first time in American history... The New Deal appears to have accomplished what the Socialists, the IWW, and the Communists never could approach. It has drawn a class line across the face of American politics'.

Although it needs to be placed in a larger context, Lubell's interpretation of the 1940 presidential election makes a good deal of sense. Workers' enthusiastic identification with Franklin Roosevelt was, in many instances, entirely compatible with a class-conscious view of American society and politics. At a time when a lively and combative sense of 'us' versus 'them' prevailed among millions of American workers, the overwhelming majority regarded the patrician FDR as one of 'us'. This was true not only of the allegedly conservative immigrant groups in the ethnic enclaves around Detroit and Pittsburgh, but of militant miners in the coalfields and radicalised maritime workers on the Pacific coast. At the local and state levels, electoral politics sometimes continued to fragment the working-class vote; it seemed to accentuate the heterogeneity of American workers and the unevenness of their consciousness. Roosevelt was the one political figure who was consistently able to transcend these tendencies. In the electoral arena, at least, he galvanised and unified working-class sentiment in a way that the leadership of organised labour could only dream of.

An examination of the Amalgamated Clothing Workers (ACW), one of the most important CIO affiliates, will demonstrate, first, the depth and character of working-class attachment to FDR; second, the way in which a fiercely independent union, with a strong tradition of left-wing political commitment, became wedded not only to Roosevelt but to the Democratic Party; and third, how the New Deal served to hasten the integration of major sections of the working class into the mainstream of American society. Integration into the American mainstream had, to some degree, been the goal of CIO unions like the Amalgamated Clothing Workers all along. But as an insurgent movement that successfully challenged some of the world's most powerful corporations, and an industrial union federation that included a leadership cadre of deeply committed left-wingers and a mass base of millions, the CIO also contained within itself the seeds of an American social democracy. The fact that those seeds failed to take root and grow is well known. The reason for that failure continues to divide historians and other students of American society.

In the course of the 1930s, Sidney Hillman, the dynamic and influential president of the Amalgamated, developed especially close ties to the Roosevelt administration, and by 1940 the entire ACW leadership was passionately committed to FDR's re-election. Without it, they argued, not only the continued economic well-being of American workers, but the survival of organised labour, and even of democratic institutions in general, would be placed in serious jeopardy.

This unashamed allegiance to a representative of one of the mainstream political parties was relatively new in the Amalgamated. Forged out of the struggles of twenty-six nationality groups against sweatshop conditions in the men's clothing industry, and led from the outset by Hillman, who had twice been imprisoned for revolutionary activity in Tsarist Russia, the Amalgamated had long been proud of its reputation for independence and innovation. Reflecting the cultural traditions of its Jewish members, the union had a longstanding commitment to socialism and labour-party politics. But while paying lip-service to such sentiments, Hillman had endeavoured for many years to build a cross-class alliance in which the independent initiative of labour would be augmented by the enlightened self-interest of liberal employers and the expertise and influence of progressive reformers.

The Depression had sorely tested the mettle of the ACW and its needle-trades constituency. However, with the coming of the Roosevelt presidency the Amalgamated prospered, adding 50,000 new members in 1933 alone and significantly expanding the union's geographical reach. During FDR's first term, the key indicators in the men's clothing industry improved dramatically, and Hillman himself flourished as a presidentially-appointed member of various New Deal agencies. From this position of bureaucratic responsibility, he lost all patience with left-wing and liberal critics of the Roosevelt administration, whom he dismissed as 'dreamers' who would 'destroy' what labour had built up over the years while they waited for the 'revolution'.

In April 1936 Hillman met the members of the Amalgamated's General Executive Board and tried to bring them into line with the new realities of American politics as he perceived them. Since its founding in 1914, the ACW had never formally endorsed a candidate for the presidency of the United States. Now, however, in the face of what Hillman would characterise as 'the most important presidential campaign of this century', there could be no clinging to the union's socialist past. Since the coming of the Roosevelt administration, he declared, something new had happened. 'We have participated in making the labour policy of this administration.' To Hillman, it was obvious that '[our gains] would have been totally impossible' without the New Deal and FDR. With Roosevelt in the White House, 'and with this group of people in the CIO', he said, 'we could really get somewhere'.

Hillman's argument called the day. A month later, at the ACW's convention, the General Executive Board and the Committee on Political Action recommended that the union actively support efforts to promote 'independent political action for labour'. But, in a major break with tradition, they also recommended that the Amalgamated officially endorse FDR's bid for re-election. 'This endorsement is limited to the support of President Roosevelt', the resolution declared, 'and does not apply to any other candidates on the Democratic ticket'. When some of the union's 'doctrinaires' objected to supporting a representative of a 'capitalist' political party, one delegate after another rose to announce that the accomplishments of the Roosevelt presidency, and the threat of fascism, required a new direction. 'It was through Roosevelt that we organized in Connecticut and got better conditions', said Stella Gedja. Today, said August Bellanca of New York City, 'the question is not Franklin Roosevelt or the Socialist Party; the question is concentration camps or liberty'.

Others argued that whatever the convention delegates decided, the ACW's greatly expanded membership would vote for Roosevelt anyway.

On strike; neckwear
workers in Pennsylvania,
October 1936 – an echo
of the class-conscious
activism that
characterised politics in
the 30s.

'The membership', Hillman had reminded the executive board earlier, 'is just a cross section of the country... We could vote to support the Socialist Party, but our members would still vote Tammany'. As painful as this realisation was, Hillman did not shrink from its implications. 'The membership', he said, 'is closer to realities.' As Abraham Chatman, a member of the General Executive Board from upstate New York, warned, 'nine thousand organized clothing workers in the City of Rochester, whether you decide for or against this resolution, are going to vote for Franklin D. Roosevelt'; and the same would be true 'in Buffalo, in Utica, in Syracuse, and everywhere'.

Although a New York City delegate counselled that it was time to 'lay our traditions aside' and 'be realistic in these matters', many speakers expressed the belief that endorsing Roosevelt was not incompatible with the union's longstanding goal of building a labour party. Sarah Borinsky of Baltimore, who had 'always voted the Socialist ticket since the time when I was eligible to vote', argued that now it was necessary to support Roosevelt, because he would help enact the social legislation that workers desired. But after the election, she said, 'we hope for a labour party that will enable us to legislate these things for ourselves'.

As FDR's second term evolved and ultimately hedged on its commitment to social reform – even as Roosevelt found it politically necessary to distance himself from the CIO – Hillman swallowed hard and declared unequivocally that the President 'has kept faith with the people'. In January 1940 he announced that the Amalgamated would gladly support Roosevelt again should he decide to run for a third term. In the face of clear evidence to the contrary, he declared: 'Has there been any retreat from the policies and programs of... the New Deal? There has been none'.

The Amalgamated Convention in May 1940 became an emotional demonstration of support for Roosevelt's re-election. When the Committee on Political Action recommended the drafting of the president for a third term, bedlam broke out on the convention floor. The delegates paraded around Madison Square Garden, stamped their feet, and chanted 'We Want Roosevelt', for more than an hour. In the subsequent discussion of the committee's recommendation, the attitude expressed toward FDR was one of awe and even worship. Nicholas Firello, of Minersville, Pennsylvania, declared that 'mere words cannot be used in eulogizing this great humanitarian', but many of his fellow delegates were willing to try. For Ida Warhof, of

Cincinnati, 'God ha[s] blessed America with Franklin Delano Roosevelt'. For others, he was not only 'our beloved President', but 'that great leader of humanity', 'the greatest spokesman for democracy the world over', and even 'that great humanitarian Messiah'. Almost overcome by the euphoric demonstration on the president's behalf, Sam Smith of Chicago told his fellow delegates:

I heard you yell and holler and stamp, 'We Want Roosevelt.' And in my very ears there echoes the sound of the words, and the valleys and mountains, the lakes and the oceans, and the very earth and the high heavens echo it. They seem to cry out to me, 'Give Us Roosevelt.'

The contrast between the 1936 and 1940 conventions is instructive. In 1936, the delegates had enthusiastically supported FDR, and had expressed respect and affection for him and his record. For the great majority the clear priority had been Roosevelt's re-election. But the tone of the discussion had been much less worshipful, and many delegates had also argued that endorsing FDR was entirely compatible with the union's historic commitment to independent political action. In 1940, however, there was little if any mention of a labour party. The final convention resolution on political action called only for 'vigorous participation by organized labour in the political life of the nation'.

Len De Caux, a left-winger and Lewis partisan, was at the 1940 convention in his capacity as editor of the *CIO News*. At every chance, he recalled:

'...with or without pretext, the band struck up 'God Bless America,' and all joined in singing it. The delegates... sang fervently, and with relish, sucking in deeply the sweetness of the repeated 'God Bless America, my home sweet home!'

De Caux found it 'too emotional for my taste'. But in retrospect at least, he understood the source of the delegates' fervour. Like Hillman, 'these were mostly long-Americanized Jewish immigrants. They had come from countries of anti-Semitism, feudal backwardness, political despotism'. With the Amalgamated as their weapon, and Roosevelt as their patron on high, they had fought despotic American employers and won a better life for themselves. Now Hitler was conquering the countries of their birth and annihilating their kinsfolk and co-religionists. It was a grim moment, but they could take comfort from the fact that 'their America was defended by Roosevelt in the White House, with Hillman at his side. Their emotions overflowed in this song'.

De Caux's recollection touches on a point of fundamental importance. Hillman and his executive board could shape the convention resolutions to their specifications, but they couldn't supply the emotional fervour that flowed from the delegates. In the minds of these immigrants and children of immigrants, the CIO, the New Deal, and above all Roosevelt, had made it possible for them to enter the mainstream of American life. As a woman from Georgia put it, 'This little union book gave me the right to citizenship in my industry, and this little union book also demonstrates that I am in partnership with the President of the United States'. In the face of that kind of sentiment, any talk of repudiating Roosevelt, from the Left or the Right, was bound to come up against a stone wall.

Even though Roosevelt and the New Deal were instruments of cultural integration, the process was one that involved bitter contention between and within social classes. What is striking about the thirties, in industry after industry, is that beyond questions of wages, hours, and union recognition, the very meaning of America and Americanism was at stake. People who had lived on the margins of American society, who had been victimised for generations by nativism and anti-Semitism and class prejudice, were finally standing up and saying to the self-appointed keepers of the national seal, '*We* are Americans, too'. More than that, they were implying that their industrial and political adversaries were downright un-American'. In Thomas Bell's novel *Out of This Furnace*, set in the steel towns of western Pennsylvania, steelworker Dobie Dobrejcak suddenly realised that even though he and his fellow CIO organisers were not Protestant, middle-class, and Anglo-Saxon, they were 'thinking and talking like Americans'. 'Maybe not the kind of American that came over on the *Mayflower*', he reflected, but 'Made in U.S.A.' nonetheless.

I'm almost as much a product of that mill down there as any rail or ingot they ever turned out... If I'm anything at all, I'm an American, only not the kind you read about in history books or that they make speeches about on the Fourth of July; anyway, not yet.

To seize the mantle of Americanism, then, was not incompatible with a continuing consciousness of social and political division rooted in the class experience of workers, from the New York City garment district to the steel mills of western Pennsylvania. But having chosen to justify themselves and their struggles in these terms, workers and their unions would soon run up against an enormous obstacle when the international conflict between the United States and the Soviet Union, and the domestic ravages engendered by McCarthyism, recast the debate over Americanism in ways that were sharply disadvantageous to the forces of working-class insurgency. Indeed, the Cold War and McCarthyism would change the meaning of the struggle between 'us' and 'them' in basic ways. As Walter Dean Burnham has reminded us, the results of the Second World War, and of the national liberation struggles in the Third World thereafter, 'were to create a kind of worldwide sectionalism', meaning that domestic 'vertical conflict' over the allocation of the fruits of American society was increasingly superseded by 'horizontal conflict' between the people of the United States on the one hand and the Soviet Union and the emerging nation states of the Third World on the other. Insofar as this conflict was pitched in terms of a Manichean struggle between good and evil, says Burnham, its 'restricting effects on the development of political alternatives at home were, and remain, enormous'.

For organised labour, this development would indeed have enormous consequences several years before Joseph McCarthy seized the centre stage of domestic hysteria in February 1950. As early as 1946, 'Red-baiting' was used to devastating effect in heading off 'Operation Dixie', an aggressive CIO campaign designed to organise the South and thereby undercut the regional and racial inequality that had haunted the labour movement and would continue to do so for years to come. Soon thereafter, in 1949-50, the CIO expelled eleven of its own unions – comprising about 20 per cent of the industrial union federation's total membership – because the leaders of those unions were allegedly 'dominated' by the Communist party. At the same time, in the United Auto Workers, the largest and most important union in the CIO, a decade of vibrant and often chaotic multi-party democracy came to an end with the triumph of Walter Reuther and the subsequent purge of the union's sizable left wing. 'Americanism', once again, had become a weapon of exclusion and an instrument for the imposition of narrow ideological conformity. Although the experience of class would continue to be distinctive, more than ever before the articulation of the political and social aspirations of workers would be confined within the straitjacketing framework of Cold War dogma.

This narrow framework would have an especially significant impact in the realm of electoral politics. In regard to the possibility of independent labour politics in the 1930s and beyond, the issue must be addressed not only in terms of the role of the trade union leadership in shortcircuiting such a development but also from the standpoint of the electoral behaviour of workers, especially in those instances where there seemed to be a possibility of translating working-class insurgency at the 'point of production' into political power. Here the record of the thirties – in industrial cities and towns such as Detroit, Akron, and Aliquippa (Pennsylvania) – reveals the unevenness of workers' consciousness and the continuing fragmentation of the labour vote at the local level.

Perhaps a more unified, patient, and ideologically independent trade union leadership could have changed this pattern. But there always seemed to be a crisis at hand propelling labour into the arms of the Democrats. (Often, the crisis was the prospect of a Republican electoral victory.) For nearly a decade after 1940, progressive unionists would recommend 'consideration of the possible need of a new labour party later on', as three CIO officials put it in 1943. But when the moment of truth came, the 'new labour party' was always a project for the future. And by 1950 'later on' had apparently become 'never'.

The role of Hillman and his ACW lieutenants in this regard is crystal clear and somewhat ironic. As recently as 1934 it had been commonplace for delegates to the Amalgamated's biennial convention to call for the formation of 'a Labour party completely divorced from the old political parties'. But by 1936 there was a growing sense that the union's objectives – in the economic and electoral arenas – should be essentially defensive, and that only Roosevelt could serve as labour's sword and shield in the struggle to ward off capitalist reaction. At the 1936 convention, when a delegate from New York City declared that the Amalagamated should support FDR in order to 'save our bread and butter and try to avoid fascist rule in America', he received a standing ovation. By 1940 Dorothy Bellanca, an ACW vice-president, was arguing that 'Roosevelt does not need us; it is we who need Roosevelt'. And, according to his premier biographer, Hillman himself was more willing than ever 'to trust the fate of labour to Roosevelt, to in effect become the President's campaign manager within the CIO, precisely because both the CIO and the New Deal had lost the initiative'.

This trend was by no means limited to the Amalgamated. As the President's second term unfolded, there was an increasingly clear tendency within labour's ranks to argue that working people owed far more to Roosevelt than he owed them, and a belief that labour's gains were more the result of FDR's benevolence than of the workers' own initiative through their unions. Clearly, Franklin Roosevelt was the one figure who could transcend the fault-lines of division within local and state Democratic parties and an increasingly contentious labour movement. His magnetism reinforced the legitimacy of the existing political system and deepened the electoral habits and practical ties that bound workers and their unions more closely to the Democratic Party.

But there must have been more than FDR's unifying presence at work, because the upset victory of Harry Truman on a populistic platform in 1948 indicates that the working-class vote was holding solid for the Democrats, even in the absence of his charismatic predecessor.

By 1948, Roosevelt had been dead for three years; the Republicans were determined to recapture the White House after sixteen years in the political wilderness; and virtually no one gave the seemingly inept Truman a chance of defeating GOP nominee Thomas E. Dewey. But he did, mainly by casting himself as the defender of the New Deal and the rights of labour. And once again the overwhelming support of workers played a vital role in the Democrats' success. Much of Truman's strength was in the cities, among the urban working classes. This was especially true of union members, who were both much more likely to vote and much stronger supporters of Truman than were non-union workers.

Truman's victory in 1948 played a major role in undermining the recurring dream of independent labour politics. After Roosevelt's death and Truman's accession, elements of organised labour had seriously contemplated the formation of a third party. But while labour hesitated, other forces – including the Communists – formed the Progressive Party. The tarring of the Progressives and their presidential candidate, Henry Wallace, with the red brush, at a time when Cold War hysteria was approaching a fever pitch, served further to 'delegitimise' third-party politics. Had Truman lost the election, at least the Progressives could have claimed the power to punish their anti-communist liberal tormentors. Instead, they became a symbol of fuzzy-minded idealism, left-wing isolation, and ignominious failure. With Truman's victory, and the Progressives' defeat, the marriage of labour to the Democratic party would become an apparently permanent feature of American political life.

Was the marriage 'barren' (as some historians have claimed)? To place this question in historical perspective, let us look once again at the sentiments of rank-and-file clothing workers on the eve of the 1940 presidential election. As the day of decision drew near, the Amalgamated sponsored a 'Write-a-Letter-to-Roosevelt' campaign among its members, and published the ones it judged best in a pamphlet entitled *The People Speak: Letters from Clothing Workers*. Almost entirely, the letters focused on immediate but vital concerns such as income, physical health, and old-age pensions. Mrs C. Londen, of Cincinnati, declared: 'I am a factory worker's wife and am voting for President Roosevelt's re-election because we are free of debts for the first time in twenty-three years of married life. I have purchased my first ready-made coat, and attended my first big-league ball game since his election. O. H. Schneider, also of Cincinnati, wrote that 'I thought a vacation was only for the rich before Roosevelt'. Now 'I take a vacation every year... [and] do not have to worry about old age. I feel secure'. Thanks to the ACW and the Roosevelt administration, it seemed to Har-

ry Wolfe of Philadelphia that 'a miracle happened to me and my family'. He reported working fewer hours, making 'a fine living', and enjoying better health. 'Roosevelt... made possible our dream come true'.

What these statements reveal, of course, is that the New Deal created a new relationship between the federal government and the American people. It not only built the foundations of the welfare state; it also asserted that government had an important role to play in the management of the economy and in safeguarding the economic wellbeing of the majority of Americans. The Democratic Party became the 'party of government' and, in circumstances of unprecedented post-war prosperity, government delivered an expanding package of benefits – pensions and medical insurance for the elderly, home loans and educational assistance for veterans, compensatory payments for unemployed workers and so on. Together, the trade unions, the Democratic Party, and the New Deal welfare state helped to soften the edges of inequality in an expanding economy, and to integrate workers into the mainstream of a consumer capitalist culture.

But the post-war consensus on the role of government in managing the economy and providing for the public welfare emerged only after sharp contention in which a number of alternatives on the left and the right were defeated. The clearest Left alternative, which historians have characterised as labour-liberal, or social-democratic, or social-Keynesian, envisaged a much more aggressive and systematic role for the state in mitigating the inequality rooted in the operation of the capitalist market. Important CIO leaders like Hillman (who died in 1946) and his youthful counterpart, Walter Reuther of the UAW, believed that, in order to achieve a more just and equitable social order, the management of the economy must become a tripartite venture involving the leaders of labour, capital, and 'the public'. The potential political base of this social-democratic vision was the unionised workforce in the basic industries of the North and the hitherto unorganised labour force, white and black, of the South.

This policy orientation had been implicit in the intellectual premises of the New Deal by 1938, but for many reasons it was to suffer a crushing defeat in the aftermath of the Second World War. The leadership of capital, with few exceptions, rejected it as a dangerous infringement of management's 'right to manage'. The rulers of the South thwarted Operation Dixie. The federal government, especially at the Congressional level, turned sharply to the right and punished labour with the Taft-Hartley Act which imposed restrictions on the political activities of unions. And important sections of the trade-union leadership spurned this tripartite vision of industrial governance and opted

Banner carried in the 1938 Labour Day parade in Toledo, Ohio, depicting John L. Lewis, leader of the United Mine Workers and the CIO, who became so disenchanted with Roosevelt that he called upon workers to vote Republican in the 1940 election.

instead for collective bargaining free – as much as possible – from state interference. Even among many New Deal liberals the 'statism' of the late 1930s had given way to a renewed faith in the benevolence of a corporate-dominated 'economy of abundance'. Meanwhile, in elections at the local and state level, the working-class political constituency upon whose behalf the bold new programme was to have been implemented continued to divide along ethnic and, increasingly, racial lines.

With the collapse of the tripartite vision, the most innovative sectors of labour and capital chose to create instead a kind of private welfare state through the operation of carefully controlled collective bargaining. After a pioneering agreement between General Motors and the United Auto Workers in 1948, the great breakthrough came with the so-called 'Treaty of Detroit' in 1950. In exchange for a five-year contract, and a no-strike pledge for its duration, GM gave the UAW automatic cost-of-living increases, additional wage guarantees pegged to annual increases in productivity, vacations, pensions, and generous medical insurance plans. For the Auto Workers and the unions that followed their lead, it was a dazzling achievement. Walter Reuther exulted that collective bargaining was creating a 'whole new middle class'. What he apparently failed to anticipate was that an ideologically straitjacketed labour movement, basing itself upon a more affluent and secure blue-collar 'middle class', would be

less and less likely to function as a mass social force nurturing within itself an alternative vision of the future. As Steve Fraser has noted, the emergence of the new social contract embodied in the Treaty of Detroit meant that 'the struggle over Nelson, power and property … was superseded by the universal quest for more – goulash capitalism'.

Gradually, perhaps inevitably, this quest for more within a privatised domain reduced the commitment of organised labour to an expanded welfare state, exacerbated the reality of material inequality within an increasingly segmented labour market, and served to diminish the sense of solidarity between relatively secure and well-paid sectors of the working class and their less privileged, often non-white brothers and sisters. This inequality, and declining commitment to social solidarity, would become painfully obvious in the 1960s, when the black freedom movement turned northward and began to make demands that challenged the precarious status and security of white working-class Americans – many of them second-generation members of the CIO unions – in the realms of employment, education, and housing. It was in the mid-1960s, when their hardwon 'turf' was threatened, that these blue-collar workers and many other so-called 'middle Americans' helped make the politics of racial backlash an enduring feature of American life. Insofar as the Democratic Party embraced and supported the struggle for black equality, its relationship to the white majority of organised labour's rank-and-file constituency became more and more tenuous; while government, and the 'party of government', were increasingly perceived as part of the problem rather than part of the solution to society's ills. Ironically, the day would come when the fading memory of Roosevelt would be invoked more effectively by a Republican president who challenged the New Deal order than by those members of FDR's own party who claimed to be his rightful heirs.

FOR FURTHER READING:
Robert S. McElvaine, ed., *Down & Out in the Great Depression: Letters from the Forgotten Man* (University of North Carolina Press, 1983), and *The Great Depression: America, 1929-1941* (Times Books, 1984); Arthur M. Schlesinger, Jr., et al, *History of American Presidential Elections, 1789-1968*, vol. IV (Chelsea House, 1971); Len De Caux, *Labour Radical – From the Wobblies to CIO: A Personal History* (Beacon Press, 1970); Melvyn Dubofsky and Warren Van Tine, eds., *Labour Leaders in America* (University of Illinois Press, 1987); Walter Dean Burnham, *The Current Crisis in American Politics* (New York: Oxford University Press, 1982); Steve Fraser and Gary Gerstle, eds., *The Rise and fall of the New Deal Order, 1930-1980* (Princeton University Press, 1989).

1940 AMERICA

ON THE EVE OF CONFLICT

Lewis Lord

America was ready for a blowout when 1940 finally rolled in, and so were New York's Finest. For New Year's Eve, the cops planted a signal box at Broadway and 45th Street, a wondrous innovation that told pedestrians when to stop and when to walk. At midnight, a 300-pound ball on a Times Square flagpole lit the numbers 1-9-4-0, informing 1¼ million revelers that the worst decade in their memory was history. In Chicago's Palmer House, couples got in the groove with Tommy Dorsey, "the Sentimental Gentleman of Swing." At the nearby Hotel Sherman, jitterbuggers kicked out with Tommy's brother Jimmy, "the World's Greatest Saxophonist." And the *Chicago Tribune,* "The World's Greatest Newspaper," went to press with an editorial that summed up the hopes of Americans everywhere: "We have a peaceful New Year's. Let's keep it."

World War II was 4 months old, but no one called it that. It was Europe's war, and if the *Tribune* and a majority of the American public had their way, that was what it would remain. On this side of the Atlantic, people were fox-trotting to "Oh Johnny, Oh," a rising hit on the Lucky Strike Hit Parade, and reading a column headlined ED SULLIVAN PICKS THE STARS OF '40. "Ronald Reagan, former Midwestern sports announcer, has had a solid year of 'B' pictures," Sullivan reported, and is ripe for stardom along with Ingrid Bergman, Lana Turner and a dozen others. But, the columnist counseled, "it is you, the movie fan, who will order the fates of all these young players. So be kind to the kids in 1940."

With the Great Depression entering its 11th year and 1 in 5 workers still out of work, a helping hand remained in vogue. A box-office smash that New Year's was "Mr. Smith Goes to Washington," with Jimmy Stewart in the role of an earnest young senator appealing for "a little bit of plain, ordinary kindness—and a little looking out for the other fella, too." Yet Franklin D. Roosevelt, whose New Deal had spent seven years looking out for the little fella, knew that America now faced a bigger problem. The President sat in the Oval Office, an unfiltered Camel in his cigarette holder, a fountain pen in his hand, going through seven drafts of his seventh state-of-the-union address. "It becomes clearer and clearer," he wrote,

"that the future will be a shabby and dangerous place to live in—yes, even for Americans to live in—if it is ruled by force in the hands of a few."

In January, that looked like a big if. True, Hitler had crushed Poland, but most Americans felt sure that he would never beat Britain and France. Certainly he seemed in no hurry to try. What the world had now, many scoffed, was a "phony war." But soon everything changed. In the spring, while Americans hummed "When You Wish Upon a Star" from Walt Disney's "Pinocchio," the Nazis turned their "sitzkrieg" into a blitzkrieg. They smashed Denmark and Norway in April, conquered Holland and Belgium in May, occupied Paris in June. By summer, America was mobilizing for a war it still hoped to stay out of. And with the buildup, the Depression at last began to fade, vanishing for good a few score Sundays later at a faraway place called Pearl Harbor.

For much of 1939 and '40, patrons strolled the New York World's Fair wearing I HAVE SEEN THE FUTURE buttons. Technology in the next two decades, the "World of Tomorrow" exhibits promised, would deliver not only television and air-conditioned homes but also slum-free cities, cars that could cross the country in 24 hours and cures for cancer and traffic congestion. In truth, the most revolutionary changes would stir in only a year or two and would occur not in technology but in society. Nylon stockings and garbage disposals were on the way; so, too, was a life for women outside the home. Blacks soon would demand roles in the war effort, a harbinger of the civil-rights movement. No one was aware that that very year America was exiting its sheltered adolescence and entering a "world of tomorrow" the futurists never imagined.

"It is here! A car without a clutch pedal . . . a car that never needs shifting . . . the most modern car in the world!"
—Advertisement introducing the 1940 Oldsmobile with Hydra-Matic Drive.

America a half-century ago was a land of porch swings, roadside zoos and knock-knock jokes. Middle-class families drove $793 Hudsons and $897 Nash Arrow-Flights and lived in $6,500 houses bought at 4½ percent interest. The sound of a coal shovel scraping a cellar floor was as common as the whiff of mothballs in an upstairs closet. Little boys rat-a-tat-tatted their "Gangbusters" machine guns, just as the crime fighters did on CBS's Wednesday-night radio show. Little girls cuddled "Dorothy dolls" with red shoes like those Judy Garland wore in "The Wizard of Oz," a Technicolor movie that was up for a slew of Oscars. And mothers dreaded summer for fear of polio, the mysterious disease that left toddlers and teenagers on crutches or cocooned in iron lungs and the man in the White House in steel braces from heel to hip.

Pan American's "Yankee Clipper" was starting its transatlantic flights—23 hours from New York's LaGuardia, the world's busiest airport, to Lisbon—but a poll showed most people would rather stay home, even if their expenses were paid. Fifteen cents bought a gallon of gasoline at a "filling station." A movie was a "picture show," seen by adults for a quarter and by kids under 12 for a Mercury-head dime, and a viewer with luck could win a set of china on "Dish Night" or $5 on "Bank Night." Few if any conversations ended with "Have a nice day," but plenty began with "What's cookin', good lookin'?"

Heroes were both real and imaginary. *Daily Planet* reporter Clark Kent retreated to phone booths to peel down to his Superman get-up, but teenager Billy Batson became the decade's No. 1 comic-book wonder—Captain Marvel—by just saying "Shazam!" Bob Feller's fastball was a marvel. During his season-opening no-hitter, an opposing batter beefed about a called strike. "What was wrong with it?" the umpire asked. "It sounded high," the batter replied.

First Lady Eleanor Roosevelt was America's social conscience, the most admired and most ridiculed woman in the land. (WE DON'T WANT ELEANOR EITHER, declared buttons at the GOP convention.) Her "My Day" column ran in 135 dailies, and *Movie & Radio Guide* rated only one person—her husband—as a stronger radio personality. But according to the *Ladies' Home Journal,* the typical 20-year-old female dreamed of becoming someone far different: "The American Glamour Girl," ideally a looker like Ann Sheridan, whose "luscious contours"—bust 34 inches, waist 23 inches, hips 34½ inches—made her Hollywood's "Oomph Girl."

The zipper was a hot item. Among men, it reduced chances of someone calling out "1 o'clock"—the signal that a trouser fly was open. Among women, it prevented "gap-osis," Madison Avenue's term for a slip glimpsed between buttons on a dress. Most men wore caps or hats, but beards were sights to gawk at. A set of roadside signs posted by a shaving-cream maker summed up attitudes regarding the hirsute; WITH GLAMOUR GIRLS / YOU'LL NEVER CLICK / BEWHISKERED / LIKE A BOLSHEVIK / BURMA-SHAVE.

The shopping cart, invented three years earlier by Oklahoma City grocer Sylvan Goldman, was catching on. An ad in the *Mobile* (Ala.) *Register* described the experience that awaited housewives at Mobile's new A&P supermarket. "You don't carry a cumbersome basket. You roll a carriage. And when you have everything you need, you wheel the carriage to a cashier's desk where your order is checked and packed for you." But not everyone liked what was happening at A&P and the other chain stores that were locating across America. Forty-four percent of the public felt that chains should either pay a special tax or be outlawed, because they threatened the family-owned stores that lined every Main Street. For months, Congress pondered taxing multistate chain stores out of business. A&P rescued the industry and itself by hiring public-relations wizard Carl Byoir, who spread the word that chains saved consumers money.

Big business may have been suspect, but government was trusted as a friend. "Do you favor government ownership of banks?" one poll asked. Half said yes. "Should the federal government provide free medical care for those unable to pay?" It should, replied 4 out of every 5. "Would you favor or oppose a law requiring all private citizens owning pistols or guns to register with the government?" Eighty percent liked the idea. When people thought of government, they rarely thought of taxes. The floor on the lowest income tax bracket was $3,000 a year. Most earned less than half that and thus paid no tax at all. A married person with a net income between $3,000 and $4,000 was taxed $8. One who made $5,000—average for a doctor or lawyer—paid $80. Nine of every 10 income-tax dollars came from a sliver of the population—280,000 families—with incomes over $10,000. Their tax rates ranged from 4 percent up to 68 percent. By and large, they were the people who referred to Roosevelt as "that man."

Popular music actually was popular, enjoyed by parents and kids alike. Teenagers in saddle oxfords paid 50 cents for the latest 78-rpm records, such hits as Glenn Miller's "Pennsylvania 6-5000" and Dinah Shore's "The Nearness of You." Grownups packed the jive joints on New York's West 52nd Street, where Bud Freeman and Teddy Wilson held forth. There, on the "Street of Swing," a couple could wreck a $5 bill in an evening of dining and dancing.

Mickey Mouse donned a magic cap in Disney's "Fantasia" and, with help from Bach, Beethoven and conductor Leopold Stokowski, turned lowbrows into highbrows, at least for 2½ hours, including intermission. Philcos and Zeniths picked up the Metropolitan Opera on Saturdays and the NBC Symphony on Sundays. Soprano Lily Pons, who could trill on a 16th note and take a scale from middle C to the F sharp above high C, reigned as the "trapeze artist of the Met." Arturo Toscanini ruled the NBC Symphony, except for a few concerts when Bruno Walter filled in. Walter had been Germany's best conductor until Hitler ran him off.

A different sound was taking hold in the heartland. Today, it's called "country." Then, to devotees and detractors alike, it was "hillbilly music," and millions tuned in on Saturday nights to savor every foot-stomping moment. From Chicago, they heard WLS's National Barn Dance, starring the Hoosier Hot Shots and Lulu Belle and Scotty. From Nashville's WSM came the Grand Ole Opry, with NBC picking up the half-hour sponsored by Prince Albert Smoking Tobacco (7 percent of cigarette smokers rolled their own, mostly "with good P.A."). The Opry's Roy Acuff, of "Wabash Cannonball" fame, soon would be known wherever the U.S. military went. "To hell with Roosevelt!" Japanese soldiers would shout to Marines dug in on Okinawa. "To hell with Babe Ruth! To hell with Roy Acuff!"

"Let Jesus lead you and Roosevelt feed you."
—A black minister to his congregation.

Sociologists in the late '30s and early '40s were studying Americans the same way they had examined islanders in the Pacific. And every place they looked—from the mythical "Middletown" (which was actually Muncie, Ind.) to "Yankee City" (Newburyport, Mass.) to "Cottonville" (Indianola, Miss.)—they reached the same conclusion: American communities were sharply divided by class. Nearly every aspect of life—the kind of home you lived in, the church you attended, what you studied in high school, whether you went to college, whom you married, the work you did, the health care you got—was determined by which social class you belonged to, upper, middle, or lower. Or, for that matter, which ethnic group you were born into.

On the bottom dwelled most of the 13 million blacks, or Negroes, as they were called until the 1960s. Three of every 4 lived in the South, where laws dictated an American apartheid, from separate restrooms, restaurants and water fountains to segregated courtrooms, buses and theaters. Schools were separate but hardly equal; 350,000 black teenagers lived in 425 counties that operated high schools only for whites. Custom banned biracial handshakes or any other act that implied mutual respect. Whites did the voting, and a Mississippi favorite, Theodore Bilbo, was asking the U.S. Senate for $1 billion to ship every black to Africa.

The South had no monopoly on racism. In stores in the

nation's capital, blacks could buy dresses but could not try them on. Blacks grumbled among themselves, but few whites saw a problem. Segregation was hardly an issue, and integration not yet a goal. A year earlier, a poll explored a topless-swimsuit controversy—2 out of 3 Americans, it concluded, felt that men should not hit the beach bare chested—but not until 1942 did polltakers examine "the race question" in detail. They found a segregation-minded nation: 66 percent for separate schools, 69 percent for separate restaurants, 84 percent for separate neighborhoods.

Barely 10,000 millionaires existed in America—compared with 1.5 million today—and only one, Metro-Goldwyn-Mayer President Louis B. Mayer, made as much as $1 million in yearly pay. But few Americans dreamed of becoming millionaires. Most, the polls showed, would be happy with half of what Tom Wright made running a department store in Burlington, Vt. His $5,000 salary sent a son to the University of Pennsylvania's Wharton School and three daughters to liberal-arts colleges. A Cadillac and a summer place on Lake Champlain were paid for, as was a home in town—a 15-room Victorian with crystal chandeliers, stained-glass windows and a cherry staircase.

An air of "we're not poor" formality prevailed among much of the middle class. Ads told housewives that happy marriages relied on gleaming bathrooms, dust-free living rooms and on-time evening meals set on tablecloths free of "tattletale gray." The husband usually did his part by showing up for dinner in a coat and tie, even in August. After all, manual workers went around in open-necked shirts with short sleeves. Jeans appeared only on laborers, cowboys and children. Good posture was essential. "Sit up straight," many a mother nagged her offspring. "Do stand up straight." With a bit of backbone, many felt, you could get ahead.

The 1940 census suggested progress, despite the Depression. Among 132 million Americans, 1 of every 5 owned a car, 1 in 7 had a phone, and 15 percent of the college-age kids were in college. No other country did better. Yet for millions, conditions remained basically as they were in 1937, when Roosevelt found "one third of a nation ill-housed, ill-clad, ill-nourished." From FDR's 1940 White House Conference on Children in a Democracy emerged this grim snapshot of American life: "More than a quarter of all families of the Untied States have yearly incomes of under $750; a half of all families of the United States have an income of less than $1,160 and two thirds of all U.S. families have incomes of less than $1,500 a year. A third of the nation's families cannot afford even an 'emergency level' diet. More than half cannot provide a maintenance level of food."

One of every 4 kitchens still lacked refrigeration, either an old-time icebox or a new electric wonder like the $99.95 Crosley Shelvador. Six of every 10 homes had no central heat. Kerosene lamps lit 3 of every 4 farm homes. One in 3 families got by without an indoor toilet. And 2 of 5 had no bathtub or shower. A shampoo every week or two was considered frequent. Women controlled their hair with twice-a-year permanents and curling irons. Men kept theirs ruly by adding oil.

With the first clinical use of penicillin still a year away, bacterial infections remained a scourge. Tuberculosis killed twice as many people as car wrecks did, and pneumonia and flu were almost as deadly. New Deal health programs cut infant-mortality rates sharply, but thousands of children still died from measles, whooping cough and diphtheria. Hookworm and pellagra plagued the South, and rotten teeth were seen almost everywhere. Of the first million men called for the draft, nearly 40 percent failed their physicals, and dental problems were the No. 1 cause of rejection. Dentures were common even among people in their 30s, like Clark Gable, who was seen on movie screens all year long telling Scarlett O'Hara he didn't give a damn. Years later, tests would show that fluoridated water could cut cavities.

The automobile and the New Deal's home-mortgage policies were pulling the middle class into the suburbs, a land occupied a decade earlier mainly by farmers and the well-to-do. The urban cores that remained—the "blighted areas"—were being left mostly to blacks, migrants from Appalachia and first and second-generation immigrants. Among the 8 million American families on relief were the O'Briens of Brooklyn—a man, a woman and five children who lived in a clean but crude cold-water flat that cost $19 of the $66 they got in welfare each month. The father and two sons slept on one broken-down bed, the mother and two daughters on another, and a baby girl in a baby carriage. For food, they relied on items from the federal surplus-commodities depot, Grade B milk, a few eggs, a pound of butter, a pound of prunes, whatever the government made available every other week. They kept putting off the baby's christening; they had no Sunday clothes to wear to mass.

Seventy million people—over half the population—lived on farms or in towns with fewer than 10,000 inhabitants. There, a little went a long way. One family—Nels and Anna Handevidt and their children in Minnesota's corn country—thrived on $1,000 a year and a cupboard laden with produce and meat canned in Mason jars. They had no desire to live anywhere else, especially now that rural electrification was lighting their home and powering their new refrigerator, toaster and waffle iron.

But many farmers saw scant hope of a better life. They were the 47 percent of the farming population who farmed someone else's land, often ending the crop year deeper in debt. Tenancy was on the rise across America, but nowhere was it more common than in the South. Among Dixie's farmers, 1 of every 2 whites and 3 of every 4 blacks were tenants or sharecroppers. Henry and Estelle Bracey, a black couple near Vicksburg, Miss., were not atypical. With help from two mules and a big family of pickers and hoehands, the Braceys cleared $26 in cash from a year of cropping a few acres of their landlord's cotton plantation. They and their children and grandchildren shared four beds in a three-room shack. The kids never saw a movie or heard a radio. But they knew religion. Every Sunday the Braceys, all 16 of them, walked 2 miles to church.

Millions of white sharecroppers in the South shared the same yoke, except the land they worked was often poorer. Many existed in gully-ravaged hill country, eating corn bread and beans, wearing shirts and dresses made of flour sacks and using snuff as a toothache remedy. Children skipped school on frosty days for lack of shoes. The five-month school year was common; it freed youngsters for farm work. Rural education outside the South also was in sad shape. Several million kids attended 130,000 one-room schools, many in abandoned stores or tents. Only 1 in 4 rural adults in their 20s possessed a high-school diploma. Half of the young adults in the cities had one.

The dust storms that turned much of the heartland into wasteland had faded by '40, but the westward tide of $10 jalopies laden with "Okies," "Arkies" and assorted Depression victims kept coming. "They were not farm men any more, but migrant men," wrote John Steinbeck in *The Grapes of Wrath*, the 1939 bestseller that became a 1940 Hollywood hit. "Eyes watched tires, ears listened to clattering motors, and minds struggled with oil, with gasoline, with the thinning rubber between air and road . . . water in the evening was the yearning, and food over the fire." Most were bound for California, a state that was a year away from becoming the third most populous of the 48. Out there, a good grape picker could earn $1.25 a day, of which 95 cents might be subtracted as rent on a tar-paper shanty with no plumbing and a dirt floor.

"Today, women's work is done . . . faster, easier and infinitely better . . . by modern mechanical servants."

4. GREAT DEPRESSION TO WORLD WAR II

—Ad for the Bendix Home Laundry, the first automatic clothes washer.

As America headed into 1940, author Norman Cousins proposed a cure-all for the nation's economic ills. Ten million people were out of work, he noted, and 10 million of the people who had jobs were women. "Simply fire the women, who shouldn't be working anyway, and hire the men. Presto! No unemployment. No relief rolls. No depression." Many people deemed that a splendid idea. Pollsters a year earlier posed this question: "Do you approve of a married woman earning money in business or industry if she has a husband capable of supporting her?" Four of every 5 said no.

Women were reminded relentlessly, by Hollywood, by Madison Avenue, even by their own magazines, that a caress was better than a career. In a revealing series titled "How America Lives," the *Ladies' Home Journal* profiled 16 families, including the Wrights, O'Briens, Handevidts and Braceys. There were 16 husbands and 16 wives, and, except for the spouse who picked cotton, not one wife worked outside the home. The *Journal* concluded this about the typical homemaker: "Sometimes she wonders vaguely whether she might not have been a career woman if marriage and motherhood had not come along . . . But she wouldn't really change for the world!"

What kind of career might a woman pursue? Law remained an overwhelmingly male enclave, except for the secretaries, and so did medicine, but for the nurses. Yet a fourth of the nation's work force was female and had been since the boom years of the '20s. Women tended dime-store counters, cotton-mill looms and telephone switchboards (but the New York Telephone Company wouldn't hire Jewish women as operators; it said their arms were too short to operate the equipment). Women made most of America's shirts and dresses, half of its coats and suits, a fifth of its cigars. No one knew how many women did piecework at home, hooking rugs, addressing envelopes and shelling nuts, but at least 2 million toiled as servants in other people's houses. An Indianapolis woman spent 63 hours a week handling one family's cooking, laundry, cleaning and child care. Her total weekly pay came to $5.

Whatever the job, a woman usually earned less than a man. The first woman cabinet member, Frances Perkins, opposed wage differentials, but a fourth of the minimum-wage codes created by her Labor Department in 1938 dictated more money for men. "Skirt Operators, Female," for instance, collected 80 cents an hour, a dime less than "Skirt Operators, Male." Sometimes women attained better jobs, but usually with the understanding that they would remain single, like Miss Perkins. Three fourths of the school systems refused to hire married women as teachers. Lawmakers in 26 states debated whether to bar them from state jobs. Nor could they expect a hand from organized labor. In a perfect world, one union leader explained, "the married woman will find her place in the home caring for children, which is God's greatest gift to women and her natural birthright."

Ed Sullivan was right. Ronald Reagan did become a star in 1940, as a dying Notre Dame football player named George Gipp. When Pat O'Brien, as Coach Knute Rockne, urged the Fighting Irish to "win just one for the Gipper," tears gushed in theaters across the land, and Reagan, at 29, was a "B" actor no more. Roosevelt also was correct. The world did become a dangerous place even for Americans, and the nation soon was spending billions to meet the peril. By December, defense plants were hiring nearly every skilled worker they could find. In two more years, the leader of Hoboes of America, Inc., would report that most of its 2 million members were either in uniform or in war industries. The few still riding the rods, he said, were not hoboes. "They're just bums."

The War Manpower Commission would ask women to do their part by filling in for departing warriors. Soon, 1 of every 3 workers would be female. In 1944's political conventions, both parties expressed their thanks by including the equal-rights amendment in their platforms. But all that most Rosie the Riveters wanted were jobs at home when peace and their husbands returned. Not until the '60s—a generation after women proved they could do "men's work"—would the move toward workplace equality gain force.

One group of Americans had to plead for roles in the war effort. "The Negro is ready—with his sleeves rolled up and his chest bared," a Harlem daily reported. "Give him something to do." Only under federal pressure did many industries hire blacks. One Indiana ordnance plant set aside a production line for black workers; in air-raid drills, they would rush to a room marked BOMB SHELTER—COLORED ONLY. At the peak of war production in 1943, 1 million blacks earned defense-industry paychecks. Nearly all, including the skilled, held unskilled jobs, but it was a breakthrough nevertheless. Progress was no less grudging in the military, with black soldiers in all-black units and black sailors mostly in the kitchen. But many thousands eventually saw combat, and more than 1 million emerged as veterans, including 250,000 who would go to college under the GI Bill of Rights. Few could be content to follow a white man's mule again, or to ride in the back of a bus.

As "Dr. New Deal," Roosevelt gave the bottom third some help and a lot of hope. As "Dr. Win the War," he would deliver far more. Rich and poor would remain, but the gap between them would narrow. America, as historian Geoffrey Perrett noted, would "at last become what it said it was and what it had so long wanted to be—a middle class nation: an economic and social democracy." Yet in 1940 none of this was inevitable. "Some few doubters among us," FDR told the country, were asking whether America's story was coming to an end. He answered: "We Americans of today—all of us—we are characters in the living book of democracy. But we are also its author. It falls upon us now to say whether the chapters that are to come will tell a story of retreat or a story of continued advance."

An American Tragedy:

THE INTERNMENT OF JAPANESE-AMERICANS DURING WORLD WAR II

"Of the more than 110,000 people who were interned by our government [during World War II], more than 60% were U.S. citizens. Over 40,000 of those interned were under the age of 19, and 99.3% of those 40,000 were native-born citizens."

Norman Y. Mineta

Rep. Mineta (D.-Calif.) is a member of the Public Works and Transportation Committee, the Select Committee on Intelligence, and the Science and Technology Committee.

FEBRUARY, 1984, marked a dark anniversary for the U.S. In February, 1942, the President of the United States signed an executive order which commanded the U.S. Army to "relocate" and "intern" 110,000 Americans of Japanese ancestry. To many Americans, the internment means little, but to more than 110,000 American citizens and law-abiding residents, the internment meant years of undeserved imprisonment and impoverishment.

I was one of those Americans. I had committed no crime and, as a 10-and-a-half-year-old child, I presented little threat to my country. Yet, I was taken from my home and incarcerated by the U.S. Army shortly after America entered World War II.

On Feb. 19, 1942, Pres. Franklin Roosevelt signed Executive Order 9066, an action which instituted an imprison-by-background policy for the U.S. government. As a result, all Americans of Japanese ancestry living on the West Coast were "relocated" and then "interned" in prison camps. We were not incarcerated because we had committed a crime, but because our ethnic background alone rendered us suspect.

The executive order swiftly uprooted my family, and it eventually separated us. My parents had to sell or store our possessions. Leaving San Jose, Calif., I boarded the train wearing my Cub Scout uniform, a uniform which I hoped would help show that I was an American. The soldier guarding us on the train was lenient enough to let me wave good-bye to my friends.

Leaving our homes, we were first sent to the Santa Anita Racetrack in southern California. The racetrack was euphemistically called a government "Assembly Center," but it was our first prison camp. There, for six months, we slept in horse stables and showered in horse paddocks. Then, after half a year, my government, the U.S. government, "relocated" my family again.

We were from California, and we were unprepared for the frigid weather which the Wyoming winters offered. We were moved into unfinished barracks, buildings with floors which allowed the cold winds to rush through our rooms, and we quickly became aware of the fact that there were not enough provisions for the 12,000 people who lived in our internment camp.

I spent two years living in that camp. Indeed, the word "camp" was and is a euphemism. Some government officials said that the internment was being conducted for the protection of those who were interned. However, our "camp" in Heart Mountain was surrounded with barbed wire, and the army guards in the watch-towers pointed their machine guns in at us and not out towards the cold, barren land which surrounded us. Those guards were preventing escape, rather than attack—and we were living in a prison, not in a congenial camp.

Thus, 110,000 of us were imprisoned, and more than 40,000 of us were imprisoned not as adults, but as children. Often, too, our families endured both separation and incarceration; in the latter months of the war, many families were split up, as some family members were allowed to leave while others were forced to stay.

For years, important facts about the internment remained shrouded in mystery. After World War II ended, many of us who had been interned wanted merely to work at recovering our professional and community positions; we spent decades rebuilding what our own government had taken from us.

During that time, almost nobody clamored for review, least of all Americans of Japanese ancestry. One crucial reason for that was that nearly all of us were hampered by unwarranted shame. We were not eager to review a

Reprinted from *USA Today Magazine*, May 1984, pp. 89-93. Copyright 1984 by Society for the Advancement of Education.

Soldiers patrol Santa Anita Racetrack in California, where Japanese-Americans were temporarily detained before being sent to permanent camps.

nightmare in which our own government had labelled us as subversives.

Yet, with the maturing of the children and grandchildren of those who were interned, questions and indignation began to resurface. How could the U.S. government have locked up more than 100,000 people purely on the basis of ethnic background?

To help answer that question, to investigate the details of the internment, and possibly to recommend retrospective action, the U.S. Congress formed the Commission on Wartime Relocation and Internment of Civilians. The members of that distinguished, bipartisan commission were jointly appointed by the President, by the Speaker of the House, or by the President Pro Tem of the Senate.

In 1983, the Commission completed a year and a half of investigations with a report concluding that the internment was prompted not by the exigencies of national security, but by "war hysteria," "racial prejudice," and a "failure of political leadership." Indeed, the evidence overwhelmingly indicates that the war served as a rationalization, as an excuse to unleash long-lasting bigotry as a guide to policy.

For several decades before World War II, there had existed strong anti-Asian sentiments. Prejudice against Americans of Asian ancestry was especially prevalent in America's western states, where immigrants were seen as competitors in farming, as well as other occupations. There were groups in California who were well-known for insisting that quotas be placed on the number of Japanese allowed to enter the U.S. each year, and, in 1924, they were successful in persuading Congress to pass a bill prohibiting any Japanese from emigrating to our country.

War hysteria and racial prejudice

As a result of Japan's strategic attacks on Pacific forces in December, 1941, rumors spread that there would next be an invasion of the west coast of the U.S. by Japanese troops. Three days after the attack on Pearl Harbor, Attorney General Francis Biddle appealed to the citizens of the U.S. to be fair to the ethnic Japanese here in America. Yet, the virulent racism against anybody of Japanese ancestry persisted, and it soon determined Federal policy.

Lt. Gen. John L. DeWitt was responsible for the security of the western part of the U.S. He was able to wield great authority over the area and did little to calm the rumors of espionage activity allegedly conducted by American citizens and residents of Japanese ancestry.

Two weeks after the attack on Pearl Harbor, DeWitt recommended to the War Department that, because the west coast of the U.S. was a "Theatre of Operations," all "alien subjects of enemy nations" should be removed to interior areas of the country. The words "enemy nations" of course implied that the U.S. was threatened by people of Italian and German background as well as Americans of Japanese ancestry. Yet, DeWitt wanted to "relocate" only the ethnic Japanese. (There were 58,000 people of Italian heritage, 23,000 people of German ancestry, and 40,000 people of Japanese ancestry in the states DeWitt was discussing, but DeWitt's recommendation included the assertion that there were approximately 40,000 "enemy aliens" on the West Coast.)

DeWitt supported his recommendations with false rumors—rumors which were contradicted by facts available and evident at the time. For example, DeWitt claimed that ethnic Japanese on the West Coast were signalling Japanese ships out in the Pacific Ocean. After investigating the charge, the chairman of the Federal Communications Commission branch in

Right: At the Civil Control Stations, internees were registered and assigned family numbers. (Note the tag on child at the right of photo, which indicates family identification number.) **Below:** Child awaiting evacuation. **Bottom:** Over 18,000 Americans of Japanese ancestry were interned at Tule Lake Camp, located in northern California near the Oregon border, from May 27, 1942, through March 20, 1946.

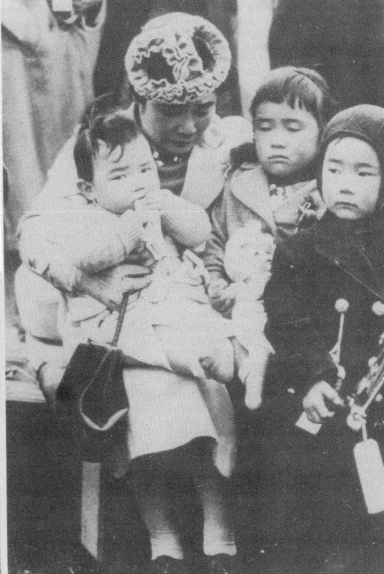

Clem Albers/War Relocation Authority

San Francisco specifically said that no such signalling had occurred.

DeWitt also said that American citizens and residents of Japanese ancestry had stockpiled numerous rounds of ammunition and weapons. Late in December, 1941, "enemy aliens" in the western states were required to surrender short wave radios, cameras, binoculars, and various weapons. After an investigation of the General's claims, the FBI noted that the weapons found were mainly of the type that any citizen might possess, and that one of the reasons for the large number of weapons confiscated was because the roundup included items collected from a sporting goods store and a general merchandise warehouse.

In fact, there was a chronic problem in 1942 with securing undistorted information. In February of that year, FBI director J. Edgar Hoover noted in a memorandum to Attorney General Francis Biddle that the Western Defense Command (WDC), under the direction of DeWitt, was unskilled at gathering information, since "hysteria and lack of judgment" warped their operations. Even Maj. Gen. Joseph Stillwell, who served under DeWitt as the person in charge of southern California, noted that the intelligence gathering by the WDC did nothing to calm rumors. Writing about the San Francisco headquarters of the WDC, Stillwell said, "Common sense is thrown to the winds and any absurdity is believed."

Actually, a number of organizations investigated the charges of espionage and sabotage by American citizens and residents of Japanese ancestry, including the FBI, U.S. Naval Intelligence, and Pres. Roosevelt's own personal sources. All of these groups reported that there was no evidence indicating that Americans of Japanese ancestry posed a threat to the U.S.

In fact, the absence of reason for suspicion was so clear that even J. Edgar Hoover—a man seldom noted for his unwavering protection of individuals' rights—said that the U.S. government had no justification for relocating or interning the ethnic Japanese in America.

Despite the conclusions of all these groups, DeWitt relentlessly launched verbal attacks on American citizens and residents of Japanese ancestry. DeWitt testified before a Congressional committee that he did not trust the ethnic Japanese in our country. He claimed that American citizens of Japanese ancestry would always be loyal to Japan. When asked about Americans of German and Italian descent, DeWitt commented:

You needn't worry about the Italians at all except in certain cases. Also, the same for the Germans except in individual cases. But we must worry about the Japanese all the time *until he is wiped off the map*. Sabotage and espionage will make problems as long as he is allowed in this area—problems which I don't want to have to worry about.

The hatred continued to mount. In California, the State Personnel Board voted to prohibit the state civil service from hiring any person whose ethnicity was that of a country with whom the U.S. was at war. Again, the rule sounded as if it applied to people of Italian and German ancestry as well as to those of Japanese ancestry, but the prohibition only prevented the hiring of Americans of Japanese ancestry.

During the first week of February, 1942, the army identified 12 "restricted areas" in the U.S. "Enemy aliens" who resided in those areas were required to observe a curfew, travel only to and from work, and remain within five miles of their homes.

Following this action, a number of Members of Congress from the western U.S. sent a letter to Pres. Roosevelt urging the removal of all ethnic Japanese from strategic areas in California, Oregon, and Washington. DeWitt's final report on the situation quickly followed the request of the western Congressional delegation. DeWitt offered plenty of warped logic in the report, including that demonstrated by his statement that "the very fact that no sabotage has taken place to date is a disturbing and confirming indication that such action will be taken." DeWitt recommended the removal and detention of all American citizens and residents of Japanese ancestry.

The War Department was unable to prove any of the allegations that American citizens and residents of Japanese ancestry were a threat to the defense of the West Coast states. Nevertheless, with neither proof nor supportive military analysis, Secretary of War Henry L. Stimson recommended to Pres. Roosevelt that an exclusion of West Coast ethnic Japanese be pursued.

Attorney General Biddle informed the President that, if an exclusion order was to be constitutional, it must be supported by some type of military necessity, so it became essential for the Administration to create a rationale which would explain why it was circumventing the clause of the Constitution which guarantees due process of law.

The Administration's solution was to assert that there was "fifth column" activity—espionage and sabotage by some Americans or residents of Japanese ancestry. It used these unfounded assertions as justification for the removal of more than 110,000 loyal Americans of Japanese ancestry from their homes. Despite the fact that they lacked any evidence substantiating such charges, military and political leaders acceded to the widespread racism. Instead of guarding against bigotry, they yielded to it. Leaders chose to urge the President to evacuate all Americans of Japanese ancestry from the West Coast.

On Feb. 19, 1942, Pres. Roosevelt signed Executive Order 9066, which allowed the Secretary of War, or his designee, to establish military areas and to remove whomever he wanted. The following day, DeWitt was appointed the military commander responsible for carrying out the mandate of the executive order. DeWitt designated the entire western half of California, Oregon, and Washington as a "military area," and ordered, "in the interest of military necessity," that all people of Japanese ancestry were to be removed from those areas.

While Executive Order 9066 provided for the evacuation of American citizens and residents of Japanese ancestry from various areas of the U.S., the order stipulated no particular penalty if the order was not followed. In other words, there was no authority to enforce the executive order. The War Department hastily drafted legislation which would delegate the necessary authority to the Justice Department and sent this proposal to Congress. At this point, Congress had an opportunity to question both the constitutionality and logic of the executive order; instead, Members of Congress quickly passed the proposal (Public Law 77-503) and sanctified the presidential proclamation.

In passing P.L. 77-503, Congress was giving the War Department authority over civilians, despite the fact that our courts remained open and that martial law had not been declared. Our Constitution had never allowed the military to assume authority over the citizens of our country. The Supreme Court reaffirmed this in the case *Ex Parte Milligan,* a case which took place during the U.S. Civil War and which affirmed the constitutional principle that the military shall have limited jurisdiction over American citizens.

The abridgement of rights remains startling. Not only law-abiding residents, but tens of thousands of U.S. citizens were summarily incarcerated without due process of law. Of the more than 110,000 people who were interned by our government, more than 60% were U.S. citizens by birth. Over 40,000 of those interned were under the age of 19, and 99.3% of those 40,000 were native-born citizens. What kind of outcry would there be today if more than 50,000 young citizens were incarcerated for several years without having committed any crimes.

This was our country

To this day, many people mention the Japanese attack on Pearl Harbor as if it somehow justified the internment. When I talk with some antagonists about this issue, they sometimes rear back with indignation and charge, "but *you* attacked us!" Such references neglect the simple fact that the internees were not Japanese nationals; we were a group made up of native-born American citizens and law-abiding residents. We were not the enemy. We were Americans.

Obviously, now is not the first time that many have overlooked that fact. In 1942, U.S. government officials chose to paste over our residency and citizenship with the labels "enemy alien" and "non-alien." In so doing, these officials pasted over our identity as individuals who deserved the most fundamental protections of our Constitution.

Despite the color of our hair and skin, despite the shape of our eyes, the U.S. was our country. I remember how my parents reminded us of that fact. Just before our family was evacuated, my father brought us together in the living room of our home in San Jose, Calif., and told us about rumors that all people of Japanese ancestry who were not born in America could be expatriated in exchanges for U.S. POW's. My sisters, my brother, and I understood the possible ramifications; if the rumor was accurate, our parents would be separated from us and sent back to Japan. Yet, even then, our father said, "No matter what happens, *this* is your home."

That episode now reminds me of more than the internment's breach of our citizenship. Recalling my parents—the wartime loyalty they displayed and the trauma they needlessly endured—now serves to remind me that the internment constituted a shattering assault on our fundamental legal rights as residents and citizens of the U.S.

During the internment, our President, Congress, and Supreme Court all used ethnic background as a standardized measure of patriotic loyalty. Our government thus abridged the fundamental right of each person to be judged as an individual. Thus, even if we lacked the overwhelming evidence gathered by the Commission on Wartime Relocation—evidence that there *never* was a "fifth-column" threat—the violation of rights inherent to the internment would still leave that policy worthy of our condemnation.

Some now shrug off the fact that Americans of Japanese ancestry never presented a threat to American security. Instead of denying anybody's identity as an American, these apologists may concede that the internment was an ill-conceived action which caused unnecessary suffering; but then they disregard that condemnation by saying, "we *all* suffered during the war."

Of course, America was at war and, as Americans, we all joined together to defend our country and we all accepted the sacrifices that defense entailed. Indeed, Americans of Japanese ancestry contributed mightily to the allied war effort. The 101st Battalion/442nd Regimental Combat Team was comprised only of Americans of Japanese ancestry—many of whom volunteered from relocation camps. It became the most highly decorated military unit in the history of the U.S. Army, and it was unmatched in the proportion of casualties from which it suffered. Americans of Japanese ancestry also served with extraordinary distinction in the Military Intelligence Service.

Yet, the internment went beyond the demands faced by all U.S. citizens during the war. The internment cost us three years of our lives and much more—not to further the defense of our country, but to cater to crass racial prejudice and political cowardice.

Those who retrospectively lump together all wartime suffering make a mistake easily highlighted by analogy. During World War II, when one American citizen robbed another, the war itself did not render the thief innocent. Nor did the war make the victim's loss just. The internment amounted to a situation in which thousands of American citizens and residents were robbed by their own government—needlessly robbed of freedom, property, opportunity, and honor.

By lumping together all forms of wartime misery, many ignore the fact that the internment was a domestic act of theft and not an international expression of war. Simply put, the internment never involved combat or conflict between wartime enemies. It involved the unjust, racist, and opportunistic imprisonment of Americans by Americans.

Redress

Several of us in Congress introduced the Civil Liberties Act of 1983, legislation which proposes that the U.S. government issue a formal apology for the internment and offer some compensation, or reparation payment, to each of the surviving internees.

This Congressional initiative precisely follows the recommendations issued by the special Commission on Wartime Relocation and Internment of Civilians. Concluding that the internment was a blatant violation of civil rights, rather than a necessary defense of American security, the Commission has said that reparations are in order.

An increasing consciousness of the internment's basic injustices has left widespread agreement that the internment was wrong. Today, then, the largest remaining controversies about the internment surround questions about whether it is wise now to seek reparations for a 40-year-old injustice.

One often-voiced hesitation about the payment of reparations is that it would set us off on what lawyers refer to as the "slippery-slope" of precedent. "If we offer reparations for this," some ask, "will the American government be liable for all past government injustices?" Those asking that question should note that the courts and the American government have already provided far more generous precedents for Federal redress. In some cases, such as those affecting American Indians who unjustly lost property, several hundred people have collectively received several million dollars.

Furthermore, both the Commission recommendation and the Civil Liberties Act of 1983 limit the realm of recipients to those who actually were interned, so that paying reparations in this case would provide no precedent for an endless, generation-hopping quest to redress for all historical injustices.

A few have said they wish to see reparations determined in the courtroom and not in Congress, but these people have forgotten that the sudden internment seldom allowed for the derivation of tidy contracts or the careful collection of documents; if there had been time then, perhaps trials would be appropriate now.

Finally, some people simply recoil at the figure of $1,500,000,000. However, after adjusting for inflation and an annual interest rate of only three per cent, economists working for the Commission estimated that the total monetary value of the *material* losses suffered by the interned amounts to between $2,500,000,000 and $6,200,000,000 in 1983 dollars.

That figure, of course, does not include even an estimate of the immense value lost in the years of forfeited freedom. Given the scope of these losses, the proposal for compensation of $1,500,000,000 is modest. With these figures available, it should be clear that the drive to offer reparations to survivors of America's internment camps involves the pursuit of equal justice, rather than the arrangement of special advantage.

If you are skeptical about reparations, try to guess the amount of money which would prompt you into an agreement to sacrifice most of your property. Ask yourself how much money it would take to make you go willingly into a prison camp for two or three years. Finally, ask yourself how you would feel if this country incarcerated you and your family solely because of your ethnic background. Would you seek redress?

Rosie the Riveter Remembers

For millions of women, consciousness raising didn't start in the 1960s. It started when they helped win World War II.

For warehousing, at left, particularly strong and tall women were selected from the 1942 Boeing work force.

Interviews by Mark Jonathan Harris, Franklin D. Mitchell, Steven J. Schechter

URING THE FIRST three years of World War II, five million women covered their hair, put on "slacks," and at the government's urging went to work in defense plants. They did every kind of job, but the largest single need was for riveters. In song, story, and film, the female patriot, "Rosie the Riveter," was born. Many of the new recruits had worked in service trades—as maids, cooks, or waitresses. Many more had never worked at any paying job. Practically none of them had ever made as much money.

How they felt about resentful male co-workers, race and sex prejudice, and their own new self confidence is revealed in these interviews with ex–defense workers.

WINONA ESPINOSA: RIVETER AND BUS DRIVER

N JULY 1942 I left Grand Junction, Colorado, where I grew up, and came to San Diego with my brother-in-law and my sister. I was nineteen and my boyfriend had joined the Army and was in Washington State. In my mind San Diego sounded closer to Washington than Colorado, and I thought that would make it easier for

BOEING COMPANY ARCHIVES

us to see each other. I also wanted to do something to help the country get the war over with and I knew there were a lot of defense jobs in San Diego.

I applied for a job at Rohr Aircraft, and they sent me to a six-week training school. You learned how to use an electric drill, how to do precision drilling, how to rivet. I hadn't seen anything like a rivet gun or an electric drill motor before except in Buck Rogers funny books. That's the way they looked to me. But I was an eager learner, and I soon became an outstanding riveter.

At Rohr I worked riveting the boom doors on P-38s. They were big, long, huge doors that had three or four thicknesses of skins, and you had to rivet those skins together. Everything had to be precise. It all had to pass inspection. Each rivet had to be countersunk by hand, so you had to be very good.

I found the work very challenging but I hated the dress. We had to wear ugly-looking hairnets that made the girls look awful. The female guards were very strict about them too. Maybe you'd try to leave your bangs sticking out, but they'd come and make you stick them back in. You looked just like a skinhead, very unfeminine. Then you had to wear pants —we called them slacks in those days —and you never wore them prior to the war. Finally, all the women had to wear those ugly scarves. They issued them so they were all the same. You couldn't wear a colorful scarf or bandanna.

I worked at Rohr for almost a year, then, when I got married and pregnant, I went back to Grand Junction for a while.

When I came back, I went to work for the San Diego Transit driving buses and streetcars. I just saw a sign on a bus downtown one day that said, "I need you," and I went and applied. I hadn't even been driving very long. I only learned to drive a car after I got to San Diego, and I didn't know anything about driving a big vehicle like that. But the war really created opportunities for women. It was the first time we got a chance to show that we could do a lot of things that only men had done before.

The transit company had a three-month school. They had classroom lessons and training in the field. You had to learn the automotive aspects of the bus so that if it broke down you could call in to tell the mechanic what was wrong so he could come and fix it. You also had to learn all the bus routes.

I drove buses and streetcars for about two and a half years. In fact I was driving a bus the day the war ended. I let everybody ride my bus free that day.

INEZ SAUER:
CHIEF CLERK, TOOLROOM

I WAS THIRTY-ONE when the war started and I had never worked in my life before. I had a six-year-old daughter and two boys, twelve and thirteen. We were living in Norwalk, Ohio, in a huge home in which we could fit about two hundred people playing bridge, and once in a while we filled it.

I remember my first husband saying to me, "You've lived through a depression and you weren't even aware that it was here." It was true. I knew that people were without work and that lots of people were having a hard time, but it never seemed to affect us or our friends. They were all the same ilk—all college people and all golfing and bridge-playing companions. I suppose you'd call it a life of ease. We always kept a live-in maid, and we never had to go without anything. Before the war my life was bridge and golf and clubs and children. One group I belonged to was a children's improvement group. I sat one night at the meeting and looked around at the group of women—there must have been thirty of us sitting there —and each one of us had maids, and our children were all at home with the maids. We were discussing how to improve our children, and they would have been far better off if we'd been home taking care of them.

When the war broke out, my hus-band's rubber-matting business in Ohio had to close due to the war restrictions on rubber. We also lost our live-in maid, and I could see there was no way I could possibly live the way I was accustomed to doing. So I took my children home to my parents in Seattle.

The Seattle papers were full of ads for women workers needed to help the war effort. "Do your part, free a man for service." Being a D.A.R., I really wanted to help the war effort. I could have worked for the Red Cross and rolled bandages, but I wanted to do something that I thought was really vital. Building bombers was, so I answered an ad for Boeing.

My mother was horrified. She said no one in our family had ever worked in a factory. "You don't know what kind of people you're going to be associated with." My father was horrified too, no matter how I tried to impress on him that this was a war effort on my part. He said, "You'll never get along with the people you'll meet there." My husband thought it was utterly ridiculous. I had never worked. I didn't know how to handle money, as he put it. I was nineteen when I was married. My husband was ten years older, and he always made me feel like a child, so he didn't think I would last very long at the job, but he was wrong.

They started me as a clerk in this huge toolroom. I had never handled a tool in my life outside of a hammer. Some man came in and asked for a bastard file. I said to him, "If you don't control your language, you won't get any service here." I went to my supervisor and said, "You'll have to correct this man. I won't tolerate that kind of language." He laughed and laughed and said, "Don't you know what a bastard file is? It's the name of a very coarse file." He went over and took one out and showed me.

So I said to him, "If I'm going to be part of this organization, I must have some books, something that shows me how I can learn to do what I'm supposed to do." This was an unheard-of request. It went through channels, and they finally brought me some large, classified material that showed all the tools and machinery needed to build the B-17s. So gradually I educated myself about the various tools and their uses, and I was allowed to go out and roam around the machine area and become acquainted with what they were doing. The results showed on my paycheck. Eventually I became chief clerk of the toolroom. I think I was the first woman chief clerk they had.

The first year, I worked seven days a week. We didn't have any time off. They did allow us Christmas off, but Thanksgiving we had to work. That was a hard thing to do. The children didn't understand. My mother and father didn't understand, but I worked. I think that put a little iron in my spine too. I did something that was against my grain, but I did it, and I'm glad.

Since I was the chief clerk, they gave me the privilege of coming to work a half-hour early in the morning and staying over thirty to forty minutes at night. Because I was working late one night I had a chance to see President Roosevelt. They said he was coming in on the swing shift, after four o'clock, so I waited to see him. They cleared out all the aisles of the main plant, and he went through in a big, open limousine. He smiled and he had his long cigarette holder, and he was very, very pleasant. "Hello there, how are you? Keep up the war effort. Oh, you women are doing a wonderful job." We were all thrilled to think the President could take time out of the war effort to visit us factory workers. It gave us a lift, and I think we worked harder.

Boeing was a real education for me. It taught me a different way of life. I had never been around uneducated people before, people that worked with their hands. I was prudish and had never been with people that used coarse language. Since I hadn't worked before, I didn't know there was such a thing as the typical male ego. My contact with my first supervisor was one of animosity, in which he stated, "The happiest day of my life will be when I say good-bye to each one of you women as I

My mother warned me when I took the job that I'd never go back to being a housewife. She was right.

usher you out the front door." I didn't understand that kind of resentment, but it was prevalent throughout the plant. Many of the men felt that no woman could come in and run a lathe, but they did. I learned that just because you're a woman and have never worked is no reason you can't learn. The job really broadened me. I had led a very sheltered life. I had had no contact with Negroes except as maids or gardeners. My mother was a Virginian, and we were brought up to think that colored people were not on the same economic or social level. I learned differently at Boeing. I learned that because a girl is a Negro she's not necessarily a maid, and because a man is a Negro doesn't mean that all he can do is dig. In fact, I found that some of the black people I got to know there were very superior —and certainly equal to me—equal to anyone I ever knew.

Before I worked at Boeing I also had had no exposure to unions. After I was there awhile, I joined the machinists union. We had a contract dispute, and we had a one-day walkout to show Boeing our strength. We went on this march through the financial district in downtown Seattle.

My mother happened to be down there seeing the president of the Seattle First National Bank at the time. Seeing this long stream of Boeing people, he interrupted her and said, "Mrs. Ely, they seem to be having a labor walkout. Let's go out and see what's going on." So my mother and a number of the people from the bank walked outside to see what was happening. And we came down the middle of the street—I think there were probably five thousand of us. I saw my mother. I could recognize her—she was tall and stately—and I waved and said, "Hello, Mother." That night when I got home, I thought she was never going to honor my name again. She said, "To think my daughter was

marching in that labor demonstration. How could you do that to the family?" But I could see that it was a new, new world.

My mother warned me when I took the job that I would never be the same. She said, "You will never want to go back to being a housewife." At that time I didn't think it would change a thing. But she was right, it definitely did.

I had always been in a shell; I'd always been protected. But at Boeing I found a freedom and an independence I had never known. After the war I could never go back to playing bridge again, being a clubwoman and listening to a lot of inanities when I knew there were things you could use your mind for. The war changed my life completely. I guess you could say, at thirty-one, I finally grew up.

RACHEL WRAY: HAND RIVETER, GROUP LEADER, MECHANIC

I GREW UP ON a farm in northeastern Oklahoma, knowing nothing but the Depression. My father lost the farm, and we moved to town just when I was starting junior high school. I lived there until the eleventh grade, when I was forced to quit school to go to work.

When I was nineteen I fell in love with a boy from Oklahoma. George was also from a depressed area and joined the Navy to get ahead. He was stationed in California, and I decided to come and join him. I felt there would be more opportunity in California, and I was determined that I was going to have a different life.

I had twenty-five dollars when I left Oklahoma. I answered an ad in the paper looking for riders to California and paid twelve dollars for the trip. I arrived here with twelve dollars to my name and lived with friends until I could get work.

I got a job as a pastry cook at a restaurant in Whittier, a very exclusive place. I was making fifteen dollars (and board) a week and was very proud of myself. George and I were planning to marry. Then Pearl Harbor was attacked, and his ship was sent out to fight in the Pacific.

After he left I knew I had to make it on my own. I saw an ad in the paper announcing the opening of a school for vocational training in aircraft. I was looking for the opportunity to learn something else, and I wanted to earn more money. I worked during the day cooking and went to school at night studying bench mechanics and riveting, how to read blueprints and use different aircraft tools.

After about three months the instructor said, "There's no use in you spending any more time here. You can go out and get a job." He gave me my graduation slip, and I went down to San Diego to look around, because George's mother lived there. I went to Convair, which was Consolidated Aircraft then, and they hired me.

I was one of the first women hired at Convair and I was determined that I wasn't going to lose the job and be sent back to working as a pastry cook. Convair had a motto on their plant which said that anything short of right is wrong, and that stuck with me. I went to work in the riveting group in metal-bench assembly. The mechanics would bring us the job they had put together, and we would take the blueprints and rivet what they brought us.

They would always put the new people with another person, a "leadman." The man I went to work for was really great. He saw my determination and he would give me hard jobs to do. The other girls would say, "Joplin, don't give her that, I'll do it." But he would say, "I'm going to break her in right, I'm going to do it the hard way." He told me later that he had made a mistake and been too easy with the other girls.

I tackled everything. I had a daring mother who was afraid of nothing: horses, farm implements, anything,

so maybe I inherited a little bit of that from her. I remember my brother, who was in the Air Corps at the time, and his friends laughed at me one day thinking I couldn't learn this mechanical stuff. I can still see them, but it only made me more determined. I think it probably hurt their pride a little bit that I was capable of doing this.

Pretty soon I was promoted to bench-mechanic work, which was detailed hand riveting. Then I was given a bench with nothing to do but repair what other people had ruined. I visited a man recently who's seventy-four years old, and he said to my daughter, "All we had to do was foul up a job and take it to her and she'd fix it."

I loved working at Convair. I loved the challenge of getting dirty and getting into the work. I did one special riveting job, hand riveting that could not be done by machine. I worked on that job for three months, ten hours a day, six days a week, and slapped three-eighth- or three-quarter-inch rivets by hand that no one else would do. I didn't have that kind of confidence as a kid growing up, because I didn't have that opportunity. Convair was the first time in my life that I had the chance to prove that I could do something, and I did. They finally made me a group leader, although they didn't pay me the wage that went with the job, because I was a woman.

Our department was a majority of women. Many of the women had no training at all, particularly the older women. We had women in our department who were ex-schoolteachers, -artists, -housewives, so when we could give them a job from the production line, the job would have to be set up for them. I'd sit them down and show them how to use the drill press, the size drill to use, the size of screws, the kind of rivets, whether it was an Army rivet or a Navy rivet—a Navy rivet was an icebox rivet, the Army rivet was not—and so on. Then I would go back and check to see if the riveting was okay, and if there were any bad rivets, they had to take

them out. Most of the time I had to take them out myself. As a group leader that's what I did, and I did it at the same time I was doing my job as a bench mechanic. There were four male group leaders and myself. Theoretically we should have been classified as group leaders and paid for that type of work, but we were not. I felt that was discrimination and that we were being used by the company and fought against it.

Shortly after I went to work at Convair I was chosen by the people in our work group to sit on the wage-review board. The company had automatic wage reviews, and when I first started, those were the only raises that we received. The women were lucky, though, if we got a five-cent-an-hour increase on a review. Some of the women got three cents, some of the women even got two cents, and some of the women were passed over. To us it seemed that the men's pay automatically went up, and ours didn't. I was fortunate enough to get raises later, even a ten-cent raise, and I actually had an assistant foreman come up to me and say, "Don't say anything to the other girls about getting a raise." I told him, "I don't discuss my personal wages, but how about the other women who are deserving too?" So on the wage board I fought for the other women as much as I fought for myself. The highest-paid women at that time were making around $.80 an hour, but the men were probably making $1.15 to $1.50 an hour for identically the same work. In fact, there was a lot of feeling that the women were producing more work than the men on final assembly and on the bench because of their agility with their hands.

Some of the things we did change. For example, they were forced to classify you because of your work. And somewhere in the back of their minds they had the idea that they were not going to make a woman anything but a B-mechanic. As a B-mechanic you could only go to $1.00 an hour, and they were determined that no woman would ever become an A-mechanic or an A-riveter. But we really fought

167

that and we proved to them by bringing them on the job that we were doing A-mechanic work and producing more than the men. So I got my A-mechanic classification and a raise to $1.15 an hour.

I also sat on the safety board the whole time I was at Convair, for the safety requirements they demanded of women were more unreasonable than what they demanded of men. In the beginning we had caps and uniforms we were supposed to wear, but the women rebelled at that. We felt that we could be safe and wear the clothes we wanted. Eventually the company did become a little more relaxed about dress, so we won some victories there too.

ADELE ERENBERG: MACHINIST

WHEN THE WAR started, I was twenty-six, unmarried, and working as a cosmetics clerk in a drugstore in Los Angeles. I was running the whole department, handling the inventory and all that. It felt asinine, though, to be selling lipstick when the country was at war. I felt that I was capable of doing something more than that toward the war effort.

There was also a big difference between my salary and those in defense work. I was making something like twenty-two to twenty-four dollars a week in the drugstore. You could earn a much greater amount of money for your labor in defense plants. Also it interested me. I had a certain curiosity about meeting that kind of challenge, and here was an opportunity to do that, for there were more openings for women.

So I went to two or three plants and took their test. And they all told me I had absolutely no mechanical ability. I said, "I don't believe that." So I went to another plant, A.D.E.L. I was interviewed and got the job. This particular plant made the hydraulic valve system for the B-17. And where did they put women? In the burr room. You sat at a workbench, which was essentially like a picnic table with a bunch of other women,

and you worked grinding and sanding machine parts to make them smooth. That's what you did all day long. It was very mechanical and it was very boring. There were about thirty women in the burr room, and it was like being in a beauty shop every day. I couldn't stand the inane talk. So when they asked me if I would like to work someplace else in the shop, I said I very much would.

They started training me. I went to a blueprint class and learned how to use a micrometer and how to draw tools out of the tool crib and everything else. Then one day they said, "Okay, how would you like to go into the machine shop?"

I said, "Terrific."

And they said, "Now, Adele, it's going to be a real challenge because you'll be the only woman in the machine shop." I thought to myself, well, that's going to be fun, all those guys and Adele in the machine shop. So the foreman took me over there. It was a big room, with a high ceiling and fluorescent lights, and it was very noisy. I walked in there, in my overalls, and suddenly all the machines stopped and every guy in the shop just turned around and looked at me. It took, I think, two weeks before anyone even talked to me. The discrimination was indescribable. They wanted to kill me.

My attitude was, "Okay, you bastards. I'm going to prove to you I can do anything you can do, and maybe better than some of you." And that's exactly the way it turned out. I used to do the rework on the pieces that the guy on the shift before me had screwed up. I finally got assigned to nothing but rework.

Later they taught me to run an automatic screwing machine. It's a big mother, and it took a lot of strength just to throw that thing into gear. They probably thought I wasn't going to be able to do it. But I was determined to succeed. As a matter of fact I developed the most fantastic biceps from throwing that machine into gear. Even today I still have a little of that muscle left.

Anyway, eventually some of the

men became very friendly, particularly the older ones, the ones in their late forties or fifties. They were journeymen tool and die makers and were so skilled that they could work anywhere at very high salaries. They were sort of fatherly, protective. They weren't threatened by me. The younger men, I think, were.

Our plant was an open shop, and the International Association of Machinists was trying to unionize the workers. I joined and worked to try to get the union in the plant. I proselytized for the union during lunch hour and I had a big altercation with the management over that. The employers and my leadman and foreman called me into the office and said, "We have a right to fire you."

I said, "On what basis? I work as well or better than anybody else in the shop except the journeymen."

They said, "No, not because of that, because you're talking for the union on company property. You're not allowed to do that."

I said, "Well, that's just too bad, because I can't get off the grounds here. You won't allow us to leave the grounds during lunch hour. And you don't pay me for my lunch hour, so that time doesn't belong to you, so you can't tell me what to do." And they backed down.

I had one experience at the plant that really made me work for the union. One day while I was burring, I had an accident and ripped some cartilage out of my hand. It wasn't serious, but it looked kind of messy.

They had to take me over to the industrial hospital to get my hand sutured. I came back and couldn't work for a day or two because my hand was all bandaged. It wasn't serious, but it was awkward. When I got my paycheck, I saw that they had docked me for time that I was in the industrial hospital. When I saw that I was really mad.

It's ironic that when the union finally got into the plant, they had me transferred out. They were anxious to get rid of me because, after we got them in, I went to a few meetings and complained about it being a Jim Crow

I walked into the machine shop, in my overalls. Suddenly the machines stopped, and every guy looked at me.

union. So they arranged for me to have a higher rating instead of a worker's rating. This allowed me to make twenty-five cents an hour more, and I got transferred to another plant. By this time I was married. When I became pregnant I worked for about three months more, then I quit.

For me defense work was the beginning of my emancipation as a woman. For the first time in my life I found out that I could do something with my hands besides bake a pie.

SYBIL LEWIS: RIVETER, ARC WELDER

WHEN I FIRST arrived in Los Angeles, I began to look for a job. I decided I didn't want to do maid work anymore, so I got a job as a waitress in a small black restaurant. I was making pretty good money, more than I had in Sapulpa, Oklahoma, but I didn't like the job that much; I didn't have the knack for getting good tips. Then I saw an ad in the newspaper offering to train women for defense work. I went to Lockheed Aircraft and applied. They said they'd call me, but I never got a response, so I went back and applied again. You had to be pretty persistent. Finally they accepted me. They gave me a short training program and taught me how to rivet. Then they put me to work in the plant riveting small airplane parts, mainly gasoline tanks.

The women worked in pairs. I was the riveter and this big, strong white girl from a cotton farm in Arkansas worked as the bucker. The riveter used a gun to shoot rivets through the metal and fasten it together. The bucker used a bucking bar on the other side of the metal to smooth out the rivets. Bucking was harder than shooting rivets; it required more muscle. Riveting required more skill. I worked for a while as a riveter with this white girl when the boss came around one day and said, "We've decided to make some changes." At this point he assigned her to do the riveting and me to do the bucking. I

wanted to know why. He said, "Well, we just interchange once in a while." But I was never given the riveting job back. This was the first encounter I had with segregation in California, and it didn't sit too well with me. It brought back some of my experiences in Sapulpa—you're a Negro, so you do the hard work. I wasn't failing as a riveter—in fact, the other girl learned to rivet from me— but I felt they gave me the job of bucker because I was black.

So I applied to Douglas Aircraft in Santa Monica and was hired as a riveter there. On that job I did not encounter the same prejudice.

I worked in aircraft for a few years, then in '43 I saw an ad in the paper for women trainees to learn arc welding. The salary sounded good, from $1.00 to $1.25 an hour. I wanted to learn that skill and I wanted to make more money, so I answered the ad and they sent me to a short course at welding school. After I passed the trainee course, they employed me at the shipyards. That was a little different than working in aircraft because in the shipyard you found mostly men. There I ran into another kind of discrimination; because I was a woman I was paid less than a man for doing the same job.

I was an arc welder, I'd passed both the Army and Navy tests, and I knew I could do the job, but I found from talking with some of the men that they made more money. You'd ask about this, but they'd say, "Well, you don't have the experience," or, "The men have to lift some heavy pieces of steel and you don't have to," but I knew that I had to help lift steel too.

They started everyone off at $1.20 an hour. There were higher-paying jobs, though, like chippers and crane operators that were for men only. Once, the foreman told me I had to go on the skids—the long docks alongside the hull. I said, "That sounds

pretty dangerous. Will I make more than $1.20 an hour?" And he said, "No, $1.20 is the top pay you'll get." But the men got more.

It was interesting that although they didn't pay women as much as men, the men treated you differently if you wore slacks. I noticed, for example, that when you'd get on the bus or the streetcar, you stood all the way, more than the lady who would get on with a dress. I never could understand why men wouldn't give women in slacks a seat. And at the shipyards the language wasn't the best. Nobody respected you enough to clean up the way they spoke. It didn't seem to bother the men that you were a woman. During the war years men began to say, you have a man's job and you're getting paid almost the same, so we don't have to give you a seat anymore or show the common courtesies that men show women. All those niceties were lost.

I enjoyed working at the shipyard —it was a unique job for a woman —and I liked the challenge. But it was a dangerous job. The safety measures were very poor. Many people were injured by falling steel. Finally I was assigned to a very hazardous area and I asked to be transferred into a safer area. I was not granted that. They said you have to work where they assign you at all times. I thought it was getting too dangerous, so I quit.

The war years had a tremendous impact on women. I know for myself it was the first time I had a chance to get out of the kitchen and work in industry and make a few bucks. This was something I had never dreamed would happen. In Sapulpa all that women had to look forward to was keeping house and raising families. The war years offered new possibilities. You came out to California, put on your pants, and took your lunch pail to a man's job. This was the beginning of women's feeling that they could do something more. We were trained to do this kind of work because of the war, but there was no question that this was just an interim period. We were all told that when the war was over, we would not be needed anymore.

FRANKIE COOPER: CRANE OPERATOR

THE FIRST JOB I had lasted only a month. The foreman was sort of a frantic-type person and wanted me to start my machine at ten minutes to seven, and I refused. I told him I've only been here a month and I'm already making my quota and I have no intention of starting my machine early. He said, "You know I can fire you," and I said, "You know I don't care." So he fired me.

Then I heard of an opening at American Steel for a crane operator, on a small ten-ton crane. I applied for it and got it. Then I had to learn it. The men said, "You won't learn it. Women can't do that job." But they were wrong. I think I was the fourth woman hired in the mill. It wasn't an important or dangerous job, just moving gun mounts and gun barrels around and cleaning up the floor in what they called the Navy building. The important work was inside the foundry, where they poured the steel. It was all men in the foundry. You had to have seniority to run one of those fifty-ton cranes because there was so much responsibility involved.

One day there was a terrible accident at the plant. One of the crane operators lost a load of steel, poured it all over. It just streamed everywhere, put a lot of lives in danger. After the accident they took him to the doctor and he was examined carefully. They found that he was losing his eyesight, that he couldn't see that far away in the brightness to pour the steel. They had to take him off the crane and needed an immediate replacement. They looked around and there wasn't anyone but women. The men they still had were on jobs where they couldn't be replaced.

By this time I had moved up to operating a fifty-ton crane and I had learned the language of the foundry, the sign language with which you communicate to your rigger or chainman. So they offered the job to me, and I took it. Pouring steel was the hardest job in the mill, and the men said, "It's too big a responsibility for a woman. She'll never last." But I did.

The hardest part for me was sanding the rails. The rails are what the wheels of the crane run on. They're way up in the air over the concrete floor and they have to be sanded every eight-hour shift, because if your rails get too slick, your hook will slide. That was the first time I had a crane with railings before, and when I found out that the operators had to sand them, I was almost scared to death. I thought, "I can't do that. I can't look down at that concrete and put this little bucket of sand up and down. I just can't do it." And one of the men said, "Well, that'll get her. She'll never sand them tracks." That's what made me sand them. After that I

An intent riveter, above, is reflected in the dorsal fin she is building at Douglas's Long Beach plant.

An integrated riveting team, above, at work at a Douglas Aircraft plant.

had to. I had to show them I could do it.

It took a while to be accepted. We had a big coke stove and we'd gather around it to get warm. On occasion, when I had time to come down and take my breaks, the men would stand so close together around the stove that there wasn't room for me. So I just leaned up against the wall. The wall was warmer than where they were standing anyway because it had absorbed the heat from all the hours the fire had been going. So I would lean up against the wall and laugh at their jokes. And I would offer them a doughnut if I had one and so forth. So actually I made the overtures. And after a while they began to accept me.

During the war the morale inside the plants was extremely high. Not just myself, but everybody, gave everything they had. They wanted to do it. Today you don't sit around and talk about patriotism while you're drinking a beer, but you did back then. I mean you had a neighbor next door—maybe he lived states and states away—and if you were like me, often you couldn't understand what he said, but you had this great thing in common. You were all pulling together for one great war effort.

I was never absent, and I wasn't unique in that. There was very little absenteeism where I worked. If I woke up in the morning and I didn't feel too good and I really didn't want to work, I could make myself go by thinking, "What about those boys who are getting up at five o'clock, maybe haven't even been to bed? Maybe they're leaning their chin on a bayonet just to stay awake on watch. I don't even know their names. They don't even have faces to me, but they're out there somewhere overseas. And I'm saying that I don't feel like going to work today because I've got a headache?" That would get me out of bed and into work. And by the time I'd stayed there a couple of hours, it was okay. I was going to make it. So I never stayed at home.

There was only one really difficult problem with working. That was leaving my two-and-one-half-year-old daughter. When a mother goes away from home and starts to work for her first time, there is always a feeling of guilt. Any mother that has ever done this has had this feeling. I couldn't cope with it at first.

I relate so much with women who are trying to get into nontraditional jobs today, because during the war we had those jobs out of necessity, and then after the war they were no longer there. Women have actually had nontraditional jobs since the first wagon train went across the country. When they arrived at the place where they wanted to settle, they helped cut the logs, they helped put them together, they helped put the mud between the log cabins, and they made a home and had their babies inside. And everytime a war comes along, women take up nontraditional work again. During the Civil War they worked in factories, they helped make musket balls, they made clothing for the troops, and they kept the home fires burning the way they always have. World War I came along and they did the same thing. After the war was over, they went back home. World War II, it was exactly the same thing, but the women were different in World War II: they didn't want to go back home, and many of them haven't. And if they did go back home, they never forgot, and they told their daughters, "You don't have to be just a homemaker. You can be anything you want to be." And so we've got this new generation of women.

These interviews are excerpted from The Homefront: America During World War II *by Mark Jonathan Harris, Franklin D. Mitchell, and Steven J. Schechter.*

From the Cold War to the Reagan Revolution

President Franklin D. Roosevelt had hoped to create a peaceful postwar world through continued collaboration of the "Big Four" (the United States, the Soviet Union, Great Britain, and China) working within the United Nations. Cracks began appearing in the Grand Alliance even before the fighting had ended. Disputes over Eastern Europe and other areas drove a wedge between the Soviets and their allies. This condition, which became known as the "cold war," soon came to tint the lenses through which Americans viewed most foreign policy issues. As time wore on, some believed it was only a matter of time before another war erupted. Mutual fear and suspicion fueled a potentially catastrophic arms race between the two superpowers.

During the years following V-J Day, the United States suffered (or appeared to suffer) a number of setbacks in foreign affairs. The Soviets tightened the screws on Eastern European nations, initiated the Berlin blockade, and exploded their first atomic device. China "fell" under Communist domination and in June 1950 the United States found itself in a war again when North Korea invaded South Korea. Bewildered and frustrated, many Americans became receptive to the message presented by Senator Joseph R. McCarthy and others. The real problem, they said, was that Communists and "fellow travelers" had become deeply entrenched in America's government and other institutions, and were working to subvert the national interests. The only way to get the United States on the right track was to root out these subversives wherever they were found.

Dwight D. Eisenhower's enormous popularity and his promise to end the Korean War resulted in a landslide victory for the Republicans in 1952. The 1950s became to many the decade of conformity and do-nothing government. Actually, there was a good deal of ferment over a variety of issues. A landmark Supreme Court decision against racial segregation in 1954, for instance, set the stage for what later became a massive struggle over civil rights.

The 1960s began calmly enough. John F. Kennedy's election seemed to promise a more vigorous government, but no radical departures from what had gone before. Kennedy's assassination cut short his tenure, and Lyndon B. Johnson inherited the whirlwind. Smoldering discontent over the Vietnam War and social injustices broke out openly on college campuses and in cities across the nation. Many young people joined what they called the "counterculture," which rejected the American society as brutal and dehumanizing. By 1968 domestic upheavals had destroyed Johnson's presidency.

Richard M. Nixon won the 1968 election in part because he had promised to end the Vietnam War. He also profited from a backlash against the counterculture's contempt for American values and morals. Nixon modified but did not dismantle Johnson's "Great Society," and helped regularize relations with the Soviet Union and with the People's Republic of China. Nixon's accomplishments were overshadowed by the onset of a series of scandals that drove him from office. His successor, Gerald Ford, was perceived as a mere time-server, and Jimmy Carter ran for president as an outsider who promised to restore decency and compassion to government. A man of considerable gifts, Carter nonetheless came to appear too small for the job as a number of issues—the Iranian hostage crisis, for instance—undermined his effectiveness.

By the end of the 1970s the high fervors of the previous decade had dissipated. "Hippies" traded in their sandals and candles for three-piece suits, and movements for racial and sexual equality lost momentum though very real gains had been made. The stage was set for the "Reagan Revolution." Ronald Reagan promised to get government "off people's backs" at home and to restore the nation's pride and influence abroad. Federal programs in a variety of fields were cut back or closed down, and agencies dealing with matters such as the environment were staffed with people whose commitment to their tasks was dubious at best. Reagan vastly increased military spending while cutting taxes, and in the process the national debt was enormously increased. Relations with the Soviet Union, which earlier he had dubbed the "evil empire," improved considerably during his second term. Through it all Reagan remained popular despite a number of scandals within his administration, such as the Iran-Contra affair. The long-range effects of his "revolution" have yet to be tallied.

"The Ike Age" deals with the years of Dwight D. Eisenhower's presidency. A view commonly held at the time was that Eisenhower was a passive executive who spent most of his time playing golf and bridge while subordinates ran the store. The article surveys the revisionist view of Eisenhower as a far more effective president.

"The Forgotten War" and "Lessons From a Lost War" examine two examples of cold war confrontations. "Rebels Without a Cause? Teenagers in the '50s" examines attitudes of young people to provide insight to the uncertainties that Americans grappled with during the 1950s. "Trumpet of Conscience: A Portrait of Martin Luther King, Jr." describes the greatness of this martyr in the struggle for equality in America. "The New Indian Politics" provides an account of new strategies American Indians have adopted in their own struggle. "Reappraising the Presidency of Lyndon B. Johnson" tries to present a balanced view of this dynamic leader who was discredited by the Vietnam War. "A Change in the Weather" analyzes the Reagan Revolution and discusses issues that will have to be dealt with in the future.

Looking Ahead: Challenge Questions

The Korean War, if not forgotten, has not loomed large in American memory. Discuss the impact of that conflict on relations between the United States and its allies with the Soviet Union. Do the same for the Cuban missile crisis. Why did the Vietnam War cause so much dissension within the United States?

Analyze the career and contributions of Reverend Martin Luther King, Jr. What were Lyndon B. Johnson's accomplishments as president?

Discuss the Reagan Revolution. What were its goals and how well did it succeed? What was its legacy in foreign and domestic policies?

THE FORGOTTEN WAR

*Still unsung after 40 years, the Korean
conflict left an enormous legacy that has
changed the very course of the world*

It was both postscript to the last war and prologue to the next, a brutal struggle that began on a monsoon-drenched morning 40 years ago this week and raged up and down a remote, ravaged Asian peninsula for 37 months. It was the cold war suddenly turned hot, Communism's boldest "war of national liberation" and the United Nations' first—and probably last—"police action." When it finally ended in stalemate, at a bleak "truce village" in a no man's land called Panmunjom, it had involved 22 nations, claimed 5 million lives and set off political and economic tremors that reverberate still.

Yet four decades after it began, the Korean War remains as hazy in America's memory as the mist-shrouded mountains that were its killing fields. Where, for example, is a memorial worthy of those who fell at Pork Chop Hill and Heartbreak Ridge, or during the retreat from the Chosin Reservoir? What colleges tutor the young about "The Korean War: Its Origins and Objectives"? And why is the war's best-known work of art a television sitcom called "M*A*S*H," which was really an allegory about Vietnam?

Slowly, those who have inherited this forgotten war are beginning to realize the size of its lien on posterity. It encouraged seven American Presidents to draw lines against Communist subversion from Vietnam to El Salvador, drew an Atlantic America irreversibly into Asia and helped catapult what had been a declining military establishment to the forefront of American foreign policy. If the Berlin Wall was the symbol of the division of Europe, the border between the two Koreas is its Asian counterpart. When they met two weeks ago in San Francisco, Mikhail Gorbachev and South Korean President Roh Tae Woo may have started a thaw that could someday eliminate the most visible remaining vestige of the cold war: The division of Korea.

Moreover, in this spring of reconciliation in Asia, both Beijing and Moscow are taking new steps toward diplomatic rapprochement with Seoul, a government that Communism's twin giants had tried to destroy in 1950 and in the 40 years since have ignored, denounced and sought to subvert. Even the relentless enmity between the U.S. and Kim Il Sung's Stalinist regime has begun to soften. American diplomats and Pyongyang's representatives have quietly been holding a series of getting-to-know-you meetings that last month resulted in the North Koreans' turning over the remains of five American servicemen who had died in Pyongyang's nightmarish prison camps. "For the first time in four decades," exults South Korea's Lee Hongku, a special assistant to Roh and a former Minister of Unification, "we can look forward with great expectations."

That it has taken almost four decades for such expectations to materialize is a measure of the epic changes wrought by the Korean conflict. The struggle not only saved the southern half of the Korean peninsula from Communist despotism (though not from anti-Communist authoritarianism), but set it on the road toward prosperity and a still precarious democracy. It also helped transform Japan into a technological superpower that is America's most formidable economic competitor. It so chilled relations between the U.S. and the new People's Republic of China that Chinese children born during the war are instantly recognized by such given names as "Resist America" and "Aid Korea."

The war's effects were felt far from its battlefields. Worried that Korea was only a diversion in advance of a Soviet attack on Berlin, the Truman administration sent four U.S. divisions to Europe to bolster the two already on occupation duty and began pressing to transform occupied West Germany into a rearmed anti-Communist bastion.

A model war

At the same time, Korea wrenched a Eurocentric America's attention back to the Pacific, where some of it has remained, uneasily, ever since. After World War II, the U.S. had begun losing interest in the Orient; the Truman administration was even creeping toward a modus vivendi with "Red China." "Asia is outside the reach of the military power, the economic control, and the ideological influence of the Western World," columnist Walter Lippmann wrote.

While there now is evidence that the conflict opened a rift that later became a chasm between China and the Soviet

Union, at the time it reinforced the image of monolithic Communism on the march, a perception that dogged American policymakers for years. It raised a protective U.S. umbrella over Taiwan, enabling it to survive as an unloved but thriving diplomatic orphan, and it focused America's attention on other likely targets of Communist aggression. One stood out: French Indochina.

More than any other event, the Korean War transformed the cold war from a political and ideological struggle into a military one. In so doing, it was a catalyst not only for the postwar policy of containment, but also for the creation of what Dwight D. Eisenhower dubbed "the military-industrial complex." Defense outlays soared from a planned $14 billion in fiscal 1951 to $54 billion in fiscal 1953.

Even more striking was the militarization of America's foreign-aid program: In fiscal 1950, military aid accounted for only 12 percent of America's aid budget; by 1960, the military's share of foreign aid was 41 percent. In *The Making of America's Soviet Policy,* Ernest R. May put it this way: " ... before mid-1950, containment seemed to involve primarily an effort to create economic, social and political conditions assumed to be inhospitable to Communism, whereas from mid-1950 on, the policy seemed primarily one of preserving military frontiers behind which conditions unsuited to subversion could gradually evolve." With mixed results, later administrations tried to do in South Vietnam, Iran, El Salvador, the Philippines and elsewhere what Truman had done in South Korea—to hold off the Communists and hope democracy could develop.

At the same time, as historian Arthur M. Schlesinger has argued, in dispatching troops to Korea without first asking Congress to declare war, Truman continued to expand the powers of the Presidency and set the White House on a collision course with Congress and with critics of administration policies. An internal White House paper from 1951 eerily presaged Vietnam and later Oliver North's Iran-Contra defense. "The circumstances of the present crisis," the paper said, "make any debate over prerogatives and power essentially sterile, if not dangerous to the success of our foreign policy."

Korea also introduced a fundamental contradiction that was to plague American foreign policy throughout the cold war. On one hand, played out as it was against a backdrop of virulent anti-Communism at home, the war encouraged a succession of American politicians to vow to defeat Communist aggression wherever it appeared. On Sept. 30, 1950, three months after the North Korean attack, Truman enshrined containment as policy by sign-

---

Washington's missing memorial

Let us now praise forgotten men . . .

And some there be, which have no memorial; Who are perished, as though they had never been.

—Ecclesiasticus

About 1.5 million Americans served in Korea, 54,000 died there and more than 100,000 were wounded or reported missing. They are the forgotten warriors, neglected by a nation that only eight years before showered their brothers with ticker tape after World War II.

Not until 1986 did Congress decree that the soldiers of Korea should have a monument in Washington. The Korean War Memorial will sit on the Mall just across the Reflecting Pool from the Vietnam Veterans' Memorial. But it will not have the cathartic healing power of the black granite wall across the way. Vietnam's veterans were caught in the cross fire over whether their war was just, and their wall corrects that injustice. Korea's veterans have simply been ignored. Forty years later, the new memorial will honor them. But can it force us to remember them?

Words born in action—a Korean War glossary

Bug-out: Unauthorized retreat.

Chicoms: Chinese Communists.

Chopper: Helicopter.

Gook: Derisive slang for Koreans; a corruption of the Korean *han'guk saram,* which means "Korean."

Hooch: Small house or hut.

MASH: Mobile Army Surgical Hospital.

NAPALM: (Naphthene plus Palmitate) Jellied-gasoline bombs.

R and R: Rest and Recreation. Time away from the front; in-country for GI's, Tokyo for officers.

ROK's: Republic of Korea troops.

KATUSA's: Korean soldiers attached to U.S. Army units.

---

ing National Security Council paper 68 which, in language foreshadowing John Kennedy's inaugural address a decade later, declared that given the rise of Soviet power, "the nation must be determined, at whatever cost or sacrifice," to defend democracy "at home and abroad." But defending the autocratic Syngman Rhee could hardly be considered serving the cause of democracy.

Fire on the right

On another level, though, the stalemate in Korea was a reminder that in the Atomic Age (the U.S.S.R. announced its first successful nuclear test less than three months before the war began), there were compelling reasons not to let wars escalate. This new concept of "limited war," however, did not suit Gen. Douglas MacArthur, who pushed to end the war by carrying it to China with nuclear weapons. In March, 1951, an increasingly emotional MacArthur openly challenged Truman's concept of limited war in a letter to Representative Joseph Martin, a leading member of the China lobby: "Here in Asia is where the Communist conspirators have elected to make their play for global conquest," he wrote. "If we lose the war to Communism in Asia the fall of Europe is inevitable . . . We must win. There is no substitute for victory."

There also was no substitute for obeying orders. Truman finally fired MacAr-

thur for insubordination, but that did not end the debate about how vigorously Communism should be "rolled back." The ouster of the outspoken anti-Communist general encouraged demagogues like Wisconsin's Senator Joseph McCarthy to bluster that Communist sympathizers were at work in the highest ranks of the Truman administration. Thirteen years later, after the fiasco at the Bay of Pigs and with the U.S. heading into another "limited war" in Asia, Senator Barry Goldwater echoed MacArthur, telling the 1964 Republican convention that "extremism in the defense of liberty is no vice." The man who introduced Goldwater, Ronald Reagan, finally carried the conservative torch into the White House.

By demonstrating that it was easier for the U.S. to contain naked aggression than subversion, that wars of national liberation were best fought with stealth, obfuscation and patience, Korea also hastened the onset of a new kind of cold warfare. The frustrating struggle divided Americans and as the foreign policy consensus eroded, a succession of Presidents tried to cloak some of their efforts to contain Communism—in Guatemala, Iran, Cuba and Nicaragua, for example—in secrecy.

Given this far-reaching legacy, what is most surprising about the Korean War is that it has been so completely forgotten. Almost as many Americans fell in Korea (54,000) as would die in Vietnam a generation later (58,000), but the Korean

5. COLD WAR TO THE REAGAN REVOLUTION

War never gained the same hammerlock on the nation's emotions. To those who had won unconditional surrenders from Germany and Japan, battling to a draw with North Korea and China was anything but memorable. "Korea," says retired U.S. Army Col. David Hackworth, who fought both there and in Vietnam, "was like the 49ers tying Stanford two weeks after winning the Super Bowl."

At first, though, the Americans were fortunate to fight the North Koreans to a tie, finally halting the invasion outside the port city of Pusan. "We sent in troops who'd had almost no training," recalls former Secretary of State Dean Rusk, then assistant secretary for Far Eastern affairs. "Had the North Koreans kept coming," says Rusk, "they could have overrun the entire peninsula."

MacArthur rebounded brilliantly, staging an amphibious landing at Inchon, just west of Seoul, and sending the North Koreans reeling back across the 38th parallel. Triumphant, MacArthur flew off to Wake Island in the mid-Pacific to meet with Truman.

In a hut near the airfield runway, the imperious five-star general assured the homespun former World War I artillery captain that the war would be over by Christmas. If the Chinese were foolish enough to intervene, MacArthur arrogantly predicted, the U.S. Air Force would embark on "the greatest slaughter in military history." Instead, the Chinese routed the United Nations forces so completely that a despairing MacArthur told Washington that unless the U.S. attacked China, it would risk an Asian Dunkirk. "In one cable," Rusk recalls, "he talked about the loss of morale of his troops, when he was talking about his own morale. He was clearly in a state of depression."

Without a word

But led by Lt. Gen. Matthew B. Ridgway, 56, a paratroop hero, the U.S. Eighth Army began moving northward again, inflicting huge casualties on the overextended Chinese. There was little sentiment for crossing the 38th parallel a second time, however. Truce negotiations began on July 10, 1951, but went nowhere fast. On one occasion, both delegations sat staring at each other for 2 hours and 11 minutes without uttering a word. The seesaw war of trenches and numbered hills finally came to a silent, coldly formal conclusion on the morning of July 27, 1953, almost exactly where it had begun three years before.

For all its ups and downs, Korea engaged only a small fraction of the nation. Truman extended the draft, raised taxes and imposed wage-and-price controls, but compared with World War II five years before, the domestic sacrifices were modest. Compared to Vietnam, which was nightly theater in living color, Korea was a map in the morning paper and the black-and-white photographs of David Douglas Duncan and others. As Ohio's Senator John Glenn, who as a Marine combat pilot in Korea shot down three MiG's, explains: "Korea didn't come into every American life the way Vietnam did because you didn't have blood flowing out of your TV set every night."

There is another reason why Korea never had the same mesmerizing effect as Vietnam: It did not set off what in essence was a domestic civil war. Perhaps that is because the generation that fought in Korea, the generation of Levittown and William H. Whyte, Jr.'s *The Organization Man,* had grown up amid a crusade against foreign evils—not, as its rebellious children did, during a civil-rights crusade against evils at home.

Forty years later, as the scars of Vietnam heal and the cold war recedes, there is a discernible connection between the sacrifices at Pork Chop Hill and the birth of fragile democracies in Prague, Warsaw, Budapest and in Seoul itself. Containment worked. America and its allies paid a heavy price to stop Communist aggression in Korea. But given the final outcome, history no doubt will conclude it was a price worth paying.

The revisionist view of Eisenhower.

The Ike Age

Stephen E. Ambrose

Stephen E. Ambrose is professor of history at the University of New Orleans. He is the author of *The Supreme Commander* (Doubleday), *Rise to Globalism* (Penguin), and 10 other books on recent American history. He is currently at work on a full-scale biography of Eisenhower.

> For all the jokes about golf playing, he did a far, far better job of handling that office than anyone realized.
>
> —Ronald Reagan on
> Dwight D. Eisenhower

Since Andrew Jackson left the White House in 1837, 33 men have served as president of the United States. Of that number, only four have managed to serve eight consecutive years in the office—Ulysses Grant, Woodrow Wilson, Franklin Roosevelt, and Dwight Eisenhower. Of these four, only two were also world figures in a field outside politics—Grant and Eisenhower—and only two had a higher reputation and broader popularity when they left office than when they entered—Roosevelt and Eisenhower.

Given this record of success, and the relative failure of Ike's successors, it is no wonder that there is an Eisenhower revival going on, or that President Reagan and his staff are attempting to present themselves as the Eisenhower administration resurrected. Another major reason for the current Eisenhower boom is nostalgia for the 1950s —a decade of peace with prosperity, a 1.5 percent annual inflation rate, self-sufficiency in oil and other precious goods, balanced budgets, and domestic tranquility. Eisenhower "revisionism," now proceeding at full speed, gives Ike himself much of the credit for these accomplishments.

The reassessment of Eisenhower is based on a multitude of new sources, as well as new perspectives, which have become available only in the past few years. The most important of these is Ike's private diary, which he kept on a haphazard basis from the late 1930s to his death in 1969. Other sources include his extensive private correspondence with his old military and new big business friends, his telephone conversations (which he had taped or summarized by his secretary, who listened in surreptitiously), minutes of meetings of the cabinet and of the National Security Council, and the extensive diary of his press secretary, the late James Hagerty. Study of these documents has changed the predominant scholarly view of Eisenhower from, in the words of the leading revisionist, political scientist Fred Greenstein of Princeton, one of "an aging hero who reigned more than he ruled and who lacked the energy, motivation, and political skill to have a significant impact on events," to a view of Ike as "politically astute and informed, actively engaged in putting his personal stamp on public policy, [who] applied a carefully thought-out conception of leadership to the conduct of his presidency."

The revisionist portrait of Ike contains many new features. Far from being a "part-time" president who preferred the golf course to the Oval Office, he worked an exhausting schedule, reading more and carrying on a wider correspondence than appeared at the time. Instead of the "captive hero" who was a tool of the millionaires in his cabinet, Ike made a major effort to convince the Republican right wing to accept the New Deal reforms, an internationalist foreign policy, and the need to modernize and liberalize the Republican party. Rather than ducking the controversial issue of Joseph McCarthy, Eisenhower strove to discredit the senator. Ike's failure to issue a public endorsement of *Brown v. Topeka* was not based on any fundamental disagreement with the Warren Court's ruling, but rather on his understanding of the separation, the balance, of powers in the US government—he agreed with the decision, it turns out, and was a Warren supporter. Nor was Ike a tongue-tied general of terrible syntax; he was a careful speaker and an excellent writer who confused his audiences only when he wanted to do so.

Most of all, the revisionists give Eisenhower high marks for ending the Korean War, staying out of Vietnam, and keeping the peace elsewhere. They argue that these achievements were neither accidental nor lucky, but rather the result of carefully conceived policies and firm leadership at the top. The revisionists also praise Ike for holding down defense costs, a key factor in restraining inflation while maintaining prosperity.

Altogether, the "new" Ike is an appealing figure, not only for his famous grin and winning personality, but also because he wisely guided us through perilous times.

"THE BLAND leading the bland." So the nightclub comics characterized the Eisenhower administration. Much of the blandness came from Ike's refusal to say, in public, anything negative about his fellow politicians. His lifelong rule was to refuse to discuss personalities. But in the privacy of his diary, parts of which have just been published with an excellent introduction by Robert H. Ferrell (*The Eisenhower Diaries*, W. W. Norton), he could be sarcastic, slashing, and bitter.

In 1953, when Ike was president and his old colleague from the war, Winston Churchill, was prime minister, the two met in Bermuda. Churchill, according to Ike,

> has developed an almost childlike faith that all of the answers to world problems are to be found merely in British-American partnership.... He is trying to relive the days of World War II. In those days he had the enjoyable feeling that he and our president were sitting on some rather Olympian platform ... and directing world affairs. Even if this picture were an accurate one of those days, it would have no application to the present. But it was only partially true, even then, as many of us who ... had to work out the solutions for nasty local problems are well aware.

That realistic sense of the importance of any one individual, even a Churchill or a Roosevelt, was basic to Eisenhower's thought. Back in 1942, with reference to MacArthur, Ike scribbled in his diary that in modern war, "no one person can be a Napoleon or a Caesar." What was required was teamwork and cooperation.

Although Lyndon Johnson, John F. Kennedy, Hubert Humphrey, and other Democratic senators of the 1950s catch hell from time to time in Ike's diary, he reserved his most heartfelt blasts for the Republicans (he never expected much from the Democrats anyway). Thus, Ike wrote of Senator William Knowland of California, "In his case there seems to be no final answer to the question 'How stupid can you get?'" In *Eisenhower the President* (Prentice-Hall), William Bragg Ewald Jr., a former Eisenhower speechwriter, records that when Republicans urged Ike to convince Nelson Rockefeller to take the second place on a 1960 ticket with Richard Nixon, Ike did so, rather half-heartedly, and then reported on Rockefeller: "He is no philosophical genius. It is pretty hard to get him in and tell him something of his duty. He has a personal ambition that is overwhelming." Eisenhower told Nixon that the only way to persuade Rockefeller to run for the vice presidency was for Nixon to promise to step aside in Rockefeller's favor in 1964.

IKE DIDN'T like "politics," and he positively disliked "politicians." The behind-the-scenes compromises, the swapping of votes for pork-barrel purposes, the willingness to abandon conviction in order to be on the popular side all nearly drove him to distraction. His favorite constitutional reform was to limit congressional terms to two for the Senate and three or four for the House, in order to eliminate the professional politician from American life.

Nor did Ike much like the press. "The members of this group," he wrote in his diary, "are far from being as important as they themselves consider," but he did recognize that "they have a sufficient importance ... in the eyes of the average Washington officeholder to insure that much government time is consumed in courting favor with them and in dressing up ideas and programs so that they look as saleable as possible." Reporters, Ike wrote, "have little sense of humor and, because of this, they deal in negative criticism rather than in any attempt toward constructive helpfulness." (Murray Kempton, in some ways the first Eisenhower revisionist, recalled how journalists had ridiculed Ike's amiability in the 1950s, while the president actually had intelligently confused and hoodwinked them. Kempton decided that Eisenhower was a cunning politician whose purpose was "never to be seen in what he did.")

The people Ike did like, aside from his millionaire friends, were those men who in his view rose above politics, including Milton Eisenhower, Robert Anderson, and Earl Warren. Of Milton, Ike wrote in 1953, "I believe him to be the most knowledgeable and widely informed of all the people with whom I deal.... So far as I am concerned, he is at this moment the most highly qualified man in the United States to be president. This most emphatically makes no exception of me...." Had he not shrunk from exposing Milton to a charge of benefiting from nepotism, Ike would have made his younger brother a member of his cabinet.

In 1966, during an interview in Eisenhower's Gettysburg office, I asked him who was the most intelligent man he had ever met, expecting a long pause while he ran such names as Marshall, Roosevelt, de Gaulle, Churchill, Truman, or Khrushchev through his mind. But Ike never hesitated: "Robert Anderson," he said emphatically. Anderson, a Texan and a Democrat, served Ike in various capacities, including secretary of the navy and secretary of the treasury. Now Ewald reveals for the first time that Eisenhower offered Anderson the second spot on the Republican ticket for 1956 and wanted Anderson to be his successor. Anderson turned down the president because he thought the offer was politically unrealistic.

Which inevitably brings up the subject of Richard Nixon. Eisenhower's relations with Nixon have long been a puzzle. Ike tried to get Nixon to resign during the 1952 campaign, but Nixon saved himself with the Checkers speech. In 1956 Ike attempted to maneuver Nixon off the ticket by offering him a high-level cabinet post, but Nixon dug in his heels and used his connections with the right wing of the party to stay in place. And in 1960, Ike's campaign speeches for Nixon were distinctly unenthusiastic. Still, Eisenhower and Nixon never severed their ties. Ike stuck with Nixon throughout his life. He often remarked that Nixon's defeat by Kennedy was one of his greatest disappointments. And, of course, his grandson married one of Nixon's daughters. Sad to say, neither the diary nor the private correspondence offers any insights into Eisenhower's gut feelings toward Nixon. The relationship between the two men remains a puzzle.

SOME WRITERS used to say the same about the Eisenhower-Earl Warren relationship, but thanks to Ike's diary, Ewald's book, and the correspondence, we now have a better understanding of Eisenhower's feelings toward Warren personally, and toward his Court. In December 1955, Jim Hagerty suggested that if Ike could not run for a second term for reasons of health, Warren might make a good nominee. "Not a chance," Ike snapped back, "and I'll tell you why. I know that the Chief Justice is very happy right where he is. He wants to go down in history as a great Chief Justice, and he certainly is becoming one. He is dedicated to the Court and is getting the Court back on its feet and back in respectable standing again."

Eisenhower and Warren were never friends; as Ewald writes, "For more than seven years they sat, each on his eminence, at opposite ends of Pennsylvania Avenue, by far the two most towering figures in Washington, each playing out a noble role, in tragic inevitable estrangement." And he quotes Attorney General Herbert Brownell as saying, "Both Eisenhower and Warren were very reserved men. If you'd try to put your arm around either of them, he'd remember it for sixty days."

Ike had a great deal of difficulty with *Brown v. Topeka*, but more because of his temperament than for any racist reasons. He was always an evolutionist who wanted to move forward through agreement and compromise, not command and force. Ike much preferred consensus to conflict. Yet Ewald argues that he privately recognized the necessity and justice of *Brown v. Topeka*. Even had that not been so, he would have supported the Court, because—as he carefully explained to one of his oldest and closest friends, Sweed Hazlett, in a private letter—"I hold to the basic purpose. There must be respect for the Constitution—which means the Supreme Court's interpretation of the Constitution—or we shall have chaos. This I believe with all my heart—and shall always act accordingly."

Precisely because of that feeling, Eisenhower never made a public declaration of support for the *Brown v. Topeka* decision, despite the pleas of liberals, intellectuals, and many members of the White House staff that he do so. He felt that once the Supreme Court had spoken, the president had no right to second guess nor any duty to support the decision. The law was the law. That Ike was always ready to uphold the law, he demonstrated decisively when he sent the US Army into Little Rock in 1957 to enforce court-ordered desegregation.

Despite his respect for Warren and the Court, when I asked Eisenhower in 1965 what was his biggest mistake, he replied heatedly, "The appointment of that S.O.B. Earl Warren." Shocked, I replied, "General, I always thought that was your best appointment." "Let's not talk about it," he responded, and we did not. Now that I have seen the flattering and thoughtful references to Warren in the diary, I can only conclude that Eisenhower's anger at Warren was the result of the criminal rights cases of the early 1960s, not the desegregation decisions of the 1950s.

As everyone knows, Ike also refused publically to condemn Senator McCarthy, again despite the pleas of many of his own people, including his most trusted adviser, Milton. Ike told Milton, "I will not get into a pissing contest with that skunk."

The revisionists now tell us that the president was working behind the scenes, using the "hidden hand" to encourage peaceful desegregation and to censure McCarthy. He helped Attorney General Brownell prepare a brief from the Justice Department for the Court on *Brown v. Topeka* that attacked the constitutionality of segregation in the schools. As for McCarthy, Greenstein writes that Eisenhower,

> working most closely with Press Secretary Hagerty, conducted a virtual day-to-day campaign via the media and congressional allies to end McCarthy's political effectiveness. The overall strategy was to avoid *direct mention* of McCarthy in the president's public statements, lest McCarthy win sympathy as a spunky David battling against the presidential Goliath. Instead Eisenhower systematically condemned the *types* of actions in which McCarthy engaged.

Eisenhower revisionism is full of nostalgia for the 1950s, and it is certainly true that if you were white, male, and middle class or better, it was the best decade of the century. The 1950s saw peace and prosperity, no riots, relatively high employment, a growing GNP, virtually no inflation, no arms race, no great reforms, no great changes, low taxes, little government regulation of industry or commerce, and a president who was trusted and admired. Politics were middle-of-the-road—Eisenhower was the least partisan president of the century. In an essay entitled "Good-By to the 'Fifties—and Good Riddance," historian Eric Goldman called the Eisenhower years possibly "the dullest and dreariest in all our history." After the turmoil of the 1960s and 1970s—war, inflation, riots, higher taxes, an arms race, all accompanied by a startling growth in the size, cost, and scope of the federal government—many Americans may find the dullness and dreariness of the 1950s appealing.

Next to peace, the most appealing fact was the 1.5 percent inflation rate. The revisionists claim that Ike deserved much of the credit for that accomplishment because of his insistence on a balanced budget (which he actually achieved only twice, but he did hold down the deficits). Ike kept down the costs by refusing to expand the New Deal welfare services—to the disgruntlement of the Republican right wing, he was equally firm about refusing to dismantle the New Deal programs—and, far more important, by holding down defense spending.

This was, indeed, Ike's special triumph. He feared that an arms race with the Soviet Union would lead to uncontrollable inflation and eventually bankrupt the United States, without providing any additional security. In Ike's view, the more bombs and missiles we built, the less secure we would be, not just because of the economic impact, but because the more bombs we built, the more the Soviets would build. In short, Ike's fundamental strategy was based on his recognition that in nuclear warfare, there is no defense and can be no winner. In that situation, one did not need to be superior to the enemy in order to deter him.

The Democrats, led by Senator John F. Kennedy, criticized Ike for putting a balanced budget ahead of national defense. They accused him of allowing a "bomber gap" and, later, a "missile gap" to develop, and spoke of the need to "get America moving again." Nelson Rockefeller and Richard Nixon added to the hue and cry during the 1960 campaign, when they promised to expand defense spending. But as long as Eisenhower was president, there was no arms race. Neither the politicians nor the military-industrial complex could persuade Eisenhower to spend more money on the military. Inheriting a $50 billion defense budget from Truman, he reduced it to $40 billion and held it there for the eight years of his tenure.

Holding down defense costs was a longstanding theme of Ike's. As early as December 1945, just after he replaced George Marshall as army chief of staff, he jotted in his diary, "I'm astounded and appalled at the size and scope of plans the staff sees as necessary to maintain our security position now and in the future." And in 1951, before he became a candidate, he wrote in his diary that if the Congress and military could not be restrained about "this armament business, we will go broke and still have inefficient defenses."

President Eisenhower was unassailable on the subject. As one senator complained, "How in hell can I argue with Ike Eisenhower on a military matter?" But as Ike wrote in 1956 to his friend Hazlett, "Some day there is going to be a man sitting in my present chair who has not been raised in the military services and who will have little understanding of where slashes in their estimates can be made with little or no damage. If that should happen while we still have the state of tension that now exists in the world, I shudder to think of what could happen in this country."

One reason why Ike was able to reduce the military in a time of great tension was his intimate knowledge of the Soviet military situation. From 1956 on, he directed a series of flights by the U-2 spy plane over the Soviet Union. He had personally taken the lead in getting the U-2 program started, and he kept a tight personal control over the flights— he gave his approval to the individual flights only after a thorough briefing on where in the USSR the planes were going and what the CIA wanted to discover. Here too the revisionists have shown that the contemporary feeling, especially after Francis Gary Powers was shot down in 1960, that Ike was not in charge and hardly knew what was going on inside his own government is altogether wrong. He was absolutely in charge, not only of broad policy on the use of the U-2, but of implementing details as well.

The major factor in Eisenhower's ability to restrain defense spending was keeping the peace. His record here is clear and impressive—he signed an armistice in Korea less than half a year after taking office, stayed out of Vietnam, and managed to avoid war despite such crisis situations as Hungary and the Suez, Quemoy and Matsu, Berlin and Cuba. The revisionists insist that

the credit must go to Ike, and they equally insist that Eisenhower, not Secretary of State John Foster Dulles, was in command of American foreign policy in the 1950s. Dulles, says Greenstein, "was assigned the 'get tough' side of foreign-policy enunciation, thus placating the fervently anti-Communist wing of the Republican party." Ike, meanwhile, appeared to be above the battle, while actually directing it on a day-to-day basis.

"In essence, Eisenhower used Dulles." So writes Robert Divine, one of America's leading diplomatic historians, in his provocative new book, *Eisenhower and the Cold War* (Oxford University Press). Divine concludes that "far from being the do-nothing President of legend, Ike was skillful and active in directing American foreign policy." All the revisionists agree that the contemporary idea that Dulles led Ike by the nose was a myth that Eisenhower himself did the most to encourage. Nevertheless, Eisenhower did have a high opinion of his secretary of state. Divine quotes Ike's comment to Emmet Hughes on Dulles: "There's only one man I know who has seen *more* of the world and talked with more people and *knows* more than he does—and that's me."

The quotation illustrates another often overlooked Eisenhower characteristic—his immense self-confidence. He had worked with some of the great men of the century—Churchill, Roosevelt, Stalin, de Gaulle, Montgomery, and many others—long before he became president. His diary entry for the day after his inauguration speaks to the point: "My first day at the president's desk. Plenty of worries and difficult problems. But such has been my portion for a long time—the result is that this just seems (today) like a continuation of all I've been doing since July 1941—even before that."

Ike's vast experience in war and peace made him confident in crises. People naturally looked to him for leadership. No matter how serious the crisis seemed to be, Ike rarely got flustered. During a war scare in the Formosa Straits in 1955, he wrote in his diary, "I have so often been through these periods of strain that I have become accustomed to the fact that most of the calamities that we anticipate really never occur."

IKE'S self-confidence was so great that, Greenstein writes, he had "neither a need nor a desire" to capture

headlines. "He employed his skills to achieve his ends by inconspicuous means." In foreign policy, this meant he did not issue strident warnings, did not—in public—threaten Russia or China with specific reprisals for specific actions. Instead, he retained his room for maneuver by deliberately spreading confusion. He did not care if editorial writers criticized him for jumbled syntax; he wanted to keep possible opponents guessing, and he did. For example, when asked at a March 1955 press conference if he would use atomic bombs to defend Quemoy and Matsu, he replied:

> Every war is going to astonish you in the way it occurred, and in the way it is carried out. So that for a man to predict, particularly if he has the responsibility for making the decision, to predict what he is going to use, how he is going to do it, would I think exhibit his ignorance of war; that is what I believe.

As he intended, the Chinese found such statements inscrutable, as they had in Korea two years earlier. When truce talks in Korea reached an impasse in mid-May 1953, Ike put the pressure on the Chinese, hinting to them that the United States might use atomic weapons if a truce could not be arranged, and backing this up by transferring atomic warheads to American bases in Okinawa. The Chinese then accepted a truce. As Divine writes, "Perhaps the best testimony to the shrewdness of the President's policy is the impossibility of telling even now whether or not he was bluffing."

Nearly all observers agree that one of Ike's greatest accomplishments was staying out of Vietnam in the face of intense pressure from his closest advisers to save the French position there or, after July 1954, to go in alone to defeat Ho Chi Minh. Ike was never tempted. As early as March 1951 he wrote in his diary, "I'm convinced that no military victory is possible in that kind of theater." And in a first draft of his memoirs, written in 1963 but not published until 1981 by Ewald, Ike wrote:

> The jungles of Indochina would have swallowed up division after division of United States troops, who, unaccustomed to this kind of warfare, would have sustained heavy casualties until they had learned to live in a new environment. Furthermore, the presence of ever more numbers of white men in uniform probably would have aggravated

rather than assuaged Asiatic resentments.

That was hardheaded military reasoning by General Eisenhower. But President Eisenhower stayed out of Vietnam as much for moral as for military reasons. When the Joint Chiefs suggested to him in 1954 that the United States use an atomic bomb against the Vietminh around Dien Bien Phu, the president said he would not be a party to using that "terrible thing" against Asians for the second time in less than a decade. And in another previously unpublished draft of his memoirs, he wrote:

> The strongest reason of all for the United States refusal to [intervene] is that fact that among all the powerful nations of the world the United States is the only one with a tradition of anti-colonialism. . . . The standing of the United States as the most powerful of the anti-colonial powers is an asset of incalculable value to the Free World. . . . Thus it is that the moral position of the United States was more to be guarded than the Tonkin Delta, indeed than all of Indochina.

Ike's international outlook, already well known, is highlighted by the new documents. He believed that the bonds that tied Western Europe and the United States together were so tight that the fate of one was the fate of the other. In May 1947, one year before the Marshall Plan, he wrote in his diary, in reference to Western Europe:

> I personally believe that the best thing we could now do would be to post 5 billion to the credit of the secretary of state and tell him to use it to support democratic movements wherever our vital interests indicate. Money should be used to promote possibilities of self-sustaining economies, not merely to prevent immediate starvation.

Ike also anticipated Kennedy's Alliance for Progress. Historian Burton Kaufman, in the narrowest but perhaps most important study reviewed here, *Trade and Aid: Eisenhower's Foreign Economic Policy* (Johns Hopkins University Press), concludes: "Not only did Eisenhower reorient the mutual security program away from military and toward economic assistance, he was also the first president to alter the geographical direction of American foreign aid toward the developing world." After an exhaustive examination, Kaufman also gives Ike high marks for resisting Nel-

son Rockefeller and others who wanted the president to enourage private investment overseas through tax breaks, while reducing or eliminating all forms of public foreign aid. Kaufman's basic theme is "the transition of a foreign economic program based on the concept of 'trade not aid' when Eisenhower took office to one predicated on the principle of 'trade and aid,' with the emphasis clearly on the flow of public capital abroad, by the time he left the White House."

That Ike himself was in charge of this transition, Kaufman leaves no doubt. That Kaufman likes Ike is equally clear: the foreign aid and trade program, Kaufman writes, "demonstrates the quality and character of Eisenhower's intellect and the cogency and forcefulness of his arguments in defense of administration policy. Finally, it emphasizes Eisenhower's flexibility as president and his capacity to alter his views in response to changing world conditions."

Kaufman, however, is critical of Ike on a number of points. Eisenhower himself, it turns out, could be as hypocritical as the "politicians" he scorned. In his speeches, Ike espoused the principles of free trade with sincerity and conviction; in his actions, he supported a protectionist agricultural policy and made broad concessions to the protectionist forces in Congress. Kaufman reaches the conclusion that "he often retreated on trade and tariff matters; he gave up the struggle with hardly a whimper."

And, as Blanche Wiesen Cook, another of the new Eisenhower scholars (but no revisionist), points out in *The Declassified Eisenhower* (Doubleday), Ike's vision of a peaceful world was based on a sophisticated version of Henry Luce's "American Century." Cook argues that Eisenhower's "blueprint . . . involved a determination to pursue political warfare, psychological warfare, and economic warfare everywhere and at all times." Under Ike's direction, she writes, the CIA and other branches of the government "ended all pretentions about territorial integrity, national sovereignty and international law. Covert operatives were everywhere, and they were active. From bribery to assassination, no activity was unacceptable short of nuclear war."

Cook does stress the importance of Eisenhower's stance against general war and his opposition to an arms race,

but insists that these positions have to be placed in context, a context that includes the CIA-inspired and -led governmental overthrows in Iran and Guatemala, covert operations of all types in Vietnam and Eastern Europe, and assassination attempts against political leaders in the Congo and Cuba. Returning to an earlier view of Ike, Cook regards him as a "captive hero," the "chosen instrument" of the leaders of the great multinational corporations "to fight for the world they wanted."

ONE DOES NOT have to accept Cook's "captive hero" view to realize that it may indeed be time, as Kaufman indicates, to blow the whistle on Eisenhower revisionism. Ike had his shortcomings and he suffered serious setbacks. For all his openness to new ideas, he was rigid and dogmatic in his anti-communism. The darker side of Eisenhower's refusal to condemn McCarthy was that Ike himself agreed with the senator on the nature, if not the extent, of the problem, and he shared the senator's goals, if not his methods. After his first year in office, Ike made a list of his major accomplishments to date. Peace in Korea was first, the new defense policy second. Third on the list: "The highest security standards are being insisted upon for those employed in government service," a bland way of saying that under his direction, the Civil Service Commission had fired 2,611 "security risks" and reported that 4,315 other government workers had resigned when they learned they were under investigation. That was the true "hidden hand" at work, and the true difference between Ike and McCarthy—Ike got rid of Communists and fellow travelers (and many liberals) quietly and effectively, while McCarthy, for all his noise, accomplished nothing.

Thus, no matter how thoroughly the revisionists document Ike's opposition to McCarthy personally or his support for Warren, it remains true that his failure to speak out directly on McCarthy encouraged the witch hunters, just as his failure to speak out directly on the *Brown v. Topeka* decision encouraged the segregationists. The old general never admitted that it was impossible for him to be truly above the battle, never seemed to understand that the president is inevitably a part of the battle, so much so that his inaction can have as great an impact as his action. With McCarthy and *Brown v. Topeka* in mind, there is a sad quality to the following Eisenhower diary passage, written in January 1954, about a number of Republican senators whom Ike was criticizing for being more inclined to trade votes than to provide clear leadership:

> They do not seem to realize when there arrives that moment at which soft speaking should be abandoned and a fight to the end undertaken. Any man who hopes to exercise leadership must be ready to meet this requirement face to face when it arises; unless he is ready to fight when necessary, people will finally begin to ignore him.

One of Ike's greatest disappointments was his failure to liberalize and modernize the Republican party, in order to make it the majority party in the United States. "The Republican party must be known as a progressive organization or it is sunk," he wrote in his diary in November 1954. "I believe this so emphatically that far from appeasing or reasoning with the dyed-in-the-wool reactionary fringe, we should completely ignore it and when necessary, repudiate it." Responding to cries of "impeach Earl Warren," Ike wrote in his diary, "If the Republicans as a body should try to repudiate him, I shall leave the Republican Party and try to organize an intelligent group of independents, however small." He was always threatening to break with the Republican party, or at least rename it; in March 1954, he told Hagerty, "You know, what we ought to do is get a word to put ahead of Republican—something like 'new' or 'modern' or something. We just can't work with fellows like McCarthy, Bricker, Jenner and that bunch."

A favorite revisionist quotation, which is used to show Ike's political astuteness, comes from a 1954 letter to his brother Edgar:

> Should any political party attempt to abolish social security and eliminate labor laws and farm programs, you would not hear of that party again in our political history. There is a tiny splinter group, of course, that believes that you can do these things. Among them are H. L. Hunt, a few other Texas oil millionaires, and an occasional politician and businessman from other areas. Their number is negligible and they are stupid.

Good enough, but a critic would be quick to point out that Ike's "tiny splinter group" managed to play a large role in the nominations of Barry Goldwater, Richard Nixon, and Ronald Reagan. In short, although Ike saw great dangers to the right in the Republican party, he did little to counter the reactionary influence in his own organization. Franklin Roosevelt did a far better job of curbing the left wing in the Democratic party, and generally in building his party, than anything Ike did for the Republicans.

THE EISENHOWER legacy for the Reagan administration, in brief, is mixed. Reagan can choose to emphasize the darker side of Ike's foreign policy, with its emphasis on CIA activities and reflexive opposition to communism, or he can follow Ike's lead and reject any thought of general war while searching for a genuine peace. Similarly, on the domestic front he can ignore the poor and the minorities in an attempt to balance the budget and curb inflation, or he can again emulate Ike and insist on retaining a strong Social Security system backed by the federal government. He could also recall that Ike presided over the largest public works program in the history of mankind, the Interstate Highway System.

What Reagan cannot do, and still remain faithful to Eisenhower's legacy, is spend increasing sums on the military. From the end of World War II to his last day in the White House, Eisenhower resisted swollen military budgets. In January 1952 he noted in his diary his fear of "the danger of internal deterioration through the annual expenditure of unconscionable sums on a program of indefinite duration, extending far into the future." Or, as he told some members of Congress, "It is perfectly clear that you can't provide security just with a check book. You've got to be prepared to live with a series of [crises] for the next 40 years. If these people decide to put another $3 billion into the budget every time Russia tries to push, they might as well go all the way to a garrison state." The style and rhetoric of the Reagan administration might well be those of the Eisenhower administration—the quick and easy smile, low-key cabinet government on the Whig model, practical businessmen in charge, balanced budgets and lower taxes, stern opposition to communism—but so long as the Reagan people insist on expanded military expenditures the reality can never be the same. Ike's legacy means more than presidential style; he also bequeathed us a record of achievement.

Shortly after Ike left office, a group of leading American historians was asked to rate the presidents. Ike came in near the bottom of the poll. That result was primarily a reflection of how enamored the professors were with FDR and Harry Truman. Today, those same historians would compare Ike with his successors rather than his predecessors and place him in the top 10, if not the top five, of all our presidents. No matter how much one qualifies that record by pointing to this or that shortcoming or failure of the Eisenhower administration, it remains an enviable record. No wonder the people like Ike.

REBELS WITHOUT A CAUSE?

Teenagers in the '50s

Beth Bailey

Beth Bailey is Professor of Modern British History at the University of Kansas and author of the forthcoming Crime and Society in England 1880-1980 for Longman.

The United States emerged from the Second World War the most powerful and affluent nation in the world. This statement, bald but essentially accurate, is the given foundation for understanding matters foreign and domestic, the Cold War and the Age of Abundance in America. Yet the sense of confidence and triumph suggested by that firm phrasing and by our images of soldiers embracing women as confetti swirled through downtown streets obscures another post-war reality. Underlying and sometimes overwhelming both bravado and complacency were voices of uncertainty. America at war's end was not naively optimistic.

The Great War had planted the seeds of the Great Depression. Americans wondered if hard times would return as the war boom ended. (They wouldn't.) The First World War had not ended all wars. Would war come again? (It would, both cold and hot.) And the fundamental question that plagued post-war America was would American citizens have the strength and the character to meet the demands of this new world?

Post-war America appears in stereotype as the Age of Conformity – smug, materialistic, complacent, a soulless era peopled by organisation men and their (house)wives. But this portrait of conformity exists only because Americans created it. Throughout the post-war era Americans indulged in feverish self-examination. Experts proclaimed crises, limned the American character, poked and prodded into the recesses of the American psyche. Writing in scholarly journals and for an attentive general public, theorists and social critics suggested that America's very success was destroying the values that had made success possible. Success, they claimed, was eroding the ethic that had propelled America to military and industrial supremacy and had lifted American society (with significant exceptions seen clearly in hindsight) to undreamed-of heights of prosperity.

At issue was the meaning of the American dream. Did the American dream mean success through individual competition in a wide-open free market-place? Or was the dream only of the abundance the American market-place had made possible – the suburban American dream of two cars in every garage and a refrigerator-freezer in every kitchen? One dream was of competition and the resulting rewards. The *making* of the self-made man – the process of entrepreneurial struggle – was the stuff of that dream. Fulfillment, in this vision, was not only through material comforts, but through the prominence, social standing, and influence in the public sphere one achieved in the struggle for success.

The new-style post-war American dream seemed to look to the private as the sphere of fulfillment, of self-definition and self-realisation. Struggle was not desired, but stasis. The dream was of a private life – a family, secure, stable, and comfortable – that compensated for one's public (work) life. One vision highlighted risk; the other security. Many contemporary observers feared that the desire for security was overwhelming the 'traditional' American ethic. In the dangerous post-war world, they asserted,

First published in *History Today*, February 1990, pp. 25-31. Reproduced by kind permission of History Today, Ltd., 83-84 Berwick Street, London W1V 3PJ, England.

the rejection of the public, of work and of risk would soon destroy America's prosperity and security.

The focus for much of the fear over what America was becoming was, not surprisingly, youth. Adult obsession with the new post-war generation took diverse forms – from the over-heated rhetoric about the new epidemic of juvenile delinquency (too many rebels without causes) to astringent attacks on the conformity of contemporary youth. These critiques, though seemingly diametrically opposed, were based on the shared assumption that young people lacked the discipline and get-up-and-go that had made America great.

Perhaps nowhere in American culture do we find a richer statement of concern about American youth and the new American dream than in the debates which raged over 'going steady', an old name for a new practice which was reportedly more popular among post-war teenagers than 'bop, progressive jazz, hot rods and curiosity (slight) about atomic energy'. The crisis over the 'national problem' of going steady is not merely emblematic – an amusing way into a serious question. 'Going Steady' seemed to many adults the very essence of the problem, a kind of leading indicator of the privatisation of the American dream. Social scientists and social critics saw in the new security-first courtship patterns a paradigm for an emerging American character that, while prizing affluence, did not relish the risks and hard work that made it possible.

Certainly the change in courtship patterns was dramatic. And it was not hard to make a connection between the primary characteristics of teenagers' love lives and what they hoped to get out of American life in general. Before the Second World War, American youth had prized a promiscuous popularity, demonstrating competitive success through the number and variety of dates they commanded. Sociologist Willard Waller, in his 1937 study of American dating, gave this competitive system a name: 'the campus rating complex'. His study of Pennsylvania State University detailed a 'dating and rating' system based on a model of public competition in which popularity was the currency. To be popular, men needed outward, material signs: an automobile, proper clothing, the right fraternity membership, money. Women's popularity depended on building and maintaining a reputation for popularity. They had to *be seen* with popular men in the 'right' places, indignantly turn down requests for dates made at the 'last minute', and cultivate the impression they were greatly in demand.

In *Mademoiselle*'s 1938 college issue, for example, a Smith college senior advised incoming freshmen to 'cultivate an image of popularity' if they wanted dates. 'During your first term', she wrote, 'get "home talent" to ply you with letters, invitations, telegrams. College men will think, "She must be attractive if she can rate all that attention".' And at Northwestern University in the 1920s, competitive pressure was so intense that co-eds made a pact not to date on certain nights of the week. That way they could preserve some time to study, secure in the knowledge they were not losing ground in the competitive race for success by staying home.

In 1935, the Massachusetts *Collegian* (the Massachusetts State College student newspaper) ran an editorial against using the library for 'datemaking'. The editors proclaimed: 'The library is the place for the improvement of the mind and not the social standing of the student.' Social standing, not social life: on one word turns the meaning of the dating system. That 'standing' probably wasn't even a conscious choice shows how completely these college students took for granted that dating was primarily concerned with competition and popularity. As one North Carolina teenager summed it up:

> Going steady with one date
> Is okay, if that's all you rate.

Rating, dating, popularity, competition: catchwords hammered home, reinforced from all sides until they seemed a natural vocabulary. You had to rate in order to date, to date in order to rate. By successfully maintaining this cycle, you became popular. To stay popular, you competed. There was no end; the competitive process defined dating. Competition was the key term in the formula – remove it and there was no rating, dating, or popularity.

In the 1930s and 1940s, this competition was enacted most visibly, on the dance floor. There, success was a dizzying popularity that kept girls whirling from escort to escort, 'cut in' on by a host of popular men. Advice columns, etiquette books, even student handbooks told girls to strive to be 'once-arounders', to never be left with the same partner for more than one turn around the dance floor. On the dance floor, success and failure were easily measured. Wallflowers were dismissed out of hand. But getting stuck – not being 'cut in' on – was taken quite seriously as a sign of social failure. Everyone noticed and everyone judged.

This form of competitive courtship would change dramatically. By the early 1950s, 'cutting in' had almost completely disappeared outside the Deep South. In 1955, a student at Texas Christian University reported, 'To cut in is almost an insult'. A girl in Green Bay, Wisconsin, said that her parents were 'astonished' when they discovered that she hadn't danced with anyone but her escort at a 'formal'. 'The truth was', she admitted, 'that I wasn't aware that we were supposed to'.

This 180-degree reversal took place quickly – during the years of the Second World War – and was so complete by the early 1950s that people under eighteen could be totally unaware of the formerly powerful convention. It signalled not simply a change in dancing etiquette but a complete transformation of the dating system as well. Definitions of social success as promiscuous popularity based on strenuous competition had given way to new definitions, which located success in the security of a dependable escort.

By the 1950s, early marriage had become the goal for young adults. In 1959, 47 per cent of all brides married before they turned nineteen, and up to 25 per cent of students at many large state universities were married. The average age at marriage had risen to 26.7 for men and 23.3 for women during the lingering Depression, but by 1951 the average agte at marriage had fallen to 22.6 for men, 20.4 for women. And younger teens had developed their own version of early marriage.

As early as 1950, going steady had completely supplanted the dating-rating complex as the criterion for popularity among youth. A best-selling study of American teenagers, *Profile of Youth* (1949) reported that in most high schools the 'mere fact' of going steady was a sign of popularity 'as long as you don't get tied up with an impossible gook'. The *Ladies' Home Journal* reported in 1949 that 'every high school student… must be prepared to fit into a high-school pattern in which popularity, social acceptance and emotional security are often determined by the single question: does he or she go steady?' A 1959 poll found that 57 per cent of American teens had gone or were going steady. And, according to *Cosmopolitan* in 1960, if you didn't go steady, you were 'square'.

The new protocol of going steady was every bit as strict as the old protocol of rating and dating. To go steady, the boy gave the girl some visible token, such as a class ring or letter sweater. In Portland, Oregon, steadies favoured rings (costing from $17-$20). In Birmingham, Michigan, the girl wore the boy's identity bracelet, but never his letter sweater. In rural Iowa, the couple wore matching corduroy 'steady jackets', although any couple wearing matching clothing in California would be laughed at.

As long as they went steady, the boy had to call the girl a certain number of times a week and take her on a certain number of dates a week (both numbers were subject to local convention). Neither boy nor girl could date anyone else or pay too much attention to anyone of the opposite sex. While either could go out with friends of the same sex, each must always know where the other was and what he or she was doing. Going steady meant a guaranteed date for special events, and it implied greater sexual intimacy – either more 'necking' or 'going further'.

In spite of the intense monogamy of these steady relationships, teenagers viewed them as temporary. A 1950 study of 565 seniors in an eastern suburban high school found that 80 per cent had gone or were going steady. Out of that number, only eleven said they planned to marry their steady. In New Haven, Connecticut, high school girls wore 'obit bracelets'. Each time they broke up with a boy, they added a disc engraved with his name or initials to the chain. In Louisiana, a girl would embroider her sneakers with the name of her current steady. When they broke up, she would clip off his name and sew an X over the spot. An advice book from the mid-1950s advised girls to get a 'Puppy Love Anklet'. Wearing it on the right ankle meant that you were available, on the left that you were going steady. The author advised having 'Going Steady' engraved on one side, 'Ready, Willing 'n Waiting' on the other – just in case the boys could not remember the code. All these conventions, cheerfully reported in teenager columns in national magazines, show how much teenagers took it for granted that going steady was a temporary, if intense, arrangement.

Harmless as this system sounds today, especially compared to the rigours of rating and dating, the rush to go steady precipitated an intense generational battle. Clearly some adult opposition was over sex: going steady was widely accepted as a justification for greater physical intimacy. But more fundamentally, the battle over going steady came down to a confrontation between two generations over the meaning of the American dream. Security versus competition. Teenagers in the 1950s were trying to do the unthinkable – to eliminate competition from the popularity equation. Adults were appalled. To them, going steady, with its extreme rejection of competition in favour of temporary security, represented all the faults of the new generation.

Adults, uncomfortable with the 'cult of happiness' that rejected competition for security, attacked the teenage desire for security with no holds barred. As one writer advised boys, 'To be sure of anything is to cripple one's powers of growth'. She continued, 'To have your girl always assured at the end of a telephone line without having to work for her, to beat the other fellows to her is bound to lessen your powers of personal achievement'. A male adviser, campaigning against going steady, argued: 'Competition will be good for you. It sharpens your wits, teaches you how to get along well in spite of difficulties.' And another, writing in *Esquire*, explained the going steady phenomenon this way: 'She wants a mate; he being a modern youth doesn't relish competition.'

As for girls, the argument went: 'She's afraid of competition. She isn't sure she can compete for male attention in the open market; "going steady" frees her from fear of future failures'. The author of *Jackson's Guide to Dating* tells the story of 'Judith Thompson', a not-especially-attractive girl with family problems, who has been going steady with 'Jim' since she was fourteen. Lest we think that poor Judith deserves someone to care for her or see Jim as a small success in her life, the author stresses that going steady is one more failure for Judith. 'Now that Judith is sixteen and old enough to earn money and help herself in other ways to recover from her unfortunate childhood, she has taken on the additionally crippling circumstance of a steady boyfriend. How pathetic. The love and attention of her steady boyfriend are a substitute for other more normal kinds of success.' What should Judith be doing? 'A good deal of the time she spends going steady with Jim could be used to make herself more attractive so that other boys would ask her for dates.'

There is nothing subtle in these critiques of going steady. The value of competition is presumed as a clear standard against which to judge modern youth. But there is more here. There is a tinge of anger in these judgments, an anger that may well stem from the differing experiences of two generations of Americans. The competitive system that had emerged in the flush years of the 1920s was strained by events of the 1930s and 1940s. The elders had come of age during decades of depression and world war, times when the competitive struggle was, for many, inescapable. Much was at stake, the cost of failure all too clear. While youth in the period between the wars embraced a competitive dating system, even gloried in it, as adults they sought the security they had lacked in their youth.

Young people and their advocates made much of the lack of security of the post-war world, self-consciously pointing to the 'general anxiety of the times' as a justification for both early marriage and going steady. But the lives of these young people were clearly more secure than those of their parents. That was the gift their parents tried to give them. Though the Cold War raged it had little immediate impact on the emerging teenage culture (for those too young to fight in Korea, of course). Cushioned by unprecedented affluence, allowed more years of freedom within the protected youth culture of high school and ever-more-frequently college, young people did not have to struggle so hard, compete so ferociously, as their parents had.

And by and large, both young people and their parents knew it and were genuinely not sure what that meant for America's future. What did it mean – that a general affluence, at least for a broad spectrum of America's burgeoning middle class, was possible without a dog-eat-dog ferocity? What did *that* mean for the American Dream of success? One answer was given in the runaway best seller of the decade, *The Man in the Gray Flannel Suit*, which despite the title was not so much about the deadening impact of conformity but about what Americans should and could dream in the post-war world.

The protagonist of the novel, Tom Rath (the not-so-subtle naming made more explicit by the appearance of the word 'vengeful' in the sentence following Tom's introduction), has been through the Second World War, and the shadow of war hangs over his life. Tom wants to provide well for his family, and feels a nagging need to succeed. But when he is offered the chance at an old style American dream – to be taken on as the protégé of his business-wise, driven boss, he says no. In a passage that cuts to the heart of post-war American culture, Tom tells his boss:

> I don't think I'm the kind of guy who should try to be a big executive. I'll say it frankly: I don't think I have the willingness to make the sacrifices... I'm trying to be honest about this. I want the money. Nobody likes money better than I do. But I'm not the kind of guy who can work evenings and weekends and all the rest of it forever... I've been through one war. Maybe another one's coming. If one is, I want to be able to look back and figure I spent the time between wars with my family, the way it should have been spent. Regardless of war, I want to get the most out of the years I've got left. Maybe that sounds silly. It's just that if I have to bury myself in a job every minute of my life, I don't see any point to it...

Tom's privatised dream – of comfort without sacrifice, of family and personal fulfillment – might seem the author's attempt to resolve the tensions of the novel (and of post-war American society). But the vision is more complex than simply affirmative. Tom's boss responds with sympathy and understanding, then suddenly loses control. 'Somebody has to do the big jobs!', he says passionately. 'This world was built by men like me! To really do a job, you have to live it, body and soul! You people who just give half your mind to your work are riding on our backs!' And Tom responds: 'I know it.'

The new American Dream had not yet triumphed. The ambivalence and even guilt implicit in Tom Rath's answer to his boss pervaded American culture in the 1950s – in the flood of social criticism and also in parents' critiques of teenage courtship rituals. The attacks on youth's desire for security are revealing, for it was in many ways the parents who embraced security – moving to the suburbs, focusing on the family. The strong ambivalence many felt about their lives appears in the critiques of youth. This same generation would find even more to criticise in the 1960s, as the 'steadies' of the 1950s became the sexual revolutionaries of the 1960s. Many of the children of these parents came to recognise the tensions within the dream. The baby-boom generation accepted wholeheartedly the doctrine of self-fulfillment, but rejected the guilt and fear that had linked fulfillment and security. In the turbulence of the 1960s, young people were not rejecting the new American Dream of easy affluence and personal fulfillment, but only jettisoning the fears that had hung over a generation raised with depression and war. It turns out the 1950s family was not the new American Dream, but only its nurturing home.

FOR FURTHER READING:
Beth Bailey, *From Front Porch to Back Seat: Courtship in 20th Century America* (The Johns Hopkins University Press, 1988); Paula Fass, *The Damned and the Beautiful: American Youth in the 1920s* (Oxford University Press, 1977); James Gilbert, *A Cycle of Outrage: America's Reaction to the Juvenile Delinquent in the 1950s* (Oxford University Press, 1986); Elaine Tyler May, *Homeward Bound: American Families in the Cold War Era* (Basic Books, 1988); John Modell, *Into One's Own* (University of California Press, 1989).

**A noted biographer examines the life and legacy of
the civil rights leader who may have been the most-loved and
most-hated man in America during the turbulent 1960s.**

Trumpet of Conscience

A Portrait of
Martin Luther King, Jr.

Stephen B. Oates

*Biographer and historian Stephen B. Oates is Paul Murray
Kendall Professor of Biography and Professor of History at
the University of Massachusetts, Amherst. He is the author of
twelve books, including award-winning biographies of John
Brown, Nat Turner, Abraham Lincoln, and Martin Luther
King, Jr. His newest biography,* William Faulkner: The Man
and the Artist, *was published by Harper & Row in 1987. "This
article on Martin Luther King," writes Oates, "is dedicated to
the memory of James Baldwin, who had a powerful influence
on me in the 1960s, when I was a young writer trying to understand the complexities of American race relations."*

He was M.L. to his parents, Martin to his wife and
friends, Doc to his aides, Reverend to his male par-
ishioners, Little Lord Jesus to adoring churchwomen, De
Lawd to his young critics in the Student Nonviolent
Coordinating Committee, and Martin Luther King, Jr., to
the world. At his pulpit or a public rostrum, he seemed
too small for his incomparable oratory and international
fame as a civil rights leader and spokesman for world
peace. He stood only five feet seven, and had round
cheeks, a trim mustache, and sad, glistening eyes—eyes
that revealed both his inner strength and his vulnerability.

He was born in Atlanta on January 15, 1929, and grew
up in the relative comfort of the black middle class. Thus
he never suffered the want and privation that plagued the
majority of American blacks of his time. His father, a
gruff, self-made man, was pastor of Ebenezer Baptist
Church and an outspoken member of Atlanta's black
leadership. M.L. joined his father's church when he was
five and came to regard it as his second home. The church
defined his world, gave it order and balance, taught him

how to "get along with people." Here M.L. knew who he
was—"Reverend King's boy," somebody special.

At home, his parents and maternal grandmother reinforced his self-esteem, praising him for his precocious
ways, telling him repeatedly that he was *somebody*. By
age five, he spoke like an adult and had such a prodigious
memory that he could recite whole Biblical passages and
entire hymns without a mistake. He was acutely sensitive,
too, so much so that he worried about all the blacks he
saw in Atlanta's breadlines during the Depression, fearful
that their children did not have enough to eat. When his
maternal grandmother died, twelve-year-old M.L.
thought it was his fault. Without telling anyone, he had
slipped away from home to watch a parade, only to find
out when he returned that she had died. He was terrified
that God had taken her away as punishment for his "sin."
Guilt-stricken, he tried to kill himself by leaping out of his
second-story window.

He had a great deal of anger in him. Growing up a
black in segregated Atlanta, he felt the full range of

From *American History Illustrated*, April 1988, pp. 19-27, 52. Reprinted through the courtesy of Cowles Magazines,
publishers of *American History Illustrated*.

AP/WIDE WORLD PHOTOS

The Rev. Martin Luther King, Jr., was relatively unknown in 1955 when his oratory skills caught the attention of black leaders organizing a boycott against segregated city buses in Montgomery, Alabama. Selected as spokesman, King, seen above with wife Coretta and boycott organizer E. D. Dixon at his side at the Montgomery County Courthouse, soon rose to national prominence as a moral voice for civil rights.

southern racial discrimination. He discovered that he had to attend separate, inferior schools, which he sailed through with a modicum of effort, skipping grades as he went. He found out that he—a preacher's boy—could not sit at lunch counters in Atlanta's downtown stores. He had to drink from a "colored" water fountain, relieve himself in a rancid "colored" restroom, and ride a rickety "colored" elevator. If he rode a city bus, he had to sit in the back as though he were contaminated. If he wanted to see a movie in a downtown theater, he had to enter through a side door and sit in the "colored" section in the balcony. He discovered that whites referred to blacks as "boys" and "girls" regardless of age. He saw "WHITES ONLY" signs staring back at him in the windows of barber shops and all the good restaurants and hotels, at the YMCA, the city parks, golf courses, swimming pools, and in the waiting rooms of the train and bus stations. He learned that there were even white

and black sections of the city and that he resided in "nigger town."

Segregation caused a tension in the boy, a tension between his parents' injunction ("Remember, you are *somebody*") and a system that constantly demeaned and insulted him. He struggled with the pain and rage he felt when a white woman in a downtown store slapped him and called him "a little nigger" . . . when a bus driver called him "a black son-of-a-bitch" and made him surrender his seat to a white . . . when he stood on the very spot in Atlanta where whites had lynched a black man . . . when he witnessed nightriding Klansmen beating blacks in the streets. How, he asked defiantly, could he heed the Christian injunction and love a race of people who hated him? In retaliation, he determined "to hate every white person."

Yes, he was angry. In sandlot games, he competed so fiercely that friends could not tell whether he was playing or fighting. He had his share of playground combat, too, and could outwrestle any of his peers. He even rebelled against his father, vowing never to become a preacher like him. Yet he liked the way Daddy King stood up to whites: he told them never to call him a boy and vowed to fight this system until he died.

Still, there was another side to M.L., a calmer, sensuous side. He played the violin, enjoyed opera, and relished soul food—fried chicken, cornbread, and collard greens with ham hocks and bacon drippings. By his mid-teens, his voice was the most memorable thing about him. It had changed into a rich and resonant baritone that commanded attention whenever he held forth. A natty dresser, nicknamed "Tweed" because of his fondness for tweed suits, he became a connoisseur of lovely young women. His little brother A.D. remembered how Martin "kept flitting from chick to chick" and was "just about the best jitterbug in town."

AT AGE FIFTEEN, he entered Morehouse College in Atlanta, wanting somehow to help his people. He thought about becoming a lawyer and even practiced giving trial speeches before a mirror in his room. But thanks largely to Morehouse President Benjamin Mays, who showed him that the ministry could be a respectable forum for ideas, even for social protest, King decided to become a Baptist preacher after all. By the time he was ordained in 1947, his resentment toward whites had softened some, thanks to positive contact with white students on an intercollegiate council. But he hated his segregated world more than ever.

Once he had his bachelor's degree, he went north to study at Crozer Seminary near Philadelphia. In this mostly white school, with its polished corridors and quiet solemnity, King continued to ponder the plight of blacks in America. How, by what method and means, were blacks to improve their lot in a white-dominated country? His study of history, especially of Nat Turner's slave insurrection, convinced him that it was suicidal for a minority to strike back against a heavily armed majority. For him, voluntary segregation was equally unacceptable, as was accommodation to the status quo. King shuddered at such negative approaches to the race problem. How indeed were blacks to combat discrimination in a country ruled by the white majority?

As some other blacks had done, he found his answer in the teachings of Mohandas Gandhi—for young King, the discovery had the force of a conversion experience. Nonviolent resistance, Gandhi taught, meant noncooperation with evil, an idea he got from Henry David Thoreau's essay "On Civil Disobedience." In India, Gandhi gave Thoreau's theory practical application in the form of strikes, boycotts, and protest marches, all conducted nonviolently and all predicated on love for the oppressor and a belief in divine justice. In gaining Indian independence, Gandhi sought not to defeat the British, but to redeem them through love, so as to avoid a legacy of bitterness. Gandhi's term for this—*Satyagraha*—reconciled love and force in a single, powerful concept.

As King discovered from his studies, Gandhi had embraced nonviolence in part to subdue his own violent nature. This was a profound revelation for King, who had felt much hatred in his life, especially toward whites. Now Gandhi showed him a means of harnessing his anger and channeling it into a positive and creative force for social change.

AT THIS JUNCTURE, King found mostly theoretical satisfaction in Gandhian nonviolence; he had no plans to become a radical activist in the segregated South. Indeed, he seemed destined to a life of the mind, not of social protest. In 1951, he graduated from Crozer and went on to earn a Ph.D. in theology from Boston University, where his adviser pronounced him "a scholar's scholar" of great intellectual potential. By 1955, a year after the school desegregation decision, King had married comely Coretta Scott and assumed the pastorship of Dexter Avenue Baptist Church in Montgomery, Alabama. Immensely happy in the world of ideas, he hoped eventually to teach theology at a major university or seminary.

But, as King liked to say, the *Zeitgist*, or spirit of the age, had other plans for him. In December 1955, Montgomery blacks launched a boycott of the city's segregated buses and chose the articulate twenty-six-year-old minister as their spokesman.* As it turned out, he was unusually well prepared to assume the kind of leadership thrust on him. Drawing on Gandhi's teachings and example, plus the tenets of his own Christian faith, King directed a nonviolent boycott designed both to end an injustice and redeem his white adversaries through love. When he exhorted blacks to love their enemies, King did not mean to love them as friends or intimates. No, he said, he meant a disinterested love in all humankind, a love that saw the neighbor in everyone it met, a love that sought to restore the beloved community. Such love not only avoided the internal violence of the spirit, but severed the external chain of hatred that only produced more hatred in an endless spiral. If American blacks could break the chain of hatred, King said, true brotherhood could begin. Then posterity would have to say that there had lived a race of people, of black people, who "injected a new meaning into the veins of history and civilization."

During the boycott King imparted his philosophy at twice-weekly mass meetings in the black churches, where overflow crowds clapped and cried as his mellifluous voice swept over them. In these mass meetings King discovered his extraordinary power as an orator. His rich religious imagery reached deep into the black psyche, for religion had been the black people's main source of strength and survival since slavery days. His delivery was "like a narrative poem," said a woman journalist who heard him. His voice had such depths of sincerity and empathy that it could "charm your heart right out of your body." Because he appealed to the best

*See "The Father His Children Forgot" in the December 1985 issue of American History Illustrated.

in his people, articulating their deepest hurts and aspirations, black folk began to idolize him; he was their Gandhi.

Under his leadership, they stood up to white Montgomery in a remarkable display of solidarity. Pitted against an obdurate city government that blamed the boycott on Communist agitation and resorted to psychological and legal warfare to break it, the blacks stayed off the buses month after month, and walked or rode in a black-operated carpool. When an elderly woman refused the offer of a ride, King asked her, "But don't your feet hurt? "Yes," she replied, "my feet is tired but my soul is rested." For King, her irrepressible spirit was proof that "a new Negro" was emerging in the South, a Negro with "a new sense of dignity and destiny."

That "new Negro" menaced white supremacists, especially the Ku Klux Klan, and they persecuted King with a vengeance. They made obscene phone calls to his home, sent him abusive, sickening letters, and once even dynamited the front of his house. Nobody was hurt, but King, fearing a race war, had to dissuade angry blacks from violent retaliation. Finally, on November 13, 1956, the U.S. Supreme Court nullified the Alabama laws that enforced segregated buses, and handed King and his boycotters a resounding moral victory. Their protest had captured the imagination of progressive people all over the world and marked the beginning of a southern black movement that would shake the segregated South to its foundations. At the forefront of that movement was a new organization, the Southern Christian Leadership Conference (SCLC), which King and other black ministers formed in 1957, with King serving as its president and guiding spirit. Operating through the southern black church, SCLC sought to enlist the black masses in the freedom struggle by expanding "the Montgomery way" across the South.

The "Miracle of Montgomery" changed King's life, catapulting him into international prominence as an inspiring new moral voice for civil rights. Across the country, blacks and whites alike wrote him letters of encouragement; *Time* magazine pictured him on its cover; the National Association for the Advancement of Colored People (NAACP) and scores of church and civic organizations vied for his services as a speaker. "I am really disturbed how fast all this has happened to me," King told his wife. "People will expect me to perform miracles for the rest of my life."

But fame had its evil side, too. When King visited New York in 1958, a deranged black woman stabbed him in the chest with a letter opener. The weapon was lodged so close to King's aorta, the main artery from the heart, that he would have died had he sneezed. To extract the blade, an interracial surgical team had to remove a rib and part of his breastbone; in a burst of inspiration, the lead surgeon made the incision over King's heart in the shape of a cross.

THAT HE HAD NOT DIED convinced King that God was preparing him for some larger work in the segregated South. To gain perspective on what was happening there, he made a pilgrimage to India to visit Gandhi's shrine and the sites of his "War for Independence." He returned home with an even deeper commitment to nonviolence and a vow to be more humble and ascetic like Gandhi. Yet he was a man of manifold contradictions, this American Gandhi. While renouncing material things and giving nearly all of his extensive honorariums to SCLC, he liked posh hotels and zesty meals with wine, and he was always immaculately dressed in a gray or black suit, white shirt, and tie. While caring passionately for the poor, the downtrodden, and the disinherited, he had a fascination with men of affluence and enjoyed the company of wealthy SCLC benefactors. While trumpeting the glories of nonviolence and redemptive love, he could feel the most terrible anger when whites murdered a black or bombed a black church; he could contemplate giving up, turning America over to the haters of both races, only to dedicate himself anew to his nonviolent faith and his determination to redeem his country.

In 1960, he moved his family to Atlanta so that he could devote himself fulltime to SCLC, which was trying to register black voters for the upcoming federal elections. That same year, southern black students launched the sit-in movement against segregated lunch counters, and King not only helped them form the Student Nonviolent Coordinating Committee (SNCC) but raised money on their behalf. In October he even joined a sit-in protest at an Atlanta department store and went to jail with several students on a trespassing charge. Like Thoreau, King considered jail "a badge of honor." To redeem the nation and arouse the conscience of the opponent, King explained, you go to jail and stay there. "You have broken a law which is out of line with the moral law and you are willing to suffer the consequences by serving the time."

He did not reckon, however, on the tyranny of racist officials, who clamped him in a malevolent state penitentiary, in a cell for hardened criminals. But state authorities released him when Democratic presidential nominee John F. Kennedy and his brother Robert interceded on King's behalf. According to many analysts, the episode won critical black votes for Kennedy and gave him the election in November. For King, the election demonstrated what he had long said: that one of the most significant steps a black could take was the short walk to the voting booth.

The trouble was that most blacks in Dixie, especially in the Deep South, could not vote even if they so desired. For decades, state and local authorities had kept the mass of black folk off the voting rolls by a welter of devious obstacles and outright intimidation. Through 1961 and 1962, King exhorted President Kennedy to sponsor tough new civil rights legislation that would enfranchise southern blacks and end segregated public accommodations as well. When Kennedy shied away from a strong civil rights commitment, King and his lieutenants took matters into their own hands, orchestrating a series of southern demonstrations to show the world the brutality of segregation. At the same time, King stumped the country, drawing on all his powers of oratory to enlist the black masses and win white opinion to his cause.

Everywhere he went his message was the same. *The civil rights issue*, he said, *is an eternal moral issue that will determine the destiny of our nation and our world. As we seek our full rights, we hope to redeem the soul of our country. For it is our country, too, and we will win our freedom because the sacred heritage of America and the eternal will of God are embodied in our echoing demands. We do not intend to humiliate the white man, but to win him over through the strength of our love. Ultimately, we are trying to free all of us in America— Negroes from the bonds of segregation and shame, whites from the bonds of bigotry and fear.*

We stand today between two worlds—the dying old order and the emerging new. With men of ill-will greeting this change with cries of violence, of interposition and nullification, some of us may get beaten. Some of us may even get killed. But if you are cut down in a movement designed to save the soul of a nation, no other death could be more redemptive. We must realize that change does not roll in "on the wheels of inevitability," but comes through struggle. So "let us be those creative dissenters who will call our beloved nation to a higher destiny, to a new plateau of compassion, to a more noble expression of humaneness."

That message worked like magic among America's long-suffering blacks. Across the South, across America, they rose in unprecedented numbers to march and demonstrate with Martin Luther King. His singular achievement was that he brought the black masses into the freedom struggle for the first time. He rallied the strength of broken men and women, helping them overcome a lifetime of fear and feelings of inferiority. After segregation had taught them all their lives that they were *nobody*, King taught them that they were *somebody*. Because he made them believe in themselves and in the beauty of chosen suffering, he taught them how to straighten their backs ("a man can't ride you unless your back is bent") and confront those who oppressed them. Through the technique of nonviolent resistance, he furnished them something no previous black leader had been able to provide. He showed them a way of controlling their pent-up anger, as he had controlled his own, and using it to bring about constructive change.

THE MASS DEMONSTRATIONS King and SCLC choreographed in the South produced the strongest civil rights legislation in American history. This was the goal of King's major southern campaigns from 1963 to 1965. He would single out some notoriously segregated city with white officials prone to violence, mobilize the local blacks with songs, scripture readings, and rousing oratory in black churches, and then lead them on protest marches conspicuous for their grace and moral purpose. Then he and his aides would escalate the marches, increase their demands, even fill up the jails, until they brought about a moment of "creative tension," when

King was willing to go to jail for his belief in racial equality. He is shown here leaving the Fulton County (Georgia) Jail in handcuffs after having been convicted of a trespassing charge he incurred during participation in an October 1960 sit-in at an Atlanta department store. "You have broken a law which is out of line with the moral law," he said in explaining his philosophy, "and you are willing to suffer the consequences by serving the time."

whites would either agree to negotiate or resort to violence. If they did the latter, King would thus expose the brutality inherent in segregation and so stab the national conscience so that the federal government would be forced to intervene with corrective measures.

The technique succeeded brilliantly in Birmingham, Alabama, in 1963. Here Police Commissioner Eugene "Bull" Connor, in full view of reporters and television cameras, turned firehoses and police dogs on the marching protestors. Revolted by such ghastly scenes, stricken by King's own searching eloquence and the bravery of his unarmed followers, Washington eventually produced the 1964 Civil Rights Act, which desegregated public facilities—the thing King had demanded all along from Birmingham. Across the South, the "WHITES ONLY" signs that had hurt and enraged him since boyhood now came down.

Although SNCC and others complained that King had a Messiah complex and was trying to monopolize the civil rights movement, his technique worked with equal success in Selma, Alabama, in 1965. Building on a local movement there, King and his staff launched a drive to gain southern blacks the unobstructed right to vote. The violence he exposed in Selma —the beating of black marchers by state troopers and deputized possemen, the killing of a young black deacon and a white Unitarian minister—horrified the country. When King called for support, thousands of ministers, rabbis, priests, nuns, students, lay leaders, and ordinary people—black and white alike—rushed to Selma from all over the country and stood with King in the name of human liberty. Never in the history of the movement had so many people of all faiths and classes come to the southern battleground. The Selma campaign culminated in a dramatic march over the Jefferson Davis Highway to the state capital of Montgomery. Along the way, impoverished local blacks stared incredulously at the marching, singing, flag-waving spectacle moving by. When the column reached one dusty crossroads, an elderly black woman ran out from a group of old folk, kissed King breathlessly, and ran back crying, "I done kissed him! The Martin Luther King! I done kissed the Martin Luther King!"

In Montgomery, first capital and much-heralded "cradle" of the Confederacy, King led an interracial throng of 25,000—the largest civil rights demonstration the South had ever witnessed—up Dexter Avenue with banners waving overhead. The pageant was as ironic as it was extraordinary, for it was up Dexter Avenue that Jefferson Davis's first inaugural parade had marched, and in the portico of the capitol Davis had taken his oath of office as president of the slave-based Confederacy. Now, in the spring of 1965, Alabama blacks—most of them descendants of slaves—stood massed at the same statehouse, singing a new rendition of "We Shall Overcome," the anthem of the civil rights movement. They sang, "Deep in my heart, I do believe, We have overcome—*today*."

Then, within view of the statue of Jefferson Davis, and watched by cordons of state troopers and television cameras, King mounted a trailer. His vast audience listened, transfixed, as his words rolled and thundered over the loudspeaker: "My people, my people listen. The battle is in our hands. . . . We must come to see that the end we seek is a society at peace with itself, a society that can live with its conscience. That day will be a day not of the white man, not of the black man. That will be the day of man as man." And that day was not long in coming, King said, whereupon he launched into the immortal refrains of "The Battle Hymn of the Republic," crying out, "Our God is marching on! Glory, glory hallelujah!"

Aroused by the events in Alabama, Washington produced the 1965 Voting Rights Act, which outlawed impediments to black voting and empowered the attorney general to supervise federal elections in seven southern states where blacks were kept off the rolls. At the time, political analysts almost unanimously attributed the act to King's Selma campaign. Once federal examiners were

supervising voter registration in all troublesome southern areas, blacks were able to get on the rolls and vote by the hundreds of thousands, permanently altering the pattern of southern and national politics.

In the end, the powerful civil rights legislation generated by King and his tramping legions wiped out statutory racism in America and realized at least the social and political promise of emancipation a century before. But King was under no illusion that legislation alone could bring on the brave new America he so ardently championed. Yes, he said, laws and their vigorous enforcement were necessary to regulate destructive habits and actions, and to protect blacks and their rights. But laws could not eliminate the "fears, prejudice, pride, and irrationality" that were barriers to a truly integrated society, to peaceful intergroup and interpersonal living. Such a society could be achieved only when people accepted that inner, invisible law that etched on their hearts the conviction "that all men are brothers and that love is mankind's most potent weapon for personal and social transformation. True integration will be achieved by true neighbors who are willingly obedient to unenforceable obligations."

Even so, the Selma campaign was the movement's finest hour, and the Voting Rights Act the high point of a broad civil rights coalition that included the federal government, various white groups, and all the other civil rights organizations in addition to SCLC. King himself had best expressed the spirit and aspirations of that coalition when, on August 28, 1963, standing before the Lincoln Memorial, he electrified an interracial crowd of 250,000 with perhaps his greatest speech, "I Have A Dream," in which he described in rhythmic, hypnotic cadences his vision of an integrated America. Because of his achievements and moral vision, he won the 1964 Nobel Peace Prize, at thirty-four the youngest recipient in Nobel history.

STILL, King paid a high price for his fame and his cause. He suffered from stomachaches and insomnia, and even felt guilty about all the tributes he received, all the popularity he enjoyed. Born in relative material comfort and given a superior education, he did not think he had earned the right to lead the impoverished black masses. He complained, too, that he no longer had a personal self and that sometimes he did not recognize the Martin Luther King people talked about. Lonely, away from home for protracted periods, beset with temptation, he slept with other women, for some of whom he had real feeling. His sexual transgressions only added to his guilt, for he knew he was imperiling his cause and hurting himself and those he loved.

Alas for King, FBI Director J. Edgar Hoover found out about the black leader's infidelities. The director already abhorred King, certain that Communist spies influenced him and masterminded his demonstrations. Hoover did not think blacks capable of organizing such things, so Communists had to be behind them and King as well. As it turned out, a lawyer in King's inner circle

"On to the state capitol" is the cry as King, here flanked by Mrs. King, Dr. Ralph Bunche, and the Rev. Ralph Abernathy, officially starts the final leg of the 1965 Selma-to-Montgomery civil rights march. The interracial throng of 25,000 made its way up Dexter Avenue to the Alabama state capitol, along the same route Jefferson Davis's first Confederate inaugural parade had followed more than a century before. Many observers have called the Selma campaign—which led to passage of the 1965 Voting Rights Act—the civil rights movement's finest hour.

and a man in SCLC's New York office did have Communist backgrounds, a fact that only reinforced Hoover's suspicions about King. Under Hoover's orders, FBI agents conducted a ruthless crusade to destroy King's reputation and drive him broken and humiliated from public life. Hoover's men tapped King's phones and bugged his hotel rooms; they compiled a prurient monograph about his private life and showed it to various editors, public officials, and religious and civic leaders; they spread the word, Hoover's word, that King was not only a reprobate but a dangerous subversive with Communist associations.

King was scandalized and frightened by the FBI's revelations of his extramarital affairs. Luckily for him, no editor, not even a racist one in the South, would touch the FBI's salacious materials. Public officials such as Robert Kennedy were shocked, but argued that King's personal life did not affect his probity as a civil rights leader. Many blacks, too, declared that what he did in private was his own business. Even so, King vowed to refrain from further affairs—only to succumb again to his own human frailties.

As for the Communist charge, King retorted that he did not need any Russians to tell him when someone was standing on his neck; he could figure that out by himself. To mollify his political friends, however, King did banish from SCLC the two men with Communist backgrounds (later he resumed his ties with the lawyer, a loyal friend, and let Hoover be damned). He also denounced Communism in no uncertain terms. It was, he believed, profoundly and fundamentally evil, an atheistic doctrine no true Christian could ever embrace. He hated the dictatorial Soviet state, too, whose "crippling totalitarianism" subordinated everything—religion, art, music, science, and the individual—to its terrible yoke. True, Communism started with men like Karl Marx who were "aflame with a passion for social justice." Yet King faulted Marx for rejecting God and the spiritual in human life. "The great weakness in Karl Marx is right here," King once told his staff, and he went on to describe his ideal Christian commonwealth in Hegelian terms: "Capitalism fails to realize that life is social. Marxism fails to realize that life is individual. Truth is found neither in the rugged individualism of capitalism nor in the impersonal collectivism of Communism. The kingdom of God is found in a synthesis that combines the truths of these two opposites. Now there is where I leave brother Marx and move on toward the kingdom."

BUT HOW TO MOVE ON after Selma was a perplexing question King never successfully answered. After the devastating Watts riot in August 1965, he took his movement into the racially troubled urban North, seeking to help the suffering black poor in the ghettos. In 1966, over the fierce opposition of some of his own staff, he launched a campaign to end the black slums in Chicago and forestall rioting there. But the campaign foundered because King seemed unable to devise a coherent anti-slum strategy, because Mayor Richard Daley and his black acolytes opposed him bitterly, and because white America did not seem to care. King did lead open-housing marches into segregated neighborhoods in Chicago, only to encounter furious mobs who waved Nazi banners, threw bottles and bricks, and screamed, "We hate niggers!" "Kill the niggers!" "We want Martin Luther Coon!" King was shocked. "I've been in many demonstrations all across the South," he told reporters, "but I can say that I have never seen—even in Mississippi and Alabama—mobs as hostile and as hate-filled as I've seen in Chicago." Although King prevented a major riot there and wrung important concessions from City Hall, the slums remained, as wretched and seemingly unsolvable as ever.

That same year, angry young militants in SNCC and the Congress of Racial Equality (CORE) renounced King's teachings—they were sick and tired of "De Lawd" telling them to love white people and work for integration. Now they advocated "Black Power," black separatism, even violent resistance to liberate blacks in America. SNCC even banished whites from its ranks and went on to drop "nonviolent" from its name and to lobby against civil rights legislation.

Black Power repelled the older, more conservative black organizations such as the NAACP and the Urban League, and fragmented the civil rights movement beyond repair. King, too, argued that black separatism was chimerical, even suicidal, and that nonviolence remained the only workable way for black people. "Darkness cannot drive out darkness," he reasoned: "only light can do that. Hate cannot drive out hate: only love can do that." If every other black in America turned to violence, King warned, then he would still remain the lone voice preaching that it was wrong. Nor was SCLC going to reject whites as SNCC had done. "There have

been too many hymns of hope," King said, "too many anthems of expectation, too many deaths, too many dark days of standing over graves of those who fought for integration for us to turn back now. We must still sing 'Black and White Together, We Shall Overcome.' "

In 1967, King himself broke with the older black organizations over the ever-widening war in Vietnam. He had first objected to American escalation in the summer of 1965, arguing that the Nobel Peace Prize and his role as a Christian minister compelled him to speak out for peace. Two years later, with almost a half-million Americans—a disproportionate number of them poor blacks—fighting in Vietnam, King devoted whole speeches to America's "immoral" war against a tiny country on the other side of the globe. His stance provoked a fusillade of criticism from all directions—from the NAACP, the Urban League, white and black political leaders, *Newsweek*, *Life*, *Time*, and the *New York Times*, all telling him to stick to civil rights. Such criticism hurt him deeply. When he read the *Times*'s editorial against him, he broke down and cried. But he did not back down. "I've fought too long and too hard now against segregated accommodations to end up segregating my moral concerns," he told his critics. "Injustice *any*where is a threat to justice everywhere."

That summer, with the ghettos ablaze with riots, King warned that American cities would explode if funds used for war purposes were not diverted to emergency antipoverty programs. By then, the Johnson administration, determined to gain a military victory in Vietnam, had written King off as an antiwar agitator, and was now cooperating with the FBI in its efforts to defame him.

The fall of 1967 was a terrible time for King, the lowest ebb in his civil rights career. Everybody seemed to be attacking him—young black militants for his stubborn adherence to nonviolence, moderate and conservative blacks, labor leaders, liberal white politicians, the White House, and the FBI for his stand on Vietnam. Two years had passed since King had produced a nonviolent victory, and contributions to SCLC had fallen off sharply. Black spokesman Adam Clayton Powell, who had once called King the greatest Negro in America, now derided him as Martin Loser King. The incessant attacks began to irritate him, creating such anxiety and depression that his friends worried about his emotional health.

Worse still, the country seemed dangerously polarized. On one side, backlashing whites argued that the ghetto explosions had "cremated" nonviolence and that white people had better arm themselves against black rioters. On the other side, angry blacks urged their people to "kill the Honkies" and burn the cities down. All around King, the country was coming apart in a cacophony of hate and reaction. Had America lost the will and moral power to save itself? he wondered. There was such rage in the ghetto and such bigotry among whites that he feared a race war was about to break out. He felt he had to do something to pull America back from the brink. He and his staff had to mount a new campaign that would halt the drift to violence in the black world and combat stiffening white resistance, a nonviolent action that would "transmute the deep rage of the ghetto into a constructive and creative force."

OUT OF HIS DELIBERATIONS sprang a bold and daring project called the poor people's campaign. The master plan, worked out by February 1968, called for SCLC to bring an interracial army of poor people to Washington, D.C., to dramatize poverty before the federal government. For King, just turned thirty-nine, the time had come to employ civil disobedience against the national government itself. Ultimately, he was projecting a genuine class movement that he hoped would bring about meaningful changes in American society—changes that would redistribute economic and political power and end poverty, racism, "the madness of militarism," and war.

In the midst of his preparations, King went to Memphis, Tennessee, to help black sanitation workers there who were striking for the right to unionize. On the night of April 3, with a storm thundering outside, he told a black audience that he had been to the mountaintop and had seen what lay ahead. "I may not get there with you. But I want you to know tonight that we as a people *will* get to the promised land."

The next afternoon, when King stepped out on the balcony of the Lorraine Motel, an escaped white convict named James Earl Ray, stationed in a nearby building, took aim with a high-powered rifle and blasted King into eternity. Subsequent evidence linked Ray to white men in the St. Louis area who had offered "hit" money for King's life.

For weeks after the shooting, King's stricken country convulsed in grief, contrition, and rage. While there were those who cheered his death, the *New York Times* called it a disaster to the nation, the *London Times* an enormous loss to the world. In Tanzania, Reverend Trevor Huddleston, expelled from South Africa for standing against apartheid, declared King's death the greatest single tragedy since the assassination of Gandhi in 1948, and said it challenged the complacency of the Christian Church all over the globe.

On April 9, with 120 million Americans watching on television, thousands of mourners—black and white alike—gathered in Atlanta for the funeral of a man who had never given up his dream of creating a symphony of brotherhood on these shores. As a black man born and raised in segregation, he had had every reason to hate America and to grow up preaching cynicism and retaliation. Instead, he had loved the country passionately and had sung of her promise and glory more eloquently than anyone of his generation.

They buried him in Atlanta's South View Cemetery, then blooming with dogwood and fresh green boughs of spring. On his crypt, hewn into the marble, were the words of an old Negro spiritual he had often quoted: "Free at Last, Free at Last, Thank God Almighty I'm Free at Last."

Recommended additional reading: Let the Trumpet Sound: The Life of Martin Luther King, Jr. *by Stephen B. Oates (Harper & Row, 1982), and* A Testament of Hope: The Essential Writings of Martin Luther King, Jr. *edited by James M. Washington (Harper & Row, 1986).*

Reappraising the Presidency of Lyndon B. Johnson

Vaughn Davis Bornet

Professor Emeritus of History and Social Science Southern Oregon State College

American presidencies get reappraised, but not on a regular and predictable schedule. Anniversaries are one occasion; the occurrence of major events or trends that bring remembrance can be another. The 1960s and 1970s, years of contention and conflict, have seemed ripe for a look rooted in realism, some sympathy, a bit of humility, and, maybe, a bit of neo-patriotism. Lyndon B. Johnson's time in the White House, it seems to me, is ripe for revisionism. Already, recent years have seen some attention being given to reassessment of the "promise" of President John F. Kennedy, and the "failures" of President Richard M. Nixon. Ours has not yet been a time, however, for general change in attitude toward the importance in history of the dynamic president who served during the five years between the "martyred" JFK and the "disgraced" RMN. This is true in spite of the appearance of some specialized volumes, an overly jovial stage play, a feeble TV reenactment of the pre-presidential years, and continuing analysis of the Johnson presidential archives.

My own years spent in appraisal of President Johnson, which resulted in the book *The Presidency of Lyndon B. Johnson* (Lawrence, Kansas: the American Presidency Series of the University Press of Kansas, 1983) may (or may not) be leading to increased willingness to rethink this controversial presidency. The President Johnson sketch by Henry Graff in *The American Presidency* (New York: Scribners, 1984) has to be addressed. Those who undertake this task will simply have to reendure the emotional pain of reliving, vicariously, the divisive issues of LBJ's stormy years.

How shall we go about judging the contours of the influence of President Lyndon B. Johnson in history? By continuing to describe his personality and character quirks? Contemporary journalism doted on such an approach, and yesterday's version continues to be the fare of the mass media. Surely the time has come to get down to cases: ascertain what he sought to do; find out the extent to which he achieved what he sought; and then weigh the consequences of Johnson-induced change over time. We should appraise deeds, not concentrate interminably (and superficially) on "style." Johnson was, after all, a mover and a doer. He sought massive change, and he got it. And some changes that can be tied to this president were surely not in the national or world interest, either then or later.

While my book focused on the role of this presidency in *making a difference*, I did not ignore *the person* of the president and those around him. Still, there has been some muttering, chiefly by Alonzo L. Hamby in *The American Spectator* (June 1984) that all evaluations of this presidency must begin and end with concentration on the person of "LBJ", he of the allegedly crude personality traits and supposedly flawed character. Any such procedure will surely sell books and get acceptance for articles. But the dedicated and trained historian will certainly want to rise above this temptation and, instead, concentrate on substance—in this case, public policy and its consequences. Bibliographic essays edited by Robert A. Divine entitled *The Johnson Years* (Lawrence, Kansas: 1987, 2 vols) and a Johnson Library bibliography will help.

My methodological premise was born in yesteryear, but it seems sound today. While I had the privilege of taking a number of courses in historiography in my lifetime (historiography: the principles, theory, and history of historical writing), much of the detail I once learned has been forgotten. Nevertheless, several truisms remain imbedded in the memory. Relevant here is the concept, that in evaluating great figures of the past, emphasis should be placed on *what was done* rather than *what was said* (and the manner of the saying!). While what the great figure was like as a person has much interest, especially for those preparing full biographies, what really counts in the long run of events is what a leader did. What the leader said must be studied, of course; and what he was like in both

From *Presidential Studies Quarterly*, Summer 1990, pp. 591-602. Reprinted with permission from Center for the Study of the Presidency. Reprinted by permission.

character and personality should not be avoided. Overall, what the leader sought to do, and what he actually did do in his area of responsibility is what is really vital. It should be central in our textbook accounts.

Sixteen years have passed since the death of highly controversial President Johnson, twenty-five years since he entered office, and twenty since he left Washington for the Ranch by the Perdenales River in the Hill Country of Texas. Appraisal of his presidency in one major poll of historians showed him to be rated 10th from the top among our presidents. John F. Kennedy was three below him; Harry S. Truman just above him. It would not take much for LBJ to pass both Truman and Jackson, should a new attitude toward him somehow develop, such has occurred in Eisenhower's rise in esteem by scholars. On the other hand, only a slight increase in hostility would drop him below James K. Polk and Kennedy. (The Walter Mondale campaign of 1984, which seems never to have acknowledged his existence, did nothing to help.) The four "most controversial" presidents are said to be Richard Nixon, Herbert Hoover, Andrew Jackson, and Lyndon Johnson. These are said, as a result, to be the ones most likely to change their rankings over the decades. What chance is there for Johnson revisionism? Everything depends on the nature of "the record" as depicted by historians.

The five year Johnson presidency, late 1963 to early 1969, clearly made a difference in the United States, whatever the nature of the man (or the way he appeared to be when filtered in imagery through the media). First, of course, there was the Great Society, featuring efforts to improve education, alleviate poverty, provide financing for medical care for the aged and poor, and change a multitude of other things. Accompanying this was the long and bloody undeclared Vietnam War, ever escalating, and staggering in its consequences.

It was in the Johnson years that much that was *new* came into being. The Arts and the Humanities gained federal funding. Consumerism would be monitored by a zealous federal agency. Cabinet level departments in Housing and Transportation were created. The New Conservation and beautification program of the Johnson husband and wife team paved the way for later (and more extreme) environmentalism. A new immigration law eliminated some old abuses. The elderly could sell the homestead, free of federal taxes, up to a $100,000 maximum.

Then there were the three famous and epoch-making Civil Rights Acts of 1964, 1965, and 1968, protecting voting rights, prohibiting discrimination, and helping to achieve fairness in obtaining housing. Progress was made through executive orders in rights for women employed in the federal government. A housing law sought to put a new roof over the heads of thousands of families.

Foreign affairs saw the Soviets still deterred from a thermonuclear strike. A nuclear nonproliferation treaty was signed. Glassboro was the locale for Soviet-American talks. The president handled crises competently in Panama, Guantanamo Bay (Cuba), and—accompanied with much controversy—in the Dominican Republic. Johnson personally supervised a massive program that gave vast quantities of wheat for India, but overseas economic aid did not grow. A Puenta del Este conference (in which he took special pride) carried forward on earlier Eisenhower and Kennedy policies of cooperation toward Latin America.

When a liberal mind surveys these years it quickly zeros in approvingly on the exceedingly long lists of new legislation. Viewing these law-making successes positively, former Johnson aide Joseph Califano, Jr. alleges, "Greatness must be measured by productivity. . . . Start with George Washington and study the problems in relation to the solutions. Lyndon Johnson is in a class by himself." The conservative observer of the same record naturally emerges with overt distaste! Radicals, as usual, scoff at these efforts to "shore up capitalism." Still, all such analysts are focusing on what is *central*. None waste their time by continuing to focus judgmental powers on the person of what some dubbed "the cornpone president."

The sheer bulk of White House-backed legislation had its own fallout, then and later. Said *Time* in early 1969, "All too often, big federal spending has produced not social miracles but merely a swollen bureaucracy and the anger of those who feel cheated by the gap between promise and performance." The president's budget director told him in 1966 that "states, cities, depressed areas, and individuals have been led to expect immediate delivery of benefits from Great Society programs to a degree that is not realistic." Frustration and loss of credibility would be the result, he predicted. As to this theme, Johnson observed in his inimitable way, "It's a little like whiskey. It is good. But if you drink too much it comes up on you."

Members of the opposition party naturally had their own reservations. Senator Howard Baker astutely judged the Administration's record at the time of Johnson's death. The president, he said, "showed us what could be accomplished through government action—and what could never be accomplished through government action." While LBJ had demonstrated what "government could do for people," he had at the same time shown "what people and nations must do for themselves."

There are still observers of the modern scene who believe that causing large numbers of laws to be passed stamps one as a "socialist." Here, of course, is a concept with little merit. Looking merely at the thrust of the charge, it has to be said in refutation that the

Lyndon Johnson who represented his Austin, Texas constituency for so many years never questioned the capitalist system or its basis in the profit system. By 1969, he and his talented wife had benefited from the American way in business and economics to the extent of perhaps fifteen millions accumulated aggressively from the marketplace.

Because of Vietnam, the public naturally thinks of this controversial leader as a "wartime president." Yet he (and Secretary of State Dean Rusk) saw the overall performance quite differently. Thermonuclear war with the Soviet Union had been avoided! China had not been provoked into entering the war in Southeast Asia—as had been the case in Korea! The President could tell the Pan American Union at one point that it had been "a great privilege to work with all of you toward peace and freedom in this world." By such remarks, he clearly meant that the world in his years had been spared ultimate catastrophe. The Vietnam War, whatever its growing intensity, had played an appropriate role in deterrence. At the same time, confrontations in this hemisphere with conventional weapons (such as Kennedy's Bay of Pigs misadventure) had been avoided.

Looking more closely at the Vietnam War, an important theme (as I have tried to spell it out from archival research) is that from the very beginning on November 22, 1963, this leader was determined to "carry on" the Kennedy policies as he and the Kennedy team he carefully retained in office understood them to be. Entering office only days after Kennedy insiders acquiesced in the deposing of Diem, the long-time ruler of South Vietnam, President Johnson was repeatedly informed by the secret intelligence he was getting that Saigon was the center of a state in chaos. It was evident that there would have to be vast, sustained, imaginative, and inevitably bloody effort if the Kennedy hopes for a long-lived, viable state were to be salvaged. This truth I found to be thoroughly documented in Johnson Library manuscripts declassified after 1975.

President Kennedy, in my studied opinion, was by no means on a withdrawal course in fall, 1963, whatever loyally hopeful partisans would try to contend in later years. Already looking toward reelection in 1964, JFK abhorred the slightest appearance of another humiliation rooted in miscalculation and indecision like the Bay of Pigs. Next, Kennedy had gambled that thermonuclear war would not take place during the Cuban Missile Crisis. He had waged a secret CIA war in Laos. It seems quite incredible that Kennedy would have reacted much differently from his successor in late 1964 and the early months of 1965, at least, although how later policy toward Vietnam would have developed in his hands remains a total mystery.

Johnson did, in any case, continue in 1963–64 the Kennedy crusade to establish a democratic and independent state centered around Saigon. That state was the new homeland for perhaps a million refugees (including Catholics) from the North. At Tonkin Gulf the Kennedy-Johnson team found that its uncompromising determination to prevail led to a logical outcome: further escalation. As the shooting war developed into a major battleground for conventional armies in 1965, the president failed to define and to seek "victory" in the traditional sense. In the Johnson years the enemy's supplies from the Soviet Union, the Warsaw Pact countries, and China would not be cut off, for the President shied away from such controversial measures as those to be adopted eventually by President Nixon.

Thus Hanoi was not to be invaded. North Vietnam was to be permitted safe sanctuary in a portion of Cambodia. A multitude of enemy-serving restrictions on pilot judgment would make the off and on bombing effort ineffective, thus guaranteeing major losses of planes and the creation of the prisoner problem that would loom so large in the next decade. Henry Kissinger has put the resulting situation well. The Johnson administration undertook "a commitment large enough to hazard our global position" but executed it "with so much hesitation as to defeat their purpose."

Fallout on the home front from the Vietnam adventure was immense. It has been said, "The more the United States did to preserve an independent identity for South Vietnam, the more America's own identity changed." Here the reference is to the many consequences of that long war: the killed and wounded and their loved ones at home; the effects of the selective draft on those who submitted to it, those who gained exemption, and those who resisted or fled. Moreover, there were many side effects traceable to the quick rotation of so many hundreds of thousands of young servicemen through Southeast Asia.

America changed rapidly in the Johnson years. The social developments were major: a drug culture; a generation gap; stimulation of interest in exotic religions; changes in codes of personal conduct; some erosion of the work ethic; and, during the time of the expanded use of "the pill," changes in sexual mores that affected the traditional family as an institution. The controversial war's upheavals stimulated and accelerated many such developments (just as earlier wars had left their own indelible marks).

Because of the war that he so considerably escalated, Lyndon Johnson is considered by many to have been both an evil man and a deplored president. Here, the semantics present problems, for it was the historian Lord Acton who observed, "Great men are almost always bad men." Without endorsing or debating so dramatic a point, it needs to be said that many aspects of the leadership of this president stamp him clearly as "great" in accomplishment. His impact has been felt in many areas of American life. It was no less a person than Melville B. Grosvenor of *National Geographic* magazine who wrote to assure LBJ that he was "the greatest conservation president." For example, Johnson added 4,848,000 acres to the public domain and 44 new areas to the National Park Service. With Lady Bird's enthusiastic collaboration, the national capital was beautiful anew, and progress was made against billboard blight and visible junkyards. Path breaking legislation furthered clean air; water quality; the wilderness, wild rivers, and trails; and progress in handling solid waste disposal. LBJ's was to be the first presidential message ever given on natural beauty.

As he signed several of these historic bills on the outdoors, Johnson said, "When future historians write of this era, I believe they will note that ours was the generation that finally faced up to the accumulated problems of our American life." Thus, "We are going to preserve at least a part of what God gave us." Here in the Johnson years was planted the roots of moderate environmental action in government.

The president was to be praised in 1980 by the National Consumers League for "enhancing consumer representation in government decision-making." The National Organization for Women in one of its first resolutions said Johnson had already done by 1966 "more than any other president to focus national attention on the importance of bringing women into the mainstream of public and private employment." The drama critic of the *Washington Post* would say that his services to the arts and humanities exceeded those of *all* his predecessors in the White House put together. (An exception is Eisenhower, whose own role in the arts, including planning what became the Kennedy Center, has been overlooked.) Here, in conservation-environmentalism, consumerism, financing of the arts and humanities, and equity for employed women are four areas of Johnson-induced progress in which he was dubbed the "greatest." But there is much more.

This leader deserves to be called the "civil rights president"—that is, if the Lincoln who freed the slaves be excluded. The three major acts of the LBJ years, in 1964, 1965, and 1968 resulted, to be sure, from many factors: from nonviolent protest by Martin Luther King and others; from violence in the streets and fear of more; and from action taken by the courts, the Congress, and other presidents in earlier years. But the proximate cause of passage of these bills was the dogged, uncompromising determination and brilliant leadership of President Johnson and his determined team. Said the first black on the Supreme Court, Justice Thurgood Marshall (a Johnson appointee), "It has been rewarding to serve under a president who has led the nation to historic gains in the pursuit of equal justice under law."

While not cure-alls, the civil rights acts of the 1960s were very effective. By 1978, George Wallace could be quoted as saying, "Segregation is over. And it's better

that it is over . . . because it's never coming back." What the federal government forced on "us" had "turned out for the best." Surely it takes nothing from Lyndon Johnson to say that the struggle for racial justice and equal opportunity still is being waged in the courts and the Congress, twenty years after he left office.

The Age of Space was born in the Eisenhower-Kennedy-Johnson-Nixon decade, but credit as a rule is casually assigned to Kennedy. Actually, it was Eisenhower, with Johnson's support, who founded NASA; it was a Johnson-chaired committee that recommended Project Apollo to JFK, and the burden of its yearly funding fell to Kennedy's successor. NASA administrator James Webb did work mightily with the Congress in those years; still, his president backed him all the way against those in the science, defense, education, and anti-poverty areas who sought maximum dollars for their own causes. The successful moon landing and return came less than a year after LBJ left for Texas.

The Great Society rightly remains controversial. Goals, after all, were too often unrealistic; many ideas were untried; appropriations added up to considerable totals, but were inadequate for implementing most laws fully; administration was lackluster; too much was attempted. The major thrust may have been misdirected from the outset. Still, here was, overall, a noble effort. In 1973 it was a Republican of presidential stature who observed, "If Johnson fell short of achieving the Great Society, it was not for a lack of good intentions." Many Americans increasingly wonder how to bring about a rebirth of the Johnson era's self-starting determination to war against American poverty.

On the other hand, the Great Society of those years was something of an administrative disaster. It was in the 1980s that two well qualified researchers from the LBJ School of Public Affairs, not unfriendly to Johnson, had to conclude, "The cumulative effect of Great Society legislation was to produce far greater problems of executive structure and coordination than had existed at any other time, except perhaps during the Civil War, the Great Depression, and World War II." These problems were judged to threaten permanently the capacity of the federal administrative system to fulfill policy objectives.

At the same time, one part of the Great Society crusade—the effort to upgrade the nation's educational establishment—had dramatic effects (whatever the modest funding). The figures show this conclusively. Post secondary classrooms became community colleges; teachers colleges became diversified liberal arts colleges containing business and sometimes law enforcement programs; and many four year colleges developed into universities. Educational opportunity for minorities and the poor blossomed. Percentages of high school and college graduates greatly increased, in part due to the operation of a successful work-study program. Head Start, aimed at preschoolers, surely had beneficial effects overall, whatever the difficulty initially in proving its purely academic worth. Today it is the educational program given greatest increased support by the Bush administration. Referring to Johnson's hope (now a Bush hope) of being remembered as "the Education President," the *Chronicle of Higher Education* said in 1973, "Many observers believe he earned that title."

The well-meaning intervention by Washington in the higher education theatre had measurable fallout—consequences on which egalitarian educators have been altogether too quiet. Equality gained at the expense of freedom. Says Daniel Patrick Moynihan, "The federal government has acquired the power to shut down any university it chooses." To this, *Harpers* added, "In exchange for federal aid, universities and colleges have surrendered their independence to the government." It seems safe to say that few of the institutions now dependent on the billions in federal money can now imagine life without it. Academic freedom, in the sense of untrammeled decision-making, lost out as part of the price paid for the many buildings, library holdings, equipment, faculty training programs, and grants of every description. Efforts in the mid-1980s to cut federal grants to education (or the performing arts) met with passionate protests from those affected.

Opening wide the academic gates in the 1960s was a mixed blessing. Older faculty members can remember the higher standards in student grading and work requirements they once had (for freshmen, at least) before the draft of the 1960s and early 1970s, and the entry of an array of only partly qualified and variably motivated students, changed the higher education climate. Nor did the junior and senior years of high school escape dilution as what may well have been elitism gave way to mass education. It was, of course, an inestimable boon when the Johnson education acts gave and loaned money to keep students in school. However, some who stayed on should not have, for classroom discipline suffered through the presence of the poorly motivated. Repayment of college loan obligations was far from universal, even from successful college graduates. No doubt many factors other than Johnson legislation must have contributed to the decline in American academic standards in modern times.

The oversold War on Poverty was intended to be financed by a niggardly one percent of the federal budget of that day. Its dynamic title was modified, after several months, in a Johnson speech, to "Nationwide War on the Sources of Poverty." This was more realistic, but it also proved unattainable. In any case, the anti-poverty effort was, as a coordinated, named,

and recognized activity, Lyndon Johnson's—not Kennedy's (whatever his unformulated—and naturally unlegislated—hopes for 1964 and later). It was Theodore Sorensen, a loyal Kennedy supporter, who said, "It will be unfortunate if Johnson's massive accomplishments . . . in domestic areas remain obscured by the bitter controversies over his Vietnamese policy."

President Johnson in the overall international arena would be accused of an arrogance of power. There is something to the charge, for here was an aggressively anti-communist and pro-American, activist, president. But a kinder way of putting the concentration on advancing American interests was Walt Rostow's: the president had tried to build "a structure of world arrangements of partnership." After all, from Kennedy he had inherited treaties with 42 allies. Some 429 American "major installations" and about 2,000 minor ones were located in almost every non-Communist country. He emulated his predecessor, who had sought a powerful international posture for the United States. This Kennedy-selected vice president was providing the continuity expected in foreign affairs. Said Johnson to the Congress, "To be prepared for war is one of the most effectual means of preserving peace." This point of view remains United States policy a quarter of a century later.

The free world in Johnson's years rested under the American nuclear umbrella. Yet, said the nation's spokesman, "Peace is our mission. Strength would bring safety to all free peoples." Here were ambitious words, but this commander in chief has been accused of letting our strategic forces slide. He could have done more. The nation had a vast lead over the USSR at the beginning of 1964. The Soviets did catch up to a notable degree during his years. The balance sheet in strategic weapons at the end (1969) showed the nation with 1056 ICBMs, the USSR with 900. Submarine weapons were 650 to 75; international bombers 600 to 150 and their deliverable warheads 4,200 to 1,200. Clearly, the inexorable direction had been toward parity in numbers, but the U.S. claimed to lead in accuracy, if not in "throw weight."

There were changes of emphasis in military preparedness. The area of missiles and strategic forces declined in the budget from $10.4 to $7.6 billion; "conventional," meanwhile, grew from $17.9 to $32.4 billion. Many new or updated weapons underwent R & D, looking toward the 1970s and later. Was the nation safer at the end of those years? The basis for debate into the 1980s was laid, and the question cannot be answered definitively here. In any case, there would be no Soviet attack then or later. This was an incalculable but little noted plus.

In perspective, President Lyndon Johnson should be remembered for the seriousness of his unremitting effort, with the help of an exceptionally able team—one that history has largely forgotten—to use government to benefit people at home and abroad. At home, they used (really, considerably over-used) the federal government as lawgiver, trying to benefit and serve the people. At the same time, however, came the over-regulating of private institutions and the usurping of power from state and local governments. To this writer, and many others, here was an unwholesome use of power.

Abroad, the use of national power was also massive, as the nation cooperated with NATO, Association of Southeast Asian Nations (ASEAN), Australia and New Zealand (ANZUS) and freedom-loving countries everywhere to contain Communism, the sworn enemy of democracy and freedom, within its existing boundaries. Not as dramatic as the implementation of the SEATO treaty, this allegiance to treaty commitments was appropriate to their intents and stated purposes. In my view, the anti-communist objective of the states who had signed these treaties was absolutely the right goal to have been pursuing. (Historians and writers who do not agree should at least not take out their ire on Johnson alone, for post World War II presidents have a commonality in this matter.)

In Southeast Asia, the entire Kennedy-Johnson-Nixon effort to erect a democratic, anti-communist South Vietnamese state turned out to be abortive. It is impossible to know if events had to develop so disastrously in the later era of Watergate and of Congressional determination to prevail in the foreign policy arena. Perhaps President Johnson waged his share of the war in such a way as to point inevitably toward the ultimate 1975 collapse that lost everything for which the nation had worked and planned. This political leader did definitely fail to leave in the Democratic Party a durable inclination to shore up South Vietnam in its later time of troubles. His intentions had been honorable enough, some still admitted, but here had been an ill-advised pursuit of a major uphill war waged without declaration (just with a controversial Tonkin Gulf Resolution). The hard-to-comprehend war had lacked the traditional goal of "victory," for the enemy was never supposed to be "conquered." Democratic Party leaders of the early 1970s cannot be blamed too much, perhaps, for unwillingness to "carry on" such a conflict very long in Johnson's memory. Meanwhile, there continued the pretense that Kennedy "surely" would have turned back from support of South Vietnam as the going got tough. I would surmise, even insist, that it is not a correct reading of the Kennedy character to say that he would have abandoned South Vietnam in its 1965 hour of need.

President Johnson will be remembered for the by-products, the fallout, from the vast quantities of legislation passed skillfully with great rapidity—but without mature gestation—by a Congress where he nearly always knew how to get the votes. It takes only a little from him to say that the Congress was controlled in both houses by his own party first to last, in part because of his masterful, yet sly, political campaigning in 1964—and Republican suicide. Most other presidents who had legislative majorities left no such record of extensive law-making on behalf of basic change.

Properly associated with this Administration are many negatives: excessive bureaucratic controls that reduced freedom; and ill-considered financial policies that are still remembered as the "Guns and Butter" mythology. These set in motion the institutionalization of paralyzing inflation, acceptance of federal deficits, and climbing interest rates. The value of the consumer's dollar would slide routinely for years to come. There was in presidential speeches unrealistic over-promising. Utopia was conceptualized as imminent (especially in candidate LBJ's addresses of fall, 1964) as idealistic speechwriters, some of them left over from the "bear any burden" New Frontier speech team—were allowed to put grandiose words in this normally plain-spoken man's mouth.

Too much cannot be said, however, about the block-busting effect that Johnson's well-honed legislative skills had when amplified by a well trained White House team of assistants. Many have found LBJ far superior to any other president in this aspect of leadership—Franklin Roosevelt not excepted. What former Senate leader Johnson did so successfully was, first, to develop a program of legislation; then to forge the necessary coalitions to carry the bills; and finally to perfect the timing that would be crucial to pacing consistent achievement. He used his enormous knowledge of the congressional mind to work out practical rewards and "punishments." His were the decisions that built the congressional liaison staff into such a potent force. LBJ had a sixth sense as to who were the "whales" and who the "minnows"—the leaders and the followers. The House majority leader of that day, Carl Albert, was not the only experienced contemporary to observe that the Johnson legislative performance as president was "far greater than [Franklin] Roosevelt's."

Why, then, has Johnson the president failed utterly to get his just due? Several possibilities may be advanced. First, he is still remembered for various flaws in his character and oddities in his personality (coarseness, crudeness, and crass dissimulation, thoughtlessness, self-serving) that, well publicized, helped to make him ineligible for such stereotypes as "typical American" or "father figure." Inept on TV, where he was unaccountably stiff, he did not display anything like "the wit and wisdom" of his predecessor. Never, despite his noble task force (brain trust) effort, did this tall Texan gain the vocal respect of "intellectuals."

An astute few recognized how skewed were the real Johnson priorities as measured in dollars. From 1965 to 1973, the Office of Economic Opportunity (OEO) cost about $15 billion. Meanwhile, the Vietnam War cost

$120 billion. But the federal government at least tried to offer "butter" as well as "guns," while seeking vigorously to gain public acceptance for anti-poverty efforts.

There was a brief period when former president Lyndon Johnson was still being praised for the nature and extent of his goals, efforts, and achievements. Critic Walter Cronkite conceded at LBJ's death, for example, that Johnson had been "a zealous public servant with a compelling dream of a better America—who made enormous strides to make that dream come true." To the politician from Texas, it is quite clear, his crusades for Medicare, Medicaid, education, and better law enforcement; against poverty; for better housing and model cities; for civil rights; and for a New Conservation were infinitely more than just "politics." He had his own ethic on such matters, so that he more than "carried on" for Kennedy. The man from Johnson City had his own inner compulsions as he sought massive change in the social fabric.

Here was a *president.* This leader cared enough to work astonishingly long days, and long into the nights, in the effort to pass legislation designed at making a better America. A citizen once wrote him, after his retirement, "Vietnam blinded us, your critics, to the accomplishments you made. You were a doing, acting president. . . . History will give you your credits. It will show how short-sighted we were." (Has this been a good prediction, so far?)

The Vietnam-tortured public of later years naturally withheld its approbation as many contended that America had finally "lost a war." By the 1980s (at the time for twenty and twenty-five year memorializations of JFK's passing), TV reenactments viciously portrayed the vice president LBJ of that time as a buffoon who was utterly outclassed among the New Frontiersmen. It is TV, not historians, that can and does offer the public the recreation of the years of John and Jackie Kennedy, complete with built-in slander of LBJ. Is this in the public interest?

That such an opportunity is rooted in LBJ's frequent lack of personal self-discipline as a person does not help much. And it certainly cannot be avoided that so many who now work in their media tasks served unhappily in Vietnam, or live with some guilt, perhaps, for evading that obligation. The public needs to know historical truths that go far beyond "style" and "aspect." Johnson as a *person* was a vital matter at the time, of course. Moreover, the nature of any man who rules the White House remains fair game for biographers and dramatists. The spirit of the cynical 1967 play *Macbird* lives on in such pieces as Tom Wicker's "Hey, Hey, LBJ" for *Esquire* (December 1983). But this Administration was infinitely more than just a flawed "LBJ in action." Its activist record in laws placed on the books needs to be focused upon, first to last, for better or worse.

President Johnson was beyond any doubt a dynamic and effective political leader and lawgiver. He will long get, and deserve to get, outsized blame for the overcommitment in Vietnam and the negative consequences of his years in office. Whatever his personal flaws and official mistakes, however, he certainly was one who *tried,* first to last. At the close of my book, I ventured to observe, "He dared, cared, and shared of himself, and thereby very often carried the day." The President's many accomplishments stem in considerable measure from this fundamental trait.

What President Johnson did achieve continues to have deep meaning for the American people. In his case, revisionism by historians can justifiably be on actual *deeds*—even if it may be decided that there were too many of them, and that some, especially in his waging of unsuccessful war, worked out very poorly, whatever his hopeful intent.

We are unlikely ever again to see a leader in the White House who will be so effective a force for innovative change, much of it beneficial. In biographies, histories, and (especially) the media the time for a fresh look at President Lyndon B. Johnson is at hand. There are two good reasons: LBJ himself often said that "History will judge." It was one of the major motivations he had when he wore the hat of reformer. Second, our presidents carefully study the degree of acceptance of their predecessors when deciding where to place their energies while in office. What, we may well ask, is any president to think of history as judge if the balance of appraisal of so conspicuous a leader as Johnson fails the test of impartiality? There will not soon be a better time to start than the 1990s. After all, we are at the 25th anniversary of Johnson's second Civil Rights Act, two major Education acts, Medicare, the beginning of the Planning-Programming-Budgeting System, much environmental legislation, and a great deal more.

While remembering major deeds, however, history will not want to forget gross errors made by any president in foreign and domestic policy-making. At the same time, history will gradually come to minimize yesterday's small missteps and personal deficiencies. All who mold the mind of the public and students must soon pick up the burden of rethinking and reinterpreting the Johnson presidency for the benefit of us all.

The ultimate reassessment, all will agree, should proceed cautiously, with one eye on shifts in current standards, and the other on well-established canons of professionalism in rendering historical judgment on public figures. We must change our focus from LBJ *the person* to Lyndon B. Johnson *the president.*

Lessons from a Lost War

What has Viet Nam taught about when to use power—and when not to?

The customary reward of defeat, if one can survive it, is in the lessons thereby learned, which may yield victory in the next war. But the circumstances of our defeat in Vietnam were sufficiently ambiguous to deny the nation [that] benefit.

—Edward N. Luttwak
The Pentagon and the Art of War

Ten years after the fall of Saigon, the debacle in Southeast Asia remains a subject many Americans would rather not discuss. So the nation has been spared a searing, divisive inquest—"Who lost Viet Nam?"—but at a heavy price. The old divisions have been buried rather than resolved. They seem ready to break open again whenever anyone asks what lessons the U.S. should draw from its longest war, and the only one to end in an undisguisable defeat.

Was that loss inevitable, or could the war have been won with different strategy and tactics? Was the war fought for the right reasons? Did its aftermath prove or explode the domino theory? The questions are not in the least academic. They bear on the all-important problem of whether, when and how the U.S. should again send its troops to fight abroad.

Pondering these questions, Secretary of Defense Caspar Weinberger argues, citing Viet Nam, that "before the U.S. commits combat forces abroad, there must be some reasonable assurance that we will have the support of the American people and . . . Congress." Secretary of State George Shultz replies that "there is no such thing as guaranteed public support in advance." The lesson Shultz draws from Viet Nam is that "public support can be frittered away if we do not act wisely and effectively." And this open dispute between two senior members of the Reagan Cabinet is mild compared with the arguments among policy analysts, Viet Nam veterans and the public about what kinds of wars can be won or even deserve public support in the first place.

A number of experts doubt that the U.S. can evolve any common view of Viet Nam and its lessons for many years to come. Says Graham Martin, the last U.S. Ambassador to South Viet Nam: "I estimated at the end of the war that it probably would be at least two decades before any rational,

> "I want to rail against wind and tide, kill the whales in the ocean, sweep the whole country to save people from slavery."
> —TRIEU AU, VIET NAM'S "JOAN OF ARC" A.D. 248

> "France has had the country for nearly 100 years, and the people are worse off than at the beginning."
> —FRANKLIN D. ROOSEVELT 1944

> "Kill ten of our men and we will kill one of yours. In the end, it is you who will tire."
> —HO CHI MINH 1946

objective discussion of the war and its causes and effects could be undertaken by scholars who were not so deeply, emotionally engaged at the time that their later perceptions were colored by biases and prejudices." William Hyland, editor of *Foreign Affairs* magazine, thinks an even longer perspective may be required: "We always want to make historical judgments two days after the fact. Historians need 100 years."

But the U.S. is unlikely to have anywhere near that much time to decide what lessons to draw from Viet Nam and how to apply them. The initial impulse after the American withdrawal was to avoid any foreign involvement that might conceivably lead to a commitment of U.S. troops. Scholars differ on how seriously this so-called Viet Nam syndrome inhibited an activist U.S. foreign policy, but in any case it is fading—witness the enthusiastic approval of the Grenada invasion in late 1983 (to be sure, that was a rare case in which the U.S. was able to apply such overwhelming force that it could not have failed to win quickly). Says Maine's Republican Senator William Cohen: "The legacy of Viet Nam does not mean that we will not send our sons anywhere. It does mean that we will not send them everywhere." Even some fervent doves agree that memories of Viet Nam should not keep the U.S. from ever fighting anywhere. Sam Brown, one-time antiwar leader who now develops low-cost housing in Colorado, remains convinced that if it were not for the protests against U.S. involvement in Viet Nam that he helped organize, "we would have three or four other wars now." Even so, concedes Brown, some "wrong lessons" might be drawn, among them "the risk that we won't be prepared if our national interest is genuinely threatened."

But if the specter of Viet Nam no longer inhibits all thought of projecting U.S. military power overseas, it still haunts every specific decision. In the Middle East, Weinberger's fears of entrapment in a drawn-out conflict fought without public support caused him at first to oppose sending Marines to Lebanon and then to insist on their withdrawal after terrorist attacks left 266 U.S. servicemen dead. Shultz objected that the pullout would undercut U.S. diplomacy in the area, and still regards it as

U.S. AIR FORCE

POWER

B-52 dropping bombs on guerrillas, 1966: Was it a matter of too much force, or not enough?

One of the few propositions about Viet Nam that commands near unanimous assent from Americans is the obvious one that the U.S. lost—and a growing number would qualify even that. Richard Nixon, in his new book, *No More Vietnams,* argues that "we won the war" but then abandoned South Viet Nam after the Communist North began violating the 1973 Paris accords that supposedly ended the fighting. Though the former President's self-interest is obvious, parts of his analysis are supported even by the enemy. U.S. Army Colonel Harry Summers Jr., who considers Viet Nam "a tactical success and a strategic failure," was in Hanoi on a negotiating mission a few days before Saigon fell. Summers recalls telling a North Vietnamese colonel, "You know, you never defeated us on the battlefield." The foe's reply: "That may be so, but it is also irrelevant." In essence, the U.S. was outlasted by an enemy that proved able and willing to fight longer than America and its South Vietnamese allies.

Given the weakness of South Viet Nam, the determination of the North and the extent of the aid it could count on from the Soviet Union and neighboring China, even some hawks concede that Hanoi's victory might have been inevitable. Says Military Analyst Luttwak: "Some wars simply cannot be won, and Viet Nam may have been one of them." Nonetheless, the main lesson they would draw from the war is that the U.S. threw away whatever chance for victory it may have had through blunders that must not be repeated.

The most detailed exposition of this view comes from Colonel Summers, whose book, *On Strategy: A Critical Analysis of the Vietnam War,* has become must reading for young officers. Summers argues that the U.S. should have sealed off South Viet Nam with a barrier of American troops to prevent North Viet Nam from sending troops and matériel through Laos and Cambodia to wage war in the South. Instead, he says, the U.S. "wasted its strength" fighting the guerrillas in the South, a hopeless task so long as they were continually reinforced from the North and one that American troops had no business trying to carry out in the first place. The U.S., he contends, should have confined itself to protecting South Viet Nam against "external aggression" from the North and left "pacification," the job of rooting out the guerrillas, to the South Vietnamese. By in effect taking over the war, the U.S. sapped the initiative and ultimately the will of its Southern allies to carry out a job only they could do in the end.

Luttwak carries this analysis a step further by pouring scorn on the tactics used in the South: "The jet fighter bombing raids against flimsy huts that might contain a handful of guerrillas or perhaps none; the fair-sized artillery barrages that silenced lone snipers; the ceaseless firing of helicopter door gunners whereby a million dollars' worth of ammunition might be expended to sweep a patch of high grass." This "grossly disproportionate use of firepower," says Luttwak, was not just ineffective; it alienated South Vietnamese villagers whose cooperation against the guerrillas was vital. At least equally important, "Its imagery on television was by far the most powerful stimulus of antiwar sentiment" back in the U.S. Former CIA Director William Colby agrees that the U.S. got nowhere as long as it tried to defeat guerrillas with massed firepower and only began to make progress when it shifted to a "people's war" in which the

a mistake. But Ronald Reagan ordered the withdrawal anyway and won the approval of voters, even though critics portrayed the pullout as a national humiliation. The reason, suggests Democratic Political Analyst William Schneider, is that the President sensed the persistence of a popular attitude toward foreign military commitments that is summarized by the Viet Nam-era slogan "Win or Get Out." Says Schneider: "In Grenada we won. In Lebanon we got out. So much for the Viet Nam syndrome."

The Viet Nam experience colors almost every discussion of Central American policy. Nebraska Governor Bob Kerrey, who won a Congressional Medal of Honor and lost part of a leg fighting with the Navy SEAL commandos in Viet Nam, maintains that if memories of the ordeal in Southeast Asia were not still so strong, "we'd be in Nicaragua now." In Congress, Kerrey's fellow Democrats fret that the Administration's commitment to resist the spread of Marxist revolution throughout the isthmus could eventually bog down American troops in another endless jungle guerrilla war.

Reaganites retort, correctly, that while Viet Nam is halfway around the world and of debatable strategic importance to Washington, Central America is virtually next door, an area where U.S. interests are obvious. Moreover, the amounts Washington is spending to help the government of El Salvador defeat leftist guerrillas and to assist the *contra* rebels fighting the Marxist Sandinista government of Nicaragua are pittances compared with the sums lavished on South Viet Nam even before the direct U.S. military intervention there. Still, the Administration every now and then feels obliged to deny that it has any plan or desire to send U.S. troops to fight in Central America. Weinberger last November coupled his remarks about the necessity of popular support for any foreign military commitment with a pledge that "the President will not allow our military forces to creep—or be drawn gradually—into a combat role in Central America."

> "Master fear and pain, overcome obstacles, unite your efforts, fight to the very end, annihilate the enemy."
> —GENERAL GIAP
> 1954

> "I could conceive of no greater tragedy than for the U.S. to [fight] an all-out war in Indochina."
> —DWIGHT D. EISENHOWER
> 1954

> "You have a row of dominoes set up, you knock over the first one and [the last one] will go over very quickly."
> —EISENHOWER
> 1954

> "We do commit the U.S. to preventing the fall of South Viet Nam to Communism."
> —ROBERT MCNAMARA
> 1961

South Vietnamese carried the main burden of the fighting. By then it was too late; American public sentiment had turned irreversibly in favor of a fast pullout.

According to Hyland, "The biggest lesson of Viet Nam is that we need to have a much better notion of what is at stake, what our interests are, before we go into a major military undertaking." Weinberger voiced essentially the same thought last fall in laying down several conditions, beyond a reasonable assurance of public support, that must be met if U.S. troops are again to be sent into battle overseas: "We should have clearly defined political and military objectives, and we should know precisely how our forces can accomplish those." Other criteria: "The commitment of U.S. forces to combat should be a last resort," undertaken only if it "is deemed vital to our national interest or that of our allies," and then "with the clear intention of winning" by using as much force as necessary.

Weinberger's speech, delivered after he had talked it over with President Reagan, is the closest thing to an official Administration reading of the lessons of Viet Nam. But some rude jeers greeted the Weinberger doctrine. Luttwak, for example, called Weinberger's views "the equivalent of a doctor saying he will treat patients only if he is assured they will recover." Columnist William Safire headlined a scathing critique ONLY THE 'FUN' WARS, and New York Democrat Stephen Solarz, who heads the House Subcommittee on Asian and Pacific Affairs, pointed out, "It is a formula for national paralysis if, before we ever use force, we need a Gallup poll showing that two-thirds of the American people are in favor of it."

More important, what is a "vital interest"? To some Americans, the only one that would justify another war is the defense of the U.S. against a threat of direct attack. Decrying "this whole practice of contracting our military out just for the survival of some other government and country," Georgia Secretary of State Max Cleland, who lost an arm and both legs in Viet Nam, insists, "There is only one thing worth dying for, and that is this country, not somebody else's."

Diplomats argue persuasively that a policy based on this view would leave the U.S. to confront Soviet expansionism all alone. No country would enter or maintain an alliance with a U.S. that specifically refused to fight in its defense. But in the real world, an outright Soviet attack against a country that the U.S. is committed by treaty to defend is quite unlikely. The decision whether or not to fight most probably would be posed by a Communist threat to a friendly nation that is not formally an ally. And then the threat might well be raised not by open aggression but by a combination of military, political and economic tactics that Moscow is often adept at orchestrating and Washington usually inept at countering: the front groups, the street demonstrations, the infiltrated unions, the guerrilla units. One reason the U.S. sent troops to Viet Nam is that it lacked other alternatives to help its allies prevail against this sort of subversion. In fact, developing a capacity to engage in such political action and shadowy paramilitary activities might help the U.S. to avert future Viet Nams.

Merely defining U.S. interests, in any event, can prove endlessly complicated. Geography alone is no guide in an age of ocean-spanning missiles. Economics may be vital in some areas like the Persian Gulf, where the flow of oil must be maintained,

Y.R. OKAMOTO—LBJ LIBRARY

POLITICS

Defense Secretary McNamara brooding after troop call-up, 1965: Would Americans have backed a bigger war?

"But it will be just like Berlin. The troops will march in; the bands will play; the crowds will cheer; and in four days everyone will have forgotten. Then we will be told we have to send in more troops."

–JOHN F. KENNEDY
1961

"There just isn't any simple answer. We're fighting a kind of war here that I never read about at Command and Staff College. Conventional weapons just don't work here. Neither do conventional tactics."

—FROM GRAHAM GREENE'S *THE UGLY AMERICAN*

"You let a bully come into your front yard, the next day he'll be on your porch."

—LYNDON B. JOHNSON ON SEVERAL OCCASIONS

unimportant in others like Israel, where political and moral considerations are paramount. There may be times too when U.S. intervention, even if it seems justified, would be ineffective. Not much is heard these days of the once fashionable argument that in Viet Nam the U.S. was on the wrong side of history because it was fighting a nationalistic social revolution being waged by a regime that was, deep down, benign; Hanoi's brutality within Viet Nam and its swift move to establish hegemony over all of Indochina removed all doubt that the foe was and is not only totalitarian but imperialistic besides. Today, with the focus on Central America, the argument is often heard that economic and social misery have made leftist revolution inevitable. To those who maintain that revolution is the only way to progress, the counterargument is that whatever social and economic gains may be achieved by Communist takeovers usually carry an extremely high price tag: the establishment of tyranny.

About the only general rule that foreign-policy experts can suggest is not to have any general rule, at least in the sense of drawing up an advance list of where the U.S. might or might not fight. They still shudder at the memory of a 1950 definition of the U.S. "defense perimeter" in Asia that omitted South Korea—which promptly suffered an outright Communist invasion that took three years and 54,000 American lives to repel. Walt Rostow, who was Lyndon Johnson's National Security Adviser, recalls how the late Soviet Foreign Minister Andrei Vishinsky "told a group of Americans that we deceived them on Korea." Says Rostow: "I believe that's correct."

The decision on where American military intervention might be both necessary and effective can only be made case by case, based on a variety of factors that may be no easier to judge in the future than they were in Viet Nam: the nature and circumstances of war, the will and ability of the nation under attack to defend itself, the consequences of its loss. Any such debate is sure to revive another long buried but still unresolved controversy of the Viet Nam era: whether a Communist takeover of one country would cause others to topple like a row of dominoes. Hawks insist that this theory was vindicated by Communist triumphs in Laos and Cambodia after the fall of Saigon. Opponents point out that the Asian "dominoes" that most concerned the U.S.—Thailand, Burma, Malaysia, Singapore, Indonesia, the Philippines—have all survived as non-Communist (in several cases, strongly anti-Communist) societies. Rostow, now a professor of political economy at the University of Texas, offers a counterrebuttal. Those countries might have gone under if Saigon had fallen in 1965, he contends. The U.S. intervention in Viet Nam bought them ten years to strengthen their economies and governments and, says Rostow, "bought time that was used extremely well by Asians, especially Southeast Asians."

Be that as it may, the evidence would seem to argue against any mechanical application of the domino theory. It originated in the 1950s, when world Communism was seen as a monolithic force headquartered in Moscow, with Peking a kind of branch office. Today China, never really comfortable with its Hanoi "allies," has resumed its ancient enmity toward Viet Nam; both Washington and Peking are aiding guerrillas battling against the Soviet-backed Vietnamese in Kampuchea. That does not mean that the domino theory has lost all validity everywhere, but its applicability is also subject to case-by-case application.

The most bedeviling of all the dilemmas raised by Viet Nam concerns the issue of public support. On the surface it might seem to be no issue at all: just about everybody agrees that Viet Nam proved the futility of trying to fight a war without a strong base of popular support. But just how strong exactly? Rostow argues that the only U.S. war fought with tremendous public backing was World War II. He points out that World War I "brought riots and splits," the War of 1812 was "vastly divisive" and even during the War of Independence one-third of the population was pro-revolution, one-third pro-British and one-third "out to lunch." Rostow proposes a 60-25-15 split as about the best that can be expected now in support of a controversial policy: a bipartisan 60% in favor, 25% against and 15% out to lunch.

A strong current of opinion holds that Lyndon Johnson guaranteed a disastrously low level of support by getting into a long, bloody war without ever admitting (perhaps even to himself) the extent of the commitment he was making. Colonel Summers, who considers Viet Nam a just war that the U.S. could and should have won, insists that any similar conflict in the future ought to be "legitimized" by a formal, congressional declaration of war. Says Summers: "All of America's previous wars were fought in the heat of passion. Viet Nam was fought in cold blood, and that was intolerable to the American people. In an immediate crisis the tendency of the American people is to rally around the flag. But God help you if it goes beyond that and you haven't built a base of support."

At the other extreme, former Secretary of State Dean Rusk defends to this day the Johnson Ad-

> "In the final analysis it is their war . . . We can help them . . . but they have to win it, the people of Viet Nam."
> —KENNEDY 1963

> "We are not about to send American boys 10,000 miles away to do what Asian boys ought to be doing for themselves."
> —JOHNSON 1964

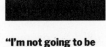

> "Hell no, we won't go!"
> —ANTIWAR CHANT 1965

> "I'm not going to be the first President who loses a war."
> —RICHARD NIXON 1969

> "Peace is at hand."
> —HENRY KISSINGER 1972

ministration's effort "to do in cold blood at home what we were asking men to do in hot blood out in the field." Rusk points out that the war began with impressive public and congressional support. It was only in early 1968, says Rusk, that "many at the grass-roots level came to the opinion that if we didn't give them some idea when this war would come to an end, we might as well chuck it." The decisive factor probably was the defection of middle-class youths and their parents, a highly articulate segment that saw an endless war as a personal threat—though in fact the burden of the draft fell most heavily on low-income youths.

Paradoxically, though, Johnson might well have been able to win public support for a bigger war than he was willing to fight. As late as February 1968, at the height of the Tet offensive, one poll found 53% favoring stronger U.S. military action, even at the risk of a clash with the Soviet Union or China, vs. only 24% opting to wind down the war. Rusk insists that the Administration was right not to capitalize on this sentiment. Says he: "We made a deliberate decision not to whip up war fever in this country. We did not have parades and movie stars selling war bonds, as we did in World War II. We thought that in a nuclear world it is dangerous for a country to become too angry too quickly. That is something people will have to think about in the future."

It certainly is. Viet Nam veterans argue passionately that Americans must never again be sent out to die in a war that "the politicians will not let them win." And by win they clearly mean something like a World War II–style triumph ending with unconditional surrender. One lesson of Viet Nam, observes George Christian, who was L.B.J.'s press secretary, is that "it is very tough for Americans to stick in long situations. We are always looking for a quick fix." But nuclear missiles make the unconditional-surrender kind of war an anachronism. Viet Nam raised, and left unsolved for the next conflict, the question posed by Lincoln Bloomfield, an M.I.T. professor of political science who once served on Jimmy Carter's National Security Council: "How is it that you can 'win' so that when you leave two years later you do not lose the country to those forces who have committed themselves to victory at any cost?"

It is a question that cannot be suppressed much longer. Americans have a deep ambiguity toward military power: they like to feel strong, but often shy away from actually using that strength. There is a growing recognition, however, that shunning all battles less easily winnable than Grenada would mean abandoning America's role as a world power, and that, in turn, is no way to assure the nation's survival as a free society. Americans, observes Secretary of State Shultz, "will always be reluctant to use force. It is the mark of our decency." But, he adds, "a great power cannot free itself so easily from the burden of choice. It must bear responsibility for the consequences of its inaction as well as for the consequences of its action."

—By George J. Church.
Reported by David S. Jackson/Austin and Ross H. Munro/Washington, with other bureaus.

THE NEW INDIAN POLITICS

Stephen Cornell

Stephen Cornell, 37, is associate professor of sociology at Harvard University. Born in Buffalo, New York, he received a B.A. from Mackinac College in Michigan (1970) and a Ph.D. from the University of Chicago (1980). His book, Return of the Native: American Indian Political Resurgence, *was published by Oxford University Press, 1990.*

On December 28, 1890, near the Badlands of South Dakota, a band of exhausted Sioux Indians, including perhaps 100 warriors and some 250 women and children, surrendered to the blue-clad troopers of the U.S. Seventh Cavalry and agreed to travel with them to the Indian agency at Pine Ridge. The joint party camped that night in freezing weather at Wounded Knee Creek, 20 miles from Pine Ridge. Surrounding the Indian tepees were nearly 500 soldiers and a battery of four Hotchkiss light artillery pieces.

The next morning, the Indian men were told to turn in their weapons. Few obeyed. The cavalrymen began to search the tepees. When they turned up few additional guns, the troops began to search the warriors themselves. Reports of subsequent events vary, but tensions ran high.

A scuffle broke out between an Indian and some soldiers. In the struggle, the warrior, intentionally or not, fired his rifle. That did it. Instantly both Indians and soldiers began firing at each other. Within moments, the Army gunners were pouring explosive Hotchkiss shells into the Indian camp.

Most of the Sioux warriors died in the opening volleys. Others, along with a large number of women and children, were shot as they fled down adjacent ravines. By the time the firing ended, nearly 200 Indians—perhaps more, the estimates vary—had been killed.

The survivors of this slaughter were among the last Indians to come under the direct administrative control of the U.S. government. Confined to reservations, they joined 300,000 others, from coast to coast, in a state of despondent dependency, sunk in poverty, wards of a white man's government that they had learned not to trust.

Eighty-two years later, on the wintry night of February 27, 1973, a group of armed Oglala Sioux from South Dakota's Pine Ridge Reservation joined forces with activists from the American Indian Movement (AIM) and seized the reservation village of Wounded Knee, the site of the 1890 massacre. They did so to protest corruption in the tribal government at Pine Ridge as well as U.S. violations of the 1868 Fort Laramie Treaty (which recognized Sioux sovereignty over much of what is now the Dakotas, Montana, Wyoming, and Nebraska). "We want a true Indian nation," said Carter Camp, an AIM coordinator, "not one made up of Bureau of Indian Affairs puppets."

Within 24 hours, a force of 250 Federal Bureau of Investigation agents, U.S. Marshals, and Bureau of Indian Affairs (BIA) police had cordoned off the village. The much-publicized siege lasted 10 weeks, punctuated by exchanges of gunfire that left two Indians dead and several men wounded on each side. In May, after lengthy negotiations, the Indians surrendered to federal authorities. The second battle of Wounded Knee was over.

The 1890 massacre brought one era to a close. The Euro-American advance across the continent was now complete. As Black Hawk, war leader of the Sauk and Fox, had said of himself a half century earlier, "He is now a prisoner to the white men; they will do with him as they wish."

86 Million Acres

The 1973 occupation also represented the culmination of an era. America's roughly 790,000 Indians still lived, for the most part, in considerable misery, afflicted by poverty, alcoholism, high unemployment, and inadequate education. But the days of dull Indian acquiescence were long gone. Beginning in the 1940s, Indians had not only been demanding a voice in federal Indian policy; increasingly, they had appropriated such a voice for themselves, forcing the surrounding society to respond. *"We talk, you listen"* was the title of a 1970 book by Sioux author Vine Deloria, Jr. And as they demonstrated at Wounded Knee, Indians did more than talk.

All in all, the path from the Wounded Knee I to Wounded Knee II traced an Indian political resurgence of striking proportions. There had always been, of course, politics *about* Indians. For the most part it was non-Indian politics, carried on in Washington, among the governors of Western states and territories, and among missionaries, reformers, and bureaucrats. The situation today is dramatically different, marked by the emergence of a new and genuinely Indian politics.

In hindsight, the turning point appears to have been the Indian Reorganization Act (IRA) of 1934. Prior to its passage, two goals had guided federal Indian policy: the acquisition of Indian lands and the cultural transformation of Indians into Euro-Americans—in a word, "assimilation." Those goals were enshrined in the Dawes Act (1887), which heralded the age of "allotment." Washington broke up much of the tribal land base, withdrawing some property from Indian ownership and distributing other, often marginal, lands to individual tribal members. "Surplus" lands, more often than not the richest, were then sold off to white settlers. Between 1887, when the Dawes Act was passed, and 1934, when allotment ceased, some 86 million acres—60 percent of the remaining Indian lands—passed into the possession of non-Indians.

Allotment, which reached a peak just before World War I, was not merely a means of appropriating Indian territory. It was part of a concerted effort to break up tribal nations, of which there were—and are—several hundred, each with a distinct history, most still with a distinct culture. This effort, like everything else on the reservations, was overseen by the Bureau of Indian Affairs, established by Secretary of War John Calhoun in 1824.

"The Indians," wrote Indian Commissioner Thomas Morgan in 1889, "must conform to 'the white man's ways,' peaceably if they will, forcibly if they must." On the reservations, BIA officials put Indian children into English-language boarding schools, dispersed village settlements, moved tribal members off communal (and on to individual) tracts of land, and took control of economic resources. Indigenous religious ceremonies, such as the Sun Dance of the Plains tribes, were outlawed.

Waiting for FDR

By the 1920s, white America's appetite for Indian lands (the best of which had already been taken) had begun to diminish. A postwar slump in farm prices helped reduce demand. Combined with the staggering extent of poverty, disease, and other social ills now apparent on the Indian reservations, these circumstances created a climate for reform.

The reform movement can be traced in part to the ideals of Progressivism and to the growing academic interest in the notion of "cultural pluralism" as a plausible alternative to the assimilation of America's ethnic groups. In 1922, when the Harding administration backed the Bursum Bill, which threatened the land and water rights of New Mexico's Pueblo Indians, a number of liberal, non-Indian organizations—the General Federation of Women's Clubs, for example—joined the Pueblos in opposing the legislation. The thriving community of artists, writers, and intellectuals around Santa Fe and Taos supported the protest. Writing in the *New York Times*, novelist D. H. Lawrence claimed that the bill played "the Wild West scalping trick a little too brazenly." The Pueblo leaders themselves, acting in concert for the first time since the Pueblo Rebellion in 1680, declared that the bill "will rob us of everything we hold dear—our lands, our customs, our traditions." After protracted debate, the Bursum Bill was defeated in Congress.

Such protests publicized the Indians' situation. But it was not until Franklin Roosevelt's election to the presidency, and his appointment of John Collier as Indian Commissioner in 1933, that a reform package won approval in Congress.

Collier, a former social worker and educator, and champion of the Pueblo cause during the 1920s, placed great faith in the power of "community." Native American communities, he was convinced, "must be given status, responsibility, and power." Backed by FDR, Collier led a drive to reorient U.S. Indian policy. The result, in 1934, was the Indian Reorganization Act.

Indian policy did an abrupt about-face. The IRA legislation not only put an official stop to allotment; it actually allocated modest funds for *expansion* of the Indian land base. It provided money (though never enough) for economic development on Indian reservations and subsidies for Indians to set up tribal business corporations. But most important, it allowed Indians into the decision-making process by making explicit the right of any Indian tribe "to organize for its common welfare" and to adopt a constitution and bylaws for that purpose. By 1936, more than two-thirds of the tribes had endorsed the IRA in special elections (although far fewer actually organized themselves under its provisions).

The mechanisms of the IRA—representative government, for example, and the business corporation—were alien to Indian tribes. Even so, during the next few years many groups took advantage of what has been called "the Indian New Deal." The majority of today's tribal councils are one result. For some groups, such as the Papago and Apache in the Southwest or the Sioux tribes on the northern Plains, these councils represented the first comprehensive political institu-

THE PRICE OF ISOLATION

The poorest county in the United States, with an annual income per capita of $2,841 (in 1982), is not in the Deep South, the Appalachians, or any of the other regions in the United States frequently associated with rural poverty. It is in South Dakota: Shannon County (pop. 11,800), site of the Pine Ridge Indian Reservation.

The poverty of Pine Ridge is shared by many Indians, especially those on the nation's 270 Indian reservations. Roughly 23 percent of all urban Indians and 33 percent of all rural Indians live below the official "poverty line"—compared with 14 percent for the entire U.S. population. In 1980, overall reservation unemployment stood at twice the national average; in some places, unemployment ranged near 80 percent.

Other statistics are even more sobering. In 1982, Indians ranked first in divorce and in deaths caused by suicide and alcohol consumption. Afflicted by poor health, family disarray, and low expectations, more than 40 percent of all Indian students entering high school drop out before graduation. No less important, note James Olson and Raymond Wilson in *Native Americans in the Twentieth Century* (1984), is the fear of many Indian parents that local public schools "alienate Native American children from tribal values." As a result, the percentage of Indians enrolled in schools is the lowest of any ethnic group in the United States.

To counter these and other difficulties, Indians on and off the reservations received roughly $2.6 billion in 1984 from federal agencies, notably the departments of Interior, Health and Human Services, Agriculture, and Education. A total that includes Social Security payments and food stamps, this amounts to $1,900 per Indian. Yet in a 1983 report, the National Tribal Chairmen's Association claimed that 70 percent of the almost $1 billion allotted to the Bureau of Indian Affairs (BIA) was spent supporting 15,000 BIA employees—or one employee for every 23 reservation Indians.

The Reagan administration has sought to reduce red tape and spur employment on Indian reservations by turning over federal programs to state, local, and tribal governments, and by encouraging private industry to invest in Indian communities. Between 1982 and 1984, Congress cut spending on Indians by 18 percent. But because almost 30 percent of all employed Indians work in public sector jobs, federal spending cuts tend to increase unemployment before they do anything else. As Peterson Zah, chairman of the Navaho, pointed out, "We don't have the people that Reagan is calling on—private sector development business people—to pick up the slack."

Those Indians who have prospered have done so primarily by leaving the reservation. Almost one-half of all Indians now reside in cities or towns, where a smaller percentage of Indians than of blacks or Hispanics live below the poverty line.

Yet few Indians adjust to urban life. Most return frequently to their reservations, where they often leave their children with relatives, and where they often choose to retire. Assimilation, the path to prosperity taken by generations of American immigrants, is an anathema to many Indians. "The pervasive fear of Indians," observes longtime Indian activist Vine Deloria, Jr., "is that they will . . . move from their plateau of small nationhood to the status of [just] another ethnic group in the American melting pot."

---

tions in their history. But their powers were limited. As an Apache leader from Arizona's San Carlos Reservation put it, "[BIA] Superintendent [James B.] Kitch was still the boss." Nevertheless, Indian groups enjoyed greater control over their own affairs, including a power of veto over some federal actions. For the first time in half a century, numerous Native American groups could also have federally recognized political organizations that could represent the tribal interests in Washington, state capitals, and the courts.

World War II as Catalyst

Another step followed. In 1944, representatives of 42 tribes founded the National Congress of American Indians (NCAI), the first major attempt to pull together Indian groups and governments in a single, supratribal organization. In the NCAI and the regional organizations that came afterwards, tribal leaders began talking to one another. The purpose of the congress, which is still active today: "to preserve Indian cultural values; to seek an equitable adjustment of tribal affairs; to secure and to preserve rights under Indian treaties with the United States; and otherwise to promote the common welfare of the American Indian." In 1948, the NCAI and other groups began a campaign designed to secure Indian voting rights—withheld at the time in both New Mexico and Arizona.*

*Both U.S. citizenship and the voting franchise came to Indians in stages. Some Indians acquired citizenship through allotment, some through military service or congressional dispensation. In 1924, the Indian Citizenship Act made citizens of all Indians born in the United States, a status that some Indians, then as now, protested as imposed against their will. Until the 1950s, some jurisdictions nevertheless denied Indians the right on the grounds that Indian lands were exempt from taxation.

If the IRA gave Indians the legal tools with which to organize, World War II gave many of them the motivation. In what the Interior Department described at the time as "the greatest exodus of Indians from reservations that has ever taken place," some 25,000 Indians joined the armed forces an saw action in Europe and the Pacific. Some 40,000 quit the economic desert of the reservations for jobs in war industries. For many Indians, experiences in the factory or on the battlefront constituted their first real exposure to the larger American society.

The identities of Native Americans have long been rooted in tribes, bands, villages, and the like, not in one's presumed "Indianness." The reservation system helped to preserve such identities and inhibited the emergence of a more inclusive self-consciousness. As a result, Indians, unlike American blacks, have had difficulty forming a common front. World War II brought Indians from different tribes into contact with one another, and with other Americans who thought of them indiscriminately as "Indians," not as Navahos or Apaches or Sioux.

It also forcefully brought home to Indians their second-class status. One Lumbee veteran told anthropologist Karen Blu: "In 1945 or '46, I applied to UNC [University of North Carolina]. I had six battle stars. They said they didn't accept Indians from Robeson County." In the Southwest, not surprisingly, it was the Indian veterans who went to court to seek voting rights. Former G.I.'s were prominent in the NCAI. In 1952, the *New York Times* reported that "a new, veteran-led sense of political power is everywhere in Indian country."

Such analyses proved premature. There had always been strong opposition to the Indian Reorganization Act, from the political Right and from politicians of all colorations in the West, partly on the grounds that it perpetuated an undesirably distinct status for Native Americans.

After the fading of the New Deal, the status of Native Americans as wards of the federal government seemed to go against the American tradition of self-reliance. Sen George Malone (R.-Nev.) complained that Indian reservations represented "natural socialist environments"—a charge echoed by Interior Secretary James Watt three decades later. Break up the tribal domains, so the argument ran, remove the protective arm of government, and cast the Indian into the melting pot and the marketplace. Everyone would benefit.

Such, in essence, was the conclusion of the so-called Hoover Commission on governmental organization, which in 1949 proposed "integration of the Indian into the rest of the population." It recommended that Indians leave the reservations and, implicitly, the tribal framework. Assimilation, the commission urged, should once again become "the dominant goal of public policy."

Ending Segregation

By the mid-1950s it was. Under "termination," as this latest turn in Washington's policy came to be called, Congress set out to dismantle the reservation system, disband tribal nations, and distribute their assets among tribal members. What Sen. Arthur V. Watkins (R.-Utah), an architect of the new policy, called "the Indian freedom program" received both liberal and conservative support. Liberal opinion during the late 1940s and '50s tended to view the problems of Indians in terms derived from the black experience and the early days of the struggle to end racial exclusion. Reservations were seen as "rural ghettoes"; termination would put an end to "segregation." As historian Clayton Koppes has noted, this view reflected the liberal emphasis on "freeing the individual from supposedly invidious group identity."

This was exactly what most Indians did not want, but Washington was not in a listening mood. Commissioner of Indian Affairs Dillon S. Myer's orders to BIA employees were explicit. "I realize that it will not be possible always to obtain Indian cooperation," he wrote in 1952. Nonetheless, "we must proceed."

During the summer of 1953, under House Concurrent Resolution 108, Congress effectively repudiated the spirit of the Indian New Deal, stipulating that Indians were to be removed from federal supervision "at the earliest possible time," with or without Indian consent. Under Public Law 280, Congress transferred to California, Minnesota, Nebraska, Oregon, and Wisconsin all civil and criminal jurisdiction over Indian reservations—previously under federal and tribal jurisdiction. Some tribal lands were broken up and sold, while many functions once performed by Washington—such as running schools and housing programs—were usually turned over to the states or other agencies.

Picking Up the Pieces

Meanwhile, to spur assimilation, Indians were urged to relocate to the cities. As Senator Watkins remarked: "The sooner we get the Indians into the cities, the sooner the government can get out of the Indian business." In 1940, fewer than 30,000 Indians were city residents; almost three-quarters of a million are today. But the government is not out of the Indian business.

That is because termination did not work. Take the case of the 3,000 Menominees in Wisconsin, one of the larger groups freed from the federal embrace. When Congress passed the Menominee Termination Act in 1954, the Menominee tribe was riding high. Poverty on the more than 200,000-acre reservation was widespread, but the tribe itself had large cash reserves and a thriving forest products industry that provided jobs and income.

With termination the Menominee reservation became a county. Tribal assets came under the control of a corporation in which individual Menominees held shares, while previously untaxed lands suddenly became subject to state and local taxes. The tribal hospital once financed by Washington was shut down, and some Menominees, faced with rising taxes and unemployment, had to sell their shares in the corporation. Before long, the corporation itself was leasing lands to non-Indians in an attempt to raise money. Soon it was selling the land in order to survive. By the mid-1960s the state and federal governments, forced to pick up the pieces, were spending more to support the Menominees than they had before termination. As more than one Menominee asked in frustration, "Why didn't they leave us alone?"

In 1969, faced with disaster, the Menominees began to fight back, organizing a major protest movement in favor of restoration of federal jurisdiction and services, preservation of the land base, and a return to tribal status. Congress acquiesced late in 1973. The Menominee Restoration Act reinstated federal services to the Menominees, and formally re-established them "as a federally recognized sovereign Indian tribe."

The assimilationist orientation of the termination policy, and Washington's complete indifference to the views of its target population, aroused Indians across the country. They saw in termination the greatest threat to *tribal* survival since the Indian wars of the 19th century.

Termination did not die officially until 1970, when President Richard Nixon repudiated it. As federal and state officials came to recognize that the policy was creating more problems than it solved, protests by Indian groups slowed. Nonetheless, some Indian groups had been irreparably harmed.

In retrospect, the chief accomplishment of termination ran directly counter to Congress's intention: It provided Indians of diverse backgrounds with a critical issue around which to mobilize. At the American Indian Chicago Conference in 1961, recalled Flathead anthropologist D'Arcy McNickle, the 500 Indians from 90 tribes who gathered for the event "had in common a sense of being under attack." The termination crisis persuaded many Indians of the utility—indeed, the necessity—of united action. Strength would be found in numbers. The category "Indian," invented and named by Europeans, was rapidly becoming the basis of a new wave of minority group politics.

Uncle Tomahawk

The tempest over termination coincided with a second development. Just as the late 1950s and early '60s were a time of change in the black movement for civil rights, they also saw the beginnings of change in American Indian Leadership and its activity. In part, the change was one of tactics. There were glimmers of the future in actions by Wallace "Mad Bear" Anderson and other Iroquois in New York State: When the New York State Power Authority in 1958 sought to expropriate a large chunk of the Tuscarora Reservation for a new water reservoir, Anderson and 100 other Indians scuffled with state troopers and riot police, attempting to keep surveyors off the property. During that same year, several hundred armed and angry Lumbee Indians in Robeson County, North Carolina, reacted to Ku Klux Klan harassment by invading a Klan rally and driving the participants away with gunfire. The harassment stopped.

The new assertiveness reflected the emergence of a new generation of Indian leaders. During the 1950s the number of Indians enrolled in college in the United States substantially increased. According to the BIA, only 385 American Indians were attending postsecondary institutions in 1932; thanks in part to the post-–World War II G.I. Bill, that number had swelled to 2,000 by 1957. On campuses, off the reservations, educated Indians from different tribes began to discover one another. That sense of discovery is apparent in Navaho activist Herbert Blatchford's description of the clubs that began to appear among Indian college students, particularly in the Southwest. "There was group thinking," he told writer Stan Steiner. "I think that surprised us the most. We had a group world view."

In 1954, Indian students began holding a series of youth conferences in the Southwest to discuss Indian issues. The largest such conference, in 1960, drew 350 Indians from 57 tribes. Some of the participants eventually turned up at the 1961 Chicago conference—and found themselves at odds with the older, more cautious tribal leaders. In *The New Indians* (1968), Steiner quotes Mel Thom, a young Paiute from Nevada who attended the conference: "We saw the 'Uncle Tomahawks' fumbling around, passing resolutions, and putting headdresses on people. But as for taking a strong stand they just weren't doing it."

Two months later, at a meeting in Gallup, New Mexico, 10 Indian activists—a Paiute, a Ponca, a Mohawk, two Nevahos, a Ute, a Shoshone-Bannock, a Potawatomi, a Tuscarora, and a Crow—founded the National Indian Youth Council (NIYC). "We were concerned with direct action," recalled Thom. It was time for Indians "to raise some hell."

They began raising hell in the Pacific Northwest. The trouble started during the early 1960s, when the State of Washington arrested Indians fishing in off-reservation waters. Though in violation of state regulations, "the right of taking fish at accustomed places" had been guaranteed by the Treaty of Point No Point and other agreements made during the 19th century be-

THE WHITE MAN'S LAW

"You tell us of your claim to our land and that you have purchased it from your State," scolded Red Jacket, chief of the Seneca, in a speech delivered 160 years ago to white speculators near Lake Geneva, New York. "How has your State, which has never owned our land, sold it to you? Even the whites have a law . . ."

White law nowadays has become a key element in each tribe's survival strategy. More than 500 Indians today hold law degrees (versus fewer than a dozen 20 years ago), and virtually all of them grapple with issues of Indian jurisprudence. Those issues involve the nature of tribal government, protection of Indian lands, freedom of religion, hunting and fishing rights, rights to water from specified rivers and lakes, and other matters.

The tangled privileges and prohibitions that govern Indian life could discourage even Felix Frankfurter, who once described Indian law as "a vast hodgepodge of treaties, judicial and administrative rulings, and unrecorded practices." Because Indian law so often rests on treaties made by Indian nations with a foreign government—the United States of America—legal actions brought by Indians often end up before the U.S. Supreme Court.

In recent years, the drive by Indians to assert their rights has been led by the Native American Rights Fund (NARF), whose 11 lawyers work out of an old college fraternity house in Denver, Colorado. NARF was founded in 1970 with help from the Ford Foundation. Now headed by John Echohawk, a Pawnee, its annual budget is roughly $3 million.

NARF has been involved in almost every significant court case concerning Indians during the past 15 years. The group's attorneys helped the Menominee of Wisconsin and the Siletz of Oregon regain their status as tribes; fought for Chippewa fishing rights in Michigan; and established a homeland for the Traditional Kickapoo in Texas. In 1983 alone NARF handled business on behalf of 75 tribes in 25 states.

Three years ago, NARF lost three important water rights cases (*Arizona v. California, Nevada v. United States,* and *Arizona v. San Carlos Apache Tribe*) before the U.S. Supreme Court. After many successes, the judicial reverses paralleled the rise of a political backlash sparked by groups such as the Interstate Congress for Equal Rights and Responsibilities. In some states, this movement has successfully contested the Indians' "special treatment" under the law. The Supreme Court of Washington, for example, has charged that the federal government, by treaty, "conferred upon tribal Indians and their descendants what amounts to titles of nobility."

Indians view their legal status not as something the white man gave them but as something the white man left them. That is why the Indian recourse to white justice will persist, seeking white support and reminding us that we are, besides much else, a nation governed by law.

—*Richard J. Margolis*

Richard J. Margolis is currently at work on a book on Risking Old Age in America, *has written widely on Indian affairs and has been an adviser to the Rosebud Sioux and Navaho tribes.*

tween various Northwestern tribes and the United States. In 1964, a new regional organization—Survival of American Indians—joined the NIYC in protests supporting Indian treaty rights. They held demonstrations at the state capital in Olympia and, more provocatively, sponsored a series of "fish-ins," deliberately setting out to fish waters forbidden to them by the state.

Equal Rights

Growing numbers of Indian tribes became involved—the Muckleshoot, Makah, Nisqually, Puyallup, Yakima, and others—and began to assert their claims in defiance of court injunctions and state actions. The protests continued into the 1970s and became more violent. In August 1970, Puyallup Indians in a fishing camp on the Puyallup River exchanged gunfire with police who had surrounded them. No one was injured, but 64 Indians were carted off to jail. A year later Hank Adams, leader of Survival of American Indians, was shot by white vigilantes as he sat in his car on the banks of the Nisqually, near Tacoma.

Adams survived, and the struggle went on. Ultimately, in 1974, a federal district court ruled in the tribes' favor on the fishing rights issue, a decision upheld by the U.S. Supreme Court five years later. But the battle is not over. In November 1984, voters in Washington approved Initiative 456, designed to undermine the Treaty of Point No Point and other similar treaties.

Jack Metcalf, a Washington state senator and author of Initiative 456, says that "the basic point is not fish—it's equal rights." But, of course, the issue *is* fish and other treaty-protected Indian resources. From the Indian point of view, it is an issue long since resolved. In the treaties they signed during the 19th century, they agreed to give to the United States most of what are now the states of Washington and Oregon as well as parts of Idaho and California. In return, the United States, among other things, recognized forever their right to fish in Northwestern waters.

Indian activism did not appear only in the countryside; it erupted in the cities as well. For many Indian migrants of the postwar period, the move from the reservation to Denver, Chicago, Seattle, and other cities merely replaced one form of poverty with another. Largely unskilled, lacking experience in the non-Indian world, victimized by discrimination in housing and jobs, Indian migrants swelled the ranks of the urban poor.

Landing on Alcatraz

They also discovered that, unlike blacks or Hispanics, they had become "invisible." In the eyes of state and local officials, urban Indians, just like reservation Indians, were the sole responsibility of the BIA. The BIA, for its part, believed that its responsibility stopped at reservation's edge. In 1963, Indians in Oakland, San Francisco, and San Jose began protesting BIA relocation policies and the failure of the Bureau to deal with urban Indian problems. They took a cue from the tactics being employed by American blacks. Observed Vine Deloria, Jr.: "The basic fact of American political life—that without money or force there is no change—impressed itself upon Indians as they watched the civil-rights movement."

The two most militant Indian political organizations took root in the cities: the American Indian Movement, founded in 1968, and Indians of All Tribes, which materialized a year later.

AIM first made its mark in Minneapolis, organizing an Indian Patrol to combat alleged police brutality in Indian neighborhoods. It soon had chapters in cities throughout the Midwest. Indians of All Tribes was founded in San Francisco in response to a specific incident. On November 1, 1969, the San Francisco Indian Center, which served the large Bay Area population, burned to the ground. There was no ready replacement for the building or the services that it provided. On November 9, a group of Indians—perhaps a dozen—landed on Alcatraz Island in San Francisco Bay, site of an abandoned federal prison, and claimed it for a new Indian center. Authorities removed them the next day. The Indians returned on November 20, now 80 strong. By the end of the month several hundred were living on the island, calling themselves Indians of All Tribes. Wary of public reaction to the use of force, federal officials pursued negotiations for 19 months. Not until June 1971, when the number of Indians on the island had dwindled and public interest had waned, did federal marshals and the Coast Guard retake "the Rock."

Alcatraz was a watershed. It drew massive publicity,

providing many Indians with a dramatic symbol of self-assertion. Said occupation leader Richard Oakes, a Mohawk: "This is actually a move, not so much to liberate the island, but to liberate ourselves." During the next five years Indians occupied Mount Rushmore, Plymouth Rock, and more than 50 other sites around the country for varying lengths of time. The wave of takeovers culminated with the seizure of the BIA headquarters in Washington, D.C., in 1972, and the Wounded Knee occupation in 1973. AIM, led by Dennis Banks and Russell Means, was a major actor in both.* All made for vivid television news stories.

The Indian activists, noted Yakima journalist Richard La Course, "blew the lid off the feeling of oppression in Indian country." They also provoked a concerted response from Washington. The FBI and the BIA began an effective infiltration campaign, directed in particular at the American Indian Movement. (AIM's chief of security, it would later be revealed, was an FBI informer.) More than 150 indictments came out of the Wounded Knee incident. Making headlines and the network evening news had its price. Conceded one AIM member in 1978, "We've been so busy in court fighting these indictments, we've had neither the time nor the money to do much of anything else."

Going to the Courts

Radical Indian action has abated since the mid-1970s. But the new Indian politics has involved more than land seizures and demonstrations. Beginning in the late 1960s, the Great Society programs opened up new links between Indian leaders and the federal government. By 1970, more than 60 Community Action Agencies had been established on Indian reservations. Office of Economic Opportunity (OEO) funds were being used to promote economic development, establish legal services programs, and sustain tribal and other Indian organizations. Through agencies such as OEO and the Economic Development Administration, tribes were able for the first time to bypass systematically the BIA, pursuing their own political agendas in new ways.

Indian activists have also turned to the courts. The legal weapon is especially potent in the Indian situation because the relationship of Native Americans to

---

*Charges against AIM leaders Banks and Means were dropped on account of misconduct by government prosecutors. Banks was convicted in 1974 of charges stemming from a riot at a Custer, South Dakota, courthouse in 1973. He fled to California and was given sanctuary by Gov. Jerry Brown, who refused extradition. Republican George Deukmejian, elected governor in 1982, was less sympathetic. Banks surrendered to South Dakota officials in 1984 and served one year in prison. He now works as an alcohol-prevention counselor on the Pine Ridge Indian Reservation in Oglala, South Dakota. Means is currently associated with the International Indian Treaty Council, a lobbying group registered with the United Nations.

the United States, unlike that of any other group in American life, is spelled out in a vast body of treaties, court actions, and legislation. In 1972, for example, basing their case on a law passed by Congress in 1790 governing land transactions made with Indian tribes, the Penobscot and Passamaquoddy tribes filed suit to force the federal government to protect their claims to more than half of the state of Maine. This action led eventually to the Maine Settlement Act of 1980, which deeded 300,000 acres of timberland to the two tribes.

Behind such actions lies an assortment of Indian legal organizations that sprang up during the 1970s, staffed by a growing cadre of Indian lawyers and supported by both federal and private funds (see box). Indeed, organizing activity of every stripe has marked the past two decades. By the late 1970s, there were more than 100 intertribal or supratribal Indian organizations, ranging from the National Indian Youth Council to the Association of American Indian Physicians to the Small Tribes of Western Washington, most with political agendas, many with lobbying offices in Washington.

Despite generally low Indian voter turnout, Indians have not ignored electoral politics. In 1964, two Navahos ran for seats in the New Mexico state legislature and won, becoming the first Indian representatives in the state's history. Two years later, 15 Indians were elected to the legislatures of six Western states. In 1984, 35 Indians held seats in state legislatures.

Of course the leverage Indians can exercise at the polls is limited. In only five states (Alaska, Arizona, New Mexico, Oklahoma, and South Dakota) do Indians make up more than five percent of the population. At the local level, on the other hand, Indians are occasionally dominant. (Apache County, Arizona, for example, is nearly 75 percent Indian.) Indians also can make a difference in particular situations. In 1963, after the South Dakota legislature had decided that the state should have civil and criminal jurisdiction over Indian reservations, the Sioux initiated a "Vote No" referendum on the issue, hoping to overturn the legislation. They campaigned vigorously among whites and were able to turn out their own voters in record numbers. The referendum passed. A similar Indian grassroots effort and high voter turnout in 1978 led to the defeat of Rep. Jack Cunningham (R.-Wash.), sponsor of legislation in Congress to abrogate all treaties between Indian tribes and the federal government.

The Finest Lawyers

If Indians lack more than limited political clout in elections, during the 1970s they found new opportunities in the economy. The 1973–74 energy crisis and rising oil prices sent the fortunes of some tribes through the roof. Suddenly, Indian lands long thought to be worthless were discovered to be laden with valuable natural resources: one-quarter or more of U.S. strippable coal, along with large amounts of uranium, oil, and gas. Exploration quickly turned up other minerals on Indian lands. For the first time since the drop in land prices during the 1920s, Indians had substantial amounts of something everybody else wanted. In an earlier time this realization would have occasioned wholesale expropriation. In the political atmosphere of the 1970s, and in the face of militant Indians, that was no longer possible. Now the tribes began demanding higher royalties for their resources and greater control over the development process. The result, for some, was a bonanza. During the 41 years between 1937 and 1978, Native Americans received $720 million in royalties and other revenues from mineral leases; during the four years from 1978 to 1982, they received $532 million.

Most of this money went to only a few tribes, much of it to meet the needs of desperately poor populations. It also had a political payoff. Michael Rogers tells the story of an Alyeska Pipeline Company representative in Alaska, who during the mid-1970s lectured pipeline workers about the importance of maintaining good relations with local Indian and Eskimo communities. "You may wonder why they are so important," the representative told his hard-hats. "They are important because they are a people, because they were here before us, and because they have a rich heritage. They are also important because they belong to regional corporations that are able to afford the finest legal counsel in the country."

What Do Indians Want?

This new Indian assertiveness, in its multiple manifestations, had a major impact on U.S. policy. In 1975, responding to "the strong expression" of Indians, Congress committed itself to a policy of "self-determination," to providing "maximum Indian participation in the government and education of the Indian people." From now on, the government was saying, it not only would attempt to listen to Indian views and honor Indian agendas but would grant to Indians a central role in the implementation of policy.

But self-determination raises an awkward, chronic question. What is it the Indians want?

According to Bill Pensoneau, former president of the National Indian Youth Council and now economic planner for the Ponca Tribe in Oklahoma, what the Indians want is "survival." In his view, it is not individual survival that is of primary concern. What is at stake is the survival of Indian *peoples*: the continued existence of distinct, independent, tribal communities.

Among other things, of course, that means jobs, health care, functioning economies, good schools, a federal government that keeps its promises. These have not been any easier to come by in recent years.

Federal subsidies to Native Americans have been cut steadily under the Reagan administration by about $1 billion in 1981–83. Cancellation of the Comprehensive Employment and Training Act program cost the Poncas 200 jobs. The Intertribal Alcoholism Center in Montana lost half its counselors and most of its beds. The Navaho public housing program was shut down.

Aside from those with lucrative mineral rights, few tribes have been able to make up for such losses of federal subsidies. With no economic base to draw on, most have found themselves powerless in the face of rising unemployment, deteriorating health care, and a falling standard of living.

But the survival question cuts more deeply even than this and reveals substantial divisions among Native Americans themselves. There are those who believe that survival depends on how well Indians can exploit the opportunities offered by the larger (non-Indian) society. Others reject that society and its institutions; they seek to preserve or reconstruct their own culture.

There are many points of view in between. Ideological divisions mirror economic and social ones. In the ranks of any tribe these days one is likely to find blue-collar workers, service workers, professionals, and bureaucrats, along with those pursuing more traditional occupations and designs for living. Most tribes include both reservation and city populations, with contrasting modes of life. The resultant Indian agenda is consistent in its defense of Indian peoples but often contradictory in its conception of how best they can be sustained. This proliferation of Indian factions, many of them no longer tribally defined, has made Indian politics more difficult for even the most sympathetic outsiders to understand.

The Indian politics of the 1960s and '70s, both confrontational and conventional, was too fragmented, the actors were too dispersed, the goals too divergent to constitute a coherent, organized, political crusade. What it represented instead was the movement of a whole population—a huge collection of diverse, often isolated, but increasingly connected Indian communities—into more active political engagement with the larger society, seeking greater control over their lives and futures. To be sure, compared with other political and social events of the period, it was only a sideshow. It did not "solve" fundamental difficulties. But in the world of Indian affairs, it was a remarkable phenomenon, surpassing in scale and impact anything in Indian-white relations since the wars of the 19th century, which finally came to an end at Wounded Knee.

A Change in the Weather

As Reagan's era recedes, compassion and Government activism regain favor

Time to look for new ideas, time to move beyond the era of self-congratulation and beer-commercial patriotism.

It happened with surreal swiftness. One moment, the pageant of Reaganism was proceeding, with brilliant fireworks over the harbor. The next moment, the Iranian scandal burst up through the floorboards. Strange blackbirds of policy flapped out of the White House basement. The Reagan Administration, the phenomenon that had defined so much of the '80s, that had given the decade its agenda and style, seemed to collapse in a bizarre shambles.

If the U.S. were a parliamentary democracy, the Reagan Government might have fallen. As it is, Ronald Reagan will remain in Washington for another 22 months. His White House is laboring to repair the damage. In time Reagan may reassert his charm. Even as a lame duck, he will have his successes, perhaps even an arms-control agreement. It is possible that Ronald Reagan has not yet exhausted his luck.

But the question is not whether Reagan can recover. The nation is beginning to look beyond Reagan now. Any President in the last half of his second term is already in the valedictory mode. The Iran affair simply hastened the process and abruptly concentrated the nation's mind. The 1988 election is coalescing. The parties are sorting out candidates and issues. There are signs of a fundamental change in the nation's political weather, a philosophical mood shift like those that seem to occur in America every generation or so.

Even without Iran, the era of Reagan was passing. It has left its indelible mark, yet its battle cry—that Government is the problem, not the so-lution—is losing force. Presidential candidates of both parties are struggling to define a new role for Government in the post-Reagan era. While seeing the need to be frugal, they are talking more and more about compassion, more active approaches to deep-rooted social problems, a new sense of community values. Reagan has done what he has done, and he has accomplished much. He presided over one of the longest periods of economic recovery in American history, a time attended by the end of inflation and of the wage-price spiral. He rolled back the writ of the Federal Government, helped to initiate tax reform, strengthened (amid some setbacks) the American posture in the world. But now one feels the ground shifting underfoot, a grinding of the tectonic plates.

"We're at the end of an Eisenhower period," says UCLA Political Sociologist Jeffrey Alexander, "and we're moving into something not unlike the 1960s. The 'era of good feeling' that Reagan presided over is ending, and people are ready for the next cycle of history, for a new period of activism and social change." But as Alexander well knows, the future never merely recycles the past. The nation cannot return to federal taxing and spending on a Great Society scale. Most candidates in 1988 will focus wistfully on new ways to engage Government, business and labor in projects to solve problems and help people. It will never again be the all-daddy Government of the New Deal, they say, but neither will it be the shrunken Reagan version. "The swing is away from what you could

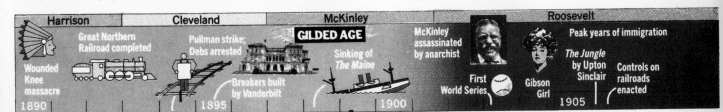

AMERICAN CYCLES Historian Arthur Schlesinger Jr. suggests that there are 30-year cycles of American history that swing between eras of liberalism and conservativism -- periods he calls Private Interest and Public Purpose.

Private Interest
Public Purpose

President's party
Republican
Democrat

> ## "People are ready for the next cycle of history, for a new period of activism and social change."

call the laissez-faire approach of Ronald Reagan to one that takes a more active, compassionate approach to those in true need," says Republican Mayor William Hudnut of Indianapolis. "It is a ground swell gaining force."

Reagan has been a master of public symbols. He worked an alchemy of nostalgia and hope, visions of the past and the future collaborating. He gave the people reassuring images of a mythic American past—the Olympic torch, the tall ships, the Statue of Liberty, the heroes in the visitors' gallery on State of the Union nights, Tom Sawyer come back to life as a yuppie—a sweet, virtuous America recrystallized by Reagan after the traumatic changes of the '60s and '70s. Reagan gave Americans the idea of a future as spacious as their past.

Some of the new American imagery is very different. It suggests something closing down, a darkness crowding in at the margins. One sees not the sunshine of Reagan's American morning but touches of Thomas Hobbes. The gloom probably is just as exaggerated as the earlier optimism. But the encroaching new images are haunting: homeless people on heating grates; the ominous national debt and the spectacle of Japanese managers moving into the American heartland to show Americans how to run things profitably; the AIDS epidemic, which is becoming an important and menacing presence in the 1988 campaign.

Another powerful image: Wall Street millionaires arrested for insider trading and taken off in handcuffs. Not long ago, the "go for it" mentality of untrammeled capitalism was a virtue in the culture of Reaganism. Now that culture is being questioned. The Rambo story, which was a cartoon of Reaganism's individualist machismo, has been discredited by the escapades of Oliver North. The enduring ghost of Viet Nam returns not in the cretinous revenge fantasies of Sylvester Stallone but in *Platoon,* a movie that confronts the ambiguous mess and tragedy of America's mission in Viet Nam. The show that has captured Broadway is *Les Misérables,* with its themes of suffering and redemption, and the injunction "Look down!"—meaning look down upon the poor, the homeless. The injunction of the Reagan years has been "Look up!"—to success, to wealth.

And of course there are the dark images of the Iranian fiasco: the President's men skulking around, with cake and Bible and guns, on ventures so goofy as to seem unhinged; the tablets of Valium that Robert McFarlane swallowed. The Iran affair destroyed Reagan's nimbus of immunity, subverted his magic. His political authority derived from the idea that Ronald Reagan believed certain simple things profoundly, with an incorruptible candor. He would bob his head, in the way he has, and smile and say, "Here I stand: I can do no other." Martin Luther washed up on the beaches of Malibu. But the Iran affair carried Reagan over into a strange, other dimension where both his candor and his principles proved

corruptible, where his powers seemed to fail. It is a powerful irony that for all the differences, the Iran affair smacks of Watergate, in the sense that the abuse of the highest power undoes the king (the highest power manipulated by little knights, stupid and zealous). That one of the most beloved American Presidents should have found himself in danger of recapitulating the fates of Richard Nixon and Lyndon Johnson is American political theater edging toward the Shakespearean.

An odd effect: Reagan's powerful connection with the American psychology now takes on a negative charge. In a way that would have seemed inconceivable not long ago, op-ed writers venture to speak well of Jimmy Carter. One senses uneasily a return of the world Americans thought they had left behind when Carter went back to Plains, Ga.

"Wise men have remarked on patterns of alternation, of ebb and flow in human history," writes Historian Arthur Schlesinger Jr. in *The Cycles of History.* Emerson observed that "the two parties which divide the state, the party of Conservatism and the party of Innovation, are very old, and have disputed the possession of the world ever since it was made . . . Innovation is the salient energy; Conservatism the pause on the last movement." But that can be tricky. Reagan in his way was no conservative and was something of an innovator, who tried, with limited success, to reverse deep-rooted Government traditions going back to the New Deal. In any case, Emerson also observed that "every hero becomes a bore at last."

What is the essence of the change that is now occurring in America?

In part it is a return from the long vacation of the Reagan years, Americans coming back from the picnic of restored nationalism and morale, a necessary pause, to discover that the old problems are still there, only in some ways worse now. The Indian summer was lovely, but the weather turned cold: Provide, provide! That holiday was paid for by more than doubling the national debt, to $2.2 trillion. Time to look for new ideas, time to move beyond the era of self-congratulation and beer-commercial patriotism. America cannot afford stupidity. It costs too much in the world. Education therefore must have a priority, and not just through more money; it needs discipline and imagination. America can no longer afford racism and a neglect of the underclass. They also cost too much. These are problems that must be solved not only as a matter of social justice (which they are) but as a question of America's long-term economic survival.

The moral ecology of American politics is altering. Issues that figured in the Reagan revolution—family values, school prayer, abortion, pornography—remain powerful. But some of them will be in collision with problems such as AIDS, homelessness, racism, toxic waste, business ethics, nuclear disarmament and the national debt—

TIME Chart by Joe Lertola, Research by Noel McCoy

Americans had a suspicion that Reaganism had gone too far in trying to rescind the compassionate functions of Government.

a more public agenda, one that veers somewhat away from religion.

The change now occurring is emphatically not a simple pendulum swing back from conservatism to New Deal liberalism. The change is more complex, more interesting. By the end of the '70s, Americans understood that from the '30s on, the welfare state had grown almost unrestrained. The left-leaning populism that bashed Big Business gave way to a right-leaning populism, one that produced tax revolts like California's Proposition 13.

That anti-Government mood prepared the way for Reaganomics and drove a wedge between the poor and the middle class. Americans in the middle detected something askew in the Government's social policies. Reagan played upon the middle-class intuition that some basic unfairness was loose in the garden of the dream. (Reagan was wise enough to know that the dream existed still and needed tending.)

"Welfare" was at least one of the things wrong. It meant a morality of entitlements, people getting something for nothing. It meant the unfairness of ordinary people paying the bill for the noblesse oblige of an élite. The Great Society eventually became institutionalized, even when the nation's economic growth flattened out and the middle class began losing ground. That dissonance helped to create Ronald Reagan. Americans bought the Reagan solution: cut welfare programs, or at least slow their rate of increase, to strengthen defense and give people more to spend through tax cuts. Says Daniel Yankelovich, the public opinion analyst: "They were uneasy about doing so because they suspected that millions of poor people would get hurt, but they accepted the Reagan approach because they agreed that something was badly amiss with the liberal theory of Government-backed entitlements. But Reagan's personal 'goodness' seemed to guarantee that it was not a Scrooge-like thing to do. As long as Reagan was credible, his solutions were acceptable."

Even before the Iran-*contra* affair, Americans had a suspicion that Reaganism had gone too far in trying to rescind the more generous work of Government: cutting Aid to Families with Dependent Children, for example, and federal funds for housing while running up the military budget from $134 billion in 1980 to $266 billion in 1986. (Although as a percentage of the gross national product, non-defense spending has declined very slightly and is still more than double defense spending.) The dream of salvation—"Get the Government off the backs of the American people and release the energies of free enterprise"—may not have been given enough time to work, but, in truth, it was never an agenda that took deep root anyway. Says Kevin Phillips, the Republican political analyst: "In the 1986 election, you saw the desire around the country for candidates who could make Government work, for defining some Government roles. It was flowing from

parts of the country where people began thinking, 'Hey, we need something from Government after all.' It was coming primarily from areas dependent on mining, timber, agriculture, energy, textiles, steel. They stopped thinking of Government as something that just took care of muggers and Detroit welfare mothers, the whole conservative rhetorical syndrome."

In a new poll for TIME by Yankelovich Clancy Shulman, people were asked whether Government spending should be increased, decreased or kept the same for various public needs. More than 70% said that funds should be increased for health care to the poor and the elderly, for cleaning up the environment and for aid to the homeless. Given a choice of spending more for the military or more for social programs, respondents preferred the social programs, 69% to 23%. More than three-fourths of those surveyed said Government "should play a more active role" in such areas as health care, poverty, housing and education. Most surprising of all, 60% said they would "support increased spending for social programs even if it would require an increase in taxes" (*see box*).

The results, though compelling, may also say something about the mood swings of the American public. Only two years ago, these same people might have said that you cannot solve problems by throwing money at them. "Americans have always expressed ambivalent desires about the role of Government," says California Pollster Mervyn Field. "We ask, Why doesn't the Government just get off our backs? And then we demand, Why doesn't the Government do something about this? Today, in several ways, the Government *is* off the public's back. Taxes are down. Inflation is down. Interest rates are down. But at the same time, our polling data show growing public anxiety about both the national and the local economies. The layoffs are hitting close to home. So are the growing numbers of the homeless. More people are now asking, Why doesn't Government do something about this?"

The Reagan revolution is not, of course, just going to evaporate. In part, it arose out of inescapable forces: a sense that Government had bloated out of control, that it was time for a period of unabashed good spirits and confidence after an era of gloom and self-doubt. "Reagan has significantly changed our attitude toward Government, away from looking toward Washington to solve our problems," says Field. A new form of Reaganism, possibly even under Democratic auspices, will have to cope with that legacy after Reagan is gone. Few Americans want to return to the Great Society style of welfare. The nation can no longer afford that kind of grand buffet, if it ever could. So the instinct for a new compassion, a word that is often heard these days as a signal of recoil against the meannesses of Reaganism, comes abruptly up against hard realities.

In a nation proud of its economic comeback, the spectacle of people sleeping on grates frays the conscience.

If Reaganism has now and then been perceived as social Darwinism, the idea that the sleekest beast with the sharpest teeth is the fittest to survive (Ivan Boesky in the skin of a panther), the new emphasis, among Republicans as well as Democrats, is upon the practice of a kind of governmental "tough love," an aggressive compassion designed to end dependencies and get people self-sufficient and back to work as quickly as possible. In the 1980s there is an acute awareness of the nation's economic limits and of the intractability of many problems.

The current push for welfare reform, led nationally by New York Senator Daniel Moynihan and Arkansas Governor Bill Clinton, is the best example of this approach. It is based on two truths: that unconditional aid leads to long-standing dependency and that the impoverished children of this nation cannot merely be abandoned. The new approach—being tried with some success in states such as Massachusetts, California, New Jersey and New York—is to require recipients to enter training and job-placement programs. In some of the proposals, the Federal Government would become the employer of last resort.

In Chicago, Aleen Zimberoff Bayard is one of the growing number of people returning to social activism but demanding "more bang for the buck." As Bayard says firmly, "People don't tolerate giveaways anymore." In 1985 Bayard and several friends started the Entertainment Action Team, whose mission is to "end hunger in Chicago through self-sufficiency." Says she: "It makes such a difference to me that I'm doing something. The team is one example of how young, socially minded people are rewriting the Reagan message." The team is auctioning off part-ownership of an Arabian horse to raise money for a café that will be a restaurant-training program for homeless teenagers. "We want to teach them job skills," says Bayard. "Our group believes people want to help themselves. We're saying, 'Money doesn't solve the problem.'"

Such programs, which owe something to Reagan's long emphasis on volunteerism, usually stress the idea that compassion is best implemented through cooperation of governments, businesses and private citizens. "We are really apolitical," says Bayard. "Fat government is the problem."

At the state level, social programs are being seen as an investment in the future. In Colorado, for example, a powerful issue in last November's gubernatorial race was how to handle an expected $434 million windfall in state tax revenues caused by federal tax reform. While the Republican nominee promised to return the money to taxpayers, Democrat Roy Romer proposed to spend it on education, highways, water projects and industrial development. He won. Says he: "I asked people, 'What's more important to you, another $18 in your pocket right now or a job for your kid when he finishes school?' The public

support for state-government investment in the economy and education is rooted in fear about where the economy is going."

In Kansas, a fortress of Reaganism, the state legislature seems to be moving leftward as the farm crisis persists. Says Richard Larimore, recently retired administrative assistant to the minority in the state senate: "The pendulum is swinging back and is already approaching the middle. In Kansas, this will probably be the last big legislative year for major economic-development programs because people are figuring out that that means giving money to the wealthy."

For years, starting in the late '60s with Lyndon Johnson, successive American Presidents have used inflation, foreign borrowing and other devices to avoid coming to terms with some fundamental problems in the nation's economy, especially the runaway spending on middle-class entitlement programs (like Social Security), the falling productivity of some industries and the resulting failure to compete in the international markets. Americans have indulged themselves in a certain denial of reality. Increasingly, however, they suffer from what is called a "cognitive dissonance" between the nominal economy and the real economy. In other words, they cannot figure out why so many are losing their jobs while 11 million new jobs have been created since 1981, why the stock market soars to record highs, and thousands of new businesses are launched every year while thousands go bust.

It would be ironic for Americans to lose their faith in a free-market economy at the very time that the rest of the world, including even socialist countries, is looking forward to the forces of market incentives and entrepreneurship. In many respects the American economy is remarkably solid, with a respectable if not spectacular growth rate of around 3% projected for 1987 and an unemployment rate significantly lower than that in most other industrialized countries. But economic reality in America is complex and contradictory. Yesterday's boom regions, like the Southwest, are suffering while yesterday's depressed areas, like the Northeast, are booming. Thirty-one states, mostly in the heartland of the nation, are in recession. Mothers and fathers know that the industries in which they have worked all their lives will not provide middle-income jobs to their daughters and sons, who may of course make their fortunes as junk-bond traders or software geniuses, but are far more likely to find "hamburger jobs" and drop into the minimum-wage sector of an increasingly bottom-heavy economy.

If Big Government was the villain of the Reagan cycle of American history, the bête noire of the new may be Big Business. In 1979, according to the pollster Lou Harris, 69% of Americans gave corporate America a favorable rating. In 1986 only 35% rated corporate America favorably. "Clearly," says Harris, "the mood about business has turned negative on a massive scale."

More than three-fourths of those surveyed say Government "should play a more active role" in such areas as health care.

This swing has been spurred by the insider-trading scandals, which find considerable resonance with Americans. Says Pollster Field: "The public doesn't distinguish between Wall Street and Big Business. I see Big Business becoming a target in 1988." Deputy Treasury Secretary Richard Darman, one of the intellectual turbines of the Reagan revolution, masterminded last year's successful push for tax reform. He has attempted to formulate a conservative populism that would save the Reagan Administration from being inextricably tied in the public mind with Big Business and Wall Street. Darman has used the term corpocracy to describe the bloated management of U.S. corporations that have resisted becoming more competitive. "Big Government isn't what is bugging everyone these days," says Darman. Instead, he sees the resentment as being directed at stagnant industries and declining education systems. Businesses that profited from tax breaks without making intelligent investments, combined with the scandals and takeovers on Wall Street, have bolstered the perception of greed run wild. One result, Darman says, "is that latent idealism is having a comeback."

These themes are being stressed by Democratic candidates, including Gary Hart, Bruce Babbitt, Joseph Biden, Richard Gephardt and Jesse Jackson. "When Rhodes scholars are arrested for insider trading, that contributes to this populist sentiment that a privileged class is getting rich at the expense of the rest of the economy," Babbitt says. Like most Democratic candidates, Babbitt is careful to focus his attacks on Wall Street and Big Business, as opposed to entrepreneurial and family businesses.

Gephardt often cites the successful Japanese management of American workers at the General Motors plant in Fremont, Calif. He wonders whether U.S. industrial failures should not be attributed to American managers rather than American workers (despite high U.S. wages compared with some of America's competitors). Babbitt adds that unlike Japanese managers, who often cut their own compensation before that of their workers, "American executives reward themselves with huge bonuses during the good times but console themselves with layoffs as soon as times turn bad."

Big Business corpulence, combined with the scandals and takeovers on Wall Street, bolsters the perception of greed run wild.

Pierre Proudhon, the 19th century French utopian, once wrote of "the fecundity of the unexpected." It is always somewhat dangerous to think that history can be foretold by studying the patterns of the past. Still, the rhythms of change in the past century have displayed uncanny regularity. Schlesinger's theory, inherited in part from his father, is that people have absorbed their formative political values by the time they reach age 18 or so. Ronald Reagan reached that age during the years of Calvin Coolidge, whose portrait now hangs in the Cabinet room in the White House. John Kennedy came of age with the New Deal and World War II. Says Schlesinger: "In general, we have 30-year cycles based on generations. Just as the 1980s were a re-enactment of the 1950s, the Eisenhower time was a re-enactment of the Harding-Coolidge time of the 1920s. So at 30-year intervals—Theodore Roosevelt in 1901, F.D.R. in '33, Kennedy in '61—we have a swing from private interest, from self-interest, to public purpose." By Schlesinger's calculation, the cyclical change now beginning should reach full momentum around 1990.

American history in the past 100 years has arranged itself in the cycles with an odd neatness. A period of economic depression, war, social change and activism has generally been followed by a spasm of reactionary backlash, followed by a time of consolidation, relative calm and prosperity.

The three decades from 1890 to the end of World War I were turbulent with industrialization. The first labor-union movement arose in idealism and turmoil and disruption. Immigrants poured in from Southern and Eastern Europe. Then came "the war to end all wars," attended by Woodrow Wilson's millennial ambitions.

Even before the war ended, Americans began recoiling from Wilson's international activism. Attorney General A. Mitchell Palmer went on witch-hunts for Bolsheviks. The Senate rejected the Treaty of Versailles. America closed down Ellis Island and slammed the door against new immigration. What followed in the '20s was the "era of good feeling," a period with some resemblance to Reagan's '80s.

The next cycle turned on the Great Depression, the New Deal and World War II, followed by the backlash of McCarthyism and the era of relative calm and prosperity during the 1950s and early '60s. Then the real '60s: turbulence, crisis, war, the rhetoric of revolution.

Reagan's election in 1980 was less a new starting point than the cresting of a conservative-populist movement that began with Richard Nixon's election in 1968. That year, the Middle American constituency struck back against the activist '60s—against antiwar protesters, against the civil rights movement and the sexual revolution, against high taxes, Government regulation, the Washington élite, the Woodstock generation. George Wallace was in full cry against "pointy-headed intellectuals." The Nixon-Agnew ticket swept into power. Watergate brought Gerald Ford's brief period of consolidation and then the anomaly of Jimmy Carter, who came to Washington campaigning against Big Government, just as Reagan did four years later.

What is the legacy that Ronald Reagan leaves?

"The Reagan revolution," observes Political Analyst Richard Scammon, "never moved as far as many on the left feared it would, or many on the right hoped it would." Just so. In American governance, the pendulum rarely makes radical swings. Change generally comes by evolution, not by sudden transformation. The only radical changes, the elections of Lincoln and F.D.R., for example, occur at times of severe national stress.

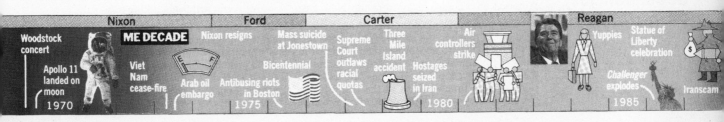

Nixon · Ford · Carter · Reagan

Woodstock concert · Apollo 11 landed on moon · 1970 · ME DECADE · Viet Nam cease-fire · Arab oil embargo · Nixon resigns · Antibusing riots in Boston · 1975 · Bicentennial · Mass suicide at Jonestown · Supreme Court outlaws racial quotas · Three Mile Island accident · Hostages seized in Iran · 1980 · Air controllers strike · Yuppies · Challenger explodes · 1985 · Statue of Liberty celebration · Irancam

The Public's Agenda

Despite six years of effort by the Reagan Administration to reduce the Federal Government's role in American life, a large majority of people still insist that Washington should be deeply involved in keeping the U.S. healthy, well housed and well educated. According to a poll taken for TIME by Yankelovich Clancy Shulman,* 77% of the public feel that in the future the Federal Government should play a more active role in such areas as health, housing, education and help for the poor. And 60% of those questioned—including 49% of Republicans—say they would support increased spending for social programs even if it meant paying more in taxes. Most critical, 56% of Americans now say they would prefer having a President in 1988 who would spend more on social needs, while only 33% would like a President who would keep such spending at current reduced levels.

Fewer than one-third of those surveyed (31%) still support increased Government spending for the military, and 69%—including 55% of Republicans—say they would spend more on social programs than on the military if they had to choose between the two. Public opinion has changed on this issue as the Reagan Administration has fulfilled its mandate: in the last year of the Carter Administration: 78% favored spending more for national defense.

The public is not entirely pleased with the Administration's tighter spending policies. The poll found that 62% of Americans are aware that there have been cutbacks in some social programs during the Reagan years; 61% of the public disapprove of them.

*The survey of 1,014 adults was taken by telephone Feb. 17-18. The potential sampling error is plus or minus 3%.

Republicans are more ambivalent, with 44% approving of the cuts and 44% disapproving. Large majorities now favor increased Government spending on health care for the elderly, nutrition programs for mothers and infants, housing for people with low or moderate incomes, more loans and grants to college students, cleaning up the environment and reducing acid-rain pollution. At the same time, those surveyed are cool toward additional spending on food stamps and the space program, with only about a third favoring increases in these areas and about the same number wanting to hold spending about where it is now.

More than a third of those surveyed want to cut spending on the President's Strategic Defense Initiative, although 49% want spending increased or kept the same. In October 1986, at the time of the Reykjavík summit, public approval for Star Wars stood at 64%.

Americans are still generally satisfied with the overall state of affairs in the country: 60% say things are going well, a drop of only two points since last September. The percentage of those citing the economy as a major problem dropped dramatically, from 50% of those polled in September 1985 to 33% today, as inflation and interest rates have withered and stock prices have leaped to record highs. Nor is there widespread concern about the federal deficit: only 12% of the people polled now consider Government spending a major problem, in contrast to 22% as recently as September 1985. For all the public attention drug abuse has received, only 9% cite it as a particular worry.

A great concern for Americans is the nation's schools: 56% agree that U.S. education is poor, and 49% say educational standards have become worse. Fully 65%, meanwhile, favor giving "substantially higher pay" to teachers to improve the schools.

Should Government spending be increased, decreased, or kept the same?

	Increased	Decreased	Kept same
Health programs for the elderly	78%	2%	18%
The environment	73%	5%	19%
Aid to the homeless	71%	5%	21%
Health services for the poor	71%	5%	22%
Nutrition programs for mothers and infants	55%	6%	34%
Reducing acid-rain pollution	54%	11%	25%
Low- and moderate-income housing	54%	11%	32%
Loans and grants to college students	52%	15%	29%
The food-stamp program	33%	24%	36%
The space program	33%	27%	34%
The military	31%	25%	38%
Star Wars	23%	35%	26%

The emphasis is on "tough love," an aggressive compassion designed to end dependencies and get people self-sufficient.

"The main achievement of the Reagan Administration," argues Norman Podhoretz, the neoconservative editor of *Commentary* magazine, "has been to move the country in a different direction, which was much more consistent with traditional American constitutional, legal and cultural values." Podhoretz distinguishes between the actual performance of the Administration and the general direction in which Reagan tried to move the nation. He has always approved of Reagan's intentions, but thinks he fell short in the performance.

After a half-century, Reagan sought to steer America on a course away from the New Deal. And yet, in doing so, he more than doubled the national debt. He was unable, or unwilling, in a term and a half to tackle middle-class entitlements, such as Social Security, Medicare and wildly excessive farm-support programs. Reagan bequeaths that burden to future Presidents.

The legacy of Reagan the great American imagist lies as much in the realm of the symbolic as in the area of hard accomplishment. One of his great achievements was to restore the morale of the American people for a time, just as he restored—for a time—a faith in the institution of the presidency and in the idea of presidential leadership. He persuaded the American people that their optimism was once again valid.

The nation in the next few years will be groping toward a new definition of itself. Now a new generation comes to power. Those marked by the formative experiences of the Depression and by World War II will leave the stage. The generation of the baby boom, which was formed by the Viet Nam era, will begin taking over.

Each party is now struggling toward its candidate, its theme. The task is harder for Republicans, who are reluctant to break abruptly with Reagan and Reaganism. Still, Congressman Jack Kemp tries to stir a "sense of activism" with ideas for a flat tax with a low rate and "enterprise zones" to bring businesses to depressed areas. Vice President George Bush, who now must ease judiciously out of the Reagan shadow and establish himself as his own man, told TIME, "There will be a reordering of priorities, and it isn't inconceivable, in the future, that there will be more emphasis [on Government's role]. I do think there is a certain feeling [concerning] tolerance, compassion, understanding, caring. I think there's a reawakening in those areas." Robert Dole, in his latest speeches, stresses the need to combine conservatism and compassion.

Gary Hart, the Democratic front runner, declares, "For all practical purposes, we have entered the post-Reagan years." But he knows that the Democrats "won't win by default, or because of some historic trend or tide. We must offer some concrete alternatives to the laissez-faire philosophy of this Administration and to its militaristic foreign policy." Most of the Democratic candidates are cautious about criticizing "militarism," for fear of being tagged antidefense, and even more cautious about advancing big-spender ideas; the national deficit is already ruinous. Hart talks about a "more important role for Government, not necessarily a larger one." Joseph Biden is somewhat more inspirational, evoking generational memories of John Kennedy and Martin Luther King Jr. and constantly quoting a hymn: "And he will raise you up on eagle's wings,/ and bear you on the breath of the dawn . . ."

Only Jesse Jackson preaches the old-time religion, a classic populism of the left. Trying to expand his coalition of the dispossessed, middle-class workers and distressed farmers, Jackson calls unashamedly for large increases in programs for education, health and public housing.

Some Democrats delude themselves that they can ignore Reagan's legacy and return to the old Democratic practice of tax and spend, as if it were still 1964. At the California Democratic Convention at the end of January, the public address system blared *Happy Days Are Here Again,* and many delegates sank into a liberal nostalgia, dreaming of a redistributed American pie. Clinton Reilly, a moderate Democrat and political consultant, listened to the rhetoric and shook his head. "One reason for Reagan's success," he said, "is that he appealed to the self-interest of the middle class. If Democrats don't learn to make the same appeal, if they only talk about the needs of the poor and don't include the middle class, they're going to lose again."

The Democrats last year recaptured control of Congress because they fielded better candidates, but also because they were more finely tuned to people's thoughts about what the Government ought to be doing. The Democrats were well in control on Capitol Hill by Christmas. With the Administration weakened, the party leaders swung into place the long-deferred Democratic agenda, items thwarted during the Reagan years: education, job training, increased research for AIDS and health care. Says Democratic Hopeful Gephardt: "I don't think people care about Government or no Government. They're willing to use Government if it is part of the solution. People want things to be solved. They want the Government to make airlines safe, to find a cure for AIDS, to prevent more Boeskys."

To be successful in the next phase of American politics, candidates and parties must come up with specific, tough-minded solutions to well-perceived problems. It will take great sifting and discipline. The recent congressional override of Reagan's veto of the clean-water bill suggested hearts in the right place (the public considers clean water a necessity, not a luxury, and is willing to sacrifice for it) but minds not yet tough enough to resist temptation (the bill was a nice display of logrolling).

A bill for emergency aid to the homeless was passed by Congress last month. That was not tough-minded either, since the $50 million to be spread around the entire country can hardly solve the problem. But the symbolism was important. In a nation that prides itself on its economic comeback from recession, the spectacle of people huddling around trash-can fires is ethically embarrassing. One makes five or ten serious moral choices (give money, pass them by, what?) on the way to work, and as many coming home, and the conscience at last is frayed. Says Massachusetts Governor Michael Dukakis, another Democratic presidential aspirant: "The conscience of the nation is beginning to be troubled. People in every city see the homeless lying around on grates, even a few blocks from the White House. And they wonder, Does this have to be?"

In the beginning, America was a blank page, in Tocqueville's phrase: no history, all potential. Today America, the oldest continuous political system in the world, has a full page of history and heavy debts to pay. The campaign of 1988 could be one of the more interesting and important in recent history. There is no incumbent; neither party has an obvious heir apparent. The nation will perform the very American act of reimagining itself.   —*By Lance Morrow.*
Reported by Laurence I. Barrett/Washington and Lawrence Malkin/Boston, with other bureaus

> The generation of the baby boom, which was formed by the Viet Nam era, will begin taking over.

New Directions for American History

Although the Reagan era closed with tinges of scandal and mounting complaints about the national debt and trade deficits, Reagan himself remained popular. Nor was there sufficient backlash to prevent the incumbent vice president George Bush from winning the presidency in 1988. Bush took several pages from Reagan's book: he wrapped himself in the American flag, promised there would be no tax increases, and accused his opponent of being "soft" on crime. Taxes have increased, as have crime rates, and in 1990 President Bush launched a major military initiative in the Middle East.

Much as politicians prefer to deal with the familiar, fundamental changes have been taking place within the United States and throughout what has become an increasingly interdependent world. "The Changing Face of a Restless Nation" descries how technological improvements, population shifts, and immigration from Asia and Latin America have altered the landscape. Various groups continue their struggles to end discrimination based on gender, race, or sexual preference. "Remember the Ladies" recounts the failure to attain passage of the Equal Rights Amendment, and "The Push for Power" treats the determination of Hispanic activists to mobilize what has become the fastest growing minority group in the nation.

Historian Paul Kennedy in 1987 published a book that raised disturbing questions about America's future. Briefly, he argued that the United States had emerged from World War II as the world's dominant economic power. In response to the perceived threat of the cold war, it assumed enormous military and economic commitments throughout the world. These commitments have continued to grow despite the fact that America's relative economic position has declined in recent years. He contends that a retrenchment of commitments is necessary to fit the new realities. "The (Relative) Decline of America" provides a brief statement of his thesis. Kennedy has been challenged by a number of critics, most of whom dispute his analyses of economic decline.

Looking Ahead: Challenge Questions

Some people used to refer to the United States as a "melting pot." Ideally, various groups would shed their ethnic and racial identities in order to become undifferentiated "Americans" of shared assumptions and values. Never really attained, the ideal itself has recently come under fire. Should ethnic and racial diversity be encouraged and emphasized, or does this raise the threat that the nation will become fragmented into a host of groups each competing for preference?

The cold war dominated American strategic thinking for decades, and exercised an enormous influence on the way the United States used its resources, both material and human. That condition has ended, but what kind of world will emerge? How can the United States use its influence to combat degradation of the environment and to relieve so much of the suffering other people endure? Can the American public be mobilized to support such endeavors? How?

Unit 6

■ DEMOGRAPHICS

THE CHANGING FACE OF A RESTLESS NATION

POPULATION SHIFTS, NOTABLY THE BABY BOOM, ARE STILL REMOLDING AMERICA

1929. It was the last year of the Jazz Age—a time of unparalleled excitement, hedonism, and growth. Buoyed by the highest standard of living the world had ever known, Americans lived it up—recklessly, if possible. Bootleggers and gangsters flourished by the thousands in the nation's capital and gunned each other down on the streets of Chicago.

Nothing was too big or too fast. While the Empire State Building and its towering companions reached triumphantly for the sky, sculptor Gutzon Borglum began to carve a granite mountain into gigantic likenesses of past Presidents. Railroads inaugurated a new air-rail service to speed impatient travelers from coast to coast in only 48 hours, with Charles A. Lindbergh himself flying the first plane. Never had America "held its liquor so well and had so much fun," wrote historian Daniel J. Boorstin.

But the great crash heralded the end of the celebration. The nation has since lived through depression, war, prosperity, and riot. The U. S. became the dominant world power. The federal government, for better and worse, was thrust into the lives of all Americans. In the past six decades, too, cities have been radically transformed, family patterns have altered, and faces from new countries have appeared on our shores.

FAMILIAR RING. The Roaring Twenties may seem like a yellowing photograph, but many of the underlying trends of the 1920s have a startlingly familiar ring. By 1929, Manhattan had become so clogged with cars that rush-hour traffic inched up Fifth Avenue at less than 3 miles per hour. Women were entering the work force in droves, and fertility continued a three-decade-long decline, leading some sociologists to warn of a society not interested in reproducing itself. Small towns died as farmers forsook the land for the cities' bright lights. Houses sprang up like weeds in the suburbs, starting the inner cities on a long spiral of decay.

Today, startling new demographic forces have sprung to the fore. Together, they are ushering in a new America. In the 1990s, the huge population bulge of postwar baby boomers will enter middle age. Increasing longevity and a declining birthrate mean the U. S. must cope with a rapidly aging population. A rise in single-parent families is helping to widen the income gap between the haves and the have-nots—and is leaving more and more children in poverty. New waves of immigration—this time from Latin America and Asia—are bringing new values and new languages to the melting pot. These immigrants already account for more than 14% of annual population growth.

Nothing has altered the American landscape more profoundly than technological change and the migrations of a restless or displaced population. In the 1930s, the Dust Bowl drove 95,000 people from Oklahoma to California. By the mid-1960s the South was well along in its economic rebirth as the Sunbelt. In the 1970s, thousands of unemployed auto workers left Detroit for Houston to seek jobs drilling for oil. Then an oil glut sent many northward once again. High-tech industry spawned new jobs in the flagging industrial Northeast.

Meanwhile, rural areas have continued their steady decline. In some parts of the Great Plains, 60% of residents' income comes in the form of federal subsidies. Kansas alone has 2,000 ghost towns, and countless other towns that haven't attracted manufacturing or service industries are fading fast. Rutgers University Professor Frank Popper suggests that after areas are abandoned, the government should step in, buy the land, and return it to its best use—as a vast prairie for the buffalo to roam.

Indeed, many of those counties have been losing population ever since the 1890s. By then, the American city had already evolved as a center of manufacturing. Pittsburgh sprouted belching furnaces to supply the nation's appetite for steel, and Chicago became "hog butcher to the world."

'BYPRODUCTS.' Farmers, made redundant by tractors and reapers, and immigrants poured into cities to work in the factories. By the turn of the century, a nation that had been 90% rural 60 years before was becoming irrevocably urban. "We woke up in 1900 with all these massive cities," says geographer Peter O. Muller of the University of Miami. "They were necessary byproducts of the industrial revolution, but they were never something that we intended."

No sooner had Americans built huge cities than people began to flee. "Unlike the major cities of Europe, South America, and Asia, America's metropolises were centers of manufacture," says Columbia University historian Kenneth T. Jackson. "No one with options wanted to live in proximity to heavy industry."

They fled on steam railroads and electric streetcars, and their speed picked up with the coming of the automobile. By 1929, suburbs such as Cleveland's Shaker Heights and Detroit's Grosse Pointe were 10 times as big as a decade earlier, and Americans owned nearly 27 million cars, trucks, and buses. "Decentralization is taking place," a senior Federal Housing Administration (FHA) official later observed. "It is not a policy, it is a reality—and it is as impossible for us to change this trend as it is to change the desire of birds to migrate."

Fueling the trend was a darker side of American life: the widespread distaste for living near people who looked different or spoke a different language. "There was a tremendous amount of white flight in the face of 'funny-looking' people," says Pennsylvania State University geographer Peirce F. Lewis. By the mid-1920s, strict immigration laws had responded to these fears by cutting off the flow from everywhere but Western Europe. But many thought that the damage had already been done. "New York," complained *The Denver Post* in 1930, "has been a cesspool into which immigrant trash has been dumped

Reprinted from *Business Week*, September 25, 1989, pp. 92-95, 98-99, 102, 106 by special permission. Copyright © 1989 by McGraw-Hill, Inc.

for so long that it can scarcely be considered American any longer."

Whether people lived in an ethnic enclave or a suburb during the 1920s, however, they had fewer children. The birthrate dropped from 27.7 babies per 1,000 people in 1920 to 21.2 in 1929. "On a farm, children provide labor at a fairly early age—and the way to be successful is to have more labor and land," says Donald J. Hernandez, chief of the Census Bureau's Marriage & Family Statistics branch. "In the industrial era, the best way to improve your life is education, which means postponing children. It also costs money to prepare for children's education." The result: fewer children and more working women.

These trends might have continued unabated. But on Oct. 29, 1929, the stock market crash started the nation's plunge into the Great Depression. "By 1931, the auto industry was operating at one-fifth capacity," reports historian William E. Leuchtenburg. "And as the great auto plants in Detroit lay idle, fires were banked in the steel furnaces on the Allegheny and the Mahoning."

PAY CUT. The migration to the cities reversed temporarily, as many of the 8 million unemployed returned to small towns. Suburban development slowed to a crawl. Banks and corporations failed. The birthrate fell lower, reaching a level not matched until 1970. Even Babe Ruth took a $10,000 pay cut in 1933.

The Depression also laid the groundwork for government policies that shaped demographic forces: It was then that Americans began to overcome their aversion to solving problems with federal money. President Franklin D. Roosevelt's alphabet-soup agencies built dams in the Tennessee Valley, subsidized farmers, wove a Social Security safety net for the elderly, and funded artists and writers. "The big change was the growing role of the government in affecting business and every other aspect of American life," explains Richard H. Jackson, a professor of historical geography at Brigham Young University.

The economy at last recovered only when the government began spending enormous sums of money on tanks and planes to fight Hitler and Japan. Military bases and defense industries in California became engines of growth for the West. With the housing industry moribund and auto makers churning out planes and tanks instead of cars, Americans' savings accumulated.

As weary GIs returned to a suddenly prosperous nation, the stage was set for a postwar consumer boom. Because the birthrate had dropped in the 1920s and '30s, the generation that came of age during the late 1940s and '50s was rela-

tively small. But despite their numbers—or perhaps because their scarcity helped boost their economic fortunes—those young men and women produced a baby boom "totally unanticipated in its duration," says Calvin L. Beale, senior demographer at the Agriculture Dept. That boom left its mark on everything from housing patterns to the current obsession with pensions.

When the government and developers considered the housing slowdown of the 1930s and 1940s together with the huge increase in families and children in the 1950s, they realized "there was a massive housing shortage," says Charles L. Leven, a Washington University economics professor. He recalls being newly married and hunting for an apartment in Chicago in 1950. "No one advertised," he says. "I went up and down streets hoping to find a sign or someone whose cousin had told them that people in their building were moving."

It was government policy that drove the suburban growth of the 1950s—and helped bring about the decline of many cities. The government responded to the housing shortage by stepping up efforts it had begun years earlier with the FHA. Before the agency was created in 1934, mortgages were limited to one-half or one-third the value of a house. With FHA-guaranteed loans, downpayments shrank to less than 10% of the price; interest rates dropped. Suddenly, thousands of families could afford houses.

Not just any house, though. The agency favored new single-family housing over older stock. And whole classes of houses, such as Baltimore's 16-foot-wide townhouses, were ineligible because they failed to meet minimum lot sizes. In addition, the FHA was dead set against what its guidelines termed "inharmonious racial or nationality groups."

Thus, in some places, the presence of a nonwhite family was enough to label an entire block "Negro" and to cut it off from FHA loans. "No agency of the U. S. government has had a more pervasive and powerful impact on the American people over the past half century than the FHA," Columbia's Jackson concluded in his book, *Crabgrass Frontier: The Suburbanization of the United States.*

To help meet the postwar demand for housing, Congress in 1944 created a Veterans Administration mortgage program similar to FHA. And it soon began pumping billions of dollars of mortgage insurance into the two plans. Housing starts jumped from 114,000 in 1944 to 1,696,000 in 1950. In a field on New York's Long Island, Abraham Levitt and his sons, William and Alfred, were completing 30 Cape Cod dwellings a day in 1947. Within a few years, so many babies were

being born in Levittown that the 17,400-house development became known as a "rabbit hutch."

DREAM HOUSES. Similar developments sprang up elsewhere—around Philadelphia, Detroit, and Los Angeles. Since buying a new house was often cheaper than renting, the percentage of American families who owned a house leapt from 44% in 1940 to 68% in 1972. "Levittown houses turned the detached single-family house from a distant dream to a real possibility for thousands of middle-class American families," wrote architecture critic Paul Goldberger.

Meanwhile, the suburban exodus had an unexpected—and disastrous—effect on the cities the new suburbanites were leaving behind. Underlying the federal housing policy was an idea called "filtering." By making suburban houses affordable to middle-class people from the cities, older city dwellings would filter down to the poor, thus solving the housing shortage for lower-income families.

That policy was "a giant mistake," says Washington University's Leven. "The problem was it worked so well. It became like the broom in *The Sorcerer's Apprentice*—you couldn't turn it off." The pent-up demand for housing was essentially satisfied by the end of the 1950s. "But we still had a mechanism that made it profitable to give up a house in the city and move to the suburbs," Leven says. "It was like throwing gasoline on a fire in terms of what it did to the inner city."

ABANDONED HOUSING. In St. Louis, for example, housing units were abandoned at the rate of three or four an hour for an entire decade. "We are the first society in history to create a surplus of housing," says Miami University of Ohio geographer James M. Rubenstein. "That's why we throw it away."

The same sad story was repeated in the South Bronx, the west side of Philadelphia, the South Side of Chicago. To make matters worse, inner cities were torn apart to make room for highways or dispiriting housing projects. Blacks migrating from the South in search of work found cities already in the midst of decay. And the inability of many blacks to live the American dream contributed to the race riots of the 1960s—Watts in 1965, Detroit in 1967.

But for those Americans who had acquired suburban homesteads—with picket fences and Kentucky bluegrass lawns—the 1950s and 1960s were a time of unparalleled prosperity. Average earnings continued to rise, industrial output increased, and the ribbons of concrete laid down by the Interstate Highway Act of 1956 enabled families to take to the road.

The new lifestyle had its costs. In a famous study of Park Forest, Ill., William H. Whyte found that racial and social homogeneity bred mindless conservatism and conformity. Many critics believe that the cost was particularly high for women and children, cut off as they were from jobs, contact with employed adults, and the stimulation that comes from diversity.

In fact, gains being made by women in narrowing the education and employment gap with men temporarily halted in the 1950s. "There's a little bit of a sense that women and men became less equal after the war," says Census Bureau demographer Suzanne M. Bianchi. "In some ways, the really strange generation is not the current one, but the one that had the baby boom."

The pattern of thousands of Ward Cleavers leaving their perfect suburban families each morning to work in the big city proved to be as ephemeral as it was aberrant. But the pattern came to an end not with the suburbanites' return to the city but with the city following them to the suburbs—in what the University of Miami's Peter Muller calls "the most important change in the history of American cities."

Driving this change was the expressway. "Once the expressways were completed, the whole advantage of a central business district was lost," explains Muller. "Any location on the expressway was just as accessible as anywhere else." The best locations, of course, were the intersections of two freeways. And it wasn't long before pioneer retailers took advantage of these new crossroads.

MALL MANIA. By the mid-1960s, giant shopping centers began springing up in such crossroads villages as King of Prussia, Pa., outside Philadelphia and Tysons Corner, Va., near Washington, to tap the vast suburban market. "Shopping centers conferred geographical cachet and prestige," says Muller. "Suddenly, sleepy backwoods areas became fashionable." It wasn't long before developers began building office buildings near the malls, and a trickle of corporate relocations turned into a flood. By the early 1970s, the suburbs surpassed the center cities in employment. The high rises in Washington's Maryland and Virginia suburbs, for example, now contain more office space than the District itself. "The suburban city is the cornerstone and infrastructure for the 21st century metropolis," says Muller.

A parallel trend has been the "Rousification" of downtown. Rouse Co. and other developers built what amount to downtown theme parks, such as Baltimore's Harbor Place. And those downtowns have shifted from being hard-core manufacturing districts to financial and service hubs, meeting places, and centers of recreation.

The transformation of the urban center has a downside, however. The disappearance of manufacturing jobs from the center city has left a legacy of the displaced and homeless. And the gentrification of former working-class neighborhoods is pushing the poor into an expanding belt between the rich center city and the prosperous outer suburbs.

While the suburbs were building, the economy remained remarkably strong. For 23 years, beginning in 1950, the average standard of living for families steadily increased. Educational levels rose. More and more women entered the workplace—and the earnings gap between the sexes shrank.

The boom seemed unstoppable, with the continued military spending of the cold war, Korea, and Vietnam pumping federal dollars into workers' wallets. Billions of dollars were spent on keeping Strategic Air Command bombers in the air, great fleets on the prowl, and battalions of soldiers in West Germany, Japan, and South Korea.

But it was too much of a good thing. And 1973 was the year that changed the face of America. It was the year when OPEC showed the world that it could dictate energy prices. It was the year that inflation began its unnerving ascent to double digits. It was the year that policymakers had little choice but to squeeze their economies to cut the use of energy and fight inflation. The nation's productivity, which had been growing about 2% a year since 1900, suddenly began to stagnate, and may just now be on the road to recovery.

Economists still debate the causes of the great productivity slide. Some pin it on the rise in energy prices that made much of America's capital equipment obsolete. Others see the culprit as the influx of the baby boomers and older women, which lowered the average experience of the labor force. Still others blame increased government regulation of business.

Whatever its cause, the productivity slump hurt the standard of living of most American families. Median family income stopped its steady rise. The percentage of people living in poverty, especially children, began to climb. The gap between rich and poor began widening.

'SWEAT FACTOR.' Still, many people fail to recognize the decline in the standard of living, because they don't consider the "sweat factor." University of Maryland economist Frank Levy, author of *Dollars and Dreams: The Changing American Income Distribution*, puts it thus: "Back in the 1950s, we had one-paycheck, three-kid families. Now we have two-paycheck, one- or two-kid families."

Witness Ralph DiOrio and Denise Fugo, owners of a chic restaurant and jazz club in a gentrifying area of Cleveland. They work full-time, have two children, and though they have a successful business, they still worry about their financial future. It's a different lifestyle from DiOrio's own family, where six children grew up in the Cleveland suburb of Garfield Heights on his father's earnings as a carpenter. "We have higher dreams and aspirations than our parents did," DiOrio says.

So do many other Americans. Can the immigrants from Latin America or the children of urban blight and rural despair—to say nothing of the beleaguered middle class—realize their dreams? In one scenario, the mix of declining birthrates and aging baby boomers will eventually produce a vast cohort of dependent elderly whose weight could crush American society.

To make matters worse, huge numbers of today's children will fail to carry America forward into the future because they grew up with the disadvantages of poverty, splintered families, and inadequate education. Tragic numbers are being destroyed by an epidemic of drugs. And with the runaway federal deficits, the government's safety net is wearing increasingly thin. Among the hardest hit have been well-funded social programs such as job training, medicaid, subsidized housing, and tuition grants.

But the picture in other crystal balls is more auspicious. The baby bust generation of the 1970s will find itself in great demand by the mid-1990s, argues University of Southern California demographer Richard A. Easterlin. With rosy economic expectations, these young adults will marry and start their families young. "The potential is there for a drastic reversal—for example, for a baby boom in the 1990s comparable to that of the 1950s," says Easterlin.

The U. S. may benefit from another powerful demographic trend on the international scene. America is not the only industrial country with an aging population. In fact, Europe and Japan are graying even faster than the U. S. Yet they have long been relatively closed societies. By contrast, America has a long heritage of welcoming immigrants, and throughout its history, the country has been reshaped and renewed by the talents, energy, and enterprise of those new citizens. They may prove to be a crucial advantage in the global economic competition of the 1990s and the early 21st century.

By John Carey in Washington

"Remember the Ladies"

Joan Kennedy Taylor

Joan Kennedy Taylor is working on a book about feminism and individualism.

*I*n March of 1776, when sentiment in the colonies was strong for independence, Abigail Adams wrote to her husband, John Adams, asking him to use his influence in any new government to change the legal status of married women. "In the new code of laws which I suppose it will be necessary for you to make," she wrote, "I desire you to remember the ladies, and be more generous to them than your ancestors. Do not put such unlimited power in the hands of husbands. Remember, all men would be tyrants if they could." Today, 200 years after the drafting of the Constitution, the legal rights of women are still ambiguous.

When Abigail Adams wrote, women's legal status was governed by British common law, which treated them as children. Politically, they had no rights at all. Economically, many occupations were forbidden to them. Their main occupation was marriage, but under common law, as the legal authority William Blackstone put it, "the husband and wife are one person in law; that is, the very being or legal existence of the woman is suspended during the marriage."

A married woman had no right to buy, sell, or manage property. She could not legally own property that she inherited or that had been hers before marriage. She did not even have the right to keep any wages she earned; they belonged to her husband. She could not sign contracts, sue or be sued, or testify in court. She had no right to her children in case of legal separation or divorce, and divorce was almost impossible for her to obtain. She was legally obliged to obey her husband, who could keep her prisoner or physically punish her, although not with excessive force.

Up from Slavery

*T*he founding of the United States did not dismantle women's common-law status. That would take a long, painful effort that has not yet been completed—some states still restrict married women's freedom to manage property, change their residence, and start businesses. Women didn't even organize to protest their status until 1848, when a Declaration of Rights and Sentiments was read aloud by Elizabeth Cady Stanton at a Woman's Rights Convention at Seneca Falls, New York.

The declaration used the format and language of the Declaration of Independence to declare it a self-evident truth that all men and women are created equal. "The history of mankind," it asserted, "is a history of repeated injuries and usurpations on the part of man toward woman, having in direct object the establishment of an absolute tyranny over her. To prove this, let facts be submitted to a candid world."

The audience was heavily composed of abolitionists, for it was in the antislavery movement that women discovered that one political right was open to them—the First Amendment right "to petition the Government for a redress of grievances." Yet they were criticized, not just for holding unpopular opinions but for being unwomanly in trying to promote *any* opinions, and many women abolitionists became aware for the first time of their subservient position. They, and the male abolitionists who worked with them, began to think and talk of women's rights as well as Negro rights.

The Seneca Falls Convention itself was organized by two women, Lucretia Mott and Elizabeth Cady Stanton, who had met at a London antislavery convention eight years before. There, they had found that they were not only forbidden to speak but were required to observe the proceedings from behind a curtain.

At Seneca Falls, Stanton also called for women's "inalienable right to the elective franchise," a demand that seemed so excessive, even to the others who had helped her draft the declaration, that only the black abolitionist Frederick Douglass would take the floor to support it. Within two years, however, women were to take the idea of suffrage so seriously that they were initiating petition campaigns for it in eight states, as well as continuing to agitate with increasing effect for property rights and marriage reform. But with the outbreak of the Civil War, women postponed such work to assist the war effort.

After Lincoln's Emancipation Proclamation, women collected almost 400,000 signatures petitioning for an amendment to abolish slavery. Once that had been accomplished with the passage and ratification of the 13th Amendment in 1865, the Anti-Slavery Society began agitating for suffrage, and a 14th Amendment was proposed and introduced in Congress. Its original purpose was to give the vote to slaves and to take it away from southerners who had fought against the Union, but for the first time in the history of the Constitution, it was proposed that the word *male* be used to characterize voters.

Abolitionist feminists were alarmed. Many abolitionists who had championed women's right to vote in the abstract were unwilling to make it a concrete political issue. Wendell Phillips, president of the Anti-Slavery Society, refused to support votes for women, arguing that "this hour belongs to the Negro." Senator Charles Sumner, a former advocate of women's rights, called the women's campaign "most inopportune." Such sentiments prevailed. Women were unsuccessful in gaining the right to vote through either the 14th or 15th amendments.

But had the 14th Amendment *inadvertently* given women the right to vote? "All persons born or naturalized in the United States," declared the amendment, "are citizens of the United States and of the State wherein they reside. No State shall make or enforce any law which shall abridge the privileges or immunities of citizens." In 1871, two members of the House Judiciary Committee signed a minority report holding that, under the amendment, women had the right to vote. The next year, Susan B. Anthony led 16 women to vote the straight Republican ticket.

On registration day, Anthony read both the 14th Amendment and the state election law to the election inspectors, pointing out that neither one prohibited women from voting. The women were allowed to register, and on election day, to vote. Although Anthony was arrested, tried, and convicted, she did not pay her fine and was never jailed for her defiance, which made it impossible for her to bring the case to the Supreme Court.

Women's only recourse was to get voters to amend the Constitution. This they succeeded in doing in 1920, after 50 years and what Carrie Chapman Catt, president of the National Woman Suffrage Association at the time, summarized as "56 campaigns of referenda to male voters; 480 campaigns to get legislatures to submit suffrage amendments to voters; 277 campaigns to get state party conventions to include woman's suffrage planks; 30 campaigns to get presidential party conventions to adopt woman's suffrage planks; and 19 campaigns with 19 successive Congresses."

One Step Forward, Two Steps Back

*W*hile women were campaigning for the vote, another issue had crept up on them: protective labor legislation. Progressive legislators had enacted a whole network of laws singling out women—laws that women were divided about.

A prime example was protective legislation to limit hours and working conditions. Such laws had been held to be a violation of men's right to contract, but in 1908, in the case of *Muller* v. *Oregon*, the Supreme Court decided that an Oregon law limiting the working hours of *women* was constitutional.

The case was the first in which sociological data persuaded the justices to modify legal principle. The brief that was filed cited reports by state commissions to prove that women are just what the common law assumed they are—frail, and in need of special protection. The rights of men—in this case, to liberty of contract—need not be available to working women, as they had traditionally not been available to married women.

Woman has always been dependent on man, said the decision, and this is natural. "Though limitations upon personal and contractual rights may be removed by legislation, there is that in her disposition and habits of life which will operate against a full assertion of those rights....Differentiated by these matters from the other sex, she is properly put in a class by herself, and legislation designed for her protection may be sustained, even when like legislation is not necessary for men, and could not be sustained."

The issue divides the women's movement to this day. An organization called the National Woman's Party, founded in 1913 to work for suffrage, became convinced that the view of women exhibited in the *Muller* decision was a threat to the idea of equal rights they had been working for. So in 1921, the party reorganized to work for the removal of all legal distinctions based on sex. At first they undertook a state-by-state campaign but soon decided to lobby instead for constitutional reform— an equal rights amendment. The amendment was introduced in Congress in 1923, and with two exceptions, substantially the same wording was submitted every year thereafter until 1972, when the ERA was finally passed by Congress and sent to the states for ratification.

From the beginning, the main opposition to the ERA was from supporters of the trade union movement. Clearly, protective labor legislation, whatever else it did, served to curb women's competition for jobs. In 1950 and 1953, the ERA was amended with a rider, urged by Eleanor Roosevelt, that would have left protective legislation intact by providing that the amendment "shall not be construed to impair any rights, benefits, or exemptions now or hereafter conferred by law upon persons of the female sex."

But it was precisely the singling out of women that the National Woman's Party opposed. So although the amended ERA twice passed the Senate, the party helped to defeat it in the House.

When Congress held hearings on the equal rights amendment in 1970 and 1971, six of the eight statements against it were submitted by organized labor, including one from the AFL-CIO. One legal expert suggested a rider to keep protective legislation intact.

During the years in which the ERA was being unsuccessfully proposed, attempts were made—also unsuccessfully—to strike down various discriminatory laws for violating the equal-protection clause of the 14th Amendment. The rationale was well expressed by scholar Bernard Schwartz, in an observation included in the record of the 1970 House hearings on the amendment by ERA foe Senator Sam Ervin: "The case law has consistently ruled that, even though women are 'persons' within the scope of the equal-protection clause, the protection which that provision affords them must be interpreted in the light of the disabilities imposed upon women at common law. Thus, as recently as 1966, a state court ruled that, until the common-law disqualification of sex is removed, women are not eligible to serve on juries—and that regardless of the equal-protection clause."

In 1971, the Supreme Court finally held that a specific classification based on sex was not "reasonable." In the years since, the Court has considered a number of challenges to statutes that differentiate on the basis of sex. "While the Court has several times struck down such statutes," comments one legal source, "those occasions have been proportionately far fewer than in suits challenging classifications based on race."

Although the Court can reverse a previous ruling, and has done so, it does not do so with abandon and generally tries to support such reversals by appealing to the "plain language" of the Constitution or to the intent of those who framed the section being interpreted. Intent is discovered by examining the debates that took place at the time the wording was adopted—the legislative history. And the legislative history of the 14th Amendment explicitly did not include women, so it would require an extremely "creative" decision to hold that the amendment applies to women.

The Slow Death of the ERA

*T*hus, the stage is set for the sad tale of the Equal Rights Amendment. Its legislative history seemed clear at the time it passed Congress. Both its supporters and its opponents agreed that it would apply only to the actions of governments; that it would *not* address private discrimination, which could only be reached by legislation that invoked Congress's power to regulate commerce; and that it would invalidate protective labor legislation that makes women less competitive in the marketplace.

In the congressional hearings, no one, not even Sam Ervin, who voiced many of the qualms that the conservative campaign against the ERA in the '70s was to pick up, thought that the amendment would expand the power of government. It would invalidate laws, not create them. In fact, Ervin feared the ERA would bring "legal chaos" because it would "merely abolish all laws making any distinction between men and women. It would not bring into existence any new laws giving us a discrimination-free society."

And feminists agreed. "ERA will not prevent discriminations by persons or by private industry," wrote Ann Scott in the pages of the popular feminist magazine *Ms.* "It will not, directly at least, change social relations. What it will do, over the long run and on a most basic level, is to prevent the government from determining the rights of women and men on the basis of sex. And that's a hell of a lot."

Then came the conservative campaign against the amendment. Not only would the ERA change social relations by driving women out of the home and into the work force and by legalizing homosexual marriage, but it was also alleged to be "a big power grab by the Federal Government." The amendment "will eliminate all-girls' and all-boys' schools and colleges," said conservative literature. It "may compel the states to set up taxpayer-financed child-care centers for all children" and "may give the Federal Government the power to force the admission of women to seminaries equally with men, and possibly force the churches to ordain women."

In response to these attacks, feminists gradually expanded their accounts of what the ERA might do. They didn't exactly *say* that the amendment would be applied to make people economically equal, but they started wearing buttons calling attention to the statistic that women earned 59 cents to a man's dollar (a misleading figure—see Jennifer Roback's "The 59-Cent Fallacy," REASON, Sept. 1984).

The ERA was supported by a broad coalition that now included many of the union forces that still wanted to expand social legislation. They thought that they could have it all—that women could be legally equal and legally different and special, all at the same time. After all, those who made blacks their constituency had pulled off that trick by changing the interpretation of the Civil Rights Act to mean present-day affirmative action with its goals and benign quotas.

So feminists started agreeing with the conservatives that the new amendment would have broad effects. Where the conservatives called it a federal power grab, Eleanor Smeal, president of the National Organization for Women (NOW), called it "a Constitutional prohibition against sex discrimination." In a letter to supporters, she said, "Unless we fight harder and in a more organized fashion than we ever have before, women will continue to be doomed to a second rate economic status of lower pay, unequal credit and inadequate job security. After all, that's what the ERA fight is *really* all about—making the lot of women really equal to the lot of men, especially when it comes to money. That's the critical litmus test of equality."

The amendment had five years to achieve ratification, and it failed to do so. The deadline was extended until 1982, and it failed again, this time permanently. Prospects for passage of a new ERA are unlikely.

The ERA was a remnant of the classical liberalism of the early abolitionist feminists, who sought equal responsibility and laws that had neither special privileges nor special restrictions for women. It could have been used as a vehicle to enunciate that philosophy to a wide audience today, but it was not. Instead, its supporters, who began by describing it correctly, came to agree with their opponents that it would engender sweeping changes in private action. And that agreement would become a self-fulfilling prophecy should the ERA pass Congress again in the near future; it has created a climate of opinion that would provide a different and malignant legislative history, one that could make all the worst nightmares of federal power grabs come true.

So the ERA is dead, but *Muller* v. *Oregon,* the cornerstone of protective legislation, has never been overruled. And the status of women is basically what state legislatures (and majority opinion) say it is. While the ERA was wending its way through the state legislatures, it became fashionable to grant women equal treatment; several states passed state equal-rights amendments to their constitutions. But the trouble with not having the Constitution view women as fully equal and independent beings is that, if the fashion changes, there is nothing to stop the laws from changing back.

Indeed, a number of feminists are now campaigning for a new kind of protective legislation, this time aimed at helping women in the workplace with laws that mandate maternity leave and provide child-care assistance. Such legislation is a pendulum that can swing either way. In *Women and Work in America*, Robert Smuts says, "The most obvious effect of the depression of the 1930s was to throw many women out of work and intensify the feeling that working women took jobs away from male breadwinners. Many state and local governments revived old bans on the employment of married women in teaching and other public jobs, and several state legislatures considered bills to prohibit the employment of wives in public industry." It could happen again.

The Push for Power

After a decade of disappointment, Hispanics try to translate their numbers into political clout

It will be months before demographers at the Census Bureau produce their portrait of who we are in the waning years of the American Century. But when the results from the 1990 count are finally in, one statistic should come as no surprise: the number of Hispanics—the nation's fastest-growing group—could be approaching 25 million, or 10 percent of the total U.S. population. Latino leaders say the census will be their community's ticket to fuller participation in American life than ever before. It seems all the more ironic, then, that the forms arriving in mailboxes across the country recently were printed only in English—another reminder that, despite their vast legions, Hispanics remain an invisible minority.

Latinos were poised to make their mark once before. "The 1980s will be the decade of the Hispanics," declared Raúl Yzaguirre, president of the National Council of La Raza, in 1978. Pollsters predicted that Hispanics would soon become a "voting time bomb." But a dozen years later, Latinos have proved largely incapable of translating their numeric strength into political and economic clout. Today Yzaguirre says, "If anything, we retrogressed in the '80s." Reagan-era cutbacks and recession pushed many Hispanics deep into poverty, while the conservative social climate permitted passage of "English Only" laws aimed at Spanish speakers. Last week, a report from Congress's General Accounting Office confirmed what Hispanics have been saying for years: the landmark 1986 immigration law, which penalized employers of illegal aliens, has produced a widespread "pattern of discrimination" against job applicants with a "foreign appearance or accent"— even citizens and green-card holders.

Disappointed by their lack of progress in the last decade, Hispanics are now determined to salvage the 1990s. Activists have adopted a grass-roots strategy that has already led to successes in school reform and political redistricting. The Latino leader-ship is looking ahead to 1992, the 500th anniversary of Columbus's discovery of the Americas. The date holds great emotional significance for Spanish-speaking Americans, and activists hope it will lure diverse Hispanics—from cosmopolitan Miami and inner-city barrios to the planting fields of California—under a single political and cultural umbrella.

But the forces that made the "decade of the Hispanics" a nonevent continue to vex the Latino community. The first problem is one of definition. The term Hispanic is an imposed label, and remains more convenient than precise: it includes Mexicans, Cubans, Puerto Ricans and others (chart) who, apart from speaking Spanish, often have little in common. And the black-white dichotomy that characterizes American thinking on minorities leaves little room for Latino concerns.

Though Latinos have had a continuous presence in this country for centuries, they have been slow to gain recognition. "Hispanic" appeared as a census term only in 1980. Relative to their numbers, they remain seriously underrepresented—there are no Hispanic senators and only 10 congressmen. A 1989 study by the Southwest Voter Registration Education Project found that Latinos vote less, attend fewer political rallies and make fewer campaign contributions than other Americans. One reason is the extreme youth of the population. Young people generally are relatively uninvolved politically; with a median age of 25, many Hispanics are also simply too young to vote. And unlike blacks, whose churches and organizations provided an institutional base for the fight against segregation, Hispanics have lacked a political superstructure and a common enemy.

The few attempts at putting together a national platform have proved ineffective.

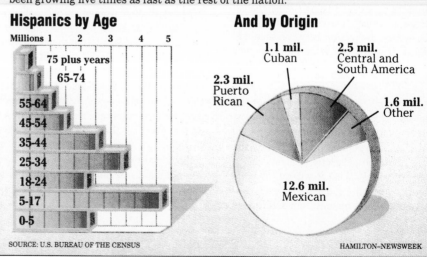

Young, Diverse and Growing

The Hispanic population, which represents about 8 percent of the U.S. total, has been growing five times as fast as the rest of the nation.

Hispanics by Age

Millions 1 2 3 4 5

75 plus years
65-74
55-64
45-54
35-44
25-34
18-24
5-17
0-5

And by Origin

1.1 mil. Cuban
2.5 mil. Central and South America
2.3 mil. Puerto Rican
1.6 mil. Other
12.6 mil. Mexican

SOURCE: U.S. BUREAU OF THE CENSUS

HAMILTON–NEWSWEEK

In 1987, political and corporate leaders headed by Henry Cisneros, then the mayor of San Antonio, Texas, presented the presidential candidates with a National Hispanic Agenda. Although the document drew attention to concerns about employment, education and housing, the group proved somewhat ineffectual on account of bickering between Mexican-Americans and Puerto Ricans. Because Mexicans represent more than 60 percent of the Hispanic population, committee members felt they should have greater control over the document. In general, the nation's various Hispanic groups have complained about having to compete for attention and scarce government and philanthropic funds.

To be sure, Latinos have made some impressive strides on the local level: they have won elections in many predominantly Spanish-speaking areas and were crucial to the victory of Harold Washington in Chicago and, more recently, David Dinkins in New York. But there hasn't yet been a break-through, national leader. Latino political aspirations suffered a serious setback in the fall of 1988, when Cisneros announced he wouldn't seek re-election, then confessed to an extramarital affair with a political fund raiser (he is still married and living with his wife). Cisneros, 42, once touted as a Democratic vice presidential candidate in 1984, had been the ethnic group's great hope. As it happened, polls a month after the scandal showed only a slight drop in his popularity and he remains, says Hispanic Rep. Bill Richardson, "our most logical leader." But his temporary fall from grace was unsettling. "There is no savior that will lead the Latino community to some political, economic and social promised land," says Segundo Mercado-Llorens, a labor official in Washington. "It depends upon a community of leaders who work together."

Latino talent: From New York to California, a new generation of Latino talent has emerged (box). Meanwhile, local leaders have set their sights close to home. "Hispanics are going to galvanize around a set of issues more than race," says Daniel Solis, head of Chicago's United Neighborhood Organization (UNO). "And because we're made up of different nationalities and different opinions, we're being forced to do it the hard way—at the grass-roots level, with local institutions." Hispanics are being elected in growing numbers to city councils and school boards—or, as one activist put it, the "front line of democracy."

Last year's school fight in Chicago, which is more than 20 percent Hispanic, illustrates the new grass-roots strategy. Angry over the city's appalling public education, busloads of Hispanics descended on the state capitol with a reform plan centered on greater parental control. They proceeded to win nearly 25 percent of the seats on newly created parent councils. Partly as a result of their efforts, some 50 principals lost their jobs. In a key legal victory, the Texas Supreme Court last year ordered a more equitable distribution of school funding—a decision that will be an automatic boost to Hispanics.

Latino leaders are now vesting their hopes for the future in the 1990 census. A vast increase in the population should bring Hispanics new funds and additional political representation. Because the 1980 census resulted in a large undercount of Hispanics—perhaps 10 percent—a number of activists have formed a program called Hágase Contar (Make Yourself Count) to ensure a more accurate picture. They have their work cut out for them. Spanish speakers have to call to request a form in their native tongue. That alone could discourage Hispanics from participating in the count.

Up for grabs: Time and numbers may be on the side of Latinos as they sail toward the 1992 anniversary. Voter registration climbed 21 percent from 1984 to 1988. At the same time, voter turnout has dropped slightly. Hispanic organizers attribute the decline to the difficulty of keeping up with a 25 percent increase in the voting-age population, though political consultants wonder whether they simply can't get out the vote. In the coming decade, some 5 million Hispanics will become eligible for citizenship, thanks in part to the amnesty program that granted legal residency to undocumented immigrants who had lived in the United States for five years. Both the Democrats and the GOP have strengthened their outreach programs to win Hispanic votes, which are viewed as being up for grabs.

But Hispanic leaders have failed to galvanize their armies before. The '90s will be a make-or-break test of their political maturity. "We either get this nation's attention," says Elaine Coronado, Quincentennial Commission director, "or we continue being perceived as a second-rate minority group." Says Cisneros: "We don't want to ever look at a decade again and say, 'Where did it go?'"

ELOISE SALHOLZ *with* TIM PADGETT *in Chicago*, DAVID L. GONZALEZ *in New York and* NONNY DE LA PENA *in Houston*

In 1945 the United States commanded a
40 percent share of the world economy; today its share is half that,
and yet our military commitments have grown dramatically. This imbalance,
which conforms to a classic historical pattern, threatens our security, both military and economic

THE (RELATIVE) DECLINE
OF AMERICA

PAUL KENNEDY
Paul Kennedy is the J. Richardson Dilworth Professor of History at Yale University.

IN FEBRUARY OF 1941, WHEN HENRY LUCE'S *LIFE* MAGAzine announced that this was the "American century," the claim accorded well with the economic realities of power. Even before the United States entered the Second World War, it produced about a third of the world's manufactures, which was more than twice the production of Nazi Germany and almost ten times that of Japan. By 1945, with the Fascist states defeated and America's wartime allies economically exhausted, the U.S. share of world manufacturing output was closer to half—a proportion never before or since attained by a single nation. More than any of the great world empires—Rome, Imperial Spain, or Victorian Britain—the United States appeared destined to dominate international politics for decades, if not centuries, to come.

In such circumstances it seemed to American decisionmakers natural (if occasionally awkward) to extend U.S. military protection to those countries pleading for help in the turbulent years after 1945. First came involvement in Greece and Turkey; and then, from 1949 onward, the extraordinarily wide-ranging commitment to NATO; the special relationship with Israel and, often contrarily, with Saudi Arabia, Jordan, Egypt, and lesser Arab states; and obligations to the partners in such regional defense organizations as SEATO, CENTO, and ANZUS. Closer to home, there was the Rio Pact and the special hemispheric defense arrangements with Canada. By early 1970, as Ronald Steel has pointed out, the United States "had more than 1,000,000 soldiers in 30 countries, was a member of 4 regional defense alliances and an active participant in a fifth, had mutual defense treaties with 42 nations, was a member of 53 international organizations, and was furnishing military or economic aid to nearly 100 nations across the face of the globe." Although the end of the Vietnam War significantly reduced the number of American troops overseas, the global array of U.S. obligations that remained would have astonished the Founding Fathers.

Yet while America's commitments steadily increased after 1945, its share of world manufacturing and of world gross national product began to decline, at first rather slowly, and then with increasing speed. In one sense, it could be argued, such a decline is irrelevant: this country is nowadays far richer, absolutely, than it was in 1945 or 1950, and most of its citizens are much better off *in absolute terms*. In another sense, however, the shrinking of America's share of world production is alarming because of the implications for American grand strategy—which is measured not by military forces alone but by their integration with all those other elements (economic, social, political, and diplomatic) that contribute toward a successful longterm national policy.

The gradual erosion of the economic foundations of America's power has been of several kinds. In the first place, there is the country's industrial decline relative to overall world production, not only in older manufactures, such as textiles, iron and steel, shipbuilding, and basic chemicals, but also—though it is harder to judge the final outcome at this stage of industrial-technological combat— in robotics, aerospace technology, automobiles, machine tools, and computers. Both areas pose immense problems: in traditional and basic manufacturing the gap in wage scales between the United States and newly industrializing countries is probably such that no efficiency measures will close it; but to lose out in the competition in future technologies, if that indeed should occur, would be even more disastrous.

The second, and in many ways less expected, sector of decline is agriculture. Only a decade ago experts were predicting a frightening global imbalance between food requirements and farming output. But the scenarios of famine and disaster stimulated two powerful responses: the first was a tremendous investment in American farming from the 1970s onward, fueled by the prospect of ever larger overseas food sales; the second was a large-scale investi-

From *The Atlantic*, August 1987, pp. 29-34, 36-38. Excerpt from THE RISE AND FALL OF THE GREAT POWERS by Paul Kennedy. Copyright © 1987 by Paul Kennedy. Reprinted by permission of Random House, Inc.

gation, funded by the West, into scientific means of increasing Third World crop outputs. These have been so successful as to turn growing numbers of Third World countries into food exporters, and thus competitors of the United States. At the same time, the European Economic Community has become a major producer of agricultural surpluses, owing to its price-support system. In consequence, experts now refer to a "world awash in food," and this state of affairs in turn has led to sharp declines in agricultural prices and in American food exports—and has driven many farmers out of business.

Like mid-Victorian Britons, Americans after 1945 favored free trade and open competition, not just because they held that global commerce and prosperity would be advanced in the process but also because they knew that they were most likely to benefit from a lack of protectionism. Forty years later, with that confidence ebbing, there is a predictable shift of opinion in favor of protecting the domestic market and the domestic producer. And, just as in Edwardian Britain, defenders of the existing system point out that higher tariffs not only might make domestic products *less* competitive internationally but also might have other undesirable repercussions—a global tariff war, blows against American exports, the undermining of the currencies of certain newly industrializing countries, and an economic crisis like that of the 1930s.

Along with these difficulties affecting American manufacturing and agriculture has come great turbulence in the nation's finances. The uncompetitiveness of U.S. industrial products abroad and the declining sales of agricultural exports have together produced staggering deficits in visible trade—$160 billion in the twelve months ending with April of 1986—but what is more alarming is that such a gap can no longer be covered by American earnings on "invisibles," which are the traditional recourse of a mature economy. On the contrary, the United States has been able to pay its way in the world only by importing ever larger amounts of capital. This has, of course, transformed it from the world's largest creditor to the world's largest debtor nation in the space of a few years.

Compounding this problem—in the view of many critics, causing this problem—have been the budgetary policies of the U.S. government itself.

A continuation of this trend, alarmed voices have pointed out, would push the U.S. national debt to around $13 *trillion* by the year 2000 (fourteen times the debt in 1980) and the interest payments on the debt to $1.5 *trillion*

Federal Deficit, Debt, and Interest (in billions)			
	Deficit	Debt	Interest on Debt
1980	$59.6	$914.3	$52.5
1983	$195.4	$1,381.9	$87.8
1985	$202.8	$1,823.1	$129.0

(twenty-nine times the 1980 payments). In fact a lowering of interest rates could make those estimates too high, but the overall trend is still very unhealthy. Even if federal deficits could be reduced to a "mere" $100 billion annual-

ly, the compounding of national debt and interest payments by the early twenty-first century would still cause unprecedented sums of money to be diverted in that direction. The only historical examples that come to mind of Great Powers so increasing their indebtedness *in peacetime* are France in the 1780s, where the fiscal crisis finally led to revolution, and Russia early in this century.

Indeed, it is difficult to imagine how the American economy could have got by without the inflow of foreign funds in the early 1980s, even if that had the awkward consequence of inflating the dollar and thereby further hurting U.S. agricultural and manufacturing exports. But, one wonders, what might happen if those funds are pulled out of the dollar, causing its value to drop precipitously?

Some say that alarmist voices are exaggerating the gravity of what is happening to the U.S. economy and failing to note the "naturalness" of most of these developments. For example, the midwestern farm belt would be much less badly off if so many farmers had not bought land at inflated prices and excessive interest rates in the late 1970s. The move from manufacturing into services is understandable, and is occurring in all advanced countries. And U.S. manufacturing *output* has been rising in absolute terms, even if employment (especially blue-collar employment) in manufacturing has been falling—but that too is a "natural" trend, as the world increasingly moves from material-based to knowledge-based production. Similarly, there is nothing wrong in the metamorphosis of American financial institutions into world financial institutions, with bases in Tokyo and London as well as New York, to handle (and profit from) the heavy flow of capital; that can only increase the nation's earnings from services. Even the large annual federal deficits and the mounting national debt are sometimes described as being not very serious, after allowance is made for inflation; and there exists in some quarters a belief that the economy will "grow its way out" of these deficits, or that government measures will close the gap, whether by increasing taxes or cutting spending or both. A too hasty attempt to slash the deficit, it is pointed out, could well trigger a major recession.

The positive signs of growth in the American economy are said to be even more reassuring. Because of the boom in the service sector, the United States has been creating jobs over the past decade faster than it has done at any time in its peacetime history—and certainly a lot faster than Western Europe has been. America's far greater degree of labor mobility eases such transformations in the job market. Furthermore, the enormous American commitment to high technology—not just in California and New England but also in Virginia, Arizona, and many other places—promises ever greater production, and thus national wealth (as well as ensuring a strategic edge over the Soviet Union). Indeed, it is precisely because of the opportunities existing in the American economy that the nation continues to attract millions of immigrants and to generate thousands of new entrepreneurs, and the capital that pours into the country can be tapped for further investment, especially in research and development. Finally, if long-term shifts in the global terms of trade are, as economists suspect, leading to steadily lower prices for foodstuffs and raw materials, that ought to benefit an economy that still imports enormous amounts of oil, metal ores, and so on (even if it hurts particular American interests, such as farmers and oilmen).

Many of these points may be valid. Since the American economy is so large and diverse, some sectors and regions are likely to be growing while others are in decline—and to characterize the whole with generalizations about "crisis" or "boom" is therefore inappropriate. Given the decline in the price of raw materials, the ebbing of the dollar's unsustainably high exchange value since early 1985, the reduction that has occurred in interest rates, and the impact of all three trends on inflation and on business confidence, it is not surprising that some professional economists are optimistic about the future.

NEVERTHELESS, FROM THE VIEWPOINT OF AMERICAN grand strategy, and of the economic foundation necessary to an effective long-term strategy, the picture is much less rosy. In the first place, America's capacity to carry the burden of military liabilities that it has assumed since 1945 is obviously less than it was several decades ago, when its shares of global manufacturing and GNP were much larger, its agriculture was secure, its balance of payments was far healthier, the government budget was in balance, and it was not in debt to the rest of the world. From that larger viewpoint there is something in the analogy that is made by certain political scientists between America's position today and that of previous "declining hegemons." Here again it is instructive to note the uncanny similarity between the growing mood of anxiety in thoughtful circles in the United States today and that which pervaded all political parties in Edwardian Britain and led to what has been termed the national efficiency movement—a broad-based debate among the nation's decision-making, business, and educational elites over ways to reverse a growing uncompetitiveness with other advanced societies. In terms of commercial expertise, levels of training and education, efficiency of production, and standards of income and (among the less well off) living, health, and housing, the number-one power of 1900 seemed to be losing its superiority, with dire implications for its long-term *strategic* position. Hence the calls for "renewal" and "reorganization" came as much from the right as from the left. Such campaigns usually do lead to reforms here and there, but their very existence is, ironically, a confirmation of decline. When a Great Power is strong and unchallenged, it will be much less likely to debate its capacity to meet its obligations than when it is relatively weaker.

In particular, there could be serious implications for American grand strategy if the U.S. industrial base continues to shrink. If there were ever in the future to be a large-scale war that remained conventional (because of the belligerents' fear of triggering a nuclear holocaust), one must wonder, would America's productive capacities be ade-

quate after years of decline in certain key industries, the erosion of blue-collar employment, and so on? One is reminded of the warning cry of the British nationalist economist Professor W. A. S. Hewins in 1904 about the impact of British industrial decay upon that country's power:

> Suppose an industry which is threatened [by foreign competition] is one which lies at the very root of your system of National defense, where are you then? You could not get on without an iron industry, a great Engineering trade, because in modern warfare you would not have the means of producing, and maintaining in a state of efficiency, your fleets and armies.

It is hard to imagine that the decline in American industrial capacity could be so severe: America's manufacturing base is simply much broader than Edwardian Britain's was, and—an important point—the so-called defense-related industries not only have been sustained by Pentagon procurement but also have taken part in the shift from materials-intensive to knowledge-intensive (high-tech) manufacturing, which over the long term will also reduce the West's reliance on critical raw materials. Even so, the expatriation from the United States of, say, semiconductor assembly, the erosion of the American shipping and shipbuilding industry, and the closing down of so many American mines and oil fields represent trends that cannot but be damaging in the event of another long, Great Power, coalition war. If, moreover, historical precedents have any validity at all, the most critical constraint upon any surge in wartime production will be the number of skilled craftsmen—which causes one to wonder about the huge long-term decline in American blue-collar employment, including the employment of skilled craftsmen.

A problem quite different but equally important for sustaining a proper grand strategy concerns the impact of slow economic growth on the American social-political consensus. To a degree that amazes most Europeans, the United States in the twentieth century has managed to avoid overt "class" politics. This, one imagines, is a result of America's unique history. Many of its immigrants had fled from socially rigid circumstances elsewhere; the sheer size of the country had long allowed those who were disillusioned with their economic position to escape to the West, and also made the organization of labor much more difficult than in, say, France or Britain; and those same geographic dimensions, and the entrepreneurial opportunities within them, encouraged the development of a largely unreconstructed form of laissez-faire capitalism that has dominated the political culture of the nation (despite occasional counterattacks from the left). In consequence, the earnings gap between rich and poor is significantly larger in the United States than in any other advanced industrial society, and state expenditures on social services claim a lower share of GNP than in comparable countries except Japan, whose family-based support system for the poor and the aged appears much stronger.

This lack of class politics despite obvious socio-economic disparities has been possible because the nation's overall growth since the 1930s has offered the prospect of individual betterment to a majority of the population, and, disturbingly, because the poorest third of American society has not been mobilized to vote regularly. But given the different birthrates of whites on the one hand and blacks and Hispanics on the other, given the changing composition of the flow of immigrants into the United States, given also the economic metamorphosis that is leading to the loss of millions of relatively high-paying jobs in manufacturing, and the creation of millions of poorly paid jobs in services, it may be unwise to assume that the prevailing norms of the American political economy (such as low government social expenditures and low taxes on the rich) would be maintained if the nation entered a period of sustained economic difficulty caused by a plunging dollar and slow growth. An American polity that responds to external challenges by increasing defense expenditures, and reacts to the budgetary crisis by cutting existing social expenditures, runs the risk of provoking an eventual political backlash. There are no easy answers in dealing with the constant three-way tension between defense, consumption, and investment as national priorities.

Imperial Overstretch

THIS BRINGS US, INEVITABLY, TO THE DELICATE RElationship between slow economic growth and high defense spending. The debate over the economics of defense spending is a heated one and—bearing in mind the size and variety of the American economy, the stimulus that can come from large government contracts, and the technological spin-offs from weapons research—the evidence does not point simply in one direction. But what is significant for our purposes is the comparative dimension. Although (as is often pointed out) defense expenditures amounted to ten percent of GNP under President Eisenhower and nine percent under President Kennedy, America's shares of global production and wealth were at that time around twice what they are today, and, more particularly, the American economy was not then facing challenges to either its traditional or its high-technology manufactures. The United States now devotes about seven percent of its GNP to defense spending, while its major economic rivals, especially Japan, allocate a far smaller proportion. If this situation continues, then America's rivals will have more funds free for civilian investment. If the United States continues to direct a huge proportion of its research and development activities toward military-related production while the Japanese and West Germans concentrate on commercial research and development, and if the Pentagon drains off the ablest of the country's scientists and engineers from the design and production of goods for the world market, while similar personnel in other countries are bringing out better consumer products, then it seems inevitable that the American share of world manufacturing will decline steadily, and likely that American economic growth rates will be slower than those of countries dedicated to the marketplace and less eager to channel resources into defense.

It is almost superfluous to say that these tendencies place the United States on the horns of a most acute, if long-term, dilemma. Simply because it is *the* global superpower, with military commitments far more extensive than those of a regional power like Japan or West Germany, it requires much larger defense forces. Furthermore, since the USSR is seen to be the major military threat to American interests around the globe, and is clearly devoting a far greater proportion of its GNP to defense, American decision-makers are inevitably worried about "losing" the arms race with Russia. Yet the more sensible among the decision-makers can also perceive that the burden of armaments is debilitating the Soviet economy, and that if the two superpowers continue to allocate ever larger shares of their national wealth to the unproductive field of armaments, the critical question might soon be, Whose economy will decline *fastest*, relative to the economies of such expanding states as Japan, China, and so forth? A small investment in armaments may leave a globally overstretched power like the United States feeling vulnerable everywhere, but a very heavy investment in them, while bringing greater security in the short term, may so erode the commercial competitiveness of the American economy that the nation will be less secure in the long term.

Here, too, the historical precedents are not encouraging. Past experience shows that even as the relative economic strength of number-one countries has ebbed, the growing foreign challenges to their position have compelled them to allocate more and more of their resources to the military sector, which in turn has squeezed out productive investment and, over time, led to a downward spiral of slower growth, heavier taxes, deepening domestic splits over spending priorities, and a weakening capacity to bear the burdens of defense. If this, indeed, is the pattern of history, one is tempted to paraphrase Shaw's deadly serious quip and say: "Rome fell. Babylon fell. Scarsdale's turn will come."

HOW IS ONE TO INTERPRET WHAT IS GOING ON? AND what, if anything, can be done about these problems? Far too many of the remarks made in political speeches suggest that while politicians worry more than they did about the nation's economic future, they tend to believe that the problems have quick and simple-minded solutions. For example, some call for tariffs—but they fail to address the charge that whenever industry and agriculture are protected, they become less productive. Others urge "competitiveness"—but they fail to explain how, say, American textile workers are to compete with textile workers earning only a twentieth of American wages. Still others put the blame for the decline of American efficiency on the government, which they say takes too much of the national income—but they fail to explain how the Swiss and the Germans, with their far higher tax rates, remain competitive on the world market. There are those who want to increase defense spending to meet perceived threats overseas—but they rarely concede that such a policy would further unbalance the economy. And there are those who want to reduce defense spending—but they rarely suggest which commitments (Israel? Korea? Egypt? Europe?) should go, in order to balance means and ends.

Above all, there is rarely any sense of the long-term context in which this American dilemma must be seen, or of the blindingly obvious point that the problem is not new. The study of world history might be the most useful endeavor for today's decision-makers. Such study would free politicians from the ethnocentric and temporal blinkers that so often restrict vision, allowing them to perceive some of the larger facts about international affairs.

The first of these is that the relative strengths of the leading nations have never remained constant, because the uneven rates of growth of different societies and technological and organizational breakthroughs bring greater advantage to one society than to another. For example, the coming of the long-range-gunned sailing ship and the rise of Atlantic trade after 1500 were not uniformly beneficial to the states of Europe—they benefited some much more than others. In the same way, the later development of steam power, and of the coal and metal resources upon which it relied, drastically increased the relative power of certain nations. Once their productive capacity was enhanced, countries would normally find it easier to sustain the burdens of spending heavily on armaments in peacetime, and of maintaining and supplying large armies and fleets in wartime. It sounds crudely mercantilistic to express it this way, but wealth is usually needed to underpin military power, and military power is usually needed to acquire and protect wealth. If, however, too large a proportion of a state's resources is diverted from the creation of wealth and allocated instead to military purposes, that is likely to lead to a weakening of national power over the long term. And if a state overextends itself strategically, by, say, conquering extensive territories or waging costly wars, it runs the risk that the benefits ultimately gained from external expansion may be outweighed by the great expense—a problem that becomes acute if the nation concerned has entered a period of relative economic decline. The history of the rise and fall of the leading countries since the advance of Western Europe in the sixteenth century—that is, of nations such as Spain, the Netherlands, France, Great Britain, and, currently, the United States—shows a significant correlation over the long term between productive and revenue-raising capacity on the one hand and military strength on the other.

Of course, both wealth *and* power are always relative. Three hundred years ago the German mercantilistic writer Philip von Hornigk observed that "whether a nation be today mighty and rich or not depends not on the abundance or security of its power or riches, but principally on whether its neighbors possess more or less of it."

The Netherlands in the mid-eighteenth century was richer in absolute terms than it had been a hundred years earlier, but by that stage it was much less of a Great Power, because neighbors like France and Britain had more power and riches. The France of 1914 was, absolutely, more powerful than the one of 1850—but that was little consolation when France was being eclipsed by a much stronger Germany. Britain has far greater wealth today than it had in its mid-Victorian prime, and its armed forces possess far more powerful weapons, but its share of world product has shrunk from about 25 percent to about three percent. If a nation has "more of it" than its contemporaries, things are fine; if not, there are problems.

This does not mean, however, that a nation's relative economic and military power will rise and fall in parallel. Most of the historical examples suggest that the trajectory of a state's military-territorial influence lags noticeably behind the trajectory of its relative economic strength. The reason for this is not difficult to grasp. An economically expanding power—Britain in the 1860s, the United States in the 1890s, Japan today—may well choose to become rich rather than to spend heavily on armaments. A half century later priorities may well have altered. The earlier economic expansion has brought with it overseas obligations: dependence on foreign markets and raw materials, military alliances, perhaps bases and colonies. Other, rival powers are now expanding economically at a faster rate, and wish in their turn to extend their influence abroad. The world has become a more competitive place, and the country's market shares are being eroded. Pessimistic observers talk of decline; patriotic statesmen call for "renewal."

In these more troubled circumstances the Great Power is likely to spend much more on defense than it did two generations earlier and yet still find the world to be less secure—simply because other powers have grown faster, and are becoming stronger. Imperial Spain spent much more money on its army in the troubled 1630s and 1640s than it had in the 1580s, when the Castilian economy was healthier. Britain's defense expenditures were far greater in 1910 than they were, say, at the time of Palmerston's death, in 1865, when the British economy was at its relative peak; but did any Britons at the later date feel more secure? The same problem appears to confront both the United States and the Soviet Union today. Great Powers in relative decline instinctively respond by spending more on security, thereby diverting potential resources from investment and compounding their long-term dilemma.

After the Second World War the position of the United States and the USSR as powers in a class by themselves appeared to be reinforced by the advent of nuclear weapons and delivery systems. The strategic and diplomatic landscape was now entirely different from that of 1900, let alone 1800. And yet the process of rise and fall among Great Powers had not ceased. Militarily, the United States and the USSR stayed in the forefront as the 1960s gave way to the 1970s and 1980s. Indeed, because they both interpret international problems in bipolar, and often Manichean, terms, their rivalry has driven them into an ever-escalating arms race that no other powers feel capable of joining. Over the same few decades, however, the global productive balances have been changing faster than ever before. The Third World's share of total manufacturing output and GNP, which was depressed to an all-time low in the decade after 1945, has steadily expanded. Europe has recovered from its wartime batterings and, in the form of the EEC, become the world's largest trading unit. The People's Republic of China is leaping forward at an impressive rate. Japan's postwar economic growth has been so phenomenal that, according to some measures, Japan recently overtook the Soviet Union in total GNP. Meanwhile, growth rates in both the United States and the USSR have become more sluggish, and those countries' shares of global production and wealth have shrunk dramatically since the 1960s.

IT IS WORTH BEARING THE SOVIET UNION'S DIFFICULTIES in mind when one analyzes the present and future circumstances of the United States, because of two important distinctions. The first is that while it can be argued that the U.S. share of world power has been declining faster than the Soviet share over the past few decades, the problems of the United States are probably nowhere near as great as those of the Soviet Union. Moreover, America's absolute strength (especially in industrial and technological fields) is still much greater than that of the USSR. The second is that the very unstructured, laissez-faire nature of American society (while not without its weaknesses) probably gives the United States a better chance of readjusting to changing circumstances than a rigid and *dirigiste* power has. But its potential in turn depends upon a national leadership that can understand the larger processes at work in the world today and perceives both the strong and the weak points of the country's position as the United States seeks to adjust to the changing global environment.

Although the United States is at present still pre-eminent economically and perhaps even militarily, it cannot avoid the two great tests that challenge the longevity of every major power that occupies the number-one position in world affairs. First, in the military-strategic realm, can it preserve a reasonable balance between the nation's perceived defense commitments and the means it possesses to maintain those commitments? And second, as an intimately related question, can it preserve the technological and economic bases of its power from relative erosion in the face of the ever-shifting patterns of global production? This test of American abilities will be the greater because America, like Imperial Spain around 1600 or the British Empire around 1900, bears a heavy burden of strategic commitments, made decades earlier, when the nation's political, economic, and military capacity to influence world affairs seemed so much more assured. The United States now runs the risk, so familiar to historians of the rise and fall of Great Powers, of what might be called "imperial overstretch": that is to say, decision-makers in Washington must face the awkward and enduring fact that the total of the United States's global interests and obligations is nowadays far too large for the country to be able to defend them all simultaneously.

To be sure, it is hardly likely that the United States would be called upon to defend all of its overseas interests simultaneously and unilaterally, unaided by the NATO members in Western Europe, Israel in the Middle East, or Japan, Australia, and possibly China in the Pacific. Nor are all the regional trends unfavorable to the United States with respect to defense. For example, while aggression by the unpredictable North Korean regime is always possible, it would hardly be welcomed by Beijing—furthermore, South Korea has grown to have more than twice the population and four times the GNP of the North. Also, while the expansion of Soviet forces in the Far East is alarming to Washington, it is balanced by the growing threat that China poses to the USSR's land and sea lines of communication in that area. The recent sober admission by Secretary of Defense Caspar Weinberger that "we can never afford to buy the capabilities sufficient to meet all of our commitments with one hundred percent confidence" is surely true; but it is also true that the potential anti-Soviet resources in the world (the United States, Western Europe, Japan, China, Australasia) are far greater than the resources lined up on the USSR's side.

Despite such consolations, the fundamental grand-strategic problem remains: the United States today has roughly the same enormous array of military obligations across the globe that it had a quarter century ago, when its shares of world GNP, manufacturing production, military spending, and armed-forces personnel were much larger than they are now. In 1985, forty years after America's triumph in the Second World War and more than a decade after its pull-out from Vietnam, 526,000 members of the U.S. armed forces were abroad (including 64,000 afloat). That total is substantially more than the overseas deployments in peacetime of the military and naval forces of the British Empire at the height of its power. Nevertheless, in the opinion of the Joint Chiefs of Staff, and of many civilian experts, it is simply not enough. Despite a near-trebling of the American defense budget since the late 1970s, the numerical size of the armed forces on active duty has increased by just five percent. As the British and the French military found in their time, a nation with extensive overseas obligations will always have a more difficult manpower problem than a state that keeps its armed forces solely for home defense, and a politically liberal and economically laissez-faire society sensitive to the unpopularity of conscription will have a greater problem than most.

Managing Relative Decline

ULTIMATELY, THE ONLY ANSWER TO WHETHER THE United States can preserve its position is *no*—for it simply has not been given to any one society to remain permanently ahead of all the others, freezing the patterns of different growth rates, technological advance, and military development that have existed since time immemorial. But historical precedents do not imply that the United States is destined to shrink to the relative obscurity of former leading powers like Spain and the Netherlands, or to disintegrate like the Roman and Austro-Hungarian empires; it is too large to do the former, and probably too homogeneous to do the latter. Even the British analogy, much favored in the current political-science literature, is not a good one if it ignores the differences in scale. The geographic size, population, and natural resources of Great

Britain suggest that it ought to possess roughly three or four percent of the world's wealth and power, all other things being equal. But precisely because all other things are never equal, a peculiar set of historical and technological circumstances permitted Great Britain to possess, say, 25 percent of the world's wealth and power in its prime. Since those favorable circumstances have disappeared, all that it has been doing is returning to its more "natural" size. In the same way, it may be argued, the geographic extent, population, and natural resources of the United States suggest that it ought to possess 16 or 18 percent of the world's wealth and power. But because of historical and technological circumstances favorable to it, that share rose to 40 percent or more by 1945, and what we are witnessing today is the ebbing away from that extraordinarily high figure to a more natural share. That decline is being masked by the country's enormous military capability at present, and also by its success in internationalizing American capitalism and culture. Yet even when it has declined to the position of occupying no more than its natural share of the world's wealth and power, a long time into the future, the United States will still be a very significant power in a multipolar world, simply because of its size.

The task facing American statesmen over the next decades, therefore, is to recognize that broad trends are under way, and that there is a need to manage affairs so that the relative erosion of America's position takes place slowly and smoothly, unaided by policies that bring short-term advantage but long-term disadvantage. Among the realities that statesmen, from the President down, must be alert to are these: that technological and therefore socioeconomic change is occurring in the world faster than it has ever before; that the international community is much more politically and culturally diverse than has been assumed, and is defiant of simplistic remedies offered by either Washington or Moscow for its problems; that the economic and productive power balances are no longer tilted as favorably in America's direction as they were in 1945. Even in the military realm there are signs of a certain redistribution of the balances, away from a bipolar and toward a multipolar system, in which American economic and military strength is likely to remain greater than that of any other individual country but will cease to be as disproportionate as it was in the decades immediately after the Second World War. In all the discussions about the erosion of American leadership it needs to be repeated again and again that the decline is relative, not absolute, and is therefore perfectly natural, and that a serious threat to the real interests of the United States can come only from a failure to adjust sensibly to the new world order.

Just how well can the American system adjust to a state of relative decline? Already, a growing awareness of the gap between U.S. obligations and U.S. power has led to questions by gloomier critics about the overall political culture in which Washington decision-makers have to operate. It has been suggested with increasing frequency that a country needing to reformulate its grand strategy in the light of the larger, uncontrollable changes taking place in world affairs may be ill served by an electoral system that seems to paralyze foreign-policy decision-making every two years. Foreign policy may be undercut by the extraordinary pressures applied by lobbyists, political-action committees, and other interest groups, all of whom, by definition, are prejudiced in favor of this or that policy change, and by the simplification of vital but complex international and strategic issues, inherent to mass media whose time and space for such things are limited and whose raison d'être is chiefly to make money and only secondarily to inform. It may also be undercut by the still powerful escapist urges in the American social culture, which are perhaps understandable in terms of the nation's frontier past but hinder its coming to terms with today's complex, integrated world and with other cultures and ideologies. Finally, the country may not always be helped by the division of decision-making powers that was deliberately created when it was geographically and strategically isolated from the rest of the world, two centuries ago, and had time to find a consensus on the few issues that actually concerned foreign policy. This division may be less serviceable now that the United States is a global superpower, often called upon to make swift decisions vis-à-vis countries that enjoy far fewer constraints. No one of these obstacles prevents the execution of a coherent, long-term American grand strategy. However, their cumulative effect is to make it difficult to carry out policy changes that seem to hurt special interests and occur in an election year. It may therefore be here, in the cultural and political realms, that the evolution of an overall American policy to meet the twenty-first century will be subjected to the greatest test.

Nevertheless, given the considerable array of strengths still possessed by the United States, it ought not in theory to be beyond the talents of successive Administrations to orchestrate this readjustment so as, in Walter Lippmann's classic phrase, to bring "into balance . . . the nation's commitments and the nation's power." Although there is no single state obviously preparing to take over America's global burdens, in the way that the United States assumed Britain's role in the 1940s, the country has fewer problems than had Imperial Spain, besieged by enemies on all fronts, or the Netherlands, squeezed between France and England, or the British Empire, facing numerous challengers. The tests before the United States as it heads toward the twenty-first century are certainly daunting, perhaps especially in the economic sphere; but the nation's resources remain considerable, *if* they can be properly utilized and *if* there is a judicious recognition of both the limitations and the opportunities of American power.

Index

Credits/ Acknowledgments

Cover design by Charles Vitelli

1. Reconstruction and the Gilded Age
Facing overview—National Archives. 25—Frederic Remington, *The Fall of the Cowboy, 1895,* oil on canvas, 25 x 35 ¹/₈ in., 1961.230, Amon Carter Museum, Fort Worth. 27—Reproduction from the Collections of the Library of Congress. 30—The Bettmann Archive. 32—Courtesy of the State Historical Society of Missouri, Columbia. 37—Chicago Historical Society.

2. Emergence of Modern America
Facing overview—National Archives. 57—Library of Congress/ Imagefinders, Washington, D.C. 58—California Museum of Photography, University of California, Riverside. 62—California Museum of Photography, University of California, Riverside. 80, 81, 82, 83—Courtesy of the author.

3. Progressivism to the 1920s
Facing overview—Courtesy of The New York Historical Society, New York City. 122-123, 125-126, 128, 130-134—Photographs from the Collections of Henry Ford Museum and Greenville Village.

4. Great Depression to World War II
Facing overview—Library of Congress. 146, 149—Labor-Management Documentation Centre, Cornell University. 153—The Archives of Labor and Urban Affairs, Wayne State University. 160-161—Clem Albers/War Relocation Authority.

5. Cold War to the Reagan Revolution
Facing overview—United Nations.

6. New Directions for American History
Facing overview—New York Stock Exchange staff photograph by Edward Topple.

ANNUAL EDITIONS ARTICLE REVIEW FORM

■ NAME: _____ DATE: _____

■ TITLE AND NUMBER OF ARTICLE: _____

■ BRIEFLY STATE THE MAIN IDEA OF THIS ARTICLE: _____

_____

_____

_____

_____

■ LIST THREE IMPORTANT FACTS THAT THE AUTHOR USES TO SUPPORT THE MAIN IDEA:

_____

_____

_____

_____

_____

_____

■ WHAT INFORMATION OR IDEAS DISCUSSED IN THIS ARTICLE ARE ALSO DISCUSSED IN YOUR TEXTBOOK OR OTHER READING YOU HAVE DONE? LIST THE TEXTBOOK CHAPTERS AND PAGE NUMBERS:

_____

_____

_____

_____

_____

_____

■ LIST ANY EXAMPLES OF BIAS OR FAULTY REASONING THAT YOU FOUND IN THE ARTICLE:

_____

_____

_____

_____

■ LIST ANY NEW TERMS/CONCEPTS THAT WERE DISCUSSED IN THE ARTICLE AND WRITE A SHORT DEFINITION:

_____

_____

_____

_____

_____

*Your instructor may require you to use this Annual Editions Article Review Form in any number of ways: for articles that are assigned, for extra credit, as a tool to assist in developing assigned papers, or simply for your own reference. Even if it is not required, we encourage you to photocopy and use this page; you'll find that reflecting on the articles will greatly enhance the information from your text.

ANNUAL EDITIONS:
AMERICAN HISTORY, Vol. II
Reconstruction Through the Present
Article Rating Form

Here is an opportunity for you to have direct input into the next revision of this volume. We would like you to rate each of the 35 articles listed below, using the following scale:

1. **Excellent: should definitely be retained**
2. **Above average: should probably be retained**
3. **Below average: should probably be deleted**
4. **Poor: should definitely be deleted**

Your ratings will play a vital part in the next revision. So please mail this prepaid form to us just as soon as you complete it.
Thanks for your help!

Rating	Article	Rating	Article
	1. The First Chapter of Children's Rights		20. 'Give Us Roosevelt': Workers and the New Deal Coalition
	2. Clara Barton: Founder of the American Red Cross		21. 1940: America on the Eve of Conflict
	3. The Winning of the West Reconsidered		22. An American Tragedy: The Internment of Japanese-Americans During World War II
	4. The Haymarket Bomb		23. Rosie the Riveter Remembers
	5. Upward Bound		24. The Forgotten War
	6. The Cycle of Reform		25. The Ike Age
	7. Hope, Tears, and Remembrance		26. Rebels Without a Cause? Teenagers in the '50s
	8. Our First Southeast Asian War		27. Trumpet of Conscience: A Portrait of Martin Luther King, Jr.
	9. The Gospel of Andrew Carnegie		28. Reappraising the Presidency of Lyndon B. Johnson
	10. Cleaning Up the Dance Halls		29. Lessons From a Lost War
	11. George Washington Carver: Creative Scientist		30. The New Indian Politics
	12. Theodore Roosevelt, President		31. A Change in the Weather
	13. Angel Island: The Half-Closed Door		32. The Changing Face of a Restless Nation
	14. Rose Schneiderman and the Triangle Fire		33. "Remember the Ladies"
	15. The Unknown Hollywood		34. The Push for Power
	16. The Saint-Mihiel Salient		35. The (Relative) Decline of America
	17. Citizen Ford		
	18. Jazz: Red Hot & Cool		
	19. How Hollywood Fixed an Election		

(Continued on next page)

ABOUT YOU

Name_____ Date_____

Are you a teacher? ☐ Or student? ☐

Your School Name _____

Department _____

Address _____

City_____ State _____ Zip _____

School Telephone # _____

YOUR COMMENTS ARE IMPORTANT TO US!

Please fill in the following information:

For which course did you use this book? _____

Did you use a text with this Annual Edition? ☐ yes ☐ no

The title of the text? _____

What are your general reactions to the Annual Editions concept?

Have you read any particular articles recently that you think should be included in the next edition?

Are there any articles you feel should be replaced in the next edition? Why?

Are there other areas that you feel would utilize an Annual Edition?

May we contact you for editorial input?

May we quote you from above?

AMERICAN HISTORY, Vol. II 11th Ed.
Reconstruction Through the Present

BUSINESS REPLY MAIL

First Class   Permit No. 84   Guilford, CT

Postage will be paid by addressee

The Dushkin Publishing Group, Inc.
Sluice Dock
DPG **Guilford, Connecticut 06437**

No Postage
Necessary
if Mailed
in the
United States